Also by Edward Giobbi *Italian Family Cooking*

EAT RIGHT, EAT WELL — THE ITALIAN WAY

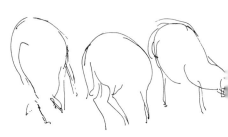

Illustrations by Edward Giobbi from his Italian sketchbooks — 1951

EAT RIGHT,
EAT WELL—
THE ITALIAN WAY

Edward Giobbi and Richard Wolff, M.D.

ALFRED A. KNOPF   NEW YORK   1988

THIS IS A BORZOI BOOK PUBLISHED BY ALFRED A. KNOPF, INC.

Copyright © 1985 by Edward Giobbi and Richard Wolff, M.D.

LIBRARY OF CONGRESS CATALOGING IN PUBLICATION DATA

Giobbi, Edward.
    Eat right, eat well — the Italian way.

    Includes index.
    1. Low-fat diet — Recipes.   Low-cholesterol diet —
Recipes.   3. Cookery, Italian.   I. Wolff, Richard.
II. Title.
RM222.2.G535   1985   641.5′63   84-47893
ISBN 0-394-53071-3

Manufactured in the United States of America
Published May 17, 1985
Reprinted Twice
Fourth Printing, January 1988

To the Giobbi children—
Gena, Lisa, and Cham—
may they have long, healthy lives
I would like to thank Craig Claiborne and Pierre Franey for their encouragement and friendship over the many years, and our editor, Judith Jones, who made this book possible.

To Nancy—and our children
Alice, David, Judith, and Amy
I gratefully acknowledge the very special help of Barbara Cholakos, Norma Casner, Adele Dronsick, Francis Fine, Eugene Kennedy, Judith Jones, Judith Krzynowek, Amy Wolff, and Nancy Wolff—and of the friends and family members who, by suspending some of the demands but none of the support of friendship, afforded me the luxury of a comfortable environment in which to work.

CONTENTS

Introduction   *Edward Giobbi*   **3**

Introduction   *Richard Wolff, M.D.*   **4**

I   Antipasto   **15**

II   Soups   **40**

III   Pastas   **69**

IV   Rice, Polenta, Gnocchi   **151**

V   Fish   **173**

VI   Poultry   **239**

VII   Meats   **288**

VIII   Vegetables   **337**

IX   Salads   **408**

X   Sauces   **425**

XI   Desserts   **443**

XII   Breakfasts, Breads and Pizzas, Snacks, and Cheese   **457**

XIII   Appendixes   **471**

    1. Risk Factors   **473**

    2. Ideal Weight, Dieting, and the Caloric Equivalents of Various Activities   **474**

    3. Characteristics of Fatty Acids   **478**

    4. Calculating Nutrients   **480**

    5. Menu Selection   **482**

    Advice from E.G. about Some Essential Italian Ingredients   **503**

    Index   **505**

EAT RIGHT, EAT WELL—THE ITALIAN WAY

An Introduction by
EDWARD GIOBBI

I am of Italian origin and—not surprisingly—I love to eat. My family and I enjoy good food every day and we take pleasure in the whole ritual of eating. We have never been on a diet; we have never had weight problems. And none of us has had a heart attack or shown any signs of heart disease. One may well wonder then why I was moved to write this book.

The truth is that the recipes in this book represent the kind of food I have always loved. When Dick Wolff, one of Boston's leading cardiologists at Beth Israel Hospital, first approached me about collaborating on a low-cholesterol, low-fat cookbook, I had some misgivings because I was afraid that I might have to make too many compromises to meet his requirements and that the quality of my cooking might suffer. But to my delight I discovered that the adjustments I had to make were minor, and over the nine or ten years that I have been creating dishes using Dick's guidelines, everyone who has eaten my food has been impressed at how delicious it is.

I started cooking when I first got an apartment in Manhattan. As a fledgling artist I was poor so I had to cook economically, using little meat. I'd never heard of cholesterol then, but Mama had always said that fats and sweets weren't good for us so instinctively I patterned my cooking on her ways. Then I went to Italy to study and spent a lot of time in the Marches area, where my family came from. There I learned how much one could do with foods low in fat, using small amounts of good fruity oil instead of butter, and emphasizing fresh fruits and vegetables and herbs. (Cream was expensive—you had to go to the big city to buy it—and eggs were a luxury, reserved for Sunday, maybe, to enrich a homemade pasta dough.) This was real Italian food—and it was delicious.

After I returned to America four years later, I was appalled at the amount of fat the average American consumed. I remember that in the late forties, some army research showed that many American soldiers who died in battle already had clogged arteries, the beginning of heart disease. The more I thought about it, the more I realized that not only were we doing ourselves harm by the way we were eating, but also that the usual American diet wasn't really very appetizing. How much better it is when you let the fresh, clean taste of the food come through rather than smother dishes in butter and cream. And how much more delicious just a little meat or fresh fish is, preceded by a light pasta, than having a half-pound steak dominate the meal. But at that time it was practically un-American to knock steak.

Years later I met Dick Wolff. He, too, loved to eat and he was so delighted at the way the dishes I prepared for him tasted that he wanted to know all my secrets. He, in turn, shared his knowledge about the use of polyunsaturated oil, which he will explain. It took me about a year to work out that fundamental change in my own cooking—mainly the use of a polyunsaturated oil in conjunction with a good olive oil*—but by now it has become second nature and I'm convinced my food hasn't lost anything. In fact, it has gained because almost everything I make now tastes lighter and fresher.

So this book is full of the kind of cooking I believe in, and I hope it will convince other Americans that they can eat better and live longer. This is the cooking I live by—and, I can assure you, I live well.

EDWARD GIOBBI

An Introduction by
RICHARD WOLFF, M.D.

I regard eating as one of the great pleasures of life. It is a pleasure I have no intention of giving up myself or of asking others to. I have tried to make this unmistakably clear to my patients—both those searching for ways to avoid heart disease and those suffering from it—when advising them to make certain changes in life style, particularly in eating habits. Yet I have been met almost invariably with a reflex response which assumes that if it is a diet we're talking about, it cannot be enjoyable. I have done my best to emphasize the positive aspects: the pleasure from feeling well and vigorous, the satisfaction that comes from a bit of self-denial, and the prospect of a longer and healthier life. I have even passed along what I know about foods with little and acceptable fat and have shared some small culinary triumphs, such as my substitute for sour cream, an "acceptable" cheesecake, and a multipurpose dough good for pies, strudel, and cookies. But what I have needed to be able to recommend is a cookbook full of recipes so appealing that the users would not feel in the least deprived. Until now, no such cookbook has existed. Long ago I even started to think of writing one myself, but I knew that I wasn't enough of a cook to take on the challenge. It would take someone who was genuinely creative in the kitchen, who was grounded in the basics of good cooking yet innovative,

---

*For important information about olive oils in cooking, see p. 503.

and who was experienced enough to follow the guidelines I could lay out and come up with an endless variety of such delicious dishes that anyone feasting on them would actually prefer them for their taste. But where was I to find anyone so gifted? Then I met Ed Giobbi.

It was nine or ten years ago. My friends Varujan and Marilyn Boghosian* were very impressed with the way their friend, the painter Ed Giobbi, cooked because his Italian-style food was always so light. Knowing of my interest, both personal and professional, in that kind of food, they invited us both to dinner. Ed cooked — and the dinner was excellent. Afterward he and I started talking about the cookbook I had in mind, and we talked whenever we met over the next few years, each time coming a little bit closer to committing ourselves to the work involved. Finally the challenge of creating superb recipes while obeying the requirements of fat and cholesterol restriction proved irresistible to Ed, and I saw in the project the realization of my old dream of being able to offer people a way to better health without their having to sacrifice pleasure. If our book was good — as I knew it could be — we would even make a significant contribution to the change in American eating habits that is already under way and that, in my opinion, is one of the principal factors responsible for the falling incidence of coronary heart disease† observed in the last decade. I viewed it as an opportunity to have a good influence over the health of many more people — children as well as adults — than I could possibly have reached within the course of my own medical practice.

We started working together; Ed devised recipes with reduced and acceptable fats, while I started to organize the data needed to explain the whys and wherefores. After enough was on paper to show our thoughts, we sought out Judith Jones, who agreed to edit the book. With her encouragement and skillful guidance, the work has proceeded to fruition; without her it would have withered on the vine.

One of the dividends of working on this book has been the opportunity to watch Ed at work in the kitchen and to enjoy eating his food. I have noted repeatedly that his creations are light and that the intrinsic flavors of the ingredients are never suppressed by an excess of salt. Although I have

---

*Varujan is Professor of Art at Dartmouth College and a skilled amateur cook; several of his recipes are included in this book. Marilyn was formerly the nurse in charge of the operating room at Boston's Peter Bent Brigham Hospital; she ran it with an iron hand and a soft heart.

†Coronary heart disease is the kind of heart disease in which trouble starts in the coronary arteries, the blood vessels through which oxygen and nutrients are carried to the heart muscle. Over the course of years there is a gradual buildup within these arteries of material — including cholesterol — which narrows or blocks the arteries so that there is severe limitation or complete cutoff of blood supply to a portion of the heart. The results are repeated bouts of pain in response to physical or emotional stress (angina pectoris), or the common form of heart attack (myocardial infarction), or sudden and unexpected death.

not made a major issue of salt restriction,* this is a good place for me to state my very strong belief that most people should reduce their intake and that Ed's recipes are helpful in that they accentuate the natural good taste of fresh, flavorful ingredients and therefore require less salt.

While we were writing this book some significant changes were taking place in the general public's attitude toward cholesterol. When we started there were still a lot of doubters around who tried to minimize the importance of cholesterol, suggesting that not all the evidence was really in and that so many other factors undoubtedly contributed to a high cholesterol level in the blood that it was useless to change one's diet in the attempt to lower it. I think that this kind of skepticism was engendered largely by wishful thinking — after all, who wants to give up all those rich foods we have come to love? But although I and other heart specialists had long believed in what the existing data had told us, we had to admit that we did not have the ultimate proof. This admission made it harder not only to convince patients who were already in trouble to adhere to a strict low-fat, low-cholesterol diet, but to persuade healthy Americans that they, too, should adopt at least some modest changes in their eating habits.

Then on January 12, 1984, the National Heart, Lung, and Blood Institute announced the results of one of the most extensive research projects ever conducted by the medical profession — a ten-year study of nearly four thousand men in twelve major medical centers. For the first time there was conclusive evidence that lowering cholesterol reduces the risk of a fatal heart attack. In February there was additional significant news: this time the American Cancer Society pointed out that reducing the amount of animal fat in one's diet also lowers the risk of cancer.

The news brought forth a spate of newspaper and magazine articles extolling the virtues of cholesterol reduction. But many of the stories omitted mention of non-dietary risk factors that I shall go into later and, in addition, failed to make clear that the cholesterol content of various foods is neither the only nor the most important determinant of blood cholesterol levels. To lower those levels, several aspects of the diet must be controlled — calories, cholesterol, total fat, saturated fat, and the ratio of polyunsaturated to saturated fat (the P:S ratio). Some newspapers published tables showing that a particular food had a few more milligrams of cholesterol in a standard amount than another food without mentioning to readers that the difference of a few milligrams was unimportant, that the standard amount might not reflect the size of customary servings, or that the total and relative amounts of polyunsaturated and saturated fats were far more important. You will realize as you read on that what matters is not

---

*When sodium (salt) intake is reduced, potassium intake is almost inevitably increased. The suggestion has been made recently that it is the increase in potassium rather than the limitation of sodium that causes lowering of the blood pressure. Medical researchers are currently looking at this and, as well, at the possible beneficial effects of calcium supplements.

only the cholesterol and fat count of an individual dish—whether it is a recipe from this book or another source—but the balance of that particular dish in a whole day's intake of food, as well as the care you devote to reducing other risk factors. We stress that, in the final analysis, *you* must be in charge of your own well-being and that you should try to be alert to adjustments which may be recommended by the American Heart Association and other advisory bodies as new research is carried on.

In the final analysis, the aim of dietary manipulation is to prevent heart attacks and strokes by slowing down or even reversing the buildup of cholesterol and other substances in the walls of arteries so that the blood can flow more freely. To prevent such gradual buildup it is necessary to follow certain recommendations designed to control cholesterol, total fat, saturated fat, and the P:S ratio in the food we eat. This book provides hundreds of delicious recipes that make it possible for you to follow these recommendations. It may be that you are finally convinced by the medical evidence that you and your family should be eating more sensibly. If so, use the recipes in this book and you will be on your way. The breakdowns that follow each recipe will give you specific data on cholesterol, total fat, and the P:S ratio so that you can design a diet that meets your requirements.

It is not possible to identify one number that represents a safe, acceptable, and attainable level of cholesterol for everyone. For one individual starting with a level of 210 milligrams per hundred millileters, we might aim for the "ideal" of 150. For another starting at 310, a reduction to 210 would be most gratifying. In both cases, there would be a significant reduction in the risk of developing coronary disease. This sort of reduction in risk is available *by choice* to the vast majority of people in developed Western societies who are walking around with unnecessarily high cholesterol levels. In my opinion the medical laboratories have done the people a great disservice by adopting as their "top normals" figures for cholesterol that are much too high.* Many doctors, in their acceptance of these figures, have acquiesced in their patients' continued maintenance of levels that expose them to double or triple the risk they might otherwise have. I believe that most people given these facts would opt for a reduction of risk, particularly if it could be accomplished without diminishing the pleasure

---

*The method of establishing a normal range of a biologic measurement most often used by medical laboratories is to test it in a group of randomly chosen subjects large enough to permit reasonable certainty that it is representative of the population at large. Then, by appropriate statistical formulas, it is possible to predict the variation of the measurement within the entire population. "Normal" is generally defined as the range which includes 95 percent of the members of the population. The lowest 2.5 percent and the highest 2.5 percent are considered abnormal by definition. By this criterion, a cholesterol value of about 310 ("about" because to some extent the measurement is age dependent) is the dividing line between normal and abnormally high. But the existence of coronary heart disease in epidemic proportions among the 95 percent of the population presumed to be normal tells us at once that the dividing line at 310 does not help us to

they get from food. Very simply, that's what this book is all about: the provision of a diet that reduces risk without reducing pleasure.

Before we discuss specific recommendations, we should explain some terms: proteins; carbohydrates, including fiber—the indigestible portion of plants; and fats, including cholesterol, fatty acids, and triglycerides.

Food, along with the water we drink and the air we breathe, provides the energy (calories) required for living and the building blocks from which we manufacture tissues needed for growth and replacement. The three main classes of food are proteins, carbohydrates, and fats (also called lipids). Each gram of protein or carbohydrate supplies approximately four calories, each gram of fat about nine calories. There are 454 grams in one pound.

Proteins are long and complex chains of individual units called amino acids. The sequence of the amino acids determines the specific characteristics of an individual protein.

Carbohydrates are sugars existing singly or in groups of two or more. Glucose and fructose, names familiar to all, are simple sugars—that is, each molecule is composed of a single sugar and is called, therefore, a *mono*saccharide. When two sugars are chemically linked, the molecule is called a *di*saccharide. Sucrose (cane sugar) is such a molecule; it is composed of one glucose and one fructose. Chains of more than two sugar molecules are called *poly*saccharides. Some polysaccharides, like the fiber in cotton and wood, are both indigestible by humans and insoluble in water. They are, as a consequence, chemically inactive when ingested. Other fibers, although indigestible, do dissolve in water and can, therefore, enter into the chemical combination with other substances in the intestines. When they combine with bile acids they form a complex which is excreted in the stool. This has the beneficial effect of eliminating the bile acid building blocks of cholesterol, thereby lowering the blood cholesterol level. It is the solubility in water of oat bran which accounts for its cholesterol-lowering effect, an effect not shared by wheat bran which is insoluble. Digestible polysaccharides, the starches, are the main source of calories in bread, rice, potatoes, cereals, and pasta. Years ago it was axiomatic that "fat burns in the carbohydrate fire." Then carbohydrates in general and starches in particular became scapegoats in the battle against

---

discriminate between normal and abnormal if by those terms we mean absence or presence of coronary heart disease (or risk).

Another method is the one used in the Framingham study. Subjects were assigned to groups on the basis of their serum cholesterol levels and the groups were compared with one another over the ensuing years. The lower the cholesterol level of the group, the fewer were the number of coronary "events." It was possible to detect differences in the frequency of events associated with differences in serum cholesterol of as little as 10 milligrams per hundred milliliters. It is more reasonable, therefore, to speak of the *risk* associated with the cholesterol level than to attempt to find a sharp division between normal and abnormal values. The data indicate that for progressively lower amounts of serum cholesterol there is progressively less risk, perhaps down to a level of 150 milligrams per 100 milliliters, but certainly down to 180 milligrams per 100 milliliters.

obesity. Recently, however, the amount of dietary carbohydrate considered desirable has been revised upward and the trend has been to recommend that this be in the form of complex starches rather than simple sugars. As I am writing, new findings suggesting that this view may be overly simplistic are being mulled over by cardiologists, diabetologists, and nutritionists; and the final answers are not yet in. It does appear, however, that what Ed told me years ago and I regarded as Italian chauvinism may turn out to be true after all: pasta may have some very special properties that make it nutritionally preferable to rice, potatoes, and bread.

Of the many classes of fats two are of special interest to us: cholesterol and triglycerides. Cholesterol is a waxy substance that is both manufactured by our bodies and derived from food of animal origin; it is in particularly high concentration in eggs, brains, and other organs such as the liver, kidneys, heart, and thymus. It is present in every one of our cells and is essential to human life. Accordingly, it is not its mere presence but an excess of it that concerns us. Such an excess is produced by the food we eat; and it is effectively reduced by limiting the amount of both cholesterol and total fat in our diets, and by adjusting the amounts of polyunsaturated and saturated fats so that we consume relatively more polyunsaturated and less saturated fat. The cholesterol that is present in the blood is bound to proteins, some of which have a low density and some of which have a high density. It is not alone the total cholesterol level that is important but also the partition between the (good) high density lipoprotein cholesterol (HDL cholesterol) and the (bad) low density lipoprotein cholesterol (LDL cholesterol). A shift to more HDL cholesterol is favored by weight reduction, exercise, the moderate use of alcohol, and the avoidance of tobacco.

The other fats of concern to us because they exert a major influence upon the blood cholesterol level are the triglycerides. They exist in the form of fats and oils which differ from one another in that fats are solid and oils are liquid at room temperature. Both are composed of a molecule of glycerol to which are attached three molecules of fatty acids. Fatty acids are of three types: monosaturated, polyunsaturated, and saturated (see Appendix 3). Monounsaturated fatty acids have no effect upon the blood cholesterol level. Saturated fatty acids raise the blood cholesterol level; but polyunsaturated fat actually lowers the blood cholesterol. A given amount of polyunsaturated fatty acid, however, lowers the cholesterol only half as much as an equal amount of saturated fat raises it.

Relatively saturated mixtures tend to be of animal origin and solid; relatively unsaturated mixtures are usually of plant origin and liquid. The major exceptions to this rule are coconut oil, cocoa butter, palm kernel oil, and palm oil which, although of plant origin, are even more highly saturated than beef and mutton tallow, lard, and butter fat.

Fish and shellfish fats or lipids tend to be more unsaturated than meat fats, but until recently data on proximate compositions have been frequently unavailable or incomplete. New work, though not yet universally accepted, suggests that the lipids present in fatty fish — at least those found in cold waters — have some fatty acids different from those found in the meat of land animals, and that these fatty acids are very effective in lowering cholesterol levels and in preventing or slowing the progress of atherosclerosis.

Let us turn now to the specific dietary recommendations — essentially those of the American Heart Association and of the Senate Select Committee on Nutrition and Human Needs, 1977. They are:
1. The limitation of cholesterol to 300 milligrams or less per day*
2. The limitation of fat so that no more than 30 percent of the day's calories are derived from fat (I would be even happier at 25 percent)
3. The partition of fats such that
   a. No more, and preferably less, than one third is saturated
   b. An equal amount and preferably more is polyunsaturated, i.e., the ratio of polyunsaturated to saturated fat (the P:S ratio) is at least 1:1
   c. The balance is monounsaturated

The Achievement and Maintenance of Ideal Weight

Ideal weight is defined differently by various authorities. I favor stricter standards than those recommended by the Metropolitan Life Insurance Company; both sets are given in Appendix 2 along with suggestions for achieving and maintaining ideal weight. Whatever criterion is adopted for ideal weight it is apparent that the number of calories required to maintain that weight is dependent upon the level of activity. Exercise not only makes one look better, feel better, and be healthier, it increases the number of calories burned and, therefore, allows one to eat more without gaining weight. Appendix 2 contains a table of the energy expended per minute in various activities.

The Limitation of Dietary Cholesterol

There is no cholesterol at all in plants; and animal products vary greatly in their contents (see Appendix 4). Certain foods have so much that an average serving exceeds the daily total average allowance of 300 milligrams. These foods are best eliminated entirely from the diet; we have not used them in any of the recipes. They include brain, kidneys, liver, tongue, and sweetbreads. The yolk of one large egg at 252 milligrams of cholesterol falls within the 300-milligram limit, but it does not by itself constitute a full serving; accordingly we have not used egg yolks or whole eggs in any of the recipes.

---

*The maximum dietary cholesterol permitted depends upon the eater's weight:

Weight in pounds	Cholesterol allowance in milligrams
100	200
125	250
150	300
175	350
200	400

The limitation of cholesterol to 300 milligrams a day is a very simple matter both because it is easy to calculate and therefore to limit the amount ingested, and because controlling the total fat and the P:S ratio will almost automatically guarantee that the daily cholesterol ration is not exceeded. There are, however, a few foods that are low in fat yet high in cholesterol, namely shrimp, which has 150 milligrams of cholesterol and only 0.8 grams of fat in a 100-gram edible portion; chicken gizzard, which has 145 milligrams of cholesterol and 2.7 grams of fat in 100 grams; and squid, with perhaps 200 milligrams of cholesterol and 0.9 grams of fat. It is, therefore, possible to get too much cholesterol even though the fat intake is very low. We do allow the use of shrimp, gizzard, and squid in limited amounts but we stress the necessity of careful calculation of the cholesterol ration on any day that these foods are eaten. We regard the current values for the cholesterol content of squid as tentative; they are being reexamined by chemists at the U.S. Bureau of Fisheries.

The Limitation and Partition of Fat

It is not so easy to limit the total fat of the diet to 30 percent or less of its calories and to fulfill the requirements we have set forth for the division into saturated, polysaturated, and monounsaturated components, namely not more and preferably less than one third of the fat to be saturated, an equal or greater amount to be polyunsaturated, and the remainder to be monounsaturated. It is not enough to devise a group of recipes which fulfill these requirements, nor is it necessary to eliminate all from the diet which do not. What is essential is that an entire day's food and every day's food furnish nutrients within the limits discussed.

What Ed has done in these recipes is to select ingredients for both flavor and nutritional balance. He has shown that mixing good, fruity oils with polyunsaturated oils in the right proportions permits the elimination of butter without loss of appeal. In fact the final product frequently has a delightful lightness that is not present when butter is used. With this one simple principle he has given us an enormous variety of dishes. Many of them — recognizable by the facts that 30 percent or less of their calories are derived from fat, that the saturated fat is 10 percent or less, and that the P:S ratio is 1:1 or greater — can be used without further ado by those following our caveats strictly. Other dishes, about which one or more of these statements cannot be made, are nevertheless improvements over most similar foods even though they are not ideal. You need not hesitate to include them in your meals, but it is advisable to familiarize yourself with the procedures and examples for calculating nutrients given in Appendixes 4 and 5. Those who wish to reap maximum benefit from the control of their fat and calorie intake need to be aware of what they are actually eating by informing themselves of the constituents of various recipes and by reading the labels of packaged foods. They can then act upon two very simple rules:

1. Inclusion in a recipe or mention on a label of any ingredient known to be high in cholesterol automatically eliminates the food containing that ingredient from the diet. These ingredients have already been listed.
2. Inclusion in a recipe or mention on a label of a fat known to be highly saturated automatically eliminates the food containing that fat from the diet. As already mentioned, fats which are naturally highly saturated are coconut oil, palm kernel oil, palm oil, and cocoa butter. Other oils which have been hydrogenated by man are also undesirable. Vegetable oil and vegetable shortening are frequently made with coconut or palm oil; they are best avoided. We also exclude coconuts and macadamia nuts from our list of acceptable foods.

These two simple rules go far toward limiting the intake of cholesterol and controlling the P:S ratio, particularly if most of the dishes are selected from this cookbook. They do not, however, prevent the fat calories from exceeding any selected limit, be it 25 percent, 30 percent, or 35 percent. This needs to be separately and consciously controlled. One obvious way to do it is to eliminate from the diet any recipe having more than the allowed percentage of fat calories you settle on, but if you do that, you'll miss the best part of this book. Look, for example, at these sauces, which all go well with fish. They contain fats accounting for 77 to 93 percent of their calories.

Salsa al pistaccio	86 percent
Pesto di magro	91 percent
Almond sauce	79 percent
Sauce for fish	93 percent
Salsa alla noci #1	89 percent
Salsa alla noci #2	77 percent
Salsa di menta #2	92 percent

If you cut them out you miss some very good eating—and you do it unnecessarily. After all, nobody makes a meal of salsa di menta. Rather, a serving of it might be used to dress up an eight-ounce (raw weight) portion of haddock and the combination would have 439 calories of which 43 percent were from fat. Further reduction of fat to or below the 30 percent level would be accomplished by the judicious selection of the remainder of the day's food.

Some specific suggestions are presented in the breakfast chapter; and Appendix 5 gives an example of how a menu may be selected together with the calculations involved. With a little calculation you can even work into the menu dishes in which there is a modest excess of saturated over polyunsaturated fat, including dishes utilizing red meat or cheese.

In summary, we have indulged our passion for good food and we have done it with recipes and meal planning designed to lower blood cholesterol levels. Your choices become almost limitless if you follow the methods of calculating nutrients and compensating appropriately as outlined in Appendixes 4 and 5.

Important as dietary cholesterol and fats are in determining the blood cholesterol level, they are by no means the only factors affecting the risk of heart attack.* Obesity, smoking, stress, lack of exercise, high blood pressure, and diabetes have all been implicated; and studies are under way to determine whether modification of these factors diminishes the number of heart attacks or postpones them to an older age. Suffice it to point out here that although the final results of controlling risk factors are not yet available, enough is already known to permit some general advice to the people at large.

1. Do not smoke. Smoking is an independent risk factor associated with cancers in several body locations as well as with heart disease. We believe that the oft-repeated plaint "It's so hard to give up smoking" serves the purposes of the tobacco industry very well. As long as this is conventional wisdom, a built-in excuse for smokers exists and they are discouraged from even trying to give up their habits; or, afraid that they will fail, they do not make a real commitment to give up smoking, but hedge their announced intention as "I'll try" rather than "I shall." It is much harder to make the *commitment* to give up smoking than it is to give up smoking.

2. Find out whether you have high blood pressure (hypertension); if you do, get it under control with your doctor's help. It is thought that salt is important in causing or increasing the severity of hypertension and that the average diet is too high in salt (sodium) content; efforts to reduce this are to be encouraged.

3. Find out whether you have diabetes (sugar diabetes, diabetes mellitus); if you do, get it under control with your doctor's help. Many authorities feel, as is the case with salt, that the sugar content of the average diet is too high and should be reduced. This is demonstrably true for some people; for the rest there is no harm and perhaps a benefit from such a reduction.

4. Make exercise a regular part of your life. Difficult as it may be to find the time, make the commitment that you will exercise, if not daily, at least three times a week. If you are not accustomed to exercise, especially if you are over 40, it is wise for you to discuss an exercise prescription with your doctor. The sense of well-being that results from proper exercise comes as a revelation to those who try it.

5. Try to control the amount of emotional stress in your life and to limit time-urgency, aggressiveness, and competitiveness, the hallmarks of so-called type A behavior. For comfort alone this is worthwhile; in addition, it is probable that such behavior modification influences whatever risk is associated with stress, but to what extent is unknown.

6. Eat sensibly. The average American diet is generally considered to contain too many calories, too much salt, too much sugar, too much fat (accounting for 40 percent or even 45 percent of the calories), and too high a ratio—about 2.5:1—of saturated to polyunsaturated fat. There can be no

---

*For a quantitative assessment of some of the risk factors you are referred to Appendix 1.

doubt that a high cholesterol level and obesity are important risk factors that can be changed by altering the diet; and that the amount of change depends upon the extent to which the diet is altered. This book gives you options. You may use our recipes to replace a few of your habitual high-fat dishes, many of them, or all of them. Those of you who wish to be strict will find specific instructions in Appendixes 4 and 5. The vigor with which you pursue cholesterol and weight control (and risk control) is up to you. You can verify the results by a blood test and by simply stepping onto a scale. Childhood is the best time to adopt or instill good eating habits, but adulthood is not too late. Once adopted, they should be maintained for life to reduce the risk of both cardiovascular disease and cancer.

Remember, you have it within your power to improve your own health. If you have diabetes or high blood pressure, you will need skilled professional advice. Smoking, physical inactivity, and type A behavior you can correct on your own. You can look forward to the hope that at some future time even heredity may be vanquished by genetic engineering. But the joyous message of this book is that you don't have to wait even one day to start improving your diet and reducing your risk. We think you will get more rather than less enjoyment from our recipes and you can apply the principles to adapt an endless array of your own favorites. Eat well, eat right, and enjoy both better food and better health.

The nutritional summaries following the recipes have been calculated with data from numerous sources (including U.S. Department of Agriculture Handbooks 8, 8-1, 8-2, 8-4, 8-5, 54, and 456; National Oceanic and Atmospheric Administration Technical Memorandum NMFS F/SEC-11; Bowes and Church's *Food Values of Portions Commonly Used*, J. B. Lippincott Co.; Marian Morash's *The Victory Garden Cookbook*, Alfred A. Knopf; and the food data bank at the University of Massachusetts, Amherst). The data in all these sources are approximate only. Accordingly, our data are also approximate; but they are as accurate as we could make them.

And now, buon appetito. Remember:

The nutritional summary after each recipe is for the whole recipe. Data for one portion are the amounts given divided by the number of servings (% total and sat. fat are the same for individual servings as for the entire recipe, however).

When two alternate ingredients, e.g. "safflower or sunflower oil," or alternate amounts are listed, our calculation is based on the former; and when optional ingredients are listed, they are not included in the nutritional summary.

The total fat listed in the nutritional data after each recipe includes other classes of fats, e.g. phospholipids, and is therefore usually more than the sum of the sat., mono., and poly. triglycerides.

I   ANTIPASTO

Italians rarely serve appetizers before dinner. The idea of sipping cocktails and eating a variety of rich appetizers is completely foreign to them. Even wine is not served before dinner. The most you are apt to be offered is an aperitivo—usually something bitter to stimulate the appetite.

We stopped serving appetizers with drinks many years ago after I realized that our guests were gorging themselves with food and drink before dinner, and then, when they were at the table, they just pushed their food around. So we have a very short cocktail period now with no food at all.

If you want an antipasto, serve it at the table as a first course and select it very carefully so that you achieve a proper balance with the courses that are to follow. Sometimes just crisp chilled celery hearts served with the simple pinzimonio dip that our family always enjoyed (page 36) make an adequate antipasto. Obviously you can get as elaborate as you wish, but you should always keep in mind the rest of the meal.

Some antipasto dishes can make an excellent lunch—tuna with beans and roasted pepper, for instance, or a frittata or a fish salad—and some go well as an accompaniment to a main course—for instance, roasted peppers with meats or a few stuffed clams with fish. By the same token, there are many seafood recipes, salads, and vegetable dishes that would make a fine antipasto, so look through those chapters for other ideas. But whatever you do, remember to pay attention not only to the overall richness but also to variety in terms of color, shape, and texture.

I find that a selection of coldcuts such as prosciutto and salami, along with tuna, anchovies, and cheese, to say nothing of an assortment of pickled vegetables, is much too heavy, particularly if a pasta course is going to follow. You will find that in better Italian restaurants a slice of melon or fresh figs topped with a paper-thin slice of prosciutto is preferred over a plate laden with coldcuts that looks as though it had been dragged through a butcher shop.

Your antipasto selection should be light, with a minimal amount of oil and vinegar. It should prepare you for your second course—not heartburn.

The aforementioned kind of gross antipasto, so often touted as typically Italian, is another unfortunate offspring of Italo-American cooking, which I as an Italo-American refuse to identify with. E.G.

It often happens that Ed and I arrive at the same conclusions for complementary reasons. What his sense of balance tells him turns out to be nutritionally as well as aesthetically valid. I agree with him wholeheartedly that little or none is preferable to lavishness in appetizers; and that cheeses and coldcuts are particularly objectionable. R.W.

SHELLFISH ON TOAST
Crostini di Mare alla Genovese

Serves 6 as an appetizer (use smaller slices of toast); 4 as a main course.

2 squid, about 1 pound
6 cherrystone clams
1 pound mussels
2 tablespoons olive oil
1 teaspoon safflower oil
2 cloves garlic, finely chopped
Hot pepper flakes to taste
2 tablespoons chopped Italian parsley
2 tablespoons wine vinegar
1 cup chopped tomatoes, fresh if possible (drain if canned)
Salt to taste
1 pound fresh sea scallops
4 to 6 slices French or Italian bread

Garnish: Finely chopped Italian parsley

Clean squid (page 215) and cut in ¼-inch-thick slices. Wash and scrub clams and mussels.

Heat the two oils in a medium skillet or shallow saucepan, then add garlic. Sauté about 30 seconds. Add squid, hot pepper flakes, and parsley and cook over high heat, stirring often, for 3 to 5 minutes. Add wine vinegar, cover, and cook over moderate heat about 5 minutes. Add tomatoes, clams, mussels, and salt, if desired. Cover, lower heat, and cook until clam and mussel shells open. Remove as they open (when they are cool, remove flesh and throw away shells). Remove cover and reduce sauce by half over high heat, stirring often. Add scallops and cook over high heat, tossing often. Cook about 3 or 4 minutes, until scallops are tender. Add shelled clams and mussels. Cover and turn off heat.

Toast bread. Serve a portion of shellfish mixture on each slice of toast. Garnish with finely chopped Italian parsley.

Calories	Cholesterol mg	Protein gm	Carbohydrate gm	Total fat gm	%	Sat fat gm	%	Mono gm	Poly gm
1183	771.0	139.5	57.4	38.7	29	4.0	3	20.3	5.6

These figures do not include the toast.

SQUID AND SHRIMP ON A SKEWER
Spiedini di Frutti di Mare

This recipe was sent to me years ago by my mother, who lives in one of the great fishing ports in Italy — San Benedetto Del Tronto. We like to serve it as a first course with stuffed clams or mussels, and another hot fish dish such as fried whiting or scallops cooked in pesto.

Serves 6.

1/2 pound bone squid, about 3 medium squid, cleaned (page 215)*
1/2 pound medium fresh shrimp, shelled and deveined
3 tablespoons olive oil
1 teaspoon safflower oil
Salt and freshly ground black pepper to taste
Hot pepper flakes or a dash Tabasco sauce to taste
2 tablespoons finely chopped Italian parsley
2 tablespoons finely chopped fresh mint
2 cloves garlic, finely chopped
3/4 cup dried breadcrumbs
2 tablespoons lemon juice or wine vinegar for basting

Garnish: Lemon wedges

*See page 214 for information about the two types of squid available in the market.

Cut squid in strips about 1 1/4 inches wide, reserving tentacles. Wash shrimp well in cold water and drain thoroughly. Place squid (including tentacles) and shrimp in a mixing bowl with 2 tablespoons of the olive oil, the safflower oil, salt, pepper, hot pepper flakes, parsley, mint, and garlic, and mix well. Now add breadcrumbs and mix thoroughly. Wrap a piece of squid around each shrimp. Spear the wrapped shrimp onto a skewer, inserting squid tentacles between 2 pieces of the wrapped shrimp. Repeat until skewer is full, then fill a second skewer—you will need two about 12 to 15 inches long.

Broil over hot coals until golden brown or under a preheated broiler, basting with lemon juice and remaining 1 tablespoon olive oil. It will take about 25 minutes under a hot broiler. This recipe is best over coals.

Serve immediately with lemon wedges.

Calories	Cholesterol mg	Protein gm	Carbohydrate gm	Total fat gm	%	Sat fat gm	%	Mono gm	Poly gm
953	484.0	57.4	65.8	50.8	47	4.9	5	31.4	6.1

SQUID AND SCALLOPS ON A SKEWER
Spiedini di Frutti di Mare

Serves 6 as an appetizer.

1 pound bone squid, cleaned and cut into
   2-inch-wide strips (page 215)
About 1/2 pound sea scallops, walnut-sized pieces
3 tablespoons olive oil
1 tablespoon safflower oil
Salt and freshly ground black pepper to taste
1 teaspoon minced garlic
2 tablespoons finely chopped Italian parsley
8 tablespoons breadcrumbs

Garnish: Lemon wedges

Mix squid and scallops with the oils, salt, pepper, garlic, and parsley. Stir in breadcrumbs. Roll a strip of squid around each piece of scallop. Spear these as well as the tentacles onto skewers, as in the preceding recipe. Broil over hot coals or under a preheated broiler for about 20 minutes, turning on all sides, depending on size of squid. Serve with lemon wedges or with one of the fish sauces (pages 427–42).

Calories	Cholesterol mg	Protein gm	Carbohydrate gm	Total fat gm	%	Sat fat gm	%	Mono gm	Poly gm
1052	574.0	78.0	56.4	59.0	42	5.6	5	32.9	12.5

OYSTERS WITH PESTO
Ostriche al Pesto

Serves 2 to 3; 1 as a first course.

1 tablespoon olive oil or 2 tablespoons peanut oil
1 teaspoon safflower oil
1 cup thinly sliced mushrooms
Salt and freshly ground black pepper to taste
6 medium oysters in shell
6 teaspoons pesto (page 426)

Heat the oils in a small skillet, then add mushrooms, salt, and pepper. Cook over medium heat until mushrooms begin to brown and all juices are cooked out.

Open the oysters and leave on the half shell, loosening the flesh. Drop 1 teaspoon of pesto on each oyster, then spread a heaping teaspoon of cooked mushroom on top of the pesto, completely covering the oyster.

Bake in a preheated 450° oven about 6 minutes.

Calories	Cholesterol mg	Protein gm	Carbohydrate gm	Total fat gm	%	Sat fat gm	%	Mono gm	Poly gm
320	42.0	9.9	6.5	28.6	79	2.7	7	16.9	6.2

OYSTERS IN GREEN SAUCE
Ostriche con Salsa Verde

Serves 2 to 4 as a first course.

1 tablespoon olive oil or 2 tablespoons peanut oil
1 teaspoon safflower oil
2 tablespoons finely chopped onion
1 cup packed fresh spinach
1 teaspoon finely chopped Italian parsley
1 tablespoon pine nuts
1 tablespoon breadcrumbs
Salt and freshly ground black pepper to taste
1 teaspoon dry sherry
8 medium oysters

Heat the oils in a small skillet, then add onion. As onion begins to brown, add spinach, parsley, pine nuts, breadcrumbs, salt, pepper, and sherry. Cover and simmer over low heat about 5 minutes. Then remove and put in a food processor or pound with mortar and pestle to purée.

Open oysters on half shell, loosening the flesh. Spread 1 teaspoon of stuffing evenly over each oyster so that the oyster is covered completely.

Bake in a preheated 450° oven about 6 minutes. Serve hot.

Calories	Cholesterol	Protein	Carbohydrate	Total fat		Sat fat		Mono	Poly
	mg	*gm*	*gm*	*gm*	*%*	*gm*	*%*	*gm*	*gm*
315	58.0	14.3	13.9	22.9	64	2.1	6	12.5	4.3

STUFFED CLAMS I—MARCHES STYLE
Cozze alla Marchigiana

For a festive antipasto, we like to serve these stuffed clams with several varieties of other shellfish, such as scallops with pesto or stuffed oysters, for example. The same recipe may be made with fresh mussels (some people prefer stuffed mussels to stuffed clams). I have also made it with fresh oysters on the half shell with success. Incidentally, clams are much easier to open if they have been chilled on ice.

Serves 4 as a first course.

16 littleneck clams
1/2 cup breadcrumbs
1/2 teaspoon dried oregano
2 tablespoons finely chopped Italian parsley
2 tablespoons freshly grated Parmesan
   or Romano cheese
2 tablespoons olive oil
2 tablespoons safflower oil
Freshly ground black pepper to taste
4 tablespoons dry white wine or sherry

Open clams and loosen the flesh from the shells, reserving the liquid. Discard the top shells and place the open clams in a baking pan.

Mix together the breadcrumbs, oregano, parsley, cheese, the two oils, and pepper. Sprinkle the mixture generously over each clam.

Strain the reserved clam juice and sprinkle over stuffed clams. Sprinkle 2 tablespoons of the wine over the clams and pour the rest into the bottom of the baking pan.

Broil under high heat of preheated broiler. When the breadcrumbs begin to brown, baste with the liquid in the baking pan and cook 30 seconds longer.

Serve immediately.

Calories	Cholesterol	Protein	Carbohydrate	Total fat		Sat fat		Mono	Poly
	mg	*gm*	*gm*	*gm*	*%*	*gm*	*%*	*gm*	*gm*
916	124.0	35.8	57.1	60.0	58	7.0	7	23.4	22.4

STUFFED CLAMS II—MARCHES STYLE
Cozze alla Marchigiana

This stuffing could also be used for mussels and oysters.

Serves 3 to 4 as an appetizer.

12 cherrystone or littleneck clams, well iced
1 teaspoon minced garlic
1 tablespoon finely chopped Italian parsley
1 tablespoon olive oil
1 tablespoon safflower oil
1 cup coarsely chopped tomatoes, fresh if possible
    (drain if canned)
Salt and freshly ground black pepper to taste

Open clams on the half shell. Mix the remaining ingredients thoroughly. Place a generous amount on each clam and broil close to heat until tops begin to brown. Serve immediately.

Calories	Cholesterol mg	Protein gm	Carbohydrate gm	Total fat gm	%	Sat fat gm	%	Mono gm	Poly gm
457	105.0	25.9	22.9	29.3	56	2.6	5	12.3	10.7

STUFFED CLAMS III—GENOA STYLE
Cozze alla Genovese

By stuffing clams this way, you can make them go further.

Serves 4 as an appetizer; 12 stuffed clams.

6 cherrystone clams, well iced
3 tablespoons pesto (page 426), diluted with
    3 tablespoons warm water
1/2 cup fresh breadcrumbs
Freshly ground black pepper to taste
Dry sherry or port wine

Carefully open the clams with a sharp knife. Cut each clam in half—you should have some clam on both half shells. Loosen the flesh on both sides, spoon a little pesto over, top with breadcrumbs, pepper liberally, and sprinkle sherry or port on top. Place clams on a baking sheet. Broil clams close to heat in a preheated broiler until breadcrumbs are browned. Serve hot.

Calories	Cholesterol mg	Protein gm	Carbohydrate gm	Total fat gm	%	Sat fat gm	%	Mono gm	Poly gm
273	53.0	15.1	19.4	14.8	48	1.3	4	7.9	3.0

FISH SALAD I
Insalata di Pesce

This is also good as a main course.

Serves 4 to 6 as an appetizer.

3 medium squid, split and cleaned (page 215)
12 mussels
1 bay leaf
1/2 cup dry white wine
1/2 pound sea scallops
1 slice white fish such as cod or striped bass,
    about 1 1/2 inches thick
Hot pepper flakes to taste
1 teaspoon dried oregano
1 tablespoon chopped fresh mint
2 tablespoons finely chopped Italian parsley
1 teaspoon minced garlic
2 tablespoons olive oil
1 tablespoon safflower oil
Juice of 1 lime or lemon

Garnish: Lemon wedges

Boil cleaned squid for 5 to 8 minutes. Drain, let cool, then slice in strips about 1/4 inch wide and put in a bowl. Steam mussels open. Remove flesh from shells and add to squid. Bring to a boil in a saucepan about 2 cups of water, the bay leaf, and wine. Add scallops and cook 3 or 4 minutes. Remove with a slotted spoon, reserving the liquid. Let the scallops cool, then slice them and add to squid and mussels. Put the slice of fish in the scallop water and boil gently until fish is cooked—about 4 to 5 minutes. Remove the fish from the liquid, cool, then remove bones and skin, cut in pieces, and add to the other seafood. Combine the remaining ingredients and carefully toss with the seafood. Let sit at least 1 hour. Serve at room temperature with lemon wedges.

Calories	Cholesterol mg	Protein gm	Carbohydrate gm	Total fat gm	%	Sat fat gm	%	Mono gm	Poly gm
1338	1063.0	170.9	27.5	48.1	32	4.8	3	21.4	12.3

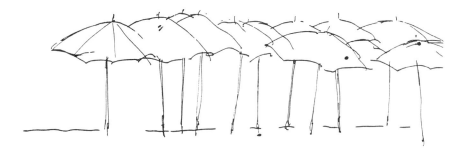

FISH SALAD II
Insalata di Pesce

Serves 4 to 6.

1/2 pound shrimp
1 cup small pasta, such as shells, tubettini, elbows,
   cooked and drained
2 slices fresh codfish about 1 1/2 inches thick, or red
   snapper, bass, or haddock, cooked as in preceding recipe
1/2 pound squid, prepared as in preceding recipe
Juice of 1 lemon
2 tablespoons extra virgin olive oil
1 tablespoon safflower oil
2 tablespoons chopped fresh mint
2 cloves garlic, finely chopped
1 tablespoon finely chopped Italian parsley
3 cups loosely packed rucola (arugola), picked and washed,
   or a mixture of salad greens (Bibb, endive, leaf)

Boil shrimp in water to cover 3 minutes, then cool and shell. Mix all ingredients except rucola together and gently toss.

Serve either on a bed of rucola or serve rucola on side of fish salad — in that case, toss rucola in an oil-and-lemon dressing.

This recipe should be cooled to room temperature to serve. Do not refrigerate.

Calories	Cholesterol mg	Protein gm	Carbohydrate gm	Total fat gm	%	Sat fat gm	%	Mono gm	Poly gm
1455	832.0	183.1	88.7	46.4	26	4.8	3	21.4	12.3

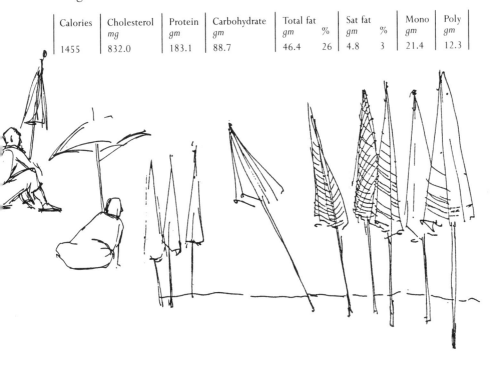

MUSSEL AND SCALLOP SALAD
Insalata di Frutti di Mare

We like this recipe as part of a fish antipasto, which might include stuffed clams or mussels, fried whitebait, or perhaps sardelle in saor (in carpione — see page 28).

Any variety of shellfish can be used in this recipe, including clams, crabmeat, shrimp, lobster, etc.

Serves 6.

1 cup dry white wine
3 cloves garlic, finely chopped
2 tablespoons finely chopped Italian parsley
1 teaspoon dried oregano
2 pounds mussels, scrubbed well and washed
1/2 pound sea scallops

The dressing
2 cloves garlic, finely minced
1 teaspoon dried oregano
Hot pepper flakes to taste
Juice of 1 lemon
2 tablespoons finely chopped Italian parsley
   or fresh mint
Very little salt
2 tablespoons extra virgin olive oil
1 teaspoon safflower oil

Put the wine, garlic, parsley, oregano, and mussels in a pot, cover, and cook until mussels open. Remove the mussels, scrape out the flesh and reserve, discarding the shells. Bring mussel broth to a boil, then add scallops and boil for several minutes. Remove scallops with a slotted spoon. Cut into slices 1/8 inch thick.

Combine scallop slices and mussels in a mixing bowl and add the dressing ingredients, mixing everything gently. Let stand for several hours and serve as a first course or part of an antipasto. Try not to refrigerate — it tastes better at room temperature.

Calories	Cholesterol mg	Protein gm	Carbohydrate gm	Total fat gm	%	Sat fat gm	%	Mono gm	Poly gm
803	212.0	74.7	38.3	38.1	42	4.0	4	20.3	5.6

SCALLOP SALAD
Insalata di Canestrelli

As a main luncheon course, this is particularly good served with a fresh tomato salad.

Serves 6 as an appetizer.

1/2 pound sea scallops
1 tablespoon olive oil
1 tablespoon safflower oil
2 cloves garlic, crushed (skins discarded)
Salt and freshly ground black pepper to taste
Juice of 1 1/2 lemons
2 cups thinly sliced whole scallions
1 1/2 tablespoons finely chopped Italian parsley
2 small to medium potatoes, boiled, peeled,
    and sliced
6-ounce jar artichoke hearts packed in oil,
    drained and chopped
Salt and freshly ground black pepper to taste

Wash and dry scallops. Heat the oils in a medium skillet and add the garlic. When it browns, remove and discard. Add scallops, salt, and pepper, and, stirring and tossing constantly, cook over high heat about 1 minute. Add juice of 1/2 lemon, continue cooking over high heat for 1 more minute, and then remove from heat. When scallops cool, cut in slices so that they are in rounds.

Mix all the remaining ingredients with the scallops and serve at room temperature.

Calories	Cholesterol mg	Protein gm	Carbohydrate gm	Total fat gm	%	Sat fat gm	%	Mono gm	Poly gm
724	79.0	46.6	72.8	28.2	34	2.6	3	12.3	10.7

SHRIMP AND PEPPER SALAD
Insalata di Gamberi e Peperoni

I use fresh shrimp with their heads still on for this recipe. They are found in New York City in Chinatown or on Ninth Avenue just below 42nd Street. We have also been able to get them in Provincetown, Massachusetts, and in Florida.

We used to buy live shrimp in bait stores in Florida — to our amazement they were cheaper than frozen shrimp. If you are fortunate enough to find whole fresh shrimp, always cook them with their heads on, since the body juices will remain inside the shrimp if it is intact.

It is important to use a very thin pasta so as not to overwhelm this dish—let the pasta serve more as a bridge between the roasted peppers and the shrimp.

Serves 4 as a first course.

1/2 pound shrimp, with shells on
2 large sweet red peppers, about 1 pound*
1/4 pound capellini (break pasta in half)
1 tablespoon coarsely chopped fresh mint
1 teaspoon finely chopped garlic
1 tablespoon finely chopped fresh ginger
4 tablespoons thinly sliced whole scallions
Juice of 1/2 lemon
2 tablespoons extra virgin olive oil
1 teaspoon safflower oil

*Green peppers may be used, but red are better.

Steam the whole shrimp for about 2 minutes; do not overcook—they will be cooked when they turn pink. Let cool, then remove and discard shells and heads.

In the meantime, roast peppers over a gas flame (see instructions for roasting peppers, page 365). When cool, remove charred skin and seeds and slice the peppers. Add peppers to shrimp.

Cook pasta in rapidly boiling water (it will cook in several minutes). Drain.

Add pasta to shrimp and peppers, along with the rest of the ingredients, and gently mix. Serve at room temperature. Do not refrigerate.

Calories	Cholesterol mg	Protein gm	Carbohydrate gm	Total fat gm	%	Sat fat gm	%	Mono gm	Poly gm
975	236.0	48.8	118.3	35.5	32	4.0	4	20.3	5.6

SMOKED FISH SALAD
Insalata di Pesce Affumicato

Any combination of smoked fish will work in this recipe—eel, whitefish, etc.

Serves 4 generously.

1 smoked trout
1/2 pound smoked sturgeon
2 medium potatoes, boiled, cooled, peeled, and sliced
Juice of 1 lemon
1/2 tablespoon good mustard
1 teaspoon small capers
1 tablespoon extra virgin olive oil

2 1/2 teaspoons safflower oil
1/2 cup thinly sliced whole scallions
2 tablespoons finely chopped Italian parsley or
    fresh coriander
Freshly ground black pepper to taste

Skin trout by cutting through it on the back with a sharp knife and then pulling off skin. Remove flesh from bones, cut in pieces, and place in a bowl. Cut sturgeon in pieces 1/4 inch thick and about 1 inch long and discard any bones. Combine with the trout and potatoes. Put lemon juice, mustard, capers, and oils in a small bowl and whip until well blended. Mix the dressing, scallions, parsley or coriander, and black pepper carefully with the fish and serve at room temperature.

Calories	Cholesterol mg	Protein gm	Carbohydrate gm	Total fat gm	%	Sat fat gm	%	Mono gm	Poly gm
1180	339.0	125.0	41.2	55.4	41	9.2	7	16.4	9.3

GREEN BEAN AND SQUID SALAD
Insalata di Fagiolini e Calamari

The two most common squid are summer squid and bone squid. Summer squid are thin, shiny, and have a purple tint to them; the taste is stronger than bone squid. Bone squid are larger, but just as tender. The flesh is white and is thicker, sweeter, and much more desirable than that of summer squid. I might add that summer squid costs less.

We prefer the long Italian or Chinese fresh green beans, which are about 1/4 inch thick and as long as 18 inches. If they aren't available, tender fresh green beans are fine.

Serves 4 to 6.

1 1/2 pounds squid, preferably bone squid
2 crushed bay leaves
2 tablespoons wine vinegar
1 1/2 pounds green beans
2 teaspoons minced garlic
3 tablespoons minced Italian parsley or
    fresh coriander
4 tablespoons olive oil
1 tablespoon safflower oil
2 tablespoons chopped fresh mint
Juice of 1 1/2 to 2 lemons
Freshly ground black pepper to taste
Hot pepper flakes to taste (optional)
Salt to taste

Split open squid, clean, and remove outer skin. Cut off the tentacles below eyes; push out beak. Wash well and place in a medium pot. Cover with water, add bay leaves and vinegar, and boil about 20 minutes, depending on thickness of squid. Drain and allow to cool.

In the meantime, clean beans, pick off ends, and cut into 2-inch pieces. Cook uncovered in boiling salted water until tender but not overcooked. Drain and allow to cool. In the meantime, cut squid in strips ¼ inch wide and about 3 inches long, cutting the tentacles into sections. Mix with the beans and the rest of the ingredients. Serve at room temperature.

Calories	Cholesterol mg	Protein gm	Carbohydrate gm	Total fat gm	%	Sat fat gm	%	Mono gm	Poly gm
924	748.0	57.1	16.6	70.9	68	7.1	7	43.2	10.4

SARDINES IN A VINEGAR SAUCE
Sardelle in Carpione

Every time I have this dish of fresh sardines that are fried and then soaked in a dressing with raisins, I am reminded of the time I was living in Florence as an art student in 1953. Several paintings of mine had been accepted for exhibition in the II Mostra Internazionale Pittura Americana in Bordighera, close to the French border in Liguria, and an American friend, who was also exhibiting, decided to go with me to see the exhibition. In those days I was living on fifty dollars a month, so we hoped to spend as little money as possible.

We took the train to Bordighera, planning, as was usual, to buy tickets on the train. But the conductor never appeared and it wasn't until we passed Genoa that we finally saw him checking and selling tickets. We were almost at our destination, so we decided we could get away with not paying. We managed to avoid the conductor, and were very pleased with ourselves as we stepped down from the train onto the platform of the railroad station in Bordighera.

As we approached the exit gate we saw, to our dismay, a conductor collecting tickets from the passengers. We hurriedly backtracked, walked around the building, and were climbing a gate when we heard, "Signori!" behind us. I turned, and my heart was in my throat as a beautifully uniformed policeman approached us and asked us if we were American. Yes, we were, we said, in the worst Italian we could conjure, hoping to seem ignorant. He asked us to follow him to the stationmaster's office, where we were politely greeted with such questions as, "Are you Americans? Are you artists?" At this point the color returned to my face, because I knew Italians loved artists. Oh yes, yes we are artists (our Italian was returning quickly now). Are you exhibiting in the Bordighera exhibition? Yes we are (by now my Italian was back to normal). "Please wait a moment," he said, and he made a phone call. About five minutes later a very personable man in his late twenties, who introduced himself as the P.R. man of the Bordighera exhibition, arrived. He expressed his delight at meeting us and said the town of Bordighera would be very pleased if we would be its guests. He drove us to a very pleasant pensione then to a restaurant for lunch, explaining that this restaurant was famous for a local specialty he thought we should try. It was served as an appetizer, and it was called sardelle in carpione (called saor in the Genoa area). I have never tasted it since in Italy, but the dish was so good it haunted me for a long time. At that stage of my young life I didn't know enough about cooking to be able to analyze and reproduce it — it was like a miracle, because I had never tasted anything like it before. But finally, in 1970, I came across this ancient recipe — really a way of preserving fish — in an Italian book. To this day I have a very warm place in my heart for the town of Bordighera — more for the recipe and the hospitality than anything else.

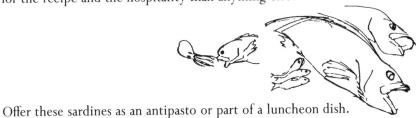

Offer these sardines as an antipasto or part of a luncheon dish.

Serves 4.

2 tablespoons olive or vegetable oil
1 large onion, thinly sliced
1 1/2 cups white wine vinegar
4 tablespoons yellow raisins, soaked in warm water
1 pound fresh sardines
Flour for dredging
Corn oil for frying
Salt and freshly ground black pepper to taste
Hot pepper flakes to taste (optional)

Heat olive or vegetable oil in a medium skillet, then add onion and cook, uncovered, until it begins to brown. Add vinegar and raisins and boil gently for 5 minutes.

In the meantime, dust sardines lightly in flour. In a small skillet heat about 3/4 inch corn oil over high heat. When hot, gently add sardines a few at a time and lightly brown on both sides. Repeat until all fish are fried. Blot on paper towels.

Place a layer of sardines on the bottom of a small deep dish about the length of one of the fish. Pour some of the dressing over fish, add salt, pepper, and pepper flakes if you wish. Repeat, building up layers of fish and sauce until used up. Put in cool place, but do not refrigerate.

Calories	Cholesterol mg	Protein gm	Carbohydrate gm	Total fat gm	%	Sat fat gm	%	Mono gm	Poly gm
1504	495.0	89.4	80.9	95.0	56	13.4	8	24.3	18.1

TRIPE SALAD
Insalata di Trippa

Serve this as an appetizer by itself or as part of an appetizer with roast peppers and stuffed olives or mushrooms.

Serves 4 to 6.

3/4 pound honeycomb tripe
2 bay leaves
1 medium onion with 4 cloves stuck in it
8 peppercorns
Salt to taste
1 small cauliflower
2 tablespoons white wine vinegar
2 teaspoons olive oil
2 teaspoons safflower oil
1 tablespoon finely chopped Italian parsley
1 clove garlic, minced
Salt and freshly ground black pepper to taste

Place the tripe, bay leaves, onion, peppercorns, and salt in a small soup pot and cover with water. Boil gently, covered, about 1 hour. Drain and let tripe cool.

Cut flowerets off main stem of cauliflower and slice the large flowerets in half. Steam or blanch the cauliflower until just tender—do not overcook. Drain and let cool.

When the tripe is cool, slice in strips 1/2 inch wide and 2 inches long. Combine the vinegar, oils, parsley, and garlic; add salt and pepper. Pour dressing over tripe and cauliflower. Mix thoroughly.

Calories	Cholesterol mg	Protein gm	Carbohydrate gm	Total fat gm	%	Sat fat gm	%	Mono gm	Poly gm
674	231.0	78.2	32	25.8	34	5.4	7	11.0	7.5

STUFFED OLIVES ASCOLI STYLE
Olive Farcite all' Ascolana

I have never tasted this recipe anywhere in Italy except Ascoli and its immediate environs, where my mother and father were born. Ascoli is a fascinating city, situated at the end (or the beginning, depending on where you came from) of the most direct route through the Apennine Pass connecting Rome with the Adriatic Sea. This picturesque road is called Via Salaria (The Way of Salt) because the Romans, who built it and named it, harvested salt from the salt beds in the Adriatic. I used to bicycle to Ascoli often when I was living with my relatives as a student, and I found the city unusually beautiful, even by Italian standards.

The food around Ascoli is wonderful and light, especially admired by Romans, who love the mountains and sea around the city. Ascoli is particularly famous for its large green olives, supposedly the best in Italy, known as olive verde Ascolane. In Ascoli they are often served with fried meats and vegetables, but they can be stuffed and offered as an appetizer or simply as an accompaniment to broiled or fried meat.

Serves 4 to 6.

2 tablespoons safflower oil
1/2 onion, finely chopped
1/2 pound lean veal, from leg or shoulder
3/4 pound chicken breast, skin removed
Salt and freshly ground black pepper to taste
3 tablespoons sweet marsala or sherry
1 teaspoon tomato paste
2 tablespoons water
Grated rind of 1 lemon
1 egg white, lightly beaten
1 tablespoon finely chopped Italian parsley
1/2 teaspoon nutmeg
36 large green olives pickled in brine
2 egg whites, lightly beaten
About 1 1/2 cups fresh breadcrumbs
Corn oil or vegetable oil for shallow-frying

Heat the safflower oil in a medium skillet, then add onion, and, as it begins to brown, add veal, chicken, salt, and pepper. Turn up heat and quickly brown chicken and veal. Add marsala, cover, lower heat, and cook several minutes. Remove cover and turn up heat. As wine cooks out, add tomato paste and water. Cover and lower heat and cook about 6 minutes. Scoop out meat, cut in pieces, then put through a grinder along with the onion and juices, or grind up in a food processor.

Place ground meat in a mixing bowl and stir in lemon rind, egg white, parsley, nutmeg, more salt and pepper, and mix well.

Pit olives with a sharp knife by cutting flesh from pit in a continuous strip, much like peeling an orange, so that the flesh is in one piece. Discard pits and soak flesh in cold water for 15 minutes. Take a heaping teaspoon of the stuffing and form into a nutmeg shape. Now stuff each olive by forming the strip of flesh around the filling, then mold the olive back into its original shape. Repeat until all olives are used up.

Roll stuffed olives in beaten egg white, then roll in breadcrumbs. Heat about 1 1/2 inches oil in a small to medium skillet. When oil is hot, carefully place some of the olives — don't crowd them — in oil and lightly brown on all sides. Remove with tongs and blot on paper towels. Repeat.

Serve hot or at room temperature. I prefer them hot.

Calories	Cholesterol mg	Protein gm	Carbohydrate gm	Total fat gm	%	Sat fat gm	%	Mono gm	Poly gm
1751	388.0	144.9	116.4	71.0	36	13.1	7	25.7	21.4

STUFFED MUSHROOMS WITH VEAL AND WALNUTS
Funghi Ripieni

Serves 3 to 6.

6 large mushrooms
¼ cup ground lean veal
2 tablespoons breadcrumbs
½ teaspoon thyme
1 tablespoon ground walnuts or other nuts such as pecans, pine nuts, etc.
3 tablespoons dry sherry or white wine
Salt and freshly ground black pepper to taste
1 tablespoon olive oil mixed with 1 teaspoon safflower oil

Remove the stems from the mushrooms and save for another recipe. Wash and dry caps.

In a small bowl mix veal, breadcrumbs, thyme, ground nuts, 1 teaspoon of the sherry, salt, and pepper. Stuff mushroom caps with this mixture. Place in a small baking dish so that they fit snugly. Pour the rest of the sherry over mushrooms, then sprinkle the oil mixture on top, cover, and bake in a preheated 400° oven about 15 minutes.

Calories	Cholesterol mg	Protein gm	Carbohydrate gm	Total fat gm	%	Sat fat gm	%	Mono gm	Poly gm
496	46.0	20.1	19.2	27.2	48	4.6	8	13.3	8.0

STUFFED MUSHROOMS WITH RAISINS AND SHERRY
Funghi Ripieni

Serves 4 as a vegetable; 2 as a first course.

4 to 6 large mushrooms
1 tablespoon olive oil
1 tablespoon safflower oil
2 tablespoons finely chopped onion
1 tablespoon finely chopped Italian parsley

3 tablespoons breadcrumbs
1 tablespoon yellow raisins
Salt and freshly ground black pepper to taste
Dry sherry

Separate stems from mushroom caps and chop stems. Heat the oils in a small skillet, then add onion and chopped mushroom stems. Sauté over moderate heat until onion begins to brown. Turn off heat. Mix in parsley, breadcrumbs, raisins, salt, and pepper. Stuff mushroom caps with this mixture. Bake mushrooms in a preheated 450° oven about 15 minutes. Sprinkle with dry sherry. Cook another 5 minutes. Serve hot.

Calories	Cholesterol mg	Protein gm	Carbohydrate gm	Total fat gm	%	Sat fat gm	%	Mono gm	Poly gm
376	0	5.6	26.9	28.5	67	3.1	7	12.0	11.5

CAPONATA SICILIAN STYLE
Caponata alla Siciliana

The first time I ever tasted pear in caponata, the famous Sicilian eggplant appetizer, was at the home of an Italian artist friend in Rome, who was an excellent cook. He served caponata with fresh pear on rigatoni and it was excellent (see variation following recipe).

Caponata should be served at room temperature and can be used as an appetizer, part of an appetizer platter, or a vegetable course. It is excellent with broiled meat or fish.

Serves 6.

1 medium to large eggplant, about 1 pound
5 tablespoons olive oil
1 tablespoon safflower oil
Salt and freshly ground pepper to taste
1 cup coarsely chopped celery
2 medium onions, coarsely chopped, about 2 cups
1½ cups coarsely chopped tomatoes, fresh if possible (drain if canned)
4 tablespoons wine vinegar
1 tablespoon sugar
3 tablespoons pine nuts
4 tablespoons capers
7 green olives, rinsed in cold water, sliced, and pitted
1 ripe firm pear, cut into ¾-inch pieces
7-ounce can Italian-style* tunafish (optional)

*Italian-style tunafish is packed in olive oil. If you use American-style, packed in water, drain off water and mix in 1 tablespoon olive oil.

Peel eggplant with a sharp knife and cut in ¾-inch slices. Heat 3 tablepoons olive oil and 1 tablespoon safflower oil in a medium to large skillet. Add eggplant, salt, and pepper. Cook over high heat, stirring often until edges of eggplant begin to brown.

Remove eggplant with a slotted spoon. Add 2 tablespoons more olive oil to the skillet and, when hot, add celery. Cook over medium heat about 5 minutes. Add onions and continue cooking until onion edges begin to brown. Add tomatoes, salt, and pepper, cover, and cook over medium heat about 6 or 7 minutes. Return eggplant to skillet and simmer covered over low heat about 5 minutes.

In the meantime, heat vinegar in a small saucepan, add sugar, and mix. Add pine nuts, capers, and sliced green olives and cook about 30 seconds; then add to eggplant mixture. Cover and simmer 5 minutes, stirring occasionally. Add pear and cook 3 or 4 minutes.

A can of tuna packed in oil, simply broken up, can be added to the caponata if you like.

Variation: If you want to use this recipe on pasta, I suggest using 2 cups tomatoes instead of 1½ cups. It would be sufficient for 1½ to 2 pounds pasta, enough for 8 servings.

Calories	Cholesterol mg	Protein gm	Carbohydrate gm	Total fat gm	%	Sat fat gm	%	Mono gm	Poly gm
1327	0	22.6	107.1	94.7	63	10.9	7	57.6	17.1
with tuna:									
1897	108.0	70.5	107.1	135.3	63	17.7	8	59.3	32.8

EGGPLANT APPETIZER
Antipasto di Melanzane

Serves 4.

¼ cup oil (2 tablespoons safflower oil,
   2 tablespoons olive oil)
1 medium eggplant, cut into ½-inch cubes
1 medium onion, chopped
1 sweet red pepper, chopped
16-ounce can tomatoes, or 1 pound fresh tomatoes
3 cloves garlic, minced
½ cup chopped Italian parsley
¼ cup lemon juice
¼ cup lime juice
½ teaspoon nutmeg
Hot pepper flakes to taste
Salt to taste
1 teaspoon basil
1 teaspoon dried oregano

1 teaspoon marjoram
1 teaspoon thyme
1 teaspoon rosemary

Heat oils in a skillet; then brown eggplant cubes. Remove with a slotted spoon and reserve. Add onion and pepper to the skillet and sauté over moderate heat, uncovered, until onion is translucent.

Return eggplant to skillet along with the tomatoes, 2 of the minced garlic cloves, parsley, lemon juice, lime juice, nutmeg, and hot pepper flakes. Cover and simmer 15 minutes, stirring occasionally. Add the remaining clove of chopped garlic, salt, and herbs and cook 5 more minutes.

Serve at room temperature with toasted bread.

Calories	Cholesterol mg	Protein gm	Carbohydrate gm	Total fat gm	%	Sat fat gm	%	Mono gm	Poly gm
851	0	17.6	151.8	58.8	61	6.0	6	23.0	22.4

"LITTLE ORANGES"—RICE BALLS
Arancini

These can be bought on boats and trains all over southern Italy—like hotdogs. Here I serve them with a sauce or wedges of lemon as an attractive first course. There is another arancini recipe in the rice chapter (page 166).

Serves 2; 4 balls.

2 tablespoons minced Italian parsley
1 egg white, lightly whipped
3 tablespoons marinara sauce (page 430)
Salt and fresh ground black pepper to taste
2 cups cooked rice (page 160)
Breadcrumbs
2 egg whites, lightly beaten
Corn oil for shallow-frying

Mix the parsley, the lightly whipped egg white, marinara sauce, salt, and pepper with the rice. Take one quarter of the rice mixture and form into a ball, working breadcrumbs and some of the beaten egg whites into the ball as you are shaping it. Keep working breadcrumbs in until the ball firms up. Make 3 more with the remaining rice mixture.

Heat 3/4 inch corn oil in a small skillet. When oil is hot, gently put in balls. Turn gently with tongs and fry until balls are golden brown on all sides. Blot on paper towels. Serve hot. Additional sauce or lemon wedges may be served with arancini.

Calories	Cholesterol mg	Protein gm	Carbohydrate gm	Total fat gm	%	Sat fat gm	%	Mono gm	Poly gm
620	0	21.5	112.8	7.4	11	0.7	1	2.5	2.6

PINZIMONIO

This is the only dip served with raw vegetables in our home. It is usually accompanied by other antipasto. I think you will find this simple sauce most refreshing with celery and fennel.

Serves 3.

Celery and fennel stalks, cut into manageable sections
4 tablespoons extra virgin olive oil
1 teaspoon safflower oil
1 tablespoon kosher salt or 2 teaspoons table salt
1 teaspoon freshly ground black pepper
Juice of 1/2 lemon (optional)

Chill the celery and fennel in ice water.

Combine all the ingredients for the sauce in a small deep bowl and mix thoroughly.

The dip is usually placed in a common bowl, but small individual bowls may be used instead. Simply dip celery and fennel pieces into the sauce and munch.

Calories	Cholesterol mg	Protein gm	Carbohydrate gm	Total fat gm	%	Sat fat gm	%	Mono gm	Poly gm
521	0	0.2	–	58.6	99	6.4	11	41.9	6.9

OPEN–FACED OMELET WITH ASPARAGUS AND SPINACH
Frittata di Asparagi

I admit I was prejudiced about Egg Beaters (I couldn't believe that a substitute product for eggs could be good—and the name put me off), but Dick Wolff asked me to try them and I was surprised to find the results most satisfying. A frittata made with Egg Beaters is not as good as one made with fresh eggs—the texture is different and the taste a little bland—but we enjoyed this dish and recommend it.

Good as an appetizer, it also makes an excellent lunch with crusty bread and a green salad.

Serves 4.

4 tablespoons olive oil
1 teaspoon safflower oil
2 medium onions, sliced, about 2 cups
3 cups fresh asparagus cut into 1-inch pieces
4 cups fresh spinach, about 1/2 pound,
    washed and chopped*

2 8½-ounce containers Egg Beaters (equivalent of
   8 large eggs), defrosted
Salt and freshly ground black pepper to taste

*Any combination of vegetables can be used in a frittata —
eggplant, zucchini, potatoes, peppers, etc. Just be certain the
vegetables are cooked before you mix them with the eggs.

Heat 2 tablespoons of the olive oil and the safflower oil in a medium skillet, add onions, and cook several minutes. Add asparagus and cook, uncovered, over medium heat about 5 minutes. Add spinach, cover, and cook about 5 minutes. Remove vegetables with a slotted spoon. Let cool, then mix in with defrosted Egg Beaters and salt and freshly ground black pepper to taste. Heat remaining 2 tablespoons olive oil in skillet, then pour in vegetable-and-egg mixture. Lower heat and cover.

Cook 12 to 15 minutes, or until eggs are cooked. The proper way to make a frittata is to flip it over after 6 or 7 minutes. However, I don't recommend trying this with Egg Beaters, since they are looser in texture than eggs. Cut the frittata in wedges and serve hot or at room temperature.

Calories	Cholesterol mg	Protein gm	Carbohydrate gm	Total fat gm	%	Sat fat gm	%	Mono gm	Poly gm
1047	0	70.4	67.6	59.8	50	6.3	5	41.8	6.9

FAVA BEAN APPETIZER
Antipasto di Fave

The best way to serve this fava bean appetizer is in a small bowl or as a garnish. To eat fava beans you have to remove the tough outer skin, but everyone does this at table and then enjoys the tender bean. Offer at room temperature.

Serves 6 to 8.

4 cups dried fava beans (broad beans), soaked overnight
2 cloves garlic, skins on
2 bay leaves
1 stalk celery with leaves, cut into 3 sections
1 small onion
Salt and freshly ground black pepper to taste
3 tablespoons olive oil
1 tablespoon safflower oil
Hot pepper flakes to taste
½ cup good wine vinegar
1 tablespoon coarsely chopped garlic
1 cup broth reserved from beans

Drain fava beans. Put in a soup pot (an earthenware pot is best) with garlic cloves, bay leaves, celery, onion, pinch of salt and pepper, and cover with about 1 ½ inches cold water. Simmer over low heat for 2 ½ to 3 hours. Let cool. In the meantime, make sauce by mixing the oils with the pepper flakes, black pepper, vinegar, and garlic.

Drain beans and reserve 1 cup of the liquid (the rest of broth can be used as a soup). Stir into the sauce.

Place fava beans in a deep container. Add sauce and let marinate at least 3 hours or, even better, overnight.

Calories	Cholesterol mg	Protein gm	Carbohydrate gm	Total fat gm	%	Sat fat gm	%	Mono gm	Poly gm
2426	0	142.5	341.3	63.6	23	6.6	2	31.3	13.4

WALNUT SPREAD ON GRILLED BREAD
Crostini con l'Aglio

As an appetizer, serve about 3 to a plate. But crostini are also good as a garnish for broiled fish and meats.

Serves 2.

10 walnuts, shelled and coarsely chopped
1 teaspoon chopped garlic
1 tablespoon olive oil
1 tablespoon safflower oil
1 tablespoon chopped Italian parsley (optional)
Salt and freshly ground black pepper to taste
6 small slices Italian or French bread

Put all ingredients except bread in a food processor and purée, or crush to a pastelike consistency with a mortar and pestle.

Toast bread, spread on walnut paste, and broil under preheated broiler until paste begins to brown. Serve warm.

Calories	Cholesterol mg	Protein gm	Carbohydrate gm	Total fat gm	%	Sat fat gm	%	Mono gm	Poly gm
673	0	11.6	40.6	53.3	70	4.8	6	15.3	27.1

ROMAN GARLIC BREAD I
Bruschetta

The garlic bread that is commonly served in America (bread heated with butter and garlic) to my knowledge is never served in Italy. We much prefer bruschetta to the American version of garlic bread, and serve it as an appetizer or in the place of bread.

Serves 4.

4 slices good crusty bread
1 tablespoon extra virgin olive oil mixed with
   1 teaspoon safflower oil
1 clove fresh garlic

Toast bread to a golden brown on both sides. Spread oil on one side of the bread, then rub with garlic.

Calories	Cholesterol mg	Protein gm	Carbohydrate gm	Total fat gm	%	Sat fat gm	%	Mono gm	Poly gm
553	0	13.4	71.3	23.4	37	2.8	4	12.8	5.3

ROMAN GARLIC BREAD II
Bruschetta

This bruschetta recipe is popular in Rome and is often served where pizza is offered. Obviously, it is best when garden-fresh tomatoes are available.

Serves 2 to 4.

4 medium slices French or Italian bread
1 clove garlic, more if necessary
1 tablespoon olive oil* mixed with 1 teaspoon
   safflower oil
1 medium firm ripe tomato, thinly sliced
Salt and freshly ground black pepper to taste

*A good rich olive oil, such as Saica brand or Madre Sicilia.

Cut bread slices about 1/2 inch thick. Toast bread to a golden brown on both sides.
   Rub one side of bread with garlic. Place slices of toasted bread, garlic side up, on a tray. Spoon oil on bread slices, add tomato slices, salt, and pepper, and return to broiler to heat close to the flame for about 1 minute. Serve immediately.

Calories	Cholesterol mg	Protein gm	Carbohydrate gm	Total fat gm	%	Sat fat gm	%	Mono gm	Poly gm
566	0	15.1	77.7	23.7	37	2.8	4	12.8	5.3

II   SOUPS

If I had to select a favorite daily food, it would be soup, especially hot soup. For me a bowl of soup acts as a tranquilizer, relaxing my insides much the way a hot bath relaxes my muscles and preparing me in a wonderful way for the food to come. I have read that some cardiologists claim hot soup is good for the heart because it relaxes the digestive system, allowing the heart to work at a more leisurely pace, and I believe this. We all know the medicinal value of a good hot, clear beef, chicken, or fish broth when illness strikes.

The variety of Italian soups is endless, and many of them are prepared without fat of any kind. My mother made excellent soups, as did my aunts in Italy. Her favorite was clear chicken or beef broth made mostly with bones. I remember that one day when she was busy in the kitchen, she asked me to add some salt to the soup, which was gently boiling on the stove. I knew she hadn't tasted the soup, so I asked her how she knew it needed salt. Her reply was simple and direct: "Can't you smell it?"

She was always extremely careful to skim off all the fat from her soup. To strain it she used a linen cap she had made that fit perfectly over the strainer.

When using pasta or rice in soup, cook the pasta or rice in a separate pot of boiling water, then drain, and spoon portions into individual soup bowls before adding the hot broth. Or if you are cooking the pasta or rice in the soup, add exact amounts in proportion to the number of cups of soup you will be serving and time the cooking so the soup is ready to serve as soon as the pasta or rice is done. In other words, the pasta and rice should not be allowed to sit in the soup—there is nothing more unpleasant than tasting overcooked pasta or rice in a soup. If you have any clear broth left over, keep it refrigerated and boil it for about 15 minutes every three days. This will kill the bacteria and the broth will keep for a long time. Needless to say, if pasta or rice is in the broth, it will become a gelatinous mess.

When adding salt to soup, use it sparingly in the beginning, then taste for salt toward the end of the cooking and correct the seasoning if necessary. Because there is a certain amount of evaporation during cooking, if you don't undersalt at the start, your broth will inevitably be too salty when it has cooked down. E.G.

Folklore contains some truths of which "medical science" has no satisfactory understanding. I do not for a moment believe that soup is good for the heart because it relaxes the digestive system; nor do I for a moment doubt the medicinal power with which Ed's Italian mother and my Jewish mother endowed it. It is soothing and warming, it pleases the palate, it permits the recapture of nutrients that might otherwise drain away, it provides water and needed salts, and it tends to sterilize things cooked in it. And its whole is greater than the sum of its parts. R.W.

CHICKEN BROTH
Brodo di Pollo

The best soup is made from old laying hens or roosters. The Italians like to quote a saying that, like most sayings, has a double meaning. *"Pollo vecchio fa buon brodo"* — "Old chickens make good soup."

I always use the juice of a fresh lemon in beef or chicken broth before serving. It enhances the broth and takes the place of grated cheese.

Yields about 2 1/2 quarts.

3- to 4-pound chicken, preferably a soup chicken
4 quarts water
2 carrots (optional)
2 large onions
2 stalks celery
2 bay leaves
1 leek, washed
Salt and freshly ground black pepper to taste
Juice of 1 lemon

Truss the chicken and put it with all other ingredients except lemon juice into a large pot and simmer gently for 2 1/2 to 3 hours, skimming the surface often. Remove chicken* and set aside. Remove vegetables and set aside. The vegetables can be served with the chicken or discarded. The fat must be removed from soup. Either chill broth until it jells and remove fat from top or strain hot broth through a clean white cloth. The soup is now ready to be used as stock or consommé. Add lemon juice after fat is removed and check seasoning for salt and pepper.

Variation: For a sweeter taste, add 2 carrots and 2 parsnips.

*Chicken can be served after soup course or on a different occasion. Serve it with one of the sauces for boiled meat on pages 427–42.

Provided the fat is carefully removed, the small amount of nutrients can be disregarded, so you need not be concerned with the calorie, cholesterol, and fat content in this recipe.

CHICKEN DUMPLING SOUP
Brodo di Gnocchetti di Pollo

Serves 4.

1 cup finely chopped cooked chicken
2 egg whites
1 tablespoon grated lemon rind
1/2 teaspoon nutmeg
2 tablespoons minced Italian parsley
Salt and freshly ground black pepper to taste
Flour
2 quarts chicken broth
Juice of 1/2 lemon

Mix the chopped chicken, egg whites, lemon rind, nutmeg, parsley, salt, and pepper together in a bowl. After mixing well, shape dumplings about 1 1/2 inches long and roll them in flour.

In the meantime, bring broth to a gentle boil, then add lemon juice and half the dumplings, spooning them in one at a time. Cover and simmer about 3 to 4 minutes.

Remove 3 or 4 dumplings with a slotted spoon, place in a soup dish, pour broth over dumplings, and keep warm while you cook the remaining dumplings in the same way.

Calories	Cholesterol mg	Protein gm	Carbohydrate gm	Total fat gm	%	Sat fat gm	%	Mono gm	Poly gm
355	111.0	54.4	15.1	7.5	19	2.2	5	2.6	1.4

ROMAN EGG DROP SOUP
Straciatella alla Romana

The original recipe includes whole eggs and grated cheese. I have omitted the egg yolks and cheese and find the recipe to be lighter and quite delicious.

Serves 3.

4 cups chicken broth
2 cups chopped and washed fresh spinach
2 egg whites, beaten
1 tablespoon grated lemon rind
Salt and freshly ground black pepper to taste

Bring broth to a boil. Add spinach and boil gently for several minutes. Mix egg whites with lemon rind and salt and pepper. Lower heat, stir in egg whites, and cook for a minute so the egg whites set.

Calories	Cholesterol	Protein	Carbohydrate	Total fat		Sat fat		Mono	Poly
	mg	gm	gm	gm	%	gm	%	gm	gm
66	0	10.9	5.7	0.4	5	–	–	–	–

DUCK SOUP
Brodo di Anitra

Serves 8.

1 fresh duck, about 5 pounds, minus breast*
2 medium white turnips
2 stalks celery
2 large carrots, scraped
2 bay leaves
1 large leek or 2 small ones
1 medium onion
Salt and freshly ground black pepper to taste

*With a sharp knife remove breasts and reserve (use for duck breast recipe, page 284).

Put duck in a soup pot, cover with about 2 inches cold water. Add the rest of the ingredients, cover, and bring to a boil. Lower heat to a steady boil and cook about 2 to 2½ hours. Let cool, drain. Set duck aside. When cool, separate fat and bones from meat. Return meat and carrots, turnips, and leeks to pot, discarding onions and celery. Remove fat from broth; the easiest way is to allow fat to congeal by putting soup in refrigerator overnight. Skim off fat and discard.

Cooked rice or fine pasta can be added to broth.

Calories	Cholesterol	Protein	Carbohydrate	Total fat		Sat fat		Mono	Poly
	mg	gm	gm	gm	%	gm	%	gm	gm
794	239.0	73.8	61.4	25.7	28	5.9	7	5.9	5.9

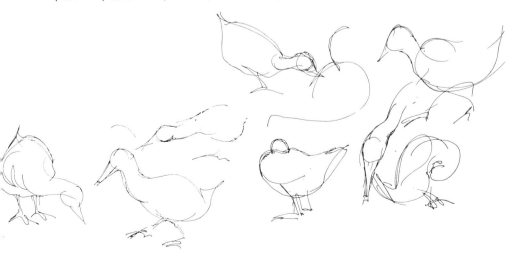

SOUP SPRING STYLE
Zuppa Primavera

This recipe is best when all the ingredients are fresh — they are all spring vegetables, hence the name.

Serves 4 to 6.

1 tablespoon olive oil
1 tablespoon safflower oil or 2 tablespoons peanut oil
1/2 cup finely chopped onion
1 cup chopped tomatoes, fresh if possible (drain if canned)
1 tablespoon finely chopped Italian parsley
4 cups water
1 cup fresh shelled peas, about 3/4 pound
1 cup diced potatoes, about 1/2 inch square
4 tablespoons Carolina long-grain rice
1 1/2 cups asparagus cut into 1-inch pieces
1 cup coarsely chopped whole scallions
Salt and freshly ground black pepper to taste

Heat the two oils in a medium pot. Add onion and sauté until it begins to brown. Add tomatoes and cook over moderate heat about 5 minutes. Add parsley and water, cover, and bring to a boil. Add peas and potatoes. Boil gently for about 5 minutes. Add rice and cook about 6 minutes. Add asparagus, scallions, salt, and pepper, and boil gently until rice is done — about 5 to 6 more minutes.

Calories	Cholesterol mg	Protein gm	Carbohydrate gm	Total fat gm	%	Sat fat gm	%	Mono gm	Poly gm
859	0	27.7	130.1	29.4	30	3.0	3	11.5	11.2

FRESH PEA SOUP
Minestra con Piselli Freschi

The beauty of this recipe is its simplicity and delicate springlike taste. It has been a favorite in our home since my childhood. Only fresh peas should be used. The pasta that is usually used in this dish is a small square egg noodle about 1/4 inch square and called quadretti, "little squares." I have replaced the quadretti with a pasta made from semolina with no eggs.

Serves 6.

3 tablespoons olive oil
1 tablespoon safflower oil
1 medium onion, chopped
1 stalk celery, chopped

1 cup peeled, seeded, and chopped fresh tomatoes
1 carrot, chopped
5 cups water
1 tablespoon fresh basil or 1 teaspoon dried
2 cups fresh peas, about 2 pounds unshelled
Salt and freshly ground black pepper to taste
5 tablespoons small pasta, such as coralini or stellette
1 tablespoon chopped Italian parsley

Heat the two oils. Add onion and, when it wilts, add celery and sauté until onion begins to brown. Add tomatoes and cook over moderate heat 5 minutes. Add carrot, water, and basil. Cook, covered, over moderate heat 20 minutes.

In the meantime, shell the fresh peas and add to broth. Cover and cook about 20 minutes. Add salt and black pepper to taste.

Add pasta and parsley. Cook pasta until al dente, and serve.

Calories	Cholesterol mg	Protein gm	Carbohydrate gm	Total fat gm	%	Sat fat gm	%	Mono gm	Poly gm
999	0	28.6	103.3	56.7	50	5.5	5	32.8	12.6

ABOUT MINESTRONE

People often ask me for the "classic" minestrone recipe, but there is none. Every region, every city, every town, and practically every family in Italy has its own version. In Genoa, for instance, pesto is used in the traditional regional minestrone. Ada Boni, in *Il Talismano della Felicita,* gives us thirty-one different minestrone recipes. The combinations and variations of vegetables used in minestrone are endless. The important factor, and the deciding factor, in making a good minestrone is that fresh seasonal vegetables be used, so, naturally, the ingredients of minestrone will change with the seasons.

SPRING MINESTRONE
Minestrone di Primavera

This light soup can be made with a variety of vegetables, such as asparagus, lima beans, green beans, etc.

Serves 6.

1 tablespoon olive oil
1 tablespoon safflower oil or 2 teaspoons vegetable oil
1/2 cup coarsely chopped onion
1/2 cup coarsely chopped tomatoes,
    fresh if possible (drain if canned)
1/2 cup chopped carrots
1 cup chopped green cabbage
1 cup peas, fresh if possible
4 cups water
3 whole scallions, chopped
1/2 cup diced potatoes
1 cup coarsely chopped mushrooms (optional)
1 tablespoon chopped Italian parsley
1 teaspoon basil
Salt and freshly ground black pepper to taste
Pasta or rice (optional)

Heat the oils in a small soup pot, then add onion. Cook, uncovered, over moderate heat. When onion begins to brown, add tomatoes. Cook for several minutes, then add the rest of the ingredients except pasta or rice. Cover and boil gently 20 to 25 minutes.

At this point small pasta, such as tiny shells or tubettini, or rice may be added. First cook pasta or rice in a separate pot. When cooked, drain and put some in the bottom of each soup plate. Ladle soup over pasta or rice.

Calories	Cholesterol	Protein	Carbohydrate	Total fat		Sat fat		Mono	Poly
	mg	gm	gm	gm	%	gm	%	gm	gm
544	0	17.2	57.3	29.2	47	3.0	5	11.5	11.2

ZUCCHINI SOUP
Minestra di Zucchini

This delicate soup can be made with rice or very thin pasta (angel's hair) instead of croutons.

Serves 4.

6 cups chicken or beef broth
1 tablespoon minced Italian parsley
1 tablespoon chopped fresh basil

2 cups diced zucchini
1 cup fresh corn, about 1 ear corn
Salt and freshly ground black pepper to taste
3 cups toasted croutons
4 egg whites, lightly beaten

Bring the stock to a boil, then add parsley, basil, zucchini, corn, salt, and pepper. Boil gently about 10 minutes, until corn is cooked. Meanwhile, sauté cubes of fresh or stale bread in a little vegetable oil till golden all over. Remove to a plate.

Lightly beat the egg whites, then add them to the soup. Mix and boil gently for several minutes. Turn off heat and let soup set for several minutes. Ladle soup into soup bowls, top with croutons.

Calories	Cholesterol mg	Protein gm	Carbohydrate gm	Total fat gm	%	Sat fat gm	%	Mono gm	Poly gm
918	0	31.1	86	52.6	50	6.0	6	30.5	8.4

If 4 angel's hair nests are substituted for the croutons and oil, the figures are:

624	0	35.6	116.5	3.2	5	–	–	–	–

GREEN VEGETABLE SOUP
Minestrone Verde

Serves 6.

1/2 cup chopped green cabbage
1 medium onion, chopped
1/2 cup chopped celery
1/2 cup chopped broccoli
1/2 cup green beans cut into 1-inch pieces
1/2 cup diced zucchini
2 tablespoons chopped Italian parsley
2 tablespoons chopped fresh basil
4 cups water
1 medium potato, diced
2 tablespoons olive oil
1 tablespoon safflower oil
Salt and freshly ground black pepper to taste
1/2 cup ditalini pasta or other small-cut pasta
2 tablespoons pesto (page 426)

Put all ingredients except the pasta and pesto in a pot and bring to a boil. Cover and boil gently about 1 hour. Add pesto and turn off the heat.

Bring a large pot of water to a boil, add the pasta, and cook until al dente—do not overcook. Drain and rinse in cold water. Add to the minestrone. Serve at room temperature with garlic bread (page 39).

Calories	Cholesterol mg	Protein gm	Carbohydrate gm	Total fat gm	%	Sat fat gm	%	Mono gm	Poly gm
934	0	19.1	101	52.4	49	5.8	5	27.4	14.5

MINESTRONE GENOA STYLE I
Minestrone alla Genovese

A summer soup to be served at room temperature.

Serves 4 to 6.

1 1/2 quarts water
1 carrot, chopped
1 stalk celery, diced
1/2 cup fresh shelled cranberry beans (shell beans)
1/2 cup green beans cut into 1-inch pieces
1 cup chopped green cabbage
1 small onion, chopped
Salt and freshly ground black pepper to taste
1/2 cup fresh shelled fava beans (broad beans) or green peas*
1/2 cup diced zucchini
1/2 cup diced potatoes
1/2 cup tubettini pasta or small elbows
2 to 3 teaspoons pesto (page 426)

*Lima beans or "lady peas" (page 364) may also be substituted for the fava beans.

Put water and all the vegetables except fava beans or peas, zucchini, and potatoes in a soup pot. Add salt and pepper, cover, and boil gently about 1 hour. In the meantime, blanch fava beans (or peas) in boiling water. Remove tough outer skin from fava beans and discard. Add fava beans (or peas), zucchini, and potatoes to soup. Continue cooking 5 or 6 minutes. Add pasta and cook until it is al dente, about 7 minutes. Add pesto and mix well. Turn off the heat and allow to cool. Serve at room temperature.

Calories	Cholesterol mg	Protein gm	Carbohydrate gm	Total fat gm	%	Sat fat gm	%	Mono gm	Poly gm
547	0	23.3	100.5	5.4	9	0.4	1	2.0	0.8

MINESTRONE GENOA STYLE II
Minestrone alla Genovese

Serve this soup at room temperature with garlic bread (page 39).

Serves 4.

4 cups water
1/2 cup fresh shelled cranberry beans (shell beans) or
   1/2 cup dried white beans soaked in water overnight
1/2 cup chopped celery
2 cups chopped green cabbage
1 cup sliced white turnips
1 medium potato, peeled and cut into 1/2-inch cubes
1 medium tomato, chopped
Salt and freshly ground black pepper to taste
2 teaspoons pesto (page 426)

Place all the ingredients except the pesto in a soup pot, cover, and boil gently about 1 hour.

Purée the soup by putting it through a food mill or food processor. Correct the seasoning and let the soup cool.

Blend the pesto into the soup well and serve.

Calories	Cholesterol mg	Protein gm	Carbohydrate gm	Total fat gm	%	Sat fat gm	%	Mono gm	Poly gm
362	0	15.8	62.3	5.1	12	0.4	1	2.0	0.8

FAVA BEAN AND ZUCCHINI SOUP
Zuppa di Fave e Zucchini

Serves 4 to 6.

1 tablespoon olive oil
1 tablespoon safflower oil
1 medium onion, finely chopped
4 tablespoons minced tomatoes
1 tablespoon chopped Italian parsley
4 cups water
2 cups fresh fava beans (broad beans)
   (canned may be used)
1/2 cup thinly sliced whole scallions
1 medium potato, peeled and cut into 1/2-inch cubes
1/3 cup finely chopped celery with greens
1 cup diced zucchini
2 tablespoons chopped fresh basil or 1 teaspoon dried
4 tablespoons rice
Salt and freshly ground black pepper to taste

Garnish: Finely chopped Italian parsley

Heat the two oils in a medium soup pot and add onion. When onion wilts, add tomatoes and parsley. Cover and cook over low heat about 5 minutes. Add water, fava beans, scallions, potato, and celery. Cover and boil gently about 20 minutes. Add zucchini, basil, rice, salt, and pepper, cover, and cook, stirring frequently, until rice is tender but not overcooked.

Garnish with finely chopped Italian parsley.

Calories	Cholesterol mg	Protein gm	Carbohydrate gm	Total fat gm	%	Sat fat gm	%	Mono gm	Poly gm
946	0	34.2	134.1	29.5	27	1.5	1	10.3	0.9

RUCOLA SOUP
Minestra di Rughetta

Rucola, or rocket as it is known to the seed growers, is very easy to grow. Plant in early spring, plant second planting in summer, and third planting in September. It will die only in a hard freeze. Rucola has a peppery flavor and is most commonly used in salads. It is mildest in the late spring, strongest in midsummer. Judge the quantity of rucola used according to the intensity of taste. The amount called for here is for the mild variety.

Serves 6 to 8.

4 tablespoons olive oil
2 tablespoons safflower oil
2 medium onions, chopped
2 cloves garlic, chopped
4 cups tightly packed rucola (arugola), stems and all
6 1/2 cups water
4 1/2 cups cubed potatoes
Salt and freshly ground black pepper to taste

Heat the two oils in a pot, then add onions. When onions wilt, add garlic. Before garlic takes on color, add the rest of the ingredients. Bring to a boil, cover, lower heat, and simmer about 20 minutes. Put in a blender or food processor and purée.

Calories	Cholesterol mg	Protein gm	Carbohydrate gm	Total fat gm	%	Sat fat gm	%	Mono gm	Poly gm
1419	0	23.8	153.7	82.9	51	8.2	5	45.2	23.2

SCALLOP SOUP
Zuppa di Canestrelli

Serves 6 to 8.

1 tablespoon safflower oil or 3 teaspoons peanut oil
2 tablespoons olive oil
1 medium onion, finely chopped
2 cloves garlic, minced

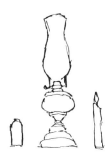

2 tablespoons finely chopped Italian parsley
1/2 cup dry white wine (optional)
6 cups water
1 bay leaf
1 stalk celery with leaves, cut into 3-inch lengths
1 medium leek, washed and cut into 3-inch lengths
2 pounds fresh fish frames and/or fish heads from
     haddock, cod, striped bass, red snapper, etc.,
     washed, gills removed
3/4 cup rice or fine pasta
3 cups broccoli, cut into bite-sized flowerets
1 pound sea scallops, washed and cut into bite-sized pieces
Juice of 1/2 lemon
Salt and freshly ground black pepper to taste

Garnish: Thinly sliced scallions

To make fish stock, heat the two oils in a medium soup pot, then add onion. When onion begins to brown, add garlic, then parsley and wine. Cover and simmer about 5 minutes. Add water, bay leaf, celery, leeks, and fish frames and/or heads. Cover and boil gently about 30 minutes. Remove fish and strain broth.*

Return broth to the soup pot, bring to a boil, and add rice or pasta; cook about 5 minutes. Add broccoli, scallops, lemon juice, salt, and pepper. Cover and continue cooking over low heat until rice is cooked. Serve hot, garnishing each plate of soup with thinly sliced scallions.

*Remove flesh from fish head or frame and return to soup for a thicker soup or reserve and make fish salad. Use one of fish sauces on fish (see pages 427–42).

Calories	Cholesterol mg	Protein gm	Carbohydrate gm	Total fat gm	%	Sat fat gm	%	Mono gm	Poly gm
933	159.0	84.0	136.2	1.9	2	4.8	5	21.4	12.3

The calculation does not include flesh from head or frame.

SCALLOP AND PEA SOUP
Canestrelli e Piselli in Brodo

Serves 6.

8 cups fish stock (see preceding recipe)
2 cups fresh or frozen peas
1/2 cup rice
1/2 pound scallops (sea scallops will do; cut large scallops
     into 1/4-inch slices)
2 tablespoons chopped Italian parsley or fresh coriander
Juice of 1/2 lemon

Bring stock to a boil, then add peas. When stock returns to a boil, add rice. Stir and boil gently about 6 minutes.

Add scallops, parsley, and lemon juice. Cover and cook until rice is tender.

Calories	Cholesterol mg	Protein gm	Carbohydrate gm	Total fat gm	%	Sat fat gm	%	Mono gm	Poly gm
884	80.0	67.8	145.5	2.6	3	–	–	–	–

LOBSTER SOUP
Brodo di Aragosta

This is a most satisfying soup, which we enjoy as a special dividend when we make lobster américaine. The broth can be served clear or with rice or thin pasta. The thin pasta we generally use is called capellini, or thin hair, which usually comes in small flat balls. One ball per serving is about right. If you want to use rice, 2 tablespoons rice per person is fine. The broth can also be used as a stock, particularly for making risotto.

Yields 10 cups, serving 6 as soup.

Shells and juices from lobster américaine
   (page 188)
1 leek, washed and cut in 3-inch lengths
1 medium onion
2 bay leaves
1 stalk celery, cut into 3-inch lengths
1 medium carrot
Very little salt
2 teaspoons chopped Italian parsley
2 quarts water
6 nests capellini or 12 tablespoons rice

Put all ingredients except capellini or rice in a soup pot. Bring to a boil, cover, and boil gently 2 hours.

Drain, discarding the solid ingredients, and return the broth to the pot to heat.

Put pasta nests in the boiling broth, stir, and cook until the nests have opened up—about 2 minutes. To serve, scoop pasta out of the soup into warm bowls and ladle the soup on top. Serve with a fork and spoon.

If using rice, sprinkle it into the boiling broth, cover, and simmer about 10 minutes, until rice is done.

Calories	Cholesterol mg	Protein gm	Carbohydrate gm	Total fat gm	%	Sat fat gm	%	Mono gm	Poly gm
558	0	18.9	113.7	1.8	3	–	–	–	–

SKATE WING SOUP
Zuppa di Razza

Skate resembles a ray fish, with a pencillike body with two flat wings attached that are covered with a tough skin, which must be removed by the fishmonger. The wing is about 1½ inches thick at its thickest, and that is the only part of the skate used.

Serves 4.

1 medium onion, chopped
2 tablespoons minced Italian parsley
2 tablespoons olive oil
1 tablespoon safflower oil
2 cloves garlic, chopped
1 cup peeled and chopped fresh tomatoes
6 cups water
1 skate wing (approximately 1 pound), top skin removed
    and meat cut into 3-inch pieces
1½ pounds fresh peas, about 1¾ cups (frozen may be used)
Fine pasta, such as capellini, 1 nest per person,
    or ⅓ cup rice
Salt and freshly ground black pepper to taste

Sauté onion and parsley in the two oils in a medium soup pot until onion becomes translucent. Add garlic, sauté for several minutes, stirring occasionally. Add tomatoes, bring to a boil, then add water and skate. Bring to a boil, add peas, and cook gently 30 minutes. Remove skate, keep warm, and add capellini or rice. Cook until al dente. Add salt and pepper to taste. Put some pasta or rice in each soup plate, add some skate, and pour broth on top. Serve with a spoon and fork.

Variation: Instead of peas, use cauliflower, cut into bite-sized pieces, and cook 10 minutes along with 2 cups small pasta in the soup (omitting the capellini).

Calories	Cholesterol mg	Protein gm	Carbohydrate gm	Total fat gm	%	Sat fat gm	%	Mono gm	Poly gm
1190	83.0	66.5	131	44.7	33	4.8	4	21.4	12.3

FISH SOUP
Zuppa di Pesce

Serves 4.

4 tablespoons olive oil
2 teaspoons safflower oil
1 medium onion, coarsely chopped
2 cloves garlic, finely chopped
3 cups chopped tomatoes, fresh if possible
    (drain if canned)
1 tablespoon chopped fresh oregano or
    1 teaspoon dried
1 tablespoon chopped fresh mint
2 tablespoons finely chopped Italian parsley
Hot pepper flakes to taste (optional)
1½ pounds white fish, such as red snapper,
    bass, cod, etc.
½ cup dry white wine
1½ pounds monkfish, cut into 2-inch pieces*
12 mussels, scrubbed
8 cherrystone clams
½ pound shrimp, with shells on
2 cups fresh bread cut into ½-inch cubes

Garnish:
2 whole scallions, cut into 1-inch pieces
2 tablespoons finely chopped Italian parsley

*If you cannot find monkfish, skate may be used, or chicken of
the sea (blowfish), or another firm white-fleshed fish.

Heat 2 tablespoons of the olive oil and 1 teaspoon of the safflower oil in a
medium saucepan, then add onion. When onion begins to brown, add
garlic and cook about 1 minute. Add tomatoes, oregano, mint, parsley, and
hot pepper flakes, cover, and simmer 10 minutes. In the meantime, remove
head from fish and take off gills, or have your fishmonger do this. Wash the
head well. Cut body of fish into 4 sections and set aside.

Add fish head to the onion-tomato mixture, cover, and boil gently 20
minutes. Strain, using cheesecloth or a colander.

Return broth to saucepan, discarding cooked fish head and pulp, add
wine, bring to a boil, and add monkfish. When broth returns to a boil, add
mussels and clams. Cover and boil until mussels and clams begin to open.
Add fish sections and shrimp. Cook about 5 minutes, until fish is done.

To make croutons, heat remaining olive oil and safflower oil in a medium
skillet, then add bread cubes and sauté over medium heat, turning often,
until bread begins to brown.

Put some shellfish, shrimp, and fish sections in each soup bowl. Pour some broth over them, sprinkle with scallions and parsley. Top this with some croutons and serve immediately.

Calories	Cholesterol	Protein	Carbohydrate	Total fat		Sat fat		Mono	Poly
	mg	gm	gm	gm	%	gm	%	gm	gm
1510	728.0	195.7	52.6	52.1	30	4.8	3	21.4	12.3

PEA SOUP
Minestra di Piselli

This is a heavier pea soup than the one on page 44, because it uses dried peas and rice.

Serves 6 to 8.

> 2 tablespoons olive oil
> 2 tablespoons safflower oil
> 2 medium onions, chopped
> 2 cloves garlic, chopped
> 1 cup split peas
> 6 cups water
> 1/2 cup sliced carrots
> 1 stalk celery, chopped
> 1 bay leaf
> Salt and freshly ground black pepper to taste
> 1 cup cooked rice (page 160) or croutons

Heat the two oils in a soup pot, add onions, then garlic. When onions wilt (do not burn the garlic), add all the rest of the ingredients except the rice. Boil gently 2 hours, stirring often.

Put some warm cooked rice on the bottom of the soup plates, then add hot soup.

Calories	Cholesterol	Protein	Carbohydrate	Total fat		Sat fat		Mono	Poly
	mg	gm	gm	gm	%	gm	%	gm	gm
1488	0	56.3	194.3	57.4	34	5.2	3	24.6	21.5

PASTA AND CORN SOUP MARCHES STYLE
Zuppa di Pasta e Granturco alla Marchigiana

Serves 4.

1 tablespoon butter
1 tablespoon safflower oil
1 small onion, minced
2 cups corn kernels, preferably fresh, although frozen
     will do
4 cups water
3/4 cup small pasta, such as small elbows, tubettini, etc.
Salt and freshly ground black pepper to taste
2 tablespoons minced Italian parsley

Heat the butter and oil in a small pot, then add onion. Sauté until onion wilts, then add corn and water. Boil gently 15 minutes. Add pasta and salt and pepper to taste. Boil gently until pasta is al dente. Add parsley and serve.

Calories	Cholesterol mg	Protein gm	Carbohydrate gm	Total fat gm	%	Sat fat gm	%	Mono gm	Poly gm
835	31.0	17.3	103.2	29.4	31	7.8	8	6.2	12.0

BEAN SOUP WITH RICE
Zuppa di Fagioli alla Romana

We first tasted this particular soup in Rome in 1972, in a favorite trattoria. It is served at room temperature.

Many Italians, especially Romans, prefer a few drops of good oil over each portion of bean soup just before serving instead of grated cheese. I too prefer good olive oil to cheese in bean soup.

Serves 6 to 8.

2 cups dried cannellini beans (white beans),
     soaked overnight
2 bay leaves
Salt and freshly ground black pepper to taste

The Sauce
1 tablespoon olive oil
1 tablespoon safflower oil
1 medium onion, chopped
2 cups coarsely chopped tomatoes, fresh if possible
     (drain if canned)
1/2 cup chopped celery

2 tablespoons finely chopped fresh basil or 1 teaspoon dried
2 cloves garlic, coarsely chopped

2 cups cooked rice (page 160)

Garnish: 6 to 8 teaspoons extra virgin olive oil

Drain beans and put them in a medium pot, preferably one of terracotta. Pour in enough cold water to cover beans by 1 1/2 inches. Add bay leaves, salt, and pepper. Cover, bring to a boil, then lower heat and boil gently about 1 hour.

In the meantime, make the sauce. Heat the two oils in a small pot and add onion. As onion begins to brown, add the rest of the sauce ingredients. Cover and simmer 15 minutes. Run through a food mill or food processor and purée. Add to beans and continue cooking 1 to 1 1/2 hours, until beans are tender.

Put several tablespoons warm cooked rice in small deep bowls. Add beans with broth and let cool. Serve at room temperature. Pour about 1 teaspoon good olive oil over each bowl before serving.

Calories	Cholesterol mg	Protein gm	Carbohydrate gm	Total fat gm	%	Sat fat gm	%	Mono gm	Poly gm
2331	0	96.2	341.5	70.4	27	6.6	2	39.8	13.2

Calculation includes 1 teaspoon olive oil on each of 8 servings.

LENTIL SOUP ABRUZZI STYLE
Zuppa di Lenticchie Abruzzese

Serves 6 to 8.

2 cups dried lentils, washed and drained
5 cups water
1 bay leaf
1 teaspoon thyme
1 teaspoon basil
1 teaspoon marjoram
1 onion, finely chopped
Salt and freshly ground black pepper to taste
12 roasted chestnuts
3 tablespoons olive oil
1 tablespoon safflower oil
1 tablespoon tomato paste, diluted in 1 cup warm water
4 tablespoons chopped Italian parsley
8 slices bread, toasted (page 39)*

*The original recipe calls for thin slices of bread fried in oil, but I prefer toasted bread.

Put lentils, water, bay leaf, thyme, basil, marjoram, onion, salt, and pepper in a pot, cover and boil gently about 1 hour, or until lentils are tender.

In the meantime, score chestnuts on concave side with a sharp knife and roast them in a preheated 450° oven about 12 minutes. Let them cool just till you can handle them, then peel off and discard skins. Chop the nuts and set aside. Heat oils in a small skillet, add chestnuts, simmer for a minute or so, add diluted tomato paste, parsley, salt, and pepper. Cover and simmer several minutes. Add this mixture to the lentils. Cover and simmer 10 minutes.

Place a piece of toasted bread in each soup plate and pour the lentil soup over the bread.

Calories	Cholesterol mg	Protein gm	Carbohydrate gm	Total fat gm	%	Sat fat gm	%	Mono gm	Poly gm
3132	0	127.3	420.3	106.9	30	11.2	3	58.4	23.3

Roman Garlic Bread I (page 39) used.

CORN SOUP WITH CHICKEN
Sopa de Mazorca con Pollo

This Mexican dish is a lovely recipe, very easy to make and most satisfying.

Serves 8.

3-pound chicken, trussed
About 8 cups water
1 medium onion
1 leek, washed and trimmed
1 bay leaf
1 tablespoon coriander seeds
1 stalk celery, cut into 4 pieces
2 carrots
Salt and freshly ground black pepper to taste
2 cups chopped tomatoes, fresh if possible
   (drain if canned)
5 ears fresh corn

Garnish: Chopped fresh coriander or Italian parsley

Place chicken in a soup pot and add water, onion, leek, bay leaf, coriander seeds, celery, carrots, salt, and pepper. Cover and bring to a boil. Cook over medium heat, partially covered so that soup boils gently, about 1 1/4 hours. Add tomatoes. Cover and continue cooking about 45 minutes.

Shave fresh corn off cob (you should have about 3 cups).

Remove chicken and let cool. Strain broth and remove all fat. Return broth to soup pot and bring to a boil. Add the corn, cover, and boil about 5 minutes.

Meanwhile, remove the chicken meat from the bones. Discard fat, skin, and bones. Break up the chicken meat with your hands and add to the soup. Cook 5 minutes. Serve hot, garnished with fresh chopped coriander or parsley.

Variation: To make a heartier soup, cook 1 cup rice (page 160). Add cooked rice to soup just before serving.

Calories	Cholesterol mg	Protein gm	Carbohydrate gm	Total fat gm	%	Sat fat gm	%	Mono gm	Poly gm
1065	421.0	133.4	83.4	25.5	21	6.5	5	8.8	4.5

SOUP FLORENTINE STYLE
Zuppa Fiorentina

Serves 6.

2 cups fresh shelled cranberry beans (shell beans)
2 cloves garlic
1 teaspoon rosemary
Salt and freshly ground black pepper to taste
2 tablespoons safflower oil or vegetable oil
1 medium onion, finely chopped
2 cups chicken or beef broth or water
1 cup chopped tomatoes, fresh if possible
   (drain if canned)
2 cups broccoli cut into bite-sized flowerets
2 tablespoons chopped fresh basil or
   1 teaspoon dried
1/2 cup rice

Put the beans in a medium saucepan with the garlic, rosemary, salt, and pepper, and cover with water (about 1 inch over the tops of the beans). Cover and boil gently 1 hour.

Meanwhile, heat the oil in a medium soup pot and add the onion. When onion browns, add the rest of the ingredients except the rice and cook 30 minutes. Add the cooked beans and their liquid, cover, and boil gently another 30 minutes. Add about 1/2 cup rice and continue to cook until the rice is al dente.

Serve hot, or at room temperature.

Variation: To make the soup looser, cook rice separately. Serve 2 or 3 tablespoons rice in each soup bowl, then ladle soup over rice.

Calories	Cholesterol mg	Protein gm	Carbohydrate gm	Total fat gm	%	Sat fat gm	%	Mono gm	Poly gm
1118	0	41.6	169.6	30.2	24	2.2	2	4.0	19.6

BEAN SOUP FRANKOWITCH
Zuppa di Fagioli alla Frankowitch

This recipe was named after Mr. Frankowitch, an American expatriot who moved to Rome right after World War II, aspiring to be a famous movie director in Italy's exciting new film industry. During his many years in Rome he often dined in a small trattoria in Rome called Nino's, and one of his favorite dishes served there was zuppa di fagioli.

Unfortunately, fate was not kind to Mr. Frankowitch, and his talents were never fully acknowledged in Rome. After a few decades there he decided to return to the States. Before leaving for America he visited his friend, Nino, and lamented the fact that Rome still did not know his name. He asked his friend if he would name a dish on the menu after him. Why not? So Nino named Mr. Frankowitch's favorite dish zuppa di fagioli alla Frankowitch. It is the only place it is known as such, and when we dined at Nino's several years ago, we had this zuppa di fagioli alla Frankowitch.

It is so easy to make this recipe with dried beans and they are so much better than canned beans that I really don't know why one wouldn't make it that way.

The original recipe calls for a grated cheese garnish, but I have found finely chopped Italian parsley a perfectly adequate substitute.

Serves 6.

2 cups dried white beans, preferably cannellini or
    Great Northern, or 2 cans Progresso
    cannellini beans
5 cups cold water
3 cloves garlic
2 bay leaves
1 tablespoon crushed rosemary
Salt and freshly ground black pepper to taste

The flavored oil
2 tablespoons olive oil
1 tablespoon safflower oil
2 cloves garlic, minced
Hot pepper flakes to taste (optional)

8 to 10 slices French or Italian bread

Place dried beans in a bowl, cover with water, and soak overnight. Drain. Place beans in a soup pot, preferably terracotta, add the water, garlic, bay leaves, rosemary, salt, and pepper. Bring to a boil, then cover and boil gently about 2½ hours, or until beans are tender. Stir occasionally.

Remove half the beans with a slotted spoon. Set aside and keep warm. Place remaining beans with their broth in a food processor or food mill and purée.

To make the flavored oil, heat the oils, garlic, and pepper flakes in the soup pot. As garlic begins to take on color, add the reserved whole beans and bean purée. Mix well and remove from heat, keeping the pot covered.

Toast slices of French or Italian bread. After bread is toasted, sprinkle with olive oil, then rub garlic on each slice. Place toasted bread on the bottom of the soup plates and pour the hot bean soup on top.

To serve the toasted bread as an appetizer or side dish, place 1 piece of toast on a flat dish and pour over just enough of the bean mixture to cover bread.

Calories	Cholesterol mg	Protein gm	Carbohydrate gm	Total fat gm	%	Sat fat gm	%	Mono gm	Poly gm
2828	0	112.0	399.0	83.0	26	8.4	3	41.2	12.5

TUSCAN BEAN SOUP
Ribollita

Ribollita means to reboil. I have had many variations of this Tuscan dish. This is one of the better recipes.

Serves 6.

1 cup dried cannellini or Great Northern beans
6 cups water
2 tablespoons olive oil
1 tablespoon safflower oil
1 medium onion, finely chopped
1 teaspoon minced garlic
1 cup finely chopped celery
2 tablespoons finely chopped Italian parsley
2 medium carrots, finely chopped
2 cups chopped fresh tomatoes, run through a
    food mill to remove seeds
Salt and freshly ground black pepper to taste
4 cups thinly sliced Savoy cabbage or green cabbage
6 slices French or Italian bread, sprinkled with
    olive oil, then toasted and rubbed with garlic

Soak the beans in 2 cups of the water overnight.

Heat the two oils in a medium soup pot and add the onion. As onion begins to brown, add garlic, celery, and parsley. Sauté for several minutes, tossing often. Add carrots and tomatoes, and cook about 5 minutes. Add the remaining 4 cups water, drained beans, salt, and pepper. Bring to a boil, cover, and boil gently about 1 hour.

Turn up heat and add cabbage. When soup boils, lower to a simmer, cover, and cook 1 hour.

Remove about half the beans and cabbage and purée in a food processor or put through a food mill. Return to the pot and simmer about 5 minutes.

Place a slice of toasted bread in each soup bowl and ladle soup into the bowls.

Calories	Cholesterol mg	Protein gm	Carbohydrate gm	Total fat gm	%	Sat fat gm	%	Mono gm	Poly gm
2021	0	74.1	283.2	65.7	29	5.6	2	32.9	12.5

LENTIL AND BEAN SOUP
Minestra di Lenticchie e Fagioli

Serves 4 to 6.

2 tablespoons peanut oil
1 cup finely chopped onion
1 teaspoon minced garlic
2 tablespoons tomato paste
1 carrot, coarsely chopped
1 stalk celery, coarsely chopped
5 cups water
1 cup lentils, washed
1 bay leaf
1 teaspoon basil
1 teaspoon crushed rosemary
1 cup cooked dried cannellini beans (white beans)
    (page 82) or 1 cup canned cannellini beans
1 cup small pasta, such as coralini, tubettini,
    small shells, etc.

Garnish: Thinly sliced whole scallions or chopped onions

Heat the oil in a soup pot and add onion. When onion begins to brown, add garlic and tomato paste. Cook for a minute or so. Add the rest of the ingredients except the pasta, beans, and garnish. Cover and boil gently about 45 minutes. Add beans and cook another 15 minutes.

Cook pasta in boiling salted water until done al dente. Drain and spoon some pasta into the bottom of each soup bowl. Ladle soup over the pasta. Garnish with thinly sliced scallions or finely chopped onions.

Calories	Cholesterol mg	Protein gm	Carbohydrate gm	Total fat gm	%	Sat fat gm	%	Mono gm	Poly gm
1786	0	71.0	294	31.6	15	4.6	2	12.4	8.6

LIMA BEAN SOUP

Serves 8.

2 cups dried lima beans, soaked in cold water overnight
5 cups water
2 medium onions, chopped
2 cloves garlic, chopped
1 bay leaf
1 teaspoon marjoram
1 stalk celery, chopped
2 carrots, chopped
1 cup small pasta, such as tubettini

Garnish: Chopped Italian parsley

Drain the soaked lima beans. Put all the ingredients except pasta and parsley in a deep pot and boil gently, covered, 2 to 2½ hours. Stir often. The beans shouldn't fall apart.*

Boil pasta in boiling water to cover until al dente. Drain and put several tablespoons cooked pasta on the bottom of each soup plate. Ladle the hot soup over the pasta and serve, garnished with chopped Italian parsley.

*A piece of dried cheese rind boiled along with the rest of the ingredients will make the soup even better.

Calories	Cholesterol mg	Protein gm	Carbohydrate gm	Total fat gm	%	Sat fat gm	%	Mono gm	Poly gm
1364	0	95.4	359.5	7.8	4	–	–	–	–

BEAN AND CORN SOUP
Minestra di Fagioli e Granturco

This is the only Italian recipe I know of other than polenta where corn is used in a recipe (but I have since devised one of my own; see page 58). I have had this dish in my grandfather's home in Italy, but never anywhere else. I have substituted vegetable oil for the pork fat and skin originally used.

Serves 4.

2 tablespoons olive oil or 1 tablespoon safflower oil
½ medium onion, minced
4 tablespoons chopped fresh tomatoes
2 cups corn, preferably frozen, although fresh may be used
3 cups water
1½ cups fresh shelled cranberry beans (shell beans)
Salt and freshly ground black pepper to taste
2 tablespoons chopped Italian parsley

Heat the oil in a small soup pot, add onion, and cook over moderate heat. When onion begins to brown, add tomatoes. Simmer several minutes; then add corn, water, beans, salt, pepper, and parsley. Cover and boil gently for about 1 hour, until beans are tender, adding more water if soup gets too thick.

Calories	Cholesterol mg	Protein gm	Carbohydrate gm	Total fat gm	%	Sat fat gm	%	Mono gm	Poly gm
1006	0	43.0	152.0	32.5	28	3.4	3	21.6	3.6

CHICK PEA SOUP I
Minestra di Ceci

Serves 8.

2 cups dried chick peas (ceci beans)*
2 cups cannellini beans (white beans)*
6 cups water
2 cloves garlic, finely minced
1/2 cup finely chopped carrots
1 cup finely chopped celery
1 cup chopped tomatoes, fresh if possible
    (drain if canned)
1 1/2-ounce package dried boletus mushrooms
2 cups chopped Swiss chard
1 bay leaf
Salt and freshly ground black pepper to taste
3 tablespoons olive oil
1 teaspoon safflower oil
8 slices toasted Italian or French bread

Garnish: Finely chopped Italian parsley

*Or you may use a 20-ounce can each of ceci beans and cannellini beans, adding beans when indicated in recipe.

Soak the dried beans in separate bowls for 24 hours in cold water, adding 1 teaspoon bicarbonate of soda to the chick peas. Drain, wash, cover the chick peas with water, and cook, covered, 4 hours.

Drain the cannellini beans. Cover with cold water and boil slowly until cooked, about 2 hours.

Put the 6 cups water in a soup pot and add the garlic, carrots, celery, tomatoes, mushrooms, Swiss chard, bay leaf, salt, and pepper. Cover and boil gently 1 hour. Add the drained, cooked chick peas, cover and boil 30 minutes. Drain the cannellini beans, add them to the soup, and cook 20 minutes. Add the two oils, cover, and boil gently 20 more minutes.

Place toast on bottom of each soup plate. Ladle soup over toast. Garnish with the Italian parsley.

Calories	Cholesterol mg	Protein gm	Carbohydrate gm	Total fat gm	%	Sat fat gm	%	Mono gm	Poly gm
2427	0	92.3	350.0	72.9	26	7.1	3	34.5	15.7

CHICK PEA SOUP II
Zuppa di Ceci

Serves 3 to 4.

20-ounce can chick peas (ceci beans), drained
1 1/2 cups water
1 teaspoon minced garlic
1 teaspoon crushed rosemary
Salt and freshly ground black pepper to taste
1/2 cup small pasta, such as tubettini, elbows, etc.
1 teaspoon safflower oil
1 tablespoon excellent olive oil

Garnish: 1 tablespoon finely chopped Italian parsley

Put all ingredients except pasta, oils, and parsley in a soup pot. Simmer about 20 minutes. Add pasta and cook until it is almost al dente. Add safflower oil. When pasta is al dente, stir in olive oil.

Garnish each bowl of soup with parsley.

Calories	Cholesterol mg	Protein gm	Carbohydrate gm	Total fat gm	%	Sat fat gm	%	Mono gm	Poly gm
904	0	40.7	140.7	21.5	21	2.2	2	10.4	4.5

LENTIL AND CHICK PEA SOUP
Minestra di Lenticchie e Ceci

We like to serve this hearty soup on a raw spring day when the fresh peas are in season.

Serves 6.

1 tablespoon olive oil
1 teaspoon safflower oil
1 medium onion, finely chopped
2 cloves garlic, skins on
2 cups chopped tomatoes, fresh if possible (drain if canned)
4 cups water
¾ cup dried lentils
1 cup chopped leeks
1 bay leaf
Salt and hot pepper flakes or freshly ground black pepper
   to taste
2 cups chick peas (ceci beans) (precooked; see page 64)
   or 20-ounce can chick peas, drained
1 cup fresh peas, 1 pound, or 1 cup frozen
2 tablespoons finely chopped fresh mint
1 cup small pasta, such as tubettini, small shells, small
   bows, elbows, etc.

Heat the oils in a medium soup pot, then add onion. When onion begins to brown, add garlic, tomatoes, water, lentils, leeks, bay leaf, salt, and either hot pepper flakes or black pepper. Bring to a boil and cover. Lower heat to a gentle boil and cook 45 minutes. Add chick peas, fresh peas, and mint, cover, and simmer about 30 minutes.

Cook pasta separately in boiling water. Drain when al dente, spoon some into the bottom of each soup plate, then add soup.

Calories	Cholesterol mg	Protein gm	Carbohydrate gm	Total fat gm	%	Sat fat gm	%	Mono gm	Poly gm
1948	0	98.9	323.3	29.5	13	2.2	1	10.4	4.5

VEAL BALLS IN SOUP
Polpette di Vitello in Brodo

This delicate handy soup is a meal in itself.

Serves 4 as a main course; 6 as a first course.

½ pound lean ground veal
Salt and freshly ground black pepper to taste
1 egg white, lightly beaten

Dash nutmeg
1 teaspoon grated lemon rind
1 teaspoon finely chopped Italian parsley
6 cups chicken or beef stock
1/2 cup Carolina long-grain rice
Juice of 1/2 lemon
6 cups coarsely chopped fresh spinach

In a bowl mix the veal, salt and pepper, egg white, nutmeg, lemon rind, and parsley. Work with your hands until the mixture is well blended. Form balls the size of walnuts — you should have about 20.

Bring the stock to a boil. Add rice and cook about 5 minutes. Add veal balls and lemon juice; cover and boil gently about 10 minutes. Add spinach and boil another 5 minutes. Serve hot.

Calories	Cholesterol mg	Protein gm	Carbohydrate gm	Total fat gm	%	Sat fat gm	%	Mono gm	Poly gm
745	161.0	66.4	89.0	12.8	15	5.5	6	5.0	0.2

VEAL AND CABBAGE SOUP
Minestrone di Cavolfiore e Vitello

This hearty soup is a meal in itself. It contains little fat and is very delicate.

Serves 4 to 6.

1 cup shredded green cabbage
2 tablespoons finely chopped fresh basil or
    1 teaspoon dried
1/2 cup chopped celery
1 medium onion, finely chopped
About 6 cups water
Salt and freshly ground black pepper to taste
3/4 pound ground lean veal
1 tablespoon finely chopped Italian parsley
1 egg white, lightly beaten
1 medium potato, peeled and diced
Juice of 1/2 lemon
1/4 cup rice

Garnish: Chopped Italian parsley

Put cabbage, basil, celery, onion, water, salt, and pepper in a medium soup pot. Cover and boil gently 1 hour.

Meanwhile, mix the veal, parsley, egg white, more salt and pepper together in a bowl. Scoop up some of the mixture and form balls about 1 inch in diameter — you should have about 25. After the soup has boiled for 1 hour, add veal balls, diced potato, and lemon juice. Cook about 20 minutes. Add rice and continue to cook until the rice is tender, about 10 minutes.

Serve the soup hot, garnished with Italian parsley.

Calories	Cholesterol mg	Protein gm	Carbohydrate gm	Total fat gm	%	Sat fat gm	%	Mono gm	Poly gm
864	242.0	83.6	88.0	18.1	18	8.3	8	7.5	0.3

III   PASTAS

One of the great recent satisfactions I have experienced has been the rehabilitation of pasta. For decades I have had to listen to a lot of nonsense about pasta being fattening with no nutritional value—a food for the poor and blue collar workers.

In January 1977, I contributed to an article in *Harper's Bazaar* extolling the virtues of pasta as a nutritional diet food. The theme of the article was eat pasta 7 days a week and lose 5 pounds a week. The pasta sauces I suggested were light and interesting.

Since then, pasta has been more or less accepted as a food, when properly cooked, that can qualify as a diet food and can provide important nutrients such as carbohydrates, protein, and fat in the right proportions.

The hard durum wheat yields a yellow flour called semolina, which is very much like fine cornmeal and contains more proteins and vitamins than regular flour, as well as a good selection of other essential amino acids. Semolina contains thiamin, riboflavin, niacin, and iron; it has a low calorie count and a very low fat content.

Unlike Americans and Italo-Americans, Italians do not drench their pasta in heavy meat sauces. Most of the sauces are very light, more often than not meatless, and they usually include vegetables, such as asparagus, peas, mushrooms, spinach, peppers, etc.

The major complaint one hears from Americans about light sauces, such as vegetable and fish sauces, is that they aren't substantial enough to cling to the pasta. There are several ways to offset this problem, if it is a problem. One is to partially cook the pasta in water, then drain it and finish cooking it in a shallow saucepan along with the vegetables and/or fish and whatever liquid you have added to the sauce components so that the pasta will help thicken the liquid a little and absorb some of its flavor. The second way accomplishes the same goal—but even more so. It is the result of an exciting discovery I made: Pasta can actually be cooked from scratch with only raw vegetables in a large shallow heavy pan and just enough moisture—either water or stock—to keep it from sticking, adding more liquid as needed. It takes only about 10 minutes, everything is done in one pot, and during the cooking the pasta drinks in the flavorful vegetable juices and, in turn, the starch in the pasta really thickens these juices, thus creating a delicate sauce. The final method is to purée the vegetables in their liquid as one does with the tomatoes in marinara sauce (page 430). You will find a number of recipes in this chapter using these different techniques.

In Italy, *pasta alla macchiato* means a pasta that has just enough sauce to stain it (*macchiare* means "to stain"), and it is a very popular way of serving pasta. The reason it is enjoyed is that good pasta has its own very definite, delicate taste, so one wants to complement that taste, not destroy its identity with a thick sauce. Today in America pasta is enjoying a popularity never before imagined, but you should remember that the pasta itself must be of superior quality; it should be cooked properly; and it shouldn't be drowned in a heavy sauce.

In my opinion there is a tremendous difference between domestic and imported pasta. I have tested many American brands side by side with Italian pastas and I have found that when I cook American pastas, invariably when I taste them for doneness, just before they are supposed to be ready, they have a slippery coating on the outside while the core is still too hard. If I boil them a minute or so more, then the pasta becomes soft throughout—that is, overcooked—so it is impossible to achieve the al dente texture—"just firm to the bite"—that is desirable. As a matter of fact, even when overcooked, a good Italian pasta will not have the unpleasant sogginess American pasta has; different ones vary according to the brand, some being worse than others. I realize that imported varieties are still not available throughout the country, so I suggest that you at least compare domestic brands and select what is best in your area. In the Northeast I have found Ronzoni and Prince to be somewhat superior to others. However, if you like really good pasta I strongly recommend that you get one of the better Italian brands even if you have to send for it mail order. I have listed below my favorites in order of my preference, all of which I have tested under exactly the same conditions:

> Gerrardo di Nola
> De Cecco
> Pastificio del Verde, Fara San Martino*
> La Molisana
> Mennucci
> Nola
> Spiga
> Spiga Doro

One more word about a new pasta—at least as far as America is concerned—that is now available. It has no name, just the manufacturer's label, De Cecco. The strands are about 1/3 inch wide with curled edges and they are formed into loose nests packed in standard boxes. The pasta is thin

---

*Fara San Martino is the name of the town in Abruzzo where De Cecco and Pastificio del Verde produce their pasta.

and made from semolina. It resembles an egg noodle but it isn't made with eggs, so it is an excellent pasta to use in recipes that call for fettuccine. In fact, I personally prefer it to fettuccine because it is lighter. If you prepare a light sauce, such as a fish sauce, for it, then be sure to cook this pasta for the last 3 or 4 minutes of its total cooking time right in the sauce. E.G.

For many years virtually the only pasta I remember hearing of was spaghetti, and the adjective "Italian" preceded it as often as not, though much of what passed in restaurants as "Italian spaghetti" was a gratuitous insult to Italian cuisine. In recent years, however, the availability of a large variety of shapes and sizes has resulted in the popularization of the generic term "pasta." At the same time, recipes for pasta have also proliferated. This is a particular boon to the cholesterol-watching meal planner, who can select from an almost endless catalogue of recipes relatively low in total fat, saturated fat, and cholesterol. R.W.

FARFALLE (BUTTERFLIES) WITH PESTO
Farfalle al Pesto

The difference between a sauce and a pesto is that pesto is usually made with a mortar and pestle (although a food processor is often used today) and the ingredients are usually raw. This pesto uses pine nuts, but there is another one in the sauce chapter (page 426) that uses walnuts.

This is a lovely combination of two raw sauces—pesto and primavera—and the marriage is very successful.

Serves 8.

The pesto sauce
4 tablespoons excellent olive oil
1 tablespoon safflower oil
2 teaspoons chopped garlic
4 tablespoons pine nuts
Salt and freshly ground black pepper to taste
4 cups tightly packed fresh basil leaves
2 tablespoons chopped Italian parsley

The primavera sauce
1 clove garlic, chopped
2 cups chopped fresh ripe tomatoes
1 cup basil leaves
1 tablespoon chopped Italian parsley
2 tablespoons olive oil
1 teaspoon safflower oil
Salt and freshly ground black pepper to taste

2 cups French-cut fresh green beans
2 cups sliced potatoes
1 1/2 pounds farfalle pasta or a similar cut pasta,
    such as shells

Blend all ingredients for pesto with a mortar and pestle or in a food processor.

Put all ingredients for the primavera sauce in a food processor and blend.

Bring about 5 quarts salted water to a boil, then add beans and potatoes. When water returns to a boil, add pasta. Stir often, and drain when pasta is al dente. Reserve about 1 cup cooking water and mix this with 1 cup pesto. Toss with the pasta, then the primavera sauce. Blend and serve.

Calories	Cholesterol mg	Protein gm	Carbohydrate gm	Total fat gm	%	Sat fat gm	%	Mono gm	Poly gm
3696	0	108.7	616.2	86.2	21	7.7	2	49.3	13.8

TRENETTE WITH PESTO
Trenette al Pesto

Trenette, which is flat like linguine but broader, is a pasta shape rarely found in America, though I have found the De Cecco brand of it on several occasions in New York City. Linguine has been used as a substitute but I find it too thin. The pesto has a tendency to thicken when served on thin pasta. To my mind some of the cut pastas, like small shells, bows, etc., are more suited to pesto sauce.

Serves 6.

1 large potato, cut in half, then sliced
2 cups French-cut fresh green beans
Salt to taste
1 pound pasta—trenette, linguine, or cut pasta
4 tablespoons or more pesto (preceding recipe or one for
    pesto on page 426)
2 large ripe tomatoes, cut into ½-inch cubes

Garnish: Cubed tomatoes

Bring a large pot of water to a boil. Add potatoes, green beans, and salt; when water returns to a boil, add pasta. Stirring occasionally, cook until pasta is al dente. Drain and reserve 4 tablespoons water. Mix this water with the pesto in a small bowl. Toss with the pasta, potatoes, and beans. More pesto may be used if desired.

Serve on hot plates, garnishing each mound of pasta with some cubed tomatoes.

Calories	Cholesterol mg	Protein gm	Carbohydrate gm	Total fat gm	%	Sat fat gm	%	Mono gm	Poly gm
2049	0	68.8	402.0	17.6	8	1.1	1	6.9	2.2

PASTA WITH EGGPLANT
Pasta con le Melanzane

The use of eggplant in pasta is of southern Italian origin, especially Sicilian. Old eggplants tend to be bitter, but young fresh ones are always sweet.

Serves 6.

2 medium eggplants, sliced ¼ inch thick
Salt
4 tablespoons olive oil
Freshly ground black pepper to taste
1 tablespoon safflower oil or vegetable oil
1 clove garlic, finely chopped
4 cups chopped tomatoes, fresh if possible (drain if canned)
3 tablespoons chopped fresh basil or 1½ teaspoons dried
Hot pepper flakes to taste
1 pound spaghettini

Garnish: Finely chopped Italian parsley

Cut eggplant slices in half, then spread on a counter or cookie tray. Sprinkle with salt. Let stand 15 minutes. Wash and pat dry slices. Meanwhile, preheat oven to 500° to 550°.

Place eggplant slices in 1 layer on a cookie tray (you will need to use 2 trays). Sprinkle about 1 tablespoon olive oil over slices on each tray, salt and pepper them, and bake. When bottom of eggplant begins to brown, flip each slice over with a spatula and brown the other side. Repeat until all slices are browned.

Meanwhile, heat remaining 2 tablespoons olive oil and the other oil in a large skillet. Add garlic, and as it begins to color, add tomatoes, basil, salt, and hot pepper flakes or black pepper. Cover and simmer 10 minutes.

Cook pasta in a large amount of boiling salted water until almost al dente. About 2 minutes before pasta is ready, drain, add to sauce, and cook, mixing often, for several minutes until pasta is cooked.

Put portions of pasta on individual plates and arrange eggplant slices around the rims.

Garnish each serving with Italian parsley.

Calories	Cholesterol mg	Protein gm	Carbohydrate gm	Total fat gm	%	Sat fat gm	%	Mono gm	Poly gm
2387	0	68.9	387.0	61.6	23	6.0	2	23.0	22.4

PENNE WITH SPINACH
Penne con Salsa di Spinaci

This simple sauce, which you can practically make while the pasta boils, has a lovely creamy consistency when combined with the almost cooked pasta. It is good to make when spinach is abundant. We tend to identify green sauces with basil and summer, but this one can bring a touch of summer to the colder months.

Serves 6.

1 pound fresh spinach, washed
3 tablespoons good olive oil*
1 teaspoon safflower oil
2 medium onions, coarsely chopped
3 anchovy fillets, coarsely chopped
1 1/2 cups chicken or beef stock
Salt and freshly ground black pepper to taste
1 pound penne, or other cut pasta such as ziti, bows, etc.

*If cheese is desired, use 1 1/2 tablespoons safflower oil and 2 tablespoons olive oil in the sauce. These will compensate for 6 tablespoons grated Parmesan cheese to be served on pasta.

Boil the spinach in a pot of boiling water for 1 minute; drain and let cool. When spinach is cool, squeeze out liquid.

In the meantime, heat the oils in a large skillet or shallow saucepan, add onions, and sauté uncovered until they begin to brown. Add chopped anchovy fillets and cook a minute or so. Add spinach, stock, salt, and pepper. Cover and simmer 10 minutes. In the meantime, cook pasta in boiling salted water. Put the spinach sauce in a food processor and purée to a creamy consistency.

Drain pasta and toss in sauce. Serve on heated plates immediately.

Calories	Cholesterol mg	Protein gm	Carbohydrate gm	Total fat gm	%	Sat fat gm	%	Mono gm	Poly gm
2346	7.0	79.0	387.2	53.4	20	5.4	2	32.0	6.3

PASTA COOKED IN A GREEN SAUCE
Pasta in Salsa Verde

Serves 4.

1 pound asparagus
3 tablespoons olive oil
1 teaspoon safflower oil
1 medium onion, coarsely chopped
Salt and freshly ground black pepper to taste
1 pound fresh tomatoes*
1 clove garlic, crushed (skins discarded)
4 or 5 leaves fresh basil or 1 teaspoon dried
1 cup chicken or beef stock
3/4 pound pasta such as bows, penne, shells,
    cooked al dente

Garnish: Finely chopped Italian parsley

*I used fresh plum tomatoes in this recipe, but any type of fresh ripe tomato will do.

Wash asparagus well, remove tough ends, and cut into 2-inch lengths. Heat 2 tablespoons of the olive oil and the safflower oil in a medium skillet, add asparagus and onion, salt and pepper lightly, and sauté over low to moderate heat until they begin to brown. Set aside.

In the meantime, boil the tomatoes in rapidly boiling water about 2 seconds. Remove them from the water and peel, then cut in half and gently squeeze out seeds. Cut the tomato halves into slices about 1/4 inch thick (about 1 1/2 cups).

Heat the remaining tablespoon olive oil in a small skillet, add garlic, and when it takes on color remove it and add tomatoes, basil, salt, and pepper. Cook over high heat, stirring often, about 10 minutes.

Put asparagus, onion, and stock in a food processor or food mill and purée.

Toss cooked pasta in the asparagus sauce, then serve garnished with tomato sauce. Sprinkle each portion with chopped Italian parsley.

Calories	Cholesterol mg	Protein gm	Carbohydrate gm	Total fat gm	%	Sat fat gm	%	Mono gm	Poly gm
1948	0	61.9	310.0	51.1	23	4.9	2	31.6	5.9

PASTA PRIMAVERA

I feel that something should be said about "pasta primavera," perhaps the most popular pasta recipe in America today and certainly the most misunderstood.

In 1973 my good friends John Vernges and Sirio Maccioni came out to Katonah to visit us to see if I would contribute a pasta recipe for their new restaurant, Le Cirque, in New York City. I made a variety of pasta recipes, concentrating on pasta with vegetables and pasta with fish and my favorite pasta dish, "pasta primavera," which was then unknown to New York restaurants. I had always enjoyed pasta primavera in Florence and in Rome when it was in season—in May and June and sometimes on into the summer; it was something we always looked forward to. The first tomatoes are harvested there in May, and the recipe is beautifully simple—fresh unrefrigerated garden-ripe tomatoes cut in 1/2-inch cubes, freshly chopped fresh basil, finely chopped Italian parsley, very good olive oil, finely chopped garlic, salt, and freshly ground black pepper.

Spaghettini was the pasta usually used. The pasta is cooked al dente, drained very well, tossed with the rest of the ingredients, garnished with extra parsley, and served immediately.

I have always found it a bit awkward, however, to twirl the pasta and at the same time pick up some of the tomato and basil and parsley and garlic. So I decided to run the sauce through a food mill (today it would be a food processor) to purée it, which works out very well. Jon Vergne and Sirio Maccioni liked the recipe and put it on their menu. Then Jon Vergne added one more ingredient: pine nuts. The dish was an instant success and the critics raved. The timing had been perfect, because the great interest in pasta and vegetable combinations was just beginning.

As winter approached, fresh tomatoes and fresh basil were no longer around, so the recipe was adjusted to make use of whatever fresh vegetables were available. Gradually cream was added and the recipe became what it is today.

The success of the dish was so great that it wasn't long before other restaurants soon added it to their menus, in most cases adding more cream and more vegetables, until the pasta often looked as though it had been dragged through the vegetable garden.

I would like to emphasize that the pasta primavera that is so popular in America today is not of Italian origin but was created in Le Cirque restaurant. There is no doubt in my mind that the recipe will eventually end up in Italy—perhaps with fewer vegetables.

PASTA PRIMAVERA I

This recipe should be made only when fresh tomatoes and basil are in season.

Serves 4 to 6.

1 pound spaghettini, imported if possible
4 cups chopped fresh garden-ripe tomatoes,
    at room temperature
2 cloves garlic, finely chopped
3 tablespoons superior olive oil
1 tablespoon safflower oil
2 tablespoons slivered fresh basil
2 tablespoons chopped Italian parsley
Salt and freshly ground black pepper to taste

Boil pasta in rapidly boiling water. In the meantime, place the rest of the ingredients in a food processor or food mill and purée.

When pasta is cooked al dente, drain well by shaking the pasta in a colander so that all the water drains off. Toss with the raw tomato sauce and serve immediately.

Calories	Cholesterol mg	Protein gm	Carbohydrate gm	Total fat gm	%	Sat fat gm	%	Mono gm	Poly gm
2363	0	67.6	381.8	61.3	23	5.6	2	32.9	12.5

SPAGHETTINI PRIMAVERA II

As in all primavera recipes, all ingredients must be garden fresh and unrefrigerated. In this recipe the tomatoes are not blended, but remain in pieces.

I like bruschetta (page 39) served with this dish as a summer lunch.

Serves 2 to 4.

3/4 pound spaghettini
2 cups fresh garden-ripe tomatoes cut into 3/4-inch pieces,
    at room temperature
3 tablespoons fresh basil cut into thin strips
2 cloves garlic, minced
1 tablespoon chopped Italian parsley
Salt and freshly ground black pepper to taste
Juice of 1/2 lemon
Grated lemon rind of 1/2 lemon
2 tablespoons excellent olive oil
1 tablespoon safflower oil

Cook pasta in boiling water until al dente, drain well. Add the rest of the ingredients and toss.

Calories	Cholesterol mg	Protein gm	Carbohydrate gm	Total fat gm	%	Sat fat gm	%	Mono gm	Poly gm
1725	0	48.1	277.7	45.6	23	4.8	2	21.4	12.3

PASTA PRIMAVERA III

A delightful summer dish that, like the others, should be made only when the ingredients are garden fresh.

Serves 3 to 4.

2 tablespoons pine nuts
2 cups chopped fresh garden-ripe tomatoes,
    at room temperature
1 tablespoon olive oil
1 tablespoon safflower oil
Salt and freshly ground black pepper to taste
1 clove or more garlic
¾ pound linguine or spaghettini
2 cups coarsely chopped rucola (arugola)

Put pine nuts, tomatoes, oils, salt, black pepper, and garlic in a food processor and blend. Cook pasta in boiling water until done al dente. Drain well, toss in sauce, add rucola, mix well, and serve.

Calories	Cholesterol mg	Protein gm	Carbohydrate gm	Total fat gm	%	Sat fat gm	%	Mono gm	Poly gm
1666	0	52.3	278.3	37	20	2.8	1	14.9	11.5

SPAGHETTINI PRIMAVERA GENOA STYLE
Spaghettini Primavera all Genovese

This is another variation of pasta primavera, popular in Liguria. Only garden-fresh tomatoes should be used.

Serves 4 to 6.

2 pounds fresh garden-ripe tomatoes, at room temperature
1 pound white onions, thinly sliced
4 tablespoons chopped fresh basil
4 tablespoons good olive oil
1 tablespoon safflower oil
Salt and freshly ground black pepper to taste
1 pound spaghettini

Pierce tomatoes with a fork and plunge in boiling water. Leave for several seconds, then remove. Peel and core the tomatoes and cut them in slices. Mix together with the onions, basil, oils, salt, and pepper and let stand for an hour or two. Do not refrigerate.

Boil spaghettini in boiling salted water until cooked al dente; then drain well and gently toss with the tomato mixture.

Calories	Cholesterol mg	Protein gm	Carbohydrate gm	Total fat gm	%	Sat fat gm	%	Mono gm	Poly gm
2644	0	73.9	416.2	75.3	25	8.4	3	41.2	14.5

V. BOGHOSIAN'S PASTA PRIMAVERA

This is a very good variation of pasta primavera, which differs from traditional versions in that the tomatoes are just lightly cooked with some garlic beforehand.

Serves 4 to 6.

4 medium to large fresh garden-ripe tomatoes
1 pound spaghettini
3 tablespoons olive oil
1 teaspoon safflower oil
2 cloves garlic, thinly sliced
Salt and freshly ground black pepper or hot pepper flakes
    to taste
About 4 tablespoons chopped fresh basil

Dip tomatoes in boiling water for a few seconds, then remove skin and chop coarsely.

Cook pasta in rapidly boiling water about 5 minutes. Meanwhile, heat the oils in a medium to large skillet. Add garlic, and as it takes on color, add the tomatoes, salt, and pepper. Cook, stirring, over high heat 3 minutes. Add basil.

Drain pasta when done al dente and add to skillet with sauce. Toss pasta in the sauce over high heat for a minute or less.

Calories	Cholesterol mg	Protein gm	Carbohydrate gm	Total fat gm	%	Sat fat gm	%	Mono gm	Poly gm
2176	0	57.3	370.0	52.3	21	4.8	2	31.5	6.1

SPAGHETTI WITH OIL AND GARLIC
Spaghetti Aglio e Olio

A number of years ago Craig Claiborne and Pierre Franey and some Italian friends and I were dining in an excellent restaurant in Rome that specialized in food from Emilia.

The owner was a charming man who was as enthusiastic about food as one can possibly be. He said that the great Italian cookbook writer Carnacina frequently dined at his restaurant and that his favorite dish was spaghetti aglio e olio. So the owner gave us the recipe: The pasta is boiled and drained, put into soup plates with oil and garlic on top (about 1 tablespoon olive oil and 1/2 teaspoon chopped garlic per serving). Another soup plate is put on top, then the two are turned over so that the chopped garlic rests on the bottom of the plate with the steamy pasta on top, and so that its aroma penetrates the pasta and those who don't eat garlic do not have to eat it.

The gentleman who owned the restaurant became very emotional as we discussed the different types of pasta that traditionally went with certain sauces. He had very strong feelings on the subject of this particular recipe. I remember that the discussion ended when, with great aplomb, he took an orator's pose and said, "*Questa e la morta degli spaghetti*" — "This is the death of spaghetti." He meant that this recipe is the ultimate recipe for spaghetti. It is essential that the pasta be the best quality available, preferably imported, that the oil be of the finest quality, and the garlic fresh.

SPAGHETTI WITH GARLIC AND OIL SAUCE GARNISHED WITH MUSHROOMS
Spaghetti Aglio e Olio

Serves 4 to 6.

1 pound spaghetti or spaghettini
1 pound mushrooms, sliced
4 tablespoons olive oil*
2 tablespoons safflower oil*
4 fat cloves garlic, finely chopped
Hot pepper flakes to taste (optional)
3 tablespoons minced Italian parsley

*More oil may be used if needed.

Cook pasta in a large pot of boiling water. In the meantime, sauté mushrooms in 2 tablespoons of the olive oil and 1 tablespoon of the safflower oil until all moisture cooks out.

When the pasta is cooked, drain, reserving about 1/2 cup cooking water. Heat remaining oil, and add garlic, then hot pepper as soon as garlic begins to color. Add pasta, half the reserved pasta water, and toss pasta for about 30 seconds. Add parsley, mix well. Serve pasta with the mound of cooked mushrooms on top.

Calories	Cholesterol mg	Protein gm	Carbohydrate gm	Total fat gm	%	Sat fat gm	%	Mono gm	Poly gm
2538	0	70.3	361.9	88.0	31	8.2	3	45.2	23.2

VERMICELLI WITH OIL, GARLIC, AND ANCHOVY
Vermicelli Aglio e Olio

Although pasta is almost always served separately from the main course in Italy, I find a portion of this recipe goes very well on the same plate with a slice of broiled fish, such as Mako shark or swordfish.

Serves 2 to 3.

1/2 pound vermicelli or spaghettini
2 tablespoons olive oil
1 teaspoon safflower oil
2 cloves garlic, minced
1 salted anchovy (page 503), washed, boned, and chopped,
    or 4 anchovy fillets packed in oil, chopped
Hot pepper flakes to taste

Garnish:
1 tablespoon finely chopped Italian parsley
1/4 cup toasted breadcrumbs*

*To toast breadcrumbs, mix well with 1 teaspoon safflower oil, then lightly toast under broiler, shaking occasionally, taking care not to burn them.

Boil pasta in a large pot of salted water. Meanwhile, heat the two oils in a medium skillet, then add garlic, anchovies, and hot pepper. Stir, and as garlic takes on color, add about 1/2 cup of the pasta cooking water, mixing well. When pasta is almost cooked (about 2 minutes before it is done al dente), drain and add to anchovy-and-garlic sauce. Stirring often, cook until most of the liquid has cooked away. Garnish with parsley and garnish each plate with toasted breadcrumbs.

Calories	Cholesterol mg	Protein gm	Carbohydrate gm	Total fat gm	%	Sat fat gm	%	Mono gm	Poly gm
1224	9.0	33.0	178.6	40.7	29	5.0	4	21.3	9.5

PENNE WITH ASPARAGUS AND MUSHROOMS
Penne con Asparagi

Serves 6.

2 tablespoons olive oil
1 tablespoon safflower oil
1 pound asparagus cut into 1 1/2-inch pieces,
    tough ends removed
Salt and freshly ground black pepper to taste
2 cups sliced mushrooms (not too thin)
1 recipe marinara sauce (page 430)
1 pound penne or other tubular pasta, such as ziti, rigatoni

Garnish: Chopped Italian parsley

Heat the two oils in a skillet and sauté the asparagus. Add salt and pepper and cook over medium heat, stirring often, about 5 minutes—do not overcook. Remove with a slotted spoon and set aside.

Add the mushrooms to the oil, salt and pepper again to taste, and sauté over high heat. When mushrooms begin to brown, remove and add to marinara sauce. Simmer in sauce 5 minutes, then add asparagus and simmer another 5 minutes.

Meanwhile, cook the pasta until al dente. Drain well and mix with the sauce, then garnish with parsley.

Calories	Cholesterol mg	Protein gm	Carbohydrate gm	Total fat gm	%	Sat fat gm	%	Mono gm	Poly gm
2926	0	86.9	439.8	94.7	28	9.0	3	54.1	17.6

PASTA WITH BEANS
Pasta e Fagioli

This recipe is also very good with Italian-style tunafish (a 7-ounce can) added to the sauce just before serving.

Serves 6.

4 cups fresh shelled cranberry beans (shell beans) or
    2 cups dried cannellini, cranberry,
    or Great Northern beans*
1 small carrot
2 3-inch stalks celery
1 bay leaf
Salt and freshly ground black pepper to taste
3 tablespoons olive oil
1 tablespoon safflower oil

1 teaspoon or more finely chopped garlic (I prefer more)
Juice of 1 lemon
1 teaspoon marjoram
2 cups chicken or beef broth
2 tablespoons finely chopped Italian parsley
1 pound pasta, such as bows, penne, or ziti

Garnish: Finely chopped Italian parsley

*Two 1-pound 4-ounce cans cannellini beans may be substituted, in which case skip the first two steps of the recipe — preparing the beans. Add them when you pour in the broth.

If using dried beans, soak overnight in water to cover.

Place beans in a saucepan, cover with water about 1 inch above beans, add carrot, celery, bay leaf, salt, and pepper to taste. Cover and boil gently until tender — about 2 hours for dried beans, 1 hour for fresh ones. Drain beans after they are cooked. Discard liquid, vegetables, and bay leaf.

In a medium skillet or saucepan heat the two oils. Add garlic and as soon as it takes on color, add lemon juice, then the beans, marjoram, broth, and parsley. Cover and simmer over low heat about 5 minutes.

Purée beans and liquid in a food processor or food mill to a creamy sauce the consistency of an average tomato sauce. Add more stock if needed.

Cook pasta in boiling salted water. Drain when al dente. Toss in sauce and serve. Garnish each portion with finely chopped parsley.

Calories	Cholesterol	Protein	Carbohydrate	Total fat		Sat fat		Mono	Poly
	mg	gm	gm	gm	%	gm	%	gm	gm
3415	0	138.5	555.9	65.3	17	6.6	2	31.3	13.9

PASTA WITH BROCCOLI
Pasta e Broccoli

Serves 6.

2 cups diced potatoes
6 cups broccoli cut into bite-sized pieces
2 tablespoons olive oil
1 tablespoon safflower oil
1 medium onion, finely chopped
1 teaspoon minced garlic
1 teaspoon marjoram
Salt and freshly ground black pepper to taste
1 pound tubular pasta, such as penne or rigatoni
Some broth

Cook potatoes and broccoli together for several minutes in several cups of boiling water. Drain, reserving 2 cups water.

Heat the oils in a medium skillet and cook onion until translucent. Add garlic, broccoli, potatoes, marjoram, reserved water, salt, and pepper. Cover and simmer over medium heat until potatoes dissolve, about 20 minutes.

In the meantime, cook pasta in boiling water. Drain pasta when al dente, reserving a little of the cooking water. Mix the pasta with the sauce. If sauce is too thick, loosen with broth or the warm water reserved from pasta.

Calories	Cholesterol mg	Protein gm	Carbohydrate gm	Total fat gm	%	Sat fat gm	%	Mono gm	Poly gm
2592	0	79.6	456.3	47.6	16	4.8	2	21.4	12.3

LINGUINE WITH BROCCOLI
Linguine con Broccoli

This is a variation on the broccoletti di rape recipe on page 85 that I created using broccoli instead. It is also very tasty.

Serves 3 to 4.

1 bunch fresh broccoli, or 1 pound broccoli di rape
6 tablespoons olive oil
2 tablespoons safflower oil
2 tablespoons coarsely chopped garlic
Hot pepper flakes to taste (optional)
About 2½ cups water
½ pound linguine or spaghettini, imported if possible,
    broken into 2-inch lengths
Salt and freshly ground black pepper to taste

Cut off broccoli flowerets and peel the stems. Cut flowerets into 2-inch lengths, slicing large ones in halves or quarters. Wash and set aside.

Put oils, garlic, and hot pepper in a large skillet. Turn up heat. When oil gets hot, add broccoli, 1 cup of the water, and the uncooked pasta. Stir thoroughly to combine ingredients—if the pasta is not mixed well at the beginning it will stick together. Add salt and pepper and stir, then cover. Cook over moderate heat, stirring often and taking care that the pasta does not stick together and to the bottom of the pot. Add more water if needed. Cook about 10 minutes, until al dente. Serve hot.

Calories	Cholesterol mg	Protein gm	Carbohydrate gm	Total fat gm	%	Sat fat gm	%	Mono gm	Poly gm
1898	0	38.3	186.6	111.8	52	11.2	5	65.8	25.0

PASTA WITH FRESH TOMATOES AND BROCCOLI
Pasta con Salsa di Pomodoro Fresco e Broccoli

Serves 4 to 5.

1/2 pound cut pasta, such as farfalle, shells, or penne
2 cups broccoli cut into bite-sized pieces
1 tablespoon good olive oil
1 tablespoon safflower oil
2 cloves garlic, minced
Hot pepper flakes to taste
8 dried black olives, pitted and sliced
2 cups fresh plum tomatoes, sliced in wedges
4 tablespoons chopped fresh basil

Garnish: 2 tablespoons finely chopped Italian parsley

Bring a large pot of water to a boil and add pasta. Put a colander with the broccoli over the boiling water, cover, and steam.* Stir the pasta occasionally.

In the meantime, heat the oils in a medium skillet, then add garlic, hot pepper flakes, olives, and tomatoes. Cook over high heat for several minutes, stirring often. Add basil, cover, and simmer. When broccoli is tender, add to sauce and continue cooking pasta until it is al dente, then drain and mix with the sauce. Garnish with parsley.

*The broccoli could be steamed in a separate pot if convenient.

Calories	Cholesterol mg	Protein gm	Carbohydrate gm	Total fat gm	%	Sat fat gm	%	Mono gm	Poly gm
1299	0	39.8	207.6	37.1	25	3.2	2	16.5	11.1

SPAGHETTINI WITH BROCCOLETTI DI RAPE
Spaghettini con Broccoletti di Rape

In 1971 we were in Germany, and we took a train from Frankfurt to Munich. The train was half empty and I looked around for a friendly face in our car. There was only one, and I knew from his black hair and sad eyes that the man was Italian. I introduced myself in Italian, then asked him if he was indeed Italian. He smiled, said yes, and asked me to sit down. It was clear from his accent that he was from Naples. It appeared that he was a factory worker in Germany and he missed his family and Napolitano cooking. I don't think we had talked more than three minutes before we were on the subject of food. He became more animated as he described his favorite dishes.

He asked me if I had tasted pasta with rape. I said I had and how I made it by cooking the pasta and rape together in a large pot of boiling water. Then, when the pasta was al dente, I drained it and tossed it with oil and minced garlic.

He looked at me with pity and shook his head. And I knew immediately I was about to get another great recipe.

He proceeded to describe in the most poetic way the following recipe, in perhaps the most expressive language in the Western world — the Napolitano dialect. He explained in detail how to prepare this simple, lovely dish, but I just could not believe it was possible to cook raw pasta with raw vegetables in a very small amount of water. I was convinced, though, when he clasped his hands, rolled his eyes, and exclaimed in his beautiful Napolitano dialect, "*E cosie buon ce famale!*" — "It's so good it hurts!"

I have to admit I get great satisfaction from collecting unknown family recipes from friends and strangers. It is like a treasure hunt for me. And though this one seemed to break all the rules, I knew it had to be good.

Serves 4.

2 cloves garlic, chopped
Hot pepper flakes to taste
3 tablespoons olive oil
1 tablespoon safflower oil
Water
¾ pound imported spaghettini, broken into 2-inch lengths
8 cups rape (page 348), cleaned and cut into 2-inch pieces*
Salt to taste

*Broccoli can be used instead of rape, but it should be blanched first in boiling water.

In a large pot sauté the garlic and hot pepper in the two oils. As soon as garlic begins to color, add 1 cup water; when it comes to a boil, add the spaghettini and a pinch of salt and stir well. When water returns to a boil again, add rape, stirring the mixture often as it cooks over medium to low heat and adding more water as is needed. Cook until pasta is tender — about 10 to 12 minutes. Taste for salt. When cooked, all the water should be incorporated into sauce. Serve immediately.

Calories	Cholesterol mg	Protein gm	Carbohydrate gm	Total fat gm	%	Sat fat gm	%	Mono gm	Poly gm
1811	0	49.7	268.0	59.3	29	6.6	3	31.3	13.4

PASTA WITH RAPE
Pasta con le Rape

Serves 6.

2 cups cleaned and chopped broccoli rape (page 348), or
   broccoli flowerets

2 cups marinara sauce (page 430)
1 pound tubular pasta, such as penne, rigatoni, ziti, etc.

Garnish: 2 cups toasted croutons (page 54)

Blanch rape or broccoli in boiling water. Drain and add to sauce. Cook in covered pot for 20 minutes. In the meantime, cook pasta in salted boiling water. Drain pasta when done al dente and toss with sauce.

Serve on individual plates. Garnish with croutons.

Calories	Cholesterol mg	Protein gm	Carbohydrate gm	Total fat gm	%	Sat fat gm	%	Mono gm	Poly gm
2510	0	72.4	411.8	63.0	22	6.5	2	36.1	8.6

RAPE WITH ORECCHIETTE ("LITTLE EARS")
Broccoletti di Rape con Orecchiette

Serves 4 to 6.

Salt to taste
1 pound orecchiette pasta
1½ pounds rape, washed and chopped (page 348)*
4 tablespoons olive oil
1 tablespoon safflower oil
3 or more cloves garlic, finely chopped
Hot pepper flakes to taste
6 anchovy fillets, chopped

*Fresh broccoli cut into bite-sized pieces can be used instead of rape.

Bring 6 quarts water to a boil, add salt and pasta. Stir and cook about 5 minutes, then add rape. Cook until pasta is al dente. Drain, reserving 1 cup water.

In the meantime, heat the oils in a large skillet, then add garlic, hot pepper, and anchovies. Cook over high heat until garlic begins to color. Add pasta with rape along with some of the reserved water. Cook over high heat, stirring often, about 1 minute.

Serve immediately on hot plates.

Calories	Cholesterol mg	Protein gm	Carbohydrate gm	Total fat gm	%	Sat fat gm	%	Mono gm	Poly gm
2538	13.2	86.1	382.8	77.6	27	8.0	3	43.8	14.3

SPAGHETTI WITH CAULIFLOWER
Spaghetti chi Vruoccoli Arriminata

This recipe is of Sicilian origin and has a lovely delicate flavor.

Serves 4.

2 tablespoons olive oil
1 teaspoon safflower oil
2 cloves garlic, finely chopped
4 cups chopped tomatoes, fresh if possible (drain if canned)
2 tablespoons finely chopped Italian parsley
2 tablespoons yellow raisins, soaked in warm water
    15 minutes and drained
2 tablespoons pine nuts
Salt and freshly ground black pepper to taste
Hot pepper flakes to taste (optional)
1 1/4 pounds cauliflower flowerets
3/4 pound spaghetti

Garnish: Chopped Italian parsley

Heat the oils in a medium skillet or shallow saucepan. Add garlic. When it takes on color, add tomatoes. Cover and cook over moderate heat for 5 minutes. Add parsley, drained raisins, pine nuts, salt, pepper, and optional hot pepper flakes. Cover and simmer over low to moderate heat for 10 minutes. In the meantime, blanch cauliflower in boiling water for 1 minute. Drain, then cut the flowerets into bite-sized pieces and add them to the sauce. Cover and continue cooking for 5 to 8 minutes. Cook pasta in rapidly boiling water until done al dente, then drain well.

Toss pasta with sauce and serve hot, garnished with chopped parsley.

Calories	Cholesterol mg	Protein gm	Carbohydrate gm	Total fat gm	%	Sat fat gm	%	Mono gm	Poly gm
2003	0	71.9	334.8	43.2	19	3.6	2	23.9	5.8

PENNE WITH CAULIFLOWER
Penne e Cavolfiore

Serves 6 to 8.

1 medium cauliflower
3 cloves garlic, chopped
3/4 cup finely chopped onion
4 tablespoons olive oil mixed with 2 tablespoons
    safflower oil
2 cups chopped tomatoes, fresh if possible, put through
    a food mill and drained.

1 teaspoon dried oregano
4 tablespoons chopped Italian parsley
Salt and freshly ground black pepper to taste
Hot pepper flakes to taste (optional)
2 cups sliced mushrooms
1/4 cup yellow raisins
2 7-ounce cans Italian-style tunafish
    (drain, break up, set aside)
3/4 pound penne, rigatoni, or any tubular pasta

Cut off cauliflower flowerets. Wash them and cook in boiling salted water for not more than 4 or 5 minutes — they should be firm. Drain and set aside.

Sauté garlic and onion in 4 tablespoons of the oil. When onion wilts, add tomatoes, oregano, 2 tablespoons of the parsley, salt, pepper, and optional hot pepper flakes. Cover and simmer over low heat.

In a skillet sauté mushrooms in the remaining 2 tablespoons oil until they are tender, then add to simmering sauce along with the raisins. Cook 10 minutes more, taste for salt and pepper. Add tuna, mix well, then turn off heat.

Preheat oven to 350°. Meanwhile, cook pasta in boiling salted water about 5 minutes. Drain, pouring 1/4 cup pasta water into a deep 4-quart ovenproof dish. Add the pasta and the sauce and toss with the pasta water. Cover and bake about 10 minutes. Depending on the type of pasta used, pasta should be al dente; if not, bake a few minutes more. Sprinkle some of remaining parsley on each portion when serving.

Calories	Cholesterol mg	Protein gm	Carbohydrate gm	Total fat gm	%	Sat fat gm	%	Mono gm	Poly gm
3114	221.0	170.4	346.4	116	33	15.7	4	51.0	29.0

PASTA WITH EGGPLANT AND WALNUTS
Pasta con Melanzane e Noci

Serves 6 to 8.

2 tablespoons olive oil
1 tablespoon safflower oil
1 eggplant, about 1 1/2 pounds, cut into 1/2-inch-thick slices,
    then cut into manageable pieces (about 7 or 8 cups)
Salt and freshly ground black pepper to taste
2 cups marinara sauce (page 430)
22 to 25 walnuts, shelled and chopped
1 pound cut pasta, such as penne, shells, ziti, etc.
2 tablespoons finely chopped Italian parsley
About 3/4 cup breadcrumbs (mix with 1 tablespoon
    safflower oil)

Heat the two oils in a large skillet, then add eggplant, salt, and pepper. Cook over medium heat, tossing occasionally, until eggplant begins to brown. Turn off heat and set aside.

Blend the tomato sauce in a food processor or run through a food mill. Pour sauce into a food processor with walnut meats and blend. Or blend some of the sauce with walnuts using a mortar and pestle, then combine crushed walnut meats with the rest of sauce.

Preheat oven to 450°. Cook pasta in a large pot of boiling water until almost done, draining about 5 minutes before cooking is completed. Put drained pasta in an ovenproof dish with sauce, mixing well. Add cooked eggplant and mix; then add parsley, top with breadcrumbs, cover, and bake about 15 to 20 minutes.

Remove dish from oven, broil under high heat a minute or two to brown breadcrumbs.

Variation: An alternative to baking is to cook pasta until done al dente, then toss with sauce and eggplant, cover with breadcrumbs, and toast crumbs under broiler.

Calories	Cholesterol mg	Protein gm	Carbohydrate gm	Total fat gm	%	Sat fat gm	%	Mono gm	Poly gm
3639	0	97.1	479.6	152.7	37	12.2	3	50.0	64.1

PASTA WITH GREEN TOMATOES I
Pasta con i Pomodori Verdi

This unusual recipe was described to me by a painter friend who lives in Rome. It had been served to him by an Italian painter who was from southern Italy. I had never heard of the recipe before and was delighted to find a pasta recipe using green tomatoes, since it seems that those of us who grow tomatoes seem to have an abundance of green tomatoes that never ripen at the end of the season.

Serves 4 to 6.

3 tablespoons olive oil
3 teaspoons safflower oil
1 medium onion, finely chopped

1 teaspoon finely chopped garlic
4 large green tomatoes, thinly sliced, about 8 cups
2 tablespoons finely chopped Italian parsley
3 tablespoons coarsely chopped fresh basil
1/2 to 1 cup chicken or beef stock
Salt and freshly ground black pepper to taste
1 pound bucatini pasta
6 tablespoons grated Pecorino Romano cheese or
     Parmesan cheese*

Garnish: Finely chopped Italian parsley

*The only Pecorino cheese available in America is Pecorino Romano, a blend of ewe's milk I personally do not like. The Pecorino cheese that is made by farmers in central and southern Italy is far superior, but unfortunately is not exported from Italy.

Heat the two oils in a medium saucepan or skillet. Add onion and simmer over moderate heat until it begins to brown. Add garlic, simmer a minute or so, then add tomatoes. Cover and simmer over medium to low heat for 5 minutes. Add parsley, basil, 1/2 cup stock, salt, and pepper. Cover and simmer over medium to low heat, adding more stock if sauce becomes too dry. Cook for 30 minutes.

When tomatoes are nearly done, cook pasta al dente. Drain well and toss with sauce. Add cheese, mix, and serve immediately.

Garnish with chopped Italian parsley.

Calories	Cholesterol mg	Protein gm	Carbohydrate gm	Total fat gm	%	Sat fat gm	%	Mono gm	Poly gm
2770	36.0	93.1	453.8	72.3	23	12.6	4	33.7	13.4

PENNE WITH GREEN TOMATOES II
Penne con i Pomodori Verdi

This recipe was given to me by an old friend from Abruzzi. It is another excellent way to use green tomatoes. The dish can be frozen successfully, but do not bake before freezing.

Serves 4 to 6.

4 egg whites
Salt and freshly ground black pepper to taste
2 pounds green tomatoes (medium to large), cut into
     1/2-inch slices
Flour for dredging
Vegetable oil for shallow-frying
1 pound penne or rigatoni
1/2 recipe marinara sauce (page 430)

Lightly beat egg whites, salt, and pepper. Dip tomato slices into egg whites one at a time and then dust with flour. Set aside.

Pour vegetable oil (I prefer corn oil) ¾ inch deep into a medium skillet. Heat and check for correct temperature by flicking a few specks of flour into it (oil should boil violently when flour hits). With a slotted spoon place tomato slices in the hot oil a few at a time. Brown slightly on both sides, remove, and place between paper towels. Repeat until all tomato slices are cooked. Salt to taste.

Cook pasta in a large pot of boiling water for 5 minutes, then drain.

Put one quarter of the marinara sauce in the bottom of a deep ovenproof dish. Place a layer of tomato slices on the sauce, then a layer of pasta. Repeat until all tomato slices and pasta are used up.

Preheat oven to 350° and bake, covered, for 20 minutes. If there is too much liquid, remove cover so some can cook away.

Calories	Cholesterol mg	Protein gm	Carbohydrate gm	Total fat gm	%	Sat fat gm	%	Mono gm	Poly gm
2434	0	90.3	426.8	40.1	14	3.4	1	18.3	7.8

PASTA WITH MUSHROOMS AND NUTS
Pasta con Funghi e Noci

Serves 4 to 6.

¾-ounce package dried boletus mushrooms, or 1 pound
    fresh mushrooms, sliced*
3 tablespoons olive oil
1 tablespoon safflower oil
1 medium onion, finely chopped
Salt and freshly ground black pepper or hot pepper flakes
    to taste
¾ cup imported dry marsala
2 cups chopped, peeled tomatoes, fresh if possible
    (drain if canned)
2 tablespoons chopped fresh basil or 1 teaspoon dried
1 pound pasta, any cut (I use spaghettini)

Garnish:
10 shelled and chopped walnuts, about ½ cup
2 tablespoons finely chopped Italian parsley

*If you use fresh mushrooms instead of dried, slice them thinly and sauté in vegetable oil until they begin to dry out, then add to the sauce at the same time you would the soaked, dried mushrooms.

Soak the dried mushrooms in ½ cup warm water for 15 minutes; then drain, reserving the liquid.

Meanwhile, heat the two oils in a medium skillet or saucepan and add the onion. When onion turns translucent, add mushrooms. Season with salt and pepper and sauté until onion begins to brown. Add marsala, cover, lower heat, and simmer until marsala cooks out. Then add tomatoes, basil, and liquid from mushrooms. Cover and simmer about 30 minutes.

When tomatoes are nearly done, boil pasta in boiling water. When cooked al dente, drain well and toss in sauce. Dish out servings in soup plates. Garnish each portion with nuts and chopped parsley. Serve immediately.

Calories	Cholesterol mg	Protein gm	Carbohydrate gm	Total fat gm	%	Sat fat gm	%	Mono gm	Poly gm
2672	0	73.3	402.7	86.6	29	8.4	3	35.1	29.3

PASTA WITH CHESTNUTS AND MUSHROOMS
Pasta con Castagne e Funghi

This is an interesting pasta recipe that children seem to have a special fondness for, perhaps because of the sweetness of the marsala.

Serves 3 to 4.

14 fresh chestnuts
1 tablespoon butter
1 tablespoon safflower oil
2 tablespoons finely chopped shallots
2 cups sliced mushrooms
6/8-ounce package dried boletus mushrooms, soaked
    in water for 15 minutes, or 2 cups sliced wild
    fresh mushrooms
1/2 cup stock
1/4 cup sweet marsala (imported Florio) or sweet sherry
Salt and freshly ground black pepper to taste
3 tablespoons finely chopped Italian parsley
1/2 pound cut pasta, such as farfalle, penne, etc.

Garnish: Chopped Italian parsley

With a sharp knife cut a slit in fresh chestnuts and boil in boiling water to cover for 12 to 15 minutes. Let chestnuts remain in hot water while you cut off outer shell and remove skin of a chestnut at a time. (They are much easier to work with when hot.) Then coarsely chop all the chestnuts.

Heat butter and oil in a medium skillet, add shallots, and sauté for several minutes. Add both fresh and dried mushrooms with their water and the chopped chestnuts, cover, and simmer 5 minutes. Add the stock, marsala, salt, pepper, and parsley, cover, and simmer over low heat.

In the meantime, cook the pasta in 4 to 6 quarts salted water in a large pot until al dente.

Drain well and toss in sauce that has been simmering while pasta was cooking. Serve immediately in hot bowls garnished with chopped Italian parsley.

Calories	Cholesterol mg	Protein gm	Carbohydrate gm	Total fat gm	%	Sat fat gm	%	Mono gm	Poly gm
1402	32.0	38.7	243.4	30.0	19	7.5	5	5.4	10.4

VERMICELLI WITH MUSHROOMS AND WINE
Vermicelli alla Carrettiera

Serves 4 to 6.

5 tablespoons olive oil mixed with 1 tablespoon
 safflower oil
2 medium onions, finely chopped
4 cups sliced mushrooms
5 tablespoons dry white wine
2 tablespoons minced Italian parsley
1 teaspoon dried oregano
3 cloves garlic, minced
Salt and freshly ground black pepper to taste
2 cups fresh breadcrumbs
1 pound vermicelli or spaghettini

Garnish:
Finely chopped Italian parsley
Toasted breadcrumbs

Heat 3 tablespoons of the oil in a medium skillet and add onions. When onions become translucent, add mushrooms and cook over high heat until liquid cooks out. Add wine, parsley, oregano, and garlic, cover, and simmer for 5 minutes. Add salt and pepper.

Put breadcrumbs on a tray and sprinkle over them the remaining oil, salt, and pepper; then mix well. Place under broiler and brown.

Cook pasta in boiling water until al dente, then drain. Place equal portions of pasta on each plate, then ladle the mushroom-and-onion mixture in a mound on top. Garnish with parsley and a generous amount of toasted breadcrumbs.

Calories	Cholesterol mg	Protein gm	Carbohydrate gm	Total fat gm	%	Sat fat gm	%	Mono gm	Poly gm
2875	0	78.3	432.7	90.5	28	10.2	3	51.1	15.6

SPAGHETTI NORCIA STYLE
Spaghetti alla Nursina

This dish is best with wild mushrooms. The original recipe calls for fresh boletus, or porcini as they are called in Italy.

Serves 4 to 6.

3/4 pound spaghetti
2 tablespoons olive oil or 3 tablespoons vegetable oil
1 tablespoon safflower oil
6 cups sliced mushrooms, about 3/4 pound (without stems)
8 anchovies, chopped
Hot pepper flakes to taste
1 teaspoon minced garlic
2 tablespoons dry white wine

Garnish: Finely chopped Italian parsley

Cook spaghetti in boiling lightly salted water (use less salt than usual because of salt content in anchovies).

Meanwhile, heat oils in a medium skillet, add mushrooms, and cook over high heat until they exude their moisture; then add anchovies, hot pepper, and garlic. Cook, stirring, for several minutes, then stir in white wine and remove from heat. Drain pasta when cooked al dente. Mix with mushroom sauce in a hot serving bowl. Garnish with a generous amount of parsley.

Calories	Cholesterol mg	Protein gm	Carbohydrate gm	Total fat gm	%	Sat fat gm	%	Mono gm	Poly gm
1854	35.0	66.4	273.3	52.5	25	7.4	4	24.3	14.2

FARFALLE WITH WHITE TRUFFLES
Farfalle al Tartufi Bianchi

This is a recipe in which we've been considerably freer with saturated fat. After all, how often does one eat white truffles?

Serves 4 to 6.

2 tablespoons butter
2 tablespoons safflower oil
2 cups sliced white or yellow onions
1/2 cup chopped shallots
Salt and freshly ground black pepper to taste
3 cups tomatoes, fresh if possible, put through a food mill and drained
1 pound farfalle pasta (butterflies), imported or homemade
1 cup half-and-half cream
1/4 teaspoon grated nutmeg

Garnish:
Freshly grated Parmesan cheese*
1 medium white truffle

*I have observed that often people tend to believe more grated cheese is better than less. Grated cheese used in excess will over-whelm any sauce, let alone a delicate sauce. The white truffle has a very distinctive delicate flavor, more of an odor than a taste, so a light touch with the cheese is suggested here.

Heat butter and oil in a medium saucepan, add onions, shallots, salt, and pepper and cook over moderate heat until onions begin to brown. Add tomatoes and continue cooking, stirring often, so that sauce boils gently for about 45 minutes. Put sauce in a food processor and blend. Pour into a large skillet.

Cook pasta in rapidly boiling salted water. Drain pasta before it is completely cooked, about 2 minutes before desired doneness.

In the meantime, bring sauce to a boil and add cream and nutmeg. When sauce boils, add drained pasta and cook over high heat until it is tender but not overcooked, stirring constantly.

Serve on hot plates. Add a little grated Parmesan (not too much) and some truffle shavings, which are shaved on the blade side of your cheese grater. Serve immediately.

Calories	Cholesterol mg	Protein gm	Carbohydrate gm	Total fat gm	%	Sat fat gm	%	Mono gm	Poly gm
2803	179	84.2	413.6	90.1	28	33.4	10	22.2	21.1

V. BOGHOSIAN'S PASTA WITH HOT PEPPER SAUCE
V. Boghosian's Pasta al l'Arrabbiata

Ten years ago I would have never recommended an American canned tomato over an imported Italian. When my friend Boghosian insisted that Hunt's put out a superior canned tomato to most of the imported Italian brands, I was skeptical to say the least. To my surprise, he was right, and I do not hesitate to say that Hunt's whole tomatoes (without added purée) are superior to most imported brands. My objection to tinned American tomatoes was that they were tasteless, and it seemed to me they were not ripe tomatoes. Hunt's uses a ripe, sweet tomato and makes an excellent sauce.

Serves 4 to 6.

2 10½-ounce cans Hunt's whole tomatoes, or
    4 cups fresh ripe tomatoes
3 large cloves garlic, cut into large pieces
4 tablespoons olive oil
1 tablespoon safflower oil
1 small dried hot pepper, seeds removed
Salt to taste
1 pound pasta — spaghetti, spaghettini, or any
    cut pasta, such as penne, ziti, etc.
2 cups thinly sliced mushrooms

Garnish: Chopped Italian parsley

Pass tomatoes through a food mill and set aside. In a medium to large skillet sauté garlic in the oils until it begins to take on color. Add tomatoes. When sauce begins to boil, add hot pepper and simmer about 5 minutes over moderate heat, uncovered, stirring often. Add salt to taste. Pick out garlic pieces and crush them, then return to sauce. Remove hot pepper from sauce and discard. Lower heat and simmer, uncovered, about 30 minutes.

Cook pasta al dente, drain, and add to sauce in skillet, stirring over high heat for a minute or so. Place a portion of the raw sliced mushrooms in each plate, add sauced pasta, and serve. Garnish with fresh chopped Italian parsley. The heat from the pasta will bind the mushroom flavor to the pasta.

Calories	Cholesterol mg	Protein gm	Carbohydrate gm	Total fat gm	%	Sat fat gm	%	Mono gm	Poly gm
2456	0	66.9	379.5	74.8	27	7.7	3	42.4	13.9

SPAGHETTI WOODSMAN STYLE
Spaghetti alla Boscaiola

This was always made in Italy with wild mushrooms — hence the name.

Serves 6 to 8.

6 tablespoons olive oil
2 tablespoons safflower oil
3 large cloves garlic, crushed (skins discarded)
4 cups chopped tomatoes, fresh if possible
    (drain if canned)
Salt and freshly ground black pepper to taste
About 24 ounces mushrooms, thinly sliced
1 to 1 1/2 pounds spaghetti
2 7-ounce cans Italian-style tunafish drained

Garnish: Finely chopped Italian parsley

Heat 3 tablespoons of the olive oil and 1 tablespoon of the safflower oil in a medium saucepan. Add crushed garlic cloves and brown. When garlic is brown, remove and discard. Add tomatoes, salt, and pepper. Cover and simmer for 15 minutes.

In the meantime, in another skillet heat the remaining 3 tablespoons olive oil and 1 tablespoon safflower oil, then add mushrooms, salt, and pepper. Cook, stirring often, until all liquid has evaporated. Set aside and keep warm.

Cook pasta in a large pot of boiling salted water about 6 minutes. Drain. Bring tomato sauce up to a boil and add pasta to it. Stirring frequently, cook until pasta absorbs sauce and is al dente. Mix in the tunafish. Place pasta on heated plates, put a generous amount of mushrooms on each portion and sprinkle parsley on top.

Calories	Cholesterol mg	Protein gm	Carbohydrate gm	Total fat gm	%	Sat fat gm	%	Mono gm	Poly gm
4541	433.0	212.2	578.7	147.9	29	18.6	4	71.6	30.8

SPAGHETTI WITH ONIONS AND MILK
Spaghetti con le Cipolle e Latte

I found this recipe in a very old Italian cookbook and it is a winner.

Serves 4 to 6.

3 1/2 tablespoons safflower oil
2 tablespoons olive oil
1 1/2 pounds onions, thinly sliced, about 7 cups
1 pound spaghetti

1 cup tomatoes, fresh if possible, put through a food mill
    and drained
1 cup milk
Salt and freshly ground black pepper to taste
6 tablespoons freshly grated Parmesan cheese*

*Finely chopped Italian parsley can be used instead of Parmesan
cheese.

Heat the oils in a wide skillet or saucepan, then add onions. Simmer over
medium heat until onions are translucent.

At this point bring a large pot of salted water to a boil, then add pasta and
cook in rapidly boiling water.

After you've put in the pasta, add tomatoes and milk to onions, cover,
and gently boil. Add salt and a generous amount of black pepper. The milk
will curdle when combined with tomatoes but do not worry.

After the pasta has cooked 5 minutes, drain and add to sauce in skillet.
Finish cooking the pasta in the sauce, stirring constantly. The sauce will
now become velvety smooth because of the starch in the pasta. Cook until
pasta is al dente, taste for salt, and add more milk to pasta if sauce becomes
too tight.

Serve immediately on warm plates, topping each serving with a little
grated cheese.

Calories	Cholesterol mg	Protein gm	Carbohydrate gm	Total fat gm	%	Sat fat gm	%	Mono gm	Poly gm
2938	51.0	90.5	437.0	98.7	30	18.5	6	30.6	37.8

SPAGHETTI WITH ONIONS
Spaghetti con Cipolle

Serves 6 to 8.

5 tablespoons olive oil
2 tablespoons safflower oil
8 cups thinly sliced onion
Salt and freshly ground black pepper to taste
2 cups beef stock, or 2 cubes beef bouillon dissolved
    in 2 cups boiling water
1 teaspoon marjoram
1½ pounds spaghetti or spaghettini
4 tablespoons chopped Italian parsley

Heat the oils in a large skillet. Add onion, salt, and pepper, cover, and
simmer over low heat for 30 minutes. Add beef stock and marjoram, cover,
and simmer over low heat for 2 hours, stirring occasionally.

Cook pasta in a large pot of boiling water until done al dente. Drain, mix in with onion in skillet and cook over moderate heat about 1 to 2 minutes, stirring constantly. Mix in parsley and serve hot.

Calories	Cholesterol mg	Protein gm	Carbohydrate gm	Total fat gm	%	Sat fat gm	%	Mono gm	Poly gm
3699	0	99.4	586.7	103.7	25	11.2	3	53.5	25.1

PASTA SHELLS WITH PEAS
Orecchiette con Piselli

Serves 4 to 6.

2 cups snow peas, ends and strings removed
Salt and freshly ground black pepper to taste
1 tablespoon peanut oil
1 cup peas, fresh if possible
2 tablespoons safflower oil
2 tablespoons butter
1 teaspoon minced garlic
3/4 pound pasta—medium shells, bows, or
   similar-cut pasta
3 tablespoons finely chopped Italian parsley
Juice of 1/2 lemon

Sauté snow peas with salt and freshly ground pepper in a medium skillet in peanut oil, uncovered, over medium heat for several minutes, stirring often. Do not overcook.

Cook peas in boiling water until tender. Drain and add to snow peas.

Heat safflower oil and butter in a small skillet. Add garlic and simmer for a minute or so, being careful not to brown it.

In the meantime, cook pasta in boiling salted water. Drain when al dente and toss in serving bowl with butter-and-garlic mixture. Add peas, snow peas, parsley, lemon juice, and more pepper. Toss several times and serve hot.

Calories	Cholesterol mg	Protein gm	Carbohydrate gm	Total fat gm	%	Sat fat gm	%	Mono gm	Poly gm
2065	62.0	60.7	297.1	69.0	29	17.2	7	17.9	24.1

PASTA WITH PEPPERS
Pasta al Peperoni

This delightful recipe should be made only when sweet red peppers are in season. In the Northeast, the season is from September to the end of October, and this dish is especially sweet because the peppers are vine-ripened. Peppers, unlike tomatoes, cannot be picked green in the expectation that they will eventually turn red. Peppers remain the color they are when they are picked. Red (or yellow) peppers are simply green peppers that were allowed to ripen. Green peppers are unripe peppers.

Serves 4 to 6.

3 tablespoons olive oil
1 tablespoon safflower oil
2 medium onions, thinly sliced
3 pounds sweet red peppers, in slices about 1/2 inch wide
2 tablespoons fresh basil or 1 teaspoon dried
Salt and freshly ground black pepper to taste
1 to 1 1/2 cups beef or chicken broth
1 pound pasta, preferably cut pasta, such as penne, ziti, or rigatoni

Garnish: Finely chopped Italian parsley

Heat the oils in a large skillet, add onions and peppers, and cook over high heat, stirring often, until edges of onions begin to brown. Lower heat to medium and add basil, salt, and pepper. Cook about 15 minutes, until peppers are tender. Add broth and cook several minutes more.

In the meantime, cook pasta in rapidly boiling water. While pasta is cooking, remove about 12 to 18 slices cooked pepper and reserve. Put the rest of the cooked peppers and their sauce in a food processor and purée to the consistency of a rather thick tomato sauce. If too thick, add more broth.

Drain pasta well and toss with sauce. Serve on warm plates. Place several reserved pepper slices on each pasta portion and garnish with parsley.

Calories	Cholesterol mg	Protein gm	Carbohydrate gm	Total fat gm	%	Sat fat gm	%	Mono gm	Poly gm
2736	0	82.3	473.5	64.4	21	5.5	2	32.8	12.6

SPAGHETTI WITH PEPPER SAUCE
Spaghetti con Salsa di Peperoni

Serves 4 to 6.

1 medium onion, thinly sliced
2 cloves garlic, minced
2 tablespoons olive oil
2 tablespoons safflower oil
1 1/2 sweet red or green peppers,
    seeded and sliced
Salt and freshly ground black pepper to taste
4 canned anchovy fillets, drained and cut into 1/2-inch
    pieces, or 4 salted anchovy fillets, washed and cut into
    1/2-inch pieces
3/4 cup dry white wine
Hot pepper flakes to taste (optional)
1 1/2 cups tomatoes, fresh if possible, put through a
    food mill and drained
1 tablespoon chopped Italian parsley
1 pound spaghetti

Garnish: 2 tablespoons chopped Italian parsley

Sauté onion and garlic over low heat with the oils. When onion begins to wilt add peppers, salt, and pepper. Continue cooking, stirring often, and when peppers are almost tender, add anchovies. Cook for several minutes and add wine—at this point a pinch of hot pepper flakes is desirable. Cover and simmer for several minutes. Turn up heat and cook out most of the wine. Add tomatoes and 1 tablespoon parsley and boil gently about 25 minutes.

Cook pasta in boiling water until about 3 minutes before desired doneness, then drain thoroughly and add to sauce. Finish cooking pasta in sauce until al dente, stirring often. Garnish with 2 tablespoons parsley.

Calories	Cholesterol mg	Protein gm	Carbohydrate gm	Total fat gm	%	Sat fat gm	%	Mono gm	Poly gm
2442	9	70.5	398.2	63.0	23	6.4	2	24.3	22.3

SHELLS WITH POTATOES
Conchigliette con Patate

Serves 6 to 8.

2 tablespoons olive oil
1 teaspoon safflower oil
1 medium onion, coarsely chopped
1 clove garlic, coarsely chopped

2 cups chopped tomatoes, fresh if possible (drain if canned)
1 teaspoon crushed rosemary
Hot pepper flakes or freshly ground black pepper to taste
Salt to taste
1/2 pound fresh spinach, washed well
1 tablespoon extra virgin olive oil
2 medium potatoes, peeled, cut in half lengthwise and
    cut into 1/8-inch slices
1/2 pound green beans, cut into 2-inch lengths
1 pound shell pasta, or any cut tubular pasta

Heat the two oils in a medium saucepan, then add onion. When onion begins to brown, add garlic and cook about 1 minute. Add tomatoes, rosemary, hot pepper flakes or black pepper, and salt; cover, lower heat, and simmer for 20 minutes. Add spinach, cover, and simmer 10 minutes, stirring occasionally.

Remove from the heat and put vegetable mixture in a food processor or run through a food mill to purée it. Add virgin olive oil to sauce and stir.

Bring a large pot of salted water to a boil, add potatoes and green beans. When water returns to a boil, add pasta and cook until pasta is done al dente.

Drain pasta, potatoes, and beans and toss in the sauce. Serve hot.

Calories	Cholesterol mg	Protein gm	Carbohydrate gm	Total fat gm	%	Sat fat gm	%	Mono gm	Poly gm
2519	0	79.9	435.5	53.2	19	4.8	2	31.5	6.1

PENNE WITH RUCOLA PESTO
Penne con Pesto Rucola

If you enjoy the unique flavor of rucola, known in this country as arugola or rocket, you will find this recipe a joy. The potatoes tend to soften the bitter taste of the rucola.

Serves 4.

The rucola pesto
7 cups fresh rucola (arugola), washed and picked over
1 tablespoon coarsely chopped garlic
3 tablespoons pine nuts
4 tablespoons olive oil
1 tablespoon safflower oil
Salt to taste

1/2 pound tubular pasta, such as penne
3 small potatoes, peeled and sliced

Put all ingredients for the pesto in a food processor and purée to a creamy consistency. You will have 1 cup. (Preserve any pesto that is not used by adding ½ inch oil to surface and refrigerate.)

Cook pasta and potatoes in boiling salted water. When pasta is done al dente, drain, reserving 4 teaspoons cooking water. Mix water with 4 tablespoons pesto so the sauce is the consistency of heavy cream. Toss with pasta and potatoes. Serve immediately on warm plates.

Calories	Cholesterol mg	Protein gm	Carbohydrate gm	Total fat gm	%	Sat fat gm	%	Mono gm	Poly gm
1748	0	43.9	218.2	78.3	39	8.7	4	45.1	15.7

SPAGHETTI WITH RUCOLA
Spaghetti alla Rughetta

I personally like this bitter sauce, but some may find it too much so; I suggest then they use the milder spring and early summer rucola.

Serves 4 to 6.

2 cups tightly packed rucola (arugola)
3 tablespoons olive oil
1 tablespoon safflower oil
2 cloves garlic, minced
Salt and freshly ground black pepper to taste
4 tablespoons pine nuts or chopped walnut meats
1 pound spaghetti

Garnish: 1 cup chopped fresh tomatoes

Put all ingredients except spaghetti and tomatoes in a food processor and blend.

Boil spaghetti in rapidly boiling water. When al dente, drain, reserving ½ cup water to dilute rucola mixture. Toss spaghetti with that mixture and garnish each portion with tomatoes.

Calories	Cholesterol mg	Protein gm	Carbohydrate gm	Total fat gm	%	Sat fat gm	%	Mono gm	Poly gm
2343	0	68.6	357.3	69.9	26	7.0	3	36.5	15.0

LINGUINE WITH BACCALA
Linguine alla Capestranese

This recipe—a delight for all who love baccalà (salt cod)—was given to me by a friend whose father is from Genoa. His family used to prepare it on Christmas Eve. You can use toasted croutons, if you like, instead of breadcrumbs.

Serves 6.

1 medium onion, finely chopped
2 tablespoons plus 2 to 3 teaspoons olive oil
1 tablespoon safflower oil
1 1/2 pounds baccalà, presoaked (page 183)
4 cups chopped, seeded fresh tomatoes
Hot pepper flakes to taste
1 tablespoon basil
Salt and freshly ground black pepper to taste
3/4 cup walnut meats, about 15 walnuts
1 pound spaghetti or other type of pasta
1 1/2 cups breadcrumbs
3 tablespoons chopped Italian parsley

Sauté the onion in 2 tablespoons olive oil and the safflower oil in a medium saucepan. Cut baccalà in 3-inch pieces and when onion begins to brown add the baccalà and tomatoes and cook several minutes. Add pepper flakes, basil, salt, and pepper, cover, and simmer for 1 hour.

In the meantime, break walnuts into small pieces with your hands. Set aside.

When baccalà mixture is almost done, cook pasta in rapidly boiling salted water. While pasta is cooking, heat 2 teaspoons olive oil in a medium skillet and sauté walnuts. Cook several minutes, taking care not to burn. Remove walnuts with a slotted spoon and set aside. Add breadcrumbs to the hot oil and lightly brown, adding another teaspoon of olive oil if needed. Drain pasta and toss in sauce. Put a portion of pasta in individual bowls and sprinkle each with walnuts, some toasted breadcrumbs, and parsley. Serve immediately.

Calories	Cholesterol	Protein	Carbohydrate	Total fat		Sat fat		Mono	Poly
	mg	gm	gm	gm	%	gm	%	gm	gm
3846	558	282.0	438.4	102.4	23	8.8	2	33.8	36.9

SPAGHETTINI WITH TOMATO SAUCE
Spaghettini al Sugo

Serves 3.

2 tablespoons olive oil
1 tablespoon safflower oil
1 small onion, minced
1 clove garlic
1/2 cup minced celery, including leaves
Hot pepper flakes to taste
2 tablespoons minced Italian parsley
1 tablespoon minced fresh mint, spearmint
    if possible
2 cups chopped tomatoes, fresh if possible
    (drain if canned)
Salt to taste
1/2 pound spaghettini

Garnish:
Chopped Italian parsley
Croutons

Heat the oils in a skillet, then add onion and garlic. When onion is translucent, add celery, cover, and cook several minutes. Add hot pepper flakes, parsley, mint, tomatoes, and salt. Cover and simmer over low heat.

In the meantime, bring water in a 6-quart pot to a boil, add salt and spaghettini, and cook until al dente. Drain well, toss with the sauce, and serve.

Garnish with chopped parsley and croutons.

Calories	Cholesterol mg	Protein gm	Carbohydrate gm	Total fat gm	%	Sat fat gm	%	Mono gm	Poly gm
1410	0	34.5	214.2	48.0	30	4.5	3	24.5	12.2

PASTA MARINER STYLE
Pasta alla Marinara

Serves 4 to 6.

1 pound tubular pasta, such as penne, ziti, rigatoni, etc.
2 cups marinara sauce (page 430)
1 cup beef or chicken stock

Garnish: 4 tablespoons chopped Italian parsley

Cook pasta in rapidly boiling water about 5 minutes. Heat sauce with stock in a pot large enough to hold the pasta—wide rather than deep. Heat sauce to a boil; then drain pasta and add it to the sauce. Cook pasta in sauce, uncovered, over moderate heat, stirring often, until it is al dente. Garnish with parsley.

Calories	Cholesterol mg	Protein gm	Carbohydrate gm	Total fat gm	%	Sat fat gm	%	Mono gm	Poly gm
2062	0	65.1	381.6	29.5	13	2.5	1	15.8	3.0

VERMICELLI HARLOT STYLE
Vermicelli alla Puttanesca

Serves 6.

4 tablespoons olive oil
1 tablespoon safflower oil
3 cloves garlic, finely chopped
3 whole salted anchovies, washed, spine removed, and
    chopped, or 6 anchovy fillets packed in oil, chopped
Hot pepper flakes to taste
12 dried black olives, pitted and coarsely chopped
2 cups chopped tomatoes, fresh if possible (drain if canned)
2 tablespoons finely chopped Italian parsley
2 tablespoons drained capers
1 1/2 teaspoons dried oregano
1 pound vermicelli or spaghettini

Garnish: Chopped Italian parsley

Heat the oils in a medium skillet. Add garlic and chopped anchovies and sauté over medium heat until garlic begins to take on color. Add hot pepper flakes, olives, tomatoes, parsley, capers, and oregano, cover, and cook over low heat about 15 minutes.

In the meantime, boil pasta in a large pot of rapidly boiling salted water until done al dente, then drain thoroughly.

Put in a serving bowl, add sauce, and mix well. Serve portions in heated bowls, garnished with additional chopped parsley.

Calories	Cholesterol mg	Protein gm	Carbohydrate gm	Total fat gm	%	Sat fat gm	%	Mono gm	Poly gm
2505	13	67.8	371.8	78.5	28	8.1	3	43.9	14.1

SPAGHETTINI WITH ZUCCHINI BLOSSOM SAUCE
Spaghettini con Salsa di Fiori di Zucchini

Serves 4 to 6.

3 tablespoons good olive oil
1 tablespoon safflower oil
1 cup finely chopped onion
4 cups zucchini blossoms cut in half and washed*
1 1/2 teaspoons saffron, diluted in 2 teaspoons broth
1 cup chicken or beef broth
Salt and freshly ground black pepper to taste
1 pound spaghettini

Garnish: 3 tablespoons finely chopped Italian parsley

*For description of zucchini blossoms, see page 405.

Heat the oils in a medium skillet or saucepan, then add onion. When onion wilts, add zucchini blossoms and cook for 5 minutes. Add saffron, broth, salt, and pepper, cover, and simmer for 15 minutes. In the meantime, cook pasta in boiling water. Put sauce in food processor and blend. Drain pasta, toss in sauce, and serve garnished with finely chopped parsley.

Calories	Cholesterol mg	Protein gm	Carbohydrate gm	Total fat gm	%	Sat fat gm	%	Mono gm	Poly gm
2203	0	58.8	352.9	59.7	24	5.6	2	32.9	12.5

PASTA WITH WALNUT SAUCE
Pasta con Salsa di Noci

Nuts are a wonderful substitute for cream. I have also tested this recipe with pecans and pine nuts, with equally excellent results.

Serves 4.

2 tablespoons olive oil
1 teaspoon plus 1 tablespoon safflower oil
1 3/4 cups chopped onion
2 cloves garlic, minced
2 cups tomatoes, fresh if possible, run through a food mill and drained
1 teaspoon dried oregano
Salt and freshly ground black pepper to taste
1 tablespoon butter
4 cups thinly sliced mushrooms
3/4 pound pasta, any cut
10 walnuts, about 1/2 cup shelled

Heat the olive oil and 1 teaspoon of the safflower oil in a medium saucepan; then add onion and cook over moderate heat until onion begins to brown. Add garlic, simmer about 1 minute; then add tomatoes, oregano, salt, and pepper, cover, and simmer for 20 minutes over low heat.

In the meantime, heat butter and remaining 1 tablespoon safflower oil in a medium skillet and add mushrooms, salt, and pepper. Cook, uncovered, over high heat, stirring often, until mushrooms begin to brown. Set aside and keep warm.

In the meantime, cook pasta in rapidly boiling salted water until al dente. While pasta is cooking, blend sauce and walnuts in food processor until the sauce reaches a creamy consistency. Drain pasta, toss in sauce, and garnish each portion with the cooked mushrooms.

Calories	Cholesterol mg	Protein gm	Carbohydrate gm	Total fat gm	%	Sat fat gm	%	Mono gm	Poly gm
2317	31.0	66.0	316.9	88.6	34	14.2	5	29.0	32.0

It is the high ratio of polyunsaturated to saturated fat in both the safflower oil and the walnuts that allows the use of highly saturated butter in this recipe without violating the requirements that 10 percent or less of the calories come from saturated fat and that there be at least as much polyunsaturated as saturated fat. The fact that more than 30 percent of the calories are from fat stems from the amount of fat needed for the recipe to "work"; this would not be altered by substituting another fat or oil for the butter.

SPAGHETTI WITH RICOTTA
Spaghetti con Ricotta

I first tasted this dish in Rome. The recipe was altered to suit this book, and the result is another example of how to produce a low-fat recipe with the proper balance of unsaturated oil and cheese.

Serves 6.

2 1/3 tablespoons safflower oil
1 medium onion, coarsely chopped
3/4 pound fresh spinach
1/2 cup chicken or beef broth
1 pound spaghetti
1 cup fresh ricotta (whole milk or skim milk)*
Salt and freshly ground black pepper to taste

Garnish: Diced fresh tomatoes, or finely chopped Italian parsley, or croutons

*If part skim milk ricotta is used, use 4 teaspoons safflower oil instead of 2 1/3 tablespoons.

Heat oil in a medium skillet or saucepan, add onion, and sauté over moderate heat. Cook until onion begins to brown. Add spinach and broth, cover, and lower heat. Simmer for about 10 minutes.

In the meantime, cook pasta in rapidly boiling water. Purée the spinach-and-onion mixture with ricotta in a food processor or run through a food mill. The sauce should be the consistency of heavy cream—add more hot broth if needed. Add salt and a generous amount of freshly ground black pepper. Toss pasta in sauce and serve on hot plates.

Garnish each portion with diced fresh tomatoes, or finely chopped Italian parsley, or toasted croutons.

With whole milk ricotta

Calories	Cholesterol mg	Protein gm	Carbohydrate gm	Total fat gm	%	Sat fat gm	%	Mono gm	Poly gm
2614	124.0	101.8	390.0	70.8	24	23.2	8	12.4	24.8

With skim milk ricotta

Calories	Cholesterol mg	Protein gm	Carbohydrate gm	Total fat gm	%	Sat fat gm	%	Mono gm	Poly gm
2406	76	102.1	395.1	44.8	16	13.7	5	7.7	14.2

RIGATONI WITH GORGONZOLA
Rigatoni al Gorgonzola

Serves 6.

1 pound asparagus
4 tablespoons safflower oil
Salt to taste
1 pound rigatoni or a similar-cut pasta
1/2 pound fresh imported Gorgonzola cheese*
1 1/2 cups chicken or beef broth
Freshly ground black pepper to taste
2 cups cubed fresh ripe tomatoes,
    at room temperature
Finely chopped Italian parsley

*Use fresh imported Gorgonzola. The color should be a creamy white laced with light green. This cheese yellows as it ages—do not use old cheese.

While water for pasta is heating, wash asparagus well and cut in pieces about 2 inches long. Heat 2 tablespoons of the safflower oil in a medium skillet, add asparagus, and cook over moderate heat until tender but crisp. Set aside.

When water comes to a boil, add salt and pasta, stir, and boil until halfway cooked—about 5 minutes. Heat remaining 2 tablespoons safflower oil in a medium, shallow saucepan, add Gorgonzola, broth, and a generous amount of freshly ground black pepper. Cover and simmer over moderate heat until cheese dissolves, stirring often. When pasta is cooked al dente, drain and add to cheese sauce; turn up heat and stir constantly until sauce thickens. Serve immediately on heated plates. Top each portion with some asparagus, some parsley, and some cubed tomatoes. Sauce will thicken as it cools.

Variation: I like to add 2 or 3 tablespoons brandy to the sauce as it is simmering, but try the recipe without the brandy the first time.

Calories	Cholesterol mg	Protein gm	Carbohydrate gm	Total fat gm	%	Sat fat gm	%	Mono gm	Poly gm
3242	245.0	130.1	380.9	134.2	36	41.5	11	18.2	41.9

VERMICELLI WITH BREADCRUMBS
Vermicelli con la Mollica

Serves 4 to 6.

1 small onion, chopped
1/2 cup chopped celery
3 tablespoons olive oil
1 tablespoon safflower oil
6 anchovy fillets, chopped
2 1/2 cups chopped tomatoes, fresh if possible
   (drain if canned)
Salt and freshly ground black pepper to taste
1 pound vermicelli or spaghettini

Garnish:
1 cup breadcrumbs, freshly made if possible
2 tablespoons chopped Italian parsley

Sauté onion and celery in 1 tablespoon of the olive oil and the safflower oil. When onion wilts, add anchovies. When anchovies dissolve, add tomatoes, salt, and pepper, cover, and simmer for about 30 minutes, stirring occasionally.

Cook pasta in a large pot of salted water. Meanwhile, brown breadcrumbs in a skillet with remaining 2 tablespoons olive oil. When pasta is cooked, drain, toss in sauce, and cover with breadcrumbs and parsley.

Calories	Cholesterol mg	Protein gm	Carbohydrate gm	Total fat gm	%	Sat fat gm	%	Mono gm	Poly gm
2657	18.0	72	437	67.7	22	7.6	3	35.6	14.5

VERMICELLI CALABRIA STYLE
Vermicelli Piccanti alla Calabrese

Serves 2 to 4.

1/2 pound vermicelli or spaghettini
2 tablespoons olive oil
1 tablespoon safflower oil
3 salted anchovies, washed, spine removed, and chopped,
  or 6 good canned anchovies, chopped
Hot pepper flakes to taste
1 teaspoon minced garlic
1 tablespoon finely chopped Italian parsley
2 cups chopped fresh tomatoes

Garnish: 1 tablespoon finely chopped Italian parsley

Cook the pasta in 4 or 5 quarts of boiling water. Meanwhile, heat the oils in a small skillet; then add anchovies and hot pepper. Sauté over low heat until anchovies dissolve. Add garlic and 1 teaspoon of the parsley. When garlic begins to brown, add 3 tablespoons of the pasta water and cook several minutes. Add tomatoes and cook 1 more minute; then turn off heat. Drain pasta when al dente and toss in a serving bowl with sauce.
  Garnish with parsley.

Calories	Cholesterol mg	Protein gm	Carbohydrate gm	Total fat gm	%	Sat fat gm	%	Mono gm	Poly gm
1295	13.0	38.4	192.6	46.7	32	5.8	4	22.1	13.0

PASTA SEA AND MOUNTAINS
Pasta Mare e Monti

This recipe was sent to me by my mother, who lives now in San Benedetto Del Tronto, Italy. Fresh wild mushrooms are used in the original recipe, but I find the combination of fresh domestic mushrooms and dried wild mushrooms works very well.

Serves 4 to 6.

1 dozen fresh cherrystone clams
3 tablespoons olive oil
1 tablespoon safflower oil
1/2 pound fresh mushrooms, sliced
1/2-ounce package dried boletus mushrooms,
  soaked in 1 cup warm water for 20 minutes
3 cloves garlic, minced

Hot pepper flakes or freshly ground black pepper to taste
Salt to taste
3 tablespoons brandy
1 teaspoon dried oregano
1 pound linguine

Garnish: 4 tablespoons finely chopped Italian parsley

Open the clams, remove flesh, straining and reserving the juice. Chop clams and set aside.

Heat the oils in a medium skillet, add fresh mushrooms, and sauté over high heat. As edges begin to brown, add dried mushrooms, without their liquid, and garlic; cook until garlic begins to color. Add pepper, salt, brandy, and oregano; then lower heat and simmer until brandy cooks out. Add clam broth and turn off heat.

In the meantime, cook linguine in rapidly boiling salted water until it is about 3 minutes before desired doneness.

Pour sauce into a large skillet and bring to a boil. Drain pasta and put it in the skillet, tossing it constantly while cooking over high heat, until pasta absorbs clam broth. At this point the pasta should be al dente. Add clams. Toss several times and garnish with parsley. Serve immediately on hot plates.

Variation: An alternative to this recipe is to sauté the mushrooms separately and use them as a garnish.

Calories	Cholesterol	Protein	Carbohydrate	Total fat		Sat fat		Mono	Poly
	mg	gm	gm	gm	%	gm	%	gm	gm
2447	105.0	89.7	376.8	62.6	23	6.6	2	8.0	39.2

PASTA WITH MUSSELS, SQUID, AND SCALLOPS
Penne con Frutti di Mare

Serves 6.

1 cup dry white wine
4 cloves garlic, finely chopped
4 to 5 tablespoons finely chopped Italian parsley
1½ teaspoons dried oregano
Hot pepper flakes to taste (optional)
1 pound mussels, scrubbed
3 tablespoons olive oil
1 teaspoon safflower oil
1 pound squid, cleaned and cut into ½-inch strips
    (page 215)
2 cups chopped tomatoes, fresh if possible
    (drained if canned)
2 tablespoons minced fresh basil
2 cups fresh peas, blanched and drained
1 pound pasta, such as penne, ziti, rigatoni, etc.
3 tablespoons brandy
½ pound sea scallops, cut into bite-sized pieces

Garnish: Finely chopped Italian parsley

Put ½ cup of the wine, 1 chopped clove garlic, 1 tablespoon of the parsley, ½ teaspoon of the oregano, hot pepper flakes, and mussels in a saucepan, cover, and cook over high heat until mussels open. Remove flesh, set aside, and discard shells. Put broth through sieve and reserve.

Heat the two oils in a large skillet or saucepan; then add remaining garlic, 2 tablespoons of the parsley, and optional hot pepper. Simmer for about 1 minute. Add squid and cook over high heat about 3 minutes. Add the other ½ cup wine and cook, uncovered, over high heat until half the wine cooks out. Add tomatoes, basil, the remaining 1 teaspoon oregano, and the remaining parsley, bring to a boil, cover, lower heat, and simmer for 10 minutes. Add peas and continue simmering over medium to low heat an additional 20 minutes.

In the meantime, cook pasta in boiling water about 5 minutes. Drain, add to sauce along with brandy, scallops, mussels, and broth. Cook, uncovered, over high heat, stirring constantly, until pasta is al dente.

Serve on hot plates garnished with parsley.

Calories	Cholesterol mg	Protein gm	Carbohydrate gm	Total fat gm	%	Sat fat gm	%	Mono gm	Poly gm
3142	645.0	175.4	421.8	57.9	16	4.9	1	31.6	6.0

SPAGHETTINI WITH CLAMS AND ANCHOVIES
Spaghettini con Vongole e Acciughe

Serves 6.

1 1/2 dozen cherrystone clams (see opening
    clams, page 116)
1 1/2 pounds spaghettini or linguine
3 tablespoons olive oil
1 tablespoon safflower oil
1 teaspoon minced garlic
6 anchovies, chopped
1/2 cup dry white wine
1 teaspoon dried oregano
2 tablespoons minced Italian parsley
Hot pepper flakes to taste

Garnish: Finely chopped Italian parsley

Open clams, remove flesh, and strain and reserve the liquid. Slice clams and set aside separately.

Cook pasta in boiling salted water. When pasta is almost al dente, drain. In the meantime, heat the oils in a large skillet and add garlic. As garlic begins to color, add anchovies, wine, clam broth, oregano, parsley, and hot pepper flakes. Bring to a boil; then add the drained pasta and toss constantly until the pasta absorbs the liquid. Add clams, toss about 30 seconds, and serve, garnished with parsley.

Calories	Cholesterol mg	Protein gm	Carbohydrate gm	Total fat gm	%	Sat fat gm	%	Mono gm	Poly gm
3350	186.0	130.3	537.7	69.9	18	6.6	2	31.3	13.4

PASTA WITH CLAMS AND ZUCCHINI
Pasta con Vongole e Zucchini

This is a recipe I put together with some of my favorite ingredients. I think it works very well. I like the idea of the baked zucchini with clams. Their individual delicacies seem to complement each other, and you will find that baked zucchini is much more delicate than fried. I have had some unpleasant experiences in Italian restaurants, where I found, to my dismay, that very often fried zucchini was too oily. Zucchini has a tendency to absorb oil, like a blotter, and care should be taken when cooking it.

Serves 2 generously.

6 cherrystone clams (see opening clams, below)
2 small zucchini, sliced entire length into strips
   1/4 inch wide
1/2 pound spaghettini or linguine
1 tablespoon good olive oil
1 tablespoon safflower oil
2 cloves garlic, minced
Hot pepper flakes to taste (optional)
1 tablespoon minced fresh ginger
2 tablespoons finely chopped Italian parsley

To open clams, hold clam, convex side up. Slip the side of a knife along the opening and gently pry it open. Chop flesh and set aside. Reserve liquid separately.

Preheat oven as high as it will go — 450° to 500° — for about 10 minutes. Put zucchini strips on slightly oiled tray and bake. When bottom of strips brown, flip them over with a spatula. When tops are brown, remove from oven. Cut strips in half crosswise to make manageable pieces.

In the meantime, cook pasta in rapidly boiling salted water until pasta is almost al dente.

While pasta is cooking, heat the oils in a skillet or wok; then add garlic and hot pepper. As garlic begins to color, add ginger, clam broth, and 1 teaspoon of the parsley. Bring to a boil. Drain pasta and add to clam broth mixture. Cook over high heat, stirring constantly, until pasta absorbs juice. Add clams, lower heat, and toss, about 1 minute.

Place pasta in heated bowls. Add zucchini and remaining parsley.

Calories	Cholesterol mg	Protein gm	Carbohydrate gm	Total fat gm	%	Sat fat gm	%	Mono gm	Poly gm
1232	53.0	44.7	188.2	31.2	22	3.0	2	11.5	11.2

PASTA WITH MUSHROOMS, ASPARAGUS, AND CLAMS
Pasta con Funghi, Asparagi, e Vongole

Serves 4 to 6.

12 cherrystone clams (see opening clams, above)
3 tablespoons safflower oil
4 cups thinly sliced mushrooms*
Salt and freshly ground black pepper to taste
1 pound linguine or spaghetti
6 cups asparagus cut in 1 1/2-inch lengths
3 tablespoons olive oil
1 teaspoon minced garlic
Hot pepper flakes to taste (optional)
4 tablespoons minced Italian parsley

*We prefer to use wild mushrooms, if available.

Open clams, chop flesh and set aside. Reserve liquid separately.

Heat the safflower oil in a medium skillet, then add mushrooms. Sauté over medium to high heat, add salt and black pepper, and stir constantly. When mushrooms begin to brown, turn off heat and set aside.

Cook pasta in a large pot of boiling salted water, stirring occasionally. Sauté asparagus in a medium skillet with 2 tablespoons of the olive oil. When asparagus begins to brown, turn off heat and set aside.

Heat the remaining 1 tablespoon olive oil in a 12-inch skillet. Add garlic, and as it begins to turn color, add clam broth and pepper. Cook several minutes at this point. When the pasta is cooked al dente, drain and add it to garlic-and-clam broth. Turn up heat; mix well. Add raw clams, parsley, salt and pepper, and optional pepper flakes; mix well. Serve pasta on heated plates and garnish with the cooked mushrooms, sautéed asparagus, and minced parsley. Serve immediately.

Calories	Cholesterol mg	Protein gm	Carbohydrate gm	Total fat gm	%	Sat fat gm	%	Mono gm	Poly gm
2882	105.0	111.0	404.2	91.1	28	7.8	2	36.9	32.1

RIGATONI WITH SHELLFISH AND BRANDY
Rigatoni con Frutti di Mare al Brandy

This recipe uses mussels, cherrystone clams, and scallops, but any combination of shellfish is fine — try oysters, for instance.

Serves 8.

2 tablespoons olive oil
1 tablespoon safflower oil
1 medium onion, finely chopped
4 tablespoons finely chopped Italian parsley
3/4 pound sliced mushrooms, or 1/2 pound sliced
    mushrooms and 3/4-ounce package dried boletus
    mushrooms, soaked in warm water 15 to 20 minutes
Salt and freshly ground black pepper to taste
Hot pepper flakes to taste (optional)
2 teaspoons or less minced garlic
4 cups chopped tomatoes, fresh if possible,
    run through a food mill and drained
2 tablespoons finely chopped fresh mint
    or 1 teaspoon dried
1 dozen mussels, scrubbed and washed
1 dozen cherrystone clams
1 pound rigatoni
1/4 cup brandy
1/2 pound sea or bay scallops

Heat the oils in a saucepan, then add onion, 2 tablespoons of the parsley, fresh mushrooms, and drained dried mushrooms. Cook, uncovered, over moderate heat. Add salt, pepper, and optional hot pepper flakes. Cook until liquid evaporates, then add garlic and cook several more minutes. Add tomatoes and mint. Cover and simmer 20 minutes.

Add mussels to the sauce, cover, and cook until they open. Remove mussels, and let cool. Meanwhile, add clams; while they are cooking, remove mussel flesh and discard shells. When clams open, remove, cool, and scrape out flesh, discarding shells. Cut clams in slices, discard tough mussel connections, and mix the two together.

Preheat oven to 450°.

Boil pasta for 5 minutes in rapidly boiling salted water. Drain and place in deep ovenproof dish. Add sauce, clams, mussels, brandy, and the remaining 2 tablespoons parsley. Cover tightly and bake, stirring often, for about 20 minutes, until pasta is al dente. The scallops should be added about 10 minutes before end of cooking.

Serve immediately in hot bowls.

Calories	Cholesterol mg	Protein gm	Carbohydrate gm	Total fat gm	%	Sat fat gm	%	Mono gm	Poly gm
2886	307.0	156.4	432.9	54.2	17	4.8	1	21.4	12.3

TOMASSO'S ANGEL'S HAIR
Capelli d'Angelo alla Tomasso

Serves 6 to 8.

1 medium fish head or carcass from bass, cod,
   red snapper, etc.
6 tablespoons olive oil
2 tablespoons safflower oil
3 cloves garlic, minced
1/2 green pepper, chopped
4 cups plum tomatoes
2 tablespoons chopped Italian parsley
1 tablespoon fresh basil or 1 teaspoon dried
Hot pepper flakes to taste (optional)
Salt to taste
1 pound angel's hair or fidelini (imported if possible)

Garnish: Chopped Italian parsley

Remove gills from fish. Wash well and drain. Heat the oils in a saucepan, add garlic and green pepper. When garlic begins to color, add tomatoes, parsley, basil, hot pepper flakes, and salt. Simmer gently, covered, for 15 minutes.

Add fish head, cover, and boil gently for 30 minutes. Remove fish head, and after it cools, take off the white flesh and return to sauce. Discard rest of head.

Boil pasta in rapidly boiling water, stirring often, about 4 or 5 minutes. In the meantime, put sauce in a wide saucepan or skillet — about 12 inches in diameter — and bring to a boil (it should be boiling by the time pasta is drained). Finish cooking pasta in the sauce over medium heat, constantly tossing, until al dente. Sprinkle 1 teaspoon chopped Italian parsley on each serving.

Calories	Cholesterol mg	Protein gm	Carbohydrate gm	Total fat gm	%	Sat fat gm	%	Mono gm	Poly gm
1942	50.0	86.3	385.8	115.5	52	11.2	5	65.0	25.0

PASTA WITH FISH HEAD SAUCE
Pasta con Sugo di Testa di Pesce

This is quite different from the preceding recipe in that the pasta is cooked in the fish broth and then asparagus is added for texture and color and its own delicate flavor.

Serves 6.

> 1 leek, washed and cut into 4-inch lengths
> 2 carrots
> 2 stalks celery, cut into 3- to 4-inch lengths
> 1 medium onion
> 2 bay leaves
> 4 quarts water
> About 3 pounds fish heads or carcass from striped bass, cod, red snapper, etc.
> 3 tablespoons olive oil
> 1 tablespoon safflower oil
> 1 tablespoon minced garlic
> Hot pepper flakes to taste
> 3 cups asparagus cut into 1-inch pieces
> 1 pound spaghettini
> Salt to taste

Boil leek, carrots, celery, and onion with bay leaves in the water for about 20 minutes. Add fish heads and boil another 20 minutes. Strain broth. Pick edible flesh from heads and set aside. Discard vegetables and inedible parts of fish heads.

Heat the two oils in a large skillet; add the minced garlic, hot pepper flakes, and asparagus, and sauté for several minutes.

Bring fish broth to a boil, add pasta, and cook until almost al dente. Check for salt. Drain, reserving 1 cup broth.

Heat up the asparagus again and then add fish, the 1 cup broth, and pasta.

Cook over moderate heat, tossing constantly, for several minutes. Serve immediately.

Calories	Cholesterol mg	Protein gm	Carbohydrate gm	Total fat gm	%	Sat fat gm	%	Mono gm	Poly gm
2696	220.0	144.2	363.2	70.8	23	7.6	2	32.3	13.4

PASTA FISHERMAN STYLE
Pasta alla Pescarese

Serves 6.

2 tablespoons olive oil
1 tablespoon safflower oil
2 teaspoons chopped shallots
1 teaspoon chopped garlic
Hot pepper flakes to taste
3 cups peeled, chopped tomatoes, fresh if possible
    (drain if canned)
1 teaspoon dried oregano
1 cup fresh peas, cooked 3 or 4 minutes
2 teaspoons chopped fresh basil or 1 teaspoon dried
Salt to taste
1 pound white fish fillet such as scrod, striped bass,
    red snapper, cut into 1-inch cubes
1 pound any tubular cut pasta, such as elbows, shells, etc.
2 teaspoons brandy or good bourbon (optional)

Garnish: Finely chopped Italian parsley

Heat the oils in a medium to large skillet or saucepan and add shallots. When shallots begin to get translucent, add garlic and hot pepper. When garlic begins to brown, add tomatoes, oregano, peas, basil, and salt. Cover and simmer for 15 minutes. Add fish and continue cooking, uncovered, for several minutes.

In the meantime, cook pasta a little less than al dente; then drain well. Add to sauce, turn up heat, add brandy, and cook over high heat a minute or two.

Garnish with parsley.

Calories	Cholesterol mg	Protein gm	Carbohydrate gm	Total fat gm	%	Sat fat gm	%	Mono gm	Poly gm
2724	250.0	155.6	365.1	79.1	26	4.1	1	22.6	11.6

TOMASSO'S LINGUINE WITH LOBSTER SAUCE I
Linguine con Salsa d'Aragosta alla Tomasso

The lobsters used for the pasta sauce may be served after the pasta as a main course or used for warm lobster salad (page 420). The lobster shells, heads, etc. make an excellent soup (page 52).

Serves 10.

5 cups chopped ripe plum tomatoes, fresh if possible (drain if canned)
5 tablespoons olive oil
2 tablespoons safflower oil
4 cloves garlic, minced
3/4 cup finely chopped Italian parsley
1 cup finely chopped green pepper
4 tablespoons fresh basil or 2 tablespoons dried
Hot pepper flakes to taste (optional)
Salt and freshly ground black pepper to taste
3 live medium lobsters
2 pounds linguine or spaghettini

Garnish: Chopped Italian parsley

Put the tomatoes through a food mill to purée; set aside.

Heat the oils in a skillet large enough to hold the lobsters. Add garlic, tomatoes, parsley, green pepper, and seasonings. When the tomatoes come to a boil, gently add live lobsters, cover, and simmer over low heat about 1 hour. Turn lobsters in sauce occasionally.

Remove lobsters from sauce and set aside.

Cook pasta in a large pot of boiling salted water about 6 minutes. Drain. In the meantime, remove half the sauce. Add drained pasta to boiling sauce, turn up heat, and finish cooking pasta in sauce, stirring constantly and adding more sauce as needed, until done al dente.

Serve pasta on hot plates. Add more sauce if necessary. Garnish with chopped Italian parsley.

Calories	Cholesterol mg	Protein gm	Carbohydrate gm	Total fat gm	%	Sat fat gm	%	Mono gm	Poly gm
4566	0	129.7	740.4	108.2	21	9.7	2	55.5	24.1

LINGUINE WITH LOBSTERS II
Linguine all'Aragosta

Serves 6.

3 medium cooked lobsters (page 189)
4 quarts lobster stock made from lobster shells (page 52)
1 pound linguine or spaghettini
4 tablespoons olive oil
1 tablespoon safflower oil
3 cloves garlic, minced
1 teaspoon dried oregano
Hot pepper flakes to taste
¼ cup brandy
Salt and freshly ground black pepper to taste (optional)

Garnish: Minced Italian parsley

Remove the shells (save for soup) from the lobsters and extract the meat. Cut into bite-sized pieces.

Bring the lobster stock to a rolling boil and add pasta. In the meantime, heat the oils in a large skillet, add garlic, and when hot add lobster meat, oregano, pepper flakes, brandy, salt if needed, and freshly ground black pepper (optional). Cook over high heat for a minute or two, stirring often. Drain pasta while still firm, reserving 1 cup of the lobster stock. Add pasta to skillet with lobster meat plus about ¼ to ½ cup lobster stock. Cook over high heat, stirring constantly, about 2 minutes, adding more stock if necessary. Garnish each serving with 1 tablespoon parsley.

Calories	Cholesterol mg	Protein gm	Carbohydrate gm	Total fat gm	%	Sat fat gm	%	Mono gm	Poly gm
2908	450.0	156.7	353.7	84.5	26	7.1	2	43.1	13.7

FETTUCCINE WITH SMOKED SALMON
Fettuccine al Salmone Affumicato

We decided we should have at least one pasta recipe in which we were not concerned with cholesterol. I did not have to ponder long to make this selection—a rich, elegant dish that can stand up to any pasta recipe I know.

Salmon ends are excellent for this recipe. They are available in most stores that sell smoked salmon and are half the price of sliced salmon. I'm certain that this pasta dish was created out of leftover shreds when smoked salmon became so popular in Italy during the prosperous Sixties.

I have had this dish garnished with Iranian black caviar and I have had it garnished with thinly sliced white truffles. It is also very elegant as is.

Serves 6.

2 tablespoons butter
1 pound thinly sliced smoked salmon cut in strips
3 tablespoons good Cognac
1 pound fettuccine
2 cups (1 pint) half-and-half cream
1 teaspoon grated nutmeg
Freshly ground black pepper to taste

Garnish: Freshly grated imported Parmesan cheese

Heat butter in a large skillet, add salmon, and sauté several minutes, tossing frequently. Add Cognac and simmer several minutes more.

While salmon is simmering, cook pasta in a large pot of boiling salted water. When pasta is almost al dente, drain.

Add cream and nutmeg to the salmon, turn up heat, and bring to a boil. Now add pepper and the pasta and toss constantly over high heat, until sauce thickens, about 2 minutes. Serve immediately on warm plates and garnish with Parmesan cheese.

Calories	Cholesterol mg	Protein gm	Carbohydrate gm	Total fat gm	%	Sat fat gm	%	Mono gm	Poly gm
3557	841.0	176.6	348.2	146.2	36	70.6	17	47.7	4.2

FARFALLE WITH SMOKED SALMON
Farfalle al Salmone Affumicato

Serves 6.

1 1/2 tablespoons butter
2 1/2 tablespoons safflower oil
1 medium onion, finely chopped
4 cups sliced fresh wild mushrooms or 4 cups sliced
    cultivated mushrooms or 3/4-ounce package
    dried boletus mushrooms, soaked in tepid water
    for 30 minutes
1/2 pound smoked salmon ends, thinly sliced,
    or 1/2 pound salmon shreds
3 tablespoons brandy
6 tablespoons chicken or beef broth
Freshly ground black pepper to taste
1 pound farfalle (butterflies) or similar-cut pasta

Garnish: 2 tablespoons finely chopped Italian parsley

Heat butter and oil in a large skillet, then add onion and fresh mushrooms. Cook, uncovered, until liquid from mushrooms cooks out. If dried mushrooms are used, drain and reserve liquid. Cook the mushrooms about

5 minutes, then add liquid and cook until liquid cooks out. Add salmon, cook several minutes; add brandy, cook until brandy cooks out; then add stock and black pepper and simmer about 5 minutes.

In the meantime, cook pasta in boiling salted water. When done al dente, drain and add to skillet with salmon and mushrooms. Toss for a minute or so. Serve immediately.

Garnish with parsley.

Calories	Cholesterol mg	Protein gm	Carbohydrate gm	Total fat gm	%	Sat fat gm	%	Mono gm	Poly gm
2690	157.0	116.6	372.0	79.2	26	18.6	6	17.6	25.2

PERCIATELLI WITH SARDINES
Perciatelli con le Sarde

This recipe was given to me by a Sicilian who owns a vegetable stand on Ninth Avenue in New York City, although I adapted it to use part safflower oil. He sometimes had wild fennel during the winter months, and you can probably find it in special green markets.

Serves 6 to 8.

1 pound wild fennel
6 tablespoons olive oil
3 tablespoons safflower oil
3 cloves garlic, minced
Hot pepper flakes to taste (optional)
2 tablespoons tomato paste
1/2 cup hot water
1 pound fresh sardines, cleaned and boned
Salt and freshly ground black pepper to taste
2 tablespoons pine nuts
2 tablespoons yellow raisins
1 pound perciatelli, or any tubular pasta

Garnish: Chopped Italian parsley

Boil fennel in 4 quarts water for 15 to 20 minutes. Remove it and reserve liquid. When fennel is cool, squeeze out excess liquid and chop.

Heat the oils in a skillet, then add garlic and hot pepper. As soon as garlic takes on color, add tomato paste mixed with the hot water and simmer for several minutes. Add sardines, salt and pepper, pine nuts, and raisins and simmer for 5 minutes. Add fennel and simmer, covered, for 10 minutes.

Cook pasta in the water the fennel was cooked in. When done al dente, drain and toss pasta in the sauce. Garnish with chopped Italian parsley, drizzling a little more olive oil on top if desired.

Calories	Cholesterol	Protein	Carbohydrate	Total fat		Sat fat		Mono	Poly
	mg	gm	gm	gm	%	gm	%	gm	gm
3721	508.0	161.5	384.2	169.2	40	21.6	5	70.4	44.7

LINGUINE WITH SCALLOPS AND PESTO
Linguine con Cappesante

Serves 2 to 3.

1/2 pound linguine
3 tablespoons olive oil
1 tablespoon safflower oil
1/2 pound sea scallops, sliced 1/4 inch thick
Salt and freshly ground black pepper to taste
Flour for dredging
1 clove garlic, minced
3 tablespoons dry white wine
1/2 teaspoon dried oregano
3 tablespoons pesto (page 426)
About 3 tablespoons warm water

Bring to a boil a large pot of salted water, add pasta, stir frequently, and cook until almost done al dente before cooking the scallops.

Meanwhile heat the oils in a medium skillet. Salt and pepper the scallop slices; then dust each in flour. Carefully add them one by one to the hot oil. When lightly brown, add garlic, wine, and oregano. Cook over high heat until wine cooks out — scallops should cook only 1 to 2 minutes in all.

When pasta is done, drain, reserving 3 tablespoons water to blend with the pesto. Add pesto and scallops to pasta, mix well, and serve hot.

Calories	Cholesterol	Protein	Carbohydrate	Total fat		Sat fat		Mono	Poly
	mg	gm	gm	gm	%	gm	%	gm	gm
1692	80.0	69.2	190.3	72.9	38	8.2	4	40.3	24.8

SPAGHETTINI WITH SKATE WING SAUCE
Spaghettini al Sugo di Razza

Here is another recipe that yields two courses, if you wish. After the skate wing has given its flavor to the pasta sauce, it can be served intact, bones and all, with a green salad as a second course. Or you can comb out the flesh from the skate wing bones with a fork and add it to the pasta to make a hearty single-course dinner.

Serves 6.

3 tablespoons olive oil
2 teaspoons minced garlic
1/2 cup chopped green pepper
4 cups chopped tomatoes, fresh if possible (drain if canned)
Hot pepper flakes to taste (optional)
1 teaspoon dried oregano
1 tablespoon dried basil
2 tablespoons finely chopped Italian parsley
Salt and freshly ground black pepper to taste
1/2 pair skate wings, about 3 pounds, tough surface skin
    removed, then cut into 3-inch-wide sections
1 pound spaghettini

Garnish: Chopped Italian parsley

Heat 1 tablespoon of the oil in a medium saucepan; then add 1 teaspoon of the garlic. As garlic begins to color, add green pepper, tomatoes, hot pepper flakes, oregano, basil, parsley, and salt and pepper. Cover and simmer about 15 minutes. Add skate wing and simmer gently about 45 minutes.

Remove skate wing and keep warm. Put sauce in a food processor and blend.

Cook pasta in a large pot of boiling salted water. As pasta is cooking, heat the remaining 2 tablespoons olive oil in a large skillet, then add remaining garlic. As garlic takes on color, add sauce and bring to a boil. When the pasta is almost cooked, drain and add to sauce. Cook over high heat, tossing constantly, until pasta is al dente.

Garnish with chopped Italian parsley.

Calories	Cholesterol mg	Protein gm	Carbohydrate gm	Total fat gm	%	Sat fat gm	%	Mono gm	Poly gm
2282	0	69.4	388.2	48.2	19	5.4	2	29.7	3.3

PASTA WITH SQUID
Farfalle con Calamari

This squid pasta is delicately flavored with the feathery greens of fennel bulbs, which most people usually throw out.

Serves 4 to 8.

2 tablespoons olive oil
1 tablespoon safflower oil

1 pound squid, cleaned and cut into ½-inch-wide strips
   (for cleaning, see page 215)
2 cloves garlic, finely chopped
Hot pepper flakes to taste
¾ cup dry white wine
1 teaspoon dried oregano
Salt to taste
¾ pound fresh spinach, picked over and well washed
About 1 pound feathery greens from fennel tied in a
   bundle (optional)
¾ pound pasta, such as farfalle or penne

Heat the oils in a medium skillet, then add squid. Cook over high heat until liquid cooks out and squid begins to stick. Add garlic and hot pepper and cook about 1 minute. Then add the wine and oregano, lower heat, and cook until wine cooks out. Add salt and spinach. Cook over moderate heat for 5 minutes, then set aside covered.

In the meantime, bring 5 quarts water to a boil in a large pot, add fennel greens, and cook for 20 minutes. Remove fennel and discard. Add salt and pasta and cook until done al dente. Drain. Toss the pasta with the spinach and squid and cook over high heat for several minutes, stirring constantly. Serve immediately.

Calories	Cholesterol mg	Protein gm	Carbohydrate gm	Total fat gm	%	Sat fat gm	%	Mono gm	Poly gm
1935	499.0	91.2	281.8	47.9	22	4.8	2	21.4	12.3

FARFALLE MARINER STYLE
Farfalle alla Marinara

The sauce in this recipe is unusually sweet and light, excellent both as a first course or a main luncheon course.

Serves 8.

3 live blue hardshell crabs
3 large squid, about 9 to 10 inches long

The stuffing
1 pound fillet of whiting or other white fish, such as
    cod, bass, haddock, etc.
2 tablespoons chopped Italian parsley
1 teaspoon chopped garlic
Salt and freshly ground black pepper to taste
1 egg white, lightly beaten

1 tablespoon safflower oil
3 tablespoons finely chopped garlic
1/2 medium green pepper, finely chopped
2 tablespoons chopped Italian parsley
Hot pepper flakes to taste (optional)
6 cups tomatoes, fresh if possible, put through a food
    mill and drained
1 to 1 1/2 pounds farfalle pasta
3 tablespoons brandy

Garnish: Chopped Italian parsley

Remove top of crab shells by lifting flap, then slowly drive a wide knife between bottom and top shell. Twist knife and pry off top shell and discard. Remove gills and rinse. You may kill the crabs first by plunging them in boiling water for a few seconds.

Pull tentacles with head from body of squid. Cut tentacles off just before eyes, force out beak and discard. Clean squid by removing everything inside of tube. Pull skin off squid. Wash inside of tube and outside of tube well. Set aside. Repeat with the 2 remaining squid.

To make the stuffing: Remove skin and bones from fish. Chop fillets with a sharp knife. Add 2 tablespoons parsley and garlic and chop a little more with the fish. Put in a bowl and blend well with salt, freshly ground black pepper, and lightly beaten egg white. Stuff the squid with this mixture. Sew opening of tube with needle and thread, then sew on tentacles.

Heat oil in a medium saucepan. Then add garlic. As garlic begins to take on color, add chopped green pepper, parsley, hot pepper flakes, tomatoes, and salt to taste. Bring to a boil, then add crabs, cover, and simmer for 45 minutes. Add squid and cook another 15 to 20 minutes.

Remove squid and crabs. Cut squid in 1/2-inch-thick rounds and set aside, keeping warm.

Cook the farfalle in boiling salted water about 5 to 6 minutes. Drain. In the meantime, pour about 3 to 4 cups sauce into a large skillet. Bring sauce to a boil, add drained pasta and brandy, and cook, uncovered, over high heat, adding more sauce as needed and stirring often. Cook until pasta is al dente.

Serve pasta on hot plates. Top with sliced rounds of stuffed squid and garnish with chopped parsley. Serve crabs whole as a decorative garnish.

Calories	Cholesterol mg	Protein gm	Carbohydrate gm	Total fat gm	%	Sat fat gm	%	Mono gm	Poly gm
3911	1499.0	407.0	424.1	54.0	12	5.6	1	6.5	9.8

PASTA WITH SHRIMP AND PESTO
Pasta con Gamberi al Pesto

Serves 6.

2 cups firmly packed fresh basil
3 tablespoons coarsely chopped Italian parsley
6 tablespoons extra virgin olive oil
4 teaspoons safflower oil
1 tablespoon coarsely chopped garlic
4 tablespoons pine nuts
4 tablespoons freshly grated Parmesan cheese*
Salt and freshly ground black pepper to taste
1 pound cut pasta, such as penne, bows,
    medium-sized shells
2 cups peeled, sliced potatoes
3/4 pound fresh mushrooms, sliced
Hot pepper flakes to taste (optional)
3/4 pound shrimp, shelled

*In the original pesto recipes, Pecorino cheese was used instead of Parmesan.

Put in a food processor or blend with a mortar and pestle the basil, parsley, 3 tablespoons of the olive oil, 3 teaspoons of the safflower oil, garlic, pine nuts, Parmesan cheese, salt, and pepper. Blend to a creamy consistency.

Bring a large pot of salted water to a boil and add pasta and potatoes. In the meantime, heat 2 tablespoons olive oil and remaining 1 teaspoon safflower oil in a medium skillet, then add mushrooms, salt, and pepper. Cook over high heat, stirring often. When mushrooms begin to brown, remove with a slotted spoon and set aside.

Heat the remaining 1 tablespoon olive oil in the skillet, add the optional hot pepper flakes and shrimp, and cook over high heat until shrimp turns pink.

When pasta is done al dente, drain, reserving about 4 tablespoons of the cooking water to mix with the pesto so the sauce has the consistency of heavy cream. Add pesto to the pasta, mixing well. Serve pasta and potatoes in soup plates, sprinkle some cooked mushrooms on each portion, then top each portion with some shrimp.

Serve immediately.

Calories	Cholesterol mg	Protein gm	Carbohydrate gm	Total fat gm	%	Sat fat gm	%	Mono gm	Poly gm
3296	526.0	124.6	424.6	103.8	28	12.8	3	61.7	18.9

PASTA WITH MUSHROOMS, FISH, SHRIMP, AND ASPARAGUS
Pasta, Funghi, Pesce, Gamberi, e Asparagi

Serves 6.

5 tablespoons peanut oil
2 cups sliced mushrooms
Salt and freshly ground black pepper to taste
1 teaspoon finely chopped garlic
2 cups chopped tomatoes, fresh if possible, put through
   a food mill and drained
1 tablespoon finely chopped Italian parsley
1 teaspoon dried basil
Hot pepper flakes to taste (optional)
1/2 pound white fish, such as monkfish, striped bass,
   cod, flounder, etc.
2 tablespoons coarsely chopped shallots
1 pound fresh medium asparagus, cut into 1 1/2-inch
   lengths, tough stems discarded
1/2 pound fresh shrimp, shelled and washed
1 pound cut pasta, such as penne or rigatoni

Garnish: Chopped Italian parsley

Heat 3 tablespoons of the oil in a medium skillet, then add mushrooms, salt, and freshly ground black pepper. As mushrooms begin to brown, add garlic. As garlic takes on color, add tomatoes, parsley, basil, and hot pepper flakes. Bring to a gentle boil, cover, and simmer for 20 minutes. Add fish, and cook until fish separates from bone. Let cool, remove flesh from bones, discarding them, and return flesh to sauce.

In a separate medium skillet, heat the remaining 2 tablespoons oil; then add shallots and asparagus. Cook over medium heat. As asparagus begin to brown, add shrimp. Toss over high heat until shrimp turn pink. Add tomato-and-mushroom sauce, cover, and cook over moderate heat for several minutes. In the meantime, cook pasta in rapidly boiling salted water until done al dente. Drain pasta well and toss in sauce. Garnish with parsley.

Calories	Cholesterol mg	Protein gm	Carbohydrate gm	Total fat gm	%	Sat fat gm	%	Mono gm	Poly gm
2920	455.0	155.5	390.6	78.6	24	11.8	4	31.3	20.3

PASTA WITH SHRIMP
Pasta con Gamberi

If this dish is to be served as a main course, we like the fresh asparagus cut in 2-inch lengths and sautéed in vegetable oil as a garnish on top of each portion of pasta.

Serves 6.

1 tablespoon olive oil
3 tablespoons safflower oil
1 medium onion, coarsely chopped
1 teaspoon or more minced garlic
2 tablespoons finely chopped Italian parsley
Hot pepper flakes to taste (optional)
2 cups coarsely chopped tomatoes, fresh if possible
   (drain if canned)
1 teaspoon dried oregano
Salt to taste
1 pound pasta, preferably spaghettini or linguine
1 pound fresh medium shrimp*
2 cups asparagus cut in 2-inch lengths (optional)
4 tablespoons brandy or good bourbon

Garnish: Chopped Italian parsley

*If possible, use shrimp with their heads still attached. Then remove shell but leave head attached to body. You could also use headless medium shrimp. Remove shells and wash in cold water.

Heat the oils in a medium saucepan; then add onion and cook, uncovered, over moderate heat. When onion begins to brown, add garlic, parsley, and optional hot pepper. Simmer about 1 minute. Add tomatoes and oregano, cover, and lower heat. Add salt to taste and simmer for 20 minutes.

In the meantime, add pasta to rapidly boiling water. Add shrimp to sauce and cover and cook for 5 minutes. (If you used headed shrimp remove them with a slotted spoon, pull off heads and discard. Return shrimp to pot just before pasta is added to sauce.)

If you want to add the asparagus, prepare as on page 117.

When pasta is almost cooked — about 1 minute before desired doneness — drain pasta, add to sauce with shrimp, and add brandy. Turn up heat and cook 1 minute, mixing often.

Top with the asparagus, if you like, and garnish with chopped Italian parsley.

Calories	Cholesterol mg	Protein gm	Carbohydrate gm	Total fat gm	%	Sat fat gm	%	Mono gm	Poly gm
2961	681.0	183.1	400.8	67.0	20	4.8	1	16.4	30.4

PASTA WITH BROCCOLI AND TUNA
Pasta con Broccoli e Tonno

Here is a pasta recipe that can be made ahead of time and served at room temperature as a main course.

Serves 6.

3/4 pound cut pasta, such as rigatoni, penne, ziti, etc.
4 tablespoons olive oil
4 cups fresh broccoli cut into bite-sized pieces
1 tablespoon safflower oil
1 teaspoon minced garlic
Salt and freshly ground black pepper to taste
2 tablespoons pesto (page 426)
1 cup thinly sliced whole scallions
2 9-ounce cans Italian-style or American-style tunafish
2 cups sliced fresh, ripe tomatoes
12 dried black olives, pitted and sliced (optional)
2 tablespoons finely chopped Italian parsley

Garnish: Thinly sliced whole scallions

Cook pasta al dente in boiling salted water. Drain, add 3 tablespoons of the olive oil, toss, and let cool.

Cook broccoli in boiling salted water until almost cooked. Heat safflower oil and remaining tablespoon olive oil; then add broccoli, garlic, salt, and pepper. Cook until broccoli is tender. Toss with pasta, add pesto and mix well; then add scallions, tuna, tomatoes, remaining oil, and olives. Gently toss, add parsley. Do not refrigerate. Serve at room temperature.

Garnish with thinly sliced scallions.

Calories	Cholesterol mg	Protein gm	Carbohydrate gm	Total fat gm	%	Sat fat gm	%	Mono gm	Poly gm
3222	332.0	202.8	292.7	134.0	37	19.1	5	58.3	24.1

PENNE WITH TUNA
Penne al Tonno

Serves 4 to 6.

3 tablespoons olive oil
1 teaspoon safflower oil

1 cup finely chopped onion
1 teaspoon crushed rosemary
1/2 teaspoon crushed fennel seeds
1 1/2 cups chicken or beef broth
Freshly ground black pepper to taste
2 tablespoons pine nuts
1 7-ounce can Italian-style tunafish
1 pound penne or other tubular pasta
1 tablespoon vegetable oil
1/2 pound medium asparagus, cut into 1 1/2-inch lengths
  (about 3/4 cup)

Garnish: Finely chopped Italian parsley

Heat the two oils in a medium saucepan, then add onion. Sauté over medium heat, and when onion begins to brown, add rosemary, fennel seeds, stock, and pepper. Cover and simmer about 15 minutes. Purée sauce to a creamy consistency in a food processor or put through a food mill. Return to saucepan, add pine nuts, cover, and simmer about 5 minutes. Add tuna, crush with a fork, and mix thoroughly. Remove from heat.

Cook pasta in a large pot of boiling water. Meanwhile, heat the vegetable oil in a medium skillet and sauté asparagus over medium heat, uncovered, until tender. Add to tuna sauce.

When pasta is cooked al dente, drain well and toss pasta with sauce. Garnish each portion with chopped Italian parsley and serve immediately.

Variation: Peas can be served with this recipe instead of asparagus.

Calories	Cholesterol mg	Protein gm	Carbohydrate gm	Total fat gm	%	Sat fat gm	%	Mono gm	Poly gm
2681	111.0	116.0	361.3	83.2	27	9.9	3	39.1	19.5

PENNE IN THE MANNER OF PORTO D'ASCOLI
Penne alla Porto d'Ascoli

Porto d'Ascoli is a lovely little town in central Italy by the Adriatic Sea, about three miles from where my relatives live.

Serves 4 to 6.

1 can Italian-style tunafish
1 can anchovies, chopped
1/2 cup finely chopped green olives
4 tablespoons finely chopped capers
2 medium carrots, finely chopped
4 tablespoons finely chopped fresh basil
4 tablespoons finely chopped Italian parsley
6 to 8 cloves garlic, finely chopped
1/2 medium onion, finely chopped
5 tablespoons good olive oil
2 tablespoons safflower or corn oil
1 pound penne or other tubular pasta, such as rigatoni
  or shells

Garnish: Chopped Italian parsley

Put all ingredients except the pasta and garnish in a bowl and let rest at least 2 hours.

Boil pasta until al dente. Drain, toss with mixture, and serve with additional chopped parsley.

Calories	Cholesterol mg	Protein gm	Carbohydrate gm	Total fat gm	%	Sat fat gm	%	Mono gm	Poly gm
3172	136.0	119.7	366.0	133.3	37	16.8	5	70.6	29.4

PASTA WITH SMOKED TROUT
Pasta alla Trota Affumicata

The use of "pink" sauces is quite common in Italy—sauces made with tomatoes and milk, cream, or a beciamella sauce.

Serves 6.

2 smoked trout, about 1/2 pound each*
1 pound pasta, such as gnocchi, small shells, penne, etc.
5 tablespoons safflower oil
2 tablespoons finely chopped shallots
1 cup chopped tomatoes, fresh if possible,
  put through a food mill and drained
1 cup half-and-half cream
Salt and freshly ground black pepper or
  1 teaspoon hot pepper flakes to taste
4 tablespoons brandy

Garnish:
3 tablespoons freshly grated Parmesan cheese, or
Finely chopped Italian parsley

*Any type of smoked fish may be used in this recipe.

Skin the trout, remove the bones, and cut into 1-inch pieces.

Heat salted water for pasta. When water comes to a boil, add pasta.

In the meantime, heat oil in a large skillet, then add shallots. When shallots become translucent, add tomatoes, cover, and simmer over low heat for 5 minutes. Add cream, salt and pepper, cover, and cook several minutes. (See page 99 for remarks about curdling.) Add brandy and trout, simmer for several minutes. At this point, pasta should be al dente; drain it and add to sauce with trout. Cook over medium heat for several minutes, mixing constantly until pasta is well blended with sauce.

Serve on heated plates immediately, with some grated Parmesan cheese sprinkled on each portion.

Calories	Cholesterol mg	Protein gm	Carbohydrate gm	Total fat gm	%	Sat fat gm	%	Mono gm	Poly gm
3736	355.0	170.7	365.1	158.0	37	39.4	9	28.4	50.1

PASTA BAKED IN PARCHMENT
Pasta al Cartoccio

Serves 4 to 6.

3 tablespoons olive oil
1 tablespoon safflower oil
2 cloves garlic, finely chopped
Hot pepper flakes to taste
2 cups chopped tomatoes, fresh if possible (drain if canned)
2 tablespoons finely chopped Italian parsley
1 teaspoon dried oregano
Salt to taste
1 pound mussels, scrubbed
½ pound medium shrimp, shelled
½ pound sea scallops, cut in half
3 tablespoons brandy
1 pound pasta such as farfalle, penne, etc.
Kitchen parchment paper

Garnish: Finely chopped Italian parsley

Heat oils in a large saucepan, then add garlic and hot pepper. As garlic begins to take on color, add tomatoes, parsley, oregano, and a little salt. Cover and simmer for 10 minutes. Add mussels, cover, and cook until they open. Remove mussels, scrape out flesh, discarding shells. Meanwhile, add shrimp and scallops to the sauce and cook about 30 seconds. Turn off heat. Add brandy and return mussels to the pan.

In the meantime, boil pasta in salted water for 5 minutes. Drain well, then toss in sauce.

Place a sheet of parchment about 22 inches long on the bottom of a baking tray about 15 × 10 × 2 inches. Place another sheet of parchment about 16 inches long across bottom sheet. Scoop pasta with sauce onto parchment. Place another sheet of parchment over top of pasta and crimp edges all around pasta.

Place tray in preheated 400° oven and bake about 20 minutes. Present the parchment to your guests, then unfold and serve portions, garnishing each with finely chopped Italian parsley.

Calories	Cholesterol mg	Protein gm	Carbohydrate gm	Total fat gm	%	Sat fat gm	%	Mono gm	Poly gm
2878	492.0	157.4	378	65.6	20	5.6	2	32.9	12.5

RIGATONI WITH VEAL AND ARTICHOKE HEARTS
Rigatoni con Sugo di Vitello

This recipe can be made with broccoli, cauliflower, fresh peas, fresh lima beans, and artichoke hearts, in any combination, but I would suggest using no more than two vegetables. The dish makes a complete main course — all you would need is a tossed green salad to finish the dinner nicely.

Serves 6 to 8.

2 tablespoons olive oil
1 tablespoon safflower oil or 2 tablespoons butter and
    2 teaspoons safflower oil
1½ pounds veal, from either shoulder or leg,
    cut into 1-inch pieces
Salt and freshly ground black pepper to taste
1 cup finely chopped onion
3 cloves garlic, skins on
1 medium carrot, finely chopped
3 tablespoons minced Italian parsley
1 cup dry white wine
4 cups chopped tomatoes, fresh if possible,
    put through a food mill and drained
¾-ounce package dried boletus mushrooms, soaked in
    warm water 15 minutes (optional)
6 cloves, crushed
1 tablespoon dried basil
9-ounce package frozen artichoke hearts or 2 cups small
    fresh artichokes, prepared as on page 338
10-ounce package frozen lima beans or 2 cups fresh shelled
    lima beans or 2 cups fresh peas
1½ pounds rigatoni

Garnish: Minced Italian parsley

Heat oils in a medium saucepan; then add veal, salt, and pepper, stirring often. When moisture cooks out and veal begins to brown, add onion and garlic. When onion begins to brown, add carrot and parsley; cook several minutes more, stirring constantly. Add wine, cover, lower heat, and simmer about 10 minutes. Remove cover and simmer until wine cooks out. Add tomatoes and optional mushrooms, cloves, and basil, cover, and simmer about 1 1/2 hours.

Blanch artichoke hearts and lima beans. Add to the sauce, cover, and simmer an additional 20 minutes.

Cook pasta in a large pot of rapidly boiling water. Drain when done al dente and toss with sauce. Garnish each portion with minced Italian parsley.

Calories	Cholesterol mg	Protein gm	Carbohydrate gm	Total fat gm	%	Sat fat gm	%	Mono gm	Poly gm
4697	483.0	271.4	675.7	87.3	16	21.2	4	26.4	12.9

PASTA WITH TRIPE AND WILD MUSHROOMS
Pasta, Trippa, e Porcini

This is a hearty dish. I suggest a simple salad to finish the meal.

Serves 8.

1 1/2 pounds honeycomb tripe
2 tablespoons olive oil
2 tablespoons safflower oil*
1 cup finely chopped onion
1 teaspoon finely chopped garlic
1 teaspoon crushed rosemary
1 cup dry white wine
1 bay leaf
Salt and freshly ground black pepper to taste
3/4-ounce package dried boletus mushrooms, soaked in
    warm water for 15 minutes
2 tablespoons finely chopped Italian parsley
3/4 cup chopped carrots
1 cup chicken broth
2 cups chopped tomatoes, fresh if possible,
    put through a food mill and drained
1 pound rigatoni or penne

*If you would like to serve grated Parmesan with this recipe, allow 1 additional teaspoon safflower oil for 3 tablespoons grated Parmesan for the proper fat balance.

Put the tripe in a kettle and add water to cover—about 3 quarts. Bring to a boil and cook about 10 minutes. Drain tripe and let cool. Cut off all fat from the underside of the comb and discard; then cut the tripe with a sharp knife into strips about 1/4 inch wide and 2 to 3 inches long.

Heat the oils in an ovenproof casserole, then add tripe and onion. Cook, uncovered, over moderate heat, stirring often, for 6 or 7 minutes. Add garlic and cook another minute. Add rosemary, wine, bay leaf, salt, and pepper, cover, lower heat, and cook until wine cooks out. Add drained mushrooms, parsley, carrots, chicken broth, and tomatoes, cover, and bring to a boil.

Meanwhile, preheat oven to 350°. Place tripe in the oven and bake about 1 1/2 hours.

Cook pasta in boiling water and drain when al dente. Toss well with tripe and serve immediately on hot soup plates.

Calories	Cholesterol mg	Protein gm	Carbohydrate gm	Total fat gm	%	Sat fat gm	%	Mono gm	Poly gm
2121	462.0	197.4	402.9	75.0	31	12.8	5	29.8	22.4

PASTA WITH CHICKEN BREASTS
Pasta con Petti di Pollo

Serves 6 to 8.

1 whole chicken breast, cut into strips about
    1/2 inch wide and 3 inches long
1 teaspoon minced garlic
1 tablespoon soy sauce
Freshly ground black pepper to taste
Juice of 1/2 lemon
3 tablespoons olive oil
1 tablespoon safflower oil
Salt to taste
3 medium potatoes, peeled and cut into
    bite-sized pieces
1 pound tubular pasta, such as ziti, rigatoni, or penne
6 cups broccoli cut into bite-sized pieces
3 tablespoons pesto (page 426)

Marinate cut-up chicken breasts with garlic, soy sauce, pepper, and lemon juice for several hours.

Heat the oils in a saucepan. Remove chicken from marinade and cook for several minutes over high heat. Add marinade and cook, tossing, for 10 seconds or more. Turn off heat and set aside.

Bring a large pot of water to a rolling boil and add salt and potatoes. When water returns to a boil, add pasta. Stir, cook about 4 minutes, then add broccoli and cook until pasta is done al dente. Drain. Reserve some of the water — 1/2 to 3/4 cup — and mix with the pesto until it has a thin saucelike consistency. Add to pasta and vegetables in a large serving bowl. Add chicken and juices and toss.

Calories	Cholesterol mg	Protein gm	Carbohydrate gm	Total fat gm	%	Sat fat gm	%	Mono gm	Poly gm
2951	121.0	119.7	433.0	79.6	24	9.2	3	41.6	17.4

TORTELLONI

The dough for this tortelloni works well with Egg Beaters, the commercial egg substitute, because the pasta does not have to be as hard as cut pasta. The recipe takes some effort but it is worth it for special occasions. The same recipe can be used for ravioli or cannelloni. See descriptions at end of recipe.

Enough to serve 8.

The dough
3 cups semolina*
1 container Egg Beaters (defrost according to directions
    on package)
Pinch salt

*All-purpose flour may be used instead of semolina. If flour is used, then about 4 cups will be needed.

Dump semolina on a bread board or counter top, make a well in the center, and pour the defrosted Egg Beaters in the center. With a fork gradually work the flour into the mixture, slowly working the mass in a circular motion. Scrape board with a pastry scraper or knife so that all the ingredients are incorporated. If dough is too sticky, add more flour; add a little water if too dry. Sprinkle the board with some flour to keep the dough from sticking, but do not add too much — this dough must remain pliable.

Knead the dough in a rolling motion, pushing the ball away from you with the heels of your hands. Work the dough this way for 15 or 20 minutes, until the dough is smooth and has a velvet-like consistency.

Flatten the ball so that it looks like a cake of cheese and rub the surface with a little olive oil to prevent drying. Place ball between two soup plates and allow dough to rest at room temperature for at least 1 hour.

The stuffing
1 pound fillet of sole
1 smoked trout, about 1/2 pound
2 egg whites, lightly beaten
2 tablespoons finely chopped Italian parsley
Salt and freshly ground black pepper to taste
1 tablespoon grated lemon rind

Poach or steam sole until opaque—about 3 minutes. Skin and bone trout. Finely chop both sole and trout and put in a small mixing bowl with egg whites, parsley, salt, pepper, and lemon rind and mix well.

After dough has rested at least 1 hour, sprinkle board with semolina or all-purpose flour. Cut ball of dough into 4 pieces. Roll one section at a time with a rolling pin on a floured board. Then run dough through the widest opening of your pasta machine. If pasta breaks up run it through again. Turn wheel to next notch and roll pasta sheet through; repeat until sheet has been run through the smallest opening. Place sheet on floured board or tabletop. Repeat until all pasta is rolled out.

With a 3-inch cookie cutter or glass cut rounds from rolled-out pasta sheets. Place a scant teaspoon stuffing in the center of each round of pasta. Fold it in half and seal the dough by pressing the edges together. Turn ends up so that they form little hats and then press the two points together. Wet edges if necessary to form seal. When the tortelloni are all filled, boil in rapidly boiling salted water about 5 minutes.

While tortelloni are cooking, make the sauce. Drain tortelloni when cooked and keep warm. Add to sauce when it is ready.

> *The sauce*
> 1 tablespoon olive oil
> 3 tablespoons safflower oil
> 3 cups sliced mushrooms
> Salt and freshly ground black pepper to taste
> 1 1/2 cups tomato purée
> 1 1/2 cups medium cream
> Dash nutmeg
> 4 tablespoons brandy

Heat the oils in a medium skillet or saucepan, then add mushrooms, salt, and pepper and cook over high heat. When mushrooms begin to brown, add tomato purée. Bring to a boil, add cream, nutmeg, salt, and pepper and cook for 5 minutes—the sauce will be curdled at this point, but don't worry. Add brandy. Pour sauce into a large skillet, bring to a boil, add tortelloni, and cook over medium to high heat about 2 minutes, gently mixing occasionally. When tortelloni is added, you will notice that the starch from the pasta will neutralize the curdling, making a smooth, creamy sauce. Serve hot.

To make ravioli, use the same recipe. Simply cut rolled-out pasta into 2-inch squares, put about 1 tablespoon filling in the center of each square. Place another square of pasta over it and press the edges together with a fork. Boil the same amount of time as tortelloni.

Preheat oven to 500°. Put cooked and drained ravioli in an ovenproof dish. Pour sauce on top and cover with foil. Bake about 8 to 10 minutes.

Serve immediately.

To make cannelloni, use the same recipe. Cut pasta into 4-inch squares and allow to dry about 45 minutes.

Boil pasta for several minutes. Drain, pour cold water over pasta squares, and carefully separate them. Place some stuffing in the center of each square and roll pasta up into a tube 1 inch in diameter. Carefully place in a shallow ovenproof dish. (Up to this point, recipe can be prepared in advance.) Pour the sauce on top, cover with foil, and bake in a preheated 400° oven about 15 minutes.

Serve immediately.

Calories	Cholesterol mg	Protein gm	Carbohydrate gm	Total fat gm	%	Sat fat gm	%	Mono gm	Poly gm
4234	352.0	236.3	475.8	133.1	36	35.0	7	34.8	31.5

GREEN LASAGNA MY WAY
Lasagne Verdi a Modo Mio

This recipe is a variation of a recipe of mine that was published in the *New York Times Magazine* in 1972, later selected as the most popular recipe of the year. I have received many requests for it since then; sometimes the recipe readers had clipped had been used so often it was no longer legible and they wanted a copy.

Because of its popularity I decided to redo the recipe to make it acceptable for this book. I am very pleased with the result, and I think you will find it a rather good low-fat lasagna recipe. It may seem complicated at first glance, but it really isn't.

Serves 12 to 14, as a first course.

The pasta
1 cup tightly packed fresh spinach leaves*
3 cups all-purpose flour
1 container Egg Beaters, defrosted (equivalent of 4 eggs)

The meat sauce
2 tablespoons olive oil
2 teaspoons safflower oil
1½ pounds ground lean veal or lean beef (top round)
Salt and freshly ground black pepper to taste
1 cup white wine
4 cups sliced fresh mushrooms
Double recipe marinara sauce (page 430)†
1-ounce package dried boletus mushrooms, soaked in warm
     water to cover for 15 minutes
½ cup water
1 teaspoon dried oregano

The beciamella sauce
1 tablespoon butter
1 tablespoon flour
1 cup skim milk
Salt and freshly ground black pepper to taste
Dash nutmeg

6 tablespoons freshly grated Parmesan cheese

*Packaged spinach lasagna (preferably imported) may be used in
this recipe, but fresh is lighter.
†In making the double recipe of marinara sauce, use 6 tablespoons plus 2 teaspoons safflower oil instead of olive oil to compensate for the cheese.

Boil the spinach for several minutes, then drain and let cool. Squeeze out
all moisture and finely chop.

Make pasta according to directions on page 139, adding chopped spinach
with the Egg Beaters. Put ball of pasta between two plates and let it rest
for at least 1 hour.

In the meantime, make the meat sauce. Heat 1 tablespoon of the olive
oil and 1 teaspoon of the safflower oil in a large skillet, then add ground
veal and salt and pepper. Cook, uncovered, over high heat, stirring often.
When veal begins to brown, add the white wine. Cover and simmer over
low heat until wine cooks out. Remove ground veal from skillet and put in
a bowl. Heat in the skillet the remaining 1 tablespoon olive oil and 1
teaspoon safflower oil, then add the fresh mushrooms. Cook, uncovered,
over high heat until mushrooms begin to brown. Remove from skillet and
add to cooked ground veal.

After the double portion of the marinara sauce has been made and put through a food mill, put it in a large saucepan and add the soaked dried boletus mushrooms and their juice, along with the ground veal mixture, water, and oregano. Cover and simmer for 2 hours, stirring often.

After the pasta dough has rested for 1 hour, cut it in 4 sections. Roll out one section of dough with a rolling pin so that it will fit in the widest opening of your pasta machine. Roll pasta, dust with flour, and continue rolling the sheet through the pasta machine until dough is run through the smallest opening. Place pasta sheet on a floured board. Repeat with the remaining 3 pieces of pasta dough. Cut all of the pasta sheets into 4-inch sections. (These are easier to handle than strips — you can work much faster.) Dust with flour, turn over occasionally, allow to dry at least 45 minutes, turning pasta sections over every so often. Dust with more flour if needed.

Now make the beciamella sauce: Heat butter in a small saucepan, then add flour and blend with a wire whisk. In a separate pot scald the milk. Add milk to flour-and-butter mixture, whisking well until sauce begins to thicken. Add salt, pepper, and nutmeg, cover, and simmer for 4 to 5 minutes, stirring occasionally.

Bring a large pot of salted water to a boil. Add one 4-inch-section sheet of pasta at a time to boiling water, and cook about 4 or 5 minutes. Drain and run cold water over pasta. Remove pasta sections from colander. Place some of the meat sauce on the bottom of a medium baking dish or tray. Add a layer of pasta, more sauce, and another layer of pasta. After the second layer of pasta, add the beciamella sauce. Repeat. Sprinkle half the Parmesan cheese on one layer, and 3 tablespoons on a second layer. Recipe can be assembled an hour or two ahead of time.

Cover lasagna. Bake in a preheated 400° oven about 20 minutes. Serve hot.

Calories	Cholesterol mg	Protein gm	Carbohydrate gm	Total fat gm	%	Sat fat gm	%	Mono gm	Poly gm
5093	543	270.8	523.8	210.4	36	42.7	7	55.1	90.9

VEGETABLE LASAGNA

This is a most satisfying lasagna recipe, which is excellent as a main luncheon course or dinner course. It is perhaps one of the lightest lasagna recipes you will have the pleasure to serve.

The original recipe calls for cream or beciamella sauce, for which I have substituted walnuts. The result is a creamy sauce without saturated fats.

If the recipe is served as a main course a mixed green salad would make a good accompaniment.

Baked slices of eggplant or zucchini can be used instead of fried eggplant, and fresh peas can be used instead of artichoke hearts, but do not use too many varieties of vegetables or one will cancel the other out.

Serves 12, as a first course.

2¼ to 2½ pounds eggplant in slices ¼ to ½ inch thick
9-ounce package frozen artichokes
4 tablespoons olive oil
2 tablespoons safflower oil
2 cups coarsely chopped onion
1 cup sliced carrots
2 cloves garlic, chopped
4 cups chopped tomatoes, fresh if possible (drain if canned)
1 teaspoon dried oregano
1 tablespoon dried basil
4 cloves
Salt and freshly ground black pepper to taste
1 pound sliced mushrooms
Corn or vegetable oil for shallow-frying
Flour for dredging
1 pound lasagna pasta, preferably imported Italian
22 walnuts, shelled, 1 cup

Sprinkle eggplant slices with salt and let them drain for 1 hour; then wash and pat dry. Blanch frozen artichokes in boiling water, then drain.

Heat 2 tablespoons of the olive oil and 1 tablespoon of the safflower oil in a medium saucepan. Add onion and carrots. When onion wilts, add garlic and cook for several minutes. Add tomatoes, oregano, basil, cloves, and salt and pepper to taste. Cover and simmer for 30 minutes, stirring occasionally. Pour into a food processor and blend. Return to pan, add artichokes, and cook 15 minutes more.

In the meantime, heat the remaining 2 tablespoons olive oil and 1 tablespoon safflower oil in a large skillet. Add the sliced mushrooms, salt, and pepper. Cook over high heat until mushrooms begin to brown. Remove from skillet and set aside.

Heat about ¾ inch corn oil in a medium skillet. Dust eggplant slices with flour a few at a time, then shake off excess. When oil is hot, add some of the eggplant slices and cook until lightly brown. Blot dry on paper towels and repeat process until all slices are browned.

Cook pasta in rapidly boiling salted water for 5 or 6 minutes. Drain, rinse in cold water. On a baking tray about 12 × 12 inches and about 3 inches deep, lay one layer of pasta, then one layer of eggplant.

Spoon off about 2 cups sauce (without artichokes) and place in food processor. Add 1 cup warm water and the walnuts. Blend to a creamy consistency. Pour some of this sauce and artichoke hearts on top of the eggplant, add another layer of pasta, spread cooked mushrooms over, add another layer of pasta, a layer of eggplant and sauce. Repeat with another layer of eggplant, sauce, and pasta until all ingredients are used up. Top with a layer of pasta with sauce. Add some water if too dense. Cover with foil and bake 30 minutes in a preheated 400° oven.

Calories	Cholesterol mg	Protein gm	Carbohydrate gm	Total fat gm	%	Sat fat gm	%	Mono gm	Poly gm
4044	0	120.2	552.3	163.3	36	13.2	3	55.6	68.2

CANNELLONI

Serves 3 to 6.

1 tablespoon peanut or safflower oil
1 small onion, chopped
½ pound veal, any cut, or stewing veal,
    cut into large cubes, or lean tenderloin
Salt and freshly ground black pepper to taste
3 tablespoons dry sherry
3 cups packed fresh spinach
¾ cup walnut meats
1 cup fresh breadcrumbs
Dash grated nutmeg
1 egg white, lightly beaten
6 cannelloni tubes
3 cups marinara sauce (page 430)

Heat oil in a small skillet. Add onion and cook a minute or two, then add veal, salt, and pepper. Cook over high heat, stirring often. When veal begins to brown, add sherry. Cover and simmer until sherry cooks out. Remove contents of pan and put through a meat grinder or food processor.

Bring a little water to a boil in a medium pot and add spinach. Cook for several minutes. Drain, let cool, and then squeeze out juice. Chop spinach and mix with the veal. Grind walnut meats in a food processor and add to the veal mixture along with the breadcrumbs, nutmeg, egg white, and salt and pepper to taste. Mix well.

Boil the cannelloni tubes in a large pot of boiling salted water about 5 minutes. Drain and let cool. Stuff shells with veal mixture.

Place in a casserole pot just large enough to hold the cannelloni tubes. Pour the sauce on top, cover, and bake in a preheated 350° oven until cannelloni is tender, 15 to 20 minutes.

Calories	Cholesterol mg	Protein gm	Carbohydrate gm	Total fat gm	%	Sat fat gm	%	Mono gm	Poly gm
2085	162	89.7	162	123.1	52	19.5	8	42.8	44.6

TIMBALE OF MACARONI
Timballo di Maccheroni

Serves 10.

Salt to taste
3 eggplants, about 4 pounds, cut into 1/4- to 1/2-inch slices
Corn or vegetable oil for shallow-frying
Flour for dredging
2 tablespoons olive oil
3 tablespoons safflower oil
2 cups coarsely chopped onion
1 cup chopped carrots
2 cloves garlic, minced
4 cups chopped tomatoes, fresh if possible (drain if canned)
1 teaspoon dried basil
2 tablespoons chopped Italian parsley
1 tablespoon butter
3/4 pound mushrooms, thickly sliced
Salt and freshly ground black pepper to taste
3 tablespoons imported sweet marsala
1 pound pasta; a smaller-cut pasta is ideal for this dish

Salt eggplant slices and allow to drain for at least 15 minutes. Wash and blot dry.

Pour about 3/4 inch corn oil into a medium skillet. Dust eggplant slices with flour and when oil is hot quickly fry the slices a few at a time to a golden brown. Remove blot on paper towels, and repeat until all are done.

Oil thoroughly an ovenproof pot or casserole, preferably with a rounded bottom, about 10 to 12 inches in diameter and 4 inches deep. Line the bottom and sides of pot with cooked slices of eggplant, reserving some for top of dish later.

Heat the olive oil and 1 tablespoon of the safflower oil in a medium saucepan. Add onion and carrots and sauté until onion begins to brown. Add garlic and sauté about 30 seconds. Add tomatoes, basil, and parsley. Cover and simmer for 20 minutes. Put through a food processor or food mill and reserve.

In the meantime, heat the butter and the remaining 2 tablespoons safflower oil in a large skillet. Add mushrooms, salt, and pepper and cook over high heat until mushrooms begin to brown. Add marsala and cook several minutes more.

Cook pasta in boiling salted water one half its usual cooking time. Drain and mix with three quarters of the sauce. Add mushrooms and mix well. Pour into the pot lined with eggplant slices. Cover with remaining slices of eggplant.

Preheat oven to 400°. Cover pot and bake about 25 minutes.

Put a flat plate over pot and turn pot over. Carefully lift up pot; the eggplant mold should drop out easily. To serve, cut wedge-shaped portions with a knife. Serve with remaining sauce.

Calories	Cholesterol mg	Protein gm	Carbohydrate gm	Total fat gm	%	Sat fat gm	%	Mono gm	Poly gm
3704	0	105.2	524.1	132.7	32	18.6	4	38.3	56.8

MACARONI WITH MEAT SAUCE
Maccheroni al Ragu

The best known "ragu" sauces in Italy contain little tomato, but use a small amount of tomato paste to give color and flavor. I have dined on some ragu sauces that contain no tomatoes at all. The dominant flavor should be the meat.

Serves 4 to 6.

2 tablespoons olive oil
1 tablespoon safflower oil
1 medium onion, finely chopped
1 cup finely chopped celery
1 pound lean ground veal or lean ground beef (top of
    the round)
Salt and freshly ground black pepper to taste
3/4 cup dry white wine
2 cups chicken or beef broth
2 tablespoons tomato paste
1 tablespoon dried basil
3/4-ounce package dried boletus mushrooms,
    soaked in warm water for 15 minutes
1 pound macaroni, any cut

Garnish: Finely chopped Italian parsley

Heat the oils in a medium skillet, then add onion and celery. Sauté over medium heat until onion begins to brown. Add veal, salt, and pepper and cook over medium heat until veal begins to brown. Add wine, cover, and simmer over low heat until wine cooks out.

In the meantime, mix in a saucepan the broth, tomato paste, basil, mushrooms, and 4 tablespoons of the liquid mushrooms were soaked in. Bring to a boil, stir until tomato paste dissolves, then add veal mixture, cover, and boil gently over low heat about 2 hours.

Cook pasta in a large pot of boiling water until done al dente, drain well, and toss in sauce.

We like to garnish each serving with finely chopped Italian parsley.

Calories	Cholesterol mg	Protein gm	Carbohydrate gm	Total fat gm	%	Sat fat gm	%	Mono gm	Poly gm
2830	322	155.5	386.5	69.5	22	15.7	5	31.4	12.8

SPAGHETTI WITH RUCOLA SALAD
Spaghetti con Insalata di Rucola

Instead of—or to supplement—the rucola, any mixture of fresh interesting salad greens can be used in this recipe. It is a lovely dish to prepare when fresh garden greens are available.

Serves 4 to 6.

8 cups fresh rucola (arugola), washed
1 pound spaghetti or spaghettini
2 teaspoons finely minced garlic
4 tablespoons olive oil
1 tablespoon safflower oil
4 to 5 tablespoons Italian wine vinegar
Salt and freshly ground black pepper to taste

Drain all moisture from rucola. Put in a salad bowl. Cook pasta al dente, then drain and add to rucola.

Mix together garlic, oils, and vinegar and toss rucola and pasta with the dressing. Add salt and pepper, and serve.

Calories	Cholesterol mg	Protein gm	Carbohydrate gm	Total fat gm	%	Sat fat gm	%	Mono gm	Poly gm
2341	0	63.4	353.9	73.8	28	7.1	3	43.2	13.4

PASTA SALAD
Insalata di Pasta

This interesting pasta recipe, which is made with raw salad greens, was given to me by an English friend who had it on the Isle of Capri.

Serves 4.

About 10 cups loosely packed salad greens (Bibb, rucola,*
    leaf lettuce, escarole hearts, radicchio, etc.)
1 pound spaghettini
3 tablespoons olive oil
1 tablespoon safflower oil
3 tablespoons good red wine vinegar, or lemon juice
1 teaspoon dried oregano
1 teaspoon minced garlic
Salt and freshly ground black pepper to taste

*You can use all rucola (arugola) if it is plentiful in your garden.

Wash and drain salad greens. Tear large leaves in half.

Boil pasta in a large pot of boiling salted water until al dente, then drain. Blend the oils, vinegar, oregano, and garlic together. Put the greens in a salad bowl and pour half the dressing over them. Add the pasta, the rest of the dressing, salt to taste, and a generous amount of freshly ground pepper. Toss.

Calories	Cholesterol mg	Protein gm	Carbohydrate gm	Total fat gm	%	Sat fat gm	%	Mono gm	Poly gm
2259	0	64.7	352.0	60.6	24	5.6	2	32.9	12.5

RIGATONI WITH BROCCOLI FOR FIFTY PEOPLE
Rigatoni con Broccoli per Cinquanta Persone

Many people have asked me for a pasta recipe for a large number of people, so I offer this simple recipe, which works very well. I was introduced to a similar dish in a favorite restaurant in Rome in 1972, and I have since made my version of the recipe for Craig Claiborne's annual New Year's Eve party for an average of 50 to 60 people. You will need a 15-quart pot, but if you don't have one, you can boil the pasta in several batches. Of course, you can make the recipe for a smaller number — just scale it down according to your needs.

Serves about 50 as part of a dinner.

5 bunches fresh broccoli, about 32 cups, cleaned and
    cut into bite-sized pieces
2 cups good olive oil
Salt and freshly ground black pepper to taste
Several tablespoons vegetable oil
5 pounds rigatoni, preferably Italian

The sauce
3 tablespoons coarsely chopped garlic
2 cups chopped fresh basil
1/2 cup chopped Italian parsley
3 cups chopped fresh tomatoes
1/2 cup olive oil
1/2 cup safflower oil

4 bunches thinly sliced whole scallions, about 6 cups
5 7-ounce cans Italian-style tunafish
1/2 cup finely chopped Italian parsley
10 to 12 ripe tomatoes at room temperature, cut into
    bite-sized pieces

Boil the broccoli in boiling salted water about 5 minutes, until broccoli is al dente — do not overcook. Drain, place in large bowls and allow to cool. Divide 1 cup of the olive oil among the bowls of broccoli and add salt and pepper.

In a 15-quart pot boil about 10 quarts salted water with several table-spoons vegetable oil. When water comes to a rolling boil, add pasta. Stir often with a fork or spoon long enough to scrape bottom of pot. Keep several quarts water boiling in another large saucepan in case of last-minute need if 15-quart pot cannot handle all the pasta. It is no problem to transfer some pasta from one pot of boiling water to another.

Drain pasta when cooked a little firmer than al dente. Drain well and allow to cool in wide serving bowls. Divide the other cup of the olive oil among the pasta, add salt and pepper, and mix so that pasta does not stick.

Make the sauce: Blend the garlic, basil, parsley, tomatoes, and oils in a food processor.

When the pasta and broccoli are cool, gently mix together—it's easier to do with your hands. Add scallions, crush tunafish with your hands, and mix with the pasta and broccoli.

Add the sauce and gently mix. Add 1/2 cup parsley and the tomatoes. Check for salt. Do not refrigerate but serve at room temperature.

*The component parts of this recipe can be made ahead of time—the pasta cooked in the morning and dressed just with the olive oil, the sauce made, and the vegetables prepared. I find it best to blanch the broccoli, however, just a little before mixing everything together so it keeps its freshness.

Calories	Cholesterol mg	Protein gm	Carbohydrate gm	Total fat gm	%	Sat fat gm	%	Mono gm	Poly gm
15579	540.0	651.0	1899.0	579.0	33	44.8	3	263.2	100

IV   RICE, POLENTA, GNOCCHI

Risotto is an ideal food as far as the goals of this book are concerned. When one cooks rice with vegetables and a little fish or meat, it becomes a complete, nourishing meal—a one-pot dish that is relatively easy to make. It is also nice served as a first course, as they do in Italy, with a small piece of meat or fish and/or a salad to follow as a second course.

Here I include both light summer risotto recipes with vegetables and fish and heavier ones that are ideal for winter menus. The recipes are in two groups. For the first, it is essential to use imported Italian rice, such as Arborio, because you must use the basic risotto cooking technique—that is, first sautéing the rice in oil, then adding liquid a little at a time and stirring constantly. When the rice has absorbed the liquid, you have a very creamy dish. Domestic rice does not hold up to this kind of treatment and would become mush.

In the second group of recipes, the rice is not always sautéed and the liquid, which can be tomatoes or stock, is added in larger quantities; less stirring is required, and the result is a looser risotto. With these recipes it is not essential to use an imported Italian rice. A good long-grain, like Carolina, will do, although frankly I prefer Arborio for both kinds of recipes.

RISOTTO MILANESE STYLE
Risotto alla Milanese

Although this recipe does not call for it, I like to serve it garnished with sautéed mushrooms, preferably wild ones. The mushrooms do not interfere with the simple elegance of the recipe.

Serves 4.

1 tablespoon butter
1 tablespoon safflower oil
1 medium onion, finely chopped
1 cup Arborio rice
½ cup dry white wine
2 cups plus chicken broth
Freshly ground black pepper to taste
½ teaspoon saffron

Heat butter and oil preferably in a heavy, medium saucepan, then add onion. When onion wilts, add rice. Cook several minutes, stirring from the bottom of the pan up. Add wine and cook, stirring frequently, until wine cooks out. Add broth, a little at a time, stirring constantly. Add pepper and saffron. Continue adding more broth as it is absorbed, stirring more or less constantly; in other words, don't leave the pot for more than a minute. Cook until rice is tender—about 15 minutes.

Calories	Cholesterol mg	Protein gm	Carbohydrate gm	Total fat gm	%	Sat fat gm	%	Mono gm	Poly gm
1053	36.0	15.5	167.9	26.0	22	7.4	6	5.8	10.1

RISOTTO COUNTRY STYLE
Risotto alla Rustica

If you want, substitute the early summer vegetables with later seasonal vegetables.

Serves 6.

2 tablespoons olive oil
1 tablespoon safflower oil
1 cup finely chopped onion
1½ cups asparagus, about 14 spears,
    cut into 1-inch pieces
1 cup fresh peas, blanched
2 cups zucchini cut into ½-inch pieces
2 cups chopped tomatoes, fresh if possible
    (drain if canned)
Salt and freshly ground black pepper to taste

1 cup cooked beans (cranberry or cannellini)*
2 tablespoons chopped fresh basil or
   1 teaspoon dried
2 cups chicken or beef broth
1 cup Arborio rice

*You can use fresh cranberry beans — cook according to directions
on page 346; dried white beans — see instructions on page 82; or
canned cannellini beans, drained and rinsed.

Heat the oils in a heavy saucepan about 8 or 9 inches wide, then add
onion. When onion begins to brown, add fresh asparagus and sauté over
moderate heat for several minutes. Add peas, zucchini, and tomatoes and
sauté over medium heat for 5 minutes. Add salt, pepper, beans, and basil
and 4 teaspoons of the broth. Cover and boil gently for 10 minutes. Add
rice, mix well, then stir in about 1/2 cup of the broth, lower heat, and boil
gently. Add a little salt, if needed. As broth is absorbed, add more, stirring
occasionally. You should add just enough liquid at a time to keep the rice
gently boiling. Cook until rice is done al dente, about 10 to 15 minutes —
at which point all the liquid should be absorbed. Serve hot.

Calories	Cholesterol mg	Protein gm	Carbohydrate gm	Total fat gm	%	Sat fat gm	%	Mono gm	Poly gm
1612	0	56.2	249.3	44.7	24	4.8	3	21.4	12.3

RISOTTO PIEDMONTESE STYLE
Risotto alla Piemontese

Serves 4.

2 tablespoons olive oil
1 tablespoon safflower oil
1 medium onion, finely chopped
1/2 cup finely chopped carrots
1/2 cup finely chopped celery
1 cup finely sliced leeks, washed
6 cups coarsely chopped fresh spinach
1/3 cup dry white wine
1 cup Arborio rice
2 cups hot chicken or beef broth
Salt and freshly ground black pepper to taste

Garnish: Chopped Italian parsley

Heat the oils in a medium saucepan, then add onion. As onion begins to
brown, add carrots, celery, leeks, and spinach; cover and simmer about
5 minutes. Add wine and cook 3 to 5 minutes. Add rice, and about 1/2 cup
of the stock, stir, add salt and pepper to taste. Cook over low to moderate
heat, adding more broth as is needed. Continue adding stock, stirring

occasionally, until rice is tender, about 10 to 15 minutes (for details, see preceding recipe). Some water may be added if stock is not sufficient.

Garnish with parsley.

Calories	Cholesterol mg	Protein gm	Carbohydrate gm	Total fat gm	%	Sat fat gm	%	Mono gm	Poly gm
1302	0	28.2	193.6	42.9	29	4.1	3	22.6	11.7

RISOTTO PADUA STYLE
Risotto alla Padovana

Serves 6.

2 tablespoons olive oil
2 tablespoons safflower oil
1 large onion, finely chopped
1 cup chopped celery
2 cups sliced fresh mushrooms or 1-ounce package dried
    boletus mushrooms, soaked in a little warm water
    for 20 minutes
1 pound ground lean veal
Salt and freshly ground black pepper to taste
1 cup dry white wine
4 tablespoons finely chopped Italian parsley
1½ cups Arborio rice
About 2½ cups chicken or beef broth
2 cups fresh peas, blanched and drained

Garnish: Chopped Italian parsley

Heat the oils in a medium saucepan, then add onion, celery, and mushrooms. Cook until onion becomes translucent. Add veal, salt, and pepper and cook over moderate heat, stirring frequently, until veal begins to brown. Add wine, parsley, and rice and cook, uncovered, mixing often until wine evaporates. Stir in about ½ cup of the broth and cook over low to moderate heat, adding more as it is absorbed by rice. Cook about 5 minutes, then add peas. Continue adding broth and stirring until rice is tender but not overcooked. Serve immediately, garnished with chopped parsley. Serve as a first course or as a vegetable course.

Calories	Cholesterol mg	Protein gm	Carbohydrate gm	Total fat gm	%	Sat fat gm	%	Mono gm	Poly gm
2554	322.0	138.3	311.7	80.1	28	16.9	6	33.0	22.8

RISOTTO WITH LEMON
Risotto al Limone

Serves 4 to 8.

2 tablespoons olive oil
1 tablespoon safflower oil
1 cup chopped onion
1 cup Arborio or Carolina long-grain rice
1 cup dry white wine
Grated rind of 1 lemon
2 cups chicken or beef broth
1 teaspoon marjoram
Salt and freshly ground black pepper to taste
Juice of 1 lemon
2 tablespoons chopped fresh basil or Italian parsley

Heat the oils in a saucepan, then add onion. When onion wilts, add rice, stirring for a minute or so. Add wine and lemon rind, stirring often, and cook until wine cooks out. Stir in ½ cup of the stock and add marjoram, salt, and pepper. Continue adding broth as needed, stirring constantly as described on page 152. Cook until rice is tender, about 10 minutes, depending on rice. Add lemon juice and basil or parsley. Mix and serve hot.

Calories	Cholesterol	Protein	Carbohydrate	Total fat		Sat fat		Mono	Poly
	mg	gm	gm	gm	%	gm	%	gm	gm
1129	0	14.7	172.1	41.4	32	4.8	3	21.4	12.3

RISOTTO MARINER STYLE
Risotto alla Marinara

This recipe and the following are two variations on the same theme. The first has a greater variety of shellfish and the second includes some pesto.

This is a delightful recipe—light, unusual, and very satisfying. It is essential that all ingredients are fresh. Crabmeat, lobster, oysters, shrimp, etc., may be used.

Serves 5 to 6 as a first course.

3 tablespoons olive oil
2 tablespoons safflower oil
1 teaspoon minced garlic
1/2 pound squid, washed and cut into 2-inch lengths, 1/2
    inch wide (page 215)
1 tablespoon finely chopped Italian parsley
1 teaspoon dried oregano
Salt and freshly ground black pepper to taste
2 cups chopped tomatoes, fresh if possible (drain if canned)
1 dozen mussels, scrubbed
1 dozen small to medium clams
1/2 pound sea scallops, cut into bite-sized pieces
1 medium onion, finely chopped
1 1/2 cups Arborio or Carolina long-grain rice
1/2 cup dry white wine
4 cups fish stock (page 51)
1 teaspoon grated lemon rind

Garnish: Finely chopped Italian parsley

Heat 1 tablespoon of the olive oil and 1 tablespoon of the safflower oil in a medium skillet, then add garlic. As garlic heats up, add squid, parsley, and oregano. Cook over high heat until all liquid cooks out. Add salt and pepper and tomatoes, cover, lower heat, and simmer for 10 minutes. Add mussels, cover, and cook over low heat until mussels open; then remove. Add clams and cook the same way until they open, then remove. Add scallops, turn up heat, and cook, uncovered, about 5 minutes. Remove flesh from mussels and clams, cut in 1/4-inch slices, and return the slices to the sauce.

Heat the remaining 2 tablespoons olive oil and 1 tablespoon safflower oil in a medium saucepan, then add onion and sauté for several minutes. Add rice and cook over medium heat, mixing constantly until onion begins to brown. Add wine. Cook, stirring, until wine cooks out. Stir in 1/2 cup of the fish stock and cook over moderate heat, stirring, until absorbed. Continue cooking, adding more stock as needed (for details, see page 152). Add salt and pepper to taste. After about 5 minutes add lemon rind. Continue adding stock as needed until rice is tender but not overcooked.

With a ladle, put a ladleful of rice in a heated soup bowl. Form a depression on top of each rice mound and pour a ladleful of tomato and shellfish mixture over it. Garnish each portion with finely chopped Italian parsley.

Calories	Cholesterol mg	Protein gm	Carbohydrate gm	Total fat gm	%	Sat fat gm	%	Mono gm	Poly gm
2189	499.0	122.3	288.7	76.3	31	7.8	3	32.9	23.5

RISOTTO WITH SHELLFISH GENOA STYLE
Risotto con Frutti di Mare alla Genovese

Serves 6 to 8.

2 pounds mussels, scrubbed*
1 dozen small clams, washed
2 cups broth (preferably mussel and clam broth), or a fish
  or chicken stock
2 cloves garlic, sliced
4 tablespoons olive oil mixed with 2 tablespoons
  safflower oil
3 cups coarsely chopped tomatoes, fresh if possible
  (drain if canned)
3 tablespoons chopped Italian parsley
Salt and hot pepper flakes or freshly ground black pepper
  to taste
2 tablespoons pesto (page 426), optional
1 cup chopped onion
2 cups Arborio or Carolina long-grain rice
1 cup dry white wine

Garnish: Chopped Italian parsley

*Other seafood may be used in this dish — scallops, squid, lobster,
etc. If squid is used, clean, cut in strips, and add with onion.

Steam mussels and clams open separately. Set aside, and when flesh cools remove from shells and chop coarsely. Strain and reserve broths. If there aren't 2 cups, add enough fish or chicken stock to make 2 cups.

Sauté garlic in 2 tablespoons of the combined oils. When garlic browns, remove with a slotted spoon and discard. To the hot oil add the tomatoes, parsley, salt, and either hot pepper flakes or freshly ground black pepper. Cover and simmer over moderate heat about 10 minutes.

Add chopped shellfish and cook, uncovered, over moderate heat for 5 minutes. Add pesto, mix well, and turn off heat.

Heat remaining 4 tablespoons oil in a fairly deep pot, add onion, and sauté until onion is limp. Add rice and cook over moderate heat, stirring constantly. When rice begins to color, add wine, salt, and freshly ground black pepper. Continue to cook over moderate heat, stirring constantly, until liquid is absorbed. Still stirring, add the broth a little at a time, as described on page 152. Cook until rice is tender but al dente.

To serve, put a mound of rice on each plate. Make a well in the mound, then pour a generous amount of shellfish and sauce into the well.

Garnish with chopped Italian parsley.

Calories	Cholesterol mg	Protein gm	Carbohydrate gm	Total fat gm	%	Sat fat gm	%	Mono gm	Poly gm
2688	215	91.2	366.4	91.3	30	9.6	3	42.8	24.6

RICE WITH EEL
Risi e Bisati

Eel lovers will enjoy this dish. It is delicate and most satisfying—an excellent winter dish.

Serves 4.

1 pound fresh eel
2 tablespoons olive oil
1 tablespoon safflower oil
Salt and freshly ground black pepper to taste
1 clove garlic, finely chopped
2 tablespoons finely chopped Italian parsley
1 bay leaf
¼ cup chopped whole scallions
Juice of 1 lemon
½ teaspoon saffron, diluted in 1 teaspoon warm water
1 cup Arborio or Carolina long-grain rice
2½ cups fish stock (page 51)

Garnish: About 1 tablespoon finely chopped Italian parsley

Have fishmonger skin eel, or do it yourself: First drive a nail into the head onto a board. With a sharp knife cut skin around head; then with a pair of pliers pull skin down. Once started, the skin will pull off very quickly. Gut eel, wash, and cut in 1-inch sections.

Heat the two oils in a shallow saucepan, add eel, salt, and pepper and cook over high heat until flesh takes on color. Add garlic, and as garlic begins to brown, add parsley, bay leaf, scallions, lemon juice, saffron, and rice. Cook for several minutes, stirring. Add about ½ cup of the stock. Cook over moderate heat, stirring often. As rice absorbs stock, add more and continue until rice in tender, as described on page 152.

Garnish with finely chopped parsley.

Calories	Cholesterol mg	Protein gm	Carbohydrate gm	Total fat gm	%	Sat fat gm	%	Mono gm	Poly gm
1854	187.0	67.7	156.4	103.6	49	18.4	9	45.2	12.3

According to the nutritional summary, this is not a dish to be heartily recommended. However, the available figures for eel almost certainly underestimate the content of polyunsaturated fat. My guess is that early indications that fatty fish is beneficial will be confirmed and that recipes like this will be approved in the future.

RISOTTO WITH FAVA BEANS (BROAD BEANS)
Risotto con le Fave

Serves 4.

2 cups fresh fava beans (broad beans)
1 tablespoon olive oil
1 tablespoon safflower oil
1 medium onion, finely chopped
3 tablespoons finely chopped celery
1 carrot, finely chopped
2 tablespoons finely chopped Italian parsley
1 cup chopped tomatoes, fresh if possible (drain if canned)
2 cups chicken or beef broth
2 teaspoons chopped fresh basil
Salt and freshly ground black pepper to taste
1 cup Arborio or Carolina long-grain rice

Garnish: 2 tablespoons finely chopped Italian parsley

Boil fava beans in water to cover for several minutes, then drain and let cool. Remove tough outer skin and reserve the beans.

Heat the oils in a medium saucepan, then add onion. When onion wilts, add celery, carrots, and parsley and sauté until onion begins to brown. Add tomatoes, cover and simmer about 20 minutes. Add ½ cup of the broth, basil, salt, and pepper; cook several more minutes, then stir in rice, cover, and, when hot, add fava beans. Continue cooking and stirring, adding more broth as described on page 152, until rice is tender.

Garnish with 2 tablespoons chopped Italian parsley.

Calories	Cholesterol mg	Protein gm	Carbohydrate gm	Total fat gm	%	Sat fat gm	%	Mono gm	Poly gm
1354	0	42.6	229.6	29.7	19	2.6	2	12.3	10.7

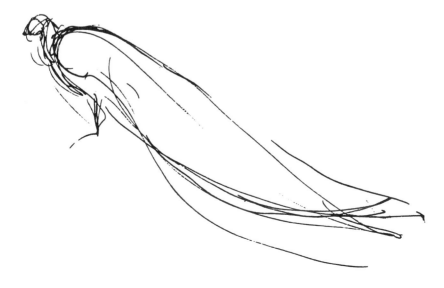

BAKED RISOTTO
Risotto al Forno

Serves 8.

9-ounce package frozen artichoke hearts
1 medium onion, minced
3 tablespoons safflower oil
1 cup peas, fresh if possible
1 cup sliced mushrooms
About 4 cups beef or chicken broth
Salt and freshly ground black pepper to taste
2 cups Arborio or Carolina long-grain rice
2 tablespoons butter or olive oil

Cook the artichoke hearts in boiling water 1 minute; drain, coarsely chop them, and set aside.

Sauté onion in safflower oil in a medium casserole. When onion begins to brown, add peas, artichoke hearts, mushrooms, 1 cup of the stock, salt, and pepper. Cover and cook gently for 20 minutes. In the meantime, in a separate pot boil 4 cups water, stir in the rice, and boil for 5 minutes. Drain and add rice to vegetable mixture. Add butter and 2 more cups stock. Cover and place in preheated 400° oven, stirring occasionally and adding more stock as is needed (at least 1 more cup). Taste for salt. The dish should be done in 10 minutes or so, depending on the rice.

Calories	Cholesterol mg	Protein gm	Carbohydrate gm	Total fat gm	%	Sat fat gm	%	Mono gm	Poly gm
2204	62	44.7	355.6	66.7	27	15.9	6	13.6	30.0

Butter was used in the calculation.

BASIC STEAMED RICE

Serves 4; about 3 cups cooked rice.

2 cups water
1 cup good-quality Carolina long-grain rice
Salt to taste

Put the water and rice along with a little salt in a small saucepan and bring to a boil. Cover tightly (put several sheets of paper towels between the lid and the pot) and simmer over low heat until all water is absorbed—about 10 minutes.

Calories	Cholesterol mg	Protein gm	Carbohydrate gm	Total fat gm	%	Sat fat gm	%	Mono gm	Poly gm
672	–	12.4	148.0	0.7	1	–	–	–	–

RICE WITH POTATOES
Riso e Patate

Serves 6.

3 tablespoons olive oil
2 tablespoons safflower or vegetable oil
1 medium onion, finely chopped
2 tablespoons finely chopped shallots
1 cup chopped tomatoes, fresh if possible (drain if canned)
1 medium potato, peeled and thinly sliced
1 tablespoon chopped fresh basil
1/2 pound mushrooms, thinly sliced
1 pound asparagus, washed and cut into 1-inch lengths
Salt and freshly ground black pepper to taste
1 cup Carolina long-grain rice
1/2 cup white wine
2 cups chicken or beef broth

Garnish: Finely chopped Italian parsley

Heat 1 tablespoon of the olive oil and 1 tablespoon of the safflower oil in a medium skillet, then add onion and shallots. Cook until onion becomes translucent, add tomatoes, potatoes, and basil, cover, and simmer about 10 minutes. Add some warm water if needed.

Remove mixture, place in a bowl, and set aside. Wipe out skillet, then add remaining 1 tablespoon safflower oil and 1 more tablespoon olive oil, mushrooms, and asparagus. Cook over medium to high heat, uncovered, until mushrooms begin to brown. Add salt and pepper. Turn off heat and set aside.

Heat remaining 1 tablespoon olive oil in a medium saucepan, add rice, stir rapidly to mix, then add wine and salt to taste. Cook over low heat, stirring often, until wine cooks out. Add some broth. Continue adding broth as needed (following directions on page 152), and after about 5 minutes, add tomato-and-potato mixture. Continue to cook, adding more broth, about 5 minutes, then add mushrooms and asparagus and continue cooking in the same way.

Garnish with parsley.

Calories	Cholesterol mg	Protein gm	Carbohydrate gm	Total fat gm	%	Sat fat gm	%	Mono gm	Poly gm
1696	0	36.7	230.2	70.7	37	7.8	4	32.9	23.5

RICE WITH TOMATOES
Riso e Pomodori

Good as is, this rice dish also makes a wonderful stuffing for tomatoes and peppers.

Serves 6.

3 tablespoons vegetable oil—safflower oil will do,
  or peanut oil
2 medium onions, finely chopped
4 cups chopped tomatoes, fresh if possible
  (drain if canned)
3 tablespoons chopped fresh basil or Italian parsley
Salt and freshly ground black pepper to taste
2 cups Carolina long-grain rice

Heat the oil in a medium skillet, then add onions. Cook over medium to high heat, and when onions begin to brown, add tomatoes, basil, salt, and pepper. Cover, lower heat, and simmer about 10 minutes.

In the meantime, add 2 cups good-quality rice to 4 cups water. When water boils, cover pot tightly and turn heat down as low as possible. Cook rice until it absorbs the water. Mix in sauce and serve in bowls as a first course or as a starch in a main course.

Calories	Cholesterol mg	Protein gm	Carbohydrate gm	Total fat gm	%	Sat fat gm	%	Mono gm	Poly gm
2022	0	39.5	360.3	44.5	19	6.9	3	18.6	12.9

RISOTTO CERTOSA STYLE
Risotto alla Certosina

Most frogs' legs arrive in the markets individually wrapped and frozen. The best imported frozen frogs' legs come from Japan. A cheaper variety is imported from India and is also good. Fresh local frogs' legs would, of course, be your first choice. In northern Italy frogs thrive in the rice fields.

Serves 6 or more.

3 tablespoons olive oil
1 tablespoon safflower oil
2 cups finely chopped leeks
1/2 cup finely chopped celery
1 cup finely chopped onion
1 cup finely chopped carrots
3 tablespoons finely chopped Italian parsley
6 pair frogs' legs
Salt and freshly ground black pepper to taste
Flour for dredging
Corn or vegetable oil
1 cup dry white wine
2 cups fresh sliced mushrooms, wild, if possible
1-ounce package dried boletus mushrooms, soaked in warm
  water for 15 minutes

2 cups chopped tomatoes, fresh if possible (drain if canned)
2 cups peas, preferably fresh, blanched
About 3 cups chicken or beef broth
2 cups Arborio or Carolina long-grain rice

Garnish: Finely chopped Italian parsley

Heat the oils in a medium saucepan, then add leeks, celery, onion, carrots, and parsley. Sauté over medium heat about 10 minutes, stirring often.

In the meantime, wash the frogs' legs and blot dry. Dust with salt and pepper and flour. Heat enough corn or vegetable oil to cover the bottom of a large skillet, then sauté frogs' legs in two batches until lightly browned. Add them to the sauce along with the wine, fresh and drained dried mushrooms, and tomatoes. Cover and cook gently about 20 minutes. Add blanched peas and cook 5 minutes more.

Remove frogs' legs and keep warm.

Remove half the sauce and set aside.

Add 2 cups of the stock to the remaining sauce and bring to a boil. Add rice, mixing well, and cook over moderate heat about 6 minutes, stirring often. Add reserved sauce and remaining 1 cup broth and continue to cook until rice is tender.

Serve rice on heated plates, garnished with frogs' legs and parsley. Serve immediately.

Calories	Cholesterol mg	Protein gm	Carbohydrate gm	Total fat gm	%	Sat fat gm	%	Mono gm	Poly gm
2823	144	112.1	439.8	65.0	20	7.2	2	32.4	16.1

RICE VALTELLINA STYLE
Risotto alla Valtellinese

Serves 6 to 8.

8 cups shredded green cabbage
1 medium onion, thinly sliced
1½ cups Arborio rice
About 3 cups beef or chicken broth
Salt and freshly ground black pepper to taste
10-ounce package frozen lima beans or 2 cups fresh
    lima beans

Garnish:
3 tablespoons butter
3 tablespoons safflower oil
3 tablespoons crumbled sage

Put cabbage, onion, rice, and stock in a pot, bring to a boil, add salt and pepper, cover, and lower heat. In the meantime, blanch the lima beans, drain, and add to cabbage-and-rice mixture. Continue to cook, stirring, adding more stock, as needed, a little at a time (see page 152 for details). When rice is cooked, turn off heat and set aside.

In a small pan heat the butter and oil. When butter melts add sage and cook for several minutes. Spoon 1 tablespoon butter-and-oil mixture over each portion. Serve hot.

Calories	Cholesterol mg	Protein gm	Carbohydrate gm	Total fat gm	%	Sat fat gm	%	Mono gm	Poly gm
1934	93	31.6	274.2	78.9	36	22.5	10	16.2	31.2

LIMA BEANS, BROCCOLI, AND RICE
Minestra di Riso

This recipe makes a delicious complete lunch dish.

Serves 6 to 8.

2 cups dried lima beans, soaked in cold water about 2 hours
6 cups water
1 tablespoon crushed rosemary
1 bay leaf
Hot pepper flakes to taste (optional)
1 medium onion, coarsely chopped
Salt and freshly ground black pepper to taste
3 cups broccoli cut into bite-sized pieces

The sauce
3 tablespoons vegetable oil (I prefer 1 tablespoon olive
    and 2 tablespoons safflower)
1 medium onion, coarsely chopped
2 cups chopped tomatoes, fresh if possible (drain if canned)
1/4 cup diced celery
3 tablespoons chopped fresh basil or 1 tablespoon dried
Salt and freshly ground black pepper to taste

1 cup Carolina long-grain rice

Drain lima beans, then put in a saucepan with 4 cups of the water, the rosemary, bay leaf, hot pepper, onion, salt, and freshly ground black pepper. Cover and boil gently for about 1 1/2 hours. Add broccoli. Cook another 20 minutes. Keep warm.

To make the sauce heat the oils in a skillet, then add onion and sauté until brown. Add the rest of the ingredients. Cover and simmer over medium heat about 20 minutes.

Cook 1 cup rice in 2 cups water (page 160). When rice is cooked, mix in the tomato sauce.

Put a serving of cooked rice on each plate. Make a well on each rice mound, pour lima-bean-and-broccoli mixture over, and serve.

Calories	Cholesterol mg	Protein gm	Carbohydrate gm	Total fat gm	%	Sat fat gm	%	Mono gm	Poly gm
2694	0	113.6	466.7	51.0	17	3.7	1	14.4	20.5

RICE AND PEAS
Risi e Bisi

Serves 4 to 6.

2 tablespoons olive oil
1 tablespoon safflower oil
1 cup finely chopped onion
1 cup sliced mushrooms (optional)
About 3 cups chicken or beef broth
2 cups fresh peas
1 cup Arborio or Carolina long-grain rice
Salt and freshly ground black pepper to taste

Garnish: 2 tablespoons minced Italian parsley

Heat the oils in a medium saucepan, then add onion. When it becomes translucent, add mushrooms and simmer until onion begins to brown. Add 1 cup of the stock and the peas, cover, and boil gently for 15 minutes. Add rice, salt, and pepper, and simmer, stirring continuously and adding more stock as needed. Cook until rice is tender but not overcooked. Sprinkle parsley on top before serving.

Calories	Cholesterol mg	Protein gm	Carbohydrate gm	Total fat gm	%	Sat fat gm	%	Mono gm	Poly gm
1341	0	34.4	202.8	42.8	28	4.1	3	22.6	11.6

Mushrooms are included in calculations.

RICE WITH TUNA
Riso al Tonno

Serves 6 to 8.

2 cups Arborio or Carolina long-grain rice
1 medium onion, chopped
4 tablespoons vegetable oil
4 tablespoons finely chopped Italian parsley
2 cups crumbled Italian-style tunafish

Garnish:
6 to 8 tablespoons grated Parmesan or Romano cheese, or
Additional chopped parsley

Put rice in a heavy saucepan and add 4 cups water. Bring to a boil, then cover tightly and cook over very low heat until rice absorbs all the water (chicken or beef broth can be used instead of water)—about 10 minutes.

Meanwhile, sauté onion in oil. Add parsley and tuna, cover, and simmer gently about 10 minutes. Toss with rice and serve.

Sprinkle 1 tablespoon freshly grated cheese over each serving or garnish with chopped parsley instead of cheese.

Calories	Cholesterol mg	Protein gm	Carbohydrate gm	Total fat gm	%	Sat fat gm	%	Mono gm	Poly gm
2668	232.0	132.6	314.3	91.2	30	17.5	6	14.6	46.0

ABOUT ARANCINI

This recipe, a variation on arancini ("little oranges"), was given to me by an Italian woman who was hawking her homemade rice balls on Mulberry Street in Little Italy in New York City. I asked her how they were made and she explained that there were two groups of rice balls on her tray. One contained a core of ground meat, light tomato sauce, and peas; the other had a core of chopped prosciutto and mozzarella.

I mentioned to her that I had never tasted rice balls in Italy prepared with ground meat, sauce, and peas or with mozzarella and prosciutto. She replied indignantly, "Mine are better." With that, I felt I owed it to her and to myself to try one. I tasted the ground meat and peas and she was right—it was excellent, in fact, better than the arancini I had tasted in southern Italy. I did think the rice was a little sticky, but that was because she did not use a good-quality rice.

The size of the rice balls generally ranges from that of a golf ball to a baseball. Her rice balls were a perfect compromise between golf ball and tennis ball size.

Arancini are usually made with boiled rice and tomato sauce. They are formed into a ball, rolled in egg and then breadcrumbs, and deep-fried.

Often a little meatball or piece of mozzarella is forced to the center of the ball. Actually, you can be creative with this dish—you can push fish into the center of the rice ball or vegetables such as cooked asparagus tips or sautéed mushrooms. For orange rice balls, which I serve as appetizers, see page 35.

RICE BALLS WITH VEAL AND PEAS
Arancini

Serves 8.

2 tablespoons safflower oil
1 small onion, finely chopped

1/2 pound ground lean veal
Salt and freshly ground black pepper to taste
1/2 cup dry white wine
2 cups chopped tomatoes, fresh if possible (drain if canned)
2 tablespoons finely chopped fresh basil or
    1 tablespoon dried
2 tablespoons finely chopped Italian parsley
1 cup fresh or frozen peas, blanched
2 cups cooked Carolina long-grain rice (page 160)
4 egg whites, lightly beaten
3/4 cup fine breadcrumbs
Corn oil for frying

Heat the oil in a medium saucepan, then add onion and cook, uncovered, until onion begins to brown. Add veal, salt, and pepper and, stirring frequently, cook, uncovered, over medium heat. When the veal begins to brown, add wine, cover, lower heat, and cook, stirring the bottom of the pan occasionally so the meat doesn't stick, until the wine cooks out. Add tomatoes, basil, parsley, salt, and pepper, cover, and boil gently for about 1 1/2 hours, stirring occasionally. Add drained blanched peas, cover, and simmer an additional 30 minutes.*

In the meantime, cook rice according to instructions on page 160 and let cool. Add 2 of the lightly beaten egg whites, salt, and pepper. Form a ball between the size of a golf ball and tennis ball. Then, with a spoon, remove some rice from the center and fill with about 1 teaspoon meat-and-pea mixture. Re-form the ball. Continue making balls—you should have 8 of them. Roll them in the remaining 2 egg whites, then in breadcrumbs, re-forming if necessary.

Pour about 1 1/2 inches corn oil in a small, deep saucepan. When oil is hot, gently place a rice ball in the oil with tongs. Cook one at a time, turning when browned on one side. When a deep golden brown, remove and blot on paper towels. Repeat until all are done.

The rice balls can be served as is or cut in half with more sauce poured over them.

*About 1/2 cup sauce and meat is needed for this recipe. I suggest you make this amount. The remaining sauce can be used on pasta, enough for 1 pound.

Calories	Cholesterol mg	Protein gm	Carbohydrate gm	Total fat gm	%	Sat fat gm	%	Mono gm	Poly gm
2028	40.0	64.0	366.5	28.6	12	3.4	1	5.9	12.3

ABOUT POLENTA

During my childhood polenta was never served in our home without inviting Vincenzo. That was the only time I saw him— perhaps three or four times a year. Vincenzo had been a widower as far back as I could remember, and since he adored polenta with a passion, his friends always invited him whenever they made it.

Vincenzo was a gentle, quiet man. He seemed very big, perhaps because I was so small, and his stomach looked as large as a 50-gallon wine barrel.

After the polenta was cooked it was spread about 1/2 inch thick on a wooden board 3 or 4 feet square. The board was made of poplar wood because it has no taste or odor, and the density of the wood allows it to retain the heat of the polenta, thus keeping the polenta warm.

A tomato sauce made with wild mushrooms, homemade sausages cut into bite-sized pieces, chicken giblets, and often squab cut in manageable pieces were all spread on top of the polenta, which was then generously dusted with homemade Pecorino cheese that my relatives in Italy sent us every 6 months.

The board was placed on the kitchen table. We would sit around it and with spoons eat the polenta and goodies in front of us. No one was allowed to pick or eat anything except what was directly in front of him. It was a delightful country way of eating polenta. We loved the intimacy and fun as children and there was a logic to it as well. The heat that the wood absorbed from the polenta, and that in turn kept the polenta warm, allowed us to eat at a leisurely pace.

I had a poplar board made for my own family 15 years ago and have enjoyed it on many occasions.

POLENTA COUNTRY STYLE
Polenta alla Campagnola

This is truly one of the warmest ways to dine with special guests that I can think of. A light second course should follow.

Serves 10.

> 3 tablespoons safflower or vegetable oil
> 4 squab, washed and trussed, rubbed with salt and pepper
> 1/2 pound chicken gizzards (remove all fat)
> 1 medium to large onion with 5 cloves stuck into it
> 1 large carrot, cut in half
> 1 pound veal bones
> 1/2 pound pork bones
> Salt and freshly ground black pepper to taste
> 1 pound mushrooms, cut in large sections
> 1 1/2 cups dry white wine
> 10 cups chopped tomatoes, fresh if possible, passed
>   through a food mill and drained
> 1 1/2-ounce package dried boletus mushrooms, soaked in
>   warm water for 15 minutes
> 3 tablespoons finely chopped Italian parsley

2 tablespoons kosher salt*
3 cups fine-ground cornmeal†

*We use kosher salt because it is sweeter than regular table salt.
†Cornmeal comes in a fine or coarse ground. Some prefer the
coarse and some the fine — it is a matter of taste. White cornmeal
is popular in the Venice area.

Heat oil in a large saucepan about 4 or 5 inches deep and wide enough so
that all the meat and bones can fit in one layer. Add the squab, chicken
gizzards, onion, carrot, bones, salt, and pepper. Brown over medium to
high heat, turning often with a wooden spoon. When squab are a golden
brown, add mushrooms and cook for several minutes. Add wine, cover,
lower heat, and, stirring often, continue to cook about 10 to 15 minutes
until wine cooks out. Add tomatoes, dried mushrooms and their liquid,
and parsley. Lower heat, cover, and simmer gently for about 3 hours.

Remove and discard bones. Remove chicken gizzards with a slotted
spoon and, when cool, slice and return to sauce. Remove squab and break
into bite-sized pieces, removing and discarding breastbone and backbone.
Add to sauce. Remove carrot and onion and purée them with some of the
sauce in a food processor, then return to the pot.

In the meantime, bring 2½ quarts water and the kosher salt to a gentle
boil. Add the cornmeal (polenta) to the water slowly by taking a handful at
a time and allowing the cornmeal to trickle from the bottom of your hand
in a slow, steady stream; stir constantly with a wooden spoon in your other
hand. Continue, stirring constantly, until all the cornmeal is used up, about
20 to 25 minutes. At this point, polenta will have the consistency of a
thick porridge.

Pour the polenta onto a wooden board 36 × 30 inches (see page 168) and
spread to a thickness of about ½ inch. Spoon on the sauce with the
gizzards, mushrooms, and squab sections. Seat guests around the board so
that each may eat the portion of polenta directly in front of him or her —
or heat plates, spread about ½ inch polenta on each plate, spoon sauce on
top with squab, and serve.

Calories	Cholesterol mg	Protein gm	Carbohydrate gm	Total fat gm	%	Sat fat gm	%	Mono gm	Poly gm
3779	982.0	242.6	449.7	118.3	28	16.6	4	24.0	40.1

GRILLED POLENTA

Serve grilled polenta with game or meats. It is particularly good with salt cod Florentine style (page 183).

Serves 6 to 9.

About 7 cups water
1 tablespoon kosher salt
2½ cups fine-ground cornmeal

Add salt to water and bring the water to a simmering boil. Take a fistful of cornmeal at a time and allow a slow trickle of cornmeal to fall into the simmering water, as you stir constantly with a wooden spoon in your other hand. Continue until all the cornmeal is used up—about 10 to 15 minutes— then cook, still stirring constantly, for another 5 to 10 minutes, depending on the consistency of the polenta. The total cooking time is about 25 minutes.

Pour the polenta into an oiled shallow pan about 8 inches square. Allow it to cool, then cut it into 9 squares with a fine wire. Brush with vegetable oil or a mixture of half safflower oil and half butter. Grill over hot coals.

Calories	Cholesterol mg	Protein gm	Carbohydrate gm	Total fat gm	%	Sat fat gm	%	Mono gm	Poly gm
1122	0	28.0	224.6	16.5	13	1.9	1	3.4	10.5

SEMOLINA GNOCCHI FROM SARDINIA
Ciciones

These gnocchi, called ciciones, are a little tough, but that is the quality of the dough. I would think a fine-ground cornmeal would do nicely in this recipe if semolina is not available.

Serves 6.

2 cups fine semolina, about ¾ pound
½ teaspoon saffron, diluted in
    ¾ cup hot water
Salt to taste
Tomato sauce, any kind

Pour semolina in a mound on a board or countertop. Make a well in the mound, work the water with saffron into the semolina with a fork, then work with hands. Knead with the palms of your hands until ball is silky, about 10 minutes.

Place the ball of dough between two plates and let it rest for 1 hour. Cut ball in quarters and roll out 1 quarter. Roll and stretch until the dough is the thickness of a pencil. Cut dough in ¼-inch rounds. Repeat with remaining quarters.

Boil the pieces of dough in boiling salted water about 12 minutes. Drain and toss in sauce.

Serve hot.

Calories	Cholesterol mg	Protein gm	Carbohydrate gm	Total fat gm	%	Sat fat gm	%	Mono gm	Poly gm
1120	0	44.0	238.6	6.7	5	–	–	–	–

These figures do not include sauce.

POTATO DUMPLINGS
Gnocchi di Patate

I tested this recipe a number of times before I finally produced the desired results—a light potato gnocchi. During a recent visit to Italy I made a lot of inquiries about a recipe for gnocchi. All of the people I talked to, including my mother, insisted that the potatoes be allowed to cool after mashing, before the flour is added to them. The secret to a light gnocchi is to use a minimal amount of flour and no eggs. I assure you that this recipe will produce the lightest gnocchi you'll ever make.

Serves 4 to 6.

1 1/2 pounds new potatoes
About 1/2 cup flour
Salt to taste
2 cups sauce, such as marinara (page 430) or pesto
  (page 426)

Garnish: Lemon wedges for fried gnocchi

Boil potatoes in their skins just until tender. Be careful not to overcook to the point the potatoes split apart. Drain and allow to cool. Peel the potatoes and put them through a potato ricer or mash with a fork. If you use a fork, be certain to mash all lumps. Spread potatoes on a countertop and allow to cool some more. When potatoes have become quite cool, bring about 4 quarts salted water to a boil. Now work the flour a little at a time into the cooled, mashed potatoes, add some salt, and form a loaf. Cut the loaf into quarters and roll out each one with your hands on a floured board until it forms a cylinder about 1/2 inch thick. With a knife cut the cylinder into pieces about 3/4 inch long. Repeat until you've used up all the dough. Slip the gnocchi into a large pot of rapidly boiling water and cook until they float on the surface of the water—no more than a minute or so. Do not overcook, as the gnocchi will fall apart if cooked too long.

Drain gnocchi and toss in sauce.

Variation: Gnocchi may be rolled into oblong shapes after they are cut and then fried in vegetable oil (I prefer corn oil) until golden brown. Blot, and add salt. Serve hot with wedges of lemon as a vegetable with a main course.

Calories	Cholesterol mg	Protein gm	Carbohydrate gm	Total fat gm	%	Sat fat gm	%	Mono gm	Poly gm
768	0	21.5	165.2	1.4	2	–	–	–	–

These figures do not include sauce.

GNOCCHI SARDEGNA STYLE
Gnocchi di Patate alla Sarda

This recipe for gnocchi with mint was given to me years ago by a young Sardinian student, who claimed the dish was a specialty of Sardinia.

The original recipe calls for a tomato sauce, but we prefer the Gorgonzola sauce.

Serves 4.

2 pounds potatoes, either new or Idaho
3 tablespoons finely chopped fresh mint
Salt to taste
3/4 cup flour
4 tablespoons safflower oil
1 cup chicken or beef broth
1/4 pound imported Gorgonzola cheese

Garnish:
Freshly ground black pepper to taste
2 tablespoons grated Parmesan cheese

Boil potatoes with skins on. Drain and let cool, then peel and put through a ricer or mash with a fork. Spread on a countertop, and let cool completely to room temperature. Add mint and salt to taste. Work in the flour, about 1/2 to 3/4 cup, and roll with your hands into 4 cylinders, as in preceding recipe. Cut cylinders into 1/2-inch-long pieces and put on a lightly floured board.

Make the sauce by heating the oil, then adding the broth. Cut up Gorgonzola, add to the broth and oil, and boil, uncovered, until Gorgonzola dissolves.

Bring a large pot of salted water to a boil, then gently add gnocchi with a spatula. When gnocchi float to the surface, they are cooked. Do not overcook, or they will fall apart. Drain in a colander.

Serve gnocchi on heated plates. Pour sauce over, grind on black pepper, and sprinkle with grated Parmesan.

Calories	Cholesterol mg	Protein gm	Carbohydrate gm	Total fat gm	%	Sat fat gm	%	Mono gm	Poly gm
2021	123.0	62.5	228.9	95.6	42	28.8	13	19.2	40.6

V FISH

The Italians prefer fish to any other food. It's not surprising, therefore, that for the most important celebration of the year—Christmas Eve—they would feast on fish.

In our house Christmas Eve was a very special occasion. My mother served seven different fish seven different ways, the seven fish representing the seven sacraments. I do not know the origin of this tradition and most Italians do not practice it.

Our children always counted the fish to be certain there were seven. Now that they are adults, they look forward to continuing the tradition when they have their own families, and so it goes.

I thought you might be interested to know what one of our typical Christmas Eve menus consisted of. This one was prepared on Christmas Eve 1982:

> Fried whitebait
> Stuffed clams with sherry
> Sautéed frogs' legs with fresh wild mushrooms and
>   white wine*
> Roasted sweet red peppers
> Linguine with crabs and skate wing sauce
> Baked striped bass with mussels, wine, and broccoli
> Endive and fennel salad
> Ellie's bread
> Vino Mio—Cabernet, 1979; Chardonnay, 1979
> Ellie's cheese pie
> Fruit, Louis Roederer Champagne, espresso, grappa

We always serve small portions and set a very leisurely pace. Everyone must be dressed properly—it was always the one occasion when the children did not resent it. We never invite more than 7 guests, because the round table we use for the occasion seats only 12 and we want everyone around one table so that we can all enjoy one another.

This chapter offers a wide selection of the kinds of fish I grew up on—squid, cuttlefish, monkfish, skate, fresh sardines, shark, and whiting, as well as more familiar varieties such as crab and swordfish.

*We consider frogs a fish. The wild mushrooms were mushrooms I had gathered and frozen.

FRESH ALBACORE OR TUNA ON A SKEWER
Spiedini di Tonno

Serves 2.

1-pound slice albacore or tuna ¾ inch thick
Juice of 1 lime
1 teaspoon olive oil
1 teaspoon safflower oil
1 teaspoon minced garlic
1 teaspoon crushed rosemary
Salt and freshly ground black pepper to taste
1 medium green pepper, cut into 4 pieces
About 12 fresh mint leaves

Garnish: Lime or lemon wedges

Wash the fish, remove tough outer skin, cut out dark red section in center of meat. Cut fish steak into 1- to 1½-inch cubes. Marinate in lime juice, the two oils, garlic, rosemary, salt, and pepper at least 2 hours.

Cook the green pepper in boiling water about 2 minutes. Drain and let the pieces cool.

Spear 1 mint leaf on a skewer, then a piece of fish, then another mint leaf. Spear 2 sections of peppers between fish sections. Prepare a second skewer the same way.

Broil over hot coals or under a preheated broiler. Cook about 4 minutes on each side under a broiler, less time over coals. Do not overcook.

Serve with lime or lemon wedges.

Calories	Cholesterol mg	Protein gm	Carbohydrate gm	Total fat gm	%	Sat fat gm	%	Mono gm	Poly gm
933	260.0	117.3	10.0	43.8	41	0.9	1	4.7	3.6

BAKED FRESHWATER BASS

Serves 2.

2 tablespoons olive oil
1 teaspoon safflower oil
1 cup sliced mushrooms
2 cloves garlic, finely chopped
½ cup dry white wine
1 cup thinly sliced scallions
3 tablespoons finely chopped Italian parsley
2 tablespoons Kikkoman mild soy sauce*
2 tablespoons coarsely chopped fresh mint

> Hot pepper flakes or freshly ground black pepper to taste
> 2 freshwater large-mouth bass, gutted, scales and gills removed, heads on, about 1 1/2 pounds each

*This soy sauce has about half the amount of salt of regular soy sauce.

Heat the oils in a medium skillet or saucepan; then add mushrooms and lightly brown. Add garlic and cook over high heat about 30 seconds. Add wine, scallions, parsley, soy sauce, mint, and pepper. Cover and simmer over moderate heat for several minutes.

Place washed fish in a baking dish so that they fit snugly and pour the sauce over them. Cover baking dish with foil and bake in preheated 500° oven for 15 minutes.

Calories	Cholesterol mg	Protein gm	Carbohydrate gm	Total fat gm	%	Sat fat gm	%	Mono gm	Poly gm
911	232.0	85.8	22.0	43.3	42	7.6	7	26.1	5.1

STRIPED BASS IN A PAPER BAG I
Spigola al Cartoccio

For those of us blessed with fresh large fish, this is an excellent recipe. Spigola is very similar to striped bass, although, frankly, it is not quite as good as our fresh striped bass.

The difference between steaming in paper and steaming in aluminum foil is that paper produces a "dry" steam, while foil produces a wet steam. Paper is especially good with foods that contain a great deal of moisture, such as fish and veal. An oiled brown paper bag can be used, but household parchment is preferable.

Serves 6.

> 4 1/2- to 5-pound striped bass, scaled, cleaned, gills removed, head on*
> 3 to 4 cloves garlic, finely chopped
> 3 to 4 tablespoons finely chopped Italian parsley
> 2 tablespoons crushed rosemary
> Salt and freshly ground black pepper to taste
> 2 sheets kitchen parchment
> 3 tablespoons olive oil mixed with 1 teaspoon safflower oil

*Any large fresh fish, such as cod, red snapper, or salmon, will do.

Wash fish in cold water. Make 3 slits in fish on each side about 4 inches apart. Stuff some of the garlic, parsley, and rosemary into the slits and rub the cavity of the fish with the mixture, plus salt and pepper. Spread remaining garlic, parsley, rosemary, salt, and pepper on both sides of fish.

Place 1 sheet of parchment on the bottom of the baking tray. (We use an oval stainless-steel platter.) The parchment sheet should be about 2 to 3 inches larger than fish. Place fish on parchment in tray and sprinkle with the oil mixture. Rub some vegetable oil on a second sheet of parchment the same size as first sheet and place over fish. Crimp the edges together all around fish.

Bake fish in preheated 500° oven about 20 minutes. Lower heat to 400° as paper begins to char and cook about 10 minutes more.

Serve with one of fish sauces on pages 426–42. It is also excellent with mint and basil pesto thinned to a creamy consistency with pan juices.

Calories	Cholesterol mg	Protein gm	Carbohydrate gm	Total fat gm	%	Sat fat gm	%	Mono gm	Poly gm
2786	1238.0	426.3	6.6	105.8	33	27.4	9	54.7	6.0

BASS IN A PAPER BAG II
Branzino al Cartoccio

Serves 4.

1 medium onion, finely chopped
6 medium mushrooms, sliced
1 tablespoon safflower oil
3 tablespoons olive oil
1 teaspoon minced garlic
Hot pepper flakes to taste (optional)
1/2 cup peeled, seeded, chopped tomatoes,
    fresh if possible (drain if canned)
1 teaspoon dried oregano
2 tablespoons capers
1 teaspoon crushed rosemary
Salt and freshly ground black pepper to taste
4 slices striped bass or other white-fleshed fish,
    1 inch thick
4 sheets kitchen parchment
4 tablespoons chopped Italian parsley

Sauté onion and mushrooms in the two oils. When onion wilts, add garlic and optional hot pepper. When garlic begins to color, add tomatoes and oregano and cook for several minutes. Add capers, rosemary, salt, and pepper, cover, and simmer for 30 minutes. In the meantime, salt and pepper the fish slices, then place 2 each on 1 sheet of parchment arranged on the bottom of a baking tray. Ladle equal amounts of sauce on top of each slice of fish, then top with 1 tablespoon chopped parsley. Place 2 sheets of parchment over the fish and crimp top and bottom edges to seal. (If you have to use paper bags, allow 1 per piece of fish.)

Place tray in a preheated 450° oven and cook about 10 minutes, spraying some water on the parchment after the first 6 minutes of cooking. Open the parchment before your guests.

Calories	Cholesterol mg	Protein gm	Carbohydrate gm	Total fat gm	%	Sat fat gm	%	Mono gm	Poly gm
1562	495.0	176.7	19.5	78.7	44	14.6	8	41.9	12.5

BROILED SPLIT FISH WITH PESTO
Pesce alla Brace con Pesto

Any small to medium fish that can be split can be used in this recipe, but I do recommend that the fish be a white-fleshed fish rather than a dark-fleshed fish.

Serves 2.

> 2 white-fleshed fish, such as rock bass, small
>   striped bass, small red snapper, etc., split
> Salt and freshly ground black pepper to taste
> 2 tablespoons pesto (page 426)
> Juice of 1 to 2 limes or lemons

Place fish on a baking tray, salt and pepper it, and spoon about 1 tablespoon pesto on top of each portion.

Bake fish, uncovered, in a preheated 450° oven until cooked, about 15 minutes. Squeeze lime or lemon juice over fish several minutes before serving.

Calories	Cholesterol mg	Protein gm	Carbohydrate gm	Total fat gm	%	Sat fat gm	%	Mono gm	Poly gm
355	155.0	53.8	4.7	12.4	31	3.3	8	5.8	1.1

BAKED SEA SQUAB (BLOWFISH)

Blowfish, sometimes called chicken of the sea or sea squab, is similar to monkfish, but it has no thin bones, only a spine. It is especially popular with children because of its sweet flesh and lack of small bones.

Serves 3.

6 sea squab
1 tablespoon chopped garlic
2 tablespoons olive oil
1 tablespoon safflower oil
2 tablespoons chopped Italian parsley or fresh coriander
2 tablespoons chopped pickled ginger or 2 tablespoons
    grated lemon rind
1/2 cup dry white wine
Salt and freshly ground black pepper to taste

Place sea squab on a baking tray large enough so they fit comfortably. Pour the rest of the ingredients over fish.

Place baking tray, uncovered, in a preheated 500° oven and bake about 10 minutes, until flesh separates from bone.

Calories	Cholesterol mg	Protein gm	Carbohydrate gm	Total fat gm	%	Sat fat gm	%	Mono gm	Poly gm
671	204.0	63.2	10.7	40.9	54	4.1	5	22.6	11.6

Nutritional data for sea squab unavailable; haddock substituted in calculation.

CATFISH IN CARPIONE
Gobione in Carpione

This recipe is usually made with small fish, such as sardines; see page 28. Gobione is a freshwater fish similar to catfish, so I decided to try the dish with catfish and it was delicious. Carpione is a vinegar-and-onion marinade popular in northern Italy.

Serves 3.

3 catfish, about 1 pound each
Salt and freshly ground black pepper to taste
Flour for dredging
Corn or vegetable oil for shallow-frying
2 tablespoons olive oil
1 teaspoon safflower oil
3 large onions, thinly sliced
4 tablespoons yellow raisins
3 tablespoons pine nuts
1 1/2 cups wine vinegar, preferably white
Hot pepper flakes to taste (optional)

If catfish aren't already cleaned, gut them, then cut the skin around the head of each one with a sharp knife, grip the head firmly and carefully with your hand, and with a pair of pliers pull skin toward the tail; with a pair of scissors cut off tail and fins. Salt and pepper fish, then dust with flour.

Heat about ¾ inch corn oil in a medium skillet. When hot, lower fish carefully into skillet and cook it till golden brown on both sides. Remove with a pair of tongs, blot with paper towels and set aside.

Discard all oil from skillet, then wash it out. Heat the oils in the clean skillet, add onions, and sauté until they begin to brown. Add raisins and pine nuts. Cook a minute or more and add vinegar and hot pepper flakes, if you like them as we do. Cover and boil gently for several minutes.

Place fish in a bowl or on a tray* so they fit snugly. Pour onion-and-vinegar mixture over fish and marinate in a cool place overnight. Serve at room temperature.

*Never store in aluminum food with vinegar or lemon or food with a high acid count.

Calories	Cholesterol	Protein	Carbohydrate	Total fat		Sat fat		Mono	Poly
	mg	gm	gm	gm	%	gm	%	gm	gm
1766	337.0	128.6	135.8	85.9	43	12.6	6	33.4	26.8

SOFTSHELL CRABS

Serves 6 as a first course.

6 softshell crabs
3 tablespoons olive oil and 1 tablespoon safflower oil, or
    4 tablespoons peanut oil
1 teaspoon minced garlic
2 tablespoons finely chopped Italian parsley or
    fresh coriander
Salt and freshly ground black pepper to taste
¼ cup dry sherry

Garnish: Lemon wedges

Have fishmonger kill the crabs just before you bring them home. Or bring them home alive and with scissors snip off fronts of crabs, where eyes protrude, which will kill them. Clean by lifting off flaps and removing gills. Wash crabs in cold water and pat dry with paper towels.

Heat oil in a large skillet, add crabs, and cook for several minutes. Turn crabs and cook several minutes more. Add garlic, parsley or coriander, salt, and pepper. As soon as garlic begins to color, add sherry, lower heat, and simmer several minutes.

Serve with lemon wedges.

Variation: Instead of the parsley and sherry, use 3 teaspoons soy sauce and 3 tablespoons freshly chopped coriander and the juice of 1 lemon.

Calories	Cholesterol	Protein	Carbohydrate	Total fat		Sat fat		Mono	Poly
	mg	gm	gm	gm	%	gm	%	gm	gm
1295	544.0	95.1	27.6	64.5	44	5.5	4	32.8	12.6

FRIED SOFTSHELL CRABS AND VEGETABLES

Serves 2.

2 large or 4 small softshell crabs
4 branches broccoli
Corn oil for shallow-frying
4 small eggplant slices or zucchini slices,
    about ¼ inch thick
4 scallions about 3 inches long
4 sugar pod peas or snow peas

The sauce
2 tablespoons good soy sauce
1 tablespoon finely chopped fresh ginger
1 teaspoon good mustard
3 tablespoons dry white wine
1 clove garlic, minced

The batter
1 cup flour
1 cup ice water
1 teaspoon baking powder
2 egg whites, lightly beaten

Prepare crabs as in preceding recipe.

Peel broccoli stems and either steam or blanch broccoli until just tender but still firm.

Mix sauce ingredients and divide into 2 small bowls.

Put about ¾ inch corn oil in a medium skillet. Mix batter ingredients together, blending until they are a creamy consistency. When oil is very hot dip vegetables, one at a time, in batter and carefully place a few in the hot oil. Brown to a light brown on all sides—do not overcook. Place on a platter with paper towels. Repeat until all vegetables are cooked.

With a slotted spoon skim off batter particles. Dip crabs in batter and carefully place in oil. Cook about 4 minutes, turning once.

Serve with vegetables with sauce bowls alongside for dipping.

Calories	Cholesterol mg	Protein gm	Carbohydrate gm	Total fat gm	%	Sat fat gm	%	Mono gm	Poly gm
1099	227.0	66.2	121.0	33.9	27	3.4	3	6.6	16.0

CRABS IN WHITE SAUCE
Moleche in Salsa Bianca

This is another recipe where the crabs—like the lobster on page 121—give their flavor to the pasta, and then you can eat the crabs as a second course.

Serves 4.

6 live blue hardshell crabs
2 tablespoons olive oil
1 tablespoon safflower oil
1 clove garlic, minced
Hot pepper flakes to taste (optional)
1 cup dry white wine
1 cup water
1 teaspoon dried oregano
1 tablespoon chopped fresh ginger
2 tablespoons finely chopped Italian parsley
Salt to taste
3/4 pound spaghettini
3 tablespoons brandy

Garnish: Minced Italian parsley

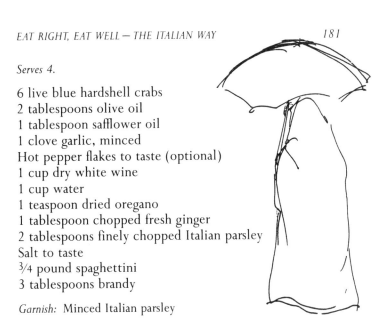

To prepare crabs, lift up bottom flaps, then pry with a medium knife to remove top shells (discard). Rinse bottom part. Heat the two oils in a medium saucepan and add garlic. As garlic begins to color, add all ingredients except crabs, spaghettini, and brandy. Bring liquid to a boil. Add crabs, cover, and simmer about 45 minutes. Taste for salt. Remove crabs from sauce.

Cook pasta in boiling salted water about 5 minutes, then drain.

Bring sauce to a boil, add pasta and brandy, and continue cooking over moderate heat, stirring often, until pasta is tender and sauce is absorbed. Garnish with minced Italian parsley.

Serve the crabs after the pasta.

Calories	Cholesterol mg	Protein gm	Carbohydrate gm	Total fat gm	%	Sat fat gm	%	Mono gm	Poly gm
1860	200.0	77.8	271.7	48.8	23	4.8	2	21.4	12.3

CUTTLEFISH VENETIAN STYLE
Sepe alla Veneziana

Serves 4.

4 tablespoons finely chopped onion
2 tablespoons olive oil
1 tablespoon safflower oil
1 teaspoon minced garlic
3 medium cuttlefish, cleaned (see directions for squid,
      page 215) and cut into lengths 2 inches × 1/2 inch
Salt and freshly ground black pepper to taste
1 tablespoon finely chopped Italian parsley
4 tablespoons dry white wine
2 tablespoons tomato paste
1 cup chicken or beef broth

Sauté onion in the two oils until translucent, then add garlic, cuttlefish, salt, pepper, and parsley. Cook, uncovered, over moderate heat, stirring constantly. When liquid cooks out, add wine, lower heat, cover, and simmer until wine cooks out. Mix tomato paste with the stock and add to pan. Cover and simmer about 30 minutes.

Serve on rice or pasta.

Calories	Cholesterol mg	Protein gm	Carbohydrate gm	Total fat gm	%	Sat fat gm	%	Mono gm	Poly gm
794	999.0	71.3	18.9	44.7	50	4.8	5	21.4	12.3

Figures for squid are used in calculations.

SALT COD WITH BROCCOLI RAPE
Baccalà con Broccoletti di Rape

This is one of the few recipes my godfather, Tomasso, cooked besides pasta dishes. It is excellent with boiled potatoes.

Friends have asked me why one would use dried salted cod (baccalà) in a recipe if fresh cod is available. The answer is simple: Aside from its distinctive flavor, dried cod does not fall apart the way fresh cod would when cooked a fairly long time. The dried cod can be stewed without destroying its identity, and as a result it makes a rich, flavorful stew.

Serves 4.

1½ pounds baccalà (salted codfish fillet), cut into
    3-inch sections
2 tablespoons olive oil
1 tablespoon safflower oil
Hot pepper flakes to taste
2 cloves garlic, finely chopped
¾ cup dry white wine
16 dried black olives
1 teaspoon dried oregano

1 1/2 pounds cleaned rape (see instructions, page 348),
  or 1 bunch broccoli

Soak codfish in a pot of cold water for 2 or 3 days, depending on thickness of fish, changing water as often as possible. Then wash and blot dry.

Place cod in a baking dish or on a tray, add oils and hot pepper, and bake in a preheated 500° oven about 5 to 10 minutes, until all moisture cooks out. Add garlic, wine, olives, and oregano and bake, uncovered, until wine cooks out. In the meantime, blanch rape and drain as soon as the water returns to boil. Add to cod. Cover and bake about 20 minutes.

Serve on hot plates.

Calories	Cholesterol mg	Protein gm	Carbohydrate gm	Total fat gm	%	Sat fat gm	%	Mono gm	Poly gm
1600	558.0	219.8	43.3	60.0	33	4.8	3	21.4	12.3

SALT COD FLORENTINE STYLE
Baccalà alla Fiorentino

We like to serve this salt cod dish with grilled polenta (page 170).

Serves 4.

3 tablespoons olive oil
1 tablespoon safflower oil
2 cups finely chopped onion
1 teaspoon minced garlic
3 tablespoons chopped Italian parsley
2 cups seeded, chopped tomatoes
2 pounds baccalà, presoaked (see preceding recipe), cut
  into pieces 2 × 2 1/2 inches
Freshly ground black pepper to taste
Flour for dredging
Corn or vegetable oil for frying

Heat oils in a medium saucepan or skillet. Add onion, and when it begins to brown, add garlic and parsley. Sauté for a minute, then add tomatoes, cover, and simmer for 20 minutes.

In the meantime, wash and blot dry the presoaked cod. Grind black pepper over the fish and dust with flour. Heat about 1/2 inch corn oil or vegetable oil in a medium skillet and when hot gently add floured pieces of baccalà and lightly brown on both sides. Remove from oil and blot on paper towels, then add to sauce. Cover and simmer over low heat for 25 minutes.

Calories	Cholesterol mg	Protein gm	Carbohydrate gm	Total fat gm	%	Sat fat gm	%	Mono gm	Poly gm
2145	738.0	271.7	53.2	88.9	36	10	4	37.9	29.4

FILLET OF FISH GENOA STYLE
Filetti di Pesce alla Genovese

Serves 3.

1 fish fillet about 1½ pounds, cut crosswise in pieces
    about 1½ inches wide
Flour for dredging
Corn oil or vegetable oil for shallow-frying
Salt and freshly ground black pepper to taste
3 tablespoons olive oil
1 tablespoon safflower oil
2 cloves garlic, minced
2 tablespoons chopped capers
Juice of 2 lemons
4 tablespoons minced Italian parsley

Dredge the fish in flour. Heat ¾ inch oil in a medium skillet. When oil is
hot, add the fish and cook about a minute on each side for thicker
fillets—less for thin. Do not overcook or let fish get too brown. As soon as
it is tender, remove from oil and blot on paper towels.

In the meantime, heat the olive oil and safflower oil in a small pan, then
add garlic. As soon as garlic begins to turn golden, add capers, lemon juice,
and parsley; cook a minute or so, then pour over hot fish.

Calories	Cholesterol mg	Protein gm	Carbohydrate gm	Total fat gm	%	Sat fat gm	%	Mono gm	Poly gm
1197	340.0	122.0	17.9	69.8	51	8.3	6	34.6	21.4

BAKED FLUKE

Serves 4.

1 fluke, about 2 pounds, or any large flatfish, such as
    yellowtail flounder*
1 tablespoon olive oil
1 tablespoon safflower oil
2 tablespoons finely chopped Italian parsley
1 teaspoon minced garlic
¼ cup fresh breadcrumbs
Juice of ½ lemon
Salt and freshly ground black pepper to taste
½ cup dry white wine

*With a sharp knife remove skin from top side of fish. Leave head
on. Your fishmonger will skin fish if requested.

Place fish in a large baking dish and add oils, then parsley, garlic, and bread-crumbs. Sprinkle lemon juice, salt, and pepper on top. Pour wine around fish. Bake in a preheated 500° oven, uncovered, until fish separates from bone easily with a fork—about 20 minutes.

Calories	Cholesterol mg	Protein gm	Carbohydrate gm	Total fat gm	%	Sat fat gm	%	Mono gm	Poly gm
511	151.0	51.9	14.6	29.9	51	2.6	4	12.3	10.7

FROGS' LEGS WITH MUSHROOMS
Rane con i Funghi

Serves 3.

2 tablespoons olive oil
1 tablespoon safflower oil
4 cups fresh wild mushrooms or sliced
    domestic mushrooms
Salt and freshly ground black pepper to taste
6 pair frogs' legs
Flour for dredging
2 cloves garlic, minced
2 tablespoons finely chopped Italian parsley
3 tablespoons brandy
4 tablespoons dry white wine
4 tablespoons chicken broth

Heat the two oils in a medium skillet, then add mushrooms and cook over high heat until they begin to brown. Add salt and pepper. Remove from oil with a slotted spoon.

Salt and pepper the frogs' legs, then dust with flour and place in skillet. When legs begin to take on color, add the garlic, mushrooms, parsley, and brandy. After a minute, add the wine and cook over high heat. When wine cooks out, add the broth and continue cooking over high heat, stirring often, for several more minutes. Serve on heated plates.

Calories	Cholesterol mg	Protein gm	Carbohydrate gm	Total fat gm	%	Sat fat gm	%	Mono gm	Poly gm
708	144.0	56.3	24.4	42.4	53	4.8	6	21.4	12.3

FROGS' LEGS IN SAUCE
Rane in Salsa

Serves 3.

3 tablespoons olive oil
1 teaspoon safflower oil
2 cloves garlic, finely chopped
1/2 green pepper, cored and chopped
9 pair frogs' legs*
1/2 cup dry white wine
1 teaspoon dried thyme
Freshly ground black pepper or hot pepper flakes to taste
     (we prefer hot pepper flakes)
2 cups chopped tomatoes, fresh if possible (drain if canned)
2 tablespoons finely chopped Italian parsley or
     fresh coriander

*Frogs' legs contain a great deal of moisture. That is why high heat is used often in this recipe. If frozen frogs' legs are used, soak in salted cold water for several hours. Drain and rinse well in cold water.

Heat the oils in a medium skillet or shallow saucepan, then add garlic and green pepper. When garlic begins to take on color, add frogs' legs and cook over medium heat until they begin to whiten. Add wine, thyme, and black pepper or hot pepper, turn up heat, and cook over high heat, gently turning legs with a spatula. Continue cooking, uncovered, over high heat until wine cooks out. Add tomatoes and parsley, cover, and cook over moderate to low heat about 15 minutes, then remove cover, turn up heat somewhat, and cook an additional 4 or 5 minutes.

Serve on steamed rice (page 160).

Calories	Cholesterol mg	Protein gm	Carbohydrate gm	Total fat gm	%	Sat fat gm	%	Mono gm	Poly gm
859	216.0	77.3	29.5	47.4	49	4.9	5	32.2	6.0

BAKED FLOUNDER WITH SCALLIONS AND GINGER

Serves 3 to 4.

1 whole flounder, about 3 pounds, or 2 smaller ones
1 teaspoon minced garlic
2 tablespoons minced fresh coriander
2 tablespoons olive oil, or 3 tablespoons peanut oil
1 tablespoon safflower oil
1 tablespoon minced fresh ginger

2 cups whole scallions cut into 2-inch lengths
Juice of 1 lemon
Salt and freshly ground black pepper to taste

Garnish: Fresh coriander and lemon wedges

Preheat oven to 500°. Place fish in a shallow baking dish. Sprinkle garlic, coriander, oil, ginger, scallions, lemon juice, salt, and pepper over fish. Cover tightly with foil and bake until fish is cooked, basting occasionally, about 25 minutes for a 3-pound fish.

Garnish with fresh coriander and lemon wedges.

Calories	Cholesterol mg	Protein gm	Carbohydrate gm	Total fat gm	%	Sat fat gm	%	Mono gm	Poly gm
811	277.0	79.4	20.6	44.6	48	4.1	4	22.6	11.6

BAKED LOBSTER
Aragosta al Forno

Serve with corn on the cob and a salad.

*Serves 2.**

2 medium live lobsters, about 2 to 2½ pounds each
2 tablespoons finely chopped Italian parsley
4 tablespoons fresh breadcrumbs
Salt and freshly ground black pepper or hot pepper flakes
   to taste
1 teaspoon minced garlic
1 tablespoon safflower or vegetable oil
1 tablespoon good olive oil
About 4 teaspoons dry sherry or vermouth

Preheat oven to 500°. With a sharp knife cut lobsters in half by driving point into head (which kills them) and forcing knife through to tail. Place split lobsters on a baking tray. Mix together the parsley, crumbs, salt, pepper, garlic, and two oils and sprinkle over lobsters. Bake, uncovered, for 10 minutes. Sprinkle with half the sherry or vermouth and continue cooking another 10 minutes. Sprinkle again with sherry, bake several more minutes, and serve.

*If vegetables such as corn on the cob, baked potato, and salad are served with lobster, half a lobster is enough for a moderate eater.

Calories	Cholesterol mg	Protein gm	Carbohydrate gm	Total fat gm	%	Sat fat gm	%	Mono gm	Poly gm
748	392.0	87.6	11.4	37.2	44	2.6	3	12.3	10.7

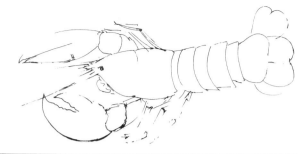

LOBSTER AMÉRICAINE
Aragosta all'Americana

Pierre Franey gave me this excellent recipe; it is a wonderful way to prepare lobster. Serve with rice. Reserve shells and any remaining sauce for lobster soup (page 52).

Serves 2 to 4.

2 1½-pound live lobsters
2 tablespoons safflower oil
2 tablespoons butter or 4 teaspoons vegetable oil
½ cup finely chopped celery
1 medium onion, finely chopped
2 tablespoons finely chopped Italian parsley
Hot pepper flakes to taste
1 to 2 cloves garlic, minced
2 cups chopped tomatoes, fresh if possible (drain if canned)
3 tablespoons brandy
½ cup dry white wine
Salt to taste

Cut lobsters in two, as described in preceding recipe. Cut tail section in two. Pull off claws.

Heat oil and butter in a large skillet. Add lobsters, with claws, and cook over medium heat, turning occasionally, until red, then remove from skillet. Add celery, onion, parsley, and hot pepper flakes and sauté, uncovered, until onion wilts. Add garlic and cook several minutes. Add tomatoes, brandy, and wine. Cover and simmer for 10 minutes. Pass sauce through a food mill, then return puréed sauce to skillet. Add salt.

Bring the sauce to a boil and return lobster to pan. Cut thorax in half. Cover and cook over moderate heat for 10 minutes. Remove cover and reduce sauce for 5 minutes.

Crack claws before serving.

Calories	Cholesterol mg	Protein gm	Carbohydrate gm	Total fat gm	%	Sat fat gm	%	Mono gm	Poly gm
969	334.0	68.5	45.4	58.1	53	15.0	14	10.8	20.8

LOBSTER WITH POTATOES
Aragosta con Patate

Serves 6.

2 3- to 3½-pound live lobsters
1 cup dry white wine
8 cups water
2 bay leaves
1 medium onion, finely chopped
¾ cup finely chopped celery
1 tablespoon finely chopped fresh ginger
1 tablespoon chopped fresh basil
Salt and freshly ground black pepper to taste
½ cup thinly sliced whole scallions
2 tablespoons chopped fresh coriander or Italian parsley
Juice of ½ lime
5 tablespoons marinara sauce (page 430)
2 potatoes, boiled, peeled, and sliced

Put lobsters in a pot so they fit tightly. Add wine, water, bay leaves, onion, celery, ginger, basil, salt, and pepper. Cover and boil about 20 minutes. Remove lobsters,* let them cool, then remove flesh, cut it into bite-sized pieces, and put them in a mixing bowl. Add scallions, coriander, lime juice, marinara sauce, potatoes, salt, and pepper. Mix gently. Serve at room temperature.

*Save broth for risotto recipe on page 157.

Calories	Cholesterol mg	Protein gm	Carbohydrate gm	Total fat gm	%	Sat fat gm	%	Mono gm	Poly gm
1094	524.0	128.0	100.0	12.0	10	0.5	1	3.2	0.6

BROILED MACKEREL
Scomberi al Ferri

Serves 3.

2-pound whole mackerel, split, head on
Juice of 1 lime
Hot pepper flakes to taste (optional)
Salt to taste

Garnish:
Juice of 1 lemon
2 tablespoons finely chopped Italian parsley
2 cloves garlic, finely chopped
2 tablespoons extra virgin olive oil

Place split mackerel on a plate and sprinkle lime juice, pepper flakes, and salt on top. Refrigerate and marinate for at least 2 hours.

In a small bowl, mix the lemon juice, parsley, garlic, and olive oil. Set aside.

Broil mackerel over hot coals about 3 to 4 minutes on each side. Garnish fish with lemon-juice-and-parsley mixture.

Variation: The fish can be served without sauce. In that case, garnish with lemon wedges. Personally, I think this sauce is divine.

Calories	Cholesterol mg	Protein gm	Carbohydrate gm	Total fat gm	%	Sat fat gm	%	Mono gm	Poly gm
1306	518	104.6	8.8	93.6	63	25.4	17	41.6	2.2

MARINATED MACKEREL
Scomberi in Saor

Serves 4 as an appetizer.

2½-pound whole mackerel, filleted, not skinned,
     cut in half crosswise
Salt and freshly ground black pepper to taste
Flour for dredging
Corn oil for shallow-frying
2 tablespoons olive oil
2 medium onions, thinly sliced
1 cup white wine vinegar
3 bay leaves
Hot pepper flakes to taste (optional)

Rinse and blot fillets dry, salt and pepper them, and lightly dust with flour. Heat about ¾ inch oil in a small skillet large enough to hold 2 sections of the fillets. When oil is hot, fry fillets flesh side down until golden brown, about 2½ minutes. Remove with a spatula, blot on paper towels, and repeat the process.

In a medium skillet heat the olive oil and onions and, when they begin to brown, add vinegar, bay leaves, and optional hot pepper flakes. Cook for 3 to 5 minutes. Place fish in a small, flat-bottomed bowl, then pour the onion-and-vinegar mixture over it and marinate overnight; it is not necessary to refrigerate.

Calories	Cholesterol mg	Protein gm	Carbohydrate gm	Total fat gm	%	Sat fat gm	%	Mono gm	Poly gm
1852	646	136.4	56.3	119.6	57	31.9	15	49.2	75

SEVICHE OF MACKEREL AND SCALLOPS

This is a Mexican specialty of marinated fish: The marinade actually penetrates the fish, giving it a "cooked" appearance and texture. We think it is an ideal recipe for this book, and although the traditional version does not call for olive oil, I like to add a few drops of extra virgin olive oil to each portion. The seviche can be served as an appetizer or main course.

Serves 5 to 6 as an appetizer, 4 as a main course.

1¹/₂ pounds mackerel, filleted, skinned, boned, and cut
    into pieces ³/₄ inch wide and 1¹/₂ inches long
¹/₂ pound scallops (if sea scallops, slice about ¹/₈ inch thick)
Juice of 3 limes
1 teaspoon dried oregano
Hot pepper flakes to taste
2 cloves garlic, finely chopped (optional)
3 tablespoons finely chopped fresh coriander
1 avocado, cut into ³/₄-inch squares
1 firm ripe tomato, cut into ³/₄-inch squares
Salt to taste

Garnish: Extra virgin olive oil (optional)

Put the mackerel, scallops, lime juice, oregano, hot pepper flakes, and garlic into a bowl and refrigerate for 24 hours. Fold in the remaining ingredients and serve, sprinkling a few drops of olive oil over each serving, if you wish.

Calories	Cholesterol mg	Protein gm	Carbohydrate gm	Total fat gm	%	Sat fat gm	%	Mono gm	Poly gm
1208	403	105.7	35.3	72.6	53	18.1	13	33	35

MONKFISH SAN BENEDETTO STYLE
Pesce Rospo alla San Benedettese

Have the fishmonger remove head and skin. Monkfish is cheap and has the consistency of lobster. It is excellent in fish stews. Serve with rice or boiled potatoes.

Serves 3.

2 tablespoons olive oil
2 tablespoons safflower oil
2 cups sliced onion
1 pepper, sliced into 1/2-inch-wide strips
1 teaspoon finely chopped garlic
4 tablespoons good wine vinegar
1 teaspoon marjoram
4 cups chopped tomatoes, fresh if possible (drain if canned)
2 tablespoons chopped Italian parsley
Salt and freshly ground black pepper or hot pepper flakes
    to taste
1 whole monkfish, skinned, cleaned, without head, about
    2 to 2 1/2 pounds

Preheat oven to 400°. Heat 1 tablespoon of the olive oil and the safflower oil in a medium skillet. When hot, add onion and cook several minutes over moderate heat. Add pepper and cook until onion begins to brown, then add garlic, cook about a minute, and add vinegar. Cover and cook several minutes. Add the marjoram, tomatoes, parsley, salt, and pepper. Cover and boil gently about 15 minutes.

Wash the fish. Place it in a baking dish that holds it snugly; then add the sauce, pour remaining 1 tablespoon olive oil over fish, and salt and pepper it. Cover and bake about 20 minutes, or until fish is tender. Remove fish from its bones and serve on toast with a generous amount of sauce. This is also good with rice or boiled potatoes.

Calories	Cholesterol mg	Protein gm	Carbohydrate gm	Total fat gm	%	Sat fat gm	%	Mono gm	Poly gm
1240	226.0	88.1	70.2	69.2	49	10.1	7	23.0	26.5

MONKFISH IN SAUCE
Pesce Rospo al Sugo

Monkfish is a highly prized fish in Italy that is very reasonably priced in America. Catfish can also be used in this recipe.

Serves 2 to 3.

1 tablespoon olive oil
1 tablespoon safflower oil or 2 tablespoons vegetable oil
1 medium onion, thinly sliced
1 pepper, preferably sweet red, thinly sliced
2 cloves garlic, finely chopped
12 dried black olives, pitted and sliced if desired
1/2 cup dry white wine
Salt and freshly ground black pepper to taste
2 cups chopped tomatoes, fresh if possible
   (drain if canned)
2 medium potatoes, boiled firm in jackets
1 1/2-pound whole monkfish, dressed

Garnish: 2 tablespoons chopped Italian parsley

Heat the oils in a medium skillet, then add onion and pepper. As onion begins to brown, add garlic and olives. As garlic takes on color, add wine, salt, and pepper; cover and cook over medium heat until wine cooks out. Add tomatoes, cover again, and simmer for 10 minutes.

Place fish in a shallow baking dish. Peel and cut potatoes in quarters and place them around fish. Pour sauce over potatoes and fish, cover, and bake in a preheated 500° oven for about 30 minutes, depending on the thickness of the fish. Serve garnished with chopped parsley.

Calories	Cholesterol mg	Protein gm	Carbohydrate gm	Total fat gm	%	Sat fat gm	%	Mono gm	Poly gm
1092	168.0	70.8	97.7	48.5	39	6.7	5	18.5	14.4

MONKFISH WITH BROCCOLI
Pesce Rospo con i Broccoli

Serves 2.

1/4 cup dry white wine
1 teaspoon minced garlic
Hot pepper flakes to taste (optional)
6 black olives, pitted and sliced
2 tablespoons minced Italian parsley
1-pound whole monkfish or other firm fish, such as catfish
1 pound broccoli, trimmed, washed, blanched, and drained
   when water returns to boil
2 tablespoons olive oil
1 tablespoon safflower oil
1 teaspoon dried thyme
3 whole scallions, cut into 1-inch lengths
Salt and freshly ground black pepper to taste

Pour the wine into a small shallow baking dish with the garlic, hot pepper, olives, and parsley. Place fish on top and distribute broccoli around fish.

Pour the two oils over fish and broccoli and sprinkle thyme and scallions on top. Add salt and freshly ground black pepper if hot pepper isn't used.

Cover the fish and bake in a preheated 500° oven about 20 minutes, or until fish is cooked,* basting occasionally with the juices.

*Cooking time will depend on quality of fish. Do not overcook.

Calories	Cholesterol mg	Protein gm	Carbohydrate gm	Total fat gm	%	Sat fat gm	%	Mono gm	Poly gm
779	112.0	53.5	26.8	52.3	59	6.5	7	25.6	13.9

MONKFISH ON A SKEWER
Pesce Rospo allo Spiedo

This is an excellent fish to skewer, because the fish is easy to bone and the meat is dense; it does not fall apart while cooking. I might add again that the price of the fish is very reasonable.

Serves 2.

1 1/2 pounds monkfish, boned and cut into large pieces
1 or 2 cloves garlic, minced
1 tablespoon olive oil
1 teaspoon safflower oil
1 teaspoon crushed rosemary
Juice of 1/2 lemon
Salt and hot pepper flakes or freshly ground black pepper
   to taste

Garnish: Lemon wedges

Put all the ingredients in a small bowl and marinate in the refrigerator for several hours.

Slip pieces of fish on a skewer and broil over hot coals, basting with marinade. Monkfish takes a little longer than most fish, about 10 minutes for this recipe. Serve immediately with lemon wedges.

Calories	Cholesterol mg	Protein gm	Carbohydrate gm	Total fat gm	%	Sat fat gm	%	Mono gm	Poly gm
492	171.0	55.1	3.5	27.8	50	5.3	9	10.4	7.6

BROILED MONKFISH
Pesce Rospo alla Griglia

The sauce for this recipe was given to me by a Japanese friend. It is wonderful for grilled fish.

Serves 3.

1½ pounds monkfish or other white-fleshed fish, such as
    striped bass, rock bass, tilefish, or red snapper
1 tablespoon soybean paste
Juice of 1 lemon
3 teaspoons safflower oil
2 cloves garlic, finely chopped
Salt and freshly ground black pepper to taste

Bone the fish and cut in large pieces. Mix all ingredients together and marinate in the refrigerator for several hours.

Broil over coals on a skewer or in a wire basket, basting with the marinade. Serve immediately after cooking.

Calories	Cholesterol mg	Protein gm	Carbohydrate gm	Total fat gm	%	Sat fat gm	%	Mono gm	Poly gm
894	374.0	126.3	9.0	36.8	36	8.0	8	1.6	16.9

MONKFISH STEW WITH PASTA
Pesce Rospo con Pasta

This recipe makes both a pasta course and a main course, so it is an easy and economical way to get two courses from one preparation. Catfish can be used instead of monkfish.

Serves 4.

3 tablespoons olive oil
1 tablespoon safflower oil
3 cloves garlic, chopped
4 cups chopped tomatoes, fresh if possible (drain if canned)
1 sweet red pepper (green will do)
3 tablespoons finely chopped Italian parsley
Salt and hot pepper flakes or freshly ground black pepper
    to taste
½ pound cleaned squid (see instructions, page 215),
    cut into ½-inch-wide strips
1½-pound whole monkfish, dressed
1 dozen mussels, washed and scrubbed
¾ pound spaghettini
3 tablespoons brandy
4 slices French or Italian bread, toasted
1 clove garlic

Garnish: Chopped Italian parsley

Heat the two oils in a large skillet. Add the garlic, and as it begins to take on color, add tomatoes, pepper, parsley, salt, and hot pepper to taste. Cover and simmer about 15 minutes. Add squid and cook about 20 minutes. Add the monkfish. Cover and cook until fish is tender, about 25 minutes, depending on size of fish. Remove squid and monkfish and keep warm. Add mussels, cover, and cook until they open, then remove and keep warm with other seafood.

Remove 2 cups sauce from the skillet and set aside. In the meantime, add spaghettini to rapidly boiling water. Cook 5 minutes, then drain. Bring the sauce in skillet to a boil, add pasta, and cook over medium heat, tossing constantly. After several minutes, add the brandy. Continue tossing until pasta is al dente—do not overcook.

Serve pasta as a first course on warm plates, each serving garnished with chopped parsley.

Add some oil to bread slices and toast them (this can be done ahead of time). Rub garlic clove on each piece of toast.

Remove flesh in chunks from monkfish, remove all but 8 of the mussels from their shells. Heat up the 2 cups reserved sauce and add monkfish pieces and mussels. Cook about 1 minute, just enough to make everything piping hot. For each serving, place a piece of toast on a plate, add one quarter of the fish and sauce to toast, garnish with 2 of the mussels left in their shells. Garnish with parsley.

Serve with a green vegetable, such as broccoli.

Calories	Cholesterol mg	Protein gm	Carbohydrate gm	Total fat gm	%	Sat fat gm	%	Mono gm	Poly gm
2752	736.0	170.2	337.3	75.4	24	9.7	3	31.3	16.5

MUSSELS COOKED IN WINE
Cozze al Vino

These mussels should either be served with small bowls of broth on the side so bread can be dunked into it, or the broth used to cook pasta; in that case, the pasta would be served first and the mussels as a second course with salad. See *Variation*.

Serves 6.

6 pounds mussels
1 teaspoon minced garlic
1/4 cup finely chopped Italian parsley
1/2 cup chopped whole scallions
Hot pepper flakes to taste (optional)
1 teaspoon dried oregano
1 cup dry white wine
3 tablespoons olive oil
1 tablespoon safflower oil
Salt* and freshly ground black pepper to taste

*Use little salt, because there is salt in the mussel liquid.

Scrub mussels under cold running water. Put all ingredients except mussels in a large pot. Bring liquid to a boil. Add mussels, cover, and cook until all mussels are open, about 8 to 10 minutes.

Drain liquid and ladle into 6 bowls. Serve mussels on a large platter separately. Dip good French or Italian bread in liquid while eating mussels.

Variation: If there is enough liquid, reserve 2 cups of it to boil thin pasta such as spaghettini or linguine in it—about 3/4 pound should be enough as a first course. When pasta is almost cooked, heat 1 tablespoon olive oil and 1 tablespoon safflower oil in a skillet, then add 1 teaspoon minced garlic. Drain pasta and stir into the oil and garlic. Take care not to brown garlic as you toss pasta over high heat. Add the reserved liquid as needed, tossing pasta until well blended. Garnish with chopped Italian parsley.

Calories	Cholesterol mg	Protein gm	Carbohydrate gm	Total fat gm	%	Sat fat gm	%	Mono gm	Poly gm
1294	396.0	115.0	43.2	71.8	49	6.6	4	31.3	13.4

BAKED FISH WITH MUSSELS AND BROCCOLI
Pesce al Forno con Cozze e Broccoli

Serves 6.

1 bunch broccoli
About 3 pounds halibut, striped bass, cod, or haddock,
    cut into 6 steaks about 1 inch thick
24 dried black olives
2 dozen mussels, well scrubbed
4 tablespoons finely chopped Italian parsley
2 cloves garlic, minced
Freshly ground black pepper or hot pepper flakes to taste
2 tablespoons olive oil
2 tablespoons safflower oil
1/2 cup dry white wine
Salt to taste

Remove broccoli flowerets. Peel stems, cut in manageable pieces, and blanch 2 minutes in boiling water along with the flowerets. Drain and set aside.

Preheat oven to 400°. Place the fish steaks in a shallow baking pan. Arrange the olives, mussels, and broccoli around the fish. Sprinkle the parsley, garlic, pepper, and both oils over fish and broccoli. Add wine and salt.

Cover the pan tightly and bake until mussels open—5 to 10 minutes. Fish should be cooked by then. Serve each fish steak with broccoli and mussels, the wine sauce poured on top.

Calories	Cholesterol mg	Protein gm	Carbohydrate gm	Total fat gm	%	Sat fat gm	%	Mono gm	Poly gm
2423	811.0	340.9	41.5	94.3	34	7.9	3	35.5	23.6

STEAMED POMPANO WITH TOMATO SAUCE

Serves 2.

Salt and freshly ground black pepper to taste
1½- to 2-pound whole pompano, cleaned, head on
1 cup marinara sauce (page 430)

Salt and pepper the pompano and place in a vegetable steamer. Cover and steam about 8 minutes, turn, and steam another 8 minutes.

Remove flesh from bone and spoon heated tomato sauce over fish.

Calories	Cholesterol mg	Protein gm	Carbohydrate gm	Total fat gm	%	Sat fat gm	%	Mono gm	Poly gm
854	209.0	74.5	12.9	54.8	56	9.8	10	10.4	12.0

BROILED POMPANO

This is delicious with pistachio sauce or other sauces on pages 426–42. Serve with broiled tomatoes and roasted peppers.

Serves 2.

1 whole pompano, large enough for 2, cleaned,
    gills removed, head on
1 clove garlic, slivered
Salt and freshly ground black pepper to taste
2 teaspoons olive oil mixed with 2 teaspoons
    safflower oil
Juice of 1 lemon

Wash pompano. Cut two slits on each side of fish. Stuff slits with garlic slivers and salt and pepper fish.

Preheat the broiler. Better still, prepare hot coals. Sprinkle the oils on fish and broil or grill. As fish begins to brown, add lemon juice and cook until fish is tender—about 4 minutes on each side. Do not overcook.

Calories	Cholesterol mg	Protein gm	Carbohydrate gm	Total fat gm	%	Sat fat gm	%	Mono gm	Poly gm
807	209.0	71.9	4.5	54.1	59	9.6	10	7.6	15.2

BROILED FRESH SARDINES
Sarde alla Graticola

A dish for the time of year when fresh sardines are available. If you can grill them over hot coals, marinating the fish first, they will taste even better. Serve with roasted peppers and broiled tomatoes.

Serves 4.

> 1 pound fresh sardines, cleaned, heads on
> 2 tablespoons olive oil mixed with 2 tablespoons safflower oil
> Salt and hot pepper flakes or freshly ground black pepper to taste
> 1 tablespoon crushed rosemary
> 2 cloves garlic, finely chopped
> 3 tablespoons minced Italian parsley
> Juice of 1 lemon

To broil: Lay fish on a flat broiling tray and cover with remaining ingredients. Preheat broiler to high. When broiler is hot, place sardines under flame and broil close to heat. Cook about 5 minutes on each side, basting with the marinade.

To grill: Lay fish on a shallow tray and cover with remaining ingredients. Let marinate about 1 hour. Prepare hot coals. Transfer fish to grill and cook about 2 minutes on each side, basting with marinade.

Calories	Cholesterol mg	Protein gm	Carbohydrate gm	Total fat gm	%	Sat fat gm	%	Mono gm	Poly gm
1232	508.0	87.9	7.0	93.2	67	14.3	10	24.6	30.5

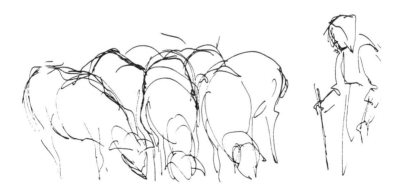

GRILLED SEA SCALLOPS
Cappe Sante alla Griglia

This is a wonderful recipe — any scallop lover will be surprised with the results. You must have a charcoal fire and a basket grill to prepare it properly.

Serves 3 as a main course; 4 as an appetizer.

1 pound bay or sea scallops; if large, cut into
    3/4-inch sections
1 clove or more garlic, finely chopped
Juice of 1 lime or lemon
1 teaspoon crushed rosemary
Salt and freshly ground black pepper to taste
2 tablespoons olive oil or vegetable oil
1 teaspoon safflower oil

Garnish: Lemon wedges

Wash and place scallops in a small bowl. Add garlic, lime juice, rosemary, salt, and pepper and refrigerate for several hours.

Add oils and mix well. Place the scallops in a basket grill and broil over hot coals, shaking often. Cook about 5 minutes, close to the coals.

Serve with lemon wedges.

Calories	Cholesterol mg	Protein gm	Carbohydrate gm	Total fat gm	%	Sat fat gm	%	Mono gm	Poly gm
662	159.0	70.0	19.1	32.6	43	3.4	5	21.1	5.2

GRILLED SEA SCALLOPS TERIYAKI

We enjoy this recipe with dried tomatoes and a green vegetable such as baked asparagus. As in the preceding recipe, the cooking should be done in a basket grill over hot coals. If you have to, you could also broil them under a very hot broiler.

Serves 2.

Juice of 1/2 lemon
1 teaspoon soybean paste
1 teaspoon teriyaki sauce
1/2 pound sea scallops
1 teaspoon minced garlic
1 teaspoon crushed rosemary
Salt* and freshly ground black pepper to taste

*Be careful not to oversalt.

Mix together the lemon juice, soybean paste, and teriyaki sauce in a small deep bowl. Add scallops, garlic, rosemary, salt, and pepper; toss. Refrigerate for several hours.

Remove scallops from sauce and place them in a wire basket for grilling or on the hot broiler. Grill over hot coals or wood embers for several minutes, basting with marinade and shaking basket often. Turn frequently under broiler.

Serve immediately on warm plates.

Calories	Cholesterol mg	Protein gm	Carbohydrate gm	Total fat gm	%	Sat fat gm	%	Mono gm	Poly gm
209	80.0	35.7	13.5	0.8	3	–	–	–	–

SCALLOPS WITH PEAS
Cappe Sante con Piselli

This is a great recipe for sea scallops; they are better than the more expensive bay scallop done this way.

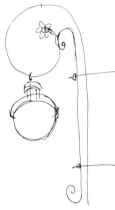

Serves 2.

1/2 pound fresh peas, about 1 cup
3 tablespoons peanut oil
1 cup sliced mushrooms
1/2 pound sea scallops, cut into slices 1/4 inch thick
Salt and freshly ground black pepper or hot pepper flakes
    to taste
Flour for dredging
1/4 cup dry white wine or dry sherry
1 teaspoon minced garlic
1 tablespoon finely chopped Italian parsley
1 teaspoon dried oregano

Cover peas with water and cook until done — about 8 minutes. Drain and set aside. Heat 1 tablespoon of the oil in a medium skillet and sauté mushrooms until moisture is cooked out. Set aside.

Spread out sliced scallops on a board and pat them dry with paper towels. Add salt and pepper, then dust with flour. Heat the remaining 2 tablespoons oil in a medium skillet. When hot, carefully add scallop slices and turn over with a spatula after a minute or so, as scallops begin to brown. After another minute sprinkle with wine, add garlic, mushrooms, parsley, oregano, and peas. Cook over high heat, turning constantly until wine cooks out, about 2 minutes or less. Serve on rice or toasted French or Italian bread.

Calories	Cholesterol mg	Protein gm	Carbohydrate gm	Total fat gm	%	Sat fat gm	%	Mono gm	Poly gm
805	80.0	52.3	49.5	42.4	46	6.9	8	18.6	12.9

BAY SCALLOPS WITH PESTO
Cappe Sante al Pesto

Serves 3 to 4 as a main course.

2 tablespoons butter
2 tablespoons safflower oil
2 cloves garlic, minced*
Hot pepper flakes to taste
1 pound bay scallops or sea scallops†
Salt to taste
2 tablespoons pesto (page 426), diluted with warm water
    to the consistency of heavy cream

*Shallots may be used instead of garlic.
†If sea scallops are used, slice scallops after they are cooked.

Heat the butter and oil in a skillet, add garlic and hot pepper. Just as garlic begins to color, add scallops and sauté, uncovered, over high heat. Add salt and pepper flakes. Cook about 4 minutes. Add pesto and stir for several minutes.
    Serve immediately.

Calories	Cholesterol mg	Protein gm	Carbohydrate gm	Total fat gm	%	Sat fat gm	%	Mono gm	Poly gm
918	221.0	71.3	18.2	61.3	59	17.7	17	15.8	23.3

ABOUT SCROD

    Many people seem to be confused about exactly what kind of fish scrod is. According to Webster's Dictionary, scrod, or schrod as it is spelled in Boston, is a young cod or the young of any of several fish, such as pollack or haddock; in other words, it is the young of the cod family. It goes on to say that scrod is boned and split for cooking.
    Young cod is usually sold as scrod, and the famous Boston scrod is young cod boned and split with the skin still on. When fresh, scrod is one of the most delightful fish sold in the Northeast. Unfortunately, one rarely finds the fillets cut in the Boston manner, with the skin left on.

SCROD FILLET WITH POTATOES
Filetti di Merluzzo con Patate

Serves 4.

4 medium potatoes, peeled and cut in half lengthwise
2 tablespoons olive oil

1 teaspoon safflower oil
1 medium onion, thinly sliced
4 tomatoes, coarsely chopped
12 dried black olives
2 tablespoons chopped fresh basil or 1 teaspoon dried
Salt and hot pepper flakes or freshly ground black pepper
    to taste
2 pounds fresh scrod fillet in one piece, or cod, striped
    bass, or any large white-fleshed fish
1 tablespoon crushed rosemary

Garnish: 1 teaspoon chopped fresh mint

Boil potatoes about 5 minutes, then drain and reserve.

Heat the two oils in a medium skillet and add onion, tomatoes, olives, basil, salt, and pepper (I prefer hot pepper flakes). Cover and simmer over moderate heat for 10 minutes.

Preheat oven to 450°.

Put fish on a baking tray and sprinkle with rosemary and salt and black pepper. Arrange potatoes around fish and pour sauce over fish and potatoes. Cover with foil and bake for 15 minutes.

Garnish with mint.

Calories	Cholesterol mg	Protein gm	Carbohydrate gm	Total fat gm	%	Sat fat gm	%	Mono gm	Poly gm
1710	450.0	180.8	142.2	44.5	23	4.4	2	28.1	5.7

BAKED SCROD WITH TOMATOES AND PEPPERS
Pesce al Forno con Pomodori e Peperoni

Serve this with rice.

Serves 3.

2 tablespoons plus 1 teaspoon olive oil
1 tablespoon safflower oil
1 medium onion, sliced
2 cups sliced green peppers
2 cups chopped tomatoes, fresh if possible
    (drain if canned)
1 teaspoon dried oregano
Salt and freshly ground black pepper to taste
1 fillet, about 1½ pounds, scrod or other white fish,
    such as sole, flounder, red snapper — preferably thick
1 teaspoon minced garlic
2 tablespoons chopped Italian parsley

Heat 2 tablespoons of the olive oil and the safflower oil in a medium skillet and add onion and peppers. Cook over moderate heat, stirring often, until onion and peppers begin to brown. Add tomatoes, oregano, salt, and pepper, cover, and lower heat. Cook about 5 minutes. Turn off heat and set aside.

Preheat oven to 500°. Wash fish and place it in a baking dish. Add remaining 1 teaspoon olive oil, garlic, salt, and pepper. Surround fish with tomato-and-pepper mixture and garnish with parsley. Cover and bake about 10 minutes. The cooking time depends on thickness of the fish.

Calories	Cholesterol mg	Protein gm	Carbohydrate gm	Total fat gm	%	Sat fat gm	%	Mono gm	Poly gm
1197	340.0	132.8	50.2	49.2	36	5.4	4	24.7	12.7

ABOUT FRESH SHAD

Shad can be had on the East Coast from Florida to Maine. The shad are available in Florida and Georgia from about January and they eventually work their way up to the Northeast by spring.

Because of the many bones in shad, it is best filleted. It is filleted in a very unusual way and ends up with three sections (all joined to skin) instead of the usual two. The bottom skin is left on in order to hold the fillets together. The people who fillet the shad are highly skilled, and apparently not many people can do it.

Shad is a rich but extremely delicate fish. I think it is best broiled (under flames or over coals), and it is a seasonal treat we very much look forward to.

BROILED SHAD

Serves 2.

1 shad fillet, about 1 pound
1 teaspoon safflower oil
Grated rind of 1 lemon
2 tablespoons finely chopped Italian parsley or
    fresh coriander
2 cloves garlic, finely chopped
1 teaspoon rosemary
Salt and freshly ground black pepper or hot pepper flakes
    to taste
Juice of 1 lemon

Heat the broiler. Meanwhile, wash the shad, pat dry, and spread open skin side down on a baking tray coated with the oil. Sprinkle the center with the lemon rind, parsley, and garlic, then fold sides of shad back over the center and sprinkle rosemary, salt, and pepper on top. Broil close to heat for 5 minutes. Add lemon juice, lower heat, and broil another 15 minutes. Check for doneness by plunging a fork into the center fillet to the bottom — the flesh will separate when cooked.

Serve immediately on heated plates.

Calories	Cholesterol mg	Protein gm	Carbohydrate gm	Total fat gm	%	Sat fat gm	%	Mono gm	Poly gm
840	250.0	85.4	7.4	50.1	52	14.0	15	14.1	3.4

MAKO SHARK

Mako shark is becoming increasingly popular along the Northeast coast. I have served it on several occasions and find it an excellent fish, quite similar to swordfish (and cheaper); in fact, it is sometimes served in restaurants as swordfish. It is lighter in color, and although the flesh is dense, it's not as dense as swordfish and its flavor is more delicate. It should be treated in the same way, preferably broiled, with lemon or lime juice and a minimal amount of oil.

Serves 2.

1-pound slice Mako shark about ¾ inch thick
Juice of ½ lemon or 1 lime
Freshly ground black pepper to taste
Salt to taste
1 tablespoon chopped fresh mint
1 tablespoon finely chopped Italian parsley
1 clove garlic, minced
2 teaspoons safflower oil

Wash fish, put it in a shallow bowl, then squeeze lemon or lime juice over it. Add pepper and marinate at least 1 hour.

Preheat broiler (or, better still, prepare hot coals) for at least 10 minutes.

Sprinkle salt, mint, parsley, garlic, and oil on fish. Broil fish close to heat until cooked — about 8 minutes, less over hot coals. Do not overcook.

Calories	Cholesterol mg	Protein gm	Carbohydrate gm	Total fat gm	%	Sat fat gm	%	Mono gm	Poly gm
630	250.0	87.6	3.5	27.2	38	5.3	7	5.5	6.8

No figures are available for shark; the calculations are based on swordfish.

SHRIMP WITH ARTICHOKE HEARTS
Scampi alla San Benedettese

Serves 6.

3 tablespoons olive oil
1 tablespoon safflower oil
2 cups sliced fresh mushrooms
Salt and freshly ground black pepper to taste
3/4-ounce package dried boletus mushrooms,
    soaked in warm water for 15 minutes
2 cloves garlic, finely chopped
1 cup thinly sliced scallions
3/4 cup dry white wine
2 tablespoons finely chopped fresh mint
1 teaspoon crushed rosemary
9-ounce package frozen artichoke hearts
1 pound large shrimp, with shells on

Heat the oils in a large skillet, then add fresh mushrooms, salt, and pepper and cook over high heat, uncovered, stirring often until mushrooms begin to brown. Drain dried mushrooms, reserving 2 tablespoons liquid. Add dried mushrooms and reserved liquid, garlic, scallions, wine, mint, and rosemary to the cooked mushrooms. Cover and cook over medium heat for about 10 minutes.

In the meantime, blanch artichoke hearts in boiling water, drain when water returns to a boil, and add to mixture in skillet. Cover and cook about 10 minutes over low to medium heat. Taste for salt. Add shrimp, turn up heat, and cook until they turn pink. Do not overcook.

Remove shells from shrimp before serving.

Calories	Cholesterol mg	Protein gm	Carbohydrate gm	Total fat gm	%	Sat fat gm	%	Mono gm	Poly gm
1038	470.0	71.2	61.7	57.6	49	5.6	5	37.9	12.5

SHRIMP WITH SQUID AND SCALLOPS
Brodetto di Frutta di Mare

Serves 4.

2 tablespoons olive oil
1 teaspoon safflower oil
1 medium onion, finely chopped
2 tablespoons finely chopped shallots
1 pound squid, cut into 1/2-inch-thick strips
    (see cleaning instructions, page 215)
1/2 cup dry white wine
1 teaspoon dried oregano

1 cup chopped tomatoes, fresh if possible (drain if canned)
Salt and hot pepper flakes or freshly ground black pepper
　　to taste
1 cup fresh or frozen peas, blanched
1/2 pound shrimp, with shells on
1/2 pound sea scallops
4 tablespoons brandy

Garnish: 2 tablespoons finely chopped Italian parsley

Heat the oils in a medium saucepan or skillet, then add onion and shallots. Cook over moderate heat until onion begins to brown. Add squid and cook over medium heat until liquid from squid cooks out. Add wine and oregano, cover, lower heat and cook until wine cooks out. Add tomatoes, salt, pepper, and peas, cover, and simmer about 15 minutes. Add shrimp, scallops, and brandy and cook over high heat until shrimp are red. Remove shells from shrimp, garnish with parsley, and serve with rice or bruschetta (page 39).

Calories	Cholesterol	Protein	Carbohydrate	Total fat		Sat fat		Mono	Poly
	mg	*gm*	*gm*	*gm*	*%*	*gm*	*%*	*gm*	*gm*
1072	814	115.4	64.8	36.8	30	4.0	3	20.3	5.6

SHRIMP WITH CHICKEN BREAST AND BROCCOLI
Gamberi, Pollo, e Broccoli Neri

This recipe seems complicated, but it is really quite simple. It is just a question of timing. The worst thing you can do is overcook the chicken and shrimp. The reason safflower oil is used here exclusively is that the shrimp have a rather high cholesterol level.

Serves 4.

1 pair boned chicken breasts, cut with the grain
　　into slices 1/2 inch wide
Juice of 1/2 lemon
2 cloves garlic, finely chopped
1/2 cup sliced scallions
Salt and hot pepper flakes or freshly ground black
　　pepper to taste
5 tablespoons safflower oil
3 cups (1/2 pound) sliced mushrooms
4 cups broccoli flowerets, blanched and drained
　　when water returns to a boil
4 tablespoons dry sherry
1/2 pound shrimp, shelled, deveined, and washed
1 1/2 cups cooked rice (page 160)

Garnish: 1 1/2 teaspoons chopped Italian parsley

Marinate the chicken strips with the lemon juice, garlic, scallions, salt, and pepper. Refrigerate for at least 2 hours.

Heat 3 tablespoons of the safflower oil in a medium skillet. Add the mushrooms, salt, and pepper and cook, uncovered, over high heat for several minutes. Add the blanched broccoli and 2 tablespoons of the sherry. Continue cooking over high heat, stirring often for several minutes. Remove from skillet and keep warm.

Heat remaining 2 tablespoons oil in the skillet and add chicken strips. Cook over high heat until chicken turns white — do not overcook. Remove from skillet, put in a bowl and keep warm. Add shrimp to skillet and cook over high heat until shrimp just turns pink. Return chicken breast to pan with shrimp, add remaining 2 tablespoons sherry, and cook over high heat, tossing, about 30 seconds. Add broccoli and mushrooms and cook over high heat another 30 seconds, tossing. Serve on rice or pasta, garnished with the parsley.

Calories	Cholesterol mg	Protein gm	Carbohydrate gm	Total fat gm	%	Sat fat gm	%	Mono gm	Poly gm
1441	356.0	89.6	100.5	74.3	45	7.1	4	9.3	51.2

BUTTERFLIED FRIED SMELTS
Frittura di Alborelle

We eat fried smelts like corn on the cob, nibbling the flesh off the bone. Serve with a green salad.

Serves 3 as a main course.

1 1/2 pounds smelts, as large as possible (about 9)
Salt and freshly ground black pepper to taste
2 cups corn or vegetable oil
Flour

Garnish: Lemon wedges

Cut smelts open from under head to tip of tail, remove and discard innards and gills but leave head on if you wish. Carefully pull out spine with bones — once started it will come out easily; leave on tail.

Wash well in cold water and pat dry. Add salt and pepper.

Heat the oil in a medium skillet until hot but not smoking (test by flicking flour into oil — oil should boil when flour is added). Dust a couple of the smelts with flour — only those that will be fried immediately, since the flour will get sticky if left on the wet fish. Fry only enough smelts at a time so that they fit comfortably in the skillet, not overlapping. Fry briefly, over high heat, just until the smelts take on a little color, less than a minute. Remove with a slotted spoon, blot on paper towels, and repeat.

For this delightful recipe to be a success, the oil must be hot, the fish must not be overcooked, and they should be served immediately.

Serve with lemon wedges.

Calories	Cholesterol mg	Protein gm	Carbohydrate gm	Total fat gm	%	Sat fat gm	%	Mono gm	Poly gm
588	202.0	69.8	9.8	28.2	42	5.8	9	9.4	10.8

BAKED RED SNAPPER

Simplicity is the essence of good design, and this is a very basic recipe that one can use for almost any fish.

Serves 2.

> 1 red snapper large enough for 2, or other white-fleshed fish, split and boned
> 3 tablespoons vegetable, safflower, or sunflower oil
> Juice of 1 lemon or lime
> 4 tablespoons fresh breadcrumbs
> 2 tablespoons minced Italian parsley
> Salt and freshly ground black pepper to taste

Wash fish. Place on a small baking tray, skin side down. Sprinkle about 1 tablespoon of the oil over fish and the juice of half the lemon. In a bowl mix the breadcrumbs, parsley, the remaining 2 tablespoons oil, and salt and pepper. Preheat the broiler and broil about 3 inches from the flame. Be careful not to burn breadcrumbs. As crumbs begin to brown, squeeze other half of lemon over crumbs. When fish separates it is done — in about 3 to 5 minutes, depending on size of fillets. Serve it with a green salad or a tomato-and-basil salad.

Calories	Cholesterol mg	Protein gm	Carbohydrate gm	Total fat gm	%	Sat fat gm	%	Mono gm	Poly gm
727	193.0	140.4	8.1	44.3	54	3.3	4	6.0	29.4

STEAMED RED SNAPPER

Any white-fleshed whole fish can be cooked this way — whiting, black bass, weakfish, trout, porgy, etc.

Serves 2.

2 small red snappers, cleaned, heads on
2 tablespoons chopped fresh coriander or Italian parsley
1 teaspoon minced garlic
Salt and freshly ground black pepper to taste
About 10 large lettuce leaves from such lettuce as Bibb,
    romaine, etc.

Wash fish. Stuff cavity with coriander and garlic. Salt and pepper outside of fish.

Blanch lettuce leaves in boiling water about 10 seconds. Run cold water in pot until lettuce leaves cool. Carefully wrap fish with lettuce leaves, leaving head exposed.

Place fish in a steamer, or on a straw or bamboo rack. Cover and steam about 15 minutes. Serve whole fish, still wrapped in lettuce leaves, with one of the fish sauces on pages 427–42. Raw sauce goes well with this recipe.

Calories	Cholesterol mg	Protein gm	Carbohydrate gm	Total fat gm	%	Sat fat gm	%	Mono gm	Poly gm
354	193.0	141.4	5.5	3.2	8	–	–	–	–

FILLETS OF SOLE WITH SNOW PEAS

Tender young cucumbers, peeled and cut lengthwise into quarters, would go beautifully with this dish.

Serves 2.

1 tablespoon peanut oil
1 small onion, finely chopped
1/2 cup dry white wine
2 cups fresh snow peas, strings removed
1/2 cup sliced scallions
1 tablespoon soy sauce
2 tablespoons chopped fresh coriander or Italian parsley
2 fillets of sole (about 6 ounces each) or any other
    white-fleshed fish

1 tablespoon olive oil
1 teaspoon safflower oil
Salt and freshly ground black pepper to taste
Juice of 1 lime or lemon
4 tablespoons fresh breadcrumbs

Preheat broiler. Heat the peanut oil in a medium skillet, add onion, and sauté until translucent. Add wine, snow peas, scallions, soy sauce, and coriander. Cook, uncovered, for 3 or 4 minutes.

Place fish in a baking dish. Add 1 teaspoon of the olive oil and the safflower oil, salt, pepper, lime juice, and breadcrumbs. Broil close to heat until fish is cooked — about 5 to 7 minutes. Do not overcook. Serve fish fillets with a generous portion of snow peas and sauce on top of each fillet.

Calories	Cholesterol mg	Protein gm	Carbohydrate gm	Total fat gm	%	Sat fat gm	%	Mono gm	Poly gm
768	171.0	68.0	46.2	35.4	40	4.6	5	16.7	8.4

FILLETS OF SOLE OREGANO
Filetti di Sogliola Oreganato

This is good with boiled potatoes and a green salad. If potatoes are used, boil and peel them, break them up with a fork, and add salt, pepper, and juices from the fish.

Serves 2.

2 fillets of sole (about 6 ounces each) or haddock,
    flounder, or cod
2 cloves garlic, minced
2 tablespoons olive oil
1 tablespoon dried oregano
Salt and freshly ground black pepper to taste
Juice of 1 lemon

Garnish:
2 tablespoons chopped Italian parsley or fresh coriander
Lemon wedges

Wash and dry fillets and place in a shallow pan. Sprinkle garlic, olive oil, oregano, salt, and pepper over them.

Preheat the broiler or oven as high as it will go. When hot, put the fish in and after several minutes add lemon juice. Basting with juices, broil until fish separates — about 5 minutes. Do not overcook. Sprinkle parsley or coriander on fish and serve with lemon wedges.

Calories	Cholesterol mg	Protein gm	Carbohydrate gm	Total fat gm	%	Sat fat gm	%	Mono gm	Poly gm
663.0	171.0	57.9	11.0	43.5	58	4.1	5	22.6	11.6

FILLETS OF SOLE POACHED IN WINE
Filetti di Sogliola Affogato

This is a very light recipe that is very satisfying. Serve with rice or boiled potatoes and a green salad.

Serves 4 as an appetizer; 3 as a main course.

1 1/2 cups fresh peas, about 1 pound, shelled
Salt to taste
8 small fillets of grey sole or lemon sole, or other thin
    white-fleshed fillets (about 20 ounces in all)
Freshly ground black pepper to taste
8 teaspoons pesto or green sauce (pages 426 and 428)
1 cup dry white wine
1 tablespoon finely chopped shallots

Put peas in a small pan, cover with water, add salt, and cook until peas are tender—about 8 minutes, depending on size of peas. If frozen peas are used, cook about 4 minutes.

In the meantime, wash fillets, pat them dry, and sprinkle with salt and pepper. Spoon 1 teaspoon pesto over each fillet, then roll it up like a jelly-roll. Pierce with a toothpick to hold roll together. Put wine, shallots, and peas in a large saucepan, bring to a boil, then gently put in the fish rolls. Simmer for several minutes until fish is cooked. Do not overcook.

Calories	Cholesterol	Protein	Carbohydrate	Total fat		Sat fat		Mono	Poly
	mg	gm	gm	gm	%	gm	%	gm	gm
808	257.0	101.8	26.3	23.4	25	1.6	2	6.4	8.0

FILLETS OF SOLE PRIMAVERA
Filetti di Sogliola Primavera

This is a delightful, light, attractive-looking dish, which I concocted, and it is extremely popular with my friends. Armando Orsini liked it so much that he put it on his menu.

Serves 4.

4 cups sliced mushrooms
2 tablespoons safflower or peanut oil
Salt and freshly ground black pepper to taste
4 fillets of lemon sole, grey sole, or flounder
    (about 6 ounces each)
Juice of 1 lime or lemon (I prefer lime)
4 teaspoons pesto (page 426), optional
2 cups chopped whole scallions
4 cups fresh ripe tomatoes cut into 1/2-inch cubes

Olive oil
4 tablespoons minced Italian parsley or fresh coriander

Sauté the mushrooms in the oil until all moisture is cooked out, then season with salt and pepper.

Preheat the oven to 500°.

Wash and pat the fish dry and place in a shallow baking dish. Squeeze lime juice or lemon juice over, add salt and pepper, and spread 1 teaspoon pesto over each fillet. Add a layer of mushrooms, a thick layer of scallions, and a layer of tomatoes so that the vegetables make a mound. Season with more salt and pepper and sprinkle with olive oil, then parsley.

Place baking dish, uncovered, in the oven and bake until fish separates when pricked with a fork—8 to 10 minutes. Serve with a wide spatula so that fish does not separate.

Calories	Cholesterol mg	Protein gm	Carbohydrate gm	Total fat gm	%	Sat fat gm	%	Mono gm	Poly gm
1277	342.0	135.5	72.5	49.2	34	4.2	3	13.1	21.3

FILLETS OF SOLE MY WAY
Filetti di Sogliola a Modo Mio

Serve with rice or potatoes. It is also good with rice with pesto sauce (page 426).

Serves 4 to 6.

6 fillets of flounder or sole (any good white fish will do)
Salt to taste
Juice of 2 limes
2 tablespoons olive oil
2 tablespoons safflower or corn oil
2 cups sliced green peppers, the slices about ½ inch wide
½ pound mushrooms, sliced
1 medium onion, sliced
1 cup chopped tomatoes, fresh if possible, with as
    little liquid as possible
2 tablespoons chopped fresh basil or
    1 teaspoon dried
Hot pepper flakes to taste (optional)

Garnish: 2 tablespoons chopped Italian parsley or fresh coriander

Put fish in a baking dish. Add salt and lime juice and set aside. Heat the two oils in a skillet. When hot, add all the remaining ingredients except the parsley. Cook over a very high flame, stirring constantly. Do not overcook—the vegetables should be crisp.

In the meantime, heat oven to 450° to 500° and put the fish in. As soon as the fish turns opaque, put a generous amount of cooked vegetables on each fillet. Return to oven about 3 or 4 minutes, and serve with parsley.

Calories	Cholesterol	Protein	Carbohydrate	Total fat		Sat fat		Mono	Poly
	mg	gm	gm	gm	%	gm	%	gm	gm
2517	513.0	189.7	58.8	65.0	23	5.2	2	24.6	21.4

POACHED LEMON SOLE IN LETTUCE LEAVES
Sogliole Affogate

Serves 2 to 3.

About 12 large lettuce leaves, from such lettuce as Bibb, romaine, etc.
2 medium fillets of lemon sole or grey sole
2 tablespoons pesto (page 426)
2 teaspoons grated lemon rind
Freshly ground black pepper to taste
$1/2$ cup dry white wine or stock
$1/2$ cup sliced whole scallions
1 tablespoon finely chopped Italian parsley

Preheat oven to 450°. Blanch lettuce leaves quickly, a few seconds, in boiling water. Remove and run cold water in the pot until lettuce leaves are cool enough to handle, then carefully remove them from the water. Using half the leaves, spread out each and overlap them so that a bed is made large enough to hold 1 fillet. Place fillet in the middle of the lettuce. Spread 1 tablespoon pesto over the fillet, then 1 teaspoon grated lemon rind, and some freshly ground pepper. Roll the fillet, jellyroll fashion, so lettuce rolls with fish. Tuck in excess ends as fillet is rolled. Repeat the same procedure with the other fillet. Place in a baking dish so that they fit snugly. Add wine, scallions, and parsley. Cover and bake about 20 minutes. Remove rolled fillets from baking dish and with a sharp knife cut them into $1^1/2$-inch-thick slices. Pour pan juices over fish.

Calories	Cholesterol	Protein	Carbohydrate	Total fat		Sat fat		Mono	Poly
	mg	gm	gm	gm	%	gm	%	gm	gm
467	171.0	62.3	17.0	16.3	31	1.1	2	4.8	6.1

ABOUT SQUID

There are two kinds of squid available in the Northeast — summer squid and bone squid. Summer squid is reddish in color, has a thin skin and a strong taste. Bone squid is usually larger, although it also appears in the markets small; it has thicker skin, is white in color, and has a more delicate taste than summer squid. I much prefer the bone squid.

To clean the squid, first remove head, then split the squid and remove insides. Pull off the skin. Wash well and cut into 1-inch strips. Cut off tentacles just below the eyes and squeeze out the beak and discard. The tentacles taste the best.

If you want to keep the tube intact for stuffing or to make round rings to fry, pull off head, then pull the insides out, carefully keeping the tubelike body intact. Remove and discard outside skin, then cut into 1/2-inch rounds. For stuffing, keep the tube intact.

A number of recipes in this and other chapters contain squid. Squid is low in total fat, but very high in cholesterol. The tentacles contain more cholesterol than the mantles, i.e., 280 to 290 mg vs. 210 to 230 mg per 100 grams of edible fish, according to measurements made at a United States Bureau of Fisheries Laboratory during the summer of 1984. These figures apply to both varieties of squid netted in Atlantic waters off the Northeast coast of the United States. Furthermore, it is probable that seasonal variations push these figures even higher at times, although dependable data on this point do not yet exist. Pending the publication of more complete data, it seems reasonable to use squid in moderation and to calculate the cholesterol content at 220 mg per 100 grams of meat, taking care to stay within the 300 mg daily ration of cholesterol from all sources. It is, of course, preferable that the tentacles be discarded. R.W.

FRIED SQUID
Calamari Fritti

The secret to the success of this dish is to be certain the oil is hot and to serve the squid immediately after frying them.

Serves 4.

Corn oil or other vegetable oil
1 pound squid, cleaned (see instructions, page 215)
Flour
Salt to taste

Garnish: Lemon wedges

Heat 3/4 inch oil in a medium skillet. In the meantime, dust about one third of the squid with flour (if you do them all at once the flour will turn to glue). Test the temperature of the oil by flicking flour into it. When the flour boils violently it is ready. Using tongs, carefully place the squid in the oil, one piece at a time, using about one third of the pieces in the first frying. The oil will boil violently and splatter, so be careful. Turn the squid after a minute. Cook for several minutes, but do not overcook—the squid should be only lightly brown. Remove squid, place on paper towels, cover with more towels, and repeat with the two remaining batches. Season with salt, add lemon wedges, and serve hot immediately. If allowed to cool, the squid will get soggy. Excellent with hot pepper sauce (pages 437–8).

Calories	Cholesterol	Protein	Carbohydrate	Total fat		Sat fat		Mono	Poly
	mg	gm	gm	gm	%	gm	%	gm	gm
342	499.0	38.1	9.9	15.7	40	1.4	4	3.8	7.2

STUFFED SQUID FLORENTINE STYLE
Calamari Ripieni alla Fiorentina

This is particularly good served with stuffed tomatoes.

Serves 3.

3 cups packed fresh spinach, blanched, drained,
    and squeezed dry
1 tablespoon finely chopped Italian parsley
2 teaspoons minced garlic
1 cup fresh breadcrumbs
1 salted anchovy, washed, boned, and chopped,
    or 2 canned anchovies
2 teaspoons olive oil
1 egg white, lightly beaten
1 teaspoon grated lemon rind
About 1/4 cup dry white wine
3 medium-sized bone squid, cleaned (see instructions,
    page 215)
1 teaspoon safflower oil
1 large bunch broccoli, cut up

Chop the spinach and mix with the parsley, 1 teaspoon of the minced garlic, the breadcrumbs, anchovy, 1 teaspoon of the olive oil, the egg white, lemon rind, and 2 teaspoons of the white wine. Stuff the squid with this mixture, sew opening closed, and sew on tentacles.

Pour the remaining 1 teaspoon olive oil and the safflower oil into a small, shallow baking dish. Roll the squid in the oil, add several teaspoons wine, cover, and bake in a preheated 350° oven for 10 minutes.

Blanch the broccoli and drain when water returns to a boil. Add broccoli to squid, sprinkle with the remaining minced garlic, cover, and bake about 15 minutes more.

Calories	Cholesterol	Protein	Carbohydrate	Total fat		Sat fat		Mono	Poly
	mg	gm	gm	gm	%	gm	%	gm	gm
759	752.0	85.1	65.0	20.5	24	1.6	2	7.1	4.2

STUFFED SQUID WITH BROCCOLI
Calamari Ripieni

Serves 4.

1 bunch broccoli, cut up and blanched*
2 tablespoons vegetable oil
1 clove garlic, minced
3 large squid, the tubular part of the body,
    about 9 inches long

The stuffing
4 tablespoons chopped Italian parsley
2 cloves garlic, minced
12 walnuts, shelled
1 anchovy fillet
2 tablespoons dry white wine
2 tablespoons olive oil
2 tablespoons safflower oil
Salt and freshly ground black pepper to taste
1 cup fresh breadcrumbs, lightly toasted

Hot pepper flakes to taste (optional)
1 tablespoon crushed rosemary
1/2 cup dry white wine

*Blanched broccoli di rape (see instructions, page 348) can be used instead of broccoli. Spinach is also sometimes used. If spinach is used, add to squid raw.

Toss blanched broccoli pieces in the vegetable oil and garlic and set aside.

Prepare squid according to directions, page 215.

Preheat oven to 400°.

For the stuffing, combine the parsley, garlic, walnut meats, and anchovy in a food processor; add the wine, olive oil, 1 tablespoon of the safflower oil, salt, and pepper, and blend. Add breadcrumbs, mix well, and stuff squid. Sew up the end of the squid, then sew on tentacles with several stitches. Spread remaining safflower oil over the bottom of the baking dish, then add squid and sprinkle with salt, hot pepper flakes, and rosemary. Bake about 10 minutes.

Add the 1/2 cup wine, sprinkle with a little oil and bake in a 350° oven until wine almost cooks out. Add broccoli to squid, cover and continue baking until broccoli is tender but not overcooked—about 10 minutes.

Cut squid into 1/2-inch slices and serve hot.

Calories	Cholesterol mg	Protein gm	Carbohydrate gm	Total fat gm	%	Sat fat gm	%	Mono gm	Poly gm
1750	1124.0	108.9	65.4	120.1	60	10.8	5	30.9	61.8

SQUID STUFFED WITH POLENTA
Calamari Ripieni

This dish is excellent with rice or polenta. I use leftover polenta for the stuffing.

Serves 4.

1 pound fillet of a white-fleshed fish, such as sole, scrod, or cod, skinned, boned, and chopped
½ cup cooked polenta (page 215), chopped
2 tablespoons finely chopped Italian parsley
1 teaspoon minced garlic
1 egg white, slightly beaten
3 anchovy fillets, chopped
Salt and freshly ground black pepper to taste
2 large squid, about 1¾ pounds, cleaned and prepared for stuffing (see instructions, page 215)*
2 tablespoons olive oil
1 tablespoon safflower oil
1 cup chopped onion
2 cups chopped tomatoes, fresh if possible (drain if canned)
1 teaspoon dried oregano
6 dried black olives, pitted
1 pound fresh peas, about 2 cups shelled, blanched and drained
Hot pepper flakes to taste

*Four smaller squid can be used.

Mix chopped fish with polenta, parsley, garlic, egg white, anchovy fillets, very little salt, and pepper. Stuff squid with this mixture. Sew up end, then sew tentacles to ends. Place stuffed squid in a baking dish and set aside.

Heat the two oils in a medium skillet and sauté onion until it begins to brown. Add tomatoes and oregano and cook over low to medium heat about 10 minutes. Add olives, peas, and hot pepper flakes, cover, and cook 3 to 5 minutes.

Pour the vegetables over the squid, cover, and bake in a preheated 500° oven about 30 minutes.

Slice into ½-inch rounds and serve hot.

Calories	Cholesterol mg	Protein gm	Carbohydrate gm	Total fat gm	%	Sat fat gm	%	Mono gm	Poly gm
1716	1114.0	184.8	106.0	56.9	29	5.9	3	25.1	13.5

SQUID WITH PEAS
Calamari in Umido

This should be served on toasted garlic bread or rice.

Serves 3 to 4.

1 pound bone squid, cleaned (see instructions, page 215)
1 tablespoon olive oil
1 tablespoon safflower oil
2 cloves garlic, minced
Salt to taste
Hot pepper flakes or freshly ground black pepper to taste
1/2 cup dry white wine
3/4 cup chopped tomatoes, fresh if possible (drain if canned)
1 cup fresh peas, blanched and drained, or 8 1/2-ounce can
    good-quality peas, or 1 cup frozen peas, blanched
1 tablespoon minced Italian parsley

Cut squid into 3/4-inch strips.

Heat the two oils in a medium skillet, then add squid, garlic, salt, and pepper. When liquid cooks out, add wine. Cover and simmer until wine cooks out. Add tomatoes, cover, and cook for 15 minutes. Add peas and cook 15 minutes more. Add parsley and turn off heat.

Calories	Cholesterol mg	Protein gm	Carbohydrate gm	Total fat gm	%	Sat fat gm	%	Mono gm	Poly gm
649	499.0	50.2	54.5	30.1	41	3.0	4	11.5	11.2

SQUID TEMPURA

Serves 4.

Corn oil or vegetable oil for shallow-frying
2 green peppers, sliced into 1/2-inch strips
2 small eggplants, preferably the long, thin Japanese type,
    cut into 1/2-inch rounds
About 12 scallions, cut into 3-inch lengths
Batter (page 388)
1 pound squid, cleaned and cut into 1/2-inch strips
    (see instructions, page 215)
Sauce (page 267)

Heat 3/4 inch oil in a medium skillet.

Dip vegetables one at a time into the batter. Carefully drop a few at a time into the hot oil and fry until very light brown—about 1 1/2 to 2 minutes. Repeat until all vegetables are cooked.

After vegetables are cooked, dip squid into the batter and fry about the same amount of time—do not overcook.* Place cooked vegetables and squid on paper towels. Serve hot with sauce as a dip.

*Squid splatter when fried, so be prepared when cooking them.

Calories	Cholesterol mg	Protein gm	Carbohydrate gm	Total fat gm	%	Sat fat gm	%	Mono gm	Poly gm
1024	499.0	67.4	140.4	18.4	16	1.4	1	3.8	7.2

ABOUT STOCKFISH

Stoccafisso and baccalà are made from the same fish—cod. The difference between the two is that baccalà is either split or filleted and salted. Stoccafisso is not salted but dried. The stoccafisso that is sold in America is rather large—2 feet or longer—but the best quality is about 1 foot long, with the spine removed before the fish is dried. Unfortunately, the smaller stoccafisso, the more desirable—and therefore the most expensive—is not available in New York.

Stoccafisso is a stronger-tasting fish than baccalà, but stoccafisso and baccalà experts prefer it to baccalà. The flesh is chewy; it is an acquired taste. We enjoy it a great deal during the winter months.

STOCKFISH ABRUZZI STYLE
Stoccafisso all'Abruzzese

Serves 4 to 6.

1½ pounds stockfish (stoccafisso)
Freshly ground black pepper or hot pepper flakes (I prefer hot pepper flakes) to taste
4 tablespoons olive oil
1 tablespoon safflower oil
24 dried black olives
1 cup chopped onion
3 cloves garlic, chopped
1½ cups dry white wine
2 teaspoons dried oregano
4 cups chopped tomatoes, fresh if possible (drain if canned)
1 bunch broccoli
5 or 6 potatoes, peeled and cut into large pieces

Cut stoccafisso with a saw into 1-inch sections and soak in cold water, changing the water as often as possible, at least 4 times a day. The best way to soak stoccafisso is in a wire basket or two colanders wired together and placed in a brook or spring, so the constant flow of water will soften the fish. Soak for 5 to 7 days, depending on the thickness of the fish. Wash fish well, pull out spine sections, and cut off fins.

Place fish skin side down in a medium, shallow baking dish. Add pepper and sprinkle with the oils. Preheat oven to 450° and bake fish, uncovered, until the edges begin to brown. Add olives and onion and continue cooking until onion wilts. Add garlic, wine, and oregano, cover, and bake until wine cooks out. Add tomatoes, cover, and cook about 45 minutes. Meanwhile, peel broccoli stems. Cut broccoli in half lengthwise from flowerets to end of stem. Wash and add to the fish along with the potatoes. Lower heat to 350°, cover, and cook an additional 30 to 45 minutes.

Calories	Cholesterol mg	Protein gm	Carbohydrate gm	Total fat gm	%	Sat fat gm	%	Mono gm	Poly gm
2690	558.0	242.7	239.7	93.1	30	9.3	3	53.7	15.7

SWORDFISH STEAK SICILIAN STYLE
Trance di Pesce Spada alla Siciliana

Serves 3.

2 tablespoons peanut oil
2 tablespoons finely chopped onion
10 dried black olives, pitted and sliced
Hot pepper flakes to taste (optional)
1/2 teaspoon minced garlic
1 cup chopped tomatoes, fresh if possible (drain if canned)
1 teaspoon dried oregano
1 tablespoon finely chopped Italian parsley
1 tablespoon capers
1 1/2 pounds swordfish steak
Salt and freshly ground black pepper to taste
Flour for dredging
Corn oil or peanut oil for shallow-frying

Heat the peanut oil in a medium skillet. Add onion and sauté for several minutes. Add olives, hot pepper flakes, and garlic and sauté for several minutes more. Add tomatoes, oregano, parsley, and capers, cover, and simmer about 20 minutes.

In the meantime, wash and pat swordfish steak dry. Season with salt and freshly ground black pepper, then dust with flour. Heat about 3/4 inch oil in a medium skillet. When oil is hot, gently add fish and lightly brown both sides. Remove from oil and blot on paper towels. Add to tomato sauce and cook about 5 to 8 minutes, turning occasionally.

Serve fish with the sauce.

Calories	Cholesterol mg	Protein gm	Carbohydrate gm	Total fat gm	%	Sat fat gm	%	Mono gm	Poly gm
1365	374.0	135.9	27.6	77.6	50	15.2	10	32.7	12.5

SWORDFISH MESSINA STYLE
Pesce Spada Messinese

Serve this tasty dish with rice or boiled potatoes.

Serves 2 or 3.

1 swordfish steak, about 2 pounds, ¾ inch thick
Salt and freshly ground black pepper to taste
Flour for dredging
3 tablespoons olive oil
1 tablespoon safflower oil
1 medium onion, thinly sliced
3 tablespoons finely chopped celery
1 teaspoon finely chopped garlic
2 cups seeded and chopped ripe tomatoes
6 green olives, pitted and sliced
5 dried black olives, pitted and sliced
1 teaspoon dried oregano
1 heaping tablespoon capers
1 tablespoon pine nuts
2 tablespoons yellow raisins, soaked in tepid water for
    15 minutes
1 bay leaf

Garnish: Finely chopped Italian parsley

Salt and pepper the fish, then dust lightly with flour. Preheat oven to 450°. In the meantime, heat 2 tablespoons of the olive oil and the safflower oil in a medium skillet. When oil is hot, add fish and cook over high heat. Turn fish over carefully with a wide spatula. When both sides of fish are light brown, remove from skillet to a plate and keep warm. Pour the remaining 1 tablespoon olive oil into the skillet, add onion and celery. When onion begins to brown, add garlic and cook for several minutes. Add tomatoes and bring to a boil. Lower heat, add both olives, oregano, capers, pine nuts, and raisins (squeeze out all moisture first), cover, and simmer about 10 minutes.

After 10 minutes put fish in an ovenproof dish. Add bay leaf and pour the sauce over the fish. Cover the fish and bake about 10 minutes. Serve hot garnished with chopped parsley.

Calories	Cholesterol mg	Protein gm	Carbohydrate gm	Total fat gm	%	Sat fat gm	%	Mono gm	Poly gm
1931	495.0	185.5	75.5	99.4	45	15.3	7	47.0	13.5

SWORDFISH STEAK MARINER STYLE
Pesce Spada alla Marinara

Serves 2.

4 teaspoons olive oil
4 teaspoons safflower oil
1 medium onion, finely chopped
1 cup chopped tomatoes, fresh if possible (drain if canned)
6 dried black olives, pitted and sliced
Hot pepper flakes to taste (optional)
1 tablespoon capers
1 tablespoon chopped fresh mint
Salt and freshly ground black pepper to taste
1 swordfish steak, about 1 pound
Flour for dredging
Juice of 1 lemon

Garnish: 1 tablespoon finely chopped Italian parsley

Heat 1 teaspoon of the olive oil and 1 teaspoon of the safflower oil in a medium skillet, then add onion. When it begins to brown, add tomatoes, olives, hot pepper flakes, capers, and mint. Cover and simmer for 10 minutes, then remove from skillet and reserve. In the same skillet heat remaining 3 teaspoons olive oil and 3 teaspoons safflower oil.

Put salt and freshly ground black pepper on the swordfish, dust lightly with flour, and add to the hot oil. Lightly brown both sides of the fish. Add lemon juice, turn fish, and add sauce. Cover and cook over moderate heat about 5 minutes. Garnish with parsley.

Calories	Cholesterol mg	Protein gm	Carbohydrate gm	Total fat gm	%	Sat fat gm	%	Mono gm	Poly gm
1060	250.0	94.3	36.4	59.1	49	9.0	7	22.8	15.5

SWORDFISH ON A SKEWER
Pesce Spada alla Spiedo

I like to prepare this recipe in our fireplace during the winter months, grilling the fish over hot wood embers. I have used pickled slices of ginger between the swordfish cubes instead of bay leaves with fine results.

Serves 3.

1½ pounds swordfish, cut into 1½-inch cubes
Juice of 1 lemon
1 teaspoon or more finely chopped garlic
1 tablespoon crushed rosemary
Freshly ground black pepper to taste
1 tablespoon olive oil
1 tablespoon safflower oil
9 bay leaves

Turn the fish in lemon juice, garlic, rosemary, pepper, and oils and refrigerate to marinate for 2 to 4 hours.

Spear a piece of swordfish, then a bay leaf on a skewer. Repeat until all fish is used up.

Grill over hot coals or under a hot preheated broiler (coals are better) for about 5 minutes on each side, for a total of 10 minutes' cooking time, basting with the marinade occasionally.

Calories	Cholesterol mg	Protein gm	Carbohydrate gm	Total fat gm	%	Sat fat gm	%	Mono gm	Poly gm
1073	374.0	131.3	8.0	54.9	45	9.4	8	19.1	10.7

POACHED TROUT
Trota in Umido

Serves 2.

2 medium trout
2 potatoes, peeled, parboiled, and cut in half
2 tablespoons minced Italian parsley
1 medium onion, coarsely chopped
2 tablespoons coarsely chopped fresh mint
2 bay leaves, chopped
1 cup dry white wine
1 cup water

The sauce
1 tablespoon safflower oil
1 tablespoon butter
1 teaspoon minced garlic or 1 tablespoon minced shallots
Juice of 1 lemon

Garnish:
2 tablespoons minced Italian parsley or fresh coriander
Salt and freshly ground black pepper to taste

Preheat oven to 500°. Wash trout and place it in a shallow baking dish. Add the rest of the ingredients. Cover with foil and bake about 20 minutes. Do not overcook; when fish is just done, remove from oven.

In the meantime, make the sauce: Heat the oil and butter, add garlic, and cook for a minute — do not brown. Add lemon juice.

Remove trout and arrange with potatoes on plates, pour sauce over both, and garnish with parsley or coriander, salt, and pepper.

Calories	Cholesterol	Protein	Carbohydrate	Total fat		Sat fat		Mono	Poly
	mg	gm	gm	gm	%	gm	%	gm	gm
1247	218.0	83.3	82.2	64.4	45	18.1	13	12.2	10.4

TROUT WRAPPED IN LETTUCE LEAVES
Trota in Foglie di Lattuga

This dish is elegant and very subtle. Any light stuffing may be used here. Serve the juices on boiled rice or boiled potatoes.

Serves 2.

Salt and freshly ground black pepper to taste
2 trout, or any small whole white-fleshed fish,
 such as whiting
1 teaspoon rosemary
2 cloves garlic, chopped
4 tablespoons chopped Italian parsley or fresh coriander
1 teaspoon chopped shallots
8 or 10 large lettuce leaves, such as bibb or escarole
1 cup dry white wine
2 tablespoons olive oil
1 teaspoon safflower oil

Salt and pepper the cavity of the fish. Sprinkle rosemary, half the garlic, half the parsley, and the shallots into the cavity.

In the meantime, cook the lettuce leaves in boiling water — about 2 minutes for Bibb or 5 minutes for escarole, drain, and let cool. Salt and pepper both sides of fish, sprinkle remaining 2 tablespoons parsley on one side of each fish. Carefully pick up the cooked lettuce leaves and gently wrap the trout in the leaves, leaving heads exposed.

Place the trout in a shallow baking dish so that they fit well. Pour wine, oils, and remaining garlic over fish. Cover tightly and bake in a preheated 450° oven about 20 minutes.

Calories	Cholesterol	Protein	Carbohydrate	Total fat		Sat fat		Mono	Poly
	mg	gm	gm	gm	%	gm	%	gm	gm
1117	187.0	76.0	18.4	70.3	55	14.0	11	28.7	5.1

FRESH TUNA GENOA STYLE
Tonno alla Genovese

This dish is a marvelous substitute for meat. It has a rich meaty flavor and yet is delicate at the same time.* It is very good with sliced fresh tomatoes.

Serves 2.

2 slices fresh tuna, about 1 pound†
Juice of ½ lemon
Salt and freshly ground black pepper to taste
Flour for dredging
1 tablespoon olive oil
1 tablespoon safflower oil
1 teaspoon minced garlic
1 anchovy fillet, chopped
2 tablespoons chopped Italian parsley
1 cup dry white wine
½-ounce package dried boletus mushrooms, soaked in warm water for 20 minutes; reserve liquid

†If the dark core of the tunafish is attached to the slice, remove and discard.

Marinate the tuna in lemon juice and refrigerate for at least 1 hour.

Remove fish from lemon juice, add salt and freshly ground black pepper, dust lightly with flour and shake off excess.

Heat oils in a medium skillet, then add tuna. Quickly brown (lightly) both sides of fish. Remove from oil and keep warm. Add the garlic, chopped anchovy, and parsley and sauté for a minute, then return tuna. Sauté for a minute or so, then add wine and mushrooms. Cover and simmer over medium heat for several minutes, turning slices occasionally. Add 2 tablespoons mushroom-soaking liquid and cook about 10 minutes. Serve fish with sauce.

*Tuna must be fresh and the slice from a good cut. Some parts of tuna are lighter than other parts, the lighter ones being the more delicate. I used to dress fresh tuna up to 300 pounds, and I found a variety of textures and tastes in the fish. Tuna is a rich fish, and small portions are recommended.

Calories	Cholesterol mg	Protein gm	Carbohydrate gm	Total fat gm	%	Sat fat gm	%	Mono gm	Poly gm
1028	261.0	118.6	28.9	46.4	40	7.3	6	16.9	10.8

TUNA LOAF
Polpettone di Tonno

I like the taste of tuna, but I don't like to be overwhelmed by it. The overly rich, dense texture of tuna is totally transformed in this light, airy dish — so much less compact than the usual meatloaf. It doesn't slice *perfectly,* but you can re-form each slice nicely on the plate when you serve it. It should be served at room temperature with a sauce — I particularly like spinach sauce — and a mixed green salad as an accompaniment. Use leftovers as a sandwich spread.

Serves 6.

3 boiling potatoes, about 1 pound
2 tablespoons olive oil
1 teaspoon safflower oil
1 large onion, finely chopped
3 egg whites, lightly beaten
1/2 cup breadcrumbs
2 tablespoons grated lemon rind
2 1/2 tablespoons finely chopped Italian parsley
Salt and freshly ground black pepper to taste
1/2 tablespoon good mustard
2 7-ounce cans Italian-style tunafish
Spinach sauce, or another sauce, such as
hot pepper or red sauce

Boil potatoes, peel, and mash in a mixing bowl. Heat the two oils in a medium skillet, add onion, and cook until it begins to brown. Add to mashed potatoes along with the rest of the ingredients, and mix well. Place mixture in the center of a piece of cheesecloth, roll up cheesecloth around it, and form a sausage shape about 3 inches wide and 10 inches long. Tie ends of cheesecloth. Place tuna roll in a steamer and steam for 20 minutes, or poach for 20 minutes in water or broth.

Remove roll from heat and allow to cool. Take off cheesecloth, cut loaf in slices about 3/4 inch thick, and serve with one of the recommended sauces.

Calories	Cholesterol mg	Protein gm	Carbohydrate gm	Total fat gm	%	Sat fat gm	%	Mono gm	Poly gm
2446	220.0	142.8	166.9	135.5	49	21.2	8	49.1	44.7

STEAMED FRESHWATER WHITEFISH
Codregone in Umido

Serve with one of the fish sauces on pages 427–42. Whitefish might very well be the best-tasting freshwater fish caught in American waters.

Serves 4.

2½- to 3-pound whole whitefish, gutted, scaled, washed, head on
Dry white wine
1 tablespoon rosemary
Salt and freshly ground black pepper to taste
2 tablespoons olive oil
1 tablespoon safflower oil
2 cloves garlic, finely chopped
3 tablespoons finely chopped Italian parsley

Garnish: Steamed vegetables (see below), with oil, finely chopped garlic, and lemon juice

Put fish on a rack on a baking tray with about ½ inch dry white wine on the bottom. Sprinkle cavity of fish with rosemary, salt, and pepper. Pour the oils over the fish and sprinkle garlic, parsley, salt, and pepper on top.

Preheat the oven to 500° for at least 15 minutes. Tightly cover the tray with foil and bake about 20 minutes, basting occasionally, until fish is cooked.

Garnish the cooked fish with steamed vegetables such as cabbage, Brussels sprouts, or broccoli that is tossed in oil, finely chopped garlic, and lemon juice.

Calories	Cholesterol mg	Protein gm	Carbohydrate gm	Total fat gm	%	Sat fat gm	%	Mono gm	Poly gm
1205	292.0	101.1	5.9	84.6	62	20.7	15	37.3	12.3

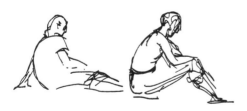

FRIED WHITING
Merluzzo Fritte

There simply isn't a sweeter fish than whiting, and it is wonderful fried. The fish must be fresh and the oil hot. This makes a wonderful lunch served with a green salad.

The heads should be left on so that the juices do not drain from the fish.

In my part of Italy whiting is called *merluzzo*, but in parts it is called *nasello*.

Serves 2.

2 medium whole whiting, cleaned, heads on, cut in
    half crosswise
Corn oil or vegetable oil for shallow-frying
Flour for dredging
Salt to taste

Garnish:
2 lemon wedges
Hot pepper sauce (pages 437–8), optional

Wash whiting and pat dry. Heat ¾ inch oil in a medium skillet. Dust fish with flour carefully, then place in the hot oil. Cook for several minutes, then gently turn over. Cook until skin firms up and becomes crusty, about 5 or 6 minutes. Salt to taste.

Remove fish from oil and blot dry. Serve with a lemon wedge and hot pepper sauce if you want to.

Calories	Cholesterol mg	Protein gm	Carbohydrate gm	Total fat gm	%	Sat fat gm	%	Mono gm	Poly gm
315	110.0	37.3	5.5	15.1	42	2.9	8	4.5	4.8

FRIED WHITING FILLETS
Filetti Fritti di Nasello

Serves 4.

4 medium whiting, cleaned and filleted
Salt and freshly ground black pepper to taste
Flour for dredging
Corn oil or vegetable oil for frying
3 egg whites, lightly beaten
About 3 cups fresh breadcrumbs

Garnish: Lemon wedges

Wash fillets and pat dry, then salt and pepper them and dust with flour. Heat the oil in a medium skillet. When oil is hot, dip each fillet in the egg whites, then roll in the breadcrumbs. Gently place fillet in hot oil. Cook as many at a time as the skillet will hold in one layer. Cook briefly on one side, about 1 minute; then turn over, cook 1 minute, and blot on paper towels. Repeat until all fillets are done. Serve immediately with one of the fish sauces on pages 427–42.

Garnish with lemon wedges.

Calories	Cholesterol mg	Protein gm	Carbohydrate gm	Total fat gm	%	Sat fat gm	%	Mono gm	Poly gm
1120	220.0	96.8	79.5	43.6	34	6.2	5	11.6	14.4

BAKED WHITING WITH ASPARAGUS
Merluzzo al Forno con Asparagi

Baked whiting with asparagus was a favorite dish that I used to prepare for my guests when I was a young painter living in Hell's Kitchen in New York City back in the 1950s. In those days whiting was 15 cents a pound and asparagus in season as low as 19 cents a pound. Then I could cook a two-course dinner for six people for $2.10. Whiting is greatly appreciated in Europe (in Italy it's very expensive), but it is much ignored in America. In my opinion it is one of the finest fish caught in the mid-Atlantic.

Serves 3 to 4.

2 large whole whiting, about 2¾ pounds fish, or 1 fish
   about that weight—striped bass, red snapper, etc.
2 tablespoons olive oil
1 tablespoon safflower oil or other vegetable oil
2 tablespoons finely chopped Italian parsley
1 tablespoon crushed rosemary
Salt and freshly ground black pepper to taste
Enough fresh asparagus for 2 people, washed and tough
   ends removed
Dry white wine

Preheat oven to 500°.

   Clean fish and leave on head but remove gills. Place fish on baking tray. Put on top the oils, parsley, rosemary, salt, and pepper. Place the asparagus around the fish. Pour enough wine into the tray so that there is about ¼ inch on the bottom. Cover with foil and bake about 25 minutes, or until fish is cooked. The cooking time depends on the size and type of fish.

Calories	Cholesterol mg	Protein gm	Carbohydrate gm	Total fat gm	%	Sat fat gm	%	Mono gm	Poly gm
1040	303.0	109.6	18.1	58.3	49	10.3	9	26.9	12.3

WHITING BAKED IN WHITE WINE
Nasello al Forno

This is delicious with roasted peppers (page 365).

Serves 2.

2 whiting, about 1 pound each, cleaned, heads left on,
   or other white-fleshed fish, such as small red snapper,
   rock bass, perch
½ cup dry white wine
1 tablespoon olive oil

1 tablespoon safflower oil
1 teaspoon minced garlic
1 tablespoon capers, preferably small
2 tablespoons finely chopped Italian parsley
Salt and freshly ground black pepper or hot pepper flakes
  (I prefer hot pepper flakes) to taste

Preheat oven to 500°–550°. Place washed fish on a baking tray so they fit snugly. Pour wine over them, then spread the rest of the ingredients over the surface of the fish, putting some of the parsley and garlic in the cavity of the fish. Cover with foil and cook until fish separates from bone when tested with a fork—about 8 minutes for whiting.

Bone the fish and serve on heated plates. Pour juices over fish before serving.

Calories	Cholesterol mg	Protein gm	Carbohydrate gm	Total fat gm	%	Sat fat gm	%	Mono gm	Poly gm
686	220.0	73.6	6.9	39.1	50	7.0	9	15.5	11.2

FISH MESSINA STYLE
Pesce alla Messinese

Serves 4.

4 slices fish about 1½ inches thick, from such fish as cod,
  striped bass, red snapper, etc.
2 medium potatoes
3 tablespoons olive oil
1 tablespoon safflower oil
1 medium onion, minced
1 clove garlic, chopped
12 dried black olives, pitted and chopped
½ cup dry white wine
1 cup chopped tomatoes, fresh if possible (drain if canned)
1 teaspoon dried oregano
2 tablespoons minced Italian parsley
2 tablespoons capers
Salt and freshly ground black pepper or hot pepper flakes
  (I prefer hot pepper flakes) to taste

Wash fish and set aside. Boil potatoes for 10 minutes. Drain, peel, and cut each potato into 3 pieces.

Heat the two oils in an ovenproof casserole; when hot, add onion and sauté for several minutes. Add garlic, olives, and wine and cook, uncovered, for several minutes. Add tomatoes, oregano, parsley, capers, salt, and pepper; cover and cook about 5 minutes. Remove half the sauce and place in a shallow pan or baking dish. Preheat the oven to 450°. Put fish and potatoes on top of the sauce. Pour the rest of the sauce over, cover, and bake about 20 minutes — or until fish is cooked.

Serve with rice.

Calories	Cholesterol mg	Protein gm	Carbohydrate gm	Total fat gm	%	Sat fat gm	%	Mono gm	Poly gm
1463	340.0	132.8	83.8	65.5	39	7.6	5	37.5	14.0

BRODETTO OF FISH MARINER STYLE
Brodetto di Pesce alla Marinara

Any variety of white-fleshed fish will do. Monkfish is especially good in this recipe. It can be used to replace shrimp.

Serves 8.

> 3 tablespoons olive oil
> 1 tablespoon safflower oil
> 1 pound cuttlefish or squid (see instructions, page 215)
> Salt and freshly ground black pepper to taste
> 1 cup thinly sliced onion
> 2 cloves garlic, finely chopped
> Hot pepper flakes to taste (optional)
> 1 tablespoon crushed rosemary
> 3 tablespoons finely chopped Italian parsley
> 1/2 cup good white wine vinegar
> 4 cups seeded, chopped tomatoes
> 4 slices white-fleshed fish, such as cod, striped bass,
>   haddock, red snapper, about 1 inch thick
> 12 mussels, scraped and brushed
> 1 pound shrimp, shelled
> 1/2 pound sea scallops
> 8 slices French or Italian bread, lightly oiled with
>   olive oil and toasted

Heat the two oils in a large skillet and add the cuttlefish, then salt and pepper. Cook over high heat until the liquid cooks out. Remove cuttlefish with a slotted spoon and reserve. Add onion to skillet. When it wilts, add garlic, hot pepper flakes, and rosemary and simmer for 1 minute. Add parsley, return the cuttlefish to the skillet, and pour in the vinegar. Cover and simmer until vinegar cooks out, about 10 minutes. Add tomatoes, cover, and simmer 15 minutes. Add fish and cook about 5 to 10 minutes, until opaque.

Remove fish slices with a spatula and reserve. Add mussels and cook several minutes, then add shrimp and scallops and cook over high heat about 3 minutes, until shrimp are tender. Remove any bones in the fish slices and return slices to stew.

To serve, place a slice of toast on a hot plate and ladle a generous amount of seafood and sauce over.

Calories	Cholesterol mg	Protein gm	Carbohydrate gm	Total fat gm	%	Sat fat gm	%	Mono gm	Poly gm
3378	1565.0	344	235	111.9	29	9.6	3	60.4	14.9

ETRUSCAN FISH STEW
Tegamaccio Etrusco

This recipe is supposed to be of Etruscan origin. It is one of the few freshwater Italian fish stews I am familiar with. I recommend catfish and perch but you could use any variety of freshwater fish.

Serves 6.

2 pounds catfish (if large, cut in sections)*
2 pounds freshwater perch
3 tablespoons olive oil
1 tablespoon safflower oil
2 medium onions, finely sliced
2 cloves garlic, finely chopped
1/2 cup dry white wine
2 cups chopped tomatoes, fresh if possible
    (drain if canned)
1 teaspoon thyme
6 slices French or Italian bread, toasted

Garnish: Chopped Italian parsley or fresh mint (optional)†

*You may find that the odor catfish expels while cooking is offensive (it is similar to dried stockfish), but the taste is delicate and most satisfying.
†I find chopped parsley or chopped fresh mint enhances this recipe, although it does not call for it.

Gut fish, scrape off scales, wash well, and set aside.
    Heat the oils in a medium skillet, then add onions and cook until they wilt. Add garlic and cook several minutes. Add wine, cover, lower heat, and cook until half the wine cooks out. Add tomatoes and thyme, cover, and cook over low to medium heat for 10 minutes.
    Place catfish in a shallow ovenproof dish, cover, and cook in a preheated 500° oven about 10 minutes. Add perch, cover, and return to oven to cook about 5 to 8 minutes, depending on the size of the fish.
    Serve hot over toast.

Calories	Cholesterol mg	Protein gm	Carbohydrate gm	Total fat gm	%	Sat fat gm	%	Mono gm	Poly gm
2046	373.0	161.8	172.1	40.1	17	10.2	4	31.3	17.0

FISH CAKES
Crocchette di Pesce

These fish cakes are very good with horseradish and tomato sauce and a green salad.

Serves 4.

> 1 pound any white-fleshed fish fillets, including
>   freshwater fish
> 3 medium potatoes, boiled, peeled, and mashed
> 1 1/2 teaspoons finely chopped Italian parsley
> 1 teaspoon minced garlic
> 2 egg whites, lightly beaten
> Salt and freshly ground black pepper to taste
> 1 1/2 cups fresh breadcrumbs
> Corn oil or peanut oil for frying

Grind the fish and place in a mixing bowl with mashed potatoes, parsley, garlic, 1 of the egg whites, salt, and pepper. Blend well, then form into 8 patties about the size of a medium-sized hamburger. Roll in the other egg white, dust with breadcrumbs, then gently pat to make the breadcrumbs adhere.

Pour about 3/4 inch oil into a medium skillet. When oil is hot, cook patties, 3 or 4 at a time, until lightly brown on both sides. Blot on paper towels and serve immediately.

Calories	Cholesterol mg	Protein gm	Carbohydrate gm	Total fat gm	%	Sat fat gm	%	Mono gm	Poly gm
1006	227.0	98.7	111.3	15.3	13	0.9	1	2.5	4.8

FRIED FISH BALLS
Polpette Fritte di Pesce

A food processor can be used to chop fish but be careful you don't liquefy the fish — fish should have texture. I prefer chopping it by hand.

Serves 4.

1 pound fish fillets (any white fish will do — cod, pollack, snapper, etc.)
2 tablespoons chopped Italian parsley
1 teaspoon minced garlic
Salt and freshly ground black pepper to taste
1 egg white, lightly beaten
About ¾ cup breadcrumbs
Corn oil or vegetable oil for frying

Garnish: Lemon wedges

Chop the fish with a sharp knife, add parsley, garlic, salt, and pepper, and continue chopping. When well blended, add the egg white and mix well. Form balls about the size of a golf ball (you should have about 8), then roll them in breadcrumbs. Heat about ¾ inch oil in a small to medium skillet. When oil is hot, add the fish balls one at a time, turning them often, and cook until golden brown. Blot on paper towels. Serve hot with lemon wedges and any fish sauce that suits your fancy.

Calories	Cholesterol mg	Protein gm	Carbohydrate gm	Total fat gm	%	Sat fat gm	%	Mono gm	Poly gm
556	227.0	82.9	19.5	13.8	22	0.9	1	2.5	4.8

FISH BALLS "AL PESTO"
Polpette di Pesce al Pesto

This recipe was sent to me by my mother in Italy. The fish balls can be steamed in a vegetable steamer, instead of boiled, if you prefer.

Serves 6.

2 pounds white-fleshed fish fillets, such as flounder, sole, etc.
2 cloves garlic, finely chopped
3 tablespoons finely chopped Italian parsley
2 egg whites, lightly beaten
Salt and freshly ground black pepper to taste
Fresh breadcrumbs (optional)
2 quarts fish or chicken stock (page 41)
⅓ cup pesto (page 426)

Chop the fish fillets as finely as possible. Put the chopped fish, garlic, parsley, egg whites, salt, and pepper in a mixing bowl and stir well. Using your hands, shape mixture into balls 1 to 1½ inches in diameter; if too wet to handle, add some fresh breadcrumbs.

Bring 2 quarts fish or chicken stock to a rolling boil. Add the balls one at a time and boil about 10 minutes. Remove with a slotted spoon. The broth may be served as a first course, with, perhaps, rice and spinach added.

Dilute the pesto in enough stock so that it has the consistency of heavy cream. Serve the fish balls hot with a generous amount of pesto spooned over them.

Calories	Cholesterol	Protein	Carbohydrate	Total fat		Sat fat		Mono	Poly
	mg	gm	gm	gm	%	gm	%	gm	gm
1112	452.0	163.1	10.3	43.2	34	3.1	2	12.7	16.2

STEAMED FISH BALLS
Polpette di Pesce in Umido

Serves 3 as a main course.

1 flounder, about 1½ pounds, filleted,
    head and bones reserved*
¼ pound fresh spinach, washed, blanched, drained,
    and chopped
1 teaspoon minced garlic
1 egg white, lightly beaten
1 teaspoon grated lemon zest (yellow part of rind)
Salt to taste

The sauce
1 tablespoon olive oil
1 tablespoon safflower oil
1 teaspoon minced garlic
2 anchovy fillets, chopped†
Fish head and bones
3 tablespoons dry white wine
1 cup chopped tomatoes, fresh if possible (drain if canned)
1 tablespoon chopped Italian parsley
Hot pepper flakes to taste

*Any white fish will do, including freshwater fish.
†We prefer salted anchovies, boned and washed, to canned anchovies (see page 503).

First make the sauce: Heat the two oils in a medium skillet or saucepan, then add minced garlic and chopped anchovy fillets. Cook until the garlic begins to take on color. Add fish head and bones and wine. Cover and simmer about 3 minutes. Add tomatoes and parsley, cover, and simmer for

20 minutes. Remove and discard bones and head. Strain sauce or blend in a food processor. Keep it warm while you prepare the fish.

Chop the fillets, add chopped cooked spinach, minced garlic, egg white, lemon zest, and salt and mix well. Form 6 balls about the size of golf balls.

Steam the fish balls in a steamer about 3 to 5 minutes.

Serve hot on a heated platter. Spoon sauce over balls and serve with steamed vegetables.

Calories	Cholesterol mg	Protein gm	Carbohydrate gm	Total fat gm	%	Sat fat gm	%	Mono gm	Poly gm
548	119.0	50.0	18.1	30.5	49	3.3	5	11.7	11.4

ABOUT FRITTO MISTO DI PESCE

Italians rarely fry fish in a batter — only a light dusting of flour. I think you will find the fish much lighter than when it is batter-dipped.

Any variety of fresh fish may be used in this recipe. Whole fish, such as whiting, can be cut in half before frying; small flounder cut into 2-inch slices; small whole fish, such as smelts, whiting, and sardines, and fillets cut into 2-inch strips, etc.

It is essential that the fish be very fresh and the oil clean and hot. I prefer to use corn oil for frying because the oil takes a high cooking temperature and when used properly is practically tasteless.

I do not advise you to prepare this for more than 4 guests the first time. The fish should be served as soon as it leaves the skillet and only 1 portion should be fried at a time. It will get soggy if allowed to stand, so your guests should eat it right away.

A skillet no larger than 10 inches in diameter is recommended. If too many fish are put into a large skillet, the oil will cool off and the fish won't fry properly. Check the temperature of the oil, as directed in the recipe, by flicking several drops of flour in oil.

ASSORTED FRIED FISH
Fritto Misto di Pesce

When fish is served in San Benedetto del Tronto, where my mother now lives, each portion of fish is served as soon as it is cooked. The cook wouldn't risk letting the fish get soggy so does not sit to eat with guests.

Serves 6.

3 medium whiting, cut in half
1 pound smelts
1 pound squid, cleaned and cut into 1-inch strips
1 pound whitebait
Flour for dredging
Corn oil for frying
Salt to taste

Garnish: Lemon wedges

Wash fish, leave heads on and remove gills. Spread flour on a piece of waxed paper.

Heat about ¾ inch oil in an 8- to 10-inch skillet. Dust a portion of all the fish in flour—only the amount of fish that can be cooked in the skillet at one time.

Flick flour into the oil; if the oil boils, it is ready. Violently shake off excess flour from fish, and place fish gently in the hot oil. Squid has a tendency to splatter, so be careful. Cook until lightly browned—do not overcook.

Remove fish from pan and lay them on a plate covered with paper towels; blot top of fish with another layer of paper towels. Then sprinkle the fried fish with salt and serve immediately with lemon wedges.

Variation: Use a combination of flounder, whiting and/or bass, and cod cut in manageable pieces.

Calories	Cholesterol mg	Protein gm	Carbohydrate gm	Total fat gm	%	Sat fat gm	%	Mono gm	Poly gm
1259	920.0	178.8	13.9	50.1	35	10.4	7	15.2	14.4

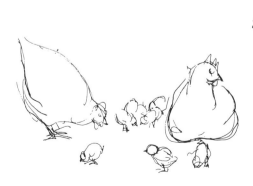

VI POULTRY

No one wants to hear about how good things used to be, but the deteriorating quality of the chickens we get today does pose a problem in cooking. The tastiest chickens are, of course, free-range or barnyard chickens that are grain fed and allowed to roam at will and eat whatever they please. When I was a student in Italy that's the kind I enjoyed, and they were the tastiest chickens I've ever eaten, particularly the ones my grandfather raised and the famous succulent yellow-skinned Val d'Arno poultry from a small area near Florence.

In this country, my parents would always buy their chickens in a Jewish poultry store, selecting live poultry and cleaning it themselves. They wouldn't have dreamt of buying a "dead chicken," and I remember as a boy that the chickens were always lean and delicious.

Now, however, the chickens available in the supermarkets and meat markets in America, as well as in Italy, are much too fat and tasteless. So I suggest that you always remove all the fat and discard it, then soak the chicken in salted water for at least 1 hour, drain, and finally wash the chicken in cold water before using.

Because old-fashioned, free-range chickens were lean, some additional fat — butter in northern Europe, salt pork in southern France and sometimes here — was used when roasting or broiling them. But today the chickens are already so laden with fat that you don't need to baste with more. It's difficult for most people to give up old habits, however, so we go on treating today's chickens as though they were the lean birds our parents and grandparents dined on. It's particularly bad to add that extra butter to a chicken, considering how much fat we already consume in our overall diets compared to previous generations.

The moral is that you should cook according to the nature of the produce at hand, not according to the way Grandma used to do it. In the

recipes that follow I've usually cooked out and discarded the excess fat and then added a wide range of different seasonings, and I think you'll find the results much more appetizing than the average chicken dish—and so much better for you. E.G.

There are a number of recipes in this chapter in which the total fat content and its distribution into saturated, monounsaturated, and polyunsaturated components are impossible to calculate accurately. I have assumed that skin and visible fat are not eaten, and that of the edible 40 percent of a dressed chicken, half is light meat and half is dark meat. R.W.

ROAST STUFFED CHICKEN

This recipe has a holiday character. It makes roast chicken, which can be ordinary, into something rather festive.

Serves 4 to 6.

1 tablespoon safflower oil or vegetable oil
1 small onion, chopped
3 large mushrooms, chopped
2 tablespoons finely chopped Italian parsley
3/4 cup fresh breadcrumbs
1 teaspoon thyme
2 tablespoons yellow raisins, soaked in warm water
    for 10 minutes and drained
1 tablespoon sweet marsala or sweet sherry
1 egg white, lightly beaten
Salt and freshly ground black pepper to taste
3 1/2-pound whole chicken
1 tablespoon rosemary
About 1 cup wine vinegar

Heat the oil in a small skillet, then add onion and mushrooms, and cook until onion wilts. Combine the mushroom-and-onion mixture with the parsley, breadcrumbs, thyme, raisins, marsala, egg white, salt, and pepper. Fill the chicken with the stuffing, sew it up, and truss. Rub salt and pepper and rosemary on chicken. Place a rack in a small baking pan just large enough to hold the chicken. Pour 1/2 cup vinegar and 1/2 cup water into the bottom of the baking pan.

Preheat oven to 500°. Roast the chicken, basting occasionally, about 1 hour and 15 minutes, turning it as it begins to brown, and add more vinegar when pan juices dry. (I use about an additional 1/2 cup.)

Calories	Cholesterol mg	Protein gm	Carbohydrate gm	Total fat gm	%	Sat fat gm	%	Mono gm	Poly gm
1163	496	149.3	54.4	36.4	27	7.8	6	10.0	14.3

A certain amount of the chicken fat and the safflower oil will inevitably find their way into the stuffing, so that we have probably underestimated both the total fat and the saturated fat. The error will be small, however, if the skin and visible fat are not eaten, and it will be much smaller or even eliminated if only white meat is eaten.

BROILED CHICKEN
Pollo allo Spiedo

This is particularly good served with country style sauce (page 440).

Serves 6.

2 chickens, split
Salt and freshly ground black pepper to taste
1 tablespoon rosemary

The basting sauce
1 cup wine vinegar
1 teaspoon finely chopped garlic

Salt and pepper both sides of the chicken, then rub with rosemary leaves.

Broil chicken over coals, about 20 minutes on each side, basting occasionally with the wine vinegar and garlic when the chicken begins to brown.

Calories	Cholesterol mg	Protein gm	Carbohydrate gm	Total fat gm	%	Sat fat gm	%	Mono gm	Poly gm
672	421.0	119.6	–	18.0	24	5.7	7	6.8	3.8

ABOUT CHICKEN BAKED IN CLAY

My wife and I have enjoyed cooking with clay ever since 1959, when we lived in Florence and I was shown how to do it by an old Florentine friend. Several years ago I was asked by my friend, Alain Sailhac, chef of Le Cirque Restaurant, if I knew anything about baking with clay. He was particularly interested in doing some game birds this way, so I told him where to buy the clay in New York City and what kind to use.

The following morning I went to Le Cirque to show Alain how to form the clay and model it. We wrapped the birds in foil after seasoning them with herbs, then applied the fresh clay and modeled it in the form of a bird.

Alain took to modeling clay as a duck takes to water, enjoying it immensely. That evening we dined on the birds at Le Cirque, and they were delicious. Chef Sailhac became so hooked on baking in clay and enjoyed modeling so much that he modeled several heads.

One day he mused about the possibility of baking veal brains in clay modeled to the shape of a human head. It sounded like a good idea at the moment, but on second thought we decided it would not be acceptable to most guests.

Cooking in clay is always fun and produces delectable results. We particularly liked doing it with the children, allowing them to paint the bird with poster colors. We would then show the painted bird to our guests, crack open the clay, and serve it forth.

CHICKEN BAKED IN CLAY
Pollo alla Zingara

The clay seals in the chicken juices and flavor in this lovely dish. Serve with roasted potatoes and baked broccoli, which can be baked in the oven at the same time.

Serves 6.

3½- to 4-pound chicken
2 cloves garlic, slivered
1 tablespoon rosemary
Salt and freshly ground black pepper to taste
Grated rind of 2 lemons
Sculptor's earth clay*
Nut Sauce or Green Sauce (pages 428 and 435), optional

*Be certain you get earth clay, not Plasticine.

Soak the chicken in cold salted water to cover for 1 to 2 hours. Drain, wash, and pat dry. Slip garlic slivers under skin over breasts. Force some rosemary under skin. Place some garlic and rosemary in the cavity of the chicken as well. Rub entire bird with salt and pepper and sprinkle on lemon zest. Wrap chicken in foil and carefully form clay over chicken, spreading it firmly and evenly. Sculpt the head of a chicken on the form—you can get as decorative as you wish. Better still, have your children do the decorating. Place the chicken in a shallow baking pan and bake in a preheated 350° oven about 45 minutes. After 45 minutes, increase heat to 400° and bake an additional 15 minutes. Look into the oven from time to time. When the clay cracks, stuff the crack with more clay in order to keep the steam from escaping. If you are using a sauce, prepare it while the chicken is baking.

To serve, crack the clay open and remove the chicken, taking care to reserve juices. Cut chicken into serving pieces. Add some of defatted chicken juices to your sauce.

Calories	Cholesterol mg	Protein gm	Carbohydrate gm	Total fat gm	%	Sat fat gm	%	Mono gm	Poly gm
799	488	139.3	4.9	21.2	23	6.6	7	7.9	4.6

BROILED CHICKEN WITH BEER SAUCE
Pollo allo Spiedo con Birra

Serves 2.

2³/4- to 3-pound frying chicken, split*
Salt and freshly ground black pepper to taste
1 cup tomatoes, peeled, seeded, chopped, and put through
  a food mill
1 cup light beer
1 tablespoon good mustard
1 tablespoon finely chopped Italian parsley
1 teaspoon crushed rosemary

*The average small fryer, or spring chicken as we called them,
weighed from 2¹/2 to 2³/4 pounds dressed. Unfortunately, it is
rather difficult to find small fryers in the average supermarket
today.

Wash the split chicken and salt and pepper it.

Heat the broiler for at least 15 minutes. Place the chicken in a baking
dish skin side down and broil close to the heat, about 8 minutes on each
side. In the meantime, boil tomatoes and beer in a small saucepan,
uncovered, over moderate heat until reduced by half. Stir the mustard,
parsley, and rosemary in, then spoon sauce over chicken. Turn chicken over
occasionally and baste with the sauce. Cook until chicken is tender and
separates from bone — a 2³/4-pound chicken takes about 45 minutes. Watch
carefully or reduce heat if the broiler seems too high.

Garnish with remaining sauce. This sauce, by the way, can be used to
baste any broiled meats.

Calories	Cholesterol mg	Protein gm	Carbohydrate gm	Total fat gm	%	Sat fat gm	%	Mono gm	Poly gm
724	384.0	113.0	11.8	27.0	33	5.2	6	6.2	3.5

GRILLED CHICKEN WITH MUSTARD
Pollo Grigliato con Senape

Serves 4.

2¹/2 tablespoons imported mustard
1 clove garlic, minced
2 tablespoons good wine vinegar
2 tablespoons minced Italian parsley
Salt and freshly ground black pepper to taste
3- to 4-pound chicken, split
Juice of 1 lemon

Combine the mustard, garlic, vinegar, parsley, salt, and pepper.

Preheat the broiler. Place chicken skin side down in a baking pan. Spoon or brush on mustard mixture. Broil about 12 minutes, fairly close to heat; then turn it over. Cook about 30 to 45 minutes in all, turning it every 10 minutes. Add lemon juice after cooking about 25 minutes.

Calories	Cholesterol mg	Protein gm	Carbohydrate gm	Total fat gm	%	Sat fat gm	%	Mono gm	Poly gm
729	418.0	121.8	9.2	20.1	24	5.7	7	6.7	3.7

CHICKEN LOMBARDY STYLE
Pollo alla Lombardia

Serves 4 to 6.

2 cloves garlic, slivered
1 roasting chicken, about 3½ pounds
Salt and freshly ground black pepper to taste
2 tablespoons rosemary
1 cup dry white wine
½ cup water
¾ cup chopped celery
1 cup minced onion
1 cup chopped carrots
3 tablespoons chopped Italian parsley
4 tablespoons olive oil
1 tablespoon safflower oil
1 cup chicken stock
½ cup chopped tomatoes, fresh if possible
  (drain if canned)
6 green olives, whole
6 black olives, dried
6 green olives, chopped

Stuff garlic slivers under skin of chicken. Truss chicken, and season with salt, pepper, and rosemary, over skin and inside cavity. Place in a casserole with the wine and water and brown in a preheated 400° oven, basting occasionally. In the meantime, sauté celery, onion, carrots, and parsley in the oils. When onion begins to brown, add chicken stock, tomatoes, and olives and cook several minutes. Add to chicken after 45 minutes, when chicken is brown.

Reduce heat to 350°; cover and cook about 30 minutes more, basting occasionally. Carve chicken and serve sauce on individual servings.

Calories	Cholesterol mg	Protein gm	Carbohydrate gm	Total fat gm	%	Sat fat gm	%	Mono gm	Poly gm
1789	494.0	147.3	47.3	101.6	50	14.8	7	58.8	18.5

CHICKEN PIEDMONTESE STYLE
Pollo alla Piemontese

Serves 4 to 6.

1 frying chicken, about 3½ pounds, cut into serving pieces

The marinade
3 cloves garlic, or 1 medium onion, sliced
Juice of 2 lemons
Rosemary (use in abundance)
Freshly ground black pepper to taste

The batter
2 tablespoons olive oil
1 tablespoon safflower oil
¾ cup warm water
¾ cup flour
½ teaspoon nutmeg
Salt and freshly ground black pepper to taste
1 egg white

Garnish: Lemon wedges

Marinate chicken in marinade for several hours or more.

Mix all ingredients for the batter, except the egg white, until well blended and allow to stand for 2 hours or more.

Drain chicken, wipe dry, and salt it all over.

Beat the egg white until rather stiff, then stir into batter. Dip each piece of chicken into the batter to coat. Oil a baking dish or tray.

Roast chicken pieces in a preheated 350° oven until tender, about 30 to 45 minutes. Serve with lemon wedges.

Calories	Cholesterol mg	Protein gm	Carbohydrate gm	Total fat gm	%	Sat fat gm	%	Mono gm	Poly gm
1510	494.0	153.7	72.1	63.2	37	11.5	7	29.5	16.7

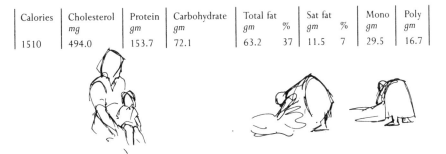

LEAN CHICKEN CANZANESE STYLE
Pollo Canzanese Magro

The original recipe includes prosciutto, but we have left it out because of its high fat content and I find the dish just as satisfactory. Serve with lemon wedges.

Serves 4.

3- to 3½-pound chicken, cut into serving pieces, all fat
   removed
3 sage leaves
2 bay leaves
1 clove garlic, minced
6 to 8 cloves garlic
1 teaspoon rosemary
12 peppercorns, crushed
Hot pepper flakes to taste (optional)
¾ cup dry white wine
¼ cup water or chicken stock
Salt to taste

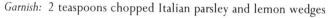

Garnish: 2 teaspoons chopped Italian parsley and lemon wedges

Soak chicken pieces in salted water at least 45 minutes. Drain and dry
chicken, then arrange in a large skillet. Add all ingredients except garnish.
Cover and simmer about 45 minutes, until chicken is cooked. When chicken
is ready, pour liquid into a bowl or defatter and remove all fat. To serve,
pour juices over chicken, garnish with parsley, and offer lemon wedges.

Calories	Cholesterol mg	Protein gm	Carbohydrate gm	Total fat gm	%	Sat fat gm	%	Mono gm	Poly gm
708	423.0	120.4	8.4	18.2	23	5.7	7	6.9	3.8

BAKED CHICKEN
Pollo al Forno

Serves 8.

2 broilers, split, about 2½ pounds each
1 cup wine vinegar
1 tablespoon coarsely chopped garlic
1 tablespoon rosemary
Salt and freshly ground black pepper to taste

Place chicken split side up in a baking dish. Add the vinegar, garlic, rosemary, salt, and pepper. Marinate at least 2 hours.
   Bake in a preheated 450° oven until chicken is tender, turning occasionally,
about 1 hour. Lower heat to 400° if chicken cooks too rapidly.

Calories	Cholesterol mg	Protein gm	Carbohydrate gm	Total fat gm	%	Sat fat gm	%	Mono gm	Poly gm
1170	704.0	199.9	17.2	30.4	23	9.5	7	11.4	6.3

CHICKEN COUNTRY STYLE
Pollo alla Campagnola

We enjoy this dish during the winter months; it is both hardy and delicate. It is best when made with an older chicken — I use a full-grown rooster. If a tough chicken is used, then allow more cooking time and add vegetables later.

Serves 8.

1 large chicken, about 4 pounds
1 bay leaf
3 stalks celery, cut into 3-inch lengths
2 cups carrots scraped and cut into 2-inch lengths
Salt and freshly ground black pepper to taste
2 cups chopped tomatoes, fresh if possible (drain if canned)
1 pound Brussels sprouts, trimmed
1 tablespoon rosemary
12 small white onions, peeled
1/2 pound mushrooms (cut large mushrooms in half)
8 medium potatoes, peeled and cut into large chunks
2 cups fresh shelled peas or a 10-ounce package frozen peas, blanched and drained
3 tablespoons chopped Italian parsley

Garnish: Finely chopped Italian parsley

Cut up the chicken, cover with cold salted water, and soak about 2 hours. Wash and drain.

Place chicken in a wide pot about 3 inches deep, so that all the chicken fits in one layer.

Add 1 cup water, bay leaf, celery, carrots, salt, and pepper and bring to a boil. Add tomatoes, cover, and boil over medium heat about 20 minutes. Add Brussels sprouts, rosemary, and onions and continue cooking 20 minutes more. Add mushrooms, potatoes, peas, parsley, salt, and pepper and cook, partially covered, about 20 minutes more, until potatoes are tender.

Garnish with parsley.

Calories	Cholesterol mg	Protein gm	Carbohydrate gm	Total fat gm	%	Sat fat gm	%	Mono gm	Poly gm
2684	564.0	232.2	366.3	31.7	10	7.6	2	9.2	5.0

CHICKEN WITH MUSHROOMS, ONIONS, AND FRESH FENNEL
Pollo con Funghi e Finocchio

Serves 6.

1 large fennel bulb, cored and cut into slices about
   1/4 inch thick
4 tablespoons safflower oil
3 1/2-pound fryer, cut into servings pieces,
   or a comparable amount of chicken parts
1 tablespoon crushed rosemary
Salt and freshly ground black pepper to taste
1 medium onion, thinly sliced
1 cup dry white wine
4 cups fresh mushrooms cut into large pieces (smaller
   mushrooms left whole)

Garnish: 3 tablespoons minced Italian parsley

Blanch fennel in boiling water, drain when it returns to a boil, and set aside.

Heat 2 tablespoons of the oil in a skillet. Add the chicken and cook, uncovered, over moderate heat, turning often. Add rosemary, salt, and pepper. When chicken is brown, drain off and discard all fat and oil. Add onion and remaining 2 tablespoons oil, and simmer until onion wilts. Add wine, cover, lower heat, and cook until wine cooks out. Add mushrooms and fennel. Cover and simmer, stirring often, until fennel is tender—about 10 minutes. Sprinkle parsley on chicken before serving.

Calories	Cholesterol mg	Protein gm	Carbohydrate gm	Total fat gm	%	Sat fat gm	%	Mono gm	Poly gm
1537	494.0	154.6	49.8	77.5	44	11.5	7	14.5	44.8

No figures available for fennel. We have used celery data instead.

CHICKEN WITH 41 CLOVES OF GARLIC
Poulet avec Quarante-et-un Gousses d'Ail

This French provincial recipe has always fascinated me — why 40 cloves of garlic? Why not 35 or 45? I decided to add an additional clove of garlic to "change" the recipe. You will be amazed at how delicate garlic cooked whole is. This recipe makes a subtle and most satisfying winter dish.

It is excellent accompanied by roasted potatoes and a green vegetable such as spinach or broccoli.

Serves 4 to 6.

3 bay leaves
2 tablespoons rosemary
41 cloves garlic, skins on
Salt and freshly ground black pepper to taste
3 1/2-pound roasting chicken
1 tablespoon thyme
2 tablespoons safflower oil
1 cup dry white wine
French or Italian bread

Preheat oven to 450°.

Put 1 bay leaf, 1 tablespoon of the rosemary, 4 cloves garlic, salt, and pepper into the cavity of the chicken, truss, and tuck the other 2 bay leaves between legs and breast. Season skin with salt, pepper, thyme, and remaining 1 tablespoon rosemary. Put the chicken in an ovenproof dish or, better still, a terracotta pot. Pour oil over chicken and surround it with remaining garlic cloves.

Bake, uncovered, about 45 minutes. Then turn the chicken on its side, continue cooking about 15 minutes; turn, and cook 15 minutes on the other side. Drain off all oil and fat and discard. Add wine, cover, and lower heat to 350°. Cook an additional 30 minutes, basting occasionally. Remove cover and bake about 10 minutes more, continuing to baste.

Toast some French bread or Italian bread. Squeeze the cooked garlic from their skins and spread on the bread. Serve with chicken, or remove garlic from skins, mash and mix with pan juices. Cut chicken in serving pieces and pour sauce over them.

Calories	Cholesterol mg	Protein gm	Carbohydrate gm	Total fat gm	%	Sat fat gm	%	Mono gm	Poly gm
1001	494.0	148.6	43.6	21.7	19	6.7	6	8.1	4.4

The bread is not included in my calculations.

CHICKEN WITH CHESTNUTS
Pollo con Castagne

This dish is good served with a green vegetable such as broccoli rape or spinach.

Serves 6.

3½-pound fryer, cut into serving pieces
2 tablespoons safflower oil
Salt and freshly ground black pepper to taste
2 cups coarsely chopped onion
1 cup sliced fresh mushrooms
¾-ounce package dried boletus mushrooms,
    soaked in warm water for 15 minutes
¾ cup dry marsala, imported if possible
1 tablespoon rosemary
2 tablespoons olive oil
14 fresh chestnuts

Garnish: 2 tablespoons finely chopped Italian parsley

Sauté the chicken in the safflower oil, add salt and pepper, and continue to cook, uncovered, over moderate heat, turning often. When chicken begins to brown, drain off and discard all fat. Add onion and mushrooms and continue cooking over moderate heat. When onion begins to brown, add marsala, rosemary, and olive oil, cover, lower heat, and cook 10 minutes. In the meantime, split each chestnut (see page 93 for instructions), and boil 5 to 8 minutes. Drain, remove shells while still hot, and split the chestnuts. Add them to the chicken, cover, and simmer 15 minutes, mixing occasionally. Add parsley and serve hot.

Variation: Fresh peas are also good in this recipe. Blanch them and add to the dish along with the chestnuts.

Calories	Cholesterol mg	Protein gm	Carbohydrate gm	Total fat gm	%	Sat fat gm	%	Mono gm	Poly gm
1432	494.0	151.4	88.2	51.0	31	9.7	6	28.7	6.2

CHICKEN WITH SAFFRON
Pollo con Zafferano

Serves 4.

1 tablespoon safflower oil
3- to 3½-pound fryer, quartered, all fat removed
4 cloves garlic, skins on
Salt and freshly ground black pepper to taste
1 cup dry white wine

1/2 teaspoon saffron, diluted in 2 teaspoons hot water
2 bay leaves
1 tablespoon rosemary
4 cloves
10 black peppercorns
Hot pepper flakes to taste

Garnish: 1 tablespoon chopped Italian parsley

Heat the oil in a skillet, then add chicken skin side down, garlic, salt, and pepper. Cook 15 minutes, uncovered, over medium heat. Turn pieces over and continue cooking. When chicken is brown, drain and discard all fat, then add wine, saffron, bay leaves, rosemary, cloves, peppercorns, and hot pepper flakes. Cover and cook until wine cooks out, about 20 to 30 minutes. Garnish with parsley.

Calories	Cholesterol mg	Protein gm	Carbohydrate gm	Total fat gm	%	Sat fat gm	%	Mono gm	Poly gm
857	494.0	141.4	16.4	21.7	22	6.7	7	8.1	4.4

CHICKEN WITH HONEY
Pollo al Miele

This recipe was given to me by an Italian woman who insisted her mother made the dish in Abruzzi and it was popular in the area, although I am not at all convinced it is of Italian origin.

This chicken is excellent with potatoes. Peel enough potatoes — 1/2 per person — then cut in half lengthwise. Add them to the roasting pan after chicken has browned and you've removed the water from the pan. Baste the potatoes with the honey mixture, adding more honey if needed.

Serves 4.

4-pound roasting chicken, all fat removed
2 cloves garlic, slivered
Freshly ground black pepper to taste
About 2 tablespoons rosemary leaves
Salt to taste
1 cup orange juice
1 tablespoon good mustard
4 tablespoons honey

Force garlic under chicken skin over breast, and put some in the cavity of the chicken. Force some pepper and rosemary under skin over breast and put some in cavity. Truss chicken, then rub with remaining rosemary and pepper and salt.

Place chicken in a roasting pan in a preheated 400° oven with about 3/4 inch water on the bottom. When chicken begins to brown, discard all liquid. Blend together the orange juice and mustard and add, lowering heat to 350°. Cook about 1 hour and 20 minutes in all, basting chicken often until sauce thickens. Add honey to chicken, and continue roasting until honey thickens and glazes chicken, about 15 minutes.

Calories	Cholesterol mg	Protein gm	Carbohydrate gm	Total fat gm	%	Sat fat gm	%	Mono gm	Poly gm
1658	564.0	173.5	173.5	27.1	14	7.6	4	9.2	5.0

This recipe is calculated with the 2 medium potatoes mentioned in the headnotes.

CHICKEN WITH SEAFOOD
Pollo con Frutta di Mare

I first heard of this recipe from a friend from my hometown who was an opera singer. He insisted it was an Italian recipe, but I had never encountered it before.

That was in 1954, when I had just returned from my student years in Italy, and I was fascinated with the idea of combining chicken with fish. (At the time I was unaware of paella and Chinese recipes combining chicken with fish.) I found to my delight that they complemented each other, and I developed a number of combinations that worked out well.

In 1955 I prepared this recipe, which is a little more elaborate, for a party of 75 people given by Walter Chrysler, Jr., in the restaurant of a friend in Provincetown. I went to the pier that morning and I was able to get all the fish I needed for the dinner by simply picking up the fish as they discarded the "trash fish" from their catch of mackerel. The "trash fish" included whiting, butterfish, squid, blowfish (now called sea squab), fluke, and small flounder among others. I then walked a short distance away along the coast and gathered all the mussels I needed. The only fish that had to be purchased for the dinner were lobsters and clams.

The event went well. We had fun arranging the trays of fish and chicken in attractive patterns. The owners of the restaurant, as well as most of the help in the kitchen, were artists. "We need more green, Ed." "I think it needs some black"—thus olives were added. And so it went as I arranged the trays, and we were pleased with the results.

Everything was fine until the guests arrived—all at once. Suddenly there was confusion, with mayhem in the kitchen. Decorating the trays with whole fish and whole lobsters had been one thing, but cutting up the fish, boning it, cutting up the lobsters and cracking the shells was something else. All of a sudden we had to serve 75 people and we were totally unprepared.

We had to handle hot lobsters with our hands in order to cut them up, then arrange a nice selection of fish and chicken on each plate, 75 of them. It finally all worked out, and of course we learned a lesson.

After that the recipe was cooked in small casseroles, for 2 to 4, and the bowls were served from the oven to the guests.

Serves 8.

3½- to 4-pound chicken, cut into small serving pieces
Salt and freshly ground black pepper to taste
2 tablespoons safflower oil
1 tablespoon rosemary
4 cloves garlic, skins on
Hot pepper flakes to taste (optional)
½ cup white wine vinegar
4 tablespoons finely chopped Italian parsley
3 tablespoons chopped fresh basil or 1 tablespoon dried
4 tablespoons chopped fresh mint
4 cups chopped tomatoes, fresh if possible
   (drain if canned)
4 tablespoons capers
2 to 3 dozen mussels, depending on size,
   washed and scrubbed
1 dozen littleneck clams, well washed
1 pound shrimp, shelled

Salt and pepper the chicken. Heat oil in a skillet and cook chicken over medium to high heat, turning often. Add rosemary and cook until chicken takes on color. Drain and discard all fat and oil, then add garlic, hot pepper, and vinegar. Cover and simmer over low heat until vinegar cooks out. Add parsley, basil, mint, tomatoes, and capers. Cover and simmer over moderate heat 10 minutes, stirring occasionally.

Remove chicken from the sauce with a slotted spoon and place in a shallow baking dish about 12 × 18 inches. Bring sauce to a boil, add mussels and clams. Cover and cook, removing mussels and then clams as soon as they begin to open. Place clams and mussels in the dish with the chicken. Pour sauce over the shellfish and chicken. Add shrimp and cover with foil.

Preheat the oven to 500° for at least 15 minutes. Place dish in oven and bake until shrimp are pink—about 3 to 4 minutes—do not overcook. Serve with rice or bruschetta (page 39).

Calories	Cholesterol mg	Protein gm	Carbohydrate gm	Total fat gm	%	Sat fat gm	%	Mono gm	Poly gm
1831	1236.0	285.2	76.8	35.7	17	7.6	4	9.2	5.0

Variations:

1. Oysters can be used. Remove from shells and add with shrimp.

2. This recipe can also be made with fish like cod, halibut, striped bass slices, monkfish, or skate wings that remain firm after cooking. It is important to use a shallow baking pan so that the fish and chicken do not overlap.

3. Lobster could be used instead of or along with the shrimp. Cut it up according to instructions on page 187 and add to the sauce when you do the shellfish.

CHICKEN WITH MUSSELS
Pollo con Muscoli

When a similar version of this recipe first appeared in my cookbook *Italian Family Cooking* in 1971, very few people had ever heard of the combination. Since then it has become more and more popular.

Serves 6 to 8.

2 tablespoons safflower oil
3-pound chicken, cut into serving pieces
Salt and hot pepper flakes or freshly ground black
  pepper to taste
2 tablespoons olive oil
2 cloves garlic, chopped
1 1/2 cups dry white wine or white wine vinegar
1 teaspoon dried oregano
1 tablespoon chopped fresh basil or 1 teaspoon dried
1 teaspoon rosemary
1 teaspoon chopped fresh mint
1 cup coarsely chopped tomatoes, fresh if possible
  (drain if canned)
1 green pepper, chopped
1/2 cup minced Italian parsley
2 pounds mussels*

*Clams or any shellfish may be used if mussels aren't available.

Heat the safflower oil in a large skillet, then add the chicken pieces and salt and pepper. Cook over moderate heat, turning chicken often until brown. Drain off all fat and oil and discard. Add the olive oil and garlic. As garlic begins to take on color, add wine, oregano, basil, rosemary, and mint, cover, lower heat, and cook for 5 minutes. Uncover, turn up heat, and cook until the wine evaporates. Add tomatoes, green peppers, and half the parsley, cover, and raise heat. When liquid boils, remove cover, and cook over moderate heat, stirring occasionally, until sauce thickens and chicken is tender—35 to 45 minutes.

In the meantime, scrub the mussels under cold running water, remove beards, and add them to chicken. Cover and cook over low heat until the mussel shells open. If sauce is too watery, remove chicken and mussels and reduce over high heat. Pour sauce over chicken and mussels, add remaining parsley, and serve immediately.

Calories	Cholesterol mg	Protein gm	Carbohydrate gm	Total fat gm	%	Sat fat gm	%	Mono gm	Poly gm
1571	554.0	167.2	42.4	52.0	29	9.3	5	26.7	7.9

STEAMED CHICKEN
Pollo al Vapore

This is a pleasant, light summer dish of warm chicken dressed with tomatoes just from the garden.

Serves 4.

3-pound frying chicken
2 cloves garlic, slivered
Salt and freshly ground black pepper to taste
1 tablespoon rosemary

The dressing
2 medium ripe tomatoes, cut in wedges
1 medium red onion, thinly sliced
3 tablespoons good red wine vinegar or juice of 1 lemon
1 teaspoon olive oil
1 teaspoon safflower oil or 3 teaspoons peanut oil

Garnish: Chopped Italian parsley or fresh basil

Slip some of the garlic slivers under the skin over breasts. Rub the whole chicken with salt, black pepper, and rosemary. Put the rest of the garlic, rosemary, and additional salt and pepper in cavity.

Truss bird and place in a steamer. If you don't have a steamer, put about 4 inches water in a 6- or 8-quart pot and put a colander in that fits snugly. Place chicken in pot and cover tightly. Steam for about 45 minutes, until chicken is tender, turning occasionally and adding more boiling water if necessary. Let cool, then either cut the chicken in serving pieces or bone it.

Gently mix all the dressing ingredients together with the chicken. Arrange in a decorative pattern on a serving plate.

Garnish with fresh parsley or basil.

Calories	Cholesterol mg	Protein gm	Carbohydrate gm	Total fat gm	%	Sat fat gm	%	Mono gm	Poly gm
895	423.0	126.2	29.9	28.0	28	6.6	6	11.0	7.4

DEVILED CHICKEN
Pollo alla Diavola

I believe this recipe is of Roman origin, although we have had it in Florence.

The chicken must be a young spring chicken weighing about 2 pounds dressed. First the chicken must be split, and then pressed with weights so that it is about 1/2 to 3/4 inch thick. We have a wonderful gadget for just this purpose — an old woodcut press. After splitting the chicken, we put it in the press, turn the wheel, and "press" until it is the right thickness. In

Italy the chickens used in this recipe are so small that one whole split chicken is served to each guest.

Serves 2.

1 spring chicken, about 2 pounds dressed, split
1 teaspoon chopped garlic
Juice of 1 lemon
Salt and hot pepper flakes to taste
2 tablespoons vegetable oil

Garnish: Lemon wedges

Marinate chicken with the garlic, lemon juice, salt, and hot pepper flakes and refrigerate for several hours.

Heat the oil in a skillet large enough to hold the chicken, then add the chicken skin side down and cook over medium heat. Occasionally slip a metal spatula under chicken to keep it from sticking, and press down on the chicken. Cover and cook until skin side browns; then turn chicken and continue cooking. Turn chicken again after about 10 minutes and continue cooking, pressing down on it every so often. Chicken done this way should be cooked in 40 minutes.*

Serve hot with lemon wedges.

*The chicken can be dusted in flour and deep-fried, but we prefer this lighter version.

Calories	Cholesterol mg	Protein gm	Carbohydrate gm	Total fat gm	%	Sat fat gm	%	Mono gm	Poly gm
714	282.0	80.8	6.9	39.3	48	6.6	8	12.2	16.9

PASTA AND CHICKEN DINNER
Pasta e Pollo

When I was a young art student in Boston, I made a similar recipe once a week. I was living with three other students and we managed to eat three meals a day, five days a week, for $3.50 each—that was in 1948. I made this recipe to get two different meals from it. Pasta with sauce was one dinner; the next day we dined on the chicken and two vegetables.

Serves 6.

3 tablespoons safflower oil or vegetable oil
1 whole chicken, about 3½ pounds, fat removed, trussed
1 pound veal or beef bones
1 large onion with 4 cloves stuck in it
Salt and freshly ground black pepper to taste
1 cup dry white wine
1 pound mushrooms, cut in half

3 cloves garlic
1 large carrot
1 piece cheese rind, scraped (optional)
8 cups chopped tomatoes, fresh if possible (drain if canned)
2 tablespoons chopped fresh basil
1 tablespoon dried oregano
1 cup water
1 pound fresh peas, about 2 cups, blanched
1½ pounds pasta

Heat the oil in a casserole, then add the chicken, bones, and onion. Lightly brown the chicken over moderate heat, turning often. Add salt, pepper, and wine. Cover, lower heat, and simmer until wine cooks out. Add mushrooms, garlic, carrot, cheese rind, tomatoes, herbs, and water, cover, and simmer for 2 hours. Add the peas and cook 30 to 45 minutes partially covered.

Remove the chicken and keep it warm to serve as the second course. Remove onion, bones, carrot, and garlic and discard. You will have enough sauce left in the casserole for 2½ to 3 pounds pasta, so put half away for another time. Boil pasta until al dente, then serve in bowls with half the sauce poured over.

Calories	Cholesterol mg	Protein gm	Carbohydrate gm	Total fat gm	%	Sat fat gm	%	Mono gm	Poly gm
3172	0	115.9	596.8	32.2	9	1.8	1	2.4	15.2

This recipe is very difficult to analyze, because an unknown amount of fat (and cholesterol) enters the sauce from both the veal bones and the whole chicken. The nutritional data given above disregard the fat from these sources. If we double the fat to 65 grams and assume that half the extra comes from chicken and half from veal bones, the data look like this:

Calories	Cholesterol mg	Protein gm	Carbohydrate gm	Total fat gm	%	Sat fat gm	%	Mono gm	Poly gm
3461	33.0	115.9	596.8	65.0	16	15.1	4	15.8	18.8

BROILED CHICKEN BREASTS I
Petti di Pollo alla Griglia

Serves 3 to 6.

3 whole boned chicken breasts, fat removed
4 tablespoons wine vinegar or juice of 3 lemons
3 cloves garlic, sliced
1 tablespoon rosemary
Freshly ground black pepper to taste
2 tablespoons chopped Italian parsley or
    fresh coriander
3 tablespoons olive oil
1 teaspoon safflower oil
Salt to taste

Garnish: Lemon wedges

Place chicken breasts in a bowl. Combine the remaining ingredients except salt, pour over chicken, and marinate at least 2 hours.

Preheat broiler for 10 minutes. Place breasts on baking dish or tray. Pour marinade over breasts and add salt. Broil close to heat about 3 to 5 minutes on each side. If breasts have skin on, broil skin side first. Do not overcook.

Serve with lemon wedges.

Calories	Cholesterol mg	Protein gm	Carbohydrate gm	Total fat gm	%	Sat fat gm	%	Mono gm	Poly gm
1077	363.0	127.6	13.2	55.9	46	8.4	7	35.4	8.0

GRILLED CHICKEN BREASTS II
Petti di Pollo alla Griglia

Serves 8.

4 whole chicken breasts, skinned and boned
Juice of 2 limes
1 tablespoon soy sauce
1 teaspoon minced garlic
2 tablespoons peanut oil
2 bay leaves
Salt and freshly ground black pepper to taste

Garnish: Lemon wedges

Put the chicken breasts in a mixing bowl and sprinkle the remaining ingredients over them. Refrigerate for several hours.

Grill breasts over hot coals about 3 minutes on each side, depending on thickness of breasts. Do not overcook.

Serve with lemon wedges.

Calories	Cholesterol	Protein	Carbohydrate	Total fat		Sat fat		Mono	Poly
	mg	gm	gm	gm	%	gm	%	gm	gm
868	484.0	169.0	7.2	13.7	14	4.4	4	5.2	2.8

CHICKEN BREASTS WITH PEPPERS, ONIONS, MUSHROOMS, AND TOMATOES
Petti di Pollo in Umido

Serves 4 to 6.

3 plump boned chicken breast halves, skin and fat removed,
    then cut into 1/2-inch strips
2 cloves garlic, chopped
Juice of 1 1/2 to 2 lemons or limes
Salt and freshly ground black pepper to taste
4 tablespoons safflower oil or 2 olive oil and 2 safflower
2 cups green peppers cut into 1/2-inch strips
2 medium onions, sliced
1 cup thinly sliced mushrooms
1 cup coarsely chopped tomatoes, fresh if possible (drain
    if canned)
Pinch hot pepper flakes
2 tablespoons chopped Italian parsley

Put the chicken breasts in a deep bowl and marinate in garlic, lemon or lime juice, salt, and pepper for at least 2 hours. Heat 2 tablespoons of the safflower oil in a skillet, then add the vegetables, hot pepper flakes, and parsley. Quickly cook vegetables, stirring often — do not overcook. Remove from skillet when vegetables are al dente.

Drain the chicken and reserve the marinade. Add remaining 2 tablespoons oil to skillet and when hot add chicken. Cook over very high heat a couple of minutes, turning often, until chicken whitens; if the meat starts to stick to the pan, add a little marinade to loosen it. Add vegetables and cook together for several minutes.

Serve with rice.

Calories	Cholesterol	Protein	Carbohydrate	Total fat		Sat fat		Mono	Poly
	mg	gm	gm	gm	%	gm	%	gm	gm
1093	182.0	77.5	57.9	61.2	49	6.1	5	10.0	40.3

CHICKEN WITH RISOTTO
Pollo in Bianco con Risotto

The original recipe is as presented, but we have found that we enjoy the dish even more when a sauce such as the horseradish and tomato one on page 432 is served with it.

You will find this recipe light, but very satisfying.

Serves 6.

1 chicken, about 4 pounds, preferably a stewing hen,
    washed, fat removed, and trussed
2 stalks celery, cut into 3-inch lengths
1 cup chopped tomatoes, fresh if possible (drain if canned)
1 medium onion, peeled, with 3 cloves stuck into it
2 carrots
2 tablespoons chopped Italian parsley
1 bay leaf
Salt to taste

The risotto
1 medium onion, chopped
2 tablespoons olive oil
1 tablespoon safflower oil
1 cup rice
Salt and freshly ground black pepper to taste
1 cup dry white wine
1½ cups reserved chicken broth
½ teaspoon nutmeg

Put the chicken in a casserole. Cover with water, then add the celery, tomatoes, onion, carrots, parsley, bay leaf, and salt. Cover, bring to a boil, and simmer gently about 2 hours, skimming occasionally.

Drain broth, remove all fat, and reserve. You should have about 8 cups.

Remove chicken, cut in large pieces, then remove bones. Set pieces aside and keep warm.

Make the risotto: Put the chopped onion and the two oils in a saucepan and sauté until translucent. Add rice, salt, and pepper, and cook, stirring often, until onion begins to brown. Add the wine and when it cooks out, add ½ cup of the broth and the nutmeg, and cook over moderate heat, stirring often. Add more stock as is needed and cook, following directions for risotto on page 152, until rice is tender.

Serve rice with chicken pieces.

Calories	Cholesterol mg	Protein gm	Carbohydrate gm	Total fat gm	%	Sat fat gm	%	Mono gm	Poly gm
2042	564.0	175.4	173.2	66.0	28	12.4	5	30.6	17.3

CHICKEN WITH PASTA AND BROCCOLI
Pollo con Pasta e Broccoli

Serves 6.

6 cups broccoli cut into bite-sized pieces
2 tablespoons safflower oil
1/2 medium onion, chopped
Hot pepper flakes to taste (optional)
4 cups chopped tomatoes, fresh if possible (drain if canned)
2 tablespoons chopped fresh basil or 1 teaspoon dried
Salt to taste
2 tablespoons good olive oil
3/4 pound cut pasta, such as ziti, penne, rigatoni
1 whole chicken breast, skin, bones, and any excess fat
    removed, cut into 1/2-inch strips
1 clove garlic, minced

Garnish: Chopped Italian parsley

Blanch broccoli in boiling water and drain.

Heat 1 tablespoon of the safflower oil in a medium skillet, then add onion. When it begins to brown, add hot pepper flakes and tomatoes. Cover, lower heat, and simmer for 15 minutes; then run the sauce through a food mill or food processor. Return to skillet, add broccoli, basil, and salt, and cover. Simmer slowly until broccoli is tender, about 8 minutes. Add the olive oil.

Boil pasta in rapidly boiling salted water until al dente. While pasta is cooking, heat remaining 1 tablespoon safflower oil in a wok or medium skillet, then quickly sauté chicken, tossing, over high heat about 1 1/2 to 2 minutes. Do not overcook. Add garlic and cook another minute or so. Add the chicken to the sauce, pour over pasta, and serve.

Garnish with parsley.

Calories	Cholesterol *mg*	Protein *gm*	Carbohydrate *gm*	Total fat *gm*	%	Sat fat *gm*	%	Mono *gm*	Poly *gm*
2292	121.0	105.9	320.0	64.4	25	6.3	2	25.9	22.5

CHICKEN BAKED IN BREAD TUSCANY STYLE
Pollo nel Pane alla Toscana

In the late 1960s I saw a picture of this dish in an Italian magazine. No recipe accompanied it, but it looked so appealing I developed my own, using our pizza dough, and everyone I have served it to has loved it.

Serves 6 to 8.

The bread
1 tablespoon dry yeast
4 cups warm water
10 to 11 cups unbleached all-purpose flour
1 tablespoon salt

$4\frac{1}{2}$- to 5-pound roasting chicken, fat removed
About 8 garlic cloves
Freshly ground black pepper to taste
4 tablespoons crushed rosemary
About $\frac{1}{2}$ cup dry white wine

To make the bread dough, put yeast in $\frac{1}{2}$ cup of the warm water and let it stand until dissolved. Dump 8 cups of the flour into a large mixing bowl, add salt, remaining water, and yeast mixture, and stir with a wooden spoon. Spread 1 cup flour on a mixing board or marble top. Remove dough from bowl and knead on board. As you work it, add more flour as needed. It will take from 1 to 2 more cups, depending on room temperature and climate. Work dough until it is smooth and manageable—about 10 to 15 minutes. Clean the mixing bowl and rub with vegetable oil. Place the ball of dough in the bowl and roll it around so that it is coated with a film of oil. Cover with cloth or plastic and keep in a warm place—near a stove is fine. Allow the dough to rise to double its bulk, which should take $1\frac{1}{4}$ to 2 hours, depending on room temperature. Then it will be ready for the chicken.

In the meantime, about an hour before the dough has finished its rising, prepare the chicken. Preheat the oven to 450°. Slip 3 to 4 slices garlic under the skin of the chicken over breasts and work in some black pepper and rosemary. Put 1 tablespoon rosemary and several cloves of garlic into the cavity, rub 1 tablespoon rosemary on surface of chicken, dust with black pepper, and truss the bird.

Place chicken in a baking pan and pour about $\frac{1}{2}$ inch water and dry white wine around. Bake, uncovered, about 45 minutes. Turn chicken over during that period and baste occasionally. Lower heat to 400° and continue to cook about 45 minutes more. Allow chicken to cool, place on a rack, and tilt to remove all liquid from cavity. Strain juices, remove all fat, and set aside. (Reserve juices as a basis for some of the sauces in Chapter X, *Sauces.*) We like to chop some onion and mushrooms, sauté them in a little vegetable oil, add pan juices, cover, and cook for about 5 minutes. If several tablespoons of pesto are added at the last minute it's even better.

Flour your work surface generously (so dough does not stick), and roll out dough until about $\frac{1}{2}$ inch thick. Place slices from 4 garlic cloves on the dough and press in firmly, then sprinkle on remaining 2 tablespoons rosemary and freshly ground black pepper. Drain chicken well. Place the chicken in the middle of the dough and fold this over the chicken, being careful not to puncture dough. Cut away excess dough, but allow to overlap for a tight seam. (Excess dough may be baked as bread rolls.) Oil a baking tray, gently place dough-wrapped chicken on it, and bake in a preheated 400° oven until bread is brown—about 20 to 30 minutes. Throw in an occasional ice cube on the oven floor so the steam will make bread crisp.

Remove from pan and place on a large platter to present to your guests. Then with a sharp knife slit bread through the middle lengthwise, spread open and remove from chicken. Put bread back into hot oven or under broiler to dry out the damp interior. Carve chicken on a platter, spoon on juices, remove bread from oven, and serve chunks of it with the chicken.

Calories	Cholesterol mg	Protein gm	Carbohydrate gm	Total fat gm	%	Sat fat gm	%	Mono gm	Poly gm
3929	635.0	259.8	544.5	69.0	15	11.5	3	19.2	24.7

The meat in a 4¹/2-pound chicken has about 1013 calories and 27.2 grams of fat. The bread adds 5010 calories and 14.1 grams of fat. There is, undoubtedly, a small amount of fat that seeps into the bread from the chicken, but the amount is small, because the chicken is roasted and drained before being placed in the bread dough. The sauce, consisting of defatted pan juices, a tablespoon of safflower oil in which are sautéed the onions and mushrooms, and 3 tablespoons pesto (page 426), adds another 411 calories and 34.7 grams of fat. The totals in the box are for chicken, sauce, and half the bread, which, in our experience, is the most that is eaten.

CHICKEN CROQUETTES
Crocchette di Pollo

Any leftover cooked meat can be used in this recipe.

Serves 4.

2 medium potatoes
2 cups boiled boned chicken
2 tablespoons chopped Italian parsley
1 teaspoon grated lemon rind
About ¹/2 teaspoon grated nutmeg
2 egg whites, lightly whipped
Salt and freshly ground black pepper to taste
Corn oil for frying
Flour for dredging

Boil potatoes with skins on until just tender, then cool, peel, and mash. Grind chicken and put in a bowl with the potatoes and remaining ingredients, except oil and flour, mixing well. Form croquettes about 2 inches long and 1 inch wide. Don't refrigerate.*

Heat about 3/4 inch oil in a small skillet. Dust croquettes with flour, then gently place a few at a time in the hot oil. Fry until golden brown on both sides. Remove and blot on paper towels. Repeat until all are done.

*If croquettes are refrigerator-cold, they will cool off the oil so that more is absorbed in frying.

Calories	Cholesterol mg	Protein gm	Carbohydrate gm	Total fat gm	%	Sat fat gm	%	Mono gm	Poly gm
1127	232.0	93.7	77.0	46.7	36	9.5	7	13.9	20.0

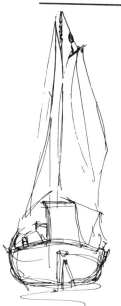

CHICKEN BREASTS WITH MUSHROOMS AND GREEN BEANS
Petti di Pollo con Funghi e Fagiolini Verdi

This dish is best made with Italian (Romano) pole beans.

Serves 4 to 6.

4 cups green beans, preferably pole beans, tops removed
    and cut in half
2 tablespoons peanut oil
4 cups mushrooms, cut in halves
2 tablespoons soy sauce
1 tablespoon chopped fresh ginger
1 whole chicken breast, boned, skinned, and cut into
    1/2-inch-thick strips
Freshly ground black pepper to taste
1 teaspoon minced garlic

Garnish: Chopped fresh coriander or Italian parsley

Blanch the beans in a large pot of boiling, salted water.

Heat 1 tablespoon of the peanut oil in a wok or medium skillet, then add mushrooms. Cook over high heat for several minutes. Sprinkle with a little of the soy sauce and cook 3 or 4 minutes. Remove mushrooms with a slotted spoon. Add blanched green beans and ginger to the skillet and cook over high heat about 3 or 4 minutes—or longer if desired—until liquid cooks out. Remove beans and mix in with the mushrooms. Heat remaining 1 tablespoon oil in the skillet, then add chicken strips, grind pepper on top, and cook over very high heat, tossing constantly, until chicken becomes white—a minute or so. Add garlic, sprinkle on remaining soy sauce, and cook for 1 more minute. Do not overcook chicken. Add to beans and mushrooms, mix, and garnish with coriander. Serve immediately.

Calories	Cholesterol mg	Protein gm	Carbohydrate gm	Total fat gm	%	Sat fat gm	%	Mono gm	Poly gm
708	121.0	60.8	44.1	32.6	41	6.7	8	13.7	9.3

CHICKEN BREASTS WITH SHRIMP AND ASPARAGUS
Petti di Pollo con gli Asparagi

Serves 4.

2 whole chicken breasts, skinned, boned, and fat removed
 (about 1 1/2 pounds)
Juice of 1 lemon
2 cloves garlic, finely chopped
2 1/2 tablespoons safflower oil
1 tablespoon olive oil
2 cups asparagus cut into 2-inch lengths
Salt and freshly ground black pepper to taste
Flour for dredging
1 cup chicken stock
1 1/2 cups thinly sliced scallions
1 tablespoon finely chopped fresh mint
1/2 pound shrimp, shelled*
3 tablespoons freshly grated Parmesan cheese

*Shucked fresh oysters can be used in place of shrimp.

Place chicken breasts in a bowl with lemon juice and garlic, and marinate at least 2 hours.

Heat the oils in a medium skillet, then add asparagus and cook, uncovered, over high heat, tossing, until tender. Remove asparagus with a slotted spoon and reserve.

Salt and pepper the chicken breasts and dust lightly with flour. Turn heat to high under skillet, add chicken breasts, and brown them, uncovered.

When both sides of the chicken breasts are lightly browned, add stock, scallions, and mint, cover, lower heat to medium, and simmer about 10 minutes. Add shrimp and asparagus. Cover, turn up heat, and cook until shrimp turn pink—do not overcook them. Sprinkle with Parmesan cheese. Turn off heat and let dish sit for several minutes. Serve on hot plates.

Calories	Cholesterol mg	Protein gm	Carbohydrate gm	Total fat gm	%	Sat fat gm	%	Mono gm	Poly gm
1270	496.0	132.4	44.8	61.2	42	9.6	7	18.2	27.7

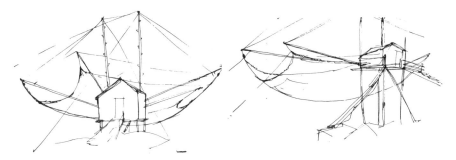

STUFFED CHICKEN BREASTS FLORENTINE STYLE
Petti di Pollo alla Fiorentina

Serves 3 to 4.

4 cups packed fresh spinach
1 egg white, lightly beaten
2 whole chicken breasts, still attached, skinned and boned
Salt and freshly ground black pepper to taste
2 tablespoons minced onion
8 dried black olives, pitted and sliced
2 anchovies, finely chopped
1 teaspoon thyme
Nutmeg
1 teaspoon rosemary
1/2 cup or more dry white wine

Bring 3 cups water to a boil, add spinach, and boil about 30 seconds. Drain, cool, and squeeze out all juice. Chop and mix with egg white.

Spread out chicken breasts and flatten skin side down between two pieces of waxed paper. Sprinkle with salt and pepper, then onion, olives, anchovies, and thyme. Spread on the spinach and add a dash of nutmeg. Roll up chicken breasts jellyroll fashion and tie at intervals to resemble thick sausages.

Preheat oven to 450°. Place breasts in a baking pan, add rosemary, salt, pepper, and 1/2 cup wine and cook, uncovered, about 50 to 60 minutes depending on size of breasts. Add more wine as needed.

Calories	Cholesterol mg	Protein gm	Carbohydrate gm	Total fat gm	%	Sat fat gm	%	Mono gm	Poly gm
592	246.0	97.1	15.0	15.5	23	2.8	4	6.8	1.8

CHICKEN BREASTS WITH EGGPLANT
Petti di Pollo con Melanzane

Serves 2.

1 small eggplant (I prefer the long, slender Japanese type)
2 tablespoons safflower oil
1 tablespoon olive oil
Salt and freshly ground black pepper to taste
1 whole boned chicken breast, split
Flour for dredging
1 teaspoon minced garlic
1/2 cup dry white wine
1 teaspoon dried oregano

1 teaspoon rosemary
2 tablespoons finely chopped Italian parsley

Preheat oven to 450°. Cut eggplant into slices about 1/4 inch thick. Coat a baking tray with 1 tablespoon of the safflower oil. Place eggplant slices on a baking tray and bake, uncovered, about 8 minutes. Then check: When bottoms begin to brown, turn over and bake for several more minutes until tops are brown. Remove from oven and set aside.

Heat remaining oils in a medium skillet. Salt and pepper the chicken breasts, dust with flour, then place in the hot oil and quickly brown on both sides. Add garlic, wine, oregano, rosemary, and parsley, cover, and simmer for several minutes. Turn off heat and transfer the chicken breasts to a small baking dish. Place the eggplant slices on top and coat with the pan juices. Cover and bake about 5 minutes.

Calories	Cholesterol mg	Protein gm	Carbohydrate gm	Total fat gm	%	Sat fat gm	%	Mono gm	Poly gm
777	121.0	47.6	24.6	46.0	52	5.3	6	14.4	22.0

CHICKEN AND CRABMEAT TEMPURA

Serves 4.

1 whole chicken breast, skinned, boned, fat removed, and
    cut with the grain into 1/2-inch-wide strips
Meat from 3 Alaska King crab claws, cut into
    2-inch-long sections
Juice of 1 lime
2 teaspoons chopped fresh coriander or Italian parsley
Salt and freshly ground black pepper to taste
1 recipe tempura batter (page 388)
Corn oil for shallow-frying
2 zucchini, cut into pieces 3 inches long and 1/2 inch wide
2 green peppers, cut into 3/4-inch-thick lengths, or about
    12 sugar snap peas

The tempura sauce:
2 teaspoons soy sauce
1 teaspoon finely chopped fresh ginger
1 teaspoon minced garlic
1 teaspoon olive oil
1 teaspoon safflower oil
4 teaspoons marinara sauce (page 430)
Juice of 1/2 lime
1 teaspoon chopped fresh coriander or Italian parsley

Mix chicken and crabmeat in a bowl with the lime juice, coriander, salt, and pepper. Refrigerate and marinate for 1 to 2 hours.

Make the tempura batter. Heat ¾ inch corn oil in a medium skillet. When oil is hot, dip vegetables one at a time in the batter and place in the oil. Fry them, turning every once in a while, about 2 minutes, or until batter is light brown. Remove and place cooked vegetables on paper towels. Repeat with more vegetables. After all are done, dip the chicken in the batter and fry, then the crabmeat. Blend together the ingredients for the sauce. Serve tempura hot with sauce on the side.

Calories	Cholesterol mg	Protein gm	Carbohydrate gm	Total fat gm	%	Sat fat gm	%	Mono gm	Poly gm
1267	234.0	91.2	133.9	38.1	26	4.2	3	12.3	15.2

CHICKEN CUTLETS
Cotolette di Pollo

These simple, delicious cutlets go well with fresh green vegetables or a green salad.

Serves 6.

3 whole chicken breasts, split, skinned, boned,
    and fat removed
Salt and freshly ground black pepper to taste
2 cloves garlic, sliced
2 lemons
2 egg whites, lightly whipped
Breadcrumbs
Corn oil or vegetable oil (not olive oil)

Flatten chicken breasts between two sheets of waxed paper with a meat pounder or flat side of a heavy knife. Salt and pepper the breasts and lay them in a deep bowl. Add garlic and juice of 1 of the lemons. Marinate in the refrigerator at least 2 hours.

Remove the breasts from the marinade and dip them in egg whites, then in breadcrumbs. In the meantime, heat about ¾ inch oil in a medium skillet.

When oil is hot (test by flipping breadcrumbs in oil; if oil boils violently, it is ready), use tongs to place each breast, one at a time, gently into the oil. Turn over after 1 minute, cooking about 2 minutes in all—don't overcook. Blot on paper towels and repeat with remaining cutlets. Serve on hot plates immediately, using remaining lemon to make wedges as a garnish.

Calories	Cholesterol mg	Protein gm	Carbohydrate gm	Total fat gm	%	Sat fat gm	%	Mono gm	Poly gm
917	363.0	137.6	27.9	25.0	24	4.7	5	7.7	9.3

CHICKEN BALLS
Polpette di Pollo

Serves 4.

1 1/2 pounds chicken breasts, skinned and boned
1 egg white, lightly beaten
1 teaspoon grated lemon rind
1 tablespoon finely chopped Italian parsley
    or fresh coriander
1 tablespoon finely chopped fresh ginger
1/2 teaspoon minced garlic
Salt and freshly ground black pepper to taste

Cut chicken in 1-inch cubes and put through the coarse blade of a meat grinder. Place in a mixing bowl with the rest of the ingredients.

Boil water in a steamer. Form mixture into 12 to 13 balls about the size of golf balls; it will be easier to form balls if you rinse your hands occasionally. Steam balls in covered container for 3 to 4 minutes. Do not overcook.

Serve with one of the boiled meat sauces in Chapter X, *Sauces*.

Calories	Cholesterol mg	Protein gm	Carbohydrate gm	Total fat gm	%	Sat fat gm	%	Mono gm	Poly gm
588	321.0	116.3	3.2	9.2	14	2.9	4	3.4	1.9

CHICKEN WINGS WITH POTATOES AND BROCCOLI
Ali di Pollo con Patate e Broccoli Neri

I am particularly fond of this recipe — the ingredients go so well together. It is excellent served with hot pepper sauce (pages 437–8) or a tomato sauce.

Serves 6.

18 chicken wings
4 cloves garlic, skins on
1 1/2 teaspoons rosemary
Salt and freshly ground black pepper to taste
About 1/2 cup water
1 large onion, finely chopped
1 cup dry white wine
1 tablespoon dried oregano
5 medium potatoes, peeled, cut into 4 sections lengthwise,
    and blanched
1 bunch broccoli, cut into bite-sized pieces and blanched
2 tablespoons safflower oil or vegetable oil

Wash chicken wings. Fold tips of wings under the large wing bone so that wings remain flat. Put them in a baking dish so that they are in one layer, add garlic, rosemary, salt, and pepper, and pour the water around them. Bake wings in a 450° preheated oven, uncovered, until they begin to brown, shaking pan occasionally so they don't stick. Drain off all fat. Add onion and continue to cook until it begins to brown, then add wine, oregano, and potatoes. Cover with foil and bake about 15 minutes more.

Add blanched broccoli, sprinkle with oil and salt, and continue to bake until potatoes are tender — about 20 minutes.

Calories	Cholesterol mg	Protein gm	Carbohydrate gm	Total fat gm	%	Sat fat gm	%	Mono gm	Poly gm
2925	495.0	199.9	190.6	149.5	45	35.7	11	49.9	45.5

The nutritional calculations for most of our chicken recipes assume that the skin and separable fat will not be consumed. The skin of chicken wings, however, is generally eaten; and although a certain amount of the fat is leached out and discarded, the fat content of the dish remains relatively high.

CHICKEN WINGS WITH MUSSELS
Ali di Pollo con Muscoli

Serves 6.

4 tablespoons safflower oil
3 cloves garlic, skins on
1 1/2 to 2 pounds chicken wings, about 16 to 18 wings
Hot pepper flakes to taste (optional)
1 tablespoon rosemary
2 cups dry white wine
1 cup chopped tomatoes, fresh if possible (drain if canned)
1 green pepper, finely chopped
2 tablespoons olive oil
1 cup thinly sliced scallions
1 teaspoon minced garlic
2 tablespoons finely chopped Italian parsley
2 pounds mussels, washed and scrubbed

Put 3 tablespoons of the safflower oil and the garlic in a large skillet along with the chicken wings, tips folded under the large wing bone, hot pepper flakes, and rosemary. Cook, uncovered, over medium heat, until wings are light brown, turning them once. Drain off all oil and fat and discard, then add 1 cup of the wine. Cover and cook over moderate heat until wine cooks out. Add tomatoes and peppers and simmer, covered, over moderate heat about 20 minutes.

In the meantime, in a separate pan heat the olive oil and remaining tablespoon safflower oil, then add scallions, minced garlic, parsley, and remaining cup of wine. Bring to a boil and add mussels. Cover and cook until mussels open. Add mussels and 1 cup of the broth to chicken wings, and cook together for several minutes.

Calories	Cholesterol mg	Protein gm	Carbohydrate gm	Total fat gm	%	Sat fat gm	%	Mono gm	Poly gm
2973	626.0	206.9	63.1	208.0	62	41.4	12	72.9	62.9

See discussion of chicken wings above.

STUFFED CHICKEN LEGS

Serves 3 to 6.

6 chicken legs with thighs attached, boned

The stuffing*
1 1/2 tablespoons olive oil
1 tablespoon safflower oil
1 medium onion, finely chopped
2 cups chopped mushrooms
1 1/2 cups fresh breadcrumbs or 1 1/2 cups cooked
    leftover polenta
2 egg whites, lightly beaten
2 tablespoons chopped pine nuts or walnut meats
3 tablespoons freshly grated Parmesan cheese
1 tablespoon finely chopped Italian parsley
Salt and freshly ground black pepper to taste
1 cup dry vermouth
1 tablespoon rosemary
2 1/2 cups fresh button mushrooms

*Any chicken stuffing can be used in this recipe.

Bone chicken legs by slowly separating with a sharp knife the flesh from the thigh bone. Do not cut through meat. Continue working with the knife, scraping against the bone to loosen the flesh until you get to within 1 inch of the bottom of the leg bone. Pull the meat back (it will be inside out now), and chop off bone, leaving bottom fragment still attached to skin. Now turn the meat back outside in.

To make the stuffing, heat the oils in a small skillet, then add onion. When onion becomes translucent, add chopped mushrooms and simmer until onion begins to brown. Transfer onion-and-mushroom mixture to a mixing bowl and add breadcrumbs, egg whites, pine nuts, cheese, parsley, salt, and pepper. Mix well.

Stuff bottom part of each leg with stuffing. Add salt and pepper, then fold thigh meat over the stuffing. Place in a baking dish so that legs fit snugly, add vermouth, rosemary, and button mushrooms around legs. Cover tightly with foil and bake in a 500° preheated oven about 30 minutes. Remove foil and bake, uncovered, about 10 minutes more, basting occasionally.

Serve with rice and a green vegetable.

Calories	Cholesterol mg	Protein gm	Carbohydrate gm	Total fat gm	%	Sat fat gm	%	Mono gm	Poly gm
1784	652.0	182.4	83.5	80.7	40	17.4	9	34.3	19.3

JOE HIRSHHORN'S CHICKEN FEET DINNER

Joe Hirshhorn had been collecting my work since 1955, but it wasn't until the early 1970s that I met him when he and his wife, Olga, came to our home several times for dinner. Soon we became fast friends.

One day, while having lunch with us in Katonah, Joe lamented the fact that in spite of his wealth he never got an opportunity to eat what he really liked. I asked him what that was, expecting to hear an exotic dish impossible to prepare. His answer was fish heads and chicken feet. I was delighted, because I adore both of them. He went on to say that when he was a child they were so poor that they lived on fish heads and chicken feet because they were free.

I have always preferred the feet to any other part of the chicken, and the sweetest meat on the fish is on and around the head.

I made a mental note about the chicken feet, deciding to start saving them for a dinner for Joe. (I did not know at the time that chicken feet are sold in Chinatown in New York City.) We had our own chickens, so every time we ate one, I saved the feet, cleaned them, and froze them. Finally we had enough for a dinner and we called up Joe and Olga and invited them over.

I decided to make something special with the chicken feet, so I cooked them with wild mushrooms. For a first course I prepared a large striped bass head, poached with herbs and vegetables, and I served it with parsley pesto (page 427).

Joe was delighted, and as all fish head eaters do, he carefully started on one side of the head, meticulously piling the bones in a neat pile on a side of the dish until the entire head was consumed, leaving only a neat mound of bones.

I served him the chicken feet as a second course with rice. He was beside himself with joy. I had a backup course for the ladies (chicken feet can be eaten only with the hands), but we all enjoyed them. The sauce was unusually sweet because of the high gelatin content in the feet and the mushrooms accented it with a smoky, musty flavor.

It was the last time the Hirshhorns had dinner with us in Katonah (they moved the next week to D.C.) and it seemed fitting that it be his favorite childhood food.

CHICKEN FEET WITH MUSHROOM SAUCE

This sauce is also excellent on pasta.

Serves 4.

3 tablespoons olive oil
1 tablespoon safflower oil
1 medium onion, coarsely chopped
1 medium carrot, thinly sliced
1 teaspoon finely chopped garlic
2 cups chopped tomatoes, fresh if possible (drain if canned)
1-ounce package dried boletus mushrooms, soaked in
$\frac{1}{2}$ cup warm water 30 minutes (optional)
12 ounces fresh mushrooms, sliced
2 bay leaves
1 teaspoon crushed rosemary
1 $\frac{1}{2}$ pounds chicken feet*
2 cups chicken broth
Salt and freshly ground black pepper to taste

*Chicken feet are usually sold skinned. If they aren't, plunge them in boiling water and remove outer skin. Cut off toenails and wash.

Heat the oils in a medium saucepan, then add onion and carrots and sauté until onion begins to brown, stirring often. Add garlic and simmer about 30 seconds. Add tomatoes, cover, and boil gently about 15 minutes. Put in a food processor or food mill and purée.

Return the sauce to the saucepan. Add dried mushrooms and their soaking liquid, fresh mushrooms, bay leaves, rosemary, chicken feet, chicken broth, salt, and pepper. Cover and simmer over low to moderate heat about 2 hours.

Serve on rice or mashed potatoes.

Variations: I have added 2 cups blanched fresh peas to this recipe and they are both attractive and tasty.

I have also cooked 1 pound blanched chicken gizzards (remove all fat) with the chicken feet and they seem to complement each other.

Calories	Cholesterol mg	Protein gm	Carbohydrate gm	Total fat gm	%	Sat fat gm	%	Mono gm	Poly gm
847	–	21.3	70.4	57.0	59	5.6	6	32.9	12.5

The nutritional data are for the ingredients other than chicken feet, for which we have no figures.

CHICKEN GIZZARDS WITH EGGPLANT
Regaglie di Pollo con Melanzane

A hearty, economical dish.

Serves 6.

1¾ to 2 pounds chicken gizzards
2 tablespoons olive oil
1 tablespoon safflower oil
1 medium onion, finely chopped
1 teaspoon finely chopped garlic
4 cups chopped tomatoes, fresh if possible (drain if canned)
1 bay leaf
2 tablespoons fresh basil or 1 teaspoon dried
1 tablespoon rosemary
Salt and freshly ground black pepper to taste
2 cups eggplant cut in ½-inch squares
    (about 1 medium eggplant)
½ to 1 cup water or chicken stock

Garnish: Finely chopped Italian parsley

Soak gizzards in cold salted water about 2 hours. Drain and wash, cover with cold water, and boil for 10 minutes. Then drain. In the meantime, heat the oils in a medium shallow pan, then add onion. When it browns, add garlic and cook a minute or so. Add tomatoes, bay leaf, basil, rosemary, salt, and pepper, cover, and boil gently for 10 minutes, mixing occasionally. Add gizzards and eggplant, cover, and boil gently.

After about 30 minutes, add ½ cup water or chicken stock. Continue cooking until gizzards are tender, about 30 to 45 minutes more. Add more water if needed.

Serve on steamed rice (page 160). Garnish with Italian parsley.

Calories	Cholesterol mg	Protein gm	Carbohydrate gm	Total fat gm	%	Sat fat gm	%	Mono gm	Poly gm
1637	1033	160.5	71.8	77.6	42	13.6	7	31.3	21.1

Chicken gizzards, like shrimp and squid, are low in fat content but high in cholesterol. They may be eaten, but they "use up" most of the daily allowance of cholesterol.

ABOUT CAPONS

My first Christmas in Italy, in 1951, was a very pleasurable experience. In those days, it was purely a family religious holiday—no gifts, no last-minute shopping, no tree ornaments, absolutely no commercialism—and I found it most refreshing.

I was fascinated with one custom. My uncle, who was the mayor of the small town we lived in, was also a building contractor; he had many friends and was well loved. It seemed that most of his friends and admirers gave him a capon at Christmas. I recall at least 30 live capons in all kinds of cages scattered about the backyard several days before Christmas. He, in turn, would give a live capon to a friend or business associate, and so it went. Some of the capons looked rather haggard, and I'm certain they had been in circulation about a week. When Christmas finally arrived, there were about 3 capons left, the others continuing their journey until their final Christmas Day fate.

At home, my own family prefers capon to turkey. I personally don't think there is any comparison between the two. As a matter of fact, I'm quite certain that once you taste capon you will lose interest in turkey.

STUFFED CAPON
Cappone Ripieno

Serves 8.

9-pound fresh capon
3 cloves garlic, slivered
2 tablespoons rosemary

The stuffing
2 tablespoons safflower oil
1 medium onion, finely chopped
1-ounce package dried boletus mushrooms, soaked
    in warm water 30 minutes, or 2 cups sliced
    fresh mushrooms
2 tablespoons yellow raisins, soaked 20 minutes and drained
4 tablespoons chopped walnuts
2 cups fresh breadcrumbs
3 egg whites, lightly beaten
1 teaspoon marjoram
2 tablespoons grated Parmesan cheese
1/4 cup finely chopped Italian parsley
Salt and freshly ground black pepper to taste

1 cup dry white wine

Wash and dry capon. Slip garlic slivers under skin over breasts and force in some of the rosemary.

To make the stuffing, heat the oil in a small skillet, add onion, and fresh mushrooms if they are used. Cook over medium to high heat, uncovered, until onion begins to brown.

If using dried mushrooms, drain and coarsely chop, then mix together with the rest of the ingredients except the wine. Add onion. Stuff the capon; if the stuffing does not all fit in the cavity, fill the area in the neck and sew skin to secure it.

Preheat oven to 450°. Place bird on a rack in a roasting pan and pour white wine and 1 cup water around it. Salt and pepper the bird and rub with more rosemary. Roast, uncovered, until bird begins to brown, basting occasionally. Lower heat to 350°, cover with foil, and continue to roast for a total of about 2 hours, adding more wine as needed.

Let capon rest at least 15 minutes before serving it.

Calories	Cholesterol mg	Protein gm	Carbohydrate gm	Total fat gm	%	Sat fat gm	%	Mono gm	Poly gm
3094	1281.0	394.1	120.1	108.2	31	21.9	6	27.4	44.2

ROAST TURKEY
Tacchino Arrosto Ripieno

Serves about 12.

The stuffing
24 fresh chestnuts
1½ tablespoons olive oil
1½ tablespoons safflower oil
3 cups finely chopped onion
1 pound mushrooms, thinly sliced
Salt and freshly ground black pepper to taste
3 cups fresh breadcrumbs
4 egg whites, lightly beaten
1 teaspoon grated nutmeg
1 cup finely chopped Italian parsley
4 tablespoons port wine

24-pound fresh turkey
4 cloves garlic, slivered
2 tablespoons rosemary
Salt and freshly ground black pepper to taste
About 4 cups dry white wine

To make the stuffing: First prepare the chestnuts. Make a slit in the shells and boil for 10 minutes. While still hot, remove shell and skin, then purée chestnuts in a food mill or food processor.

Heat the oils in a large skillet, then add onion, mushrooms, salt, and pepper, and cook over high heat until onion begins to brown. Then mix with all the remaining stuffing ingredients and set aside.

Fill the turkey cavity with the stuffing. Force the garlic slivers and some rosemary under the skin over breasts, sew skin over cavity, truss, and rub turkey all over with salt and pepper and rosemary. Place on a rack in a roasting pan with 2 cups wine and 2 cups water.

Cover and bake in a preheated 450° oven for 1 hour, until turkey is a golden brown, basting occasionally and adding more wine as is needed. Turn oven down to 350°. After 2 hours, wrap legs in foil so they don't dry out, and continue cooking, basting, for a total of 4 hours. Cover with foil, place roasting pan lid over foil, and cook 1 more hour, basting often.

Let rest about 1 hour before serving. Remove all fat from pan juices and serve clear defatted pan juices with the turkey.

Calories	Cholesterol mg	Protein gm	Carbohydrate gm	Total fat gm	%	Sat fat gm	%	Mono gm	Poly gm
9691	4537.0	1535.2	233.9	245.3	22	69.1	6	59.9	72.5

Turkey, being holiday fare, is provided in bountiful amount. It would not be unusual for a hostess to serve a 24-pound bird to 12 diners, but there would be leftovers for at least another 6 servings. Each of the 18 servings would be about 10 ounces of cooked meat, containing 252 milligrams of cholesterol.

TURKEY BREASTS NERO STYLE
Filetti di Tacchino alla Nerone

I must say, turkey breasts are not my favorite food, but they are economical and relatively low in fat and cholesterol, so, done this way, they are nice for a change.

Serves 3 to 4.

1 tablespoon butter
2 tablespoons safflower oil
16 asparagus, washed and cut into 2-inch lengths
Salt and freshly ground black pepper to taste
1¼ pounds flattened turkey breast slices,
    about 6 to 7 slices
1 egg white, lightly beaten
1 cup fresh breadcrumbs
4 bay leaves
2 tablespoons chopped shallots
4 tablespoons brandy

Heat the butter and 1 tablespoon of the oil in a large skillet, then sauté asparagus over moderate heat 5 minutes. Remove from pan and reserve.

Salt and pepper the turkey slices, dip in the egg white, then roll in breadcrumbs. In the skillet used for the asparagus, heat remaining 1 tablespoon oil and add bay leaves and turkey slices. Cook over high heat, several minutes on each side, until slices are lightly brown. Add asparagus, shallots, and brandy; then cover and lower heat. After a minute turn breasts over, cover, and cook an additional minute, until brandy cooks out.

Calories	Cholesterol mg	Protein gm	Carbohydrate gm	Total fat gm	%	Sat fat gm	%	Mono gm	Poly gm
1304	373.0	155.7	53.6	50.2	34	11.6	8	8.7	22.8

TURKEY BREASTS WITH MARSALA WINE
Filetti di Tacchino al Marsala

Here turkey breasts are used as a substitute for veal. They are good with potato loaf (page 371) and a green salad.

Serves 4.

1 tablespoon olive oil
1 tablespoon safflower oil
7 slices fresh turkey breast, about 1 1/2 pounds
Salt and freshly ground black pepper to taste
Flour for dredging
1 tablespoon finely chopped shallots
1/4 cup imported sweet marsala or sweet sherry

Garnish: 2 tablespoons finely chopped Italian parsley

Heat the oils in a skillet large enough to hold all the turkey slices in one layer. Salt and pepper turkey, then lightly dust with flour, and place in the hot oil. Cook over high heat, turning constantly, until the slices begin to brown. Add shallots and continue cooking until they begin to get translucent. Add marsala, cover, and lower heat. Cook until most of the marsala cooks out and the sauce thickens; turn turkey slices over occasionally. Serve immediately, garnished with parsley.

Calories	Cholesterol mg	Protein gm	Carbohydrate gm	Total fat gm	%	Sat fat gm	%	Mono gm	Poly gm
1111	408.0	162.5	20.6	38.2	30	6.4	5	13.5	13.9

TURKEY WING STEW
Ali di Tacchino in Umido

An economical dish that is most satisfying during the winter months.

Serves 4.

4 turkey wings
1 large onion, cut into 4 sections

2 cups chopped tomatoes, fresh if possible (drain if canned)
1 tablespoon crushed rosemary
1 cup dry white wine
4 stalks tender celery, about 3 inches long
3 cloves garlic, skins on
Salt and freshly ground black pepper or hot pepper flakes
   to taste
3 bay leaves
2 medium parsnips, peeled and cut in half
4 medium potatoes, peeled and cut in half
1 medium green pepper, cut into 1-inch-wide slices
1/3 cup water

Place turkey wings in a skillet or shallow saucepan with onion, tomatoes, rosemary, wine, celery, garlic, salt, pepper, and bay leaves. Cover and simmer over low heat about 1 hour. Add parsnips, potatoes, peppers, and water. Partially cover and cook about 1 more hour. Add more water if needed — sauce should be loose but not too much so.

Calories	Cholesterol mg	Protein gm	Carbohydrate gm	Total fat gm	%	Sat fat gm	%	Mono gm	Poly gm
691	108.0	56.7	105.3	5.1	6	0.9	1	0.5	0.8

SQUAB IN A CASSEROLE
Torresani in Tecia

This is very good with rice, potatoes, or a simple vegetable such as cabbage and potatoes and scallions.

Serves 2.

2 squab, split and washed
Salt and freshly ground black pepper to taste
2 tablespoons olive oil
1 tablespoon safflower oil
1 stalk celery, finely chopped
1 small carrot, finely chopped
1 small onion, finely chopped
1/2 cup dry white wine
1 clove garlic, finely chopped
1 cup chicken broth
1/2 teaspoon cinnamon
1 bay leaf
1 tablespoon minced Italian parsley
1 cup fresh or frozen green peas, blanched and drained

Salt and pepper the squab on both sides. Heat oils in a skillet large enough to hold squab, then brown birds over medium to high heat. When squab are brown on both sides, add celery, carrot, and onion and simmer, uncovered, until onion wilts. Add wine and garlic, cover, and simmer over medium heat until wine cooks out. Add broth, cinnamon, bay leaf, parsley, and peas, cover partially, and simmer over medium heat until sauce thickens and birds are tender—about 30 minutes.

Calories	Cholesterol mg	Protein gm	Carbohydrate gm	Total fat gm	%	Sat fat gm	%	Mono gm	Poly gm
1010	302.0	69.3	30.2	66.4	58	11.4	10	30.3	17.7

STUFFED SQUAB WITH PEAS
Piccione Ripieno

*Serves 3 to 6.**

The stuffing
2 teaspoons safflower oil
1 small onion, finely chopped
¼ pound mushrooms
1 tablespoon finely chopped Italian parsley
½ pound ground lean veal
Salt and freshly ground black pepper to taste
3 tablespoons sweet marsala or sherry
2 teaspoons yellow raisins, soaked in warm water for
    15 minutes and drained
4 tablespoons fresh breadcrumbs

3 squab
Dry white wine
1 teaspoon rosemary
Salt and freshly ground black pepper to taste
2 cups sliced mushrooms
1 tablespoon chopped shallots
2 cups fresh peas, blanched, or 10-ounce package frozen
    peas, blanched for 2 minutes
2 tablespoons chopped Italian parsley

*We have found half a squab is sufficient for a moderate eater.

To make the stuffing: Heat the oil in a small skillet, then add onion, mushrooms, and parsley. As onion begins to brown, add veal. Cook, uncovered, over high heat, stirring often. Add salt and pepper. When veal takes on color, add the marsala, cover, lower heat, and cook until liquid cooks out. Pour mixture into a bowl along with the raisins, breadcrumbs, and a little more salt and pepper. Mix well.

Wash and dry squab, stuff with mixture, and truss. Place them in a baking dish so that they fit snugly. Pour about 1/2 inch dry white wine and 1/2 cup water on the bottom of the tray.

Preheat oven to 500°. Sprinkle rosemary on the squab and salt and pepper them. Roast, uncovered, about 30 minutes, basting often and turning squab over when breasts have browned.

Remove squab and keep warm. Sprinkle mushrooms and shallots on the bottom of the baking dish and return it to the oven to cook, uncovered, about 8 to 10 minutes. Add drained peas, parsley, and the squab, cover with foil, lower heat to 350°, and roast about 15 minutes.

Calories	Cholesterol mg	Protein gm	Carbohydrate gm	Total fat gm	%	Sat fat gm	%	Mono gm	Poly gm
1496	615.0	161.3	64.2	60.5	36	16.2	10	19.4	15.1

SQUAB BAKED IN BREAD
Piccione in Pane

Serves 4 to 8.

1 tablespoon dry yeast
4 cups warm water
3 cups whole wheat flour
About 6 cups all-purpose flour
1 tablespoon salt
About 2 tablespoons vegetable oil
1 tablespoon rosemary
4 squab, washed and dried
Salt and freshly ground black pepper to taste
2 cloves garlic, sliced
3/4 cup sweet marsala

Mix yeast with water and let mixture stand about 15 minutes.

Pour the whole wheat flour and 3 cups of the all-purpose flour into a large bowl. Add salt and yeast water and stir with a wooden spoon until blended. Turn dough mixture out onto a floured board and knead, adding more all-purpose flour as needed. Knead until dough has a satin finish — about 8 to 10 minutes.

Clean and oil the bowl with about 1/2 tablespoon of the oil. Roll the ball of dough in it so that it is coated with oil, cover, and let it rise to double its bulk (about 2 hours).

Put some rosemary leaves inside the squab, along with salt, pepper, and garlic. Truss the birds.

Preheat oven to 450°. Place squab in a baking dish, pour 1 tablespoon vegetable oil over them, cover, and roast about 15 minutes. Add the marsala, cover, and roast 10 more minutes. Remove from oven. Drain off pan juices for use later.

Cut the dough into four pieces. Roll out a section large enough to encompass 1 squab on a floured board. Place squab in center of dough, fold sides over, and press overlapping ends together. Cut off excess and place in a lightly oiled pan. Prepare remaining squab in the same way. (Extra dough may be made into a loaf of bread.)

Return squab to oven and bake until bread is lightly brown—about 20 minutes.

Split loaves open and remove squab. Place bread casings under broiler and toast to dry out moist insides and serve with squab.

Remove fat from pan juices and heat till hot. Garnish squab with defatted pan juices.

Calories	Cholesterol mg	Protein gm	Carbohydrate gm	Total fat gm	%	Sat fat gm	%	Mono gm	Poly gm
4009	642.0	217.8	637.2	66.7	15	13.6	3	19.3	14.1

It is unlikely that all the bread would be eaten, thus reducing the calories but raising the percentages of total and saturated fat.

SQUAB SALAD
Insalata di Piccioncini

Pierre Franey gave me this recipe when I was visiting him in East Hampton in August 1982. You will find the dish tender and delicate if prepared properly. It is particularly good served with risotto country style (page 152).

Serves 4.

4 squab, split
1 teaspoon rosemary
1 teaspoon coarsely chopped garlic
Salt and freshly ground black pepper to taste
Interesting and colorful lettuce, such as Boston, Bibb,
    rucola (arugola), endive, radicchio
Cherry or plum tomatoes, cut in half

The dressing
1/2 cup wine vinegar
1/4 cup oil (2 teaspoons olive oil,
    1 teaspoon safflower oil)
1 teaspoon good imported mustard
Salt and freshly ground black pepper to taste
1 teaspoon finely chopped shallots

Preheat broiler. Wash split squab and pat dry. Place them skin side down on a baking tray and sprinkle with rosemary, garlic, salt, and pepper. Broil close to heat about 4 to 5 minutes. Turn squab over, add more salt and pepper, and broil close to heat another 5 minutes—the squab should be medium rare. Let them cool, then remove wings and thighs at joints and reserve. With a sharp knife remove breast from bone and slice on the bias. Reserve.

Toss the lettuce and tomatoes with a very little dressing. Salt and pepper the squab to taste. Arrange the greens and tomatoes in a graceful pattern in individual plates. Place the breast slices of 1 squab on bed of lettuce in the center of a plate. Arrange legs at bottom, wings at top, butterfly fashion. Pour some of the dressing over breast slices. Repeat with the other plates.

Serve meat at room temperature.

Calories	Cholesterol mg	Protein gm	Carbohydrate gm	Total fat gm	%	Sat fat gm	%	Mono gm	Poly gm
1300	657.0	122.7	24.4	78.7	53	16.4	11	32.2	19.0

TEAL MY WAY
Anitra a Modo Mio

Teal are very succulent small (about 1 pound) wild ducks that have practically no fat.

Serves 4.

The marinade
3 cloves garlic, crushed
1 bay leaf
Juice of 2 lemons
Salt and freshly ground black pepper to taste

4 plump teal, plucked and washed
   (discard head and feet)
1 tablespoon rosemary
2 tablespoons safflower oil
1-ounce package dried boletus mushrooms, soaked in
   warm water 30 minutes
1 cup dry white wine
3 cloves garlic, sliced
1 cup chopped tomatoes, fresh if possible (drain if canned)
2 tablespoons chopped fresh mint or 1 teaspoon dried

Combine ingredients for the marinade in a small container, add teal, and marinate in the refrigerator for 24 hours.

Remove teal from marinade, place in a small ovenproof pot so that they fit snugly, and add the rosemary and safflower oil.

Preheat oven to 450°. Roast the teal, uncovered, about 20 minutes. Drain off all fat and oil and discard. Add the wine, garlic, mushrooms, and their liquid. Cover and return to oven. Lower heat to 400° and bake until wine cooks out — about 20 minutes. Add the tomatoes and mint. Cover and roast an additional 20 minutes.

Serve on garlic toast (page 39) or with plain rice or potatoes.

Calories	Cholesterol mg	Protein gm	Carbohydrate gm	Total fat gm	%	Sat fat gm	%	Mono gm	Poly gm
1809	872.0	226.1	53.4	75.6	37	16.6	8	16.3	26.7

BROILED DUCK BREASTS
Petti di Anitra alla Griglia

Serves 2.

1 teaspoon safflower oil
1 teaspoon olive oil
Salt and freshly ground black pepper to taste
Dash rosemary
2 duck breasts, boned and skinned

Garnish: Lemon wedges

Preheat broiler for 10 minutes. Rub oils, salt, pepper, and rosemary on duck breasts.

Broil breasts about 3 minutes on each side. Slice them thinly on the bias. Serve with either lemon wedges or one of the sauces in Chapter X, *Sauces,* such as one of the honey sauces (pages 429–30).

Calories	Cholesterol mg	Protein gm	Carbohydrate gm	Total fat gm	%	Sat fat gm	%	Mono gm	Poly gm
679	368	83.1	0	36.0	47	11.4		11.7	7.0

PHEASANT WITH MARSALA, BRANDY, AND MUSHROOMS
Fagiano al Marsala

While strolling through Chinatown in New York several months ago I saw a man in a meat market plucking something that looked like a chicken. It had no head, so I asked him what it was—I knew it wasn't chicken. He knew very little English, and replied, "Wild chicken." I asked him if he had one with the feathers still on and he pulled out a large chest with about a dozen live pheasants in it. I bought one—and it was tough because I didn't hang it, but it was tasty. The pheasants you buy in meat markets, however, have always been properly hung.

Serves 4.

1 fat pheasant
Flour for dredging
3 tablespoons safflower oil
2 cloves garlic, skins on

1 tablespoon olive oil
2 tablespoons finely chopped shallots
1/2 cup dry imported marsala, Florio brand
1 teaspoon thyme
2 cups sliced fresh mushrooms, or 1 cup dried boletus
    mushrooms, soaked in warm water at least
    15 minutes
Salt and freshly ground black pepper to taste
Chicken broth (optional)
1/2 cup brandy

Garnish: 3 tablespoons finely chopped Italian parsley

Cut pheasant into serving pieces and dust with flour. Heat safflower oil in a large skillet, add pheasant, and cook, turning the pieces constantly. Add garlic, and continue to turn each piece every 3 or 4 minutes, cooking until light brown. Drain off all oil and fat. Add olive oil, then shallots, and sauté several minutes. Add marsala, thyme, mushrooms (plus soaking water if dried mushrooms are used), salt, and pepper, cover, and simmer over low heat until wine cooks out, turning pieces of pheasant occasionally. If pheasant is not tender at this point, add a little chicken broth and continue cooking 10 more minutes. Add brandy, cover, and cook over medium heat until brandy cooks out. Discard garlic and serve garnished with parsley.

Variation: Add 2 cups chopped tomatoes after adding the shallots while cooking the pheasant.

Calories	Cholesterol mg	Protein gm	Carbohydrate gm	Total fat gm	%	Sat fat gm	%	Mono gm	Poly gm
2322	1078.0	273.9	38.3	112.2	43	26.8	10	38.3	31.3

GUINEA HEN COOKED IN RED WINE
Farona al Vino Rosso

Serves 4.

1 tender guinea hen, cut into serving pieces
Salt and freshly ground black pepper to taste
Flour for dredging
3 tablespoons plus 2 teaspoons safflower oil
1 cup finely chopped onion
About 1 quart good red wine
2 tablespoons grappa or aquavit
1/2 teaspoon nutmeg
1 bay leaf
2 teaspoons butter
1-ounce package dried boletus mushrooms, soaked in
    warm water to cover for 15 minutes

Salt and pepper the guinea hen, then lightly dust with flour. Heat 3 table-spoons of the oil in a large skillet and lightly brown guinea hen on all sides. Add onion and cook, uncovered, until it begins to brown. Add about 2 cups wine and boil for several minutes. Then transfer to a casserole. Add the rest of the wine, and the grappa, nutmeg, and bay leaf.

Preheat oven to 450°. Cover and bake, covered, about 1 hour, until hen is tender.

Remove guinea hen with a pair of tongs and keep warm. In a medium skillet heat butter and remaining 2 teaspoons safflower oil, then add cooking sauce and soaked mushrooms with their liquid. Cover and simmer over low heat for 10 minutes.

Place guinea hen on a heated platter. Pour the sauce on top and serve immediately. It is excellent with rice or polenta.

Variation: Pheasant is also good prepared this way.

Calories	Cholesterol mg	Protein gm	Carbohydrate gm	Total fat gm	%	Sat fat gm	%	Mono gm	Poly gm
1449	466.0	123.3	74.2	82.1	50	8.8	5	10.8	36.3

CORNISH HENS WITH PEAS

Serves 4 to 8.

The stuffing
2 tablespoons safflower oil
1 cup finely chopped onion
2 cups chopped mushrooms
2 tablespoons sherry
1 cup freshly made breadcrumbs (about 4 slices
    toasted bread)
Salt and freshly ground black pepper to taste
2 tablespoons yellow raisins
1 teaspoon thyme
1 egg white, lightly beaten

4 Cornish hens
1 cup dry white wine
1 tablespoon rosemary
Salt and freshly ground black pepper to taste
1 medium onion, finely chopped
2 tablespoons safflower oil
2 cups chopped tomatoes, fresh if possible
    (drain if canned)
1 cup peas, preferably fresh

Preheat oven to 450°, and prepare the stuffing: Heat the oil in a small skillet and add the onion and mushrooms. Sauté until onion begins to brown, then remove to a bowl and sprinkle a little sherry over. Add the breadcrumbs, salt, pepper, raisins, thyme, and egg white and mix well. Stuff the birds with this mixture and truss them. Place in a shallow baking dish so that they fit snugly. Add wine, 1/4 cup water, rosemary, salt, and pepper. Bake, uncovered, about 1 hour.

In the meantime, sauté the finely chopped onion in the safflower oil until translucent. Add the tomatoes. Boil peas in water about 2 minutes. Drain, then add to tomatoes and onion, and cook several minutes.

Drain all fat from pan containing Cornish hens. Add tomatoes and peas. Cook, uncovered, 15 to 20 minutes.

Calories	Cholesterol mg	Protein gm	Carbohydrate gm	Total fat gm	%	Sat fat gm	%	Mono gm	Poly gm
2428	850.0	268.6	113.8	94.5	34	16.6	6	20.6	53.5

VII   MEATS

From the start we hadn't planned to include many beef recipes in this book, because it is high in saturated fat, it is expensive, particularly when you consider the amount of waste, and I find that it is the most inflexible of meats as well as being rather boring in taste. I think the more you eat well-balanced meals of pasta, soups, vegetables, and fish, the less you will crave red meat, and then, when you do eat red meat, you will need much less of it to satisfy you. Therefore, we have included here only a small selection of beef recipes, all using lean cuts.

Veal, on the other hand, is much subtler in taste and texture than beef and it is extremely versatile. It contains less saturated fat than beef, though more cholesterol, because it is the meat of a growing animal. But it is always served in small portions, and it can be prepared in countless ways to suit your needs—from a light, thin scallopini to a rolled stuffed breast. Because of its adaptability I find it a most interesting meat.

One of the problems with veal, however, is that many butchers, especially in supermarkets, do not take the trouble to separate the individual muscles—in the leg, for instance—and clean each muscle before slicing against the grain; they simply slice through everything, leaving the nerves, tendons, and gristle in the meat. A good butcher will cut veal properly, but don't expect that to happen in a supermarket, where they just don't have the time and more often than not don't care. So if you wish to enjoy good veal, I suggest you find a good butcher. If it costs a little more, just buy less.

Because lamb and pork both have a high fat content, we haven't used them often in the recipes in this chapter, and when pork is suggested only the lean cuts are recommended. But I don't think you will mourn the loss of these meats when there are so many other options to choose from.

All meats, to a lesser extent most poultry, and even many fish contain more saturated than polyunsaturated fat. When any of these foods is included in the diet, the requirement that there be at least as much polyunsaturated as saturated fat in a day's intake can be satisfied only by providing other foods—usually in the form of polyunsaturated oil—in which there is an excess of polyunsaturated over saturated fat. The amount of saturated fat in need of "neutralization" is greatest for fatty cuts of red meats. The larger the excess of polyunsaturated over saturated fatty acids in the oil you select, the less of that oil you will have to use, thus minimizing the total of calories derived from fat.

There are a number of different ways the neutralizing oil can be added to the diet. It can be part of the same recipe as the meat, poultry, or fish; it can be part of another dish in the same meal; or it can be included in another meal on the same day.

It is important that you bear in mind when you are planning meals that the lower the fat content of ingredients such as meat, poultry, and fish, and the less the excess of saturated over polyunsaturated fat, the more flexibility you allow yourself; and the more polyunsaturated the oil you use, the less of your permitted fat calories you use. R.W.

BOILED BEEF
Boeuf Saignant à la Ficelle

Boiling happens to be my favorite way of cooking beef.

In spite of my enthusiasm, however, I felt grossly inadequate writing about boiled beef, especially after reading Joseph Wechsberg's description in his delightful book *Blue Trout and Black Truffles* of the preparing and serving of boiled beef at the famed Meissl and Schadn restaurant in Vienna. I have never read such a loving, sensual description of the preparing and serving of boiled beef. The ritualistic care taken — from the feeding of the beef, the butchering of the individual cuts — and finally the preparation and serving of a particular cut of beef were delightfully and informatively portrayed.

Italian boiled meat dinners are called bollito misto (mixed boiled) and include a variety of meats, including chicken (usually a young rooster), veal, and usually parts from the head of the calf, beef, cotechino (sausage), all of which are usually served with a variety of sauces. Salsa verde is the most commonly used. Bollito misto is sometimes served with mustarda, a combination of candied fruit that is excellent with boiled meats.

Serves 6 to 8.

Vegetables (use 2 or 3 of the following):
6 to 8 medium carrots, trimmed and scraped
6 to 8 medium boiling potatoes, peeled
6 to 8 leeks, washed and trimmed
6 to 8 medium parsnips, trimmed and scraped
6 to 8 medium onions, trimmed and peeled
1 quart Brussels sprouts, trimmed
4 to 6 quarts good beef broth, strained
1 whole filet mignon, fat removed and tied as for rolled
   roast, with a 12-inch length of string at each end
Sauce (see suggestions at end of recipe)

Using a pot that will accommodate the filet, cook the vegetables in the boiling beef broth until tender, putting in those that take the longest time first, such as onions and potatoes together, then carrots and parsnips, and last, leeks and Brussels sprouts. Remove vegetables when cooked and keep warm. Lower the filet into the boiling broth, leaving the long pieces of string at the ends to hang outside the pot. Cook about 20 minutes for medium-rare meat, then lift the filet out of the broth with the strings. Remove strings and keep meat warm while you serve the broth as a first course. Reheat the vegetables in the remaining broth, slice the filet 3/4 inch thick (you should have 10 to 12 slices), and arrange the vegetables on a warm platter around the sliced meat in an attractive way. Serve with hot pepper sauce II (page 438), or nut sauce III (page 436), or mustard sauce (page 434), or green sauce Genoa style (page 429).

Calories	Cholesterol mg	Protein gm	Carbohydrate gm	Total fat gm	%	Sat fat gm	%	Mono gm	Poly gm
4359	925.0	384.6	499.6	83.1	17	35.4	7	32.6	1.4

Although the amount of beef is more than the usual recommended serving, it is very lean beef and the necessary adjustments to the rest of the diet are readily made.

BOILED BEEF WITH BEEF SOUP
Bollito di Manzo

Aside from boeuf saignant à la ficelle, my favorite boiled beef is beef shank. One of the reasons I enjoy it is that, because of its highly gelatinous content, the shank remains moist. Beef shank comes in various widths because of the construction of the lower leg; try to buy the upper cut, which has less bone and more meat.

Serves 4.

4 quarts water
1 1/2 pounds beef shank
2 pounds beef bones
2 medium to large carrots, scraped and split in half*
2 medium onions, peeled*
2 bay leaves
2 stalks celery, cut into 2-inch lengths
2 large parsnips, scraped
Salt and freshly ground black pepper to taste

*Turnips, leeks, and potatoes can also be used.

Put the water and beef shank in a large pot, cover, and boil 30 minutes, skimming off the foam from the surface every so often. Add the remaining ingredients, using only a little salt at this stage, and boil gently for 1 1/2 hours. Pour off the broth and remove all fat from it. Keep the meat and vegetables warm while you serve the broth either plain (correct seasoning) or with rice or capellini pasta with a touch of lemon juice. Then serve the meat and vegetables with green sauce (page 428), or a hot pepper sauce.

Calories	Cholesterol mg	Protein gm	Carbohydrate gm	Total fat gm	%	Sat fat gm	%	Mono gm	Poly gm
1141	347.0	124.0	94.5	25.9	20	11.3	9	10.2	0.5

BEEF ON A SKEWER
Manzo allo Spiedo

Serves 2.

1 pound good lean beef, cut into 1 1/2-inch squares (top of
   the round or flank steak)
1 tablespoon chopped fresh ginger
1 teaspoon soy sauce
1 teaspoon minced garlic
Juice of 1/2 lime
Freshly ground black pepper to taste
1 tablespoon peanut oil
6 small white onions
1 green pepper, cut in wide slices

Combine all ingredients except onions and peppers in a mixing bowl and marinate at least 3 hours.

Blanch the onions and pepper slices. Drain and let cool.

On two skewers spear a piece of beef, a slice of green pepper, then an onion. Repeat.

Preheat broiler about 15 minutes or, better still, prepare a bed of coals. Broil or grill, turning skewers occasionally, about 15 minutes under the broiler, or about 4 minutes on each side over coals.

Serve with bruschetta II (page 39) and baked eggplant (page 358).

Calories	Cholesterol mg	Protein gm	Carbohydrate gm	Total fat gm	%	Sat fat gm	%	Mono gm	Poly gm
896	394.0	103.6	24.6	39.8	39	14.7	14	17.6	4.8

GRILLED PEPPER STEAK
Bistecca di Manzo al Ferri

We suggest you serve with this pepper steak a tossed green salad or a rucola salad made with a dressing of 2 tablespoons safflower oil, 1 teaspoon wine vinegar, and salt and pepper to taste to offset the cholesterol in the beef.

Serves 2.

2 cloves garlic, finely chopped
1 teaspoon crushed rosemary
2 teaspoons safflower oil
Salt and freshly ground black pepper to taste
1/2 pound top round pepper steak*

Garnish: Lemon wedges

*Some butchers carry pepper steak already cut. To prepare it yourself, take a 1/2-pound slice top round of beef about 3/8 to 1/2 inch thick and cut into strips about 1 1/2 inches wide and 2 inches long.

Mix the garlic, rosemary, oil, a good pinch of salt, and several grinds of pepper together in a bowl; then add the steak, turning it in the marinade, and marinate for at least 2 hours.

Put the steak pieces into a basket grill and grill over hot coals about 1 1/2 minutes on each side. Serve immediately on hot plates with lemon wedges.

Calories	Cholesterol mg	Protein gm	Carbohydrate gm	Total fat gm	%	Sat fat gm	%	Mono gm	Poly gm
447	154.0	45.8	0	27.9	55	13.4	26	12.3	0.5

GRILLED FLANK STEAK
WITH WHITE BEANS
Bistecca di Manzo con Fagioli

The classic Florentine combination of grilled steak and beans is a well-known gastronomic delight—traditionally, a Porterhouse steak (Florentine cut) is grilled over coals, then salted and peppered and served with lemon wedges. The beans accompanying it are "fagioli al fiasco," but the bean recipe on page 346 will be fine. This is a delightful combination, which I enjoyed many times in Florence as a student in the early 1950s. Whenever an American friend invited me to dinner in those days, we would go to either Camilio's or Sabatini's to enjoy bistecca Fiorentina with fagioli al fiasco.

Serves 4.

2 tablespoons safflower oil
1 teaspoon good mustard
2 cloves garlic, coarsely chopped
1 teaspoon marjoram
Salt and freshly ground black pepper to taste
Juice of 1 lemon

1 flank steak, about 1¼ pounds
2 cups white beans, prepared according to recipe on
page 346

Mix all ingredients together except steak and beans. Put steak in a deep bowl and cover with the marinade; let it marinate for at least 2 hours, turning it once or twice. Spread half the marinade over one side of the steak, salt and pepper it, and grill over hot coals or under a preheated broiler about 4 minutes. Turn, spread on remaining marinade, plus salt and pepper, and grill another 4 minutes. Allow meat to rest for 5 minutes or more before serving. Cut in thin slices diagonally against the grain.

Calories	Cholesterol mg	Protein gm	Carbohydrate gm	Total fat gm	%	Sat fat gm	%	Mono gm	Poly gm
1142	296.0	104.3	85.6	62.5	48	13.5	10	21.7	21.7

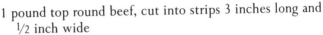

BEEF WITH SNOW PEAS

Serves 4 to 6.

1 pound top round beef, cut into strips 3 inches long and
½ inch wide
1 teaspoon minced garlic
Juice of 1 lime
1 tablespoon minced fresh ginger
Salt and freshly ground black pepper to taste
4 tablespoons safflower oil
4 cups snow pea pods
2 tablespoons minced Italian parsley or fresh coriander
1 cup thinly sliced scallions

Put the beef in a bowl with the garlic, lime juice, ginger, salt, and pepper and let it marinate for several hours.

Heat 3 tablespoons of the oil in a wide skillet, then add snow peas. Cook over high heat for several minutes, tossing. Remove peas from oil with a slotted spoon and reserve. Heat remaining 1 tablespoon oil in the same skillet. Add beef and cook over very high heat for several minutes, stirring often. Add the snow peas, parsley, and scallions and cook over high heat, tossing constantly, for another minute.

Calories	Cholesterol mg	Protein gm	Carbohydrate gm	Total fat gm	%	Sat fat gm	%	Mono gm	Poly gm
1409	309.0	109.1	95.0	72.5	45	12.2	8	15.2	39.5

BRAISED BEEF
Stracotto

Stracotto, which means "overcooked," is quite popular in Italy, from Florence north to Milan. There are many variations of this recipe. Basically, it is made with a piece of tough beef, chopped carrots, celery, onions, sometimes tomatoes, and usually a robust red wine and garlic. The meat is cooked very slowly—much like a pot roast—and, if possible, simmered in a terracotta pot from 4 to 6 hours. Since our beef is tenderer than Italian beef, 3 to 4 hours of cooking will do. The original recipe calls for pork fat and olive oil. I used safflower oil instead, to get a proper balance of polyunsaturated and saturated fats, and I think you will find the results more than satisfactory. Serve the dish with boiled potatoes.

Serves 8.

3-pound chuck or rump roast, properly tied
3 cloves garlic, slivered
Salt and freshly ground black pepper to taste
1/3 cup safflower oil
2 medium onions, coarsely chopped
2 stalks celery, coarsely chopped
2 carrots, coarsely chopped
1 cup robust red wine
2 tablespoons tomato paste
1 cup seeded, chopped tomatoes
1-ounce package dried boletus mushrooms, soaked in
   warm water for 15 minutes
2 tablespoons chopped Italian parsley

Stuff slivers of garlic into meat with some coarsely ground black pepper. Rub surface of meat with salt and pepper. Heat 2 tablespoons of the oil in a pot that will hold the meat snugly, then brown the meat on all sides over high heat. Add onions, and when they wilt, add celery and carrots and cook about 5 minutes. Add wine, cover, lower heat, and simmer until half the wine cooks out. Add tomato paste, tomatoes, mushrooms and their liquid, and parsley. Cover tightly, and simmer over as low heat as possible (liquid should just bubble) for about 4 hours. Remove meat, defat the sauce, and then blend it in a food processor or pass through a food mill. Cut meat into 1/2-inch slices and serve with the sauce.

Calories	Cholesterol mg	Protein gm	Carbohydrate gm	Total fat gm	%	Sat fat gm	%	Mono gm	Poly gm
2868	1182.0	310.0	92.6	134.5	41	39.7	12	41.7	43.6

BEEF IN WINE
Manzo al Vino

We like this recipe with bruschetta (Roman garlic bread).

Serves 5.

1 pound top round beef, cut into large chunks

The marinade
2 carrots, finely chopped
2 stalks celery, finely chopped
1 large onion, finely chopped
4 cups good robust dry red wine

1 tablespoon plus 1 teaspoon safflower oil
2 cloves garlic, chopped
1 cup seeded, chopped tomatoes
1 teaspoon tomato paste
Dash nutmeg
1 teaspoon arrowroot
3 medium potatoes, peeled and cut into 2 or 3 sections

Marinate the meat in the wine marinade for 3 days, turning occasionally. Remove beef from marinade, drain, and pat dry. Heat the oil in a medium saucepan and brown the meat over high heat. Add garlic, cook a minute more, then add the marinade with its vegetables and cook over medium to high heat until about two thirds of the liquid cooks out. Add tomatoes, tomato paste, nutmeg, and enough water to cover meat. Simmer over very low heat about 2 hours. Stir in arrowroot and potatoes, and cook slowly an additional hour, until potatoes are tender.

Calories	Cholesterol mg	Protein gm	Carbohydrate gm	Total fat gm	%	Sat fat gm	%	Mono gm	Poly gm
1534	394.0	117.8	168.2	41.0	24	11.8	7	11.5	13.9

STUFFED BEEF CUTLETS
Braciolette Ripiene

Serves 4.

4 beef cutlets from top of the round, pounded thin
Salt and freshly ground black pepper to taste
4 tablespoons minced Italian parsley
4 tablespoons chopped pine nuts
8 tablespoons yellow raisins, presoaked in warm water
1 1/2 tablespoons safflower oil
1 tablespoon butter
3/4 cup good dry sherry

Season cutlet with salt and pepper. In the lengthwise center of each cutlet spread about 1 tablespoon parsley, 1 tablespoon pine nuts, and 2 tablespoons raisins. Roll cutlet into a tube and tie with string so that it doesn't open.

Heat oil and butter in a medium skillet, add cutlets and cook over high heat, turning often. When meat is brown, add the sherry. Cover, lower heat, and simmer about 5 minutes. Serve hot.

Variation: Veal cutlets may be used.

Calories	Cholesterol mg	Protein gm	Carbohydrate gm	Total fat gm	%	Sat fat gm	%	Mono gm	Poly gm
1252	425.0	106.6	67.3	62.8	44	18.7	13	20.8	17.5

CHILI CON CARNE

Serves 6.

2 tablespoons safflower oil or peanut oil
1 1/2 cups finely chopped onion
1 cup coarsely chopped green peppers
2 cups sliced mushrooms (optional)
1 teaspoon minced garlic
1 pound lean ground beef (top of the round)
Salt and freshly ground black pepper to taste
1 cup dry white wine
2 cups chopped tomatoes, fresh if possible
    (drain if canned)
1 1/2 tablespoons chili powder
1 teaspoon dried oregano
15-ounce can red kidney beans or 2 cups
    freshly cooked beans (page 346)

Heat the oil in a skillet and add onion. When onion wilts, add peppers and mushrooms. When onion begins to brown, add garlic and cook, stirring, about 1 minute. Add the meat, turn up heat, season with salt and pepper, and sear, stirring often, until meat begins to brown. Add wine, lower heat, cover, and cook until wine cooks out. Add tomatoes, chili powder, oregano, and beans, cover, and simmer about 45 minutes.

Serve on rice or cut tubular pasta such as elbows, ziti, penne, etc.

Calories	Cholesterol mg	Protein gm	Carbohydrate gm	Total fat gm	%	Sat fat gm	%	Mono gm	Poly gm
1556	394.0	136.8	130.4	53.4	30	12.6	7	12.6	20.6

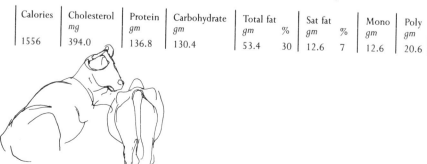

MEATBALLS
Polpette di Manzo

Yields 15 meatballs, serving 6.

1 pound lean ground beef (top of the round)
1 egg white, lightly beaten
2 tablespoons dry white wine
1 tablespoon chopped Italian parsley or fresh coriander
1 clove garlic, minced
1 teaspoon minced shallots
1 tablespoon fresh basil or 1 teaspoon dried
Salt, freshly ground black pepper, and a dash nutmeg
    to taste

The sauce
1 onion, sliced
1 tablespoon olive oil
1 teaspoon safflower oil
1/2 pound mushrooms, sliced
Salt and freshly ground black pepper to taste
2 cups chopped tomatoes, fresh if possible (drain if canned)
1 teaspoon dried oregano or basil

Garnish: Chopped Italian parsley

Mix all ingredients in a bowl and form balls about 1 to 1 1/2 inches in diameter. Place on a tray rubbed with safflower oil. Preheat oven to 450° and bake meatballs until brown, turning occasionally — about 10 minutes.

In the meantime, prepare the sauce: In a casserole sauté the onion in the oils. When onion wilts, add the sliced mushrooms, salt, and pepper, and cook over high heat until mushrooms begin to brown. Add the chopped tomatoes, oregano or basil, and meatballs. Cover partially and simmer about 20 minutes. Taste and correct the seasoning. Garnish with parsley and serve from the casserole.

Calories	Cholesterol mg	Protein gm	Carbohydrate gm	Total fat gm	%	Sat fat gm	%	Mono gm	Poly gm
1039	394.0	116.2	46.5	41.3	34	12.4	11	19.8	4.9

ESCALOPES OF GROUND BEEF
Scaloppini di Manzo Battuto

Serves 4.

2 tablespoons safflower oil
1 cup finely chopped onion
2 cloves garlic, minced
1 pound ground beef (top of the round)
2 tablespoons finely chopped Italian parsley
2 egg whites, slightly beaten
Salt and freshly ground black pepper to taste
3 tablespoons olive oil
Flour for dredging
1/2 cup vermouth

Heat safflower oil in a medium skillet, add onion, and cook until it wilts. Add garlic and cook several minutes. Remove and mix with the meat, parsley, egg whites, salt, and pepper. Form 8 patties from the mixture.

Heat the olive oil in the skillet. Dust patties with flour, add to skillet, and sauté, turning occasionally, until brown. Add vermouth, cover, lower heat, and cook until vermouth cooks out—about 10 minutes.

Calories	Cholesterol mg	Protein gm	Carbohydrate gm	Total fat gm	%	Sat fat gm	%	Mono gm	Poly gm
1381	394.0	109.4	30.6	89.3	57	18.0	11	42.3	23.9

BEEF STEW
Spezzato di Manzo

Serves 4.

2 tablespoons olive oil or 3 tablespoons peanut oil
1 tablespoon safflower oil
About 1 1/2 pounds beef, cut in 1- to 2-inch pieces (top of the round)
Flour for dredging
Salt and freshly ground black pepper to taste
3 cups thickly sliced mushrooms
1 teaspoon minced garlic
1 cup dry sherry
1 cup scallions cut into 1-inch lengths

Garnish: Finely chopped Italian parsley

Heat the oils in a medium skillet. Dust the meat with flour, then add to hot oil. Season with salt and pepper and cook over high heat, turning constantly, until meat is brown. Add mushrooms and cook until liquid dries out, turning constantly. Add garlic, toss for several minutes, then pour in sherry, cover, and lower heat. Simmer until sherry cooks out. Add scallions and simmer over low heat about 15 minutes.

Garnish with parsley. Serve with risotto Piedmontese style (page 153) and stuffed mushrooms.

Calories	Cholesterol mg	Protein gm	Carbohydrate gm	Total fat gm	%	Sat fat gm	%	Mono gm	Poly gm
1477	591	156.9	38.0	73.6	44	20.1	12	35.5	12.9

MEATLOAF
Polpettone

This meatloaf is exceptionally light and should be served with any seasonal vegetable.

Serves 5.

1 tablespoon olive oil
1 tablespoon safflower oil or 2 teaspoons vegetable oil
1 cup coarsely chopped onion
3 tablespoons coarsely chopped shallots
1 pound lean ground beef
Grated zest of 1 lemon
6 green olives, pitted and coarsely chopped
4 dried black olives, pitted and chopped
2 tablespoons finely chopped Italian parsley
1 teaspoon marjoram
2 egg whites, lightly beaten
Salt and freshly ground black pepper to taste
2 cups water
3/4 cup finely ground cornmeal

The sauce
1 tablespoon safflower oil
1 tablespoon olive oil or 2 teaspoons vegetable oil
1/2 cup coarsely chopped onion
1/2 cup chopped celery
1 tablespoon finely chopped Italian parsley
1 teaspoon minced garlic
1 cup chopped tomatoes, fresh if possible (drain if canned)
Salt to taste

Heat the oils in a medium skillet, then add the onion and shallots and sauté over moderate heat until onion begins to brown. Remove from heat. In a bowl mix together thoroughly the beef, cooked onion and shallots, lemon zest, olives, parsley, marjoram, egg whites, salt, and pepper.

Bring the water to a boil in a small saucepan, add 1 teaspoon salt, and gradually pour the cornmeal into the boiling water, stirring until the corn-meal is a creamy consistency (see polenta instructions on page 169). Add this to the meat mixture. Place the meatloaf mixture in an oiled deep loaf pan and preheat oven to 450°.

To prepare the sauce: Heat the oils in a medium skillet, add the onion, celery, and parsley, cover, and sauté over moderate heat until onion begins to brown. Then add the garlic and cook about 1 minute. Add the tomatoes and salt, cover, and simmer about 8 minutes over low heat. Pour the sauce over the meatloaf. Cover and bake about 1 hour. Remove cover and continue to bake for an additional 15 minutes.

Calories	Cholesterol mg	Protein gm	Carbohydrate gm	Total fat gm	%	Sat fat gm	%	Mono gm	Poly gm
1658	394.0	121.2	102.8	85.4	45	16.8	9	36.7	23.2

VEAL PICCATA
Piccata di Vitello

Serves 4.

8 thin slices veal from leg
Salt and freshly ground black pepper to taste
Flour for dredging
1 tablespoon butter
1 tablespoon safflower oil or 2 teaspoons vegetable oil
Juice of ½ lemon
1 tablespoon finely chopped Italian parsley
2 tablespoons dry white wine or stock

Pound veal lightly between two slices of waxed paper, then sprinkle with salt and pepper and dust lightly with flour.

Heat butter and oil in a skillet large enough to hold all the meat at once in one layer. Add veal when oil is hot. Cook over high heat, and after 30 seconds turn veal over. Then turn veal again. Do not allow to brown—total cooking time should not be more than 1½ to 2 minutes. Remove to a warm platter. Add lemon juice, parsley, and wine to the skillet. Over high heat swirl the sauce around, scraping the bottom of the skillet to loosen particles. Return the veal to the skillet and toss to heat through. Serve hot with the pan sauce spooned on top.

Variation: Use lean pork instead of veal, preferably the tenderloin. You will need 4 center-cut pork chops. Cut the tenderloin out, trim and discard fat. Butterfly each fillet, opening it up; then pound it between two pieces of waxed paper until you have a thin slice. Use the bones for stock, if you wish.

Calories	Cholesterol mg	Protein gm	Carbohydrate gm	Total fat gm	%	Sat fat gm	%	Mono gm	Poly gm
917	354.0	91.5	10.4	52.4	50	20.5	20	17.8	10.6

BROILED VEAL CUTLETS
Costolette alla Griglia

These veal cutlets are delicious with truffled sauce (page 441).

Serves 4.

4 veal cutlets, about 1 1/2 to 1 3/4 pounds
Juice of 1/2 lemon
1 tablespoon rosemary
1 clove garlic, minced
1 tablespoon olive oil
1 tablespoon safflower oil
Salt and freshly ground black pepper to taste

Combine all the ingredients with the veal and marinate for several hours.
Remove veal from the marinade and quickly broil over hot coals or under a hot preheated broiler, about 1 minute on each side. Serve on hot plates.

Calories	Cholesterol mg	Protein gm	Carbohydrate gm	Total fat gm	%	Sat fat gm	%	Mono gm	Poly gm
1207	483.0	136.1	4.8	68.4	50	22.7	17	29.5	12.0

VEAL IN A SKILLET
Vitello in Padella

Serves 4.

2 tablespoons safflower oil
2 tablespoons olive oil
3 bay leaves
1 pound veal cutlets, cut into strips 1/2 inch wide and
    3 inches long
Juice of 1 lemon
Salt and freshly ground black pepper to taste
3 tablespoons minced Italian parsley

Heat the oils with bay leaves, then add veal and cook over high heat about 3 minutes, turning constantly. Add lemon juice, salt, pepper, and parsley, toss, and cook several minutes more—be careful not to overcook. Serve immediately.
Variation: Use pork tenderloin instead of the veal.

Calories	Cholesterol mg	Protein gm	Carbohydrate gm	Total fat gm	%	Sat fat gm	%	Mono gm	Poly gm
1127	322.0	90.8	5.8	81.4	64	19.1	15	35.0	22.9

VEAL CUTLETS MILAN STYLE
Costolette di Vitello alla Milanese

The secrets to the success of this recipe are that you must have the oil very hot before adding the veal, you must not overcook the cutlet, and you must serve the veal immediately after you have removed it from the oil. When my mother cooked veal cutlets she cooked and served one cutlet at a time.

Serves 4.

4 veal cutlets, about 1/4 inch thick
Salt and freshly ground black pepper to taste
2 egg whites, lightly beaten
1 cup fresh breadcrumbs
Corn oil

Garnish: Lemon wedges

Sprinkle salt and pepper over cutlets, dip them into the egg whites, then dredge in breadcrumbs. In the meantime, heat 3/4 inch corn oil in a heavy skillet about 9 inches in diameter. It should be hot (test by sprinkling a few breadcrumbs in the hot oil; if the oil boils actively when crumbs are added, then the oil is ready). Do not allow it to smoke.

Slip 1 or 2 cutlets at a time into the hot oil. The oil should boil violently when cutlets are added. With tongs, turn the cutlets over after about 30 seconds. Cook the other side for 30 seconds, remove cutlets, blot on paper towels, and serve. Repeat. Serve with lemon wedges.

Variation: Use pork tenderloin instead of the veal, following instructions on page 300 for preparing cutlets.

Calories	Cholesterol mg	Protein gm	Carbohydrate gm	Total fat gm	%	Sat fat gm	%	Mono gm	Poly gm
867	322.0	101.3	23.3	37.5	38	14.0	11	14.1	5.9

VEAL BIRDS GENOA STYLE
Vitello all Uccelletto alla Genovese

Serves 2 to 4.

4 veal cutlets, about 4 × 5 inches
Salt and freshly ground black pepper to taste
3/4 cup fresh breadcrumbs
2 tablespoons pesto (page 426)
2 tablespoons yellow raisins, soaked in warm water
    for 15 minutes
Flour for dredging
1 tablespoon butter
1 tablespoon safflower oil

½ onion, finely chopped
2 cups mushrooms cut in half
½ cup sweet imported marsala or good sherry
2 tablespoons chopped fresh basil or
    1 teaspoon dried

Place the veal cutlets between two sheets of waxed paper and flatten them out, or have your butcher do it. Mix thoroughly salt, pepper, breadcrumbs, pesto, and raisins in a bowl. Spread stuffing over each piece of veal. Roll veal jellyroll fashion and tie securely with thin string. Dust with flour. Heat butter and oil in a medium skillet, then add veal rolls and brown over moderate to high heat.

When veal is brown, add onion and mushrooms. Cook over moderate heat until onion wilts, stirring often. Add marsala and basil, cover, and simmer over low heat about 35 to 45 minutes, until sauce thickens.

Remove strings from veal birds and serve with risotto or potato balls (page 367).

Variation: Use pork tenderloin instead of the veal.

Calories	Cholesterol mg	Protein gm	Carbohydrate gm	Total fat gm	%	Sat fat gm	%	Mono gm	Poly gm
1201	273.0	78.0	62.6	71.1	52	23.3	17	24.1	16.7

STUFFED VEAL CUTLETS
Braciolette Ripiene

Serves 4.

4 veal cutlets, pounded thin
Salt and freshly ground black pepper to taste
4 tablespoons minced Italian parsley
4 tablespoons chopped pine nuts
8 tablespoons yellow raisins, soaked in warm water
    for 15 minutes
1½ tablespoons safflower oil
1 tablespoon butter
¾ cup good sherry

Spread open cutlets. Sprinkle with salt and pepper. Spread lengthwise in the center of each cutlet about 1 tablespoon parsley, 1 tablespoon pine nuts, and 2 tablespoons raisins. Roll the cutlet up in the shape of a tube and tie with string so that it does not open. Heat oil and butter in a medium skillet, then add veal and cook over high heat, turning often. When veal is brown, add sherry, cover, lower heat, and simmer about 5 minutes. Serve hot.

Calories	Cholesterol mg	Protein gm	Carbohydrate gm	Total fat gm	%	Sat fat gm	%	Mono gm	Poly gm
1326	354.0	101.9	68.4	73.4	49	21.6	14	26.6	17.9

BROILED VEAL CHOPS I
Costolette di Vitello al Ferri

Serves 2.

2 veal chops, about 1 inch thick (loin cut, if possible)
Juice of 1 lemon
2 cloves garlic, sliced
Freshly ground black pepper to taste

Preheat broiler for 15 minutes or prepare a fire.

Place chops in a bowl with juice of $\frac{1}{2}$ lemon, garlic, and freshly ground pepper. Marinate for several hours. Remove chops from marinade and grill over hot coals. After about 2 minutes, brush with the marinade and add remaining lemon juice. Grill another 3 minutes, or until done as desired — but do not overcook.

Calories	Cholesterol mg	Protein gm	Carbohydrate gm	Total fat gm	%	Sat fat gm	%	Mono gm	Poly gm
361	161.0	36.8	5.8	20.5	50	9.9	24	9.0	0.4

BROILED VEAL CHOPS II
Costolette di Vitello al Ferri

Serves 2.

2 teaspoons safflower oil
2 cloves garlic, finely chopped
$1\frac{1}{2}$ cups chopped tomatoes, fresh if possible
 (drained if canned)
1 tablespoon capers
2 tablespoons finely chopped Italian parsley
1 red or green pepper, roasted, peeled, and sliced (see
 instructions, page 365)
2 veal chops, 1 inch thick
Salt and freshly ground black pepper to taste

Preheat broiler for 15 minutes or prepare a fire.

Heat the oil in a small skillet, then add garlic. As garlic begins to brown, add tomatoes, cover, and simmer for 10 minutes. Add capers, parsley, and roasted peppers. Cover and cook 5 more minutes.

Salt and pepper the chops; then broil, preferably over charcoal or wood embers, close to heat. Cook until light brown — about 4 minutes each side for broiler, 3 for grill. Do not overcook.

Spoon sauce over chops and serve hot.

Calories	Cholesterol mg	Protein gm	Carbohydrate gm	Total fat gm	%	Sat fat gm	%	Mono gm	Poly gm
559	161.0	45.9	28.8	30.8	48	10.7	17	10.0	7.2

GRILLED VEAL CHOPS
Costolette di Vitello alla Griglia

This recipe is similar to paillarde de veau and is best broiled over hot coals. It goes well with potatoes with celery, tomatoes, and onions (page 370) and a green salad.

Serves 4.

4 veal chops or veal steaks, 1/2 inch thick
1 tablespoon safflower oil or 2 tablespoons peanut oil
2 tablespoons olive oil
Salt and freshly ground black pepper to taste

Garnish: 4 lemon wedges

Place chops between 2 sheets of waxed paper and pound them with a meat pounder.

Place veal on grill. Brush with the oils, salt, and pepper. Grill over hot coals about 30 seconds on each side. Otherwise, preheat stove broiler and grill under high heat. Serve with lemon wedges.

Calories	Cholesterol mg	Protein gm	Carbohydrate gm	Total fat gm	%	Sat fat gm	%	Mono gm	Poly gm
682	322.0	72.4	0	41.0	53	19.8	26	18.0	0.8

VEAL CHOPS CIOCIARA STYLE
Costolette di Vitello alla Ciociara

Serves 2.

2 veal chops, about 1 inch thick (loin cut, if possible)
Salt and freshly ground black pepper to taste
Flour for dredging
1 tablespoon safflower oil
1 tablespoon butter or 2 teaspoons vegetable oil
1 medium onion, finely chopped
1 tablespoon finely chopped shallots
2 cups mushrooms cut in half
1/2 cup marsala or sweet sherry
9-ounce package frozen artichoke hearts, blanched*
3 tablespoons chicken or beef broth

*If you want to use fresh artichokes, remove all tough outer leaves, cut in quarters, and remove the chokes. Boil for 5 minutes before adding to the veal. Two medium artichokes will do.

Salt and pepper chops and dust with flour. Heat oil and butter in a medium skillet and add chops; brown both sides over high heat. Add onion and shallots. When onion begins to brown, add mushrooms and cook for several minutes, then add salt, pepper, and marsala. Bring to a boil and add drained artichoke hearts. Cover and simmer over high heat until liquid cooks out. Add broth and continue cooking about 5 minutes.

Serve with baked stuffed tomatoes.

Calories	Cholesterol mg	Protein gm	Carbohydrate gm	Total fat gm	%	Sat fat gm	%	Mono gm	Poly gm
853	182.0	50.0	58.3	46.3	48	17.3	18	14.8	10.5

SAUTÉED VEAL CHOPS
Costolette di Vitello in Padella

Serves 3.

3 veal chops, ½ inch thick
Salt and freshly ground black pepper to taste
2 egg whites, lightly beaten
Breadcrumbs
Corn oil or vegetable oil

Garnish: Lemon wedges

Place veal chops between two pieces of waxed paper and pound with a meat pounder. Rub each chop with salt and pepper. Roll in egg whites, then in breadcrumbs. In the meantime, heat ¾ inch oil in a medium skillet. Cook chops one at a time until golden brown—about 2 minutes on each side. Blot dry with paper towels and keep warm while you fry remaining chops. Serve hot with lemon wedges.

Calories	Cholesterol mg	Protein gm	Carbohydrate gm	Total fat gm	%	Sat fat gm	%	Mono gm	Poly gm
459	214.0	36.0	9.8	29.5	57	8.8	17	10.6	7.5

VEAL CHOPS WITH BROCCOLI
Costolette di Vitello con Broccoli

I have never had this recipe other than at our home. It was one of the standby veal dishes my mother made. I believe it originated in the area of Abruzzi.

Serves 4.

1 bunch broccoli
4 veal chops, about ¾ inch thick (loin cut, if possible)
Salt and freshly ground black pepper to taste
Flour for dredging

2 tablespoons safflower oil
2 cloves garlic, skins on
2 tablespoons chopped fresh basil or 1 tablespoon dried
1/2 cup dry white wine
2 cups sliced onions
1 tablespoon good olive oil
2 cups chopped tomatoes, fresh if possible (drain if canned)

Peel broccoli stems, cut into manageable sections, and break flowerets into bite-sized pieces. Blanch in boiling water, drain, and set aside.

Salt and pepper chops, then dust with flour. Heat the safflower oil in a large skillet, then add chops — they should fit snugly. Add the garlic. Brown the chops over medium to high heat, turning often.

When chops begin to brown, add wine, cover, and lower heat. Cook over moderate heat until wine cooks out. Remove chops from skillet and keep warm. Add onions with olive oil to the skillet, cover, and sauté until they begin to brown, then add tomatoes. Cover and simmer for 5 minutes. Return chops to the sauce along with the broccoli. Cover and cook over low heat for 30 minutes, basting chops and broccoli with the sauce occasionally.

Serve with rice or boiled potatoes.

Calories	Cholesterol mg	Protein gm	Carbohydrate gm	Total fat gm	%	Sat fat gm	%	Mono gm	Poly gm
1359	322.0	90.3	61.0	83.6	54	23.4	15	32.3	21.3

VEAL CHOPS WITH PEPPERS
Costolette di Vitello e Peperoni

We enjoy this recipe with boiled potatoes.

The reason red or yellow peppers are used is that they are sweeter than green peppers and they complement the vinegar, creating a sweet-and-sour combination.

Serves 2.

2 tablespoons olive oil
2 tablespoons safflower oil
3 cups sliced sweet red or yellow peppers (about 3 peppers)
Salt and freshly ground black pepper to taste
1 medium onion, thinly sliced
2 tablespoons wine vinegar
2 loin-cut veal chops, about 1 inch thick
Flour for dredging
1 teaspoon thyme
1/4 cup sweet vermouth*

*Sweet imported marsala may be used instead of vermouth.

Heat 1 tablespoon of the olive oil and 1 tablespoon of the safflower oil in a medium skillet, then add sliced peppers, salt, and pepper. Cook, uncovered, over medium heat until edges begin to brown. Add onion. When onion begins to brown, add vinegar, cover, lower heat, and cook, stirring occasionally, until vinegar cooks out. Remove peppers and reserve in a bowl. Wash and dry skillet.

Salt and pepper the chops and dust them with flour. Heat remaining 1 tablespoon olive oil and 1 tablespoon safflower oil, then add chops. Cook over high heat to lightly brown each side. Add thyme and vermouth, cover, lower heat, and cook over medium heat until vermouth cooks out. Return peppers to pan, cover, and simmer about 3 minutes.

Serve on warm dishes.

Calories	Cholesterol mg	Protein gm	Carbohydrate gm	Total fat gm	%	Sat fat gm	%	Mono gm	Poly gm
1239	161.0	50.3	89.7	76.9	55	15.1	11	33.6	21.8

VEAL CHOPS IN A PAPER BAG
Costolette di Vitello al Cartoccio

Serves 4.

4 veal chops, about 1 1/2 inches thick (loin cut, if possible), trimmed of fat
Salt and freshly ground black pepper to taste
Flour for dredging
2 tablespoons olive oil
3 tablespoons safflower oil
1 tablespoon minced shallots
1 medium onion, finely chopped
1 clove garlic, minced
2 cups thinly sliced mushrooms
1/2 cup coarsely chopped scallions
4 teaspoons sweet imported marsala or sweet sherry
1 teaspoon rosemary
4 #10 brown paper bags, oiled

Salt and pepper the veal, then dust lightly with flour.

Heat the oils in a medium to large skillet, add chops, and quickly brown both sides over high heat; then add shallots, onion, and garlic. Cook over high heat, uncovered, for several minutes. Add mushrooms and scallions and cook over high heat until moisture from mushrooms begins to dry up. Add marsala and rosemary, cover, and cook over moderate heat, turning chops occasionally. Cook until sauce thickens.*

Preheat oven to 450°. Carefully place each chop in the center of a paper bag and place on a baking tray. Carefully spoon one quarter of the mushroom sauce on top of each chop. Roll and crimp bag openings to seal them tightly. Bake about 5 to 8 minutes.

Before removing chops from bags, display them at the table. Slit each bag open and carefully slide a chop with mushroom sauce onto each plate.

*The chops can be prepared ahead of time. Then at the last minute slip them into the paper bags and bake.

Calories	Cholesterol mg	Protein gm	Carbohydrate gm	Total fat gm	%	Sat fat gm	%	Mono gm	Poly gm
1444	322.0	80.2	32.0	109.5	67	26.0	16	44.6	32.0

VEAL SHANKS IN A WINE SAUCE
Osso Buco in Bianco

I find this recipe more interesting than the more popular osso buco recipe with tomatoes, which follows.

Serves 4.

4 veal shanks, cut into pieces about 1 1/2 inches thick
Salt and freshly ground black pepper to taste
Flour for dredging
2 tablespoons peanut oil or vegetable oil
1 medium onion, finely chopped
1/2 cup dry sherry or dry white wine
2 tablespoons chopped fresh basil
1/2 cup chopped celery
1 teaspoon crushed rosemary
1 cup fresh peas
1 cup chicken or beef stock

Gremolada
1 tablespoon grated lemon rind
1 teaspoon minced garlic
2 tablespoons finely chopped Italian parsley

Salt and pepper shanks and dust with flour. Heat oil in a medium skillet, add veal, and cook over high heat, turning often, until veal is light brown. Add onion and cook several minutes, then add sherry, basil, celery, and rosemary. In the meantime, boil peas for several minutes. Drain and put aside. Cook veal until wine cooks out, then add stock. Cover and simmer over low heat for 1 hour, adding the peas during the last 30 minutes. In the meantime, make the gremolada. Mix together and add to veal. Cook, covered, about 5 minutes.

Calories	Cholesterol mg	Protein gm	Carbohydrate gm	Total fat gm	%	Sat fat gm	%	Mono gm	Poly gm
1129	322.0	108.5	56.8	52.1	41	16.4	13	23.2	8.3

VEAL SHANKS
Osso Buco

This recipe is usually served with risotto Milanese (page 152).

Serves 3.

3 tablespoons olive oil
1 tablespoon safflower oil
1 medium onion, finely chopped
3 veal shanks, cut into pieces about 1 1/2 inches thick
Flour for dredging
1 medium carrot, finely chopped
1 bay leaf
1 cup dry white wine
1 cup chopped tomatoes, fresh if possible (drain if canned)
Salt and freshly ground black pepper to taste
Beef or chicken stock (optional)

Gremolada
2 tablespoons minced Italian parsley
1 teaspoon minced garlic
1 tablespoon grated lemon rind

Heat the oils in a medium skillet or saucepan, then add onion. When onion begins to turn translucent, add veal shanks, dusted with flour, turn up heat, and lightly brown them. Add carrots, bay leaf, and wine, cover, and simmer over low heat until wine evaporates. Add tomatoes, salt, and pepper, cover and cook over low to moderate heat, turning veal shanks occasionally. Add some beef or chicken stock if moisture is needed. Cook about 30 minutes. Combine the ingredients for the gremolada. Add to veal and cook 10 more minutes.

Calories	Cholesterol mg	Protein gm	Carbohydrate gm	Total fat gm	%	Sat fat gm	%	Mono gm	Poly gm
1148	242.0	76.9	46.6	73.0	56	15.3	12	39.3	13.8

OSSO BUCO MARCHES STYLE
Osso Buco alla Marchigiana

This is a particularly light osso buco typical of the Marches, where cauliflower is produced in great abundance.

Serves 3.

2 1/2 pounds top part of veal shank cut into pieces
    1 1/2 inches thick
Salt and freshly ground black pepper to taste

Flour for dredging
2 tablespoons olive oil
1 tablespoon safflower oil
2 medium onions, finely chopped
2 cups thickly sliced fresh mushrooms
¾ cup dry white wine
1-ounce package dried boletus mushrooms, soaked in
    warm water about 20 minutes (optional)
1 tablespoon rosemary
1 bay leaf
1 cup chopped tomatoes, fresh if possible (drain if canned)
½ cauliflower, about 1 pound, cut into flowerets

Garnish: Finely chopped Italian parsley

Wash and dry veal shanks, salt and pepper them, and dust with flour.

Heat the oils in a medium skillet, then add veal shanks and lightly brown both sides over high heat. Remove from skillet and set aside.

Add onions and fresh mushrooms to the skillet and cook, uncovered, until onions begin to brown. Add veal shanks, wine, dried mushrooms if using them, rosemary, and the bay leaf, cover, and cook over low heat about 20 minutes. Add tomatoes, cover, and simmer over medium heat about 1 hour. Add cauliflower and continue cooking until cauliflower is tender, about 30 minutes.

Garnish with parsley and serve with rice, risotto, or boiled potatoes.

Calories	Cholesterol mg	Protein gm	Carbohydrate gm	Total fat gm	%	Sat fat gm	%	Mono gm	Poly gm
1534	268.0	141.4	78.5	73.5	42	18.5	11	35.8	12.2

VEAL WITH ARTICHOKE HEARTS
Spezzatino di Vitello e Carciofi

Serves 6.

1½ pounds veal cut into large chunks
    (shoulder or leg)
Juice of 1 lemon
1 pound mushrooms
5 tablespoons olive oil mixed with 4 tablespoons
    safflower oil
2 medium onions, thinly sliced
9-ounce package frozen artichoke hearts
Salt and freshly ground black pepper to taste
½ cup dry marsala or sherry
Flour for dredging

Garnish: 3 tablespoons minced Italian parsley

Marinate veal with lemon juice for several hours.

Separate mushroom caps from stems and in a skillet sauté both over moderate heat in 4 tablespoons of the oil, stirring occasionally. When mushrooms begin to brown, add onions and cook, uncovered, until onions wilt. In the meantime, put the artichoke hearts in boiling water, cook 1 minute, and drain. Add them to the skillet with salt and pepper and cook, covered, over low heat for 5 minutes. Add 1/4 cup of the marsala, salt, and pepper, cover, and simmer over low heat for 5 minutes.

Remove veal from lemon juice. Salt and pepper the pieces, then lightly dust with flour. Heat remaining 5 tablespoons oil in a skillet, then add veal. Cook over high heat, turning veal until it is lightly browned. Lower heat, add the remaining 1/4 cup marsala, cover, and simmer for 3 to 5 minutes, depending on the size of the veal pieces. Add mushroom-and-artichoke mixture to veal, cover, and simmer for several minutes. Garnish with parsley and serve hot.

Calories	Cholesterol mg	Protein gm	Carbohydrate gm	Total fat gm	%	Sat fat gm	%	Mono gm	Poly gm
2389	483.0	162.1	83.6	158.0	58	28.3	10	74.5	44.3

VEAL WITH EGGPLANT AND PEAS
Spezzatino con Melanzane e Piselli

We like this recipe served with boiled potatoes, preferably new potatoes, or rice or bruschetta (page 39).

Serves 4.

1 pound lean veal, cut into stewing-sized pieces,
    any gristle removed
Salt and freshly ground black pepper to taste
Flour for dredging
2 tablespoons olive oil
1 tablespoon safflower oil
1 medium onion, coarsely chopped
3/4 cup dry white wine
1 teaspoon crushed rosemary
1 cup chopped tomatoes, fresh if possible (drain if canned)
1 pound eggplant, cut into 1-inch squares about
    1/4 inch thick
2 cups fresh or frozen peas, blanched and drained

Garnish: 1 pound eggplant, cut into 1/4-inch slices

Salt and pepper the veal and lightly dust with flour. Heat the oils in a large skillet, add veal, and brown over very high heat, stirring often. When veal is golden brown, add onion. Cook until onion begins to brown, then add wine and rosemary, cover, and lower heat. Cook until wine cooks out. Add tomatoes, cover, and simmer over low heat, stirring often, about 45 minutes. Add cut-up eggplant and blanched peas, cover, and simmer about 30 minutes. Taste for salt.

In the meantime, place the sliced eggplant on a lightly oiled tray. Preheat oven to 500° for at least 15 minutes. Sprinkle some olive oil and salt on eggplant slices and bake until lightly brown, then turn and brown the other side. Garnish each serving of veal stew with eggplant slices.

Variation: Use pork tenderloin instead of the veal, removing all the visible fat.

Calories	Cholesterol mg	Protein gm	Carbohydrate gm	Total fat gm	%	Sat fat gm	%	Mono gm	Poly gm
1535	322.0	124.0	108.9	66.7	38	15.0	9	32.6	12.0

VEAL STEW WITH MUSHROOMS
Spezzato di Vitello

Serves 4.

3 tablespoons safflower oil
About 1½ pounds stewing veal, cut into 1- to 2-inch pieces
Flour for dredging
Salt and freshly ground black pepper to taste
3 cups thickly sliced mushrooms
1 teaspoon minced garlic
1 cup dry sherry
1 cup scallions cut into 1-inch lengths

Garnish: Finely chopped Italian parsley

Heat the oil in a medium skillet. Dust veal with flour and put into the hot oil. Add salt and pepper and cook over high heat, turning constantly, until veal is brown. Add mushrooms, stirring constantly, until liquid dries out, then add garlic and toss for several minutes. Add sherry, cover, lower heat, and simmer until sherry cooks out. Add scallions and simmer over low heat about 15 minutes.

Garnish with parsley and serve with Piedmontese risotto (page 153) and stuffed mushrooms (page 32).

Calories	Cholesterol mg	Protein gm	Carbohydrate gm	Total fat gm	%	Sat fat gm	%	Mono gm	Poly gm
1423	483.0	145.9	32.1	75.8	47	36.8	23	21.0	30.0

VEAL STEW RIATO
Stufato Riato

Serves 5.

1 cup coarsely chopped onion
1 cup coarsely chopped carrots
1 cup coarsely chopped celery
4 tablespoons safflower oil
1½ pounds stewing veal, cut into 1- to 2-inch pieces,
    trimmed of fat
Flour for dredging
Salt and freshly ground black pepper to taste
3 cups thinly sliced mushrooms
½ cup dry white wine
1 teaspoon thyme
2 cups chopped tomatoes, fresh if possible (drain if canned),
    or marinara sauce (page 430)
5 slices French or Italian bread

Garnish: Minced Italian parsley

Sauté the onion, carrots, and celery in 2 tablespoons safflower oil until tender. Remove from skillet, set aside, and in the same skillet heat the remaining 2 tablespoons oil. Dust the veal with flour, salt and pepper it, then brown it over high heat, tossing constantly. When veal has browned, add the mushrooms, wine, and thyme, cover, lower heat, and cook until most of the wine cooks out. Add sautéed vegetables, cover, and continue cooking for several minutes. Add tomatoes or tomato sauce, cover, and cook over low to moderate heat about 1 hour.

In the meantime, toast the bread and set aside. Put a slice of toast on each plate. We prefer to rub the toast with garlic before adding veal. Spoon veal and sauce over each slice of bread and garnish with parsley.

Calories	Cholesterol mg	Protein gm	Carbohydrate gm	Total fat gm	%	Sat fat gm	%	Mono gm	Poly gm
2119	483.0	166.3	147.8	91.7	38	20.8	9	23.0	39.8

VEAL STEW WITH POTATOES
Spezzato di Vitello con Patate

Serves 6 to 8.

3 medium potatoes
3 tablespoons safflower oil
1¾ pounds stewing veal, cut into 1- to 2-inch pieces,
    trimmed of fat

Salt and freshly ground black pepper to taste
2 cloves garlic, skins on
1 medium onion, sliced
1/2 cup dry white wine
1 tablespoon rosemary
1/2 cup chicken or beef stock or water, if needed
1 tablespoon extra virgin olive oil

Peel and cut potatoes into slices about 1/4 inch thick. Soak in cold water for 15 minutes, then drain and dry with paper towels.

Heat 1 1/2 tablespoons of the safflower oil in a skillet, then add veal, salt, pepper, and garlic. Cook, uncovered, over high heat, stirring often. When meat begins to brown, add onion and cook until onion wilts. Add wine and rosemary, cover, lower heat, and simmer 5 to 7 minutes.

Add potatoes and remaining 1 1/2 tablespoons safflower oil. Cover and cook over low heat. Stir often and add a little warm stock or warm water if needed to keep mixture moist. Cook until potatoes are tender, adding the olive oil for the last 5 minutes of cooking. (Some potatoes will dissolve and some will stick to skillet.) Discard garlic, and serve.

Calories	Cholesterol mg	Protein gm	Carbohydrate gm	Total fat gm	%	Sat fat gm	%	Mono gm	Poly gm
1964	563.0	172.2	96.9	95.3	42	24.5	11	32.2	32.1

VEAL WITH LENTILS AND PASTA
Vitello con Lenticchie e Pasta

This winter dish is good served with French or Italian bread. I particularly like it garnished with thinly sliced scallions or a few drops of extra virgin olive oil drizzled over each serving.

Serves 6.

1-ounce package dried boletus mushrooms, soaked
    in warm water about 15 minutes
2 pounds stewing veal, cut into 1-inch pieces
Salt and freshly ground black pepper to taste
Flour for dredging
2 tablespoons olive oil
1 tablespoon safflower oil
1 medium onion, finely chopped
1/2 pound fresh mushrooms, sliced
1 cup dry white wine
1 tablespoon rosemary
1 cup chopped tomatoes, fresh if possible (drain if canned)
3 cups chicken or beef stock
1 cup dried lentils, rinsed in cold water
3/4 cup short-cut pasta, such as ditalini, tubettini, small
    shells, elbows, etc.

Garnish: Chopped Italian parsley

Drain soaking dried mushrooms, reserving liquid and adding it to the 3 cups stock.

Salt and pepper the veal, then lightly dust with flour. Heat the oils in a large, shallow skillet, add veal, and cook over high heat, turning often, until veal is brown. Add onion and mushrooms and continue cooking over high heat. When onion begins to brown, add wine and rosemary, cover, lower heat, and cook until wine cooks out. Add tomatoes, cover, and simmer for 5 minutes. Transfer all ingredients to a stew pot and pour in the stock. Cover, bring to a boil, then lower heat and simmer gently about 1 1/4 hours.

Add lentils, cover, and continue cooking over low heat about 1 hour, stirring often (lentils have a tendency to sink to the bottom of the pot and burn easily) until tender. Add more stock if needed—the final dish should be the consistency of a thick stew.

Boil pasta until done al dente, then drain. Put equal amounts of pasta on the bottom of each soup plate and ladle veal stew on top.

Garnish with parsley.

Variation: Use lean pork from the tenderloin instead of veal.

Calories	Cholesterol mg	Protein gm	Carbohydrate gm	Total fat gm	%	Sat fat gm	%	Mono gm	Poly gm
3180	644.0	252.3	272.6	100.5	28	31.0	9	45.4	13.3

VEAL WITH WHITE BEANS
Spezzato di Vitello con Fagioli

Serves 6.

2 tablespoons olive oil
2 tablespoons safflower oil
1½ pounds stewing veal, cut into 1- to 2-inch pieces,
  trimmed of fat
2 cloves garlic, skins on
1 medium onion, finely chopped
Salt and freshly ground black pepper to taste
½ cup dry white wine
1 teaspoon rosemary
1 bay leaf
½ pound fresh mushrooms, cut in half
1 cup chopped tomatoes, fresh if possible (drain if canned)
2 cups cooked dried white beans (page 82) or 2 cups
  canned cannellini beans
¼ cup beef or chicken stock

Garnish: Chopped Italian parsley

Heat the oils in a heavy casserole, then add veal and cook over high heat, turning often. When meat begins to brown, add garlic and onion. When onion wilts, add salt, pepper, wine, rosemary, bay leaf, and mushrooms, lower heat, and simmer about 8 minutes. Add tomatoes, beans, and stock. (If canned beans are used, do not add them until veal has cooked about 45 minutes.) Cover and boil gently over low heat about 1½ hours. Garnish with chopped parsley and serve hot, with rice.

Calories	Cholesterol mg	Protein gm	Carbohydrate gm	Total fat gm	%	Sat fat gm	%	Mono gm	Poly gm
2051	483.0	165.4	95.1	97.9	42	25.7	11	41.0	23.2

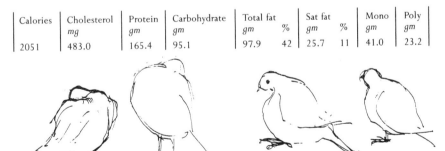

VEAL WITH POTATOES
AND ASPARAGUS
Vitello con Patate e Asparagi

This is an interesting unusual recipe that makes a rather ordinary cut of meat into a savory meal.

Serves 4.

2 tablespoons olive oil
1 tablespoon safflower oil
1 1/2 pounds stewing veal, cut into 1- to 2-inch pieces,
    trimmed of fat
1 medium onion, sliced
1 teaspoon minced garlic
2 tablespoons rosemary
Salt and freshly ground black pepper to taste
1/2 cup dry white wine
3 medium potatoes, peeled and sliced
1/2 cup chicken or beef broth or water
2 cups asparagus cut into 2-inch lengths

Garnish: 2 tablespoons minced Italian parsley

Heat the oils in a medium skillet, add veal, and brown over high heat,
turning often. When veal begins to brown, add onion, continuing to stir
often. When onion becomes translucent, add garlic, 1 tablespoon of the
rosemary, salt, and pepper. Cook for a minute, add the wine, cover, and
lower heat. Cook until wine cooks out; then add potatoes, stock or water,
cover, and cook until potatoes are tender. When potatoes are cooked, add
asparagus and salt, if needed. Cover and cook until asparagus is tender.
    Garnish with the parsley.

Calories	Cholesterol mg	Protein gm	Carbohydrate gm	Total fat gm	%	Sat fat gm	%	Mono gm	Poly gm
1960	483.0	154.6	114.0	83.8	38	24.5	11	39.4	13.1

VEAL WITH MARSALA
Spezzato di Vitello al Marsala

Serves 2.

1 tablespoon safflower oil
1 tablespoon butter
2 tablespoons chopped shallots
Salt and freshly ground black pepper to taste
1 pound lean veal from shoulder or leg, cut into julienne
    strips about 1/2 inch wide and 2 inches long
Flour for dredging
1/4 cup imported sweet marsala
1 cup sliced mushrooms (optional)

Heat oil and butter in a medium skillet; then add shallots. Salt and pepper
the veal, then dust with flour. When shallots begin to brown, add veal and
cook over high heat, turning, for a minute or two. Add marsala. (If mush-

rooms are used, sauté in 1 teaspoon vegetable oil until moisture cooks out, then add to veal when marsala is added.) Cook until sauce thickens, over high heat. Serve immediately on hot plates.

Variation: Use julienne strips of pork tenderloin instead of veal.

Calories	Cholesterol mg	Protein gm	Carbohydrate gm	Total fat gm	%	Sat fat gm	%	Mono gm	Poly gm
916	353.0	91.9	14.8	52.4	50	20.6	20	17.4	10.9

VEAL WITH PEAS AND CARROTS
Spezzatino di Vitello coi Piselli e Carote

Serves 8.

3 tablespoons safflower oil
1 large onion, coarsely chopped, about 1 cup
4 cups chopped tomatoes, fresh if possible
    (drain if canned)
2 teaspoons chopped fresh basil or 1 teaspoon dried
Salt and freshly ground black pepper to taste
2½ pounds stewing veal, cut into 1½- to 2-inch pieces
Flour for dredging
1 pound mushrooms, thinly sliced, about 4 cups
½ cup imported sweet marsala or 1 cup sherry
2 cups carrots cut into 1½-inch lengths and about
    ½ to ¾ inch thick
2 cups fresh peas (about 2½ pounds unshelled)
2 cups potatoes (about 5 potatoes) cut the same way as
    the carrots
2 tablespoons extra virgin olive oil

Heat 1 tablespoon of the safflower oil in a medium skillet, then add onion and sauté over medium heat until it begins to brown. Add tomatoes, basil, salt, and pepper, cover, and simmer gently about 10 minutes. Run sauce through a food mill or blend in a food processor.

Salt and pepper the veal and dust with flour. Heat the remaining 2 tablespoons safflower oil in large skillet (12 inches). Quickly sear a few pieces at a time over high heat, turning the veal to brown all sides; then remove to a platter. Repeat until all the veal is browned. When you have removed the last batch from the skillet, add mushrooms and cook over moderate heat, uncovered, adding 2 more tablespoons of safflower oil if needed. Cook until edges begin to brown, then add browned veal and marsala to mushrooms, lower heat, and cover. Simmer until wine is reduced, then add tomato sauce.

In a small saucepan cover carrots with water and boil 5 minutes. Add peas, cook an additional 2 or 3 minutes, then drain and add both to veal.

Cover skillet and simmer gently for 30 minutes. Add potatoes. Cover and continue simmering for 20 to 30 minutes, until carrots and potatoes are tender. Stir in the olive oil.

Serve with rice or boiled potatoes, or alone.

Calories	Cholesterol mg	Protein gm	Carbohydrate gm	Total fat gm	%	Sat fat gm	%	Mono gm	Poly gm
3645	805.0	283.9	249.0	141.9	34	40.0	10	54.6	33.8

ABOUT MEATBALLS

Here are three dishes made with meatballs, two veal and one beef. In the first, which is the lightest, the meatballs are steamed; in the second they are cooked on top of the stove with a tomato sauce; in the third, the meatballs are broiled and then cooked with a green vegetable. If you don't find ground veal in the supermarket, select a lean stewing meat and ask to have it ground. It is better ground by a high-powered machine.

STEAMED VEAL BALLS
Polpette di Vitello al Vapore

I enjoy this recipe with a pesto sauce that has been thinned with some hot broth so that it has a flowing consistency.

Served with a light vegetable sauce and a seasonal vegetable, this recipe is satisfying, light, and elegant.

Serves 4; yields about 13 balls.

1 tablespoon safflower oil or vegetable oil
1 medium onion, finely chopped
1 pound ground lean veal
1/2 teaspoon nutmeg
Salt and freshly ground black pepper to taste
1 tablespoon choppped fresh mint or
    Italian parsley
Juice of 1/2 lemon

Heat the oil in a small skillet. Sauté onion over moderate heat and cook until it begins to brown.

Mix the onion with the remaining ingredients, blending thoroughly. Form balls about the size of golf balls and steam about 8 minutes. Serve with one of sauces in Chapter X.

Variation: Use pork ground from the tenderloin instead of veal.

Calories	Cholesterol mg	Protein gm	Carbohydrate gm	Total fat gm	%	Sat fat gm	%	Mono gm	Poly gm
797	322.0	94.3	18.3	37.3	41	12.0	13	12.0	10.3

VEAL BALLS IN TOMATO SAUCE
Polpette di Vitello in Sugo di Pomodoro

This is good served with rice, potatoes, a pasta, or a vegetable.

Serves 4 as a main course with vegetables; 6 with rice or pasta.

2 tablespoons safflower oil
1 medium onion, chopped
1 clove garlic, chopped
2 cups chopped tomatoes, fresh if possible (drain if canned)
1 teaspoon dried oregano
1 tablespoon chopped Italian parsley
Salt and freshly ground black pepper or hot pepper flakes
  to taste
3/4 pound spinach
1 pound ground veal
2 egg whites, lightly beaten
1 tablespoon minced Italian parsley
4 tablespoons breadcrumbs
Grated rind of 1 lemon
1 tablespoon olive oil

Garnish: Minced Italian parsley

Heat the safflower oil in a large skillet, then add onion. When onion begins to brown, add garlic and cook about 1 minute. Add tomatoes, oregano, parsley, salt, and pepper, cover, and simmer for 30 minutes. Put sauce in a food processor and purée. Return to skillet.

To make the veal balls, boil spinach for 5 minutes in boiling water. Drain, spray with cold water, then squeeze out all water from spinach and chop. In a bowl mix veal, egg whites, parsley, spinach, breadcrumbs, lemon rind, salt, and pepper. Form balls the size of golf balls (you should have about 14). Put veal balls into the sauce, cover, and simmer 1 hour, adding the olive oil for the last 5 minutes of cooking. Garnish meatballs with parsley just before serving.

Calories	Cholesterol mg	Protein gm	Carbohydrate gm	Total fat gm	%	Sat fat gm	%	Mono gm	Poly gm
1355	322.0	120.9	68.2	66.9	43	15.1	10	23.1	21.7

MEATBALLS WITH ASPARAGUS
Polpette di Manzo con gli Asparagi

Serve this with rice steamed in stock instead of water—you will need 1 1/2 cups uncooked rice for 5 to 6 people (see page 160 for directions). Spoon some of the sauce over each portion.

Serves 5 to 6.

1 tablespoon olive oil
1 teaspoon safflower oil
1 medium onion, finely chopped
1 pound lean ground beef (top of the round)
2 tablespoons yellow raisins, soaked in warm water for
    15 minutes
Salt and freshly ground black pepper to taste
Dash nutmeg
1 cup fresh breadcrumbs
2 egg whites, lightly beaten
1 pound asparagus, washed and cut into 2-inch lengths
    (tough stems discarded)

The sauce
1 tablespoon olive oil
1 teaspoon safflower oil
1 medium onion, coarsely chopped
2 cups chopped tomatoes, fresh if possible
    (drain if canned)
1 cup chicken or beef broth

Garnish: 2 tablespoons finely chopped Italian parsley

Heat 1 tablespoon of the olive oil and 1 teaspoon of the safflower oil in a medium skillet, add the finely chopped onion, and sauté, uncovered, over moderate heat until it begins to brown. Mix together thoroughly with the rest of the ingredients except the asparagus. Form into pingpong-size balls (you should have about 20). Rub a metal tray with some vegetable oil and place meatballs on it. Broil close to the flame or bake in a high preheated oven until meatballs are golden brown, turning them over once with a spatula.

In the meantime, prepare the sauce. In a medium saucepan heat the remaining 2 tablespoons olive oil and 1 teaspoon safflower oil, then add the onion and cook until it begins to brown. Add the tomatoes and broth, cover, and simmer 15 minutes. Remove from the heat and purée the tomatoes in a food processor or a food mill.

Return the sauce to the pan, add browned meatballs, cover, and simmer for 20 minutes.

Add the asparagus to the meatballs and sauce and cook until the asparagus is done—for 10 more minutes. Garnish with parsley.

Variation: The recipe can be made with peas, or other vegetables, such as broccoli, cauliflower, or lima beans.

Calories	Cholesterol mg	Protein gm	Carbohydrate gm	Total fat gm	%	Sat fat gm	%	Mono gm	Poly gm
1598	322.0	124.9	106	75.8	42	16.2	9	43.5	9.7

VEAL PATTIES
Polpette di Vitello Buttute

Serves 4 to 5.

1½ pounds ground lean veal or top of the round beef
½ cup cooked rice
5 tablespoons finely chopped Italian parsley
2 cups finely chopped onion
2 egg whites, lightly beaten
3 tablespoons dry marsala or sherry
Salt and freshly ground black pepper to taste
2 tablespoons olive oil
1 tablespoon safflower oil
2 cups chopped tomatoes, fresh if possible,
    (drained if canned)
2 cups fresh or frozen peas, blanched and drained

Combine the veal, rice, 3 tablespoons of the parsley, 1 cup of the onion, egg whites, marsala, salt, and pepper. Form patties about 3 inches in diameter — you will have about 9 of them.

Preheat broiler. Place patties on a lightly oiled baking tray, sprinkle with vegetable oil and broil close to the flame. As patties brown, carefully turn them over with a spatula and brown the other side. They will take about 8 minutes in all.

Carefully remove patties and keep warm. In the meantime, heat the oils in a medium skillet, add remaining 1 cup onion, and cook over moderate heat until onion wilts. Add tomatoes and remaining 2 tablespoons parsley, cover, and simmer for 10 minutes. Add the peas, cover, and cook over moderate heat another 30 minutes for fresh peas, 15 minutes for frozen.

Place 2 patties on each serving plate. Spoon sauce and peas over meat. This dish is good with rice or mashed potatoes.

Calories	Cholesterol mg	Protein gm	Carbohydrate gm	Total fat gm	%	Sat fat gm	%	Mono gm	Poly gm
1847	161.0	173.9	103.5	77.6	37	20.5	10	37.6	12.2

TUNNIED VEAL
Vitello Tonnato

There are many recipes for vitello tonnato. In some cases veal is braised first and cooked in a little liquid; sometimes the meat is boiled in water, sometimes in wine. The sauces differ also. Some recipes include homemade mayonnaise, but I prefer vitello tonnato without it — and the recipe is acceptable for this book.

Serves 6.

1 large carrot, scraped and cut in half lengthwise
2 bay leaves
1 large onion with 4 cloves stuck in it
1 stalk celery with leaves, cut into 3 pieces
About 3 cups dry white wine or 1/2 wine and 1/2 water
Freshly ground black pepper to taste
2-pound piece of veal from leg, rump, or shoulder

The tuna sauce

2 salted anchovies (page 503), washed, boned, and
  chopped, or 4 canned anchovies of good quality
7-ounce can Italian-style tunafish
2 tablespoons chopped Italian parsley
Juice of 1 lemon
2 tablespoons olive oil
4 tablespoons safflower oil
2 to 3 tablespoons veal stock
Freshly ground black pepper to taste

Garnish: 2 tablespoons small capers

Put the carrot, bay leaves, onion, celery, and wine in a pot just large enough to hold veal and bring to a boil. Pepper the veal all over and wrap in cheesecloth. Tie securely and place in the pot. Lower heat, cover, and boil gently about 1 1/4 hours. Allow veal and liquid to cool.

In the meantime, prepare the tuna sauce. Put all the sauce ingredients in a food processor and blend to a creamy consistency, or blend a little at a time with a mortar and pestle.

After veal has cooled, remove cheesecloth and with a sharp knife carve veal in slices about 1/4 inch thick or less. The thickness of the slices will depend on the cut of veal used; cuts that involve more than one muscle, such as rump or shoulder, cannot be cut as thinly. Place veal slices on a platter and pour sauce over each slice. Garnish with capers. Cover and refrigerate overnight.

Calories	Cholesterol mg	Protein gm	Carbohydrate gm	Total fat gm	%	Sat fat gm	%	Mono gm	Poly gm
2333	755.0	229.3	5.2	150.4	57	38.9	15	53.6	47.0

TRIPE MILANESE STYLE
Busecca (Trippa alla Milanese)

Kidney beans or dried white beans may be used in this recipe, as well as fresh cranberry (shell) beans, but the season for fresh cranberry beans is only about 4 or 5 weeks. I find cannellini, Great Northern, or kidney beans best suited for this particular dish, because I consider it a winter recipe and dried beans seem to make the most sense.

Serves 6.

1 cup dried cannellini beans
2 cloves garlic
1 tablespoon rosemary
3 bay leaves
3 medium onions, finely chopped
Salt and freshly ground black pepper to taste
2 pounds honeycomb tripe
4 teaspoons safflower oil
3/4 cup finely chopped carrots
1 cup finely chopped celery
2 cups chopped tomatoes, fresh if possible
   (drain if canned)
1 1/2 to 2 cups chicken or beef broth
1/2-ounce package dried boletus mushrooms, soaked in
   warm water for 15 minutes (optional)
2 teaspoons sage
2 1/2-inch-long strip of Parmesan cheese skin,
   scraped (optional)
2 tablespoons extra virgin olive oil

Cover beans with about 2 inches cold water and soak overnight. Beans will expand about 3 times their bulk.

Place beans in a small pot, cover with about 1 inch cold water, and add garlic, rosemary, 1 bay leaf, 1 of the finely chopped onions, salt, and pepper. Bring to a boil, cover, and simmer 1 hour.

Cook tripe in boiling water for 5 minutes. Drain and cut off all fat from back of tripe, opposite the comb side. Then cut tripe into strips 2 inches long and 1/4 inch wide.

Heat the safflower oil in a medium skillet, add remaining 2 chopped onions, carrots, and celery. Sauté until onions begin to brown, then add tomatoes, broth, tripe, 2 bay leaves, mushrooms, sage, and Parmesan skin. Bring to a boil, cover, and boil gently about 2 hours. Add drained cooked beans, cover, and cook about 30 minutes. Fold in the olive oil.

Serve on a bed of rice or with good crusty French or Italian bread.

Calories	Cholesterol mg	Protein gm	Carbohydrate gm	Total fat gm	%	Sat fat gm	%	Mono gm	Poly gm
2295	618.0	231.1	185.6	69.1	26	14.0	5	29.9	16.1

TRIPE ROMAN STYLE
Trippa alla Romana

This recipe was given to me by a Roman friend, who said it was a typical Roman dish and that a substantial amount of fresh mint must be used.

I use a fresh wild mint growing on our property that is similar to spearmint. The mint you use should have a strong, distinctive flavor. There are many types of mints—too many of them are rather bland.

Serves 4.

1½ pounds tripe
1 tablespoon safflower oil
1 tablespoon olive oil
1 medium onion, finely chopped
1 stalk celery, finely chopped
2 tablespoons finely chopped Italian parsley
3 cups chopped tomatoes, fresh if possible (drain if canned)
Salt and freshly ground black pepper to taste
⅔ cup coarsely chopped fresh mint

Wash tripe well. Boil for 5 minutes in boiling water. Drain, remove fat from back side of tripe with a sharp knife, then cut the tripe in sections about ¼ inch wide and 3 inches long.

Heat oils in a medium saucepan, then add onion, celery, and parsley. Cook over medium heat until onion begins to brown. Add tomatoes, salt, and pepper and bring to a boil. Add tripe, cover, lower heat, and simmer about 1 hour and 20 minutes. Add mint, cover, and continue cooking an additional 40 minutes. Tripe should be tender but not overcooked.

Serve with good crusty bread.

Calories	Cholesterol mg	Protein gm	Carbohydrate gm	Total fat gm	%	Sat fat gm	%	Mono gm	Poly gm
1165	464.0	142.2	49.5	42.7	32	9.6	7	17.5	11.5

TRIPE WITH SAVOY CABBAGE
Trippa con Cavolo

This is a hearty winter stew that is both delicate and satisfying.

Serves 4 to 6.

1 pound honeycomb tripe
2 tablespoons olive oil
1 tablespoon safflower oil
1 medium onion, finely chopped
1 cup finely chopped celery
2 tablespoons finely chopped Italian parsley
3 tablespoons tomato paste, diluted in 3 teaspoons water
4 cups chicken or beef broth
2 bay leaves
2 pounds Savoy cabbage (1 small head)
8 medium to small potatoes, peeled and cut in half (cover
  with cold water)
Salt and freshly ground black pepper or hot pepper flakes
  to taste

Wash tripe. Cover and boil for 10 minutes, then drain and allow to cool. Heat the oils in a stewpot, then add onion, celery, and parsley. Sauté over moderate heat until onion begins to brown. Add diluted tomato paste and cook for several minutes, stirring often. Add 2 cups of the broth and bay leaves.

In the meantime, cut off all fat from back of tripe, then cut in 1/4-inch-wide 2-inch-long strips with a sharp knife. Add tripe to broth. Cover and boil gently for 1 hour.

Remove outer cabbage leaves and cut the rest into manageable pieces. Blanch in boiling water, drain, and let cool. Add cabbage to tripe broth after tripe has cooked for 1 hour. Add remaining 2 cups broth, cover, and boil gently for 30 minutes. Add potatoes and season with salt and pepper. Cook until potatoes are tender.

Serve in soup bowls with toasted garlic bread (page 39).

Calories	Cholesterol mg	Protein gm	Carbohydrate gm	Total fat gm	%	Sat fat gm	%	Mono gm	Poly gm
2063	309.0	138.8	259.2	53.1	23	9.2	4	25.4	12.5

HORSEMEAT STEW
Stufato di Carne di Cavallo

Fresh horsemeat is highly regarded in Italy and is more expensive there than beef.

Serves 6 to 8.

The marinade
2 cloves garlic, coarsely chopped
2 bay leaves
Freshly ground black pepper to taste
2 tablespoons rosemary
1 tablespoon basil
2 cups good dry red wine

2 to 2½ pounds boneless horsemeat, cut into large pieces*
3 tablespoons olive oil
1 tablespoon safflower oil
10 small onions, peeled
Salt and freshly ground black pepper to taste
4 carrots cut into 1-inch pieces
1 cup chopped celery
6 medium potatoes, cut in half

*Venison can be used instead of horsemeat.

Combine the garlic, bay leaves, pepper, rosemary, basil, and red wine with the meat and marinate about 12 hours. Remove meat from marinade and blot dry. Reserve the marinade.

Heat the oils in a skillet, then add meat and cook over high heat. Add onions, salt, and pepper, and continue to cook, turning meat often. When brown, add marinade, lower heat, and cook for 5 minutes. Transfer meat and contents to a casserole. Add carrots and celery, cover, and cook about 3 hours, depending on toughness of meat. Add potatoes, cover, and cook until potatoes are tender.

Calories	Cholesterol mg	Protein gm	Carbohydrate gm	Total fat gm	%	Sat fat gm	%	Mono gm	Poly gm
2679	–	217.2	239.9	90.9	30	6.6	–	31.3	13.4

Figures are available for the total fat in horsemeat but not for the partition into saturated, monounsaturated, and polyunsaturated components, and not for the cholesterol.

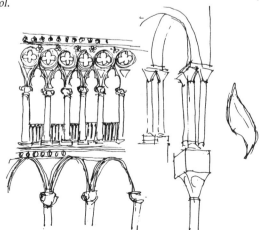

LAMB WITH ARTICHOKE HEARTS AND TURNIPS
Agnello Brodettato

We like this recipe with a green vegetable such as broccoli or spinach. It also goes well with rice.

Serves 5.

1¾ pounds lean lamb, cut into manageable pieces, preferably with bone — shank is best
Salt and freshly ground black pepper to taste
Flour for dredging
3 tablespoons safflower oil
1 cup coarsely chopped onion
1 teaspoon crushed rosemary
1 cup whole mushroom caps (optional)
¾ cup dry white wine
1 bay leaf
About ½ cup chicken or beef broth
1 pound white turnips, peeled and cut into wedges
9-ounce package frozen artichoke hearts, blanched and drained
1 bunch scallions, cut into 1-inch lengths, about 1 cup

Gremolada
Zest of 1 lemon
3 tablespoons finely chopped Italian parsley
1 teaspoon minced garlic

Salt and pepper lamb and lightly dust with flour. Heat oil in a medium skillet, add lamb, and lightly brown it. Drain off most of the oil. Then add onion, rosemary, and mushroom caps; cook until onion begins to brown. Add wine and bay leaf, and cook for several minutes. Remove to an ovenproof casserole and place in a preheated 500° oven, cover, and cook about 45 minutes.

Add broth as wine cooks out. Add turnips and cook about 15 minutes. Add artichoke hearts and scallions, cover, and cook an additional 15 minutes. Sprinkle on the gremolada, cover, and let sit about 5 minutes.

Calories	Cholesterol mg	Protein gm	Carbohydrate gm	Total fat gm	%	Sat fat gm	%	Mono gm	Poly gm
1785	561.0	174.3	83.6	87.3	43	28.3	14	22.2	30.8

BROILED OR GRILLED VENISON STEAKS
Bistecche di Cervo

Serves 3 to 6 depending on size of steaks.

3 venison steaks, about 1/2 to 3/4 inch thick
3/4 cup red wine vinegar
2 tablespoons crushed rosemary
4 cloves garlic, coarsely chopped
4 tablespoons vegetable oil, preferably 2 olive oil and
  2 safflower oil
Freshly ground black pepper to taste
3 bay leaves
Salt to taste

Garnish: Lemon or lime wedges

Marinate steaks in all the ingredients except the salt for at least 12 hours. Preheat broiler for 15 minutes or prepare a fire.

Remove steaks from marinade and salt them. Broil or cook over hot coals or in fireplace over hot embers about 2 to 4 minutes on each side, depending on desired doneness, basting with the marinade. The meat is best when medium rare. Serve hot with wedges of lemon or lime.

Calories	Cholesterol mg	Protein gm	Carbohydrate gm	Total fat gm	%	Sat fat gm	%	Mono gm	Poly gm
1399	442.0	1440	18.5	82.4	52	23.1	15	29.5	23.2

Calculations are based on 1 1/2 pounds venison.

GRILLED VENISON SCALLOPINI
Cervo alla Griglia

The secret to the success of this recipe is to have very hot coals ready and not to overcook the meat. Treat it the same as you would veal scallopini.

Serves 3.

1 pound fresh venison, cut in thin scallopini from leg
  or shoulder
3 tablespoons bourbon
1 teaspoon minced garlic
1 teaspoon crushed rosemary
1 tablespoon olive oil
1 teaspoon safflower oil
Freshly ground black pepper to taste

Combine all the ingredients in a deep bowl and marinate at least 2 hours, stirring occasionally.

Place venison slices on a grill and cook over hot coals, about 30 seconds on each side. Do not overcook.

Serve immediately on hot plates.

Variation: The venison scallopini can also be pan-fried with just a little oil. Heat oil first over high heat. Add venison and quickly cook over high heat.

Calories	Cholesterol mg	Protein gm	Carbohydrate gm	Total fat gm	%	Sat fat gm	%	Mono gm	Poly gm
572	295.0	95.3	0	18.2	28	11.4	18	4.4	0.5

ROAST RABBIT
Coniglio Arrosto

Serves 4 to 6.

3 tablespoons olive oil
1 tablespoon safflower oil
3½-pound rabbit, cut into about 10 frying pieces
1 onion, chopped
2 cloves garlic
1 cup dry white wine
1 teaspoon thyme
1 tablespoon rosemary
Salt and freshly ground black pepper to taste
20 dried black olives

Heat the oils in an ovenproof casserole, add rabbit, onion, and garlic. Brown over high heat. Add the rest of the ingredients except the olives.

Bake, covered, in a preheated 350° oven, basting rabbit occasionally, about 1¾ hours. Add olives for the last 30 minutes of cooking. Let rest for at least 15 minutes before serving.

Calories	Cholesterol mg	Protein gm	Carbohydrate gm	Total fat gm	%	Sat fat gm	%	Mono gm	Poly gm
1842	444.0	148.5	32.4	123.4	59	28.7	14	62.2	21.2

RABBIT MARCHES STYLE I
Coniglio alla Marchigiana

This is the rabbit recipe always served in my grandfather's home in Le Marche, Italy. Fresh rabbits are available in certain specialty markets, but we raise our own and find them superior to those in the markets.

This dish is delicious served with found vegetables (page 389) or rape or mixed vegetable (pages 385–8).

Serves 6.

3- to 3½-pound rabbit, skinned and cleaned
Salt and freshly ground black pepper to taste
6 cloves garlic, skins on
1 tablespoon rosemary
3 tablespoons olive oil
1 tablespoon safflower oil
4 cups dry white wine

Soak rabbit in cold salted water for at least 2 hours. Wash and dry, cut into serving pieces—small rather than large—and salt and pepper them all over. Put in a large skillet and cook until lightly brown, to cook out moisture; then add garlic, rosemary, and oils. Cook for several minutes, turning the pieces constantly.

Add ½ cup of the wine and cook, uncovered, over medium heat, tossing constantly until wine cooks out. Continue cooking, adding more wine as needed, turning rabbit pieces occasionally. It should take about 1½ hours to use up 4 cups of wine.

Let rest about 10 minutes before serving.

Calories	Cholesterol mg	Protein gm	Carbohydrate gm	Total fat gm	%	Sat fat gm	%	Mono gm	Poly gm
1590	381.0	123.2	40.5	101.5	56	24.2	13	48.9	19.2

RABBIT MARCHES STYLE II
Coniglio alla Marchigiana

This makes a very fine winter dish.

Serves 6.

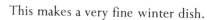

3½- to 4-pound rabbit, cut into serving pieces
Salt and freshly ground black pepper to taste
Flour for dredging
2 tablespoons olive oil
1 tablespoon safflower oil
2 cups coarsely chopped onion
½ cup good wine vinegar, preferably white
About 3 cups chopped tomatoes
1 teaspoon marjoram
2 cups celery cut into 2-inch lengths
6 small to medium potatoes, peeled and cut in half

Salt and pepper rabbit sections and dust with flour; shake off excess flour. Heat the oils in a large skillet, then carefully add the rabbit pieces and brown them over high heat. Add the onion. When onion wilts, add vinegar, lower heat, and cover. Turn rabbit pieces often, cooking until vinegar cooks out.

Then add tomatoes, marjoram, and celery, cover, and bring to a boil. Transfer rabbit and juices to an ovenproof casserole.

Cover and bake in a preheated 450° oven for about 45 minutes. Add potatoes. Lower heat to 350° and bake, covered, another 30 minutes.

Calories	Cholesterol mg	Protein gm	Carbohydrate gm	Total fat gm	%	Sat fat gm	%	Mono gm	Poly gm
2279	444.0	171.1	172.6	97.9	38	25.3	10	41.9	19.1

RABBIT HUNTER STYLE
Coniglio alla Cacciatora

This rabbit dish is particularly good served with polenta toasted over hot coals and garnished with the sauce from the rabbit. We have also served it with bruschetta (page 39) with fine results.

Serves 4.

3½-pound rabbit, skinned and cleaned
Salt and freshly ground black pepper to taste
1 tablespoon olive oil
3 tablespoons safflower oil
4 cloves garlic, skins on
Hot pepper flakes to taste (optional)
1 tablespoon rosemary
1 cup dry white wine
1 cup white wine vinegar
2 salted anchovies, washed, filleted, spine discarded,
    or 4 canned anchovy fillets
About 2 tablespoons extra virgin olive oil

Cut rabbit into serving pieces, wash well in cold water, and dry thoroughly with clean cloth towels. Salt and pepper the pieces. Place them in a large skillet, not overlapping. Cook over high heat, turning meat several times, until rabbit begins to brown. Add the two oils, garlic, hot pepper flakes, and rosemary. Cook over medium heat, turning often as rabbit takes on a golden color all over. Add wine, vinegar, and anchovies and cook about 20 minutes, until most — but not all — of the liquid cooks out. There should be enough to garnish each portion. Add the olive oil just before serving.

Rabbit seems to taste better if allowed to rest an hour or so after cooking is completed.

Calories	Cholesterol mg	Protein gm	Carbohydrate gm	Total fat gm	%	Sat fat gm	%	Mono gm	Poly gm
1951	453.0	147.6	29.6	138.1	62	30.1	14	54.5	40.9

RABBIT SAN REMO STYLE
Coniglio alla San Remese

Serves 6.

3 tablespoons olive oil
1 tablespoon safflower oil
3½-pound rabbit, cut into serving pieces
Salt and freshly ground black pepper to taste
1 onion, finely chopped
10 dried black olives, pitted and sliced
1 tablespoon rosemary
¾ cup chopped celery
2 bay leaves
2 cups good dry red wine
1 teaspoon thyme
10 walnuts, shelled and finely ground to a paste

Heat the two oils in a skillet. Add rabbit pieces and brown them over moderate heat. Add salt and pepper. When rabbit is brown, remove and set aside. Add onion, olives, rosemary, celery, and bay leaves, and simmer until onion wilts. Add rabbit and juices, wine, and thyme, cover, and cook over low heat, so that juices gently boil, about 45 minutes. Add walnut paste and cook another 10 minutes.

Calories	Cholesterol mg	Protein gm	Carbohydrate gm	Total fat gm	%	Sat fat gm	%	Mono gm	Poly gm
2083	444.0	154.0	47.0	142.2	60	29.7	13	60.8	36.6

RABBIT WITH POLENTA GENOA STYLE
Coniglio e Polenta alla Genovese

This is a most rewarding recipe, for it is both hearty and delicate—a wonderful winter dish.

Serves 6.

3½-pound rabbit, cut into large serving pieces
3 tablespoons olive oil
1 tablespoon safflower oil
1 tablespoon crushed rosemary
Salt and freshly ground black pepper to taste
1 cup dry white wine
½ pound fresh mushrooms, cut into large pieces,
    about 4 cups
¾-ounce package dried boletus mushrooms, soaked in
    warm water for 15 minutes (optional)

2 stalks celery, cut into 1-inch sections
1 1/2 cups carrots cut into 1-inch rounds
4 cups chopped tomatoes, fresh if possible (drain if canned)
1 teaspoon marjoram
Polenta (page 168)

Place rabbit pieces in a cast-iron skillet or heavy skillet and sauté over high heat to dry out, turning often, until they begin to brown. Add the oils, rosemary, salt, and pepper, and sauté over medium to high heat for several minutes. Add wine and mushrooms, cover, lower heat to medium, and cook until wine cooks out.

In the meantime, put celery, carrots, tomatoes, and marjoram in a saucepan large enough to hold rabbit pieces. Cover and gently boil till wine cooks out. Then add rabbit and the rest of the ingredients to tomato sauce. Cover partially and boil gently about 1 1/2 hours, depending on tenderness of rabbit.

Make enough polenta for 6 people. Spoon it onto heated plates, spoon sauce over polenta, and serve rabbit sections and vegetables alongside polenta.

Calories	Cholesterol mg	Protein gm	Carbohydrate gm	Total fat gm	%	Sat fat gm	%	Mono gm	Poly gm
3219	444.0	188.4	342.3	129.3	35	28.7	8	56.3	30.1

FRIED RABBIT
Coniglio Fritto

We first tasted this recipe in a restaurant in Siena. It may be served with one of the sauces for broiled or boiled meat on pages 427–42.

Serves 6.

3-pound rabbit, cut into serving pieces
Milk
Salt and freshly ground black pepper to taste
Flour for dredging
About 2 cups vegetable oil, such as corn oil
    or peanut oil

Garnish: Lemon wedges

Dry rabbit pieces and dip in milk, then salt and pepper them and dust with flour, shaking off any excess. Heat oil in a medium skillet, then carefully put in some of the rabbit sections and fry, uncovered, turning often. Cook over medium heat 10 to 15 minutes, depending on thickness of rabbit. Remove from oil and blot with paper towels; keep them warm while you cook the rest of the rabbit pieces.

Serve hot with lemon wedges.

With whole milk:

Calories	Cholesterol mg	Protein gm	Carbohydrate gm	Total fat gm	%	Sat fat gm	%	Mono gm	Poly gm
1211	384.0	127.5	27.4	61.8	45	19.9	14	21.2	13.9

With skim milk:

1203	381.0	127.5	27.5	60.9	45	19.3	14	20.9	13.9

Although rabbit has a higher percentage of total fat than the leanest cuts of beef and veal, the P:S ratio does not so overwhelmingly favor saturated over polyunsaturated fat. It is possible, therefore, to adjust the ratio to 1:1 by the addition of a relatively small amount of polyunsaturated oil; two teaspoons of safflower oil would suffice for this entire recipe.

VIII   VEGETABLES

Too many people find vegetables uninteresting because they don't use their imaginations and because they have acquired some bad cooking habits. There is still a tendency in this country to cook vegetables to death, which destroys both their taste and nutritional value. Then too often a thick sauce, such as a cream sauce or a hollandaise, or just a lot of cream and butter, is slathered on top to try to make the vegetable palatable. It doesn't really matter whether a vegetable is fresh, in season, canned, or frozen when you treat it that way.

I'm not saying that butter and cream don't complement certain vegetables, but care and discretion must be used. And to my mind the fruity flavor of a good virgin olive oil is preferable.

So respect your vegetables. Cook them lightly. Make the most of what is in season and try to bring out the identity of each vegetable.

At home we often have a vegetable dish as a main course, particularly for lunch. It is very handy, when I haven't planned a meal ahead, to go down into the garden and pick a handful of this and that and then put together an interesting combination. Even in December, when the ground is frozen, I'll find maybe some Savoy cabbage, leeks, Swiss chard, beets, parsnips, rutabagas. If you stay on a seasonal track, you won't go wrong in your combinations: winter vegetables automatically go well with one another, and spring vegetables, like dandelion or radicchio greens, the first of the onions, rucola as an herb, and new potatoes will make naturally good companions. Use potatoes in any season as a binder, mashing a little of the cooked potato for a thickener while leaving the rest in chunks, and you'll have a delicious, light but satisfying dish with its own creamy sauce to absorb the good juices—no need for butter or extra oil. E.G.

Vegetables and vegetarianism seem at first glance to provide an ideal dietary approach to the control of cholesterol. Although vegetarianism frequently results in lower cholesterol levels than meat-eating, it is not the simple solution one might imagine. For one thing, many vegetarians, so-called ovo-lacto vegetarians, eat eggs and dairy products so that they ingest not only cholesterol but also saturated fats, sometimes in considerable quantities. Other vegetarians, called vegans, avoid all animal flesh, eggs, and dairy products; but many of them use coconut and other saturated oils and nuts (including coconuts), the oils of which provide a relatively high percentage of their caloric intake. Within the past decade in the United States, some vegetarian substitutes for meat dishes have begun to appear on restaurant menus, and college caterers have recognized the need to provide sustenance for growing numbers of vegetarian students, although usually the selections have been limited, the preparation poor, and the food uninteresting.

A couple of years ago I attended a medical meeting in Bombay. Vegetarianism is so common in India that it is customary for separate meat-eating and vegetarian buffets to be set. I couldn't resist the opportunity to compare so I took a small taste of everything in both buffets. The vegetarian food was, I thought, the far more interesting of the two. It is unfortunate that similar imagination is not widely used in vegetable preparation in this country. Ed is an exception, however, and it is interesting to see how he draws on his Italian background to come up with some very delicious vegetable dishes of great originality. Not all of them avoid meat; but all avoid simply boiling vegetables to a fare-thee-well and drenching them with butter. R.W.

BAKED ARTICHOKES
Carciofi Stufati

All of the artichoke should be edible preparing it this way, but unfortunately many of the artichokes you buy in markets are apt to be too tough or too old. Look for tight heads and a rich green color; the leaves should not be dry on the outside.

Serves 4.

3 fresh artichokes, about the size of a fist
Juice of 1/2 lemon
2 tablespoons chopped Italian parsley
2 tablespoons chopped fresh mint
1 cup dry white wine
1 cup water
1 tablespoon safflower oil
2 tablespoons olive oil
Salt and freshly ground black pepper to taste

Garnish: Chopped Italian parsley

Remove several layers of outer leaves from the artichokes. With a sharp knife cut off tips about 1 inch from top. Trim stem by cutting away tough outer skin. Then quarter each artichoke lengthwise. Put in cold water with the juice of 1/2 lemon until ready to use. The lemon keeps the artichokes from discoloring.

Preheat oven to 400°. Drain artichokes and place them in a baking dish so that they fit snugly. Add the rest of the ingredients. Cover and cook about 1 hour, or until artichokes are tender. There should be a light layer of moisture when done. Garnish with chopped parsley.

Calories	Cholesterol mg	Protein gm	Carbohydrate gm	Total fat gm	%	Sat fat gm	%	Mono gm	Poly gm
528	0	13.4	28.2	41.5	69	4.1	7	22.6	11.6

In fresh artichokes the principal carbohydrate is inulin, which probably has no caloric value in humans. With storage the inulin is gradually converted to assimilable sugar so that the caloric value rises. The size of the artichokes varies considerably. In this recipe, we use artichokes that weigh about 1/3 pound each; those in artichokes with tomato and basil weigh about 1/7 of a pound each.

ARTICHOKES JEWISH STYLE
Carciofi alla Giudia

This recipe can be used as a first course or as a vegetable course. All of the artichoke is edible, and you will truly be surprised at how good this ancient Roman recipe is.

Serves 2.

2 small fresh artichokes, about the size of a fist
Juice of 1/2 lemon
Corn oil for frying
Salt to taste

Garnish: Lemon wedges

Prepare artichokes as in preceding recipe but do not quarter them.

Heat about 1 1/2 inches corn oil in a small, heavy saucepan, then carefully place one of the artichokes in an upright position and cook for about 3 or 4 minutes. Using two wooden spoons, turn artichoke over and firmly press down on it with both spoons. Cook for another 3 to 4 minutes, then turn over. Cook for several minutes again. Continue cooking and turning the artichoke until golden brown—at which point it will look like an open flower. Then flick a few drops of water into the oil to produce steam so the leaves will crisp.

Remove and blot on paper towels and cook the other artichoke in the same manner. Serve with salt and lemon wedges.

Calories	Cholesterol mg	Protein gm	Carbohydrate gm	Total fat gm	%	Sat fat gm	%	Mono gm	Poly gm
328	0	8.8	12.4	27.8	75	2.4	6	7.6	14.4

ARTICHOKES WITH TOMATO AND BASIL
Carciofi con Pomodoro e Basilico

Serves 4 as a vegetable course.

8 small fresh artichokes or 9-ounce package frozen
    artichoke hearts
4 tablespoons safflower oil
3 tablespoons olive oil
1 medium onion, chopped
2 tablespoons dry white wine (optional)
1 cup chopped tomatoes, fresh if possible (drain if canned)
2 tablespoons chopped fresh basil or 1 tablespoon dried
Salt and freshly ground black pepper to taste
2 cups bread cut in 1-inch cubes

If fresh artichokes are used, remove tough outside leaves and cut in half. If frozen artichokes are used, blanch in boiling water and drain.

Heat 1 tablespoon of the safflower oil and all the olive oil in a medium skillet, then add onion and cook several minutes. Add artichokes and cook, uncovered, over moderate heat until edges of artichokes begin to brown. Add wine, cover, and simmer for several minutes. Add tomatoes, basil, salt, and pepper and continue to cook 20 minutes more.

In the meantime, heat remaining 3 tablespoons safflower oil in a medium skillet and add bread cubes, stirring often. When croutons are golden brown, turn off heat and set aside. Serve artichokes with croutons on each portion.

Calories	Cholesterol mg	Protein gm	Carbohydrate gm	Total fat gm	%	Sat fat gm	%	Mono gm	Poly gm
1248	0	22.0	72.2	96.7	68	10.2	7	36.1	43.7

FRIED ARTICHOKE HEARTS
Cuori di Carciofi Fritti

This dish, which is excellent with fritto misto (page 389), requires small fresh artichokes, but since they're not available in most parts of America, I use frozen artichokes. They are a satisfactory substitute.

Serves 3 to 4.

9-ounce package frozen artichoke hearts
Freshly ground black pepper to taste
2 egg whites, lightly beaten
Flour for dredging

Corn oil or vegetable oil for frying

Garnish: Lemon wedges

Blanch artichoke hearts in salted water to cover. As soon as water returns to a boil, drain. Grind pepper over the artichokes, roll in egg whites, and dust with flour. In the meantime, heat 3/4 inch oil in a small skillet. When oil is hot, add artichoke hearts one at a time. Lightly brown them and then blot on paper towels. Serve hot with lemon wedges.

Calories	Cholesterol mg	Protein gm	Carbohydrate gm	Total fat gm	%	Sat fat gm	%	Mono gm	Poly gm
247	0	14.4	31.7	9.1	32	0.9	3	2.5	4.8

STEAMED ASPARAGUS
Asparagi al Vapore

Serves 2 to 3.

8 thick asparagus
1 tablespoon safflower oil
1 tablespoon butter
1 teaspoon minced garlic
Juice of 1 lemon
1 tablespoon minced Italian parsley
Freshly ground black pepper to taste

Wash asparagus well and trim off ends. Steam in a vegetable steamer about 5 to 6 minutes. Or I just put a tightly fitting colander into a pot. When water boils in pot, place asparagus in the colander, cover, and steam. Do not overcook.

Heat oil and butter. Add garlic and as soon as it begins to turn color, add lemon juice, parsley, and pepper.

Pour over hot asparagus and serve.

Calories	Cholesterol mg	Protein gm	Carbohydrate gm	Total fat gm	%	Sat fat gm	%	Mono gm	Poly gm
307	31.0	7.2	16.4	25.6	73	7.5	21	5.4	10.4

SAUTÉED ASPARAGUS
Asparagi in Padella

This dish is most successful made with the thinner asparagus — the thinner the better. And it is usually more inexpensive than the thicker asparagus.

Serves 4.

1 1/2 pounds thin asparagus
2 tablespoons peanut oil
1 tablespoon olive oil
2 cups sliced onion (optional)
Salt and freshly ground black pepper to taste

Remove tough ends from the asparagus, then wash and cut spears into 2-inch lengths. Heat oils in a medium skillet, add asparagus, and cook over high heat for several minutes. Add optional onion, salt, and freshly ground black pepper. Cook over medium to high heat, stirring often. Cook until asparagus are tender — about 5 minutes. Do not overcook.

Calories	Cholesterol mg	Protein gm	Carbohydrate gm	Total fat gm	%	Sat fat gm	%	Mono gm	Poly gm
630	0	20.4	47.7	42.1	59	6.4	9	22.3	9.7

Calculations include optional onions.

ASPARAGUS FRIED IN BATTER
Asparagi in Pastella

Serves 8 as a vegetable course.

24 to 30 asparagus spears
1 cup flour
1 egg white, lightly beaten
2/3 cup dry white wine
Salt and freshly ground black pepper to taste
Corn or vegetable oil

Cut off tough asparagus stems and wash the spears well.

Mix flour, egg white, wine, salt, and pepper and let sit at least 1 hour.

Blanch asparagus in boiling water. Drain, run cold water over them, drain, and set aside.

Pour about 3/4 inch oil in a medium skillet. When oil is hot, dip asparagus spears one at a time in batter, then gently lower into the oil and lightly brown. Do not crowd. Remove asparagus and place on paper towels. Repeat with remaining asparagus. Serve warm.

Calories	Cholesterol mg	Protein gm	Carbohydrate gm	Total fat gm	%	Sat fat gm	%	Mono gm	Poly gm
896	0	40.5	149.7	16.8	17	1.4	1	3.8	7.2

BAKED ASPARAGUS
Asparagi al Forno

I had tasted this dish only in my mother's kitchen until I started making it. Now it has become my favorite way to cook asparagus.

Serves 4 to 6.

1½ pounds asparagus
4 tablespoons coarsely chopped Italian parsley
3 tablespoons olive oil
1 tablespoon safflower oil
Salt and freshly ground black pepper to taste
2 cloves garlic, finely minced

Preheat oven to 400° to 425°. Wash asparagus well and drain. Cut off tough ends. Place asparagus in a baking tray or shallow dish and sprinkle remaining ingredients over them. Bake, uncovered, until tender but firm to the bite, 10 to 15 minutes.

Calories	Cholesterol mg	Protein gm	Carbohydrate gm	Total fat gm	%	Sat fat gm	%	Mono gm	Poly gm
635	0	14.6	27.9	55.2	76	6.6	9	31.3	13.4

GREEN BEANS VENETIAN STYLE
Fagiolini alla Veneto

Serves 4.

6 cups fresh green beans, ends removed
3 anchovies, chopped
1 tablespoon finely chopped Italian parsley
1 tablespoon olive oil
1 tablespoon safflower oil
1 clove garlic, minced
2 tablespoons lemon juice or white wine vinegar
Salt and freshly ground black pepper to taste

Boil the green beans in boiling salted water or steam them — about 5 to 7 minutes, depending on freshness. When beans are tender, drain. Put in mixing bowl, add the rest of the ingredients, and toss. Do not oversalt, because there is salt in the anchovies. Serve warm or at room temperature.

Calories	Cholesterol mg	Protein gm	Carbohydrate gm	Total fat gm	%	Sat fat gm	%	Mono gm	Poly gm
493	13.0	17.7	50.5	30.8	55	4.0	7	12.2	11.9

GREEN BEANS WITH ZUCCHINI AND POTATOES
Fagiolini con Zucchini e Patate

Serves 4 to 6.

2 tablespoons olive oil
1 tablespoon safflower oil
1 medium onion, thinly sliced
2 cups ripe chopped tomatoes
3 tablespoons chopped fresh basil
3 medium potatoes, peeled and cut into thick slices
4 cups green beans or Italian pole beans, stemmed and
    cut in half
2 cups zucchini cut in ½-inch slices
Salt and freshly ground black pepper to taste

Garnish: 2 tablespoons chopped Italian parsley

Heat the oils in a wide, shallow pan. Add onion and sauté. As it takes on color, add tomatoes and basil. Cover and simmer about 5 minutes, stirring occasionally. Add potatoes, beans, zucchini, salt, and pepper. Cover and cook over moderate heat until potatoes are tender, mixing often. Garnish with chopped parsley when serving.

Calories	Cholesterol mg	Protein gm	Carbohydrate gm	Total fat gm	%	Sat fat gm	%	Mono gm	Poly gm
1072	0	29.2	147.7	43.4	36	4.8	4	21.4	12.3

POLE BEANS WITH POTATOES AND TOMATOES
Fagiolini con Patate e Pomodori

Serves 4.

1 tablespoon olive oil
1 tablespoon safflower oil
1 medium onion, sliced
1 clove garlic, chopped
1 cup chopped tomatoes, fresh if possible
    (drain if canned)
2 tablespoons chopped fresh basil
1 tablespoon chopped Italian parsley
1 pound fresh Italian pole beans or regular green beans,*
    picked, washed, and cut in half

*If green beans aren't garden fresh, blanch them in a large pot of boiling water until water returns to a boil; then add them to sauce.

1 medium potato, sliced
Salt and freshly ground black pepper to taste

Heat the oils in a medium skillet, add onion and cook for several minutes. Add garlic, cook over low heat for several minutes. Add tomatoes, cover, and simmer for several minutes. Add basil and parsley, cover, and simmer for several more minutes. Add beans, potatoes, salt, and pepper, cover, and simmer about 20 minutes, adding a little water if needed.

Calories	Cholesterol mg	Protein gm	Carbohydrate gm	Total fat gm	%	Sat fat gm	%	Mono gm	Poly gm
626	0	17.5	79.3	28.9	41	2.6	4	12.3	10.7

GREEN BEAN RATATOUILLE
Ratatouille di Fagiolini

This recipe, which is a specialty of Domodossola, in northern Italy, should be made when all ingredients are garden fresh.

Serves 3.

1 tablespoon olive oil
1 tablespoon safflower oil or 2 tablespoons vegetable oil
1 teaspoon minced garlic
2 tablespoons finely chopped Italian parsley
2 tablespoons chopped fresh basil
4 cups green beans, ends removed, cut in half and washed
1 medium ripe tomato, chopped
1/2 cup dry red wine
Salt and freshly ground black pepper to taste

Heat the oils in a large skillet, then add garlic, parsley, and basil. As soon as garlic begins to take on color, add the rest of the ingredients, cover, and cook over low heat for 30 minutes, or until beans are tender. Serve warm.

Calories	Cholesterol mg	Protein gm	Carbohydrate gm	Total fat gm	%	Sat fat gm	%	Mono gm	Poly gm
444	0	10.7	44.6	28.2	56	3.0	6	11.5	11.2

BOILED CRANBERRY BEANS
Borlotti Lessi

Serves 3.

2 cups freshly shelled cranberry (shell) beans
1 bay leaf
2 cloves garlic
2 tablespoons fresh basil or 1 tablespoon dried
Salt to taste
1 tablespoon good olive oil
1 teaspoon safflower oil
Freshly ground black pepper to taste
1/2 onion, finely chopped

Put the beans, bay leaf, garlic, basil, and pinch of salt in a small saucepan with enough water to cover; then cover and boil about 1 hour, until beans are tender.

Drain and put beans in a serving bowl. Remove and discard garlic and bay leaf. Add oils, pepper, and onion. At this stage beans can be used as a vegetable.

Variation: Sliced ripe tomatoes added to the beans with minced parsley and lemon juice would make a very pleasant salad to be served warm or at room temperature.

Calories	Cholesterol mg	Protein gm	Carbohydrate gm	Total fat gm	%	Sat fat gm	%	Mono gm	Poly gm
522	0	26.3	66.9	19.7	33	2.2	4	10.4	4.5

BROCCOLI WITH TUNA
Broccoli con Tonno

This is excellent as a light lunch, served at room temperature.

Serves 4.

1 large head broccoli (to make 8 cups)
6 anchovies, chopped (6 packed in oil, or 3 preserved
  in salt)
3 tablespoons olive oil
1 tablespoon safflower oil
1 teaspoon minced garlic
Hot pepper flakes to taste
1 cup chopped tomatoes, fresh if possible (drain if canned)
1 7-ounce can of Italian-style tunafish, drained

Clean broccoli by peeling tough skin off stems. Cut the stems and flowerets into manageable pieces. Blanch broccoli in boiling water, then drain and set aside.

If you are using salted anchovies, wash them and then separate fillets from bone.

Heat the two oils in a large skillet, then add garlic, anchovies, and hot pepper flakes, stirring with a wooden spoon. When garlic begins to color, add tomatoes and cook over high heat, uncovered, for several minutes to reduce moisture. Add broccoli, cover, lower heat, and cook, stirring occasionally, until it is tender. Turn off heat, add tuna, mix, and serve.

Calories	Cholesterol mg	Protein gm	Carbohydrate gm	Total fat gm	%	Sat fat gm	%	Mono gm	Poly gm
1046	110.0	72.0	29.6	72.2	61	10.4	9	34.3	16.4

BROCCOLI WITH YAMS
Broccoli con Patate Dolci Americane

The combination of sweet yams and hot pepper is very pleasant in this attractive dish, the orange yam slices and green broccoli making a pleasant contrast.

Serves 4 to 6.

2 yams, about 1 1/2 pounds
1 bunch broccoli, prepared as on page 346
2 tablespoons olive oil
1 tablespoon safflower oil
3 tablespoons coarsely chopped shallots
Hot pepper flakes to taste (optional)
3/4 cup chicken or beef stock
Salt to taste

Bake yams in a preheated 450° oven until tender but firm — about 40 minutes. Blanch broccoli and drain.

Heat the two oils in a medium skillet, add shallots, and sauté. As shallots begin to brown, add broccoli, hot pepper flakes, and stock. Peel yams, cut into 1/2-inch slices, and add to broccoli. Add salt, cover, and simmer for 10 minutes.

Calories	Cholesterol mg	Protein gm	Carbohydrate gm	Total fat gm	%	Sat fat gm	%	Mono gm	Poly gm
1106	0	29.2	154.9	43.0	34	4.8	4	21.4	12.3

BROCCOLETTI DI RAPE

Broccoletti di rape is more often known in America as broccoli rab, or rabe broccoli. Rab is the southern Italian dialect term, but the correct spelling for this marvelous vegetable is broccoletti di rape — that is, if we are willing to accept the spelling of the vegetable by the great Italian cookbook writers Caranacini, Ada Boni, and Artusi, among others.

It is often incorrectly called turnip greens (rapa is the name for turnips), and perhaps some of the confusion stems from Artusi's description of broccoletti di rape, which he identifies with the turnip. Although it is possible that broccoletti di rape as we know it existed in Italy in the early part of the nineteenth century, I doubt very much that it was the same vegetable we know as broccoletti di rape today. I'm certain a great deal of cross-breeding produced the modern broccoletti di rape, with its succulent broccoli-like buds and no turnip bulb. Turnips do not produce broccoli-like buds. We grow both on our property and there is a difference.

If you grow your own broccoletti di rape, as we do, you'll notice that after the first cutting, new growth appears with smaller buds, called cimi di rape. Some Italians prefer the cimi di rape to the larger buds, but we prefer the larger buds.

Artusi describes in his *La Scienza in Cucina e L'arte di Mangiar Bene* the unpopularity of broccoletti di rape in Italy at the time. This is certainly not true now — in fact, it is by far one of the most popular vegetables in Italy today. His description convinces me that he was talking about turnip greens, not broccoletti di rape.

Serves 6.

2 pounds fresh broccoletti di rape
3 cloves garlic, finely chopped
3 tablespoons extra virgin olive oil
1 tablespoon safflower oil
Salt to taste
Hot pepper flakes to taste (optional)

Garnish: Lemon wedges

Cut flowerets about 3 inches from the top. Cut tender stems into 3-inch lengths and peel. Remove and discard any large tough leaves and any discolored leaves. Wash rape well.

Bring about 4 quarts water to a boil. Add rape and boil about 3 or 4 minutes, until tender but not overcooked. Drain well. Toss with garlic, oils, salt, and pepper flakes, mixing well. Serve hot with lemon wedges.

Calories	Cholesterol mg	Protein gm	Carbohydrate gm	Total fat gm	%	Sat fat gm	%	Mono gm	Poly gm
685	0	19.6	31.3	57.3	74	6.6	8	31.3	13.4

No figures available for rape — mustard greens have been used instead.

RAPE WITH BROCCOLI AND POTATOES
Broccoletti di Rape con Broccoli e Patate

Serves 6.

1 pound rape, 8 or 9 cups when cleaned (for preparation,
   see above)
3 medium potatoes, peeled and sliced
4 cups broccoli cut into bite-sized pieces
3 tablespoons olive oil
1 tablespoon safflower oil
1 tablespoon or less finely chopped garlic
Hot pepper flakes to taste (optional)
Salt to taste

Bring water to a boil in a medium saucepan. Add rape and potatoes. When
water returns to a boil, add broccoli and cook 4 or 5 minutes. Drain,
reserving about 1 cup water.

Heat the oils in a medium skillet, then add garlic but do not brown
it—just heat it. Add drained vegetables and hot pepper flakes. Cover and
simmer over moderate heat about 15 minutes, adding water, as needed, and
salt.

Variation: Potatoes may be omitted, in which case use 6 cups broccoli.

Calories	Cholesterol mg	Protein gm	Carbohydrate gm	Total fat gm	%	Sat fat gm	%	Mono gm	Poly gm
984	0	25.8	102.0	56.6	51	6.6	6	31.3	13.4

BROCCOLETTI DI RAPE WITH BEANS
Broccoletti di Rape con Fagioli

This is an excellent vegetable accompaniment with broiled meats and fish.

Serves 4.

1 cup dried cannellini or Great Northern beans
2 cups water
3 cups water
1 tablespoon olive oil
1 tablespoon safflower oil
Salt and freshly ground black pepper or hot pepper flakes
   to taste
1 tablespoon crushed rosemary
1 cup finely chopped onion
1 teaspoon finely chopped garlic
6 cups broccoletti di rape cut up (see directions, page 348)

Put dried beans in a small bowl, add 2 cups water, and soak overnight. Beans will triple in bulk after soaking.

Pick out and discard any discolored beans. Pour beans in a medium soup pot, preferably terracotta. Add 3 cups water and all the other ingredients except the rape, bring to a boil, cover, and boil gently about 1¼ hours, until beans are tender. Add rape and cook about 10 more minutes, then turn off heat and let stand about 10 to 15 minutes.

Calories	Cholesterol mg	Protein gm	Carbohydrate gm	Total fat gm	%	Sat fat gm	%	Mono gm	Poly gm
1007	0	61.7	136.7	32.2	28	3.0	3	11.5	11.2

BRUSSELS SPROUTS WITH POTATOES
Cavoletti di Bruxelles con Patate

Brussels sprouts can be a dreadful vegetable if not cooked properly. Try this recipe and the one that follows and you will find them most satisfying.

Serves 3 to 4.

½ pound fresh Brussels sprouts
3 medium potatoes, peeled and cut into 1-inch squares
2 tablespoons olive oil
1 tablespoon safflower oil
3 cloves garlic, finely chopped
Hot pepper flakes to taste (optional)
About 3 to 5 teaspoons reserved water
Salt and freshly ground black pepper to taste
1 teaspoon dried oregano

Remove discolored outer leaves from the Brussels sprouts and boil along with potatoes in a large pot of boiling water about 10 minutes. Drain, reserving about 3 to 5 teaspoons water.

Heat oils in a medium skillet, add garlic and hot pepper. As garlic begins to color, add drained potatoes and Brussels sprouts. Add 3 teaspoons reserved water, salt, pepper, and oregano. Cover and simmer over low heat about 10 minutes, adding more water if needed.

Calories	Cholesterol mg	Protein gm	Carbohydrate gm	Total fat gm	%	Sat fat gm	%	Mono gm	Poly gm
812	0	21.4	94.3	42.2	46	4.8	5	21.4	12.3

BRUSSELS SPROUTS WITH ANCHOVIES
Cavoletti di Bruxelles con Acciughe

Serves 4.

1 pound fresh Brussels sprouts
1 tablespoon olive oil
1 teaspoon safflower oil
2 anchovy fillets, chopped*
Hot pepper flakes to taste (optional)
1 teaspoon minced garlic
6 dried black olives, pitted and sliced
1/4 cup chicken or beef broth

*I use salted anchovies in this recipe. See instructions for washing and boning on page 503.

Remove tough outer leaves of sprouts, wash, and cook in a large pot of boiling water about 2 minutes. Drain and set aside.

Heat the oils in a medium skillet and add anchovies and hot pepper flakes. When the anchovies begin to dissolve, add the garlic and black olives. As the garlic begins to take on color, add the broth and Brussels sprouts. Cover and cook over low to medium heat about 10 minutes.

Calories	Cholesterol mg	Protein gm	Carbohydrate gm	Total fat gm	%	Sat fat gm	%	Mono gm	Poly gm
420	4.0	24.1	32.3	24.7	52	2.7	6	13.5	4.8

CABBAGE WITH POTATOES
Cavolo con Patate

You will find that Savoy cabbage — the loose-leafed curly head — is much tastier than ordinary green cabbage.

Serves 5 to 6 as a vegetable course.

1 1/2 pounds fresh cabbage, Savoy if possible
3 medium potatoes, peeled and quartered
3 tablespoons olive oil
1 tablespoon safflower oil
3 cloves garlic, lightly crushed (skins discarded)
Hot pepper flakes to taste (optional)
1 teaspoon dried oregano
Salt to taste

Garnish: 2 tablespoons finely chopped Italian parsley

Cut cabbage into 1-inch-thick wedges. Remove and discard core. Steam cabbage and potatoes in a covered container about 25 minutes.

In a medium, shallow pan, heat oils, then add garlic and hot pepper. When garlic browns slightly, either discard it or leave in pan, but discard it before serving cabbage. Add cabbage and potatoes, oregano, and salt. Cover and cook over low heat about 5 minutes. Garnish with parsley.

Variation: Use only 2 potatoes and add 1 cup chopped tomatoes.

Calories	Cholesterol mg	Protein gm	Carbohydrate gm	Total fat gm	%	Sat fat gm	%	Mono gm	Poly gm
875	0	23.5	83.2	56.0	56	5.6	6	32.8	12.7

STEAMED CABBAGE
Cavolo a Vapore

This delicate vegetable is most appealing served with a recipe such as squab with peas (page 280) or with boiled meats.

Serves 4.

> 1 small to medium head Savoy cabbage, quartered, core removed
> 3 medium potatoes, peeled and halved
> 1 tablespoon finely chopped fresh ginger
> 2 tablespoons extra virgin olive oil
> 1 tablespoon safflower oil
> 4 scallions, cut in 2-inch lengths
> Salt and freshly ground black pepper to taste

Steam cabbage and potatoes about 10 minutes. Add ginger to cabbage, forcing some between the leaves. Continue steaming until potatoes are tender. Toss with oils, scallions, salt, and pepper.

Calories	Cholesterol mg	Protein gm	Carbohydrate gm	Total fat gm	%	Sat fat gm	%	Mono gm	Poly gm
942	0	22.2	121.1	43.1	40	4.8	4	21.4	12.3

SAUERKRAUT
Crauti

I am not much of a sauerkraut fan, but this homemade recipe, which was given to me by a German friend, is delightful. The sauerkraut is very delicate because it doesn't ferment in brine. I was told by my friend that she gets the best results using glass-topped jars.

Shred green cabbage. It's very easy to do in a food processor, using the slicer blade. Each quart will require about ¾ pound of cabbage.

Put quart jars in boiling water. Remove, fill with raw cabbage, up to about 1 inch of the top of the jar. Add 1 teaspoon salt, 1 teaspoon sugar, and fill to the top with boiling water. Close jars and let them sit in a cool place for about 5 weeks before using. Sauerkraut will last for several years.

To use, drain but do not rinse the sauerkraut. It can be heated or used at room temperature with boiled or broiled meats.

Calories	Cholesterol mg	Protein gm	Carbohydrate gm	Total fat gm	%	Sat fat gm	%	Mono gm	Poly gm
97	0	4.4	19.6	0.7	6	–	–	–	–

Calculations are for 1 quart.

CAULIFLOWER MARCHES STYLE
Cavolfiore alla Marchigiana

Serves 6.

1 medium fresh cauliflower
5 tablespoons vegetable oil (4 olive, 1 safflower)
1 medium onion, thinly sliced
Hot pepper flakes to taste (optional)
Salt to taste
1/3 cup white wine vinegar
3 cups chopped tomatoes, fresh if possible
    (drain if canned)
2 tablespoons chopped Italian parsley

Cut cauliflower into flowerets, then cut large ones in half. Wash the flowerets.

Heat oil in a large skillet, then add cauliflower, cover, and sauté over medium heat. When cauliflower begins to brown, add onion, cover, and simmer until onion wilts. Add pepper flakes, salt, and vinegar, cover, and simmer until vinegar evaporates. Add tomatoes, cover, and simmer about 30 minutes, until cauliflower is tender but firm. Toss in parsley, and serve hot.

Calories	Cholesterol mg	Protein gm	Carbohydrate gm	Total fat gm	%	Sat fat gm	%	Mono gm	Poly gm
1069	0	33.6	84.6	70.9	58	8.4	7	41.2	14.5

FRIED CAULIFLOWER
Cavolfiore Fritto

The batter in this recipe is used on a variety of vegetables, such as blanched broccoli, mushrooms, peppers, and asparagus.

Serves 4.

1 cup flour
Salt and freshly ground black pepper to taste
²/3 cup dry white wine
1 egg white, lightly beaten
½ a medium cauliflower
Corn oil or vegetable oil

In a mixing bowl stir together the flour, salt, pepper, wine, and egg white, then cover and let sit for 1 hour.

Boil cauliflower flowerets about 5 minutes, then drain. Heat ¾ inch oil in a small skillet. When oil is hot, dip the flowerets one at a time into the batter with a pair of tongs, then gently place them in the hot oil and cook, turning occasionally, until they are a golden brown. Don't crowd them. Repeat the process, blotting finished flowerets on paper towels. Serve hot.

Calories	Cholesterol mg	Protein gm	Carbohydrate gm	Total fat gm	%	Sat fat gm	%	Mono gm	Poly gm
737	0	29.6	128.9	11.4	14	0.9	1	2.5	4.8

PURÉE OF CELERY ROOT

Serves 4 to 6.

1½ pounds celery root, peeled and cut into large pieces
1 tablespoon safflower oil
1 tablespoon olive oil
1 or 2 cloves garlic, minced
Salt and freshly ground black pepper to taste

Cover celery root with water and boil, covered, until fork tender. Drain and set aside.

Heat the oils in a small skillet, then add garlic and cook until it begins to color. Do not brown.

Put cooked celery root and the oil-and-garlic mixture in a food processor and purée, or use a potato ricer for the celery root and then blend in the oil and garlic. Season with salt and pepper. Serve hot.

Calories	Cholesterol mg	Protein gm	Carbohydrate gm	Total fat gm	%	Sat fat gm	%	Mono gm	Poly gm
477	0	10.7	43.2	28.9	53	3.0	5	11.5	11.2

ABOUT SWISS CHARD

Swiss chard, an often neglected vegetable in America, is very popular in Italy. It is frequently preferred over spinach for stuffings, especially for pasta stuffings.

It is a leafy summer vegetable that is easy to grow and prolific; unlike spinach, it thrives in the heat and is therefore ideal as a summer green. Its taste is delicate and I have heard Italians say it "freshens the stomach."

Swiss chard is available at the better vegetable markets. We grow a lot of it and enjoy it until a hard frost.

SWISS CHARD WITH POTATOES
Bieta con Patate

Serves 4.

3 medium potatoes, peeled and cut into 3 pieces
1 pound Swiss chard, washed and cut into large pieces
2 tablespoons olive oil
1 teaspoon safflower oil
1 small onion, coarsely chopped
2 zucchini, cut into 1-inch cubes
Salt to taste

Bring 2 quarts water to a boil, add potatoes, and cook about 5 minutes, then add Swiss chard and boil several more minutes. Drain and reserve 1/4 cup of the water.

Heat the oils in a medium shallow saucepan, add the onion, and when sizzling, add the potatoes, zucchini, Swiss chard, reserved water, and salt. Cook, covered, over moderate heat for about 20 minutes.

Calories	Cholesterol mg	Protein gm	Carbohydrate gm	Total fat gm	%	Sat fat gm	%	Mono gm	Poly gm
825	0	25.5	113.4	33.8	36	4.0	4	20.3	5.6

BAKED CUCUMBERS
Cetrioli al Forno

This is an excellent way to prepare cucumbers, especially for gardeners who seem to have more of the vegetable than they can use when it starts coming in.

Serves 2.

2 medium cucumbers
1 teaspoon olive oil
1 teaspoon safflower oil
Salt and freshly ground black pepper to taste

Preheat the oven to 450° to 500° for 10 minutes.

Peel the cucumbers and cut them into 1/4-inch slices. Lightly oil baking tray and place cucumber slices on it, not overlapping them. Sprinkle with oils, salt, and pepper. Bake, turning the cucumber slices with a spatula as their bottoms begin to brown. Cook until tops of slices begin to brown — about 8 minutes in all.

Serve hot or at room temperature.

Calories	Cholesterol mg	Protein gm	Carbohydrate gm	Total fat gm	%	Sat fat gm	%	Mono gm	Poly gm
119	0	1.7	8.1	9.3	69	1.0	7	3.8	3.8

ABOUT DANDELIONS

We look forward to early spring, when the dandelions appear and our lawn becomes a sea of yellow. We eat the greens raw in salads and cooked — a spring vegetable as popular as any other on our table. Some people think dandelion leaves should not be gathered after the flowers have blossomed, but in a temperate climate you can gather dandelion greens until mid-June, after which the days do become too hot and the sun makes the leaves bitter. Aside from the nutritional value of dandelion greens, the slightly bitter taste is most satisfying.

During a recent spring visit to Italy, practically every restaurant we dined in served cicoria in padella — sautéed dandelion greens. It is only here that the dandelion is held in some contempt, although recently more vegetable markets carry the greens in the spring.

Although it's possible to buy them, it is a lot more fun to gather your own. The best way to do so is to cut the stalk far down with a sharp knife so that you get all the leaves in one clump. It is much easier to pick and wash the greens if the leaves are still attached to the root.

Soak the greens in cold water, then pick them over carefully and cut the leaves off the root, discarding the flower, discolored leaves, and stems.

Boil dandelion greens about 20 minutes. The cooking time will depend on the size and tenderness of the greens. Drain when tender and let cool. At this point you can serve the greens as a cold vegetable with finely chopped garlic, lemon juice, and olive oil, or you can serve cicoria in padella.

DANDELION GREENS IN A SKILLET
Cicoria in Padella

Serves 6.

3 tablespoons olive oil
1 tablespoon safflower oil
3 cloves garlic, finely chopped
Hot pepper flakes to taste (optional)

2½ pounds fresh dandelion greens, washed and
    preboiled about 20 minutes (see opposite page)
Salt to taste

Garnish: Lemon wedges

Heat the oils in a medium skillet, then add garlic and hot pepper flakes. As
garlic begins to take on color, add boiled dandelion greens. Season with
salt, cover, lower heat, and cook greens about 5 to 10 minutes, tossing
often.
    Serve hot with lemon wedges.

Calories	Cholesterol mg	Protein gm	Carbohydrate gm	Total fat gm	%	Sat fat gm	%	Mono gm	Poly gm
999	0	31.1	107.0	62.1	55	5.6	5	32.9	12.5

DANDELION GREENS WITH POTATOES
Cicoria con Patate

Serves 6.

12 cups cleaned dandelion greens
2 cups diced potatoes
4 tablespoons olive oil
1 tablespoon safflower oil
3 cloves garlic, chopped
Hot pepper flakes to taste (optional)
Salt to taste

Boil dandelion greens with potatoes about 5 minutes. Drain, saving 1 cup
liquid.
    Heat the oils in a skillet, then add garlic and hot pepper. As soon as garlic
takes on color, add dandelion greens, potatoes, reserved liquid, and salt;
then cover and cook over low heat for 20 to 30 minutes. Mash potatoes
with a fork and add more oil if desired.

Calories	Cholesterol mg	Protein gm	Carbohydrate gm	Total fat gm	%	Sat fat gm	%	Mono gm	Poly gm
1264	0	31.8	125.9	74.2	52	8.4	6	43.2	14.5

PAN–FRIED EGGPLANT
Melanzane in Padella

I suggest salting eggplants for about 15 minutes if they are out of season,
then rinse and blot dry. But with fresh young eggplants salting is not necessary. I don't peel eggplants either. I find the skin holds the eggplant together
and I like the taste.

You will be surprised how tasty this simple recipe is, which goes so well with fried or broiled foods. The secret to its success is to use little oil, just enough to cover the bottom of the skillet.

Serves 3 or 4 as a vegetable course.

11 or 12 ¼-inch slices eggplant
Salt and freshly ground black pepper to taste
Flour for dredging
3 tablespoons olive oil
1 tablespoon safflower oil

Salt and pepper the eggplant slices. Lightly dust with flour, then shake off excess. Heat the oils in a medium skillet, then add eggplant slices, not overlapping them. Brown one side, turn, and brown the other side. They cook in about 3 minutes.

Calories	Cholesterol mg	Protein gm	Carbohydrate gm	Total fat gm	%	Sat fat gm	%	Mono gm	Poly gm
596	0	4.5	23.7	54.8	81	5.6	8	32.9	12.5

BAKED EGGPLANT
Melanzane al Forno

Serves 2 to 4.

2 small eggplants, the long thin Japanese strain if possible
2 tablespoons fresh breadcrumbs
1 tablespoon minced Italian parsley
1 clove garlic, finely chopped
1 teaspoon safflower oil
1 tablespoon olive oil
Salt and freshly ground black pepper to taste

Cut slits on surface of eggplants going in both directions to make a cross-hatch pattern. Mix breadcrumbs, parsley, garlic, the two oils, salt, and pepper. Blend well. With your fingers work mixture into slits on eggplants.
Preheat oven to 450°. Rub surface of a small baking tray with some vegetable oil, place eggplants on top, and bake, uncovered, about 15 to 20 minutes, depending on the size of the eggplants. Slice and serve on a platter.

Calories	Cholesterol mg	Protein gm	Carbohydrate gm	Total fat gm	%	Sat fat gm	%	Mono gm	Poly gm
237	0	3.5	15.1	18.7	69	2.2	8	10.4	4.5

EGGPLANT WITH BEANS
Melanzane e Fagioli

Serves 4 as an appetizer or vegetable course.

1 pound eggplant, cut into ¼-inch slices
2 tablespoons vegetable oil (1 olive oil and 1 safflower oil)
Salt and freshly ground black pepper to taste
1 cup cooked cannellini beans (white beans, page 82) or
    1 cup canned cannellini beans, drained
2 tablespoons finely chopped Italian parsley
Hot pepper flakes to taste (optional)
2 tablespoons wine vinegar
4 tablespoons thinly sliced whole scallions

Preheat oven to 500°. Place eggplant slices on a baking tray and sprinkle oil, salt, and pepper on top of them. Bake until eggplant begins to brown. Turn the slices over and when they begin to brown, remove from oven. Put the slices in a bowl, add remaining ingredients, and carefully mix. Let the dish rest about 2 hours before serving it, at room temperature.

Calories	Cholesterol mg	Protein gm	Carbohydrate gm	Total fat gm	%	Sat fat gm	%	Mono gm	Poly gm
563	0	19.1	57.8	29.0	45	3.0	5	11.5	11.2

EGGPLANT IN SAUCE
Melanzane in Salsa

Serve as a garnish or a vegetable; it is particularly good with broiled fish.

Serves 4 to 6.

5 small eggplants, about 1½ pounds, cut into ½-inch slices
1 tablespoon chopped Italian parsley
1 salted anchovy, rinsed and filleted, or 2 anchovy fillets
    packed in oil
1 teaspoon minced garlic
Hot pepper flakes to taste
1 teaspoon dried oregano
2 tablespoons red wine vinegar
¾ cup chopped fresh ripe tomatoes

Cook eggplant slices in boiling salted water until tender, but firm — al dente — about 3 minutes. Drain, cool in cold water, drain again.

In the meantime, make the sauce in a food processor or food mill by blending parsley, chopped anchovies, garlic, hot pepper, oregano, vinegar, and tomatoes. Pour over eggplant and let rest at least 1 hour before serving. Serve at room temperature.

Calories	Cholesterol mg	Protein gm	Carbohydrate gm	Total fat gm	%	Sat fat gm	%	Mono gm	Poly gm
237	4.0	12.1	43.4	2.7	10	–	–	–	–

BAKED FENNEL
Finocchio al Forno

This dish is sometimes served with grated Parmesan cheese, but we prefer it without cheese. The cheese has a tendency to overwhelm the delicate anise flavor.

Serves 4.

1 bulb fennel, about 1 pound
1 medium onion, finely chopped
1 tablespoon safflower oil
1 tablespoon butter
Salt and freshly ground black pepper to taste
4 tablespoons stock or water

Preheat oven to 450°. Cut fennel in half, remove core, and slice the bulb. Place in medium to small baking dish with remaining ingredients. Cover and bake for 45 minutes, then bake an additional 10 minutes uncovered.

Calories	Cholesterol mg	Protein gm	Carbohydrate gm	Total fat gm	%	Sat fat gm	%	Mono gm	Poly gm
408	31	14.6	34.1	27.0	58	7.5	16	5.4	10.4

BRAISED LEEKS AND POTATOES
Porri Brasati e Patate

Serves 3.

3 large leeks, roots trimmed, tops cut off, leaving about
    2 inches green
2 medium potatoes, peeled and cut in half
1 medium onion, sliced
1 tablespoon olive oil
1 tablespoon safflower oil or
    2 tablespoons vegetable oil
Salt and freshly ground black pepper to taste
Water

Preheat oven to 400°.

Place leeks, potatoes, onion, the two oils, salt, and pepper in a casserole with about ¼ inch water, cover, and bake about 40 minutes, or until leeks are tender—timing will depend on their size.

Calories	Cholesterol mg	Protein gm	Carbohydrate gm	Total fat gm	%	Sat fat gm	%	Mono gm	Poly gm
639	0	13.4	84.2	28.2	39	3.0	4	11.5	11.2

LENTIL STEW
Minestra di Lenticchie

This is particularly delicious when you have an abundance of dandelion greens in the spring, but other vegetables like rape, broccoli, cabbage, and potatoes can be used instead—in whatever combinations you wish. It's a good way of using bits of vegetables that may be in your refrigerator.

Serves 6.

1 cup dried lentils, washed and drained
3 cups cold water
1 medium onion, coarsely chopped
3 cups washed and chopped dandelion greens (optional)
Salt and hot pepper flakes to taste
1 pound fresh spinach, washed and drained
1 tablespoon olive oil
1 teaspoon safflower oil

Gently cook lentils, water, onion, and dandelion greens in a medium soup pot, covered, about 45 minutes. Add salt, hot pepper flakes, and spinach, then cover again and boil gently an additional 6 or 7 minutes. Stir in the oils and serve hot.

Calories	Cholesterol mg	Protein gm	Carbohydrate gm	Total fat gm	%	Sat fat gm	%	Mono gm	Poly gm
991	0	64.1	145.6	21.7	19	2.2	2	10.4	4.5

BABY LIMA BEANS (BUTTER BEANS)

Serves 6 to 8.

2 tablespoons safflower oil
2 medium onions, chopped
2 cups chopped tomatoes, fresh if possible
    (drain if canned)
4 cups fresh lima beans or 2 packages frozen lima beans
2 tablespoons minced Italian parsley
1 medium potato, peeled and diced
12 fresh okra, cut into 1/2-inch slices (optional)
Salt and hot pepper flakes or freshly ground black pepper
    to taste

Heat oil in a saucepan, then add onions. As onions begin to brown, add tomatoes and cook over medium heat about 5 minutes. Add remaining ingredients to pan along with enough water to cover them by ½ inch. Bring to a boil, cover, and boil gently about 45 to 60 minutes, until beans are tender.

Calories	Cholesterol *mg*	Protein *gm*	Carbohydrate *gm*	Total fat *gm*	%	Sat fat *gm*	%	Mono *gm*	Poly *gm*
1395	0	68.3	206.9	32.2	20	2.4	2	3.2	20.2

ABOUT MUSHROOMS

The only mushrooms I ever ate in Italy were wild, either dried or fresh. As a child in this country only wild mushrooms were served in our home, gathered by my father and canned by my mother. Today most of the mushrooms we use in our kitchen are a variety of wild mushrooms that grow on our property or nearby—morels that can be found in the spring near my wife's rock garden, puffballs that grow in our fields alongside field mushrooms, fairy ring mushrooms, and a variety of others. An edible boletus often appears on our front lawn, and oyster mushrooms grow on trees nearby. So I must admit I am prejudiced when it comes to mushrooms. I do not believe cultivated mushrooms compare at all with edible wild mushrooms. Of course, I do not recommend that anyone taste a wild mushroom unless he is absolutely certain it *is* edible.

I am aware of the fact that most people in America are not familiar with wild mushrooms, so I have tried to give the cultivated mushroom as much character as possible. But anyone who has experienced the joys of a choice wild mushroom will never again be satisfied with a cultivated mushroom. And America is blessed with an abundance of choice wild mushrooms.

Of the dried variety available, I find the Italian boletus has an excellent flavor—far preferable to the white fresh domestic mushroom, which is rather tasteless. The dried Italian boletus, however, functions more as an herb than a mushroom, because it lacks the texture needed to be used as a vegetable. If the recipe requires the texture, the "bite quality" of a wild mushroom, then I prefer to use the fresh domestic or the dried Chinese or Japanese mushrooms, which are whole and retain their identity. The thinly sliced dried Italian boletus have a tendency to dissolve for the most part while cooking.

It is often a satisfactory solution to combine fresh domestic mushrooms with Italian dried—one supplying the texture and the other the taste.

Mushrooms are used throughout this book in many, many recipes and I have included in this vegetable chapter just one simple dish for using them as a vegetable accompaniment.

SAUTÉED MUSHROOMS
Funghi Trifolati

In Italy this dish is made with fresh boletus mushrooms and it is a delight. I have made it with a variety of edible mushrooms that I have gathered (see above).

If wild mushrooms aren't available, try a combination of fresh cultivated and imported dried mushrooms, as suggested here.

Serves 4.

12 ounces mushrooms, about 4 cups
3/4-ounce package dried boletus mushrooms, soaked in
    warm water to cover for 15 minutes
2 tablespoons olive oil
1 tablespoon safflower oil or 3 teaspoons peanut oil
Salt and freshly ground black pepper to taste
1 teaspoon minced garlic
1 tablespoon finely chopped Italian parsley

Cut mushrooms in slices about 1/8 inch thick. Heat the oils in a medium skillet, then add both fresh mushrooms and dried mushrooms, drained. Cook, uncovered, over moderate heat, stirring often. Add salt and pepper. When edges of mushrooms begin to brown, add garlic and parsley. Toss several minutes more and serve hot.

Calories	Cholesterol mg	Protein gm	Carbohydrate gm	Total fat gm	%	Sat fat gm	%	Mono gm	Poly gm
438	0	12.1	27.5	32.9	66	4.0	8	20.3	5.6

FRIED ONION BLOSSOMS
Fiori di Cipolle Fritti

Unfortunately, onion blossoms are available only to gardeners who grow onions. They have a delightful taste and, like zucchini blossoms, are quite attractive when cooked. Serve them with zucchini blossoms, if possible, as a vegetable or as a first course. You will need about 2 blossoms per person.

I have tried a number of batters for onion blossoms and have found the tempura batter the most suitable.

Corn or vegetable oil for frying
1 recipe tempura batter (page 388)

Heat 3/4 inch oil in a medium skillet. When oil is hot, dip blossoms in the batter and carefully fry them till golden brown. (Onion blossoms must cook longer than zucchini blossoms, because they tend to absorb more batter.) Blot on paper towels. Serve hot.

Calories	Cholesterol	Protein	Carbohydrate	Total fat		Sat fat		Mono	Poly
	mg	*gm*	*gm*	*gm*	*%*	*gm*	*%*	*gm*	*gm*
577	0	21.6	105.8	5.9	9	0.5	1	1.3	2.4

LADY PEAS

Fresh Lady peas are not available in the Northeast, but this delicious, delicate fresh bean is common in the South. I have had Lady peas prepared in the South with salt pork or bacon, but I think you will find this method a delicious alternative to the traditional Southern recipe.

Serves 4.

4 cups Lady peas
Water or chicken stock
2 cloves garlic, minced
1 medium onion, minced
1 large potato, diced
3 tablespoons safflower or sunflower oil
Salt and freshly ground black pepper to taste
4 tablespoons chopped Italian parsley

Put all the ingredients in a pot and cover with water. Boil gently until peas are cooked, adding more water or chicken stock (which is even better) as needed. Cook until peas are tender, about 40 minutes. Most of the liquid should be cooked out by the time the peas are cooked.

Calories	Cholesterol	Protein	Carbohydrate	Total fat		Sat fat		Mono	Poly
	mg	*gm*	*gm*	*gm*	*%*	*gm*	*%*	*gm*	*gm*
1103	0	44.6	128.1	43.6	35	3.6	3	4.8	30.3

SAUTÉED SNOW PEAS

Serves 4.

2 tablespoons safflower oil
4 cups, about ¾ pound, snow pea pods, ends and
    strings removed
1 large clove garlic, minced
1 cup thinly sliced whole scallions
1 tablespoon soy sauce
Salt and freshly ground black pepper to taste
2 tablespoons chopped fresh coriander or Italian parsley

Heat oil in a medium to large skillet, then add snow peas. Cook over medium to high heat for several minutes, stirring frequently. Add garlic and scallions and cook, tossing, another minute or more. Add soy sauce, salt, and pepper and cook several minutes more, stirring often. Add coriander and turn off heat.

Calories	Cholesterol mg	Protein gm	Carbohydrate gm	Total fat gm	%	Sat fat gm	%	Mono gm	Poly gm
476	0	14.5	47.5	28.3	52	2.4	4	3.2	20.2

BLACKEYED PEAS WITH RAPE
Fagioli con l'Occhio e Rape

This is a vegetable recipe, not a soup, so the final vegetable mixture should not be soupy. I have found fresh blackeyed peas increasingly available in farmers' markets, all shelled.

Serves 4 to 6.

2 cups fresh blackeyed peas*
2 tablespoons olive oil
1 teaspoon safflower oil
3/4 cup finely chopped onion
1 teaspoon minced garlic
Hot pepper flakes to taste (optional)
About 1 1/2 cups water
Salt to taste
1 1/2 pounds rape, cleaned and cut into bite-sized pieces
   (see instructions, page 348), or 1 bunch broccoli,
   or 1 1/2 pounds fresh spinach

*If you can't find fresh ones, use dried or frozen. If dried, precook them as you would cannellini beans (page 82); if frozen, blanch in boiling water just till water comes to a boil, then drain.

Put all ingredients except rape into a medium soup pot, cover, and bring to a boil. Boil over medium heat, partially covered, about 30 minutes. Add washed rape, cover, and bring to a boil. Remove cover and boil gently about 10 minutes. If water boils out too rapidly, then cover. Serve hot.

Calories	Cholesterol mg	Protein gm	Carbohydrate gm	Total fat gm	%	Sat fat gm	%	Mono gm	Poly gm
829	0	42.3	92.4	36.4	39	4.0	4	20.3	5.6

ROASTED PEPPERS
Peperoni Arrostiti

There is a great misunderstanding about green peppers. Green peppers are unripe peppers. When peppers are ripe, they turn red or yellow, depending on the variety. It takes a pepper about two weeks to turn red, and unfortunately some rot in the process, but there is no comparison between a green pepper and a ripe pepper. The ripe peppers are much sweeter and the taste more refined.

Although green peppers are excellent in this dish, red peppers are far superior.

Serves 4 to 6.

6 large peppers, preferably red or yellow
2 cloves garlic, sliced
2 tablespoons vegetable oil (1 olive oil, 1 safflower)
1 tablespoon minced Italian parsley
Salt and freshly ground black pepper to taste

Roast peppers under a broiler with a medium flame (or, if you have them, over coals), turning constantly so that the skin blisters and chars. Only the skin should char, not the flesh of the pepper. When peppers are all blistered, remove from heat and allow to cool. Peel charred skin from peppers, but do not wash them. Cut the peppers in half lengthwise, remove core and seeds, cut into strips ½ inch wide and place them in a bowl. Toss with remaining ingredients and allow to stand an hour or so.

Remove garlic and serve at room temperature.

Calories	Cholesterol mg	Protein gm	Carbohydrate gm	Total fat gm	%	Sat fat gm	%	Mono gm	Poly gm
551	0	14.2	71.2	30.1	48	2.6	4	12.3	10.7

FRIED PEPPERS SAN BENEDETTO STYLE
Peperoni Fritti alla San Benedetto

Serves 3.

2 large sweet red peppers (green will do)
1½ tablespoons olive oil
1 teaspoon safflower oil
1 medium onion, sliced
Freshly ground black pepper to taste
1 tablespoon white wine vinegar
2 anchovies, chopped

Slice the peppers ½ inch wide and remove seeds. Heat the oils in a medium skillet, then add peppers and onion. Cook over moderate heat, uncovered. Add black pepper, and when peppers are almost cooked, or tender, add vinegar and anchovies. Continue cooking until vinegar cooks out.

Calories	Cholesterol mg	Protein gm	Carbohydrate gm	Total fat gm	%	Sat fat gm	%	Mono gm	Poly gm
405	4.0	8.8	40.0	26.7	58	2.9	6	16.3	4.9

POTATO BALLS
Coccoli di Patate

Serves 6 to 8.

4 medium Idaho baking potatoes
1 tablespoon olive oil
4 tablespoons chopped pine nuts
2 tablespoons chopped Italian parsley
1 teaspoon marjoram
Salt and freshly ground black pepper to taste
1 egg white, lightly beaten
Fresh breadcrumbs
Corn oil for frying

Boil potatoes, then peel and mash them. Mix thoroughly with olive oil, pine nuts, parsley, marjoram, salt, and pepper.

Form balls with the mixture about the size of a walnut (about 1 heaping tablespoon), roll in egg white, then in breadcrumbs.

Heat about 3/4 inch corn oil in a 9- or 10-inch skillet until hot but not smoking (oil should boil quickly when balls are added). Place balls gently in oil with tongs, not too many at a time — the pan should not be crowded. Fry until golden brown, then remove and blot on paper towels. Repeat. Serve hot.

Calories	Cholesterol mg	Protein gm	Carbohydrate gm	Total fat gm	%	Sat fat gm	%	Mono gm	Poly gm
1117	0	31.0	164.8	38.2	30	3.3	3	19.3	9.7

POTATOES BAKED WITH TOMATOES
Patate al Forno con Pomodori

Serves 6.

6 medium potatoes, peeled and sliced about 1/4 inch thick
3 medium onions, thinly sliced
2 cups chopped tomatoes, fresh if possible (drain if canned)
2 tablespoons olive oil
1 tablespoon safflower oil or 3 tablespoons peanut oil
1 teaspoon rosemary
Salt and freshly ground black pepper to taste

Place potatoes in a baking dish. Add remaining ingredients and cover.

Bake in a preheated 350° oven about 20 to 30 minutes, until potatoes are tender, stirring occasionally.

Calories	Cholesterol mg	Protein gm	Carbohydrate gm	Total fat gm	%	Sat fat gm	%	Mono gm	Poly gm
1317	0	30.6	205.8	43.0	29	4.8	3	21.4	12.3

POTATOES WITH ROSEMARY
Patate al Rosmarino

Serves about 8; half a potato per person.

Safflower or corn oil
4 medium potatoes, peeled and cut in half lengthwise
3 tablespoons rosemary
Salt and freshly ground black pepper to taste

Sprinkle enough oil in an ovenproof dish to cover the bottom and place potatoes in the dish. Add rosemary, salt, and pepper. Bake in a preheated 400° oven, turning potatoes occasionally. Cook until fork easily goes through potato — about 20 minutes.

Serve with broiled or baked meat and fish.

Calories	Cholesterol mg	Protein gm	Carbohydrate gm	Total fat gm	%	Sat fat gm	%	Mono gm	Poly gm
797	0	19.5	155.7	11.4	13	0.8	1	2.6	6.6

POTATOES WITH BROCCOLI
Patate con Broccoli

Serves 6.

4 medium potatoes, peeled and sliced 1/2 inch thick
12 cups fresh large broccoli flowerets and stems skinned
    and cut into bite-sized pieces
3 tablespoons olive oil
1 tablespoon safflower oil
2 cloves garlic, minced
Hot pepper flakes to taste (optional)
1/2 cup reserved cooking water

Boil the potato slices about 3 minutes, then add broccoli; when water returns to a boil, drain, reserving about 1/2 cup water.

Heat oils in a medium skillet, then add garlic, pepper flakes, potatoes, and broccoli and cook several minutes over high heat. Add reserved water, cover, and cook over medium heat until potatoes are tender, about 20 minutes, adding more water if needed.

Calories	Cholesterol mg	Protein gm	Carbohydrate gm	Total fat gm	%	Sat fat gm	%	Mono gm	Poly gm
1151	0	37.2	130.2	56.5	43	6.6	5	31.3	13.4

POTATOES BAKER STYLE
Patate al Forno

Serves 8.

8 medium potatoes, about 2 1/2 pounds
2 tablespoons butter
2 tablespoons safflower oil
4 cups coarsely chopped onion
1 teaspoon coarsely chopped garlic
Salt and freshly ground black pepper to taste
1 1/2 cups chicken stock
Bouquet garni (several branches of parsley, fresh thyme,
 bay leaf) in cheesecloth pouch

Slice potatoes 1/4 inch thick and soak in cold water.

Heat butter and oil in a medium skillet, then add onion and garlic. Cook until onion wilts, 3 to 5 minutes. Drain potatoes and mix well with onion and cooking juices, add salt and pepper. Put potatoes in a shallow ovenproof dish, pour in chicken stock, and bury a bouquet garni in the center of the potatoes. Bake in a preheated 400° oven, uncovered, about 1 hour.

Calories	Cholesterol mg	Protein gm	Carbohydrate gm	Total fat gm	%	Sat fat gm	%	Mono gm	Poly gm
1487	62.0	31.1	227.1	51.8	31	15.0	9	10.8	20.8

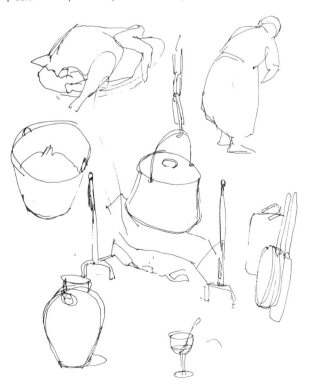

POTATOES WITH CELERY, TOMATOES, AND ONIONS
Patate con Sedano, Pomodori, e Cipolle

This simple recipe goes well with grilled meats and fish.

Serves 5 to 6.

5 medium potatoes, peeled and cut in thick slices
10 pieces of celery, about 4 inches long each
2 medium onions, sliced
2 cups chopped tomatoes, fresh if possible
   (drain if canned)
3 tablespoons vegetable oil
1 teaspoon dried oregano
Salt and freshly ground black pepper to taste
2 tablespoons finely chopped Italian parsley

Distribute all the vegetables in a shallow baking dish. Pour oil and seasonings over them and mix in. Cover and bake in a preheated 450° oven about 30 minutes, or until potatoes are tender.

Calories	Cholesterol mg	Protein gm	Carbohydrate gm	Total fat gm	%	Sat fat gm	%	Mono gm	Poly gm
1428	0	34.4	229.5	43.5	27	3.6	2	4.8	30.3

FRIED POTATOES
Patate Fritte

I first tasted potatoes fried this way in the home of an Italian relative in 1965. They are very good with broiled meats or fish.

Serves 4.

1 pound potatoes, thinly sliced
2 cups vegetable or corn oil
Salt to taste

Cover the potatoes with cold water for at least 3 hours. Drain and blot them well.

Heat the oil in a medium skillet. When hot, add about half the sliced potatoes, one slice at a time. Cook over moderate heat until potato slices begin to brown. Remove with a slotted spoon to paper towels and salt to taste. Repeat. Serve hot.

Calories	Cholesterol mg	Protein gm	Carbohydrate gm	Total fat gm	%	Sat fat gm	%	Mono gm	Poly gm
465	0	9.5	75.4	14.1	27	1.4	3	3.8	7.2

POTATO LOAF
Polpettone di Patate

Serves 4 to 5.

6 medium potatoes
2 cups sliced fresh mushrooms or 1-ounce package dried
 boletus mushrooms, soaked in warm water
 for 20 minutes
2 tablespoons olive oil
1 egg white, lightly beaten
1 tablespoon finely chopped Italian parsley
1 teaspoon minced garlic
1 teaspoon dried oregano
Salt and freshly ground black pepper to taste
1 tablespoon safflower oil or other vegetable oil
6 tablespoons fresh breadcrumbs

Boil potatoes until tender. Drain, peel, and mash them.

In the meantime, sauté mushrooms in 2 teaspoons of the olive oil until all moisture cooks out. If dried mushrooms are used, simmer in a small saucepan in their soaking liquid about 10 minutes. Drain and mix with the mashed potatoes, egg white, parsley, garlic, oregano, salt, and pepper.

Mix the safflower oil with the breadcrumbs.

Rub remaining olive oil in a small, shallow baking dish. Spread potato mixture in dish and top with the breadcrumbs. Bake, uncovered, in a preheated 400° oven about 30 minutes.

Serve immediately.

Calories	Cholesterol mg	Protein gm	Carbohydrate gm	Total fat gm	%	Sat fat gm	%	Mono gm	Poly gm
1161	0	28.5	167.1	42.5	32	4.8	4	21.4	12.3

ABOUT RADICCHIO

The vegetable radicchio has achieved a remarkable popularity in America during recent years. Virtually unknown five years ago, it is rapidly becoming America's most popular winter salad. Most of you are probably familiar with its slightly bitter, raw taste in a salad, but it is also delicious braised.

Radicchio is a winter vegetable used both as a lettuce and a cooked vegetable; it is grown in northern Italy. The two most popular types of radicchio are the radicchio di Verona, with a head from the size of a large Brussels sprout to that of a medium cabbage. The head opens like a flower and its color is a deep alizarine crimson with a white spine along the center of each leaf. Sometimes the flower resembles an open rose and is quite beautiful.

The other type is the radicchio di Treviso. It has a leaf about 3 inches long and looks more like a lily than a rose. The color ranges from light to deep alizarine crimson.

It is the larger heads of radicchio di Verona that are often used for braising and are a true gastronomic delight.

I first planted radicchio in 1965, when a friend had given me some seeds that came from Italy. I planted the seeds in July, knowing it was a winter vegetable, but hoping for a fall harvest. To my disappointment the seeds produced large rich green leaves (not red) and the plants grew quite large, about 3 feet high. The leaves were so bitter I just ignored them and let them die back in the fall. Then, to my delight, in late February little alizarine crimson buds appeared in the soil and developed into lush heads of radicchio.

I then realized what had happened. The plants had to establish a strong root, very much as a dandelion root does. After the root is established, the first head to appear is the red radicchio. If allowed to grow, the red heads open up and the leaves eventually turn green. The plant then grows 2 to 3 feet in height. I have had several cuttings from the same plants and the roots have lasted for several years.

BRAISED RADICCHIO
Radicchio Brasato

Serves 4.

1 pound radicchio, about 4 good-sized heads
3/4 cup finely chopped onion
1 cup finely chopped carrots
1 cup finely chopped celery
3 tablespoons water
Salt and freshly ground black pepper to taste
2 tablespoons extra virgin olive oil

Trim radicchio heads and cut them in quarters if they are the size of a baseball; cut in half if smaller. Wash in cold water, then remove tough core with a sharp knife.

Put chopped onion, carrots, and celery in a medium baking dish—about 10 inches wide and 3 inches deep. Pour the water over the chopped vegetables and place radicchio on top. Add salt and pepper. Cut out a piece of waxed paper the size of the pan and fit it snugly over. Bake radicchio in a preheated 400° oven about 15 minutes. Lower heat to 350° and bake an additional 20 to 30 minutes. Test doneness by putting a fork into the radicchio.

Sprinkle olive oil over the vegetables and serve warm.

Calories	Cholesterol mg	Protein gm	Carbohydrate gm	Total fat gm	%	Sat fat gm	%	Mono gm	Poly gm
549	0	15.9	56.6	30.7	49	3.6	6	19.8	2.2

No figures are available for radicchio; figures used are for dandelion greens.

ABOUT REDROOT

Green amaranth (*Amaranthus retroflexus*) is also called redroot, rough-weed, pigweed, and wild beet. Redroot is a weed that grows from Canada to Florida and from the Atlantic to the Pacific. It grows in great profusion in our vegetable garden and in the gardens of most of our friends. The weed was a curse that gave me much frustration until I learned that it was not only edible, but also tasty. I still have an abundance of redroot growing in my vegetable garden, but the fact that it is edible makes the weeding much easier, and occasionally we have a nice plate of redroot for dinner.

REDROOT

The flavor is delicate and the texture is good. Redroot is good cooked by itself or with other vegetables such as potatoes, or other weeds such as lamb's quarters, dandelion greens, or purslane.

SAUTÉED REDROOT

This is a recipe for redroot alone. The leaves can also be cooked with potatoes, or with other vegetables such as broccoli and cabbage.

Serves 4.

12 cups tightly packed redroot leaves
3 tablespoons olive oil
1 teaspoon safflower oil
3 cloves garlic, finely chopped
Hot pepper flakes to taste (optional)
3/4 cup reserved liquid
Salt to taste

Garnish: 4 lemon wedges

Wash redroot leaves and cook in boiling water about 5 minutes if leaves are large, or about 2 minutes if leaves are small. Drain and reserve 3/4 cup water.

Heat the oils in a medium skillet or shallow saucepan, add garlic and hot pepper. When garlic begins to take on color, add boiled red root leaves, reserved liquid, and salt. Cover and simmer over medium to low heat about 15 minutes.

Garnish each serving with a wedge of lemon.

Calories	Cholesterol	Protein	Carbohydrate	Total fat		Sat fat		Mono	Poly
	mg	gm	gm	gm	%	gm	%	gm	gm
607	0	24.9	30.8	47.3	69	5.8	8	30.2	6.7

No figures are available for redroot; figures used are for spinach.

COOKED BREAD WITH RUGOLA AND POTATOES
Pancotto con Rughetta e Patate

You will be surprised with this recipe, which is very tasty and unusual. Another rucola recipe for rucola lovers.

Serves 4.

> 2 or 3 medium potatoes, peeled and sliced about 1/8 to 1/4 inch thick
> 4 cups fresh rucola (arugola), cleaned and washed
> Salt to taste
> 2 slices French or Italian bread*
> 2 tablespoons olive oil
> 1 tablespoon safflower oil
> 3 cloves garlic
> Hot pepper flakes or freshly ground black pepper to taste

> *I use homemade whole-wheat bread; use 4 slices bread if slices are small.

Cover potatoes with water and boil until almost cooked. Add rucola and salt. Cover and cook about 3 minutes. Add bread and cook about 1 minute. Drain.

Heat the oils in a medium skillet, then add whole garlic cloves and hot pepper flakes if used. Brown garlic, then discard it. Add rucola-and-potato mixture and salt and black pepper, if used, and cook over high heat, turning with a flat spatula, for several minutes.

Serve immediately.

Calories	Cholesterol	Protein	Carbohydrate	Total fat		Sat fat		Mono	Poly
	mg	gm	gm	gm	%	gm	%	gm	gm
918	0	25.1	102.9	45.5	44	4.8	5	21.4	12.3

SPINACH AND POTATOES
Spinaci con Patate

Serves 4 to 6.

2 1/2 pounds fresh spinach
3 Idaho potatoes
3 tablespoons olive oil
2 tablespoons safflower oil
2 medium onions, thinly sliced
Hot pepper flakes to taste (optional)
Salt and freshly ground black pepper to taste
1 clove garlic, minced

Wash spinach in warm water, discard tough stems, drain, and set aside.

Boil potatoes to almost desired doneness. Peel and cut into slices 1/2 inch thick.

Heat the oils in a large skillet, then add onions and cook several minutes. Add potatoes and hot pepper, and cook over high heat, with a spatula turning potatoes over often. Add salt and pepper. When potatoes begin to brown, add spinach and garlic. Cover and lower heat, turning occasionally. Do not overcook spinach — it should be a bright green and enough moisture should come from it to bind potatoes. If some water is needed, add a little.

Calories	Cholesterol mg	Protein gm	Carbohydrate gm	Total fat gm	%	Sat fat gm	%	Mono gm	Poly gm
1295	0	41.4	140.5	71.1	48	7.8	5	32.9	23.5

SPINACH GENOA STYLE
Spinaci alla Genovese

Serves 4.

About 2 1/4 pounds fresh spinach
3 tablespoons olive oil
1 teaspoon safflower oil
1 small clove garlic, chopped
3 tablespoons yellow raisins, soaked in tepid water
    for 10 minutes
3 anchovies, chopped
2 tablespoons pine nuts
1 tablespoon chopped Italian parsley
Dash nutmeg
Salt and freshly ground black pepper to taste

Cook spinach in boiling water for 3 minutes. Drain. When spinach cools, squeeze out excess water and set aside.

Heat the oils in a medium skillet, then add garlic, raisins (drained), anchovies, and pine nuts and sauté for several minutes. Add spinach, parsley, nutmeg, salt, and pepper. Cover and cook over low heat for 5 to 10 minutes.

Calories	Cholesterol mg	Protein gm	Carbohydrate gm	Total fat gm	%	Sat fat gm	%	Mono gm	Poly gm
841	13.0	41.2	61.4	55.4	58	7.0	7	33.5	8.2

BAKED HUBBARD SQUASH OR ACORN SQUASH

This is a delicious and easy way to serve these winter squashes.

Serves 2.

> 2 teaspoons vegetable oil
> Salt and freshly ground black pepper to taste
> 1 clove garlic, finely chopped
> 1 Hubbard or acorn squash, cut in half lengthwise,
> seeds removed

Add oil, salt, pepper, and garlic to cut surface of squash. Preheat oven to 500°. Bake until tender, about 20 minutes, depending on size.

Calories	Cholesterol mg	Protein gm	Carbohydrate gm	Total fat gm	%	Sat fat gm	%	Mono gm	Poly gm
274	0	6.7	49.2	9.4	30	0.8	3	1.0	6.8

SPAGHETTI SQUASH

I have been told that spaghetti squash is so much like spaghetti that some people cannot tell the difference. This is simply not true—there is no comparison with a good semolina pasta, but this is excellent as a vegetable. It works very well with certain pasta sauces, such as marinara sauces and vegetable-based sauces, including pesto.

Serves 4.

> 1 spaghetti squash
> 1 tablespoon olive oil
> 1 teaspoon safflower oil
> 1 medium onion, chopped
> 1 cup chopped tomatoes, fresh if possible (drain if canned)
> 1 tablespoon fresh basil or 1 teaspoon dried
> Salt and freshly ground black pepper to taste

Put squash in a pot, cover with water, and boil about 1 hour, until fork goes in easily. Drain and let cool.

In the meantime, heat the oils in a small skillet, then add onion. When onion browns, add tomatoes, basil, salt, and pepper. Cover and simmer for 15 minutes. Run through a food mill or food processor.

When squash cools, cut it in half lengthwise. With a fork comb out the seed and top layer of pulp, t' en comb out the spaghettilike strands. Pour off any liquid. Mix the stranus 'ith the sauce and serve as a vegetable.

Calories	Cholesterol mg	Protein gm	Carbohydrate gm	Total fat gm	%	Sat fat gm	%	Mono gm	Poly gm
458	0	15.6	66.3	19.6	38	1.8	3	10.9	4.2

ABOUT FRESH TOMATOES

One often hears people lament that tomatoes do not taste the way they did "when I was a child" and they go on to describe the wonderful, succulent tomatoes they enjoyed on Grandpa's farm. Of course tomatoes purchased off-season that have been shipped from California, Texas, or Mexico in a refrigerated van are not as good as Grandpa's. For tomatoes to survive the long shipping distances, they have been picked partially green and ripened artificially, held in humidity-controlled situations to speed up or slow down maturation. Some are waxed to kill bacteria, some are gassed with ethylene to give them a bright red hue, and God knows what else is done to them.

The tomatoes I ate as a child were tomatoes from our garden. We ate them as long as the season lasted, then waited for the next season. We never ate fresh tomatoes any other time of the year—and that's the way it should be.

The tomatoes we grow today in our own vegetable garden are just as good as the tomatoes my father grew and just as good as the tomatoes my grandfather grew. If you like the taste of a fresh tomato, wait for its season. If you really enjoy fresh tomatoes, grow them yourself—it's that simple— and never refrigerate a tomato if you want to enjoy its full flavor. If you can't have a garden, try to get tomatoes in season from the farmers' markets that are now flourishing around the country.

All the recipes in this book where tomatoes are used were made with tomatoes that were either garden fresh or canned from our own garden tomatoes.

I plant 150 tomato plants a year, usually a number of varieties, some for canning (San Marzano and Cuore di Bue) because of their meaty quality, and several kinds for eating and cooking. I plant a mid-summer crop so that we have tomatoes until the winter freeze. The most suitable tomato for a fall crop is the plum tomato, San Marzano and Roma being the best known. If the tomatoes are covered during the fall evenings (I use clear plastic), you can harvest tomatoes until a hard frost.

I stake all of my tomato plants. This insures me a healthier, more plentiful crop, not to mention the fact that the staked tomatoes are easier to prune. I use natural fertilizers and I do not use pesticides. On the advice of an old Italian I dust the tomato plants with sulphur dust when green tomatoes appear. The taste of the tomato is sweeter as a result, and I imagine the sulphur dust inhibits bugs as well.

We dine on tomatoes every day while we have them, and we rarely eat fresh tomatoes after the season is over. We can about 100 quarts of tomatoes from our garden every year. All our sauces are made from our own canned tomatoes.

When used in a sauce, tomatoes should be skinned by plunging them in boiling water, then peeling off the skins. Or rub a tomato with the dull side of a knife, then pierce the skin and peel it off.

Seeds should be removed by cutting tomatoes in half, then squeezing until the seeds pop out. Or put tomato, skin and all, in a food processor and purée. I prefer this method if the recipe calls for a purée. The skins and seeds disappear in the sauce, and the skins add both color and flavor to the sauce.

The canning process is simple. We use mostly pint jars because we rarely use more than 2 cups of tomatoes in one recipe. Wash the jars, then put them in boiling water and boil for several minutes. Remove the jars and pack in peeled, cored, and sectioned tomatoes. Add 1 teaspoon salt (optional) and several fresh basil leaves. Screw on the covers, place in a large cooking pot, and cover with water. Bring the water to a boil and boil 15 to 20 minutes. Remove the jars from the pot, screw lids tight, and turn upside down to make certain the jar is sealed. (Air will audibly escape if the cap is not sealed.) Allow to cool at room temperature. Store on cellar or kitchen shelves, not in direct sunlight. Tomatoes have lasted for at least 2 years for us when done this way.

If you buy commercial canned tomatoes, be sure to get whole tomatoes in their own juice, not tomatoes in a puree or sauce. You will find the tomatoes in sauce much too assertive for the recipes in this book.

BROILED TOMATOES I
Pomodori alla Griglia

This recipe should be made only with garden-fresh tomatoes. Use as a vegetable course or antipasto.

Serves 4.

3 tablespoons fresh breadcrumbs
1 teaspoon minced garlic
1/2 teaspoon dried oregano
1 tablespoon olive oil mixed with 1 teaspoon
　　safflower oil
Salt and freshly ground black pepper to taste
2 medium firm tomatoes, not too ripe, cut in
　　half lengthwise

In a small bowl mix the breadcrumbs, garlic, oregano, oil, salt, and pepper.

Sprinkle each tomato half with the breadcrumb mixture and place tomatoes on a baking tray. Preheat broiler. Broil tomatoes, taking care not to place them too close to the heat, else the breadcrumbs will burn. Broil for about 5 minutes, until crumbs are golden brown.

Serve at room temperature.

Calories	Cholesterol mg	Protein gm	Carbohydrate gm	Total fat gm	%	Sat fat gm	%	Mono gm	Poly gm
243	0	3.9	17.3	18.9	68	2.2	8	10.4	4.5

BROILED TOMATOES II
Pomodori alla Griglia

Like the preceding recipe, this should be made only with garden-fresh tomatoes and served as a vegetable course or antipasto.

Serves 4.

2 medium tomatoes, not too ripe, cut in half lengthwise
2 cloves garlic, slivered
1 tablespoon olive oil mixed with 1 teaspoon safflower oil
1 tablespoon crushed rosemary
Salt and freshly ground black pepper to taste
4 slices French or Italian bread, toasted

Place tomatoes on a baking tray. Stuff about 3 slivers of garlic into each tomato. Pour oil over tomatoes, then add crushed rosemary, salt, and pepper.

Broil close to the flame until tomato edges begin to char.

Remove garlic and serve on toast at room temperature.

Calories	Cholesterol mg	Protein gm	Carbohydrate gm	Total fat gm	%	Sat fat gm	%	Mono gm	Poly gm
621	0	16.4	85.6	24.4	35	2.8	4	12.8	5.3

TOMATOES ON TOAST
Pomodori con Pane Tostato

A good accompaniment to broiled meats and fish. It is also a pleasant alternative to garlic bread.

Serves 4.

1 tablespoon olive oil
1 teaspoon safflower oil
1 teaspoon minced garlic
2 cups chopped fresh tomatoes (squeeze out seeds and pulp)
1 tablespoon chopped fresh basil
Salt and freshly ground black pepper to taste
4 to 6 slices French or Italian bread

Heat the oils in a medium skillet, then add garlic. As it begins to brown, add tomatoes, basil, salt, and pepper. Cover and simmer over medium heat and cook about 10 minutes.

In the meantime, toast the bread.

Remove cover from tomatoes, turn up heat, and reduce sauce until watery part cooks out. Dish onto the toast and serve immediately.

Calories	Cholesterol	Protein	Carbohydrate	Total fat		Sat fat		Mono	Poly
	mg	*gm*	*gm*	*gm*	*%*	*gm*	*%*	*gm*	*gm*
672	0	18.1	97.6	23.3	31	2.2	3	10.4	4.5

FRIED GREEN TOMATOES
Fritto di Pomodori Verdi

Serves 4.

2 egg whites, lightly beaten
Salt and freshly ground black pepper to taste
2 medium green tomatoes, sliced about 1/4 inch thick
Flour for dredging
Corn oil for frying

Add salt and pepper to egg whites. Dip tomato slices in egg whites, then dust lightly with flour. In the meantime, heat about 3/4 inch oil in a medium skillet. When hot, gently put in tomato slices, brown lightly on both sides, blot on paper towels, and serve immediately.

Calories	Cholesterol	Protein	Carbohydrate	Total fat		Sat fat		Mono	Poly
	mg	*gm*	*gm*	*gm*	*%*	*gm*	*%*	*gm*	*gm*
282	0	12.3	26.2	14.4	45	1.4	4	3.8	7.2

BAKED TURNIPS AND POTATOES
Rapa al Forno con Patate

Serves 4 to 6.

2 cups yellow turnips, peeled and sliced 1/4 inch thick
2 large potatoes, peeled and sliced 1/4 inch thick

2 cups sliced onion
3 tablespoons oli · cil
1 tablespoon safflc · er oil
2 tablespoons finely chopped Italian parsley
1 teaspoon marjoram
Salt and freshly ground black pepper to taste
5 tablespoons water (reserved from cooking potatoes
and turnips)

Put turnips and potatoes in boiling water and cook for 3 or 4 minutes. Drain and reserve 5 tablespoons water. Place the vegetables in a baking dish with the onion, oils, parsley, marjoram, salt and pepper, and reserved water. Cover and bake in a 400° preheated oven about 40 minutes, stirring occasionally. Serve hot.

Calories	Cholesterol mg	Protein gm	Carbohydrate gm	Total fat gm	%	Sat fat gm	%	Mono gm	Poly gm
1078	0	18.2	131.4	55.4	45	6.6	5	31.3	13.4

FRIED ZUCCHINI PATTIES
Crocchette di Zucchini

Serves 4 as a vegetable course.

4 cups grated zucchini
1 teaspoon peanut oil or vegetable oil
3 small potatoes, boiled and peeled
1 medium onion, finely chopped
Salt and freshly ground black pepper to taste
1 egg white, lightly beaten
Fresh breadcrumbs
Corn oil for frying

Garnish: Lemon wedges

Put grated zucchini in a colander and let it drain for several hours.
Heat oil in a medium skillet and sauté onion until translucent.
Squeeze juice out of the grated zucchini. Grate cooked potatoes on coarse side of grater. Mix zucchini, potatoes, onion, salt, and pepper together, then add egg white and mix well. With your hand pick up one quarter of the mixture, roll it in breadcrumbs, working in enough of them to form a patty. Set aside, and repeat with the rest.
Heat about ¾ inch corn oil in a medium skillet. When hot, carefully place patties in oil. Cook until golden brown on both sides. Blot on paper towels. Serve hot, garnished with lemon wedges.

Calories	Cholesterol mg	Protein gm	Carbohydrate gm	Total fat gm	%	Sat fat gm	%	Mono gm	Poly gm
486	0	17.5	71.9	14.8	27	1.8	3	4.7	6.1

GRATED ZUCCHINI WITH ONION
Zucchini Grattati alla Cipolle

This is an excellent recipe for anyone who has an abundance of zucchini during the growing season.

Serves 3.

4 small zucchini
Salt to taste
1 tablespoon olive oil
1 tablespoon safflower oil
1 cup finely chopped onion
Freshly ground black pepper to taste

Using the large holes on a grater, grate zucchini into a colander set over a saucepan. Mix a little less than a tablespoon of salt into the grated zucchini and let stand to drain for about 20 minutes. Squeeze grated zucchini in cheesecloth to extract remaining juice.

Heat the oils in a medium skillet, then add onion, and cook over moderate heat until translucent. Add grated zucchini and pepper. Cook over low to moderate heat about 5 minutes, stirring often. Cover. Cook another 8 minutes.

Calories	Cholesterol mg	Protein gm	Carbohydrate gm	Total fat gm	%	Sat fat gm	%	Mono gm	Poly gm
411	0	9.2	33.7	27.9	60	3.0	6	11.5	11.2

ZUCCHINI WITH POTATOES
Zucchini e Patate

Serves 4 to 6.

2 teaspoons olive oil
1 teaspoon safflower oil
1 large onion, sliced
1 cup chopped tomatoes, fresh if possible (drain if canned)
1 tablespoon fresh basil or 1 teaspoon dried
2 large potatoes, peeled and thinly sliced
3 small zucchini, about 4 cups, cut in half lengthwise,
    then cut into 1-inch pieces
1/2 cup thinly sliced scallions
Salt and freshly ground black pepper to taste

Heat the oils in a medium skillet, then add onion. When onion wilts, add tomatoes, basil, and potatoes, cover, and cook over low heat until potatoes are partially cooked. Add zucchini, scallions, salt, and pepper. Cover and cook over low heat about 10 minutes, or until potatoes are tender.

Calories	Cholesterol mg	Protein gm	Carbohydrate gm	Total fat gm	%	Sat fat gm	%	Mono gm	Poly gm
631	0	20.2	106.4	15.3	21	1.6	2	7.1	4.2

FRIED ZUCCHINI BLOSSOMS
Fritto di Fiori di Zucchini

Serves 5.

20 zucchini or squash blossoms
2 egg whites, lightly beaten
Salt and freshly ground black pepper to taste
Flour for dredging
Corn oil or vegetable oil for frying

Roll blossoms in egg whites. Add salt and pepper, then dust with flour. Heat about 3/4 inch oil in a medium skillet. When oil is hot, add blossoms one at a time, just enough to fit comfortably in the pan. Lightly brown them, turning them a few times. Drain on paper towels.

Calories	Cholesterol mg	Protein gm	Carbohydrate gm	Total fat gm	%	Sat fat gm	%	Mono gm	Poly gm
279	0	10.8	26.7	14.0	44	1.4	4	3.8	7.2

FRIED STUFFED ZUCCHINI BLOSSOMS
Fiori di Zucchini Imbottiti

Serves 4 as a vegetable course or as a first course.

16 zucchini blossoms
8 anchovies, cut in half
Batter (page 388)
Corn oil for frying

Stuff each zucchini blossom with half an anchovy and dip in batter. Heat 3/4 inch oil in a medium skillet. When oil is hot, carefully add zucchini blossoms and cook until light brown. Remove and blot on paper towels. Serve hot.

Calories	Cholesterol mg	Protein gm	Carbohydrate gm	Total fat gm	%	Sat fat gm	%	Mono gm	Poly gm
769	35.0	33.9	106.0	21.6	25	1.7	2	4.0	7.4

BAKED ZUCCHINI I
Zucchini al Forno

Serve as an antipasto, or as a vegetable with roasted or broiled meat and fish. If refrigerated, the zucchini will last quite a while. The same recipe can be made with eggplant.

Serves 4.

3 medium zucchini, about 12 inches long
Oil for baking tray
1 tablespoon wine vinegar
1 teaspoon minced garlic
Hot pepper flakes to taste (optional)
Salt to taste
1 teaspoon dried oregano
2 tablespoons olive oil mixed with 1 teaspoon
    safflower oil

Cut zucchini into 3-inch sections, then into slices about ¼ inch thick.

Preheat oven as high as it will go, about 450°, about 20 minutes. Rub some oil on a baking tray, place slices on top, and bake until the bottom of the zucchini is brown. Turn over and brown top. This will take about 10 minutes in all. Remove with a spatula. Place about one third of them in the bottom of a bowl, add a little of the wine vinegar, garlic, hot pepper flakes, salt, oregano, and oil. Repeat, tossing well. Serve at room temperature.

Calories	Cholesterol mg	Protein gm	Carbohydrate gm	Total fat gm	%	Sat fat gm	%	Mono gm	Poly gm
425	0	8.6	23.2	34.7	72	4.2	9	20.9	6.8

BAKED ZUCCHINI II
Zucchini al Forno

This makes a very nice substitute for eggplant Parmesan.

Serves 6.

2 tablespoons olive oil
1 tablespoon safflower oil
1 medium onion, finely chopped
2 cloves garlic, minced
4 cups chopped tomatoes, fresh if possible (drain if canned)
2 tablespoons chopped fresh basil or 1 teaspoon dried
Salt and freshly ground black pepper to taste
Corn oil or vegetable oil for frying
2½ pounds zucchini, cut into slices 3 inches long and
    ¼ inch thick

3 egg whites, lightly beaten
1 cup flour

Heat the oils in a medium skillet, then add onion. When onion begins to brown, add garlic, and as garlic takes on color, add tomatoes, basil, salt, and pepper. Cover and simmer about 30 minutes. Run sauce through a food processor or food mill.

Heat about 3/4 inch corn oil in a medium skillet. When oil is hot, dip zucchini slices in egg whites, then in flour. Shake off excess and with tongs carefully place in hot oil a few at a time. Fry until light brown, then remove with tongs and blot on paper towels. Repeat until all zucchini have been fried.

Put a layer of zucchini in an ovenproof dish — I use one 6 × 12 × 2 inches. Pour a layer of sauce over cooked zucchini, then put down another layer of zucchini; repeat process until all zucchini are used up, pouring the last of the sauce over the top layer. Cover with foil and bake in a preheated 400° oven about 45 minutes. Let rest about 30 minutes before serving. It is good also at room temperature.

Calories	Cholesterol mg	Protein gm	Carbohydrate gm	Total fat gm	%	Sat fat gm	%	Mono gm	Poly gm
1859	0	52.1	194.4	99.6	47	10.4	5	36.6	41.1

MIXED VEGETABLES I
Verdura Mista

Serves 8.

1 bunch broccoli
1 head cauliflower, cut into flowerets
3 potatoes, peeled and sliced 1/4 inch thick
3 tablespoons olive oil
1 tablespoon safflower oil
3 cloves garlic, finely chopped
2 cups chopped tomatoes, fresh if possible (drain if canned)
About 22 dried black olives
Hot pepper flakes to taste (optional)
1 tablespoon dried oregano
Salt and freshly ground black pepper to taste
1 tablespoon olive oil

Skin broccoli stems, then quarter them lengthwise; cut flowerets into large pieces. Blanch broccoli, cauliflower, and potatoes in boiling water; drain. In the meantime, heat oils in a medium skillet, then add one third of the chopped garlic. As garlic begins to color, add tomatoes, cover, and simmer for 5 minutes.

Place vegetables in a large, shallow baking dish, add the rest of the ingredients, including the remaining chopped garlic, and toss lightly, then spread tomatoes on surface, cover, and bake in a preheated 500° oven until vegetables are cooked, about 20 minutes. Do not overcook.

Calories	Cholesterol mg	Protein gm	Carbohydrate gm	Total fat gm	%	Sat fat gm	%	Mono gm	Poly gm
1463	0	44.5	139.8	98.7	59	10.2	6	52.6	15.6

MIXED VEGETABLES II
Verdura Mista

I like to serve this dish with broiled meat or fish.

Serves 6.

2 tablespoons olive oil
2 tablespoons safflower oil
3 medium onions, sliced
2 cloves garlic, chopped
Hot pepper flakes to taste (optional)
3 potatoes, sliced ½ inch thick
3 tomatoes, coarsely chopped, or 2 cups strained, chopped
    canned tomatoes
2 cups broccoli flowerets and peeled, sliced stems
2 zucchini, sliced ½ inch thick
2 sweet peppers, sliced
1 teaspoon rosemary
Salt and freshly ground black pepper to taste
2 tablespoons chopped Italian parsley

Heat the oils in a skillet or wide pot, then add onions, garlic, and hot pepper. In the meantime, boil potato slices about 5 minutes.

As onions begin to brown, add tomatoes and cook over high heat, mixing often, about 3 minutes. Lower heat, add drained potatoes and the remaining ingredients except parsley. Cover and cook over medium heat until potatoes and broccoli are tender—about 15 minutes. Add parsley just before serving.

Calories	Cholesterol mg	Protein gm	Carbohydrate gm	Total fat gm	%	Sat fat gm	%	Mono gm	Poly gm
1321	0	36.3	170.5	57.8	39	6.0	4	23.0	22.4

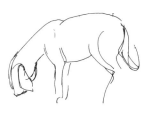

MIXED SUMMER VEGETABLES I
Insalata Mista d'Estate

Serves 6.

2 teaspoons vegetable oil, such as peanut oil or
   safflower oil
1 medium onion, coarsely chopped
2 cups eggplant cut in 1/2- to 1-inch cubes
2 cups sliced sweet peppers
2 medium potatoes, peeled and thinly sliced
2 cups chopped tomatoes, fresh if possible (drain if canned)
3 cups zucchini cut into 1-inch pieces
3 teaspoons chopped fresh basil or 1 teaspoon dried
Salt and freshly ground black pepper to taste

Heat oil in a wide skillet, then add onion, eggplant, and peppers. Cook about 10 minutes and add the rest of the ingredients. Cover and cook about 1 hour over medium heat.

Variation: If a 7-ounce can of Italian-style tunafish is mixed with about one third of this recipe and served at room temperature, garnished with finely chopped Italian parsley, it will make a very nice appetizer or enough for 4 as a main course.

Calories	Cholesterol mg	Protein gm	Carbohydrate gm	Total fat gm	%	Sat fat gm	%	Mono gm	Poly gm
733	0	28.8	126.9	12.6	15	1.6	2	4.2	2.6

MIXED SUMMER VEGETABLES II
Insalata Mista d'Estate

This is excellent with broiled fish or meat.

Serves 8 to 10.

2 tablespoons olive oil
1 tablespoon safflower oil
1 medium to large onion, sliced
4 cups eggplant cut into 1-inch cubes
4 cups zucchini cut into 1-inch cubes
4 cups peeled, chopped ripe tomatoes
2 tablespoons chopped fresh basil
Hot pepper flakes to taste (optional)*
5 dried black olives, pitted and sliced (optional)*
Salt to taste

*Although the recipe does not include hot pepper and olives, I find they enhance the dish.

Heat the oils in a medium skillet, then add onion. Cook for several minutes and add eggplant. Cook over high heat until eggplant begins to color. Add zucchini and cook for several minutes. Add tomatoes, basil, hot pepper, and olives. Cover and simmer about 10 to 15 minutes. The dish should not be stewlike, but dry enough so that it can be served easily as a vegetable. Serve hot or at room temperature.

Variation: Add a 7-ounce can of Italian-style tunafish after the dish cools. Garnish with chopped Italian parsley and serve at room temperature as a main course.

Calories	Cholesterol mg	Protein gm	Carbohydrate gm	Total fat gm	%	Sat fat gm	%	Mono gm	Poly gm
887	0	25.3	96.7	47.6	47	4.5	4	25.2	11.9

MIXED WINTER VEGETABLES
Misto di Verdura Invernale

This is a light vegetable combination that we enjoy during the winter months. We like this recipe served with one of the hot pepper relishes.

Serves 6.

2 medium potatoes, peeled and quartered
1 pound fresh Brussels sprouts, discolored leaves removed
1 small cauliflower, broken into flowerets (cut large ones
   in half)
3 tablespoons olive oil
1 tablespoon safflower oil
2 cloves garlic, minced
1 teaspoon dried oregano
Salt and freshly ground black pepper to taste

Boil potatoes until tender.

Steam Brussels sprouts and cauliflower together, cooking until Brussels sprouts are tender but not overcooked. Drain potatoes and put in a mixing bowl with cooked Brussels sprouts and cauliflower. Add the rest of the ingredients, toss, and serve warm.

Calories	Cholesterol mg	Protein gm	Carbohydrate gm	Total fat gm	%	Sat fat gm	%	Mono gm	Poly gm
945	0	41.6	102.1	57.4	53	6.6	6	31.3	13.4

VEGETABLES TEMPURA
Fritto Misto

Serves 4.

The batter
1 cup flour
1 cup ice-cold water

1 teaspoon baking powder
2 egg whites, lightly beaten

Corn or vegetable oil for frying

Fresh vegetables, such as
Broccoli (blanched)
Zucchini blossoms
Zucchini, cut in half crosswise, then quartered lengthwise
Scallions, cut into 3-inch lengths
Asparagus, cut into 3-inch lengths
Sugar snap edible pea pods or snow peas

Heat corn oil or vegetable oil in a medium skillet. When hot, dip vegetables one at a time in the batter, then carefully place in hot oil. Repeat the process. Turn and cook several minutes, until light brown. Do not overcook. Put on a platter lined with paper towels to dry out a little. Arrange cooked vegetables in a pleasing pattern on a serving plate. A bowl of soy sauce could accompany the tempura to act as a dip.

Calories	Cholesterol mg	Protein gm	Carbohydrate gm	Total fat gm	%	Sat fat gm	%	Mono gm	Poly gm
789	0	31.3	129.0	15.8	18	1.4	2	3.8	7.2

FOUND VEGETABLES
Verdura Trovata

Serves 8 or more.

About 2 pounds mixed found vegetables*
4 cups diced potatoes
3 tablespoons olive oil
1 tablespoon safflower oil
1 1/2 tablespoons minced garlic
Hot pepper flakes to taste (optional)
Salt to taste

*A variety of vegetables that seed themselves, such as rape, turnips, radicchio, or cabbage, may be used in this recipe along with wild vegetables, like purslane, redroot, and dandelion greens.

Wash and drain vegetables and chop coarsely. Put potatoes and vegetables in boiling water and boil about 4 or 5 minutes. Drain, reserving 3 cups water.
Heat the oils in a skillet, then add garlic, hot pepper, the boiled vegetables, about 1 cup reserved water, and salt. Cover and simmer over medium to low heat, adding more water as needed. Stir occasionally, crushing potatoes after they become soft. Cook about 1 hour.

Calories	Cholesterol mg	Protein gm	Carbohydrate gm	Total fat gm	%	Sat fat gm	%	Mono gm	Poly gm
1244	0	41.6	160.2	58.4	41	5.5	4	32.8	12.6

Stuffed Vegetables

STUFFED CABBAGE WITH TOMATOES
Cavolo Imbottito al Pomodoro

Serve these cabbage rolls with boiled potatoes or rice, preferably plain rice.

Serves 5 to 6.

1 medium cabbage

The stuffing
1 pound ground lean veal
1 teaspoon minced garlic
2 tablespoons yellow raisins
2 tablespoons chopped pine nuts
1 cup fresh breadcrumbs
2 egg whites, lightly beaten
2 tablespoons finely chopped Italian parsley
Salt and freshly ground black pepper to taste
1 teaspoon dried oregano

1 tablespoon olive oil
1 tablespoon safflower oil
1 medium onion, finely chopped
1 cup chopped tomatoes, fresh if possible (drain if canned)
1 cup chicken or beef broth

Garnish: Chopped Italian parsley or fresh coriander

Carefully remove cabbage leaves, blanch in boiling water, drain, and let cool. If leaves are difficult to separate, drop the whole head into boiling water first. Boil about 5 minutes, drain, and then remove leaves.

Mix the stuffing ingredients in a bowl and set aside.

Heat the oils in a medium skillet, then add onion. When onion begins to brown, add tomatoes, cover, and simmer for 5 minutes. Add broth and cook for several minutes. Reserve.

Spread out cabbage leaves. For each leaf, make a ball about the size of a golf ball from the stuffing, flatten it a bit and place it in the middle of the leaf. Fold one end of the leaf over the stuffing and roll it up. Place filled rolls seam side down on a medium baking tray so that they fit snugly. Repeat until all the meat is used up. Pour the reserved tomato-and-broth sauce over the stuffed cabbage. Cover with foil and bake in a preheated 450° oven about 1 hour.

To serve, garnish with chopped Italian parsley or fresh coriander.

Calories	Cholesterol mg	Protein gm	Carbohydrate gm	Total fat gm	%	Sat fat gm	%	Mono gm	Poly gm
1337	322.0	117.7	86.2	57.7	38	14.1	9	24.1	12.4

WHOLE CABBAGE STUFFED WITH VEAL
Cavolo Imbottito al Vitello

Serve this whole stuffed cabbage with boiled potatoes.

Serves 6.

2 tablespoons peanut oil or vegetable oil
1 onion, finely chopped
1 medium cabbage
1 pound ground lean veal
2 tablespoons yellow raisins
2 egg whites, lightly beaten
1 cup fresh breadcrumbs
Salt and freshly ground black pepper to taste
1 clove garlic, minced
1 piece cheesecloth about 18 inches square
4 cups chicken stock
1 onion, coarsely chopped
1 stalk celery, chopped

Heat the oil in a medium skillet, add finely chopped onion, and sauté until translucent.

Remove leaves from cabbage and blanch them. Drain, let them cool, then flatten them out.

In a mixing bowl combine sautéed onion, veal, raisins, egg whites, breadcrumbs, salt, pepper, and garlic. Mix well.

Spread out the cheesecloth and place 3 of the largest cabbage leaves in the center of the cheesecloth. Spread some stuffing on these leaves. Add more leaves, then more stuffing, and continue until leaves and stuffing are used up. Pull up the corners of the cheesecloth and wrap tightly around the cabbage and stuffing to form a ball. Tie corners together.

Preheat oven to 450°. Place stuffed cabbage in a casserole, add chicken stock, coarsely chopped onion, and chopped celery. Cover and bake about 1 1/2 hours, basting occasionally.

Remove cheesecloth. To serve, cut stuffed cabbage into 6 wedges.

Calories	Cholesterol mg	Protein gm	Carbohydrate gm	Total fat gm	%	Sat fat gm	%	Mono gm	Poly gm
1263	322.0	113.5	82.1	52.3	36	15.7	11	22.6	8.2

STUFFED EGGPLANT
NEAPOLITAN STYLE
Melanzane Imbottito alla Napoletano

Serves 4 as a first course; 2 as a main course.

1/2 cup rice
4 small eggplants, about 5 inches long
Salt to taste
1 tablespoon safflower or peanut oil
1/2 onion, finely chopped
1 1/2 cups chopped tomatoes, fresh if possible (drain
    if canned)
2 tablespoons chopped celery
1 tablespoon chopped fresh basil
Freshly ground black pepper to taste
1 egg white, lightly beaten
1 tablespoon finely chopped Italian parsley
1 tablespoon chopped pine nuts
8 toothpicks
1 tablespoon olive oil

Steam rice in 1 cup water (see page 160).

Preheat oven to 450°.

Cut off stem end of eggplant, cut in half lengthwise, and scoop out center, leaving about 1/2 inch flesh on all sides. Chop and reserve scooped out flesh. Sprinkle insides with salt and let sit about 15 minutes. Rinse out insides and pat dry.

Heat the safflower oil in a small skillet, then add onion. When onion begins to brown, add tomatoes, celery, basil, salt, pepper, a little water, and the scooped out eggplant. Cover and simmer for 15 minutes.

Prepare stuffing by thoroughly mixing the cooked rice with the egg white, parsley, pine nuts, salt, and pepper. Stuff each half of eggplant with stuffing. Put halves together and hold together by forcing a toothpick through both sides at each end.

Place the re-formed eggplants in a small ovenproof casserole so that they fit snugly. Pour tomato-eggplant sauce over and drizzle olive oil over all. Cover and bake about 30 minutes. These are good hot or at room temperature.

Calories	Cholesterol mg	Protein gm	Carbohydrate gm	Total fat gm	%	Sat fat gm	%	Mono gm	Poly gm
1010	0	29.9	150.2	32.9	29	3.1	3	12.8	11.6

EGGPLANT STUFFED WITH TOMATOES
Melanzane Imbottite

Serves 4.

4 small eggplants, about 1 pound
Salt to taste
1½ cups chopped fresh tomatoes
1 clove garlic, finely chopped
1 teaspoon dried oregano
1 tablespoon olive oil
1 teaspoon safflower oil
Freshly ground black pepper to taste
3 tablespoons fresh breadcrumbs mixed with 1 teaspoon
    safflower oil

Preheat oven to 450°.

Cut the eggplants in half lengthwise. Slice a bit off the bottom so that they sit upright. Score the cut surface with a sharp knife in a cross-hatch pattern. Add salt to cut surface and allow to sit about 20 minutes. Rinse and pat dry.

Put eggplants on a baking tray. In a bowl mix the tomatoes, garlic, oregano, the two oils, salt, and pepper. Spoon onto the surface of each eggplant half. Bake about 20 minutes. Add breadcrumbs to each eggplant half and bake another 15 minutes.

Serve hot or at room temperature.

Calories	Cholesterol mg	Protein gm	Carbohydrate gm	Total fat gm	%	Sat fat gm	%	Mono gm	Poly gm
420	0	10.3	41.8	24.6	52	2.6	5	10.9	7.9

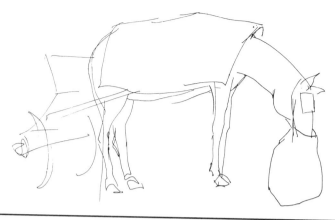

VEAL–STUFFED EGGPLANT WITH TOMATO SAUCE
Melanzane Imbottite alla Siciliana

A very good dish served with potatoes or rice, or simply a green vegetable.

Serves 6 to 9.

The sauce
2 tablespoons olive oil
1 tablespoon safflower oil
1 medium onion, chopped, about 3/4 cup
4 cups coarsely chopped tomatoes, fresh if possible
    (drained if canned)
2 tablespoons chopped fresh basil or 1 teaspoon dried
Salt and freshly ground black pepper to taste

2 medium to large eggplant
Corn or vegetable oil for frying
3 egg whites, lightly beaten
About 1 1/4 cups flour for dredging
1 1/2 pounds ground lean veal
1 egg white, lightly beaten
1 tablespoon finely chopped Italian parsley
1 teaspoon minced garlic
1 teaspoon grated lemon rind
1/2 teaspoon grated nutmeg

To make the sauce: Heat olive oil and safflower oil in a medium skillet, add onion, and sauté until it begins to brown. Add tomatoes, cover, and simmer. Add basil, salt, and pepper, cover, and simmer about 20 minutes.

In the meantime, cut the eggplants in half, then slice them lengthwise about 1/4 inch thick. Spread the slices on a tray, sprinkle with salt, and let stand about 20 minutes. Blot the slices dry. Heat about 3/4 inch corn oil or vegetable oil in a medium skillet, then dip eggplant slices in 3 egg whites, dust with flour, and lightly brown in the oil, several pieces at a time, not crowding the pan. Blot cooked eggplant slices and continue cooking remaining pieces in the same way.

Mix the veal with the 1 egg white, parsley, garlic, lemon rind, nutmeg, salt, and pepper.

Put the tomato sauce through a food mill or food processor and blend. Preheat oven to 450°.

In a deep baking dish 9 or 10 inches square, place a layer of eggplant, some sauce, another layer of eggplant and sauce. Spread all the veal mixture over eggplant, pour some sauce over veal, then a layer of eggplant. Repeat layers of eggplant and sauce until eggplant is used up, finishing with sauce. Cover and bake about 30 minutes. Let stand about 30 minutes before serving.

Calories	Cholesterol mg	Protein gm	Carbohydrate gm	Total fat gm	%	Sat fat gm	%	Mono gm	Poly gm
2804	483.0	199.0	250.5	108.8	34	24.6	8	43.0	28.9

STUFFED LETTUCE IN BROTH
Lattughe Ripiene in Brodo

Serves 4.

About 20 good-sized lettuce leaves from Boston or
    romaine lettuce
1 pound ground veal
1 medium onion, finely chopped
1 tablespoon finely chopped Italian parsley
Dash nutmeg
2 egg whites, lightly beaten
1 teaspoon grated lemon rind
Salt and freshly ground black pepper to taste
2 to 3 cups chicken or beef broth
Juice of 1/2 lemon

Wash lettuce leaves, then drop in boiling water about 30 seconds. Add cold water to pot, then remove lettuce leaves carefully and place on paper towels.

Mix veal, onion, parsley, nutmeg, egg whites, lemon rind, salt, and pepper together. Form balls to fit each lettuce leaf. Place ball near the wide end of the leaf and fold two sides toward the center, then the other two to make a package. Place lettuce packages on the bottom of a pot and add broth and lemon juice. Cover and boil gently about 10 minutes.

Serve about 5 lettuce packages in each soup bowl and pour in some broth.

Calories	Cholesterol mg	Protein gm	Carbohydrate gm	Total fat gm	%	Sat fat gm	%	Mono gm	Poly gm
757	322.0	105.3	25.8	23.8	28	10.9	13	10.0	0.4

LETTUCE STUFFED WITH CHICKEN
Lattughe Ripiene

Serves 4.

1 whole chicken breast, skin, bones, and fat removed,
   then cut into 1 1/2-inch squares

The marinade
1/2 teaspoon minced garlic (more if desired)
Juice of 1/2 lemon
Salt and freshly ground black pepper to taste
1 tablespoon finely chopped fresh ginger
3 tablespoons thinly sliced scallions

About 20 large lettuce leaves from bibb lettuce,
   romaine, etc.
Corn or vegetable oil for frying
2 egg whites, lightly beaten

Marinate chicken pieces for at least 2 hours.

In the meantime, blanch lettuce leaves. Add cold water to the pot and
carefully remove lettuce leaves. Place them on paper towels to drain. Put a
piece of chicken in the middle of each lettuce leaf, fold two sides toward
the center, then the other two sides to make a package.

Heat about 3/4 inch corn or vegetable oil in a medium skillet, When oil
is hot, roll some of the lettuce-wrapped pieces of chicken in the beaten egg
whites. Gently place them in the hot oil and fry for several minutes. Place
on paper towels and keep warm. Repeat until all are cooked. Serve
immediately.

Calories	Cholesterol mg	Protein gm	Carbohydrate gm	Total fat gm	%	Sat fat gm	%	Mono gm	Poly gm
402	121.0	52.1	8.6	17.1	37	2.8	6	4.6	8.7

STUFFED ONIONS
Cipolle Imbottite

Serves 6 as an appetizer or vegetable course; 3 as a main course.

6 medium onions
1 cup ground lean veal or beef
1 tablespoon chopped fresh basil or 1 teaspoon dried
2 tablespoons fresh breadcrumbs
Salt and freshly ground black pepper to taste
1/2 cup dry white wine or chicken broth
1 teaspoon safflower oil mixed with 1 tablespoon
   olive oil

Peel and cut off bottoms of onions so that they will stand upright. Cut off top and boil about 5 minutes. Drain and remove core.

Preheat oven to 450°. In a small bowl mix the veal, basil, breadcrumbs, salt, and pepper. Stuff onions with mixture.

Place onions in a small baking dish so they fit snugly. Pour wine over onions, then the oil mixture. Cover and bake about 25 minutes. Then bake, uncovered, another 5 minutes.

Calories	Cholesterol mg	Protein gm	Carbohydrate gm	Total fat gm	%	Sat fat gm	%	Mono gm	Poly gm
958	188.0	70.6	84.9	33.7	34	8.6	9	16.2	4.6

PEPPERS STUFFED WITH VEAL
Peperoni Ripieni di Vitello

Serves 4 as a main course.

5 tablespoons safflower or sunflower seed oil
1 pound lean stewing veal, fat removed, cut into
    1-inch cubes
Salt and freshly ground black pepper to taste
1 teaspoon rosemary
Juice of ½ lemon
4 whole peppers, preferably red but green will do
1 medium onion, chopped
2 cups chopped tomatoes, fresh if possible (drain if canned)
1 cup cooked rice (page 160)
1 egg white
2 tablespoons chopped Italian parsley
Dash nutmeg

Heat 3 tablespoons of the oil in a medium skillet, then add veal, salt, and pepper. Cook over high heat, turning veal constantly until it begins to brown. Add rosemary and lemon juice, cover, lower heat, and simmer for several minutes. Remove from the heat and grind veal and juices in a meat grinder or food processor. Set aside.

Lightly char outsides of peppers over high heat, turning until lightly blistered all over. This is just to give a nice charred taste and appearance. Cool the peppers, then cut off tops and reserve. With a sharp knife cut out seeds, leaving the peppers intact.

Sauté onion in the remaining 2 tablespoons oil until it begins to brown. Add tomatoes, salt, and pepper, cover, and simmer 10 minutes.

Mix thoroughly the rice, egg white, parsley, nutmeg, salt, pepper, ground veal, and 8 tablespoons of the tomato sauce. Stuff peppers with the mixture and put the caps back on. Set in an upright position, close together, in a small ovenproof casserole. Pour the remaining sauce over the peppers, cover, and bake in a preheated 375° to 400° oven about 30 minutes.

Calories	Cholesterol mg	Protein gm	Carbohydrate gm	Total fat gm	%	Sat fat gm	%	Mono gm	Poly gm
1939	322.0	118.3	153.8	94.4	43	17.4	8	18.0	50.9

PEPPERS STUFFED WITH TUNA
Peperoni Ripieni di Tonno

This is a dish that may be served hot or at room temperature. It goes very well with a green salad.

Serves 4.

4 medium peppers, preferably red
7-ounce can Italian-style tunafish
8 green olives, pitted and chopped
2 tablespoons chopped capers
4 anchovy fillets, chopped
8 tablespoons fresh breadcrumbs
2 teaspoons minced garlic
2 tablespoons safflower oil or other vegetable oil
2 tablespoons minced Italian parsley or fresh coriander
Freshly ground black pepper to taste
Dry white wine (optional)

Preheat oven to 450°.

Cut off tops of peppers about 1 inch down with a sharp knife. Remove seeds. Mix all remaining ingredients (except wine) in a bowl and stuff peppers with the mixture.

Put peppers in an ovenproof dish so that they fit tightly. Cover bottom with 1/2 inch dry white wine or water. Bake, uncovered, for 20 minutes.

Calories	Cholesterol mg	Protein gm	Carbohydrate gm	Total fat gm	%	Sat fat gm	%	Mono gm	Poly gm
1100	120.0	68.6	95.8	49.8	40	6.5	5	9.1	23.3

STUFFED PEPPERS MY WAY
Peperoni Ripieni a Modo Mio

Serves 6 as a main course; 12 as a vegetable course.

6 red or green sweet peppers
12 dried black olives, pitted and chopped
3 tablespoons capers
3 tablespoons raisins
3 tablespoons pine nuts
2 anchovies packed in oil or 1 salted anchovy, washed and boned, finely chopped

2 cups fresh breadcrumbs
3 tablespoons dry white wine
1 teaspoon minced garlic
2 tablespoons finely chopped Italian parsley
Salt and freshly ground black pepper to taste
1/2 cup chicken or beef broth
2 teaspoons vegetable oil

Quickly char outsides of peppers over high heat and remove skins (for details, see page 365). Cut off tops of peppers and remove seeds.

Make the stuffing by mixing all the ingredients (except broth and oil). Stuff peppers, put caps back on, and place in a deep baking dish so that they fit snugly. Pour in broth. Pour oil over peppers.

Preheat oven to 450° and bake about 20 minutes. Serve hot or at room temperature.

Calories	Cholesterol mg	Protein gm	Carbohydrate gm	Total fat gm	%	Sat fat gm	%	Mono gm	Poly gm
1178	4.0	36.4	195.1	31.7	24	2.4	2	11.3	8.8

STUFFED PEPPERS FLORENTINE STYLE
Peperoni Imbottiti alla Fiorentina

Serves 3 as a main course; 6 as an appetizer.

1/4 pound fresh spinach
1/2 pound boneless, skinless chicken breasts, coarsely ground
3 tablespoons finely chopped onion
3/4 cup fresh breadcrumbs
1 teaspoon marjoram
1 tablespoon finely chopped Italian parsley
1 egg white, lightly beaten
Salt and freshly ground black pepper to taste
3 peppers, preferably sweet red ones
1 cup marinara sauce (page 430)
1 tablespoon olive oil mixed with 1 tablespoon
    safflower oil

Wash and boil spinach about 1 minute. Drain, let cool, then squeeze out as much moisture as possible. Chop and place in a mixing bowl. Add ground chicken breast, onion, breadcrumbs, marjoram, parsley, egg white, salt, and black pepper and mix well.

Cut off tops of peppers with a sharp knife and reserve. Remove seeds. Fill peppers with the stuffing, then put them in a baking dish so that they fit snugly, pour tomato sauce around them, and pour oil on top. Replace caps on top of the peppers. Cover with foil, place in a preheated 450° oven, and bake about 45 minutes. Remove foil and cook an additional 15 minutes, basting occasionally with sauce.

Serve with rice.

Calories	Cholesterol mg	Protein gm	Carbohydrate gm	Total fat gm	%	Sat fat gm	%	Mono gm	Poly gm
1286	152.0	96.2	124.2	48.1	33	5.9	4	20.7	13.8

PEPPERS STUFFED WITH PASTA
Peperoni Ripieni di Pasta

These may be cooked ahead of time and served at room temperature. They are particularly good the next day.

Serves 4 to 6.

4 large sweet peppers, preferably red or yellow
1/2 pound pasta, either long cuts such as spaghetti,
 spaghettini, vermicelli, linguine, or small cuts
1 cup marinara sauce (page 430)
1 tablespoon capers
10 dried black olives, pitted and
 cut in slivers
2 tablespoons chopped Italian parsley
2 tablespoons olive oil mixed with 1 tablespoon
 safflower oil

Char peppers on top of the stove over low heat, following directions on page 366, turning them often. Cut the tops off and scrape out seeds, keeping peppers intact. Set aside.

Cook pasta in a large pot of boiling water until done al dente. Drain and mix with tomato sauce, capers, slivered olives, and parsley. Carefully stuff the pasta into the peppers, replace caps, and put the peppers in a deep oven-proof dish that will hold them snug and upright. Pour oil over peppers after they are in place. Preheat oven to 350°, place peppers in oven, and cook, uncovered, 15 to 20 minutes.

Calories	Cholesterol mg	Protein gm	Carbohydrate gm	Total fat gm	%	Sat fat gm	%	Mono gm	Poly gm
1842	0	46.7	272.2	64.4	31	7.1	3	34.2	14.5

STUFFED POTATOES I
Patate Ripiene

Serves 6.

6 fairly large potatoes, peeled
1 tablespoon olive oil
1 tablespoon safflower oil or peanut oil

1 medium onion, finely chopped
3 to 4 anchovy fillets, chopped
1 teaspoon minced garlic
2 cups chopped tomatoes, fresh if possible (drain if canned)
1 tablespoon minced Italian parsley
1 tablespoon chopped fresh basil or $1/2$ teaspoon dried
Salt and freshly ground black pepper to taste
1 tablespoon drained capers
6 tablespoons toasted fresh breadcrumbs

Cut the top off the narrow end of each potato, then scoop out the insides with a sharp spoon or small knife (and discard—or use in a soup) so that you have a good-sized cavity that will hold about 3 tablespoons filling. Soak potatoes in cold water.

Heat the oils in a skillet, then add onion. When it is translucent, add anchovies and garlic and sauté about 30 seconds. Add tomatoes, parsley, basil, salt, and pepper, cover, and simmer about 5 minutes. Add capers and continue simmering about 15 minutes.

Preheat oven to 400°. Drain potatoes thoroughly, cut off other end, and place upright in an oiled baking dish just large enough to hold them snugly. Put tomato mixture into the cavities and sprinkle breadcrumbs on top. Bake, covered, about 15 minutes, then continue baking, uncovered, until potatoes are tender—about 10 to 15 minutes more.

Calories	Cholesterol mg	Protein gm	Carbohydrate gm	Total fat gm	%	Sat fat gm	%	Mono gm	Poly gm
1165	7.0	30.8	193.2	30.9	23	3.5	3	11.9	11.6

STUFFED POTATOES II
Patate Ripiene al' Forno

Serves 3.

1 tablespoon safflower oil
4 tablespoons finely chopped onion
3 tablespoons finely chopped green pepper
    (about $1/2$ pepper)
4 tablespoons chopped tomatoes, fresh if possible
    (drain if canned)
1 clove garlic, minced
1 teaspoon dried oregano
Salt and freshly ground black pepper to taste
3 baking potatoes, prepared as in preceding recipe
1 tablespoon olive oil

Preheat oven to 400°. Heat the safflower oil in a small skillet, then add onion and peppers. When onion wilts, add tomatoes, garlic, oregano, salt, and pepper. Cover and cook for several minutes. Stuff potatoes with mixture. Place potatoes in a small baking dish so that they sit snugly. Sprinkle the olive oil over potatoes, salt and pepper them, then cover and bake about 45 minutes.

Serve hot or at room temperature.

Calories	Cholesterol mg	Protein gm	Carbohydrate gm	Total fat gm	%	Sat fat gm	%	Mono gm	Poly gm
796	0	16.1	118.4	28.1	31	3.0	3	11.5	11.2

STUFFED TOMATOES TRASTEVERE STYLE
Pomodori Ripieni alla Trasteverina

Serves 2.

2 tablespoons olive oil
1 tablespoon safflower oil
4 tablespoons minced onion
4 tablespoons minced celery
1 tablespoon minced Italian parsley
1 cup coarsely chopped mushrooms
2 tablespoons fresh breadcrumbs
1 egg white, lightly beaten
Salt and freshly ground black pepper to taste
2 medium to large ripe tomatoes

Heat 1 tablespoon of the olive oil and the safflower oil in a small skillet, then add onion, celery, parsley, and mushrooms and sauté over moderate heat. Cook until onion wilts. Remove to a mixing bowl. Add breadcrumbs, egg white, salt, and pepper and mix. In the meantime, cut off tops of tomatoes and hollow out insides. Reserve the pulp. Fill each tomato with the stuffing and put tops back in place.

Preheat oven to 400°. Place tomatoes in a small baking dish. Add pulp to dish. Pour remaining olive oil over tomatoes and bake, uncovered, about 20 to 25 minutes. Serve at room temperature.

Calories	Cholesterol mg	Protein gm	Carbohydrate gm	Total fat gm	%	Sat fat gm	%	Mono gm	Poly gm
446	0	7.6	12.9	41.2	81	4.8	9	21.4	12.3

ZUCCHINI–STUFFED BROILED TOMATOES
Pomodori Imbottiti

Serves 4 to 5 as a vegetable course.

1 1/2 cups shredded zucchini
4 to 5 medium ripe tomatoes

1 tablespoon safflower oil
1 small onion, finely chopped
Salt and freshly ground black pepper to taste
1 tablespoon finely chopped Italian parsley
1 cup cooked rice
1 tablespoon olive oil

Drain shredded zucchini for 30 minutes in a colander, then squeeze out juices.

Cut off tops of tomatoes (a sawtooth pattern makes an attractive presentation) and hollow out tomatoes, reserving pulp.

Heat the safflower oil in a small skillet, then add onion and cook several minutes. Add zucchini, salt, and pepper and cook over medium heat for several minutes. Add the pulp from 3 of the tomatoes and cook several minutes. Add parsley and rice and mix well.

Fill tomatoes with stuffing and place them in a small ovenproof dish. Put remaining pulp on bottom of dish. Sprinkle olive oil over tomatoes.

Preheat oven to 450°. Bake tomatoes, uncovered, about 25 minutes. Spoon pan juices over tomatoes. Preheat broiler. Broil tomatoes close to heat to slightly crust the tops of the tomatoes.

Calories	Cholesterol mg	Protein gm	Carbohydrate gm	Total fat gm	%	Sat fat gm	%	Mono gm	Poly gm
648	0	13.9	85.3	28.8	39	3.0	4	11.5	11.2

BAKED STUFFED ZUCCHINI
Zucchini Imbottiti al Forno

Serves 5.

5 zucchini, 6 to 7 inches long

The stuffing
3 tablespoons finely chopped onion
1 clove garlic, minced
1 cup cooked rice (page 160)
1/2 pound ground lean veal
1 tablespoon chopped pine nuts
1 1/2 teaspoons grated lemon rind
3 tablespoons fresh breadcrumbs
1 egg white, lightly beaten
Salt and freshly ground black pepper to taste

1 tablespoon olive oil
1 tablespoon safflower oil

Garnish: Lemon wedges

Cut zucchini in half lengthwise. Preheat oven to 400°. Scoop out center of zucchini and discard. Mix all the stuffing ingredients. Place zucchini in a baking tray so that they fit snugly and fill each zucchini with stuffing. Sprinkle oils over zucchini, cover, and bake 30 minutes. Remove cover and bake another 15 minutes. Add a little broth if too dry.

Serve with lemon wedges.

Calories	Cholesterol mg	Protein gm	Carbohydrate gm	Total fat gm	%	Sat fat gm	%	Mono gm	Poly gm
919	161.0	61.7	72.4	41.8	40	8.5	8	17.8	11.8

ZUCCHINI STUFFED WITH VEAL
Zucchini Ripiene

Serves 3 to 6.

The sauce
1 tablespoon olive oil
1 tablespoon safflower oil
1 cup finely chopped onion
1 cup chopped tomatoes, fresh if possible (drain if canned)
Salt and freshly ground black pepper to taste

¼ pound ground lean veal
3 tablespoons minced onion
Juice of ¼ lemon
1 teaspoon finely chopped Italian parsley
1 egg white, lightly beaten
3 teaspoons fresh breadcrumbs
6 zucchini, prepared as in preceding recipe

To make the sauce: Heat the oils in a small skillet, then add onion. When onion wilts, add tomatoes, salt, and pepper, cover, and simmer for 10 minutes. Preheat oven to 450°.

In a bowl mix thoroughly the veal, minced onion, lemon juice, parsley, egg white, breadcrumbs, salt, and pepper. Stuff zucchini with the mixture, then place stuffed zucchini in a shallow baking dish so that they fit snugly. Pour tomato sauce over the zucchini. Bake, uncovered, about 30 minutes, adding a little water if more moisture is needed.

Calories	Cholesterol mg	Protein gm	Carbohydrate gm	Total fat gm	%	Sat fat gm	%	Mono gm	Poly gm
635	81.0	38.5	55.4	34.3	48	5.3	7	15.0	10.8

ZUCCHINI STUFFED WITH TUNA
Zucchini Ripiene

Serves 4 to 6.

3 medium zucchini, prepared as in baked stuffed zucchini
    (page 403)
3/4 cup fresh breadcrumbs, soaked in 2 tablespoons milk
2 tablespoons finely chopped Italian parsley
Freshly ground black pepper to taste
7-ounce can Italian-style tunafish
1 teaspoon marjoram
1 tablespoon olive oil
1 tablespoon safflower oil
1 clove garlic, finely chopped
1 cup chopped tomatoes, fresh if possible (drain if canned)

Preheat oven to 400°.

In a bowl mix thoroughly the breadcrumbs, parsley, pepper, tuna, and marjoram. Fill scooped out zucchini with this mixture and place on a baking tray so they fit snugly.

In the meantime, heat the oils in a small skillet, then add the garlic. As soon as garlic starts to color, add tomatoes, cover, and simmer over low heat about 5 minutes. Spoon over the zucchini; bake, uncovered, about 20 minutes.

Calories	Cholesterol mg	Protein gm	Carbohydrate gm	Total fat gm	%	Sat fat gm	%	Mono gm	Poly gm
801	111.0	59.8	40.6	43.9	48	7.3	8	14.7	14.1

STUFFED ZUCCHINI BLOSSOMS I
Fiori di Zucca Ripieni

In my first book, *Italian Family Cooking*, published in 1971, I explained the difference between a female zucchini blossom and a male zucchini blossom.

The male blossom pollinates the female blossom, which has a small zucchini attached to it. There are always more male zucchini blossoms on a plant than female, certainly more than needed to pollinate the female blossoms. It is the male blossoms that are picked, since they do not bear fruit. The male blossoms appear at the end of a straight stem, while the female blossoms appear attached to a branch at the end of a small zucchini. If the blossom is pollinated, the zucchini will mature; if it is not pollinated, it will drop off with the blossom.

Italians harvest zucchini when they are no larger than 5 or 6 inches long, with the female blossom still attached to them. I read of a theory that the male blossom is harvested because it tastes better—but this is not true.

Both flowers taste the same. In fact, a female blossom attached to a zucchini about 2 inches long is divine cooked with zucchini (see zucchini blossoms fried in tempura batter, page 388), which can be made only if you raise your own zucchini — and in abundance. It is best to pick the blossoms in the morning, when the flowers are open.

Serves 4.

1/2 cup sliced zucchini
1/2 cup fresh green beans, cut in half
1 medium potato, diced
1 egg white, lightly beaten
1 clove garlic
1 tablespoon chopped fresh basil
1 teaspoon dried marjoram
Salt and freshly ground black pepper to taste
12 zucchini flowers (or any squash flowers,
    including pumpkin)

Boil zucchini slices, beans, and potatoes until almost cooked. Drain, and when cool squeeze out as much juice as possible. Blend with a mortar and pestle or food processor. Add the egg white, garlic, basil, marjoram, salt, and pepper. Mix well.

Remove pistils from flowers and carefully stuff each flower with the mixture.

Place blossoms on an oiled baking tray and bake in a preheated 450° oven about 20 minutes.

Calories	Cholesterol mg	Protein gm	Carbohydrate gm	Total fat gm	%	Sat fat gm	%	Mono gm	Poly gm
188	0	9.1	34.3	2.7	13	0.2	1	0.6	1.2

STUFFED ZUCCHINI BLOSSOMS ROMAN STYLE II
Fiori di Zucchini Imbottiti alla Romana

This is a popular way of serving zucchini blossoms in Rome. Piperno Restaurant in Rome is especially known for its stuffed zucchini blossoms.

Serves 4.

6 anchovy fillets, cut in half
12 zucchini blossoms*
1 tablespoon coarsely chopped Italian parsley
1/4 pound fresh skim milk mozzarella, finely chopped
Freshly ground black pepper to taste
Corn oil or vegetable oil for frying
1 1/2 cups wine batter (page 354)

*Pick blossoms in the morning while they are open. If closed blossoms are used, slit flowers and stuff them.

Place half an anchovy in each blossom. Chop parsley and mozzarella together and add pepper. Put some mozzarella mixture in each blossom—the amount used will depend on the size of the blossom. Heat about 3/4 inch oil in a medium skillet. Dip some of the stuffed blossoms in batter and deep-fry until flowers begin to brown. Blot on paper towels and repeat with another batch.

Serve hot as an appetizer or a vegetable course.

Calories	Cholesterol	Protein	Carbohydrate	Total fat		Sat fat		Mono	Poly
	mg	gm	gm	gm	%	gm	%	gm	gm
1170	85.0	248.2	109.6	55.9	42	15.0	11	14.6	16.5

STUFFED ZUCCHINI BLOSSOMS III
Fiori di Zucchini Imbottiti

Serves 4.

1 cup ground cooked chicken
1 cup fresh breadcrumbs
Dash nutmeg
1 egg white, lightly beaten
1 tablespoon finely chopped Italian parsley
Salt and freshly ground black pepper to taste
8 to 10 zucchini or squash blossoms
Corn oil for frying
1/2 recipe tempura batter (page 388)

Mix chicken, breadcrumbs, nutmeg, egg white, parsley, salt, and pepper. Carefully pack stuffing into blossoms.

Heat about 3/4 inch oil in a small skillet. When oil is hot, quickly dip flowers in batter, then carefully place them in the oil a few at a time and fry until lightly brown. Drain on paper towels. Serve hot.

Calories	Cholesterol	Protein	Carbohydrate	Total fat		Sat fat		Mono	Poly
	mg	gm	gm	gm	%	gm	%	gm	gm
821	109.0	48.8	76.5	33.9	36	4.2	5	9.3	15.4

IX SALADS

$\mathbf{M}$y feeling about salads is much the same as my feeling about vegetables: The less that is done to them, the better. I like a simple oil-and-vinegar (or lemon) dressing. Use a good wine vinegar (I make my own), and since you will be combining olive oil with safflower oil, it is particularly important that the olive oil be extra virgin, with a good fruity, assertive flavor.

For green salads, you should have a balanced mixture of greens: for a coarse texture, chicory; for crispness, Bibb lettuce; for bite, rucola or watercress; and I like the touch of bitterness that dandelion greens, endive, or radicchio gives. I prefer my greens without tomatoes and definitely without raw carrots. Tomatoes are best alone, or with onions and peppers, or with garden cucumbers.

Don't drown any salad with too much dressing and be sure to add it just before serving, since vinegar turns lettuce limp.

The salads in this chapter — that is, those that aren't leaf salads — will serve as appetizers or as accompaniments for a particular dish: for instance, the beet and potato salad goes well with boiled meats and the green bean and broccoli salad is particularly nice with broiled fish. Some of the salads are substantial enough for a main course in a summer lunch. One thing about salad — you can always eat a lot of it without feeling guilty. E.G.

The green, or garden, salad, for which Ed has given some very succinct advice, is a convenient vehicle for adjusting the diurnal balance between saturated and polyunsaturated fats. All meats and poultry, and almost all fish, have more saturated fat than polyunsaturated, and this imbalance needs to be corrected. Although many of our recipes contain within themselves enough polyunsaturated oil to achieve the desired balance, others make only a partial correction, and still others (e.g., grilled venison steak) contain only the meat with no balancing polyunsaturated oil. In such instances, polyunsaturated oil may be added to the diet in the form of a salad dressing; the other ingredients in the dressing and the greens themselves add little in the way of calories and nutrients. Remember, however, that every time you add polyunsaturated oil to balance an excess of saturated fat, you increase the overall percentage of calories derived from fat.

The other salads in this chapter are very easy to work with in meal planning. Several have no cholesterol. In almost all, there is more polyunsaturated fat than saturated fat, and the saturated fat contributes under 10 percent of the calories. R.W.

ASPARAGUS SALAD
Insalata di Asparagi

I think one of the most unpalatable eating experiences I have had in Italian restaurants in Italy as well as America is consuming soggy boiled asparagus. During our last visit to Italy, every time we ordered cold asparagus they were inedible. It is very simple to cook them so that they are green and crisp. I find the best way to prepare asparagus for a salad is to steam them.

Serves 4.

1 pound asparagus about the thickness of a pencil (tough
   ends removed)
1 clove garlic, finely chopped
1 tablespoon finely chopped fresh mint
Juice of 1/2 lemon
1 tablespoon extra virgin olive oil
1 teaspoon safflower oil
Salt and freshly ground black pepper to taste

Steam asparagus until just tender — about 3 minutes. Do not overcook, since asparagus should be crisp. Let them cool. Meanwhile, mix the rest of the ingredients.

Put the asparagus on a flat plate, pour the dressing over them, and serve at room temperature.

Calories	Cholesterol mg	Protein gm	Carbohydrate gm	Total fat gm	%	Sat fat gm	%	Mono gm	Poly gm
289	0	11.7	26.2	18.9	58	2.2	7	10.4	4.5

BROCCOLI SALAD
Insalata di Broccoli

Serves 4.

1 large bunch broccoli
2 tablespoons good olive oil
1 teaspoon safflower oil
12 dried black olives, whole or pitted
1 teaspoon minced garlic
Hot pepper flakes to taste (optional)
Salt to taste

Garnish: Lemon wedges

Peel broccoli stems. Cut flowerets with stems intact into manageable sections. Soak in salted water for 15 minutes, drain, and rinse. Steam broccoli for about 4 to 5 minutes — do not overcook. Put in a mixing bowl.

Mix remaining ingredients with broccoli. Serve with lemon wedges at room temperature.

Calories	Cholesterol mg	Protein gm	Carbohydrate gm	Total fat gm	%	Sat fat gm	%	Mono gm	Poly gm
504	0	17.4	22.7	41.2	72	5.0	9	26.5	6.2

GREEN BEAN AND BROCCOLI SALAD
Insalata di Fagiolini e Broccoli

Serves 4 to 6.

2 cups green beans
1 large bunch broccoli
1 cup thinly sliced whole scallions
10 dried black olives, pitted and sliced
1 teaspoon minced garlic
2 tablespoons good olive oil
1 tablespoon safflower oil
Salt to taste
Hot pepper flakes to taste (optional)
2 tablespoons chopped Italian parsley or fresh mint
Juice of 1 lemon

Steam the beans until tender but not overcooked. Set aside and cool. Peel the stems of the broccoli and cut lengthwise into manageable pieces, with flowerets attached. Steam broccoli until tender. Let cool.

Mix beans and broccoli together in a shallow mixing bowl or serving dish. Add the rest of the ingredients. Carefully toss and serve at room temperature.

Calories	Cholesterol mg	Protein gm	Carbohydrate gm	Total fat gm	%	Sat fat gm	%	Mono gm	Poly gm
681	0	23.3	47.5	49.5	64	5.6	7	26.6	12.8

GREEN BEAN, BROCCOLI, AND POTATO SALAD
Insalata di Fagiolini, Broccoli, e Patate

Serves 4.

3 small potatoes
About 1/2 pound green beans
About 1/2 bunch broccoli
1 tablespoon olive oil
1 tablespoon safflower oil

Juice of 1/2 lime
1/2 cup thinly sliced whole scallions
2 tablespoons chopped fresh mint
Salt and freshly ground black pepper to taste

Boil the potatoes until tender, then drain, peel, and slice them. Pick stem ends off the beans. Peel broccoli stems, separate flowerets, and, with stems attached, cut into manageable pieces.

Steam or blanch broccoli and beans until tender. Drain and let cool. Cut beans into 1-inch lengths. Combine the oils and lime juice and toss with the vegetables, scallions, and fresh mint. Add salt and pepper. Serve at room temperature.

Calories	Cholesterol mg	Protein gm	Carbohydrate gm	Total fat gm	%	Sat fat gm	%	Mono gm	Poly gm
496	0	15.8	48.0	28.5	51	3.0	5	11.5	11.2

WARM POTATO SALAD
Insalata di Patate

Serves 6.

6 medium potatoes
1 cup thinly sliced whole scallions
3 tablespoons good wine vinegar
1 tablespoon good mustard
1 tablespoon olive oil
1 tablespoon safflower oil
3 tablespoons finely chopped Italian parsley
Salt and freshly ground black pepper to taste

Wash potatoes and boil them until tender, then drain, cool, peel, and slice them. Put them in a shallow bowl along with the scallions. In a small bowl mix the vinegar, mustard, and the oils, blending well. Pour over the potatoes, add parsley, salt, and pepper and gently mix.

Do not refrigerate.

Calories	Cholesterol mg	Protein gm	Carbohydrate gm	Total fat gm	%	Sat fat gm	%	Mono gm	Poly gm
983	0	21.4	160.9	28.8	26	3.0	3	11.5	11.2

SALADE NIÇOISE

I have seen a number of variations of this recipe. In a sense, anything goes. Sometimes salade Niçoise is served with all the ingredients mixed together, but I prefer to keep the ingredients separate so that their identities are not lost.

Serves 6.

3 potatoes

The dressing for the potatoes
1 tablespoon safflower oil
1 tablespoon wine vinegar
Salt and freshly ground black pepper to taste
1 teaspoon imported mustard
1 tablespoon finely chopped Italian parsley

The salad dressing
2 tablespoons olive oil
1 teaspoon safflower oil
1 teaspoon dried oregano
1 teaspoon minced garlic
2 teaspoons wine vinegar
2 teaspoons capers

2 cups green beans
2 peppers, preferably sweet red ones
4 ripe tomatoes
1 cup sliced whole scallions
1 small onion, thinly sliced
7-ounce can Italian-style tunafish
Salt and freshly ground black pepper to taste
4 anchovies, chopped
14 dried black olives
3 small fresh cucumbers

Boil the potatoes till tender, then drain and cool. Peel and slice them. Make the potato dressing and toss the potatoes in it. Place on one section of a large serving platter.

Combine the ingredients for the salad dressing. Boil beans until tender and mix with some of the salad dressing. Place near the potatoes in a neat mound.

Roast peppers, according to instructions on page 365. Remove charred skin and seeds. Cut in 1/2-inch slices and mix with some of the salad dressing. Place on plate with potatoes and beans.

Slice tomatoes in wedges. Mix with the scallions, sliced onion, tunafish, salt, and pepper. Place in a mound on the platter.

Sprinkle the anchovies and black olives over the roasted peppers. Peel the cucumbers and cut in half lengthwise or in quarters lengthwise if too large. Toss with remaining salad dressing and arrange on the platter.

Calories	Cholesterol mg	Protein gm	Carbohydrate gm	Total fat gm	%	Sat fat gm	%	Mono gm	Poly gm
1550	119.0	72.4	91.9	100.1	57	12.7	7	30.1	32.9

Data for capers unavailable and, therefore, not included.

BEET AND POTATO SALAD
Insalata di Barbabietole e Patate

Serves 4 to 6.

4 medium fresh beets, about 2 pounds
3 medium potatoes
1 small onion, thinly sliced
2 tablespoons olive oil
1 tablespoon safflower oil
3 tablespoons red wine vinegar
1/2 teaspoon dried oregano
1 tablespoon finely chopped Italian parsley
1 tablespoon good mustard
Salt and freshly ground black pepper to taste

Cover beets with water and cook until tender. In another pot boil the potatoes (they will cook more quickly) until tender, then drain, cool, peel, and slice them. When beets are cooked (test for doneness with a fork), drain, cool, peel, and slice. Combine beets, potatoes, and onion in a shallow serving dish.

In a cup mix the oils, vinegar, oregano, parsley, and mustard, blending well. Pour over sliced potatoes, beets, and onion, add salt and pepper, and mix thoroughly. Serve at room temperature.

Calories	Cholesterol mg	Protein gm	Carbohydrate gm	Total fat gm	%	Sat fat gm	%	Mono gm	Poly gm
1010	0	21.0	138.8	42.4	37	4.8	4	21.4	12.3

BEET AND CARROT SALAD
Insalata di Barbabietole e Carote

Serves 4 to 6.

4 medium beets
6 carrots, scraped and cut into 1-inch pieces
1 teaspoon dried oregano
2 teaspoons chopped Italian parsley
1 medium onion, thinly sliced
2 teaspoons safflower oil
3 teaspoons red wine vinegar
Salt and freshly ground black pepper to taste

Boil beets and carrots together. Remove carrots when done. When beets are cooked, drain and peel them. Cut in slices. Mix the rest of the ingredients in a bowl, then add beets and carrots and toss. Serve at room temperature.

Calories	Cholesterol mg	Protein gm	Carbohydrate gm	Total fat gm	%	Sat fat gm	%	Mono gm	Poly gm
555	0	16.5	100.2	10.6	17	0.8	1	1.0	6.8

CAULIFLOWER SALAD
Insalata di Cavolfiore

Serves 4.

1 medium cauliflower
1 tablespoon olive oil
1 teaspoon safflower oil
4 anchovies packed in oil or 2 salted anchovies,
    coarsely chopped
1 tablespoon capers
6 dried black olives, slivered
1 tablespoon finely chopped Italian parsley
Salt and freshly ground black pepper to taste

Cut the cauliflower in flowerets and boil until cooked but firm. Drain and let cool. Mix all the remaining ingredients together, toss with the cauliflower, and serve.

Calories	Cholesterol mg	Protein gm	Carbohydrate gm	Total fat gm	%	Sat fat gm	%	Mono gm	Poly gm
412	9.0	22.3	29.9	25.1	54	3.3	7	14.0	5.3

TOMATO AND ONION SALAD
Insalata di Pomodori e Cipolle

Italians do not use overripe tomatoes in salads but, rather, tomatoes still on the green side. That way the tomato is firmer and does not disintegrate while being tossed and served; moreover, the slight tartness of the unripe tomato complements the vinegar or lemon dressing, and its crispness adds to the pleasure of the salad. There is nothing worse in my opinion than soggy, overripe tomatoes in a salad.

Serves 4.

3 medium semiripe fresh tomatoes
1 medium onion, thinly sliced
3 tablespoons chopped fresh basil (coriander or dill is
    also good)
4 tablespoons good wine vinegar or the juice of 1 lemon
3 tablespoons oil (2 tablespoons olive oil, 1 tablespoon
    safflower or sunflower oil)
Salt and freshly ground black pepper to taste

Core tomatoes and cut in wedges. Add the rest of the ingredients and toss gently. Do not refrigerate.

Calories	Cholesterol mg	Protein gm	Carbohydrate gm	Total fat gm	%	Sat fat gm	%	Mono gm	Poly gm
526	0	7.5	35.8	41.7	70	4.8	8	21.4	12.3

FENNEL AND TOMATO SALAD
Insalata di Finocchi e Pomodori

This is a nice early fall salad, when tomatoes are still around and fennel is just coming in.

Serves 6.

1 large fresh fennel bulb
3 firm ripe tomatoes
2 tablespoons olive oil
1 tablespoon safflower oil
3 tablespoons good red wine vinegar
Salt and freshly ground black pepper to taste

Slice fennel in thin slices, about 1/4 inch thick. Remove and discard tough core. Put in a bowl and cover with cold water for about 30 minutes.

Core and slice tomatoes.

Put all ingredients in a salad bowl and toss.

Variations: Excellent additions would be rucola, endive, or radicchio.

Calories	Cholesterol mg	Protein gm	Carbohydrate gm	Total fat gm	%	Sat fat gm	%	Mono gm	Poly gm
522	0	8.1	35.1	41.8	70	4.8	8	21.4	12.3

MUSHROOM AND TOMATO SALAD
Insalata di Funghi e Pomodori

This salad is a little more than a salad. It makes a most satisfying light lunch served with garlic bread, such as bruschetta (page 39).

Serves 4.

2 tablespoons olive oil
1 tablespoon safflower oil
1/2 pound mushrooms, cut into large pieces (I use wild mushrooms)
1 clove garlic, minced
1 teaspoon dried oregano
Salt and freshly ground black pepper to taste
Hot pepper flakes to taste (optional)
2 large firm ripe tomatoes, cut in half, sliced in 1/2-inch slices, then cut in half again

Garnish: 1 tablespoon finely chopped Italian parsley

Heat the oils in a large skillet and sauté mushrooms over high heat. When mushroom liquid cooks out, add garlic, oregano, salt, and pepper. Cover, lower heat, and simmer about 10 minutes.

Combine with tomatoes in a bowl. Check for salt, add parsley, toss again, and serve.

Calories	Cholesterol mg	Protein gm	Carbohydrate gm	Total fat gm	%	Sat fat gm	%	Mono gm	Poly gm
531	0	11.6	29.2	41.5	69	4.8	8	21.4	12.3

TUNA AND TOMATO SALAD
Insalata di Pomodori e Tonno

This salad is also good with garlic bread, such as bruschetta (page 39).

Serves 4.

3 medium semiripe tomatoes
7-ounce can Italian-style tunafish
1 1/2 tablespoons capers
1 small red onion, thinly sliced
2 tablespoons thinly sliced fresh basil
1 tablespoon thinly sliced fresh mint
10 dried black olives, pitted and sliced
2 teaspoons olive oil or 2 1/2 teaspoons peanut oil
1 teaspoon safflower oil
Juice of 1/2 lemon or lime

Mix all ingredients together in a serving bowl.

Calories	Cholesterol mg	Protein gm	Carbohydrate gm	Total fat gm	%	Sat fat gm	%	Mono gm	Poly gm
874	108.0	53.8	25.4	61.8	62	9.9	10	20.5	21.9

SALAD MARCHES STYLE
Insalata alla Marchigiana

Because of the extreme dry summer heat, there is not much of a variety of salad greens available in most of Italy during the summer months. The following is one of the most popular salads in the Marches; it should be made only when the vegetables are garden fresh.

Serves 4.

2 thin-skinned frying peppers, cut in slices 1/2 inch wide
1 red onion, thinly sliced
2 semiripe tomatoes, sliced
2 tablespoons chopped fresh basil
1 tablespoon olive oil
1 teaspoon safflower oil
1 cup rucola (arugola) (optional)
2 tablespoons red wine vinegar
Salt and freshly ground black pepper to taste

Mix all ingredients together in a salad bowl.

Calories	Cholesterol mg	Protein gm	Carbohydrate gm	Total fat gm	%	Sat fat gm	%	Mono gm	Poly gm
355	0	9.3	37.5	19.4	48	2.2	5	10.4	4.5

PURSLANE, TOMATO, AND ONION SALAD

My mother often picked a weed with a succulent oval-shaped leaf in our vegetable garden to mix with a summer salad. It was especially good mixed with garden-fresh sliced tomatoes and onions. The weed is called purslane (*Portulaca oleracea*) and it is found from the Atlantic to the Pacific. It has a mild acid taste, which goes very well in a salad with an oil-and-vinegar dressing.

This weed is very prolific and can be found in most vegetable gardens. Use only the leaves or the end of the smaller plants. It appears in our garden in June and continues to grow until a hard frost.

Purslane is also excellent cooked with other edible weeds — see recipe for found vegetables on page 389.

Serves 2.

2 firm ripe tomatoes
1 cup purslane ends and leaves, washed
½ medium onion, thinly sliced
1½ tablespoons wine vinegar
1 tablespoon extra virgin olive oil
½ teaspoon safflower oil
Salt and freshly ground black pepper to taste

Slice tomatoes, put in a bowl with the rest of the ingredients, and toss.

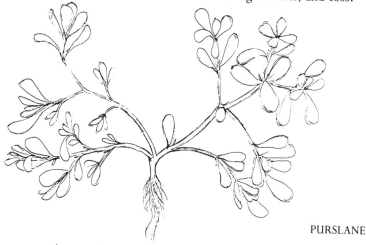

PURSLANE

Calories	Cholesterol mg	Protein gm	Carbohydrate gm	Total fat gm	%	Sat fat gm	%	Mono gm	Poly gm
255	0	5.7	23.0	16.7	58	2.0	7	10.2	2.8

CHICKEN SALAD I
Insalata di Pollo

Serves 3 to 4.

2 cups boiled chicken cut into strips
1 small onion, thinly sliced
1 medium tomato, sliced
1 tablespoon minced fresh coriander or Italian parsley
1 tablespoon vegetable oil
Juice of ½ lemon
Salt and freshly ground black pepper to taste

Toss all the ingredients together in a mixing bowl.

Calories	Cholesterol mg	Protein gm	Carbohydrate gm	Total fat gm	%	Sat fat gm	%	Mono gm	Poly gm
636	216.0	82.9	11.1	27	37	5.9	8	8.2	10.8

CHICKEN SALAD II
Insalata di Pollo

Serves 2.

Leftovers from about 1/2 chicken (broiled, roasted, or
    boiled), about 1 1/2 cups meat in pieces
1/2 cup sliced whole scallions
1 tablespoon soy sauce
Freshly ground black pepper to taste
1 tablespoon peanut oil

Remove the meat from the bones and cut into manageable pieces. Mix
with the scallions, soy sauce, pepper, and oil and serve at room temperature.

Calories	Cholesterol mg	Protein gm	Carbohydrate gm	Total fat gm	%	Sat fat gm	%	Mono gm	Poly gm
496	162.0	62.2	5.2	22.1	39	5.5	10	9.9	6.4

POTATO AND TUNA SALAD
Insalata di Patate con Tonno

Serves 3.

2 medium potatoes
2 whole scallions, coarsely chopped
7-ounce can Italian-style tunafish
1 teaspoon good imported mustard
3 tablespoons wine vinegar
3 tablespoons extra virgin olive oil
1 teaspoon safflower oil
1 1/2 tablespoons finely chopped Italian parsley
12 dried black olives
Salt and freshly ground black pepper to taste

Boil potatoes until tender. Drain and, when cool, peel and slice. Toss with
the rest of the ingredients and serve at room temperature. Do not refrigerate.
    Variation: Instead of the black olives, use 2 tablespoons drained capers.

Calories	Cholesterol mg	Protein gm	Carbohydrate gm	Total fat gm	%	Sat fat gm	%	Mono gm	Poly gm
1297	108.0	56.1	57.8	94.5	64	14.3	10	44.6	24.5

AVOCADO AND TUNAFISH SALAD
Insalata di Avogado e Tonno

Serves 3.

1 ripe avocado, peeled and sliced
1 medium firm ripe tomato, sliced
1 small onion, thinly sliced
6 dried black olives, pitted and slivered*
2 tablespoons good olive oil
1 tablespoon safflower oil
7-ounce can Italian-style tunafish
1 tablespoon chopped fresh mint or 2 tablespoons chopped
    Italian parsley
Juice of 1 lemon
Salt and freshly ground black pepper to taste

*Dried black olives, commonly known as Greek olives, are inaccurately labeled even in Italian delicatessen stores. They are, in fact, Italian olives called Gaeta olives, imported from Italy. To my knowledge, among the many Greek varieties available in America, none of them is dried.

Put all the ingredients in a salad bowl, mix gently, and serve. Do not refrigerate.

Calories	Cholesterol mg	Protein gm	Carbohydrate gm	Total fat gm	%	Sat fat gm	%	Mono gm	Poly gm
1283	108.0	54	20.4	111.1	76	17.9	12	44.2	29.8

WARM LOBSTER SALAD
Insalata di Aragosta

This is an excellent way to serve lobsters that have been used to make Tomasso's linguine with lobster sauce (page 121). Use shells and scraps to make lobster soup (page 52). Serve as an appetizer garnished with salad greens or as a main course with roasted peppers or sautéed asparagus.

Serves 4 to 6.

3 tablespoons olive oil
1 tablespoon safflower oil
2 cloves garlic, minced
3 potatoes, boiled, peeled, and sliced 1/4 inch thick
Meat from 3 medium cooked lobsters
Hot pepper flakes to taste (optional)
1/4 cup good dry sherry or brandy
3 tablespoons minced Italian parsley
Salt and freshly ground black pepper to taste

Heat the two oils in a large skillet, then add garlic. Cook, stirring often, until garlic begins to color—do not brown. Add potatoes and toss for several minutes. Add the rest of the ingredients. Cook, stirring often, until lobster is hot. Serve warm.

Calories	Cholesterol mg	Protein gm	Carbohydrate gm	Total fat gm	%	Sat fat gm	%	Mono gm	Poly gm
1264	408.0	97.6	69.4	54.6	38	6.6	5	31.3	13.4

WHITING SALAD
Insalata di Merluzzo*

This is very good with bruschetta—the toasted garlic bread that is served in Rome (page 39).

Serves 3.

> 2 medium whiting, cleaned, heads left on, or any
>   medium white fish, such as red snapper,
>   black bass, porgies†
> 2 small potatoes, boiled, peeled, and sliced
> Juice of ½ lemon or lime
> 2 tablespoons finely chopped Italian parsley or
>   fresh coriander
> 1 to 2 tablespoons chopped fresh mint, depending on
>   strength of mint (optional)
> 1 cup thinly sliced whole scallions
> 1 medium firm ripe tomato, sliced
> Salt and freshly ground black pepper to taste
> 2 tablespoons extra virgin olive oil
> 1 teaspoon safflower oil

Garnish: Lemon wedges

> *In some parts of Italy called nasello.
> †The reason it is better to leave the heads on when you steam a whole fish is that the juices remain in the fish, making it sweeter and moister.

Steam the fish. When cooked—as soon as flesh separates from bone—let them cool. Remove skin and bones and discard.

Put potatoes in a mixing bowl. Add the rest of the ingredients except fish. Mix gently, then add the fish, and toss lightly. Serve at room temperature with lemon wedges.

Calories	Cholesterol mg	Protein gm	Carbohydrate gm	Total fat gm	%	Sat fat gm	%	Mono gm	Poly gm
639	110.0	42.3	31.0	38.1	52	6.8	8	22.3	5.6

RICE SALAD I
Insalata di Riso

Serves 4 to 6.

2 cups green beans, cut in half
1 cup fresh peas
1 cup cooked rice (page 160)
2 cups cubed fresh tomatoes
1 cup thinly sliced whole scallions
2 tablespoons chopped Italian parsley or fresh basil
Juice of 1 lemon
2 tablespoons olive oil
1 tablespoon safflower oil
7-ounce can Italian-style tunafish

Steam or boil the beans until tender, then let them cool. Cook the peas until tender, then cool. Mix together the rest of the ingredients, breaking up the tunafish. Carefully mix in the beans and peas, using a fork to keep the salad light.

Variation: Early in the season use just peas and asparagus, omitting beans, tomatoes, and scallions.

Calories	Cholesterol mg	Protein gm	Carbohydrate gm	Total fat gm	%	Sat fat gm	%	Mono gm	Poly gm
1507	108.0	73.3	113.8	84.6	49	12.3	7	29.6	29.5

RICE SALAD II
Insalata di Riso

Serves 6 to 8.

1 1/2 cups rice
6-ounce jar artichoke hearts

5 tablespoons drained capers
3 tablespoons olive oil
2 tablespoons safflower oil
1 firm ripe tomato, diced
Juice of 1 lemon or lime
3 tablespoons chopped Italian parsley

Cook rice until tender—do not overcook. Drain and rinse in cold water.

Drain artichoke hearts and chop coarsely. Mix the rice and artichoke hearts with the remaining ingredients and let salad stand for an hour before serving. Serve at room temperature.

Calories	Cholesterol mg	Protein gm	Carbohydrate gm	Total fat gm	%	Sat fat gm	%	Mono gm	Poly gm
1717	0	24.8	247.8	69.0	35	7.8	4	32.9	23.5

Chart does not include data on capers.

SPRING RICE SALAD
Insalata di Riso Primavera

Peas and asparagus are spring vegetables, hence the name. This is excellent as a main course with a green salad or as a vegetable course with fried, boiled, or roasted food.

Serves 4 to 6.

1 cup fresh peas
1 cup fresh asparagus cut into 1 1/2-inch lengths
1 tablespoon safflower oil
1/2 cup cooked long-grain Carolina rice (page 160)
2 tablespoons olive oil
10 dried black olives, pitted and coarsely chopped
7-ounce can Italian-style tunafish, drained and chopped
2 tablespoons minced Italian parsley or
    fresh coriander
Salt and freshly ground black pepper to taste

Cook peas in a small pot with water to cover until tender. Do not cover them and don't overcook. Drain and let cool. Sauté asparagus in the safflower oil in a small skillet over moderate heat until tender, but not overcooked. Let cool.

In a mixing bowl combine all the ingredients, toss, and serve. Do not refrigerate.

Calories	Cholesterol mg	Protein gm	Carbohydrate gm	Total fat gm	%	Sat fat gm	%	Mono gm	Poly gm
1274	108.0	64.3	51.7	89.6	62	13.1	9	34.8	30.0

ORANGE AND OLIVE SALAD
Insalata di Arancie e d'Olive

I first tasted this recipe in my uncle's home in Abruzzi, Italy, in 1951. The salad, which is made only during the winter, when oranges are in season, is known in southern Italy, but I do not believe it is served in areas north of Rome. It's a delightful, colorful dish that is especially appreciated during the winter months. It is very good served with fried or broiled fish or meat.

Serves 4.

4 navel oranges
3 tablespoons extra virgin olive oil
1 teaspoon safflower oil
1 clove garlic, finely chopped
12 dried black olives, pitted and sliced
Salt to taste (optional)
Freshly ground black pepper to taste

Wash the skins of the oranges thoroughly. Leaving the skin on, cut oranges in slices about 1/8 to 1/4 inch thick with a sharp knife.*

Combine with the remaining ingredients and gently mix.† Serve as a salad.

*Oranges may be sliced ahead of time, but do not blend with other ingredients until ready to serve (olives will stain oranges). Do not refrigerate.
†Sometimes hot pepper flakes are used in this recipe.

Calories	Cholesterol mg	Protein gm	Carbohydrate gm	Total fat gm	%	Sat fat gm	%	Mono gm	Poly gm
738	0	6.5	68.0	53.8	64	6.8	8	36.4	7.3

The nutritional value of the orange peel is unknown.

X   SAUCES

This book has an unusual number of sauce recipes. The variety is extensive enough so that there are sauces for meats, fish, and pasta for every kind of taste. All the recipes are very low in saturated fats, none of them contains cream, and only one recipe contains butter (a butter-and-lemon dip for boiled lobster). Most of these sauces are made with herbs, vegetables, and a small amount of oil. In fact, many of them have the texture of a condiment and are used in small quantities — sometimes just a teaspoonful.

ABOUT PESTO

The traditional way to make pesto is with a mortar and pestle. The basil leaves, nuts, garlic, and parsley are added a little at a time, and as the pestle grinds the mixture, a little oil is slowly added. When all has been ground and the oil absorbed, you have a loose pesto — the consistency of heavy cream — with a rough texture. With the advent of high-speed food processors, methods have changed. It is simple to make large quantities of pesto of pretty good quality and texture with a food processor, but only a mortar and pestle can make the perfect pesto.

We have eliminated cheese from the pesto recipe because of its high saturated fat content, and we have added a mixture of safflower oil and olive oil. I think you will find the following pesto recipes excellent. In addition, there is a rucola pesto in the pasta chapter, page 103.

I have had great success with preserving pesto for over a year by packing it in a clean jar and covering it with oil (see recipe that follows). It should be kept refrigerated and the oil replaced as the pesto is used. I find this method much more satisfying than freezing it.

The first pesto in the book, the rucola pesto, calls for pine nuts, which are traditionally used in Liguria, and you don't need more than 6 tablespoons of pine nuts to make a creamy sauce. They are expensive, however, and often hard to find. Therefore, the pesto recipe that follows here uses walnuts instead; you'll note, however, that you need a full cup of walnut meats to get a properly creamy consistency.

PESTO

I have not used grated cheese in this recipe, as is traditional in pesto, but have added more nuts to compensate, and I have found it to be completely satisfactory. It is important to use a fine olive oil, preferably one like Madre Sicilia or a similar rich green oil. Or even better, use extra virgin olive oil.

Yields about 3/4 pint (enough for about 2 pounds pasta or 3 cups rice).

2 tablespoons safflower oil
4 tablespoons good olive oil
1 cup walnut meats
4 cups tightly packed fresh basil
3 tablespoons chopped Italian parsley
Salt and freshly ground black pepper to taste

Place all the ingredients in a food processor and blend. Put in a jar, add 1/2 inch oil (1/2 olive oil, 1/2 safflower oil) on top of pesto, and refrigerate. It will last all winter.

Calories	Cholesterol mg	Protein gm	Carbohydrate gm	Total fat gm	%	Sat fat gm	%	Mono gm	Poly gm
1591	0	22.0	27.5	162.1	90	13.8	8	57.2	72.8

LIGHT PESTO
Pesto di Magro

This is not a pasta sauce. It is good served with boiled or broiled meats and fish.

Yields 1/2 pint (enough for 4 servings).

2 cups fresh basil
2 cloves garlic, coarsely chopped
2 canned anchovies, chopped
2 tablespoons pine nuts
3 tablespoons olive oil
1 tablespoon safflower oil
Salt and freshly ground black pepper to taste

Purée all the ingredients with a mortar and pestle or in a food processor.

Calories	Cholesterol mg	Protein gm	Carbohydrate gm	Total fat gm	%	Sat fat gm	%	Mono gm	Poly gm
582	4.0	6.6	7.7	60.1	91	6.1	11	35.7	13.5

PARSLEY PESTO
Salsa di Prezzemolo

This pesto is delicious on fish and boiled meats as well as on pasta.

Yields 1/2 pint.

> 2 cups chopped Italian parsley
> 1 tablespoon or less chopped garlic
> 5 tablespoons pine nuts
> 5 tablespoons olive oil
> 1 tablespoon safflower oil
> Salt and freshly ground black pepper to taste

Put all ingredients in a food processor and blend to a creamy consistency.

If used on pasta, allow about 1 tablespoon per portion. Reserve some pasta water and add to pesto so that it has the consistency of light cream. To store, cover pesto with 1/2 inch oil (1/2 olive oil, 1/2 safflower oil) and refrigerate.

Variations: I have also used 2 cups fresh coriander in place of the parsley and it produces a lovely aromatic sauce.

Grated lemon rind is a good addition.

For a fish sauce, add 5 or 6 finely chopped anchovies.

Calories	Cholesterol mg	Protein gm	Carbohydrate gm	Total fat gm	%	Sat fat gm	%	Mono gm	Poly gm
917	0	13.0	15.8	93.9	90	10.7	10	57.6	17.6

ALMOND SAUCE
Salsa alle Mandorle

This is a very old Sicilian sweet-and-sour recipe for boiled or baked fish.

Yields about 1 1/4 cups.

> 15 almonds, toasted
> 1 medium onion, chopped
> 2 tablespoons olive oil
> 1 tablespoon safflower oil
> 3 tablespoons tomato paste, diluted in 1/2 cup warm water
> 1 teaspoon flour
> 10 green olives, pitted, soaked in cold water
> 1 tablespoon capers, soaked in cold water
> 1 anchovy plus 1 teaspoon safflower oil
> Salt and freshly ground black pepper to taste

Shell the almonds, blanch in boiling water 1 minute, drain, skin, and toast them in a 400° oven until light brown, about 8 to 10 minutes. Meanwhile, sauté onion in the oils. When it begins to brown, add diluted tomato paste, flour, and drained olives and capers. Cover and simmer gently about 20 minutes. Add the anchovy and almonds, simmer for several minutes, and blend in a food processor. Add salt and pepper to taste.

Serve at room temperature.

Calories	Cholesterol mg	Protein gm	Carbohydrate gm	Total fat gm	%	Sat fat gm	%	Mono gm	Poly gm
677	2.0	9.3	29.3	60.6	79	6.7	9	32.2	18.0

SAUCE FOR FISH
Salsa per il Pesce

For baked, boiled, fried fish.

Yields 1 cup.

1/2 cup dry white wine
1 clove garlic
1/2 cup walnut meats
2 tablespoons minced Italian parsley
3 teaspoons good mustard
2 tablespoons olive oil
1 teaspoon safflower oil
Salt and freshly ground black pepper to taste

Put all the ingredients into a food processor and blend, or pound to a purée with a mortar and pestle.

Calories	Cholesterol mg	Protein gm	Carbohydrate gm	Total fat gm	%	Sat fat gm	%	Mono gm	Poly gm
724	0	10.4	11.0	76.9	93	6.8	8	26.3	30.4

GREEN SAUCE
Salsa Verde

This is wonderful on boiled or broiled meats and fish.

Yields 1 1/2 cups

1 bunch scallions, coarsely chopped
1 clove garlic, chopped
1/2 small white onion
2 stalks celery, coarsely chopped
2 tablespoons chopped Italian parsley
1 medium cucumber, peeled and chopped
2 tablespoons safflower oil

1 tablespoon olive oil
Tabasco to taste (optional)
3 teaspoons prepared mustard
2 tablespoons red wine vinegar
Salt and freshly ground black pepper to taste

Put in a blender or food processor and blend.
   Variation: For a thicker sauce, add 1 boiled potato.

Calories	Cholesterol mg	Protein gm	Carbohydrate gm	Total fat gm	%	Sat fat gm	%	Mono gm	Poly gm
499	0	5.9	28.8	41.7	74	4.2	7	13.1	21.3

GREEN SAUCE GENOA STYLE
Salsa Verde alla Genovese

Serve on broiled, fried, or boiled fish.

Yields a little over 1 cup, serving 4.

2 tablespoons pine nuts (sauce also works with
   walnut meats)
1 tablespoon olive oil
1 teaspoon safflower oil
1 or 2 cloves garlic
1 whole salted anchovy fillet* or 2 canned anchovy fillets
2 cups fresh basil
1 cup chopped ripe tomatoes
Salt and freshly ground black pepper to taste

*Rinse and bone salted anchovy.

Put all ingredients in a food processor and blend. Or, using a mortar and
pestle, grind and crush pine nuts with oils and garlic, then work in the
anchovies, gradually add basil, and finally add tomatoes, salt, and pepper.

Calories	Cholesterol mg	Protein gm	Carbohydrate gm	Total fat gm	%	Sat fat gm	%	Mono gm	Poly gm
309	4.0	9.0	18.4	24.5	70	2.7	8	13.2	5.5

HONEY SAUCE I
Salsa di Miele (Salsa Pimice)

A specialty from northern Italy, sometimes called salsa delle api. Although
this sauce is normally used on boiled meats, I have had fine results with it
on roast chicken.

Serves 4 to 6.

10 walnuts, shelled
3 tablespoons loose honey
   (flowing rather than thick)
½ cup chicken or beef broth
1 to 2 tablespoons good imported mustard

Blend ingredients in a food processor, adding mustard to taste.

Calories	Cholesterol mg	Protein gm	Carbohydrate gm	Total fat gm	%	Sat fat gm	%	Mono gm	Poly gm
464	0	6.8	58.3	26.2	50	1.8	3	3.8	15.9

HONEY SAUCE II
Salsa di Miele

Excellent on game and boiled or broiled meats.

Serves 4.

1 cup fresh breadcrumbs
2 tablespoons white wine vinegar
6 walnuts, shelled
Salt and freshly ground black pepper to taste
1 teaspoon good mustard
2 tablespoons honey
¼ cup chicken or beef broth

Soak breadcrumbs in vinegar, and blend with the rest of the ingredients in a food processor.

Calories	Cholesterol mg	Protein gm	Carbohydrate gm	Total fat gm	%	Sat fat gm	%	Mono gm	Poly gm
415	0	7.8	62.1	17.0	36	1.0	2	2.3	9.5

MARINARA SAUCE
Salsa alla Marinara

We were first introduced to this wonderful sauce in 1959 when we were living in Florence and had a housekeeper from San Gimignano who made it for us. The beauty of this recipe is in the sweetness that the carrots and onions give to it—and by blending the carrots and onions in the sauce, it becomes creamy and thick without being cooked to death.

Of all the tomato sauces in this book, this one is our favorite.

The recipe appeared in *The New York Times* in the early 1960s and many times after that, including one recipe (a lasagna recipe) that was selected as the favorite recipe of the year printed in *The New York Times*. It's a wonderful base for other recipes; if made from fresh garden tomatoes it can be frozen or canned (see tomato canning recipe, page 378) with practically no negative effects. This is a truly versatile and economical sauce, not to mention the fact that it is low in saturated fat and low in calories. The original recipe contained some butter, but I have now eliminated it and the sauce is just as good.

I might add that I have never seen this sauce printed in an Italian cookbook.

Makes about 4 cups, enough for about 1 1/2 pounds pasta. Serves 6.

3 tablespoons olive oil
1 teaspoon safflower oil
1 1/2 cups sliced carrots
2 cups coarsely chopped onion
Salt and freshly ground black pepper to taste
2 cloves garlic, chopped
4 cups chopped tomatoes, fresh if possible (drain if canned)
2 tablespoons chopped fresh basil or 1 tablespoon dried
About 1/4 cup water or chicken or beef broth

Garnish: Finely chopped Italian parsley

Heat the oils in a large, shallow pan, then add carrots, onion, salt, and pepper. Sauté, uncovered, over moderate heat until onion begins to brown, then add garlic and cook about 1 minute. Add tomatoes and basil, cover, and simmer over low to medium heat for 20 minutes, stirring occasionally.

Pour sauce in a food processor and purée to a creamy consistency or force sauce through a food mill.

Return sauce to pan and add enough water or broth to make the sauce the consistency of heavy cream. Cover and simmer over low heat an additional 10 minutes.

Serve on pasta or as a tomato sauce base.

Variation: With mushrooms: Either add mushrooms to the sauce after it has been puréed or garnish each serving of pasta and marinara sauce with the browned mushrooms.

2 to 3 tablespoons vegetable oil
1 pound fresh mushrooms, sliced
Salt and freshly ground black pepper to taste

Heat the oil in a large, shallow skillet, add mushrooms, and cook over high heat, stirring often, for 5 minutes. Add salt and pepper. Continue cooking until mushrooms begin to brown. It is important to really cook the mushrooms down so that they acquire a nice nutty taste.

Calories	Cholesterol mg	Protein gm	Carbohydrate gm	Total fat gm	%	Sat fat gm	%	Mono gm	Poly gm
737	0	15.5	70.6	47.3	55	5.8	7	30.2	6.7

HORSERADISH AND TOMATO SAUCE
Salsa di Rafano e Pomodoro

The idea for this recipe was given to me by Pierre Franey. More tomato sauce may be used if the sauce is too hot for your taste.

Yields about 3 1/2 cups.

3 tablespoons olive oil
1 tablespoon safflower oil
1 medium onion, chopped
1 teaspoon minced garlic
2 cups marinara sauce (above) or any other tomato sauce
Salt and freshly ground black pepper to taste
1/2 pound fresh horseradish, cleaned and grated
(about 1 1/2 cups)

Heat the oils in a medium skillet, add onion, and cook, uncovered, over moderate heat. When onion begins to brown, add garlic. Cook for about 30 seconds, then add tomato sauce, salt, and pepper. Cover and cook for about 15 minutes. Put in a food processor or food mill and purée. Mix with the horseradish.

Refrigerate when not in use.

Calories	Cholesterol mg	Protein gm	Carbohydrate gm	Total fat gm	%	Sat fat gm	%	Mono gm	Poly gm
1069	0	16.0	79.4	78.5	65	9.5	8	46.4	16.8

MARÒ

This delightful recipe produces a beautiful green pastelike sauce that is rather remarkable for its delicacy. It should have the consistency of heavy cream. If you like it more liquid, add some broth or more oil. Use with boiled meats.

Yields 3/4 cup.

1 cup blanched, shelled fresh fava beans (broad beans),
tough outer skins removed
1 tablespoon coarsely chopped fresh mint
2 tablespoons olive oil
1 tablespoon safflower oil
Salt and freshly ground black pepper to taste

Blend all the ingredients in a food processor or with a mortar and pestle.

Calories	Cholesterol mg	Protein gm	Carbohydrate gm	Total fat gm	%	Sat fat gm	%	Mono gm	Poly gm
407	0	3.9	7.3	40.8	88	3.0	6	21.4	12.3

MINT SAUCE I
Salsa alla Menta

This thick rustic sauce is particularly good with broiled or boiled meat. The simplicity of the recipe is most appealing.

Yields 1 cup.

2 cups fresh breadcrumbs
3 tablespoons good wine vinegar
4 tablespoons chopped fresh mint (I prefer wild spearmint)
1 1/2 tablespoons chopped Italian parsley
1/2 teaspoon salt
1 teaspoon sugar

Soak the breadcrumbs in the vinegar. When soft, blend with all the remaining ingredients, using either a mortar and pestle or a food processor.

Calories	Cholesterol mg	Protein gm	Carbohydrate gm	Total fat gm	%	Sat fat gm	%	Mono gm	Poly gm
281	0	8.4	51.8	2.8	9	–	–	–	–

MINT SAUCE II
Salsa alla Menta

This sauce is more of a relish than a sauce, to be served with broiled, baked, or fried fish.

Yields about 3/4 cup.

3 tablespoons chopped fresh mint
1 tablespoon chopped Italian parsley
2 tablespoons wine vinegar
1 teaspoon finely chopped garlic
1 teaspoon sugar
Salt to taste
2 tablespoons olive oil
1 tablespoon safflower oil

Purée all the ingredients in a food processor or with a mortar and pestle until well blended.

Calories	Cholesterol mg	Protein gm	Carbohydrate gm	Total fat gm	%	Sat fat gm	%	Mono gm	Poly gm
389	0	0.6	9.1	40.6	92	4.8	11	21.4	12.3

PIERRE FRANEY'S SAUCE MOUTARDE AUX CORNICHONS

I first tasted this sauce at Pierre Franey's home. He served it on leftover broiled pork loin and it was a delight.

Yields 1 1/2 cups, serving 4 to 6.

1 tablespoon vegetable oil
1 cup coarsely chopped onion
1/4 teaspoon minced garlic
3 tablespoons white wine vinegar
2 tablespoons arrowroot
1 1/2 cups chicken or beef broth
1/2 bay leaf
1/4 teaspoon thyme
10 pickled cornichons or gherkins (in vinegar), thinly sliced
1 tablespoon good prepared mustard
Salt and freshly ground black pepper to taste

Heat the oil in a small saucepan or skillet, add onion, and cook over moderate heat until it browns. Add garlic, sauté a minute or so, then add vinegar. Cook until vinegar cooks out. Stir in the arrowroot and mix well. Add the broth and continue cooking at a gentle simmer over low heat, stirring constantly.

After about 3 or 4 minutes, add the bay leaf and thyme and cook 3 or 4 more minutes. Add the sliced gherkins, mustard, salt, and pepper and continue to simmer, uncovered, 10 more minutes.

If you are serving with leftover meat, slice the meat and combine it with the sauce in a skillet, gently cooking until the meat is hot. Serve hot with potatoes or rice.

Variation: For an onion sauce, simply eliminate the mustard and gherkins and add 1/2 cup more onion.

Calories	Cholesterol mg	Protein gm	Carbohydrate gm	Total fat gm	%	Sat fat gm	%	Mono gm	Poly gm
497	0	3.3	97.0	15.2	27	1.2	2	1.6	10.1

MUSTARD SAUCE
Salsa alla Senape

This sauce is good on poached or boiled fish as well as on leftover fish.

Yields about 3/4 cup, enough for 4 servings of fish.

2 tablespoons minced Italian parsley
2 tablespoons drained capers

2 tablespoons good imported mustard
4 anchovies, chopped
1 tablespoon olive oil
1 teaspoon safflower oil
Juice of 1/2 lemon

Put all the ingredients in a food processor and blend, or mix with a mortar and pestle.

Calories	Cholesterol mg	Protein gm	Carbohydrate gm	Total fat gm	%	Sat fat gm	%	Mono gm	Poly gm
226	9.0	5.1	6.2	21.1	82	3.0	11	10.8	4.9

Exclusive of capers, for which we have no data.

NUT SAUCE I
Intingolo di Noci

This is an excellent creamy sauce — a good example of how a creamlike sauce can be made without cream. Use it for broiled meats.

Yields 3/4 cup, serving 6.

6 walnuts, shelled
2 tablespoons pine nuts
1 cup fresh mint
2 tablespoons extra virgin olive oil
1 teaspoon safflower oil
1/4 cup warm chicken or beef stock
Pinch salt
Freshly ground black pepper to taste

Place all the ingredients in a food processor and blend to a creamy consistency.

Calories	Cholesterol mg	Protein gm	Carbohydrate gm	Total fat gm	%	Sat fat gm	%	Mono gm	Poly gm
511	0	8.4	9.0	51.9	89	5.3	9	25.2	15.9

NUT SAUCE II
Salsa alle Noci

Goes well with boiled, fried, or broiled foods.

Serves 4 to 6.

6 walnuts, shelled
1 cup fresh breadcrumbs, soaked in 4 tablespoons chicken
    or beef broth
1 clove garlic, chopped
1 tablespoon safflower oil
2 tablespoons olive oil
Juice of 1 lemon
2 tablespoons chopped Italian parsley
Salt and freshly ground black pepper to taste

Blend all the ingredients in a food processor until creamy. Add more oil if the sauce is too thick. It should have the consistency of heavy cream.

Calories	Cholesterol mg	Protein gm	Carbohydrate gm	Total fat gm	%	Sat fat gm	%	Mono gm	Poly gm
656	0.0	8.2	31.4	57.5	77	5.9	8	23.7	21.8

NUT SAUCE III
Salsa alle Noci

Good with fish, such as boiled fish, or with boiled meats.

Serves 4.

15 walnuts, shelled
1 clove garlic
1 anchovy
3 tablespoons oil (2 olive oil and 1 safflower oil)
1 tablespoon minced Italian parsley
Salt and freshly ground black pepper to taste

Purée all the ingredients with a mortar and pestle or in a food processor. Serve at room temperature.

Calories	Cholesterol mg	Protein gm	Carbohydrate gm	Total fat gm	%	Sat fat gm	%	Mono gm	Poly gm
762	2.0	10.1	9.7	79.4	92	5.9	7	27.3	36.2

PISTACHIO SAUCE
Salsa al Pistacchio

Used primarily for boiled and broiled meats, this is also excellent with chicken balls.

Serves 6.

1/4 pound plain pistachio nuts, about 1/2 cup shelled
2 tablespoons pine nuts
2 anchovies packed in oil or 1 salted anchovy, washed and boned
2 tablespoons olive oil
1 tablespoon safflower oil
3 tablespoons lemon juice
1 tablespoon chopped fresh mint
Freshly ground black pepper to taste

Put all the ingredients in a food processor and blend.

Calories	Cholesterol mg	Protein gm	Carbohydrate gm	Total fat gm	%	Sat fat gm	%	Mono gm	Poly gm
782	4.0	16.1	16.8	76.8	86	8.4	9	44.1	19.1

HOT PEPPER SAUCE I
Salsa di Peperoni Piccanti

I make large quantities of this sauce in the summer with my own fresh produce — I then can the sauce in half-pint jars and use it all winter. Put it on fish, meats, and in sauces.

Yields about 2 cups.

3 tablespoons vegetable oil (safflower or sunflower)
2 cups chopped peppers, hot and sweet*
1 medium onion, chopped
2 cloves garlic, chopped
2 cups coarsely chopped tomatoes

*The desired hotness of the sauce will depend on the combination of hot and sweet peppers you choose to use.

Heat the oil in a medium skillet, then add the peppers and onion and cook over medium heat until peppers begin to brown. Add garlic, stir, and when it begins to brown, add the tomatoes. Cover and simmer for about 30 minutes.

Let the sauce cool, then put it in a food processor and blend.

The sauce can be frozen or canned in jars (see directions for canning tomatoes, page 378).

Calories	Cholesterol mg	Protein gm	Carbohydrate gm	Total fat gm	%	Sat fat gm	%	Mono gm	Poly gm
602	0	11.7	41.4	42.5	62	3.3	5	6.0	29.4

HOT PEPPER SAUCE II
Salsa di Peperoni Piccanti

This is an unusually good hot sauce. The sauce is sweet because the peppers are not cooked. And it is hot — a little goes a long way. It's good on meat and fish, and I even like it on pasta.

Yields ³/4 pint.

8 cups fresh hot red peppers, cored and cut into 2-inch
    pieces (I used 16 red Hungarian wax peppers)
3 tablespoons safflower oil
¹/4 cup olive oil
1 tablespoon chopped garlic

Dry the peppers in an electric fruit dryer about 3 hours. They should be dry but not completely dried. They should be a bit soft — not stiff. They can also be dried in the sun or in a greenhouse; again the purpose is to "soft dry" them. Under perfect conditions this would take 2 to 3 days.

Put dried peppers in a food processor with the rest of the ingredients and blend. Pack in a pint jar, pressing down so that there are no air bubbles, and cover with ¹/2 inch oil (¹/4 inch safflower, ¹/4 inch olive).

Keep in a cool place or refrigerate. Replace the oil as it is used. If refrigerated in a glass jar, the sauce will last most of the winter.

Calories	Cholesterol mg	Protein gm	Carbohydrate gm	Total fat gm	%	Sat fat gm	%	Mono gm	Poly gm
1280	0	22.7	60.3	98.3	68	10.8	7	44.4	34.7

SPINACH SAUCE
Salsa di Spinaci

This is a light sauce that is thick and a rich green. It can be made ahead of time. Serve with boiled meats or tuna loaf.

Serves 6.

1 pound fresh spinach, washed and drained
1 tablespoon olive oil
1 teaspoon safflower oil
¹/2 cup chicken or beef broth
2 tablespoons flour
Pinch nutmeg

Salt and freshly ground black pepper to taste
1/2 tablespoon grated lemon rind

Boil spinach for several minutes and drain. Let cool and squeeze out all moisture, then chop. Heat the oils in a small saucepan, then stir in stock, flour, and nutmeg and bring to a boil.

In the meantime, purée spinach in a blender or food processor or with a mortar and pestle. Add spinach to liquid along with salt, pepper, and lemon rind. Cover and simmer for several minutes.

Calories	Cholesterol mg	Protein gm	Carbohydrate gm	Total fat gm	%	Sat fat gm	%	Mono gm	Poly gm
339	0	16.3	29.8	19.6	51	2.2	6	10.4	4.5

RAW SAUCE
Salsa Cruda

A typical northern Italian sauce for boiled or broiled meat and fish.

Yields about 1 1/2 cups.

1 clove garlic, chopped
1/2 cup roughly chopped scallions
2 tablespoons chopped fresh basil
1 tablespoon chopped Italian parsley
1 medium ripe tomato, coarsely chopped
2 tablespoons good wine vinegar
2 tablespoons olive oil
1 tablespoon safflower oil
1/2 cup rucola (arugula)
Salt and freshly ground black pepper to taste

Put all the ingredients in a food processor and blend.

Calories	Cholesterol mg	Protein gm	Carbohydrate gm	Total fat gm	%	Sat fat gm	%	Mono gm	Poly gm
430	0	3.7	15.2	41.1	84	4.8	10	21.4	12.3

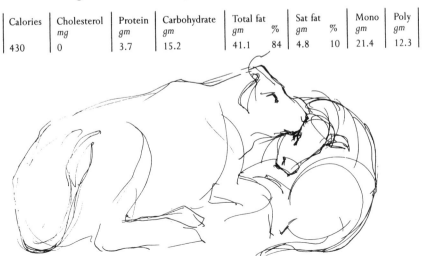

TOMATO SAUCE
Salsa di Pomodoro

This and the following country style tomato sauce are garnishes—not to be cooked with or used for pasta. Serve with boiled or broiled fish and meats.

Serves 2 to 4.

1 large tomato, cut into ½-inch-thick horizontal slices
1 tablespoon olive oil
1 teaspoon safflower oil
1 clove garlic, coarsely chopped
1 teaspoon rosemary
Salt and freshly ground black pepper to taste
1 tablespoon chopped fresh mint
1 tablespoon chopped Italian parsley
1 teaspoon finely chopped fresh ginger

Preheat the broiler.

Place the tomato slices in a baking dish. Sprinkle oils, garlic, rosemary, salt, and pepper over them. Broil close to the heat until edges of tomatoes begin to char. Put in a food processor with the mint, parsley, and ginger, and blend.

Calories	Cholesterol mg	Protein gm	Carbohydrate gm	Total fat gm	%	Sat fat gm	%	Mono gm	Poly gm
223	0	3.1	12.9	18.7	73	2.2	9	10.4	4.4

COUNTRY STYLE TOMATO SAUCE
Salsa alla Campagnola

I have found this recipe especially good on broiled chicken, as well as broiled meats.

Enough for 4 split broiled chickens.

2 large tomatoes
3 tablespoons coarsely chopped fresh basil
2 tablespoons coarsely chopped Italian parsley
1 teaspoon minced garlic
1 tablespoon olive oil or 2 tablespoons vegetable oil
1 tablespoon safflower oil
Grated rind of 1 lemon
1 tablespoon wine vinegar
Salt and freshly ground black pepper to taste

Briefly broil the tomatoes over coals or under the broiler. Peel the tomatoes, cut them in half, and squeeze out the seeds and juice. Chop into coarse pieces (you should have about 3 cups).

Put all the ingredients in a food processor and blend. Serve at room temperature.

Calories	Cholesterol mg	Protein gm	Carbohydrate gm	Total fat gm	%	Sat fat gm	%	Mono gm	Poly gm
304	0	3.2	13.1	27.6	30	3.0	9	11.5	11.2

TRUFFLED SAUCE
Salsa Tartufata

Serve this on roasted or broiled meats.

Serves 4.

1 tablespoon butter
1 tablespoon olive oil
4 tablespoons finely chopped onion
1 teaspoon minced garlic
1 tablespoon minced Italian parsley
4 tablespoons imported sweet marsala or port
1 teaspoon flour
2 tablespoons chicken or beef broth
Freshly ground black pepper to taste
2 tablespoons thinly sliced white truffles

Heat the butter and olive oil in a small saucepan, then add onion. When onion begins to brown, add garlic and parsley and cook about 10 seconds. Add marsala and flour, stir well, and add broth and pepper. Cook about 1 minute, stirring often. Turn off heat and add truffles.

Calories	Cholesterol mg	Protein gm	Carbohydrate gm	Total fat gm	%	Sat fat gm	%	Mono gm	Poly gm
265	31.0	1.1	10.5	25.0	83	8.1	27	13.7	1.4

This recipe is unusual for this book. First, it has an ingredient (truffle) for which we have been unable to find nutritional data. Second, it has butter as an ingredient. Third, it has a very high ratio (5.8:1) of saturated to polyunsaturated fat. Nevertheless, we include it — we would hate to think of someone giving you a gift of a white truffle and having it go to waste for want of a good recipe. This is not likely to happen very often, or at all, but if it does, the total amount of saturated fat can easily be compensated for by judicious choice of other menu items the day you enjoy the truffled sauce. R.W.

TUNA SAUCE
Salsa Tonnato

This sauce is a nice complement to boiled fish or meat. I like to serve it on boiled lobster and smoked fish—it's so much better than melted butter or mayonnaise!

Serves 6.

2 salted anchovies, boned and rinsed, or 4 anchovy fillets
     packed in oil
About 3½ ounces Italian-style tunafish
     (half a 7-ounce can)
2 tablespoons coarsely chopped Italian parsley
Juice of ½ lemon
2 tablespoons drained capers
1 tablespoon coarsely chopped fresh mint (optional)
3 tablespoons extra virgin olive oil
1 teaspoon safflower oil
Freshly ground black pepper to taste
3 tablespoons dry white vermouth

Chop the anchovies and mix with the remaining ingredients, using either a mortar and pestle or a food processor to make a creamy consistency.

Calories	Cholesterol mg	Protein gm	Carbohydrate gm	Total fat gm	%	Sat fat gm	%	Mono gm	Poly gm
729	63.0	27.6	5.5	66.9	81	10.2	12	34.8	15.8

ANCIENT SICILIAN SAUCE FOR BOILED FISH
Zogghiu

I enjoy this on boiled or poached fish.

Yields about ¾ cup, serving about 4.

½ cup chopped fresh mint
2 tablespoons minced Italian parsley
2 teaspoons minced garlic
2 tablespoons olive oil
2 tablespoons safflower oil
⅓ cup good white wine vinegar

Blend all the ingredients in a food processor or purée them with a mortar and pestle.

Calories	Cholesterol mg	Protein gm	Carbohydrate gm	Total fat gm	%	Sat fat gm	%	Mono gm	Poly gm
521	0	1.8	9.1	54.5	92	6.0	10	23.0	22.4

XI DESSERTS

How can I write the dessert chapter without relating a funny incident that happened in January 1973? We had just spent the morning visiting the glorious Greek temples at Paestum, on the gulf of Salerno, having driven the day before from Sicily. Our children—Gena, 13, Lisa, 11, and Cham, 9—were with us and it was about 1:30; we were famished. Several miles from Paestum, we found a very nice, rather large restaurant. What usually happened whenever we went to a restaurant was that the children would rush to the dessert table to see what was being offered. Lisa was the dessert authority, and her brother and sister always followed her advice faithfully. No one enjoyed a sweet more than Lisa. As a matter of fact, she had no interest in any other kind of food. Lisa would look, smell, touch, and savor a sweet in a ritualistic way, using all of her senses. She would eat it slowly, a bit at a time, savoring every morsel (also, perhaps, so that she would still have some left after her brother and sister finished theirs).

While Gena and Cham gave Lisa elbow room, being careful not to crowd her, Lisa looked carefully, deep in thought, anticipation on the faces of her brother and sister. With a defiant gesture she pointed to a deep brown plain chocolate cake. "That one," she said in a determined voice. Her brother and sister seemed relieved. They nodded in agreement and rushed to the table to get over the disagreeable business of eating their lunches so they could enjoy dessert.

When they had finished, Lisa called the waiter over and pointed to the dessert she wanted: "*Tre per piacere* (Three, if you please)." "Are you certain?" "Yes," replied Lisa. The waiter returned with the three slices. Hesitantly he served it to the children, then stepped back and observed. The children took a mouthful simultaneously—and spat it out simultaneously. The expressions on their faces were incredible—disgust, dismay, incredulity. Lisa's was the funniest of all, a combination of surprise and revulsion. "Yuk, what is it?" she asked.

The waiter informed her it was a Napolitano Christmas pudding made with chocolate and pig's blood. "Pig's blood!" they all shouted, and their expressions were even funnier.

I knew what it was. My mother used to make it and I liked it. But she always used sugar and walnuts, and it tasted very much like a very rich cake. But there was no sugar in this recipe and it did not taste good.

Needless to say, Lisa's reputation as dessert expert plummeted. I consoled her by explaining how fickle followers can be. You can make the right decision all your life and then make just one bad one, and your reputation goes down the drain. A chance for a second dessert (the other children selected their own this time) brought their spirits up a bit.

This dessert section has nothing as rich as chocolate cake nor as forbidding as blood pudding. The recipes are all light, and the main emphasis is on fresh seasonal fruits. E.G.

Our desserts are of two kinds. Some have so little fat — 6 percent or less of the calories — that they can offset other dishes in the diet that have a relatively high fat content. Others provide more than 30 percent of their calories as fat, but they all have P:S ratios greater than 1:1. This means that none of these desserts requires the addition of polyunsaturated fat elsewhere in the day's ration; on the contrary they "neutralize" dishes having an excess of saturated fat. R.W.

FRIED FRUIT
Fritto di Frutta

My mother used to make this recipe with apples, but she did not add ice cubes or refrigerate the batter. I borrowed the technique from the Japanese and I find the batter superior to the Italian one.

Serves 6 to 8.

The batter
1 cup all-purpose flour
1 cup cold water
2 egg whites, lightly beaten
2 tablespoons fruit liqueur
Pinch salt
1 teaspoon baking powder

2 apples
2 pears
16 strawberries
Corn or vegetable oil for frying
Powdered sugar

Mix the batter until well blended, put several ice cubes in it, and refrigerate for at least 1 hour.

Peel, core, and slice the apples and pears. Wash the strawberries. Heat about 3/4 inch oil in a small to medium skillet. When oil is hot, dip fruit in batter, a few at a time, and carefully drop coated fruit into the skillet. Fry to a golden brown. Blot on paper towels and keep warm. Repeat.

Serve hot. Dust with powdered sugar before serving.

Variations: Any variety of fresh fruit may be used, though I prefer apples and pears.

Calories	Cholesterol mg	Protein gm	Carbohydrate gm	Total fat gm	%	Sat fat gm	%	Mono gm	Poly gm
1312	0	27.6	267.3	20.8	14	1.4	1	3.8	7.2

POACHED PEACHES WITH RASPBERRY SAUCE
Pesche con Lamponi

Serves 6.

6 medium ripe, firm peaches
2¾ cups water
1½ tablespoons vanilla extract
6 cloves
1 cup plus 1 tablespoon sugar
1½ cups fresh raspberries
1 teaspoon plum brandy or kirsch

Blanch peaches in boiling water, then drain and let cool. Peel, cut in half, and remove pits.

Combine water, vanilla extract, cloves, and 1 cup of the sugar in a saucepan, bring to a boil, and boil, uncovered, over high heat about 5 minutes. Add peach halves, lower heat, and simmer 15 minutes. Put peaches and syrup in a bowl and refrigerate.

In the meantime, purée the raspberries by pushing them through a fine sieve with the back of a spoon. Discard the seeds; you should have about 1 cup sauce. Put sauce in a bowl with 1 tablespoon sugar and the plum brandy or kirsch, blend well, cover, and refrigerate. To serve, remove peach halves from syrup (discarding syrup) and place them in separate bowls or on one serving platter and pour raspberry sauce over them.

Calories	Cholesterol mg	Protein gm	Carbohydrate gm	Total fat gm	%	Sat fat gm	%	Mono gm	Poly gm
1298	0	8.0	328.2	1.7	1	–	–	–	–

FRUIT SALAD
Macedonia di Frutta

Any variety of fruit that is fresh, like pitted cherries, fresh peaches, and pineapple, can be used in this recipe.

Serves 8.

1 pear, peeled, cored, and cut into ½-inch pieces, about
   1 cup
¾ cup green grapes, peeled and seeded, cut in half
   lengthwise if large
2 apples, peeled, cored, and cut into ½-inch pieces,
   2 cups
1 banana, halved lengthwise and sliced
Juice of ½ lemon
Juice of 2 oranges
1 cup sliced strawberries
¼ cup kirsch*

*We prefer kirsch as the liqueur here, but others can be used
instead.

Combine all the ingredients except the strawberries and liqueur in a bowl
and let sit for 1 to 2 hours at room temperature. Just before serving, add the
strawberries and liqueur and toss.

Calories	Cholesterol mg	Protein gm	Carbohydrate gm	Total fat gm	%	Sat fat gm	%	Mono gm	Poly gm
721	0	7.0	180.0	5.2	6	–	–	–	–

STRAWBERRIES IN WINE
Fragole al Vino

Serves 4.

1 pint strawberries
1½ tablespoons sugar
2 cups chilled dry white wine or champagne

Wash strawberries, hull them, and cut them in slices if large, or in sections
if small. Place in a serving bowl and toss with the sugar. Cover and
refrigerate for several hours. Divide the strawberries among 4 wine or
champagne glasses, cover with wine, and serve.

Calories	Cholesterol mg	Protein gm	Carbohydrate gm	Total fat gm	%	Sat fat gm	%	Mono gm	Poly gm
590	0	2.3	64.5	1.6	2	–	–	–	–

PEACHES IN WINE
Pesche al Vino

This is the best way to serve fresh peaches in wine — each guest preparing
his own portion. Allow 1 peach per person and use regular-sized wine or
champagne glasses.

Serves 4.

4 fresh, ripe, unrefrigerated peaches*
Dry red wine†

*Peaches should be firm but ripe. Do not use overripe peaches.
†Some people prefer chilled white wine with peaches. We prefer
room-temperature dry red wine. But we do enjoy chilled champagne with peaches.

Wash the peaches and put them in a fruit bowl on the table (you could
serve other fruit as well, but just a bowl of fresh peaches is very attractive).

Give each guest a small plate and a dessert knife. You can either serve
each guest a peach or they may help themselves from the bowl. They
should peel their own peaches, then slice them and place the slices in their
own wineglass, leaving 1/2 inch space at the top. Pour the wine over the
peaches and eat immediately.

Calories	Cholesterol mg	Protein gm	Carbohydrate gm	Total fat gm	%	Sat fat gm	%	Mono gm	Poly gm
532	0	2.0	53.2	0.4	1	–	–	–	–

PEARS IN PORT
Pere al Porto

Serves 2.

2 firm ripe pears
Juice of 1 lemon
1/4 cup port
1 cup water
1/4 cup sugar
2 3-inch pieces orange rind
2-inch piece lemon peel
1 teaspoon cinnamon

Peel the pears and place them in a bowl with cold water and lemon juice.

Mix the remaining ingredients in a bowl, stirring until the sugar dissolves.
Pour into a saucepan just large enough to hold the pears. Add pears, bring
to a boil, partially cover, and simmer until pears are cooked, about 30
minutes. Allow pears to cool in syrup.

Serve cold.

Variation: The syrup can be reduced if a thicker syrup is desired. We
prefer a thin, light syrup.

Calories	Cholesterol mg	Protein gm	Carbohydrate gm	Total fat gm	%	Sat fat gm	%	Mono gm	Poly gm
473	0	3.3	120.8	1.8	3	–	–	–	–

STUFFED PEARS
Pere Ripiene

Serves 2 to 4.

1/2 cup sliced almonds,
    toasted and finely chopped*
1 tablespoon powdered sugar
2 large fresh pears, peeled and cut in half,
    or 4 canned peach halves
3 tablespoons dry marsala or sherry

*A food processor can be used to chop the almonds. Toast the almonds in a 400° oven till light brown, about 8 to 10 minutes.

Mix the chopped almonds with the sugar.

Place pear (or peach) halves in a baking dish so that they fit snugly. Stuff halves with nut-and-sugar mixture. Pour marsala on top of them. Preheat oven to 400° and bake, uncovered, 8 to 10 minutes. Serve hot.

Calories	Cholesterol mg	Protein gm	Carbohydrate gm	Total fat gm	%	Sat fat gm	%	Mono gm	Poly gm
574	0	11.7	81.0	27.4	42	2.0	3	17.2	5.1

RASPBERRY SHERBET
Sorbetto di Lamponi

This recipe can be made with strawberries or other berries. It is excellent accompanied with fresh fruit.

One of the handiest kitchen machines we have ever purchased is an electric ice cream maker called "Il Gelataio." All sorts of wonderful light sorbets can be made easily with this machine. All you do is chill the machine for 10 minutes, pour in the sherbet mixture, set the time for 20 minutes, and watch the blades churn it. However, the recipes I offer here can be made with any kind of good ice cream maker you may own. Just follow the manufacturer's instructions.

Serves 6.

1/2 cup sugar
1/2 cup water
4 cups fresh raspberries or frozen ones defrosted to
    room temperature
Juice of 1/2 lemon
1/2 cup fresh orange juice

Make a syrup by mixing the sugar and water in a small saucepan and simmering until the sugar dissolves. Allow to cool. Place syrup with the berries and fruit juices in a food processor and blend.

Pour into the container of your ice cream maker and follow the manufacturer's directions for making sherbet.

Calories	Cholesterol mg	Protein gm	Carbohydrate gm	Total fat gm	%	Sat fat gm	%	Mono gm	Poly gm
733	0	7.0	183.2	2.8	3	–	–	–	–

MANGO AND CANTALOUPE SHERBET
Sorbetto di Melone e Mango

This delicious sorbet can be served in cantaloupe halves, or with crushed fresh fruit, or slices of fresh fruit marinated in your favorite liqueur.

Serves 8.

2 medium ripe mangoes
1/2 ripe cantaloupe
1 cup plain syrup (see opposite page)

Peel, seed, and chop the mangoes. Skin, seed, and chop the cantaloupe. Purée both in a food processor or food mill, add the syrup, and mix well. Freeze in an ice cream maker according to the manufacturer's instructions.

Calories	Cholesterol mg	Protein gm	Carbohydrate gm	Total fat gm	%	Sat fat gm	%	Mono gm	Poly gm
769	0	5.1	197.0	2.1	2	–	–	–	–

WATERMELON SHERBET WITH SLICED STRAWBERRIES
Sorbetto di Melone e Fragole

Serves 8.

1 pint strawberries
4 tablespoons sweet liqueur, such as Grand Marnier
6 cups cubed watermelon, seeds removed
1 cup plain syrup (see opposite page)

Wash and slice strawberries. Place in a small bowl with the liqueur. Allow to marinate, stirring occasionally, for several hours.

In the meantime, put the watermelon in a food processor with the syrup and purée, or pass melon through a sieve and blend with syrup. Pour watermelon and syrup into an ice cream maker and freeze according to the manufacturer's instructions.

Scoop sorbet into individual serving bowls and spoon some sliced strawberries and marinade over each serving.

Serve immediately.

Variation: Less syrup and more liqueur can be used, according to taste.

Calories	Cholesterol mg	Protein gm	Carbohydrate gm	Total fat gm	%	Sat fat gm	%	Mono gm	Poly gm
965	0	7.1	207.9	3.4	3	–	–	–	–

CHAMPAGNE PEACH SHERBET
Sorbetto di Pesche alla Champagne

This recipe is wonderful for a special summer occasion.

Serves 6.

4 medium ripe peaches
2 cups good champagne, chilled
1 cup plain syrup (page 448)

Peel peaches and cut in chunks; you should have about 3 cups.

Purée peaches in a food processor. Add champagne and blend with the syrup. Freeze in an ice cream maker following the manufacturer's directions.

Calories	Cholesterol mg	Protein gm	Carbohydrate gm	Total fat gm	%	Sat fat gm	%	Mono gm	Poly gm
994	0	5.1	178.2	0.7	1	–	–	–	–

PEACH TART
Torta di Pesche

The butter in this recipe has been balanced with an equal amount of safflower oil, resulting in a crust that is softer than desired, but the recipe fits the requirement of this book. The taste is excellent, and although the dough is more difficult to manage because the safflower oil does not harden when refrigerated, with patience you will find it workable.

Serves 6 to 8.

The dough
1 1/2 cups all-purpose flour
6 tablespoons safflower oil
6 tablespoons butter
1 tablespoon sugar, or to your taste
3 tablespoons ice water
Pinch salt

The filling
5 tablespoons sugar
2 tablespoons all-purpose flour
2 pounds peaches*

The glaze
3 to 4 tablespoons peach preserves

*Any fruit can be used in this recipe — blueberries, raspberries, pears, apples, etc.

Put all the ingredients for the dough in a food processor and, using the steel blade, process until the dough forms a ball. Wrap in waxed paper and refrigerate about 30 minutes.

Dust countertop with flour and roll out the dough. Place dough in a 10-inch pie pan with a double bottom.

For the filling, mix 2 tablespoons of the sugar with the flour. Sprinkle this on the top of the piecrust.

Pierce each peach with a fork and plunge in boiling water, then peel and slice it. Add remaining 3 tablespoons sugar to the sliced peaches and carefully toss.

Arrange peaches in the dough-lined pie pan in an attractive pattern. Bake in a preheated 400° oven for 45 to 55 minutes.

Make a glaze with peach preserve (dilute with some warm water if too thick) and gently brush over peaches when tart is done.

Calories	Cholesterol mg	Protein gm	Carbohydrate gm	Total fat gm	%	Sat fat gm	%	Mono gm	Poly gm
2881	186.0	29.1	360.0	153.7	47	45.0	14	32.4	62.4

CHRISTMAS TURNOVERS
Calcionetti

This is a dessert we ate only during the Christmas holidays. I'm fairly certain the recipe is of Saracen origin. I would imagine the dough was created by an inventive Italian.

Yields about 65 turnovers.

The filling
1 cup blanched, toasted almonds*
3 tablespoons grated orange rind
1¾ cups cooked or canned chick peas (see page 64)
5 tablespoons honey
½ teaspoon cinnamon

The dough
3 cups all-purpose flour
6 tablespoons olive oil
2 tablespoons safflower oil
½ cup dry white wine
½ cup water
Pinch salt

Corn oil or vegetable oil for frying
Powdered sugar

*The almonds should be toasted in a 400° oven till light brown, about 8 to 10 minutes.

Chop the toasted almonds finely by hand or in a food processor. Add the rest of the filling ingredients and mix to a paste by hand or in a food processor.

To make the dough: Pour flour on a board or countertop. Make a well in the flour, add the oils, wine, water, and salt, and work the flour into the well gradually with a fork until the mixture thickens. Continue mixing and kneading with your hands until well blended. Roll in a ball and cut in half. Roll each half into balls. Flour a board and roll out 1 ball with a rolling pin to a circle about ⅛ inch thick or thinner.

About 1½ to 2 inches from the top of the circle put 1 teaspoon filling every 2 inches across the width of the circle. Fold the 2-inch strip from the top over filling, seal bottom edge, and with a sharp knife or pastry wheel cut out individual semicircular calcionetti, leaving about ¾ inch pastry around the edges. Seal edges with a fork and set aside on a floured board. Repeat this procedure until the circle is used up, then roll out remaining balls of dough and fill and cut out turnovers in the same way.

Heat about 1 inch oil in a medium skillet, then add calcionetti one at a time and fry until golden brown. Remove from oil with a slotted spoon and place on paper towels.

Sprinkle the calcionetti with powdered sugar.

Calories	Cholesterol mg	Protein gm	Carbohydrate gm	Total fat gm	%	Sat fat gm	%	Mono gm	Poly gm
4668	0	94.0	530.0	249.4	47	26.7	5	130.2	76.2

INDIVIDUAL CHEESECAKES (R.W.)

This dessert may be served as is, or fresh fruit or a fruit glaze may be added.

Serves 6.

1 pound 1 percent-fat cottage cheese
3/4 cup sugar
2 tablespoons cornstarch
1/4 cup low-fat buttermilk
1/4 cup Poly Perx*
1/4 cup egg whites
1/4 cup corn oil
1 teaspoon grated orange peel
1 teaspoon grated lemon peel
1 teaspoon vanilla extract
1 tablespoon lemon juice

*Poly Perx is a frozen nondairy cream substitute.

Preheat the oven to 350° and boil a kettle full of water. Process the cottage cheese in a food processor fitted with the steel blade until smooth, then add the sugar, cornstarch, buttermilk, Poly Perx, and egg whites. Again, process until smooth. With the motor running, add the corn oil through the feed tube. Finally, add the grated orange and lemon peels, vanilla, and lemon juice and process for a few more seconds. Divide the mixture among 6 11-ounce ramekins. Place the ramekins in a deep baking tray and pour boiling water into the pan to a level at or slightly below the level of the cheese mixture. Bake for 25 minutes. Remove and cool on a rack to room temperature and then refrigerate.

Calories	Cholesterol mg	Protein gm	Carbohydrate gm	Total fat gm	%	Sat fat gm	%	Mono gm	Poly gm
1614	51.0	64.9	192.0	64.7	35	9.1	5	16.5	31.1

DOUGH FOR PIECRUSTS, COOKIES, AND STRUDEL (R.W.)

Yields enough for 2-crust 8- to 9-inch pies.

1 1/2 teaspoons Jolly Joan Egg Replacer
1 1/2 tablespoons water
3 1/2 ounces evaporated skim milk
1 tablespoon corn oil
1 package (or 1 scant tablespoon) active dry yeast
Pinch salt
Pinch freshly ground black pepper
1 1/2 cups all-purpose flour
1/4 pound cold corn oil margarine

Make a smooth paste with the Egg Replacer and water. Add the evaporated skim milk and the oil, beating with an eggbeater to ensure a smooth mixture.

Stir the yeast, salt, and pepper into the flour and with a pastry cutter or two knives cut the margarine into the dry mixture to form a mixture like coarse meal. Stir in the liquid, adding a little more flour as necessary if the dough is too sticky. Form into two balls, wrap each in plastic wrap, and refrigerate for several hours or put into the freezer for 30 minutes.

Calories	Cholesterol mg	Protein gm	Carbohydrate gm	Total fat gm	%	Sat fat gm	%	Mono gm	Poly gm
1788	5.0	32.6	174.9	104.0	51	17.8	9	43.4	40.0

STRUDEL (R.W.)

Makes 2 strudels.

1 cup sugar
2 teaspoons cinnamon
1 recipe dough (above)
4 tablespoons raspberry preserves
4 tablespoons finely chopped dates
4 tablespoons finely chopped walnut meats

Mix the sugar and cinnamon together and spread it on a board. Roll out half the dough to a rectangle about 10 × 14 inches — a long side facing you. Spread 2 tablespoons of the preserves on the half of the sheet of dough closer to you, leaving 1/2-inch borders on the 10-inch sides. Sprinkle half the chopped dates and half the chopped walnuts over the portion spread with jam and roll away from you jellyroll fashion. Repeat with the second ball of dough. Place rolls on a greased cookie sheet and bake in a preheated 350° oven — about 25 to 30 minutes, until the dough is lightly browned. Remove from the oven, allow to cool for a few minutes, and slice.

Calories	Cholesterol mg	Protein gm	Carbohydrate gm	Total fat gm	%	Sat fat gm	%	Mono gm	Poly gm
2621	5	39.6	343.7	124.9	42	19.4	7	46.6	52.8

ROLLED COOKIES (R.W.)

Makes 32 cookies.

1 cup sugar
2 teaspoons cinnamon
1 teaspoon ground ginger
1/2 teaspoon ground cardamom
1 recipe dough (see opposite page)

Mix the sugar, cinnamon, ginger, and cardamom together and sprinkle half on a board. Roll half the dough into a circle about 12 inches in diameter. Slice pie fashion with a knife or pizza cutter into 16 wedges. Roll each wedge from the outside of the circle toward the center and place the cookies so formed on a greased baking sheet. Repeat with the second half of the dough, sprinkling the board with the other half of the sugar mixture. Bake in a preheated 325° oven until the cookies just start to brown.

Calories	Cholesterol mg	Protein gm	Carbohydrate gm	Total fat gm	%	Sat fat gm	%	Mono gm	Poly gm
2257	5.0	37.2	267.5	113.6	44	19.7	8	45.6	44.8

JUDITH WOLFF'S ICEBOX COOKIES

Makes about 120 cookies.

1/2 cup granulated sugar
1/2 cup brown sugar
1 cup corn oil margarine at room temperature
1/2 cup Egg Beaters
2 1/2 cups all-purpose flour
1/2 teaspoon baking soda
1/2 teaspoon cinnamon
1/2 cup chopped almonds

Mix all the ingredients together, then knead briefly. Divide the dough in half and make 2 15-inch-long rolls. Wrap in waxed paper or plastic wrap and refrigerate overnight or put in the freezer for 30 minutes.

Preheat the oven to 350°. Cut the dough into 1/4-inch slices* and place on a greased cookie sheet 1/2 inch apart. Bake for 7 to 10 minutes.

*If the dough is sliced at right angles to the length of the rolls, the yield is about 10 dozen cookies. If sliced on the bias, the yield is fewer but larger cookies.

Calories	Cholesterol mg	Protein gm	Carbohydrate gm	Total fat gm	%	Sat fat gm	%	Mono gm	Poly gm
3926	0	54.2	446.3	214.9	48	34.8	8	103.6	71.1

SPICY CARROT CAKE (R.W.)

1 1/2 teaspoons baking soda
1/4 cup warm water
2 cups grated carrots (a little over 1/2 pound)
1/2 cup low-fat yogurt
1 1/2 cups sugar
3/4 cup corn oil
1/2 teaspoon cinnamon
1/2 teaspoon ground nutmeg or a few grinds of fresh nutmeg
1/2 teaspoon ground cloves
1/4 teaspoon ground allspice
1/2 teaspoon salt
1 cup yellow raisins
1/4 cup finely chopped walnuts (optional)
1/2 cup lightly beaten egg whites
2 cups all-purpose flour

Preheat oven to 325°.

Dissolve the baking soda in the warm water and set aside. Mix together the carrots and yogurt, then add the sugar, oil, spices, and salt. Add the dissolved baking soda, the raisins, and the optional nuts. Add the egg whites, then the flour 1/2 cup at a time. Oil a 9-inch square pan and dust it with flour. Pour the batter into the pan and bake for about 1 hour, or until a cake tester comes out clean. Cool for 5 minutes and remove from the pan. Continue cooling on a wire rack.

Calories	Cholesterol mg	Protein gm	Carbohydrate gm	Total fat gm	%	Sat fat gm	%	Mono gm	Poly gm
4236	1.0	54.2	645.4	169.7	35	17.5	4	46.5	86.7

XII   BREAKFASTS, BREADS AND PIZZAS, SNACKS, AND CHEESE

Italians are not breakfast eaters. Farmers and people who do hard physical work will have a little warm food or prosciutto and fruit after several hours of labor, but they would never have a large breakfast before going to work. Personally, I cannot believe it is healthy to eat a big breakfast as soon as you get up, particularly an American breakfast of eggs, butter, pancakes, sausages or bacon, home fries, etc.; that kind of food just doesn't appeal to me first thing in the morning. And, as you will see from his analysis, Dick Wolff finds these heavy foods an unfortunate way to start the day. Fresh fruit, honest cereal, and good homemade bread make so much more sense to me. Therefore, since I care so little about breakfast, I defer to Dick Wolff for some healthful inspirations and I have confined myself to bread and pizza recipes in this chapter. I include pizzas here because I like the Italian tradition of making a pizza on baking morning—just pulling off a piece of the rising bread dough, rolling it out, and filling it with whatever might be at hand, then serving it fresh from the oven when ready. E.G.

I have taken on the challenge of breakfast not only because of Ed's lack of interest but also because on the one hand breakfast presents problems and on the other it exemplifies some of the strategies one can employ in improving one's diet. As ordinarily eaten in the United States, particularly in restaurants, breakfast is a meal in which almost all the standard items should be avoided. Eggs in any style or in pancakes, waffles, or French toast; bacon, ham, and sausages are all to be discouraged. Ready-to-eat cereals are apt to contain coconut oil or palm oil, and granolas frequently include coconut. Hot cereal is often buttered; and hot and cold cereals are served with whole milk, or, worse yet, with cream. Toast is buttered, as are muffins made with butter, eggs, and whole milk; and doughnuts are deep-fried in unacceptable fats. Danish and other pastries are rich in fats and often in eggs. Many breakfasters take whole milk or cream in coffee, though some take it black and a few with skim milk. Nondairy creamers are frequently worse than milk or cream, having a base of coconut or similar oil. A few, however, notably Poly Perx, have a P:S ratio of 2:1. Even the coffee itself (or its caffeine) has been implicated in raising blood cholesterol.

Table 1 lists the nutrients in a typical American breakfast.

TABLE 1

Food	Amount	Calories	Protein	Carbohydrate	Fat	Sat	Mono	Poly	Notes
Orange juice	6 oz.	84	1.3	19.4	0.4				
Eggs	2 large	164	13.0	1.0	11.6	3.6	5.0	0.8	
Bacon	2 slices	86	3.8	0.5	7.8	2.5	3.7	0.7	
Toast	2 slices	152	4.8	28.2	1.8	0.4	0.8	0.4	*
Butter	2 pats	72	trace	trace	8.2	4.4	2.6	0.2	
Cream	1 Tb.	32	0.5	0.6	3.1	1.7	1.0	0.1	†
TOTALS		590	23.4	49.7	32.9	12.6	13.1	2.2	

*White, enriched bread.
†Coffee cream.

Suppose this breakfast is consumed by a person weighing 154 pounds. If he utilizes 18 calories daily for every pound of weight, his 24-hour intake should be 2,772 calories — 94.5 grams of fat to provide 30 percent of his calories; not more than one third of this, or 31.5 grams, should be saturated fat, and at least that much should be polyunsaturated fat. The 590 calories in this breakfast make up 21 percent of the day's allowance — no problem here. The 32.9 grams of fat are 35 percent of the day's ration. There is nothing intrinsically unacceptable about that, but the disproportionate amount of fat for the number of calories suggests that he may run into problems later in the day — not insurmountable problems, but his choices are going to be limited. The 12.6 grams of saturated fat are 40 percent of the day's allowance — again still well within the daily limits, but the likelihood has become even greater that there will be a severe restriction of choices for the rest of the day.

When we consider alternatives, we find that there are ways of keeping the enjoyment up and the fat and calories down.

This is a good point to introduce you to a growing number of products on the market, many of which were designed originally for vegetarians. It is a matter of historical interest that the Kelloggs of cereal fame and their erstwhile employee, C. W. Post, were Seventh-Day Adventists whose vegetarianism provided the inspiration for using grains in new ways. The older products have been joined in recent years by newer ones, some again spawned by the Seventh-Day Adventist movement and others by large food concerns aware of the need for foods that do not raise blood cholesterol levels. The National Diet–Heart Study encouraged manufacturers to be creative in this area. Some of the most important products to emerge have been egg substitutes, exemplified by Egg Beaters, a frozen product that when thawed is used to prepare a scrambled egg–like dish. It is entirely devoid of fat and cholesterol. Many people find it an entirely satisfactory substitute as is; others need to add embellishments to dress it up into omelets of various descriptions; and others simply do not like Egg Beaters. Make up your own mind; if you like Egg Beaters, you have solved the egg deprivation problem. Incidentally, ½ cup, the equivalent of 2 eggs, has 60 calories versus 160 for real eggs. The product can be used in French toast, waffles, and in baking. For baking, there is another alternative, called Jolly Joan Egg Replacer, which contains arrowroot flour, potato starch, tapioca flour, modified vegetable gums, and cereal-free leavening. This product, too, is entirely free of fat and cholesterol. It is used in one recipe in this book, a pastry dough (page 454). There are many other products, such as vegetarian versions of bacon in both bits and slices, sausages, cheese foods wherein the butterfat content has been reduced with or without replacement by acceptable oils, margarines with P:S ratios of about 2:1, and nondairy creamers with similar P:S ratios, such as Poly Perx.

Let us now redesign breakfast using some of these products. Instead of bacon and eggs you can have a "cheese omelet" in which you substitute the whites of 4 eggs for the 2 whole eggs (1/2 cup Egg Beaters will work as well and hardly change the breakdowns given below), margarine for the butter, and Poly Perx for the cream. You then eliminate the bacon and add a low-fat cheeselike food such as Countdown, and, if you like, some onion. The recipe for the "cheese omelet" and the remainder of the breakfast appears on page 461. The nutritional breakdown is shown in Table 2.

TABLE 2

Food	Amount	Calories	Protein	Carbohydrate	Fat	Sat	Mono	Poly	Notes
Orange juice	6 oz.	84	1.3	19.4	0.4				*
Egg white	4	64	13.4	1.6	trace				
Safflower oil	1/2 tsp.	20	0	0	2.26	0.2	0.3	1.7	
Onion	50 grams	19	0.8	4.4					
Countdown	28.4 grams	40	6.0	3.0	1.0	0.6	0.3		
Margarine	2 pats	71	0	0	7.8	1.4		2.8	†
Toast	2 slices	152	4.8	28.2	1.8	0.4	0.8	0.4	
Poly Perx	1 Tb.	7	0	0.6	0.5	0.1	0.3	0.2	
TOTALS		457	26.3	57.2	13.8	2.7	1.7	5.1	‡

*Each egg white is 33 grams.
†Figures applicable for Fleischmann's margarine.
‡Fat, at 8.8 calories per gram, accounts for 27 percent of the calories of this breakfast. The cholesterol content is 2 mg. derived from the Countdown. This compares with 621 mg. in the bacon-and-egg breakfast.

Compared with the bacon-and-egg breakfast, there are fewer calories (16 percent of the day's allowance), less total fat (14 percent), and less saturated fat (9 percent). You have "used up," as it were, fewer of your day's ration of calories, less of the allowed fat, and even less of the permitted saturated fat; and in the process you have given yourself the opportunity to choose from a larger (and richer) menu at lunch and/or dinner.

There are other options. We will mention a few. There is the Continental breakfast, which can be adapted to consist of fruit or juice, good bread with jam, jelly, or honey and butter, plus tea or coffee with or without milk or cream. This is a relatively low-calorie, low-fat meal that can be further "improved" by substituting polyunsaturated margarine for the butter, or, better yet, using neither, and by drinking coffee or tea with Polyperx instead of cream. And there is always skim milk or fat-free cocoa for those who like it.

Fruits and fruit juices can be taken pretty much as desired, and many cereals are acceptable, among them shredded wheat, Grape-Nuts, cream of wheat, rolled oats, and cornflakes as well as cornmeal in its various guises. Labels should be read, however, because brands differ in their compositions, and some include coconut or palm oil. Fresh and dried fruits add interest to both cooked and ready-to-eat cereals, and we like the accent added to cooked cereals by spices such as ginger, nutmeg, and cinnamon.

Moreover, you don't always have to stick to an American breakfast: The customs of foreign lands and various ethnic groups may be adapted for variety. Chinese cookbooks contain recipes for congee, a kind of porridge made of mixtures of long-grain and glutinous rice and flavored with a wide variety of ingredients. Indian breakfasts may vary from fruit and sweet tea in the north to idlis, dosas (below), and hoppers in the south. The beauty of introducing completely unfamiliar foods is that you have no standard for comparision, comparison that is inevitable when, for example, Egg Beaters are substituted for real eggs. To a south Indian, coconut chutney would go with dosa as surely as mustard and relish go with that hotdog at the ball game. But when you eat dosa for the first time, your sense of taste is not yet conditioned to demand coconut chutney and it need never be. The dosa can be eaten plain or with any of a large variety of chutneys.

More characteristically American breakfasts can be eaten if desired. Pancakes or French toast can be made with egg whites or Egg Beaters and fried in nonstick pans with a minimum of approved margarine or oil. Cottage cheese with a fat content of 1 percent is good moistened with a polyunsaturated dairy dressing (below) and served with fresh, stewed, or preserved fruit if you wish. R.W.

DOSA (R.W.)

Serves 8.

The batter
1/2 cup urad dal (split black beans; available in Indian
　　grocery stores)
1 cup long-grain white rice, preferably Basmati rice
About 1 cup water
1 cup low-fat yogurt
Pinch black pepper or 1/8 to 1/4 teaspoon cayenne

To fry each dosa
1/2 teaspoon safflower oil
2 tablespoons finely chopped onion
1/2 teaspoon ground cumin (optional)

Garnish (optional):
1 to 2 teaspoons mango chutney
1 to 2 tablespoons chopped fresh coriander

Wash the dal and rice until the rinse water runs clear, then put in a glazed or stainless-steel bowl and add enough water to cover by 1 inch. Soak for 6 to 8 hours or overnight. Drain and place the dal and rice in a blender or food processor. Add ½ cup of the water and the yogurt and pepper and process until smooth. The batter will be gritty to the fingers even though it looks smooth. Add more water to make a total amount of 4 cups batter.

To make an individual dosa, heat a 9-inch nonstick pan and, when hot, add the safflower oil and the finely chopped onion. When the onion is translucent, add ½ cup of the batter (mixed with cumin if you like) and fry over medium heat until the pan releases the pancake. Turn and brown the other side. Serve as is or with mango chutney and chopped fresh coriander leaves, or any sauce or chutney you wish.

Calories	Cholesterol mg	Protein gm	Carbohydrate gm	Total fat gm	%	Sat fat gm	%	Mono gm	Poly gm
1375	17.0	50.1	235.2	26.3	17	3.8	2	3.4	13.6

LOW–FAT SOUR DAIRY DRESSING (R.W.)

Use with 1 percent-fat cottage cheese or with fresh, stewed, or preserved fruit and a piece of good bread for breakfast.

Makes about 2 cups.

2 cups 1 percent-fat cottage cheese
¼ cup buttermilk cultured from skim milk
2 tablespoons lemon juice
1 tablespoon corn oil

Put all the ingredients in a blender or food processor and blend until completely smooth, scraping down sides with spatula as necessary.

Calories	Cholesterol mg	Protein gm	Carbohydrate gm	Total fat gm	%	Sat fat gm	%	Mono gm	Poly gm
511	48.0	62.5	21.7	17.8	31	4.0	7	5.0	7.4

EGG WHITE OMELET (R.W.)

½ teaspoon safflower oil
1 small onion, finely chopped
4 egg whites, lightly beaten
1 ounce Countdown, shredded*
Salt and freshly ground black pepper to taste

*Countdown is an imitation pasteurized-process skim milk cheese spread.

Heat the safflower oil in an 8- or 9-inch nonstick skillet over a low to moderate flame. Add the onion and fry till translucent. Add half the egg whites, and when they become opaque add the Countdown. When it starts to melt, add the rest of the egg whites and salt and pepper. When the pan releases the omelet, fold it over and slide it onto a warmed plate.

Calories	Cholesterol mg	Protein gm	Carbohydrate gm	Total fat gm	%	Sat fat gm	%	Mono gm	Poly gm
143	0	20.2	9.0	3.3	20	0.8	5	0.6	1.7

ELLIE GIOBBI'S ITALIAN–STYLE BREAD

My wife, Ellie, makes all the bread we consume. She bakes several times a week.

The grain she uses comes from her grandfather's farm in Arkansas near the banks of the Mississippi River. They send us the whole grain, and Ellie grinds the wheat into flour with an electrically powered kitchen-sized stone mill.

All-purpose flour, or whole wheat flour, or whole wheat and all-purpose flour combined can be used in this recipe. This dough can also be used for pizzas.

Yields about 8 loaves 20 inches long and 3 inches wide.

2 tablespoons active dry yeast
8 cups warm water
About 16 cups flour*
2 tablespoons kosher salt or 1 1/4 tablespoons table salt

*We like 2/3 whole wheat mixed with 1/3 all-purpose flour.

Mix the yeast and water together and let sit about 5 minutes.

Pour most of the flour along with the salt into a large bowl. Add the yeast water to the flour gradually, mixing as you pour. Work the dough with your hands into a manageable ball. Remove it to a lightly floured pastry board or countertop and knead it until the ball of dough has an elastic consistency, adding more flour as needed—about 10 minutes.

Oil the bottom of the mixing bowl and roll the ball of dough in the oiled bowl until it is lightly covered with oil. Cover with a damp cloth or sheet of plastic and place bowl in a warm place. We put the bowl near our stove. Allow the dough to double its bulk—about 2 hours.

Turn the dough out and punch it down. Cut the ball into 8 pieces and form into long loaves—about 18 inches long and 2 inches wide. You can place formed loaves on oiled baking sheets or use lightly oiled French bread baking forms. Allow the loaves to double their bulk—about 1 hour.

Preheat the oven to 425°. Place the baking sheets in the oven and bake about 30 minutes.* During the first few minutes of baking, throw several ice cubes onto the oven floor occasionally to create steam, which will make the crust crisp. Remove the bread from the trays, turn them over, lower heat to 350°, and bake about 20 minutes more, or until the bread is a golden brown. Cool on racks.

To freeze bread, wrap cooled loaves in aluminum foil. To reheat, place frozen bread, still wrapped in foil, in a 500° oven. It will take about 15 minutes to heat through.

*If you line the bottom of your oven with unglazed terracotta tiles or unglazed bricks you will get a more consistent heat and a better loaf of bread.

Calories	Cholesterol mg	Protein gm	Carbohydrate gm	Total fat gm	%	Sat fat gm	%	Mono gm	Poly gm
8060	0	236	1673	27.1	3	4.2	<1	3.4	13.8

JUDITH JONES'S BASIC LOAF BREAD

Here is a basic loaf bread that can be varied by using different flours, grains, meals, and embellishments. The master recipe includes all-purpose and whole wheat flour but it could be made with all all-purpose flour, half all-purpose and half rye, as well as cornmeal, oatmeal, cracked wheat, bran, buckwheat, or millet in a ratio of about 1/2 cup to 5 to 6 cups wheat flour. Because of the cholesterol-lowering effect of oat bran (see Dr. Wolff's introduction, page 5), whole oat kernels ground in a blender or coffee grinder make a particularly healthful addition to homemade bread; try 1 cup ground oat kernels to 3 cups whole wheat flour and 3 or slightly more cups unbleached white flour in this recipe. Embellishments can include raisins, wheat germ, sunflower seeds, nuts—about 1/4 to 1/2 cup to 5 to 6 cups flour. In addition, spices like caraway, sesame, fennel, anise, and poppy seeds give zest to different kinds of loaves. Once you've mastered the basic recipe, you can play with your own combinations. Just remember that different flours and grains have a different water content, so the amount of liquid they absorb will vary. The rising time will vary too, as the heavy grains have little or no gluten potential. By the same token, do not overload a dough with too many of the heavier grains, or you will have a loaf that is too dense or too crumbly.

Makes 2 8 1/2 × 4 1/2 × 2 1/2-inch loaves.

1 package (or 1 scant tablespoon) active dry yeast
2 1/2 cups warm water
1/4 cup honey, brown sugar, molasses, or corn syrup
1/2 cup non-fat dry milk
4 tablespoons safflower oil, plus 2 to 3 more for oiling
    bowl and pans
1 teaspoon salt
3 cups whole wheat flour
3 to 4 cups unbleached all-purpose flour
1/4 cup wheat germ

Put the yeast in a large bowl and pour 1/2 cup of the warm water over it. Stir to dissolve and let stand a minute. Mix in the rest of the water, the sweetener, dry milk, oil, and salt with the dissolved yeast, blending well.

Stir in the whole wheat flour and 3 cups of the all-purpose flour, one at a time, until the dough becomes hard to stir. Turn it out onto a floured working surface and knead, adding more flour as necessary to keep it from sticking. After about 8 to 10 minutes the dough will no longer be tacky and should be smooth and elastic. Sprinkle the wheat germ over and knead in. Wash the mixing bowl, oil it, and return the dough to it, turning to coat with oil. Cover with plastic wrap and let rise until double in volume — about 1½ hours.

Turn the dough out, punch it all over, and divide in half. Oil the bread pans lightly and form the dough into 2 loaves the length of the pans. Transfer the dough to the bread pans, cover lightly with a towel, and let rise again until double in volume — about 45 minutes.

Bake the bread in a preheated 350° oven 45 minutes (if using rye, bake 10 minutes longer). Turn the loaves out onto racks and let cool.

Calories	Cholesterol	Protein	Carbohydrate	Total fat		Sat fat		Mono	Poly
	mg	gm	gm	gm	%	gm	%	gm	gm
3776	12.0	112.1	668.7	82.6	19	8.7	2	10.1	59.3

PIZZA WITH VEAL AND BROCCOLI
Pizza Rustica

This recipe makes a most satisfying lunch served with an interesting green salad.

Serves 6.

1 teaspoon active dry yeast
1 cup warm water
1 teaspoon salt
3½ cups all-purpose flour

The filling
1 tablespoon olive oil
1 teaspoon safflower oil
1 medium onion, finely chopped
½ pound mushrooms, sliced
½ pound ground lean veal or beef
Salt and freshly ground black pepper to taste
½ cup chopped tomatoes, fresh if possible
    (drained if canned)
1 teaspoon dried oregano

2 cups broccoli cut into bite-sized pieces, blanched
    and drained

Add yeast to the warm water and allow to sit for 10 minutes or more. Add salt.

Pour the flour on a table or board and make a well. Pour water-and-yeast mixture into the well slowly, mixing in the flour as you pour. Work the dough, adding more flour if needed. Knead the dough until you have a smooth, elastic ball.

Place dough in a bowl, cover with a damp towel or cloth, and put in a warm place — we put it near the stove. Allow the dough to rise until double its bulk.

In the meantime, heat the oils in a medium to large skillet, then add the onion and mushrooms. Cook over medium to high heat uncovered, stirring often, until onion begins to brown. Add the veal, salt, and pepper. Cook over medium heat, uncovered, stirring often, until veal begins to brown. Add tomatoes and oregano and cook about 5 minutes.

Lightly oil a round baking dish about 9 inches in diameter and about 1 1/2 inches deep. Punch the dough down and cut in half. Roll out one half on a floured board. Slip rolled out dough onto baking dish. Add broccoli, then spread ground veal mixture over broccoli. Roll out second half of ball and place sheet of dough on top of veal mixture. Seal the edges by pressing them together.

Preheat the oven to 400°. Bake for 15 minutes, then lower heat to 350° and bake about 30 more minutes.

Serve at room temperature or warm.

Variation: An interesting variety of fillings can be used in this recipe: Italian-style tuna with broccoli and black olives; ground veal with eggplant and onions; ground lean beef with asparagus and spinach; or any combination you might fancy.

Calories	Cholesterol mg	Protein gm	Carbohydrate gm	Total fat gm	%	Sat fat gm	%	Mono gm	Poly gm
2407	161.0	111.3	399.2	35.9	13	8.6	3	16.1	7.7

PIZZA OF ESCAROLE
Pizza di Scarola

This recipe is a Christmas Eve specialty from southern Italy.

Serves 6.

1 tablespoon yellow raisins
1 medium head escarole
4 tablespoons olive oil
2 tablespoons safflower oil
1 clove garlic, chopped
12 dried black olives, pitted and sliced
5 canned anchovies, coarsely chopped
1 tablespoon capers
2 tablespoons pine nuts
Salt and freshly ground black pepper to taste
Pizza dough (see preceding recipe)

Soak the raisins in tepid water for 15 minutes.

Chop and wash the escarole. Cook in boiling water about 5 minutes. Drain and squeeze out all the water and reserve it.

Heat in a skillet 3 tablespoons of the olive oil and 1 tablespoon of the safflower oil, then add garlic, olives, and anchovies. As soon as garlic takes on color, add escarole, raisins, capers, pine nuts, salt, and pepper (be careful of salt — anchovies and capers have salt in them). Cover and simmer over low heat for 10 minutes.

In the meantime, preheat the oven to 400°. Roll out the pizza dough so it is between 1/4 and 1/2 inch thick. Place in the oven and bake about 10 minutes, then remove and sprinkle with remaining 1 tablespoon olive oil and 1 tablespoon safflower oil and spread escarole mixture on top. Return to oven and bake at 350° about 20 minutes. Do not cook so long that the escarole dries out.

Calories	Cholesterol mg	Protein gm	Carbohydrate gm	Total fat gm	%	Sat fat gm	%	Mono gm	Poly gm
2735	11.0	65.4	391.1	101.6	33	12.5	4	52.4	29.1

ABOUT SNACKS

   Very little needs to be said about snacks. Raw vegetables are the ideal snacks. Raw fruits are equally good from the viewpoint of having negligible fat content (except for avocado), although their large sugar content makes them more caloric, reaching 275 calories per 100 grams in the case of dates and dried figs. Candied fruits are higher still. Candies, cookies, cakes, pies, nuts, and pizza are not only high but also have a significant fat content, making them undesirable snack foods. The table below gives the calories and fat content of a wide variety of snack foods. R.W.

100 grams of snack food (3½ oz. approx.)	Calories	% calories derived from fat
Almonds	598	54.2
Apple	58	0.6
Apricots, candied	338	0.2
Apricots, dehydrated	332	1.0
Avocado	167	16.4
Banana	85	0.2
Brazil nuts	654	66.9
Carbonated beverages		
Cola type	39	0
Cream soda	43	0
Fruit-flavored sodas	46	0
Ginger ale	31	0
Root beer	41	0
Cakes		
Angel food	269	0.2
Chocolate with chocolate icing	369	16.4
Pound cake	473	29.5
Sponge cake	297	5.7
Candy		
Butterscotch	397	3.4
Caramel	399	10.2
Chocolate, milk	520	32.3
Fondant	364	2.0
Hard candy	386	1.1
Jelly beans	367	0.5
Carrots	42	0.2
Cashews	561	45.7
Cheese, cheddar	398	32.2
Cherries, candied	339	0.2
Chestnuts	194	1.5
Cider, apple	47	trace
Citron, candied	314	0.3
Coconut meat, fresh	346	35.3

Cookies		
Assorted, package, commercial	480	20.2
Brownies with nuts, homemade	485	31.3
Butter, thin, rich	457	16.9
Chocolate	445	15.7
Chocolate chip, homemade	516	30.1
Coconut bars	494	24.5
Fig bars	358	5.6
Ginger snaps	420	8.9
Oatmeal with raisins	451	15.4
Raisin	379	5.3
Shortbread	498	23.1
Crackers		
Animal	429	9.4
Butter	458	17.8
Cheese	479	21.3
Graham	384	9.4
Saltines	433	12.0
Danish pastry	422	23.5
Doughnuts		
Cake type	391	18.6
Yeast-leavened	414	26.7
Figs		
Candied	299	0.2
Dried	274	1.3
Filberts (hazelnuts)	634	62.4
Frankfurter without roll	309	27.6
Gingerroot, candied	340	0.2
Grapes	69	1.0
Hamburger, regular without roll	268	21.2
Ice cream, 10% fat	193	10.6
Ice milk	152	5.1
Lemon peel, candied	316	0.3
Macadamia nuts	691	71.6
Milk, skim	36	0.1
Milk, whole	65	3.5
Mushrooms	28	0.3
Orange peel, candied	316	0.3
Oranges, raw	49	0.2
Papaya, raw	39	0.1
Peaches	38	0.1
Peanuts	568	48.4
Pears, candied	303	0.6
Pears, raw	61	0.4
Pecans	687	71.2
Pies		
Apple	256	11.1

Pies, (continued)

Blueberry	242	10.8
Cherry	261	11.3
Coconut custard	235	12.5
Lemon meringue	255	10.2
Mince	271	11.5
Pumpkin	211	11.2
Pine nuts (pignolias)	552	47.4
Pistachio nuts	594	53.7
Pizza, with cheese	236	8.3
Popcorn, oil and salt added	456	21.8
Popcorn, plain	386	5.0
Raisins, raw	289	0.2
Rolls, sweet	316	9.1
Walnuts	651	64.0

ABOUT CHEESE

Cheese is the food that results from concentrating by coagulation the protein (casein) in milk. The coagulation may be accomplished by acid, bacteria, heat, or a combination of these agents. The coagulated substances constitute the curds, and they are separated from the liquid whey. The curds may then be ripened by the action of beneficial bacteria, yeast, molds, and enzymes. Milk fat stays with the curds; and the amount varies depending upon whether whole milk, partially skimmed milk, or skim milk is used. In the manufacture of some cheeses, partially skimmed milk is used for the curd, to which additional milk fat is added later in the processing. Thus the assumption is not necessarily correct that a cheese labeled "made of partially skimmed milk" has a lower fat content than one made of whole milk. Natural cheeses are made directly from milk (curds or whey) by coagulating (curdling), stirring and heating the curd, draining the whey, collecting and/or pressing the curd, and curing the cheese by holding it for a specified time at a controlled temperature and humidity to affect flavor and texture. Pasteurized process cheese, cheese food, cheese spread, and imitation cheese are made by blending, heating, mixing, and adding foreign fats such as corn oil. It is important, therefore, to know the amount and the kind of fat in a cheese, pasteurized process cheese, cheese food, cheese spread, or imitation cheese.

The amount of fat in a given variety of cheese varies a little from batch to batch. It is generally stated as the percentage, by weight, in the cheese or in the dry matter. If it is stated in the dry matter, that figure taken together with the percentage of moisture in the cheese permits the calculation of the grams of fat per convenient unit such as per ounce (28.35 grams), per hundred grams, or per pound (454 grams).

The distribution of fatty acids into the three familiar types — saturated, mono-unsaturated, and polyunsaturated — depends upon the fat source or sources, i.e., whether from cow's, goat's, or sheep's milk or from oils such as corn, safflower, and cottonseed. Although there are variations from species to species, from breed to breed, and even within the same breed, depending upon feed, season, and other factors, we have adopted one set of figures to characterize fat from cows, sheep, and goats. We shall assume that 66 percent of the fat is saturated, 30 percent is monounsaturated, and 4 percent is polyunsaturated.

If we recall that one of the requirements of the diet is the provision of at least 1 gram of polyunsaturated fat for each gram of saturated fat, it becomes apparent that cheese obligates the addition of polyunsaturated fat to the diet. For example, an ounce of Swiss cheese has 5.0 grams of saturated fat in excess of the amount of polyunsaturated fat. To offset this by providing a similar excess of polyunsaturated over saturated fat would require about 1/2 tablespoon of safflower oil, adding both to the calorie total and to the percentage of calories derived from fat. For this reason, full fat cheeses have to be used in relatively small amounts. There are a number of strategies which may help the cheese lover.

First, lower-fat natural cheese, such as St. Otho, may be used. It is a Swiss-made cheese with a fat content of 5 percent.

Second, cheese may be used as flavoring in very small amounts, as we have done, particularly with some of the pasta recipes in this book. Stronger cheeses and finer grinds stretch the flavor further.

Next, cheeses in which the milk fat has been almost entirely removed (Countdown, with 1 percent milk fat) or in which it has been substituted for by vegetable oils, such as corn, cottonseed, etc., can be used. Careful reading of labels is, of course, essential.

Finally, it is possible to tailor combinations of cheeses for various characteristics. Low-fat cottage or farmer cheese will add bulk, Countdown will lend a melted consistency, and a strong grated cheese like Pecorino Romano will bestow flavor even in a relatively small amount.

Even high-fat cheeses may have a place in the diet. As an example, Gorgonzola cheese, with about 32 percent fat, has 9.1 grams of fat per ounce. A 1-ounce serving of Gorgonzola cheese provides the same amount of fat divided into the same proportions of saturated, monounsaturated, and polyunsaturated fatty acids as 4 1/2 ounces of lean, choice chuck steak trimmed of separable fat. The substitution could readily be made, remembering that with either the chuck steak or the Gorgonzola cheese, 2 teaspoons of safflower oil or an equivalent amount of excess polyunsaturated fatty acid in other foods would be needed to balance the saturated and polyunsaturated components.

APPENDIXES

Appendix 1
Risk Factors

There have been a number of studies, e.g., the Framingham Study, that have sought to identify as many as possible of the risk factors for coronary heart disease and to assess the contribution of each to overall risk. Some inkling as to the power of these risk factors can be obtained by considering that a 45-year-old man with a systolic blood pressure of 105 mm. of mercury, who does not have glucose intolerance (i.e., who is not diabetic), who does not smoke, and who has a serum cholesterol of 185, has 20 chances in 1000 of developing coronary heart disease in the next 8 years. If everything is the same except that he smokes cigarettes, the risk rises to 32 chances in 1000. If, in addition, he has glucose intolerance, the risk is 40 in 1000. Add a systolic blood pressure of 150 or 180, and the risks rise respectively to 69 per 1000 and 99 per 1000. A cholesterol level of 285 instead of 185 raises these figures to 158 per 1000 and 217 per 1000; and if the electrocardiogram shows enlargement of the main pumping chamber of his heart, the figures reach 284 per 1000 and 370 per 1000. If the cholesterol level is higher still, at 310, then 425 men in 1000 will be expected to have developed coronary heart disease by 8 years later. Thus, from best to worst, the risk rises from 20 to 425 per 1000! Table 1 relates risk to cholesterol level in a hypothetical, low-risk group of 45-year-old male, non-diabetic, non-smokers, with blood pressures of 105, and a high-risk group of 45-year-old male, diabetic smokers with systolic blood pressures of 180 (i.e., hypertensives) and electrocardiograms having an abnormality reflecting the hypertension. Note that the presence of additional risk factors in no way mitigates the contribution of cholesterol to overall risk.

Cholesterol mg./100 ml.	310	285	260	235	210	185
Risk of low-risk men*	60	48	39	31	25	20
Risk of high-risk men*	425	330	318	270	227	189

*Risk is defined as the number of subjects per 1000 who can be expected to develop coronary heart disease within the next 8 years.

Appendix 2
Ideal Weight, Dieting, and the Caloric Equivalents of Various Activities

There is general agreement that each of us is likely to be healthiest at an "ideal" weight; there is also widespread disagreement as to what "ideal" is. Many sets of standards are available for defining ideal or proper weight. One of the most widely used is the table published by the Metropolitan Life Insurance Company. A 1983 revision liberalized the allowable weights. The table is reprinted below (see Table 1). I prefer a stricter standard; I use a simple formula that obviates the need for a table. The formula states that a man is allowed 106 pounds for 5 feet of height, and 6 pounds more for each additional inch. A woman is permitted 100 pounds for 5 feet and 5 pounds per each extra inch. Unlike the Metropolitan Life Insurance table, this formula does not take into account variations in "frame"; to my mind this is an advantage, for, too often, the "frame" is cited as justification for the excess of flesh that hangs upon it.

Let us assume that by whatever standard is chosen, the "ideal" weight turns out to be 154 pounds (70 kilograms). I selected this weight for my example because it is the weight of the hypothetical "standard" subject most frequently referred to in medical writings. There are a number of interesting facts about this standard subject. First, the weight is standard, but the height is not. By my formula a male for whom this was the ideal weight would be 5' 8" tall, a woman 5' 10.8" tall. Second, the number of calories required by this person for various activities can be calculated in terms of calories per pound per minute or per hour or per day. It will vary from about 0.4 calorie per pound per hour for sleeping to as many as 1.6 calories per pound per hour or even more for vigorous exertion. Third, since the calorie requirement is a per pound requirement, it is obvious that a 200-pound body needs twice as many calories as a 100-pound body for the same activity performed over the same time. The interesting extension of this is that, in theory at least, anyone wishing to reduce from a stable weight to a new weight doesn't need to know anything about the caloric content of food. If, for example, he or she weighs 200 pounds and is stable at that weight, the assumption can be made that the intake of calories is just enough to maintain each and every one of those 200 pounds at the current level of activity. If a person wanted to reduce to 160 pounds, i.e., to 4/5, or 80 percent, of the 200 pounds, he would have only to reduce the portions of everything he ate by 20 percent. If he was in the habit of having 5 slices of bread in the course of 24 hours, he would reduce it to 4 slices; 5 ounces of tunafish for lunch would become 4 ounces; and a glass of milk would become 6.5 ounces instead of 8 ounces, and so on down the line for every single item eaten.

Let us assume by way of illustration that our 200-pounder has an overall activity level that calls for 15 calories per pound per day, a total of 3000 calories. For the same activity level, each pound of target weight of 160 pounds will also need 15 calories per pound per day, or 2400 calories. It matters not whether these 2400 calories are calculated by consciously deciding that the ideal weight is 160 pounds and the activity level is 15 calories per pound per day, so that the 160 must be multiplied by 15, or whether the figure is what results not from calorie counting but from eating 4/5 as much of every item as previously. The results will be the same. The energy expenditure will be 3000 calories per day; the intake will be 2400 calories per day, or 600 calories less than expended. Inasmuch as the loss of 1 pound of body weight requires a deficit of 3500 calories, it will take just under 6 days to lose 1 pound. As long as the intake is 2400 calories a day and the weight remains above 160 pounds, there will be weight loss, but the rate of loss will slow progressively. By the time the weight is down to 165 pounds the energy expenditure will be $165 \times 15 = 2475$ calories per day, only 75 calories more than the intake. It will now take 3500 divided by 75, or 46.7 days, to lose 1 pound. Despite the slowness of this approach, there are the advantages that loss is never precipitous enough to be dangerous and the same eating patterns formed at the start can be continued after the end of the period of weight loss. The extent to which calories need be limited is influenced by the level of activity. Exercise increases the number of calories burned and, therefore, the rate of weight loss (or the number of calories that can be eaten without weight gain). Table 2 lists the number of calories burned by a 154-pound subject in each minute of various activities. It is worth noting that some people who are used to inactivity and excessive food intake report that exercise actually decreases the desire for excess food.

The more vigorous the exertion and the longer its duration, the more calories are consumed. Thus, an average person sleeping burns about 1.1 calories per minute. Sitting adds 35 percent and standing 125 percent. Walking at 3, 4, and 5 miles per hour, respectively, burns 4.25, 5.5, and 8.2 calories per minute. Running at 5 miles an hour consumes 9.9 calories a minute, or 108 calories per mile. Vigorous competitive sports may require over 23 calories per minute. These figures all apply to a "standard" person weighing 154 pounds. Table 3 shows how to calculate calorie needs for that "standard" person. To derive similar figures for a particular person requires merely that one multiply the total calories by the weight in pounds of that person and divide by 154.

If you have calculated a diet designed to lose weight, but you are stable or gaining, your calculations may be right but your assumptions wrong. Eat less. Conversely, if you are losing weight on a diet you designed to remain stable or gain, eat more. Remember that the figures given are approximations only and that there is variation not only in the caloric values of various foodstuffs but from person to person. The final judge is the scale.

Table 1: 1983 Metropolitan Height and Weight Tables*

Men

Height:	Feet	Inches	Small Frame	Medium Frame	Large Frame
	5	2	128–134	131–141	133–150
	5	3	130–136	133–143	140–153
	5	4	132–138	135–145	142–156
	5	5	134–140	137–148	144–160
	5	6	136–142	139–151	146–164
	5	7	138–145	142–154	149–168
	5	8	140–148	145–157	152–172
	5	9	142–151	148–160	155–176
	5	10	144–154	151–163	158–180
	5	11	146–157	154–166	161–184
	6	0	149–160	157–170	164–188
	6	1	152–164	160–174	168–192
	6	2	155–168	164–178	172–197
	6	3	158–172	167–182	176–202
	6	4	162–176	171–187	181–207

Women

Height:	Feet	Inches	Small Frame	Medium Frame	Large Frame
	4	10	102–111	109–121	118–131
	4	11	103–113	111–123	120–134
	5	0	104–115	113–126	122–137
	5	1	106–118	115–129	125–140
	5	2	108–121	118–132	128–143
	5	3	111–124	121–135	131–147
	5	4	114–127	124–138	134–151
	5	5	117–130	127–141	137–155
	5	6	120–133	130–144	140–159
	5	7	123–136	133–147	143–163
	5	8	126–139	136–150	146–167
	5	9	129–142	139–153	149–170
	5	10	132–145	142–156	152–173
	5	11	135–148	145–159	155–176
	6	0	138–151	148–162	158–179

Reprinted through the courtesy of Metropolitan Life Insurance Company.

Table 2

Calories per minute	Activity
2 to 2½	Standing, knitting, strolling, playing cards, desk work, driving a car with "power everything."
2½ to 4	Walking at 2 mph, level cycling at 5 mph, golf using a power cart, playing piano.
4 to 5	Walking at 3 mph, level cycling at 6 mph, golf pulling a hand cart, fishing, cleaning windows.
5 to 6	Walking at 3½ mph, level cycling at 8 mph, table tennis, golf carrying clubs, dancing, doubles tennis, painting, paperhanging, light carpentry, calisthenics.
6 to 7	Walking at 4 mph, level cycling at 10 mph, skating, digging in the garden.
7 to 8	Walking at 5 mph, cycling at 11 mph, singles tennis, snow shoveling, lawn cutting with a hand mower, downhill skiing.
8 to 10	Jogging at 5 mph, cycling at 12 mph, basketball, mountain climbing, sawing hardwood, carrying an 80-pound weight, ditch digging.
10 to 11	Running at 5½ mph, cycling at 13 mph, ski touring, playing squash or handball socially, shoveling ten 14-pound shovelfuls per minute.
More than 11	Running faster than 6 mph, competitive squash or handball, shoveling ten 16-pound shovelfuls per minute.

Table 3

Activity	Time in hours or minutes		×	cal/min	=	Total calories
sleeping	8	480	×	1.1	=	528
sitting	7	420	×	1.5	=	630
standing	5	300	×	2.5	=	750
walking	2	120	×	3.0	=	360
other*	2	120	×	5.0	=	600
Total					=	2868

Might include various exercises, such as jogging at 5 mph for 30 minutes of this time and chores about the house, etc.

As a general rule, cardiovascular conditioning is more apt to result from moderate-level, continuous exertion such as cycling or jogging for 20 or more minutes than from more vigorous but intermittent bursts that use the same total amount of energy.

Appendix 3
Characteristics
of Fatty Acids

Nowadays terms like saturated and unsaturated fats, fatty acids, and triglycerides have become commonplace. Hydrogenated and homogenized are equally familiar; and even cis- and trans-isomers are occasionally spoken of in advertising copy. The following brief summary is an explanation of these terms.

A fatty acid is a chain of carbon atoms with a carboxyl group at one end. A carboxyl, or carboxylic acid group, is indicated by

$$-COOH$$

in which C stands for carbon, O for oxygen, and H for hydrogen. Each C has four binding sites, each O has two, and each H has one, indicated as follows:

$$-\overset{|}{\underset{|}{C}}- \qquad\qquad -O- \qquad\qquad -H$$

The C of the carboxyl has two of its binding sites bound to both sites of one oxygen, a third bound to one site of another oxygen, of which the other site is occupied by a hydrogen, and the last site is "available." This can be written in various ways:

$$-C\overset{\diagup O}{\underset{\diagdown O_{\diagdown H}}{}} \qquad\qquad -C\overset{\diagup O}{\underset{\diagdown OH}{}} \qquad\qquad -COOH$$

The fourth, or "available," site is joined to another carbon, thus satisfying the requirement that all the binding sites on the C are utilized. The C to which the fourth site is bound is in turn bound to another C, and it to another, and so on, so that a string of carbons exists. The example given is an 18-carbon chain.

$$-\overset{|}{\underset{|}{C}}-\overset{|}{\underset{|}{C}}-\overset{|}{\underset{|}{C}}-\overset{|}{\underset{|}{C}}-\overset{|}{\underset{|}{C}}-\overset{|}{\underset{|}{C}}-\overset{|}{\underset{|}{C}}-\overset{|}{\underset{|}{C}}-\overset{|}{\underset{|}{C}}-\overset{|}{\underset{|}{C}}-\overset{|}{\underset{|}{C}}-\overset{|}{\underset{|}{C}}-\overset{|}{\underset{|}{C}}-\overset{|}{\underset{|}{C}}-\overset{|}{\underset{|}{C}}-\overset{|}{\underset{|}{C}}-\overset{|}{\underset{|}{C}}-COOH$$

Each of these carbons has two more binding sites except the one farthest to the left, which has three. If each of these binding sites is occupied by a hydrogen, the 18-carbon fatty acid will be indicated by

$$H-\overset{\displaystyle H\ H\ H\ H\ H\ H\ H\ H\ H\ H\ H\ H\ H\ H\ H\ H\ H}{\underset{\displaystyle H\ H\ H\ H\ H\ H\ H\ H\ H\ H\ H\ H\ H\ H\ H\ H\ H}{C-C-C-C-C-C-C-C-C-C-C-C-C-C-C-C-C}}-COOH$$

or CH$_3$ · (CH$_2$)$_{16}$ · COOH. These formulas represent stearic acid. Inasmuch as all the possible sites are "saturated" with hydrogen, the acid is spoken of as a saturated fatty acid.

If, however, there were a double bond between the ninth and tenth carbons (the C of −COOH is numbered 1), the formula would look like this:

$$
\begin{array}{c}
\text{H H H H H H H H H \quad H H H H H H H H H} \\
\text{| | | | | | | | | \qquad | | | | | | | |} \\
\text{H-C-C-C-C-C-C-C-C-C=C-C-C-C-C-C-C-C-COOH} \\
\text{| | | | | | | | \qquad | | | | | | |} \\
\text{H H H H H H H H \qquad H H H H H H H}
\end{array}
$$

and we would have the 18-carbon monounsaturated fatty acid known as oleic acid. Note that the C's joined by the double bond have the hydrogens on the same side.

$$
\begin{array}{c}
\text{H H \quad H H} \\
\text{| | \quad | |} \\
\text{-C-C=C-C-} \\
\text{| \qquad |} \\
\text{H \qquad H}
\end{array}
$$

This indicates the actual arrangement within the molecule itself. There is, however, another acid, elaidic acid, differing from oleic acid only in the spatial arrangement of the hydrogens, so that they are on opposite sides of the C's joined by the double bond.

$$
\begin{array}{c}
\text{H H \qquad H} \\
\text{| | \qquad |} \\
\text{-C-C=C-C-} \\
\text{| \qquad | |} \\
\text{H \qquad H H}
\end{array}
$$

Both forms have the formula CH$_3$ · (CH$_2$)$_7$ · (CH)$_2$ · (CH$_2$)$_7$ · COOH. Such differing forms of nearly identical molecules are called geometric isomers. Those with the hydrogens on the same side are called cis-isomers. Those with hydrogens on the opposite side are called trans-isomers. The distinction needs to be made because the biologic behavior may differ depending upon the isomer, trans-isomers tending to resemble saturated fats.

If there is more than one double bond the fatty acid is called polyunsaturated. The three encountered most commonly are an 18-carbon fatty acid with two double bonds called linoleic acid, an 18-carbon fatty acid with three double bonds called linolenic acid, and a 20-carbon fatty acid with four double bonds called arachidonic acid.

Unsaturated fats tend to be liquid and saturated fats tend to be solid at room temperature. It is sometimes inconvenient for cosmetic or other reasons to have oil in a food product. Food chemists have learned that they can alter unsaturated fats by saturating them (partly or wholly) with hydrogen. The process is known as hydrogenation. A common example is the oil in peanut butter, which is hydrogenated to make it saturated. The oil, now solidified, no longer tends to separate. The product has been homogenized via the process of hydrogenation.

Appendix 4
Calculating Nutrients

$\mathbf{T}$his appendix contains instructions for calculating the nutritional breakdown of individual recipes or of a whole day's intake. The data needed for these calculations are in the table beginning on page 484; provided are the number of calories, the milligrams of cholesterol, the grams of protein, the grams of carbohydrate, the grams of fat, and the breakdown of that fat (when figures are available) into saturated, monounsaturated, and polyunsaturated components in a 100-gram (approximately 3 1/2-ounce) edible portion of each food listed. A blank means that there is less than 0.1 gram or none at all, or that data are not available.

Figure 1 shows a worksheet designed to facilitate the handling of the information. To calculate the nutritional data for a given recipe follow the steps listed below.

We have used the recipe for pasta with clams and zucchini (page 115) as an example. A nutritional summary for a whole day's food can be calculated in a similar manner by entering the data for a serving of each food eaten during the day on a separate line and adding up the columns.

Step 1: List in the column farthest to the left the ingredients called for in the recipe and the amount of each. In a given recipe the amounts may be expressed in units of weight such as grams and kilograms or ounces and pounds; in units of volume such as tablespoons, fluid ounces, or cups; or in arbitrary units such as "1 medium tomato."

Step 2: If the amount called for is not exactly 100 grams the number of grams must be determined and that number must be divided by 100 to yield a factor. The factor should be placed in parentheses alongside the ingredient and the amount. Appropriate conversion information will be found under "Amounts" for each foodstuff in the table. Thus, we learn that the meat of 4 cherrystone clams weighs 70 grams. Six clams, or 1 1/2 times as many, must weigh 1 1/2 times as much, or 105 grams. The factor for 6 clams is, therefore, 105 ÷ 100 = 1.05.

Step 3: In the table find the values for calories, protein, carbohydrate, etc., for 100 grams of raw clam meat and multiply each of these values by the factor 1.05. Enter these results on the worksheet.

Step 4: Carry out similar calculations for each ingredient in the recipe and enter the results on the worksheet.

Step 5: Add up each column and enter the totals on the worksheet and in the special box illustrated in Figure 2. A similar box summarizing the nutritional data appears after each of our recipes.

Step 6: Multiply the total grams of fat in the recipe by 8.8 (the calories per gram of fat), divide by the total calories in the recipe, and multiply by 100 to find the percentage of calories in the recipe derived from fat. Enter the percentage in Figure 2.

Step 7: Multiply the grams of saturated fat in the recipe by 8.8, divide by the total calories, and multiply by 100 to find the percentage of calories in the recipe derived from saturated fat. Enter the percentage in the special box. The special box now contains the nutritional data for the entire recipe. If it serves four, an individual serving has one quarter of each of the items listed; note, however, that the percentages of calories derived from total fat and from saturated fat respectively are the same per individual serving as for the entire recipe.

We have not listed ingredient-by-ingredient breakdowns as on the worksheets; it is a simple though time-consuming exercise to do so. In subjecting recipes from other sources or of your own invention to analysis it is necessary to go through this series of steps. Those of you who wish to analyze recipes can follow the steps outlined above utilizing data in the table on pages 484–502; and those of you who have home computers can readily use this information as the data base of a program for analyzing recipes. It is desirable to program conversions so that it is possible to enter the computer with various kinds of measurements, i.e., tablespoons, cups, grams, pounds, and units such as "1 large tomato." The computer must be told that there are 2 large, 3 medium, 8 to 9 plum, or 24 cherry tomatoes in a pound and that 1 cup = 8 fluid ounces, 1 fluid ounce = 2 tablespoons, and 1 tablespoon = 3 teaspoons. It also needs to know that 1 cup of chopped tomatoes weighs about 227 grams. The information in memory relating to the nutritional data of tomato is that 100 grams has 22 calories, 1.1 grams of protein, 4.2 grams of digestible carbohydrate, and 0.2 gram of fat. There are no data available on the breakdown of the fat into saturated, monounsaturated, and polyunsaturated components.

Figure 1

Pasta with Clams and Zucchini

Ingredient & Amount	Factor	Calories	Cholest	Protein	Carbo	Fat	Sat	Mono	Poly
6 cherrystone clams	(1.05)	84	53 mg.	11.7	6.2	0.9	—	—	—
½ lb. pasta	(2.27)	837	—	28.4	170.6	2.7	—	—	—
1 Tb. olive oil	(0.135)	119	—	—	—	13.5	1.8	9.9	1.1
1 Tb. safflower oil	(0.136)	120	—	—	—	13.6	1.2	1.6	10.1
2 cloves garlic	(0.06)	8	—	0.4	1.8	—	—	—	—
1 Tb. minced fresh ginger	(0.05)	10	—	0.3	1.9	0.2	—	—	—
2 Tb. minced parsley	(0.07)	3	—	0.3	0.5	—	—	—	—
2 small zucchini	(3.0)	51	—	3.6	9.0	0.3	—	—	—
salt	(0.0)	—	—	—	—	—	—	—	—
TOTALS		1232	53 mg.	44.7 g.	188.2 g.	31.2 g.	3.0 g.	11.5 g.	11.2 g.

Figure 2

Calories	Cholesterol	Protein	Carbohydrate	Total fat		Sat fat		Mono	Poly
	mg	gm	gm	gm	%	gm	%	gm	gm
1232	53	44.7	188.2	31.2	22	3.0	2	11.5	11.2

Appendix 5
Menu Selection

Menu selection must satisfy both appetite and the requirements that calories, cholesterol, total fat, saturated fat, and polyunsaturated fat fall within certain limits. Appetite is a highly personal matter, and, therefore, highly variable. For this reason we have avoided the rigidity of fixed menus. We prefer that you learn the few simple principles you should follow in selecting foods that appeal to you. In return for the effort of learning how to make the calculations and of making them, you gain greater latitude in menu choices.

First, by eliminating eggs, gizzard, shrimp, brains, squid, and organ meats and by using only those recipes that fulfill the recommendations for fats set forth on page 12, you do not have to concern yourself with either the cholesterol content of the diet or the P:S ratio. You need only control total calories and total fat.

Suppose the menu is for a rather sedentary 154-pound person who needs only 15 calories for each pound of weight daily, a total of 2310 calories. Of that total, 30 percent can be from fat, or 693 calories, the energy of 78.8 grams of fat (693 calories ÷ 8.8 calories per g. = 78.8 g.). Let us suppose that our subject starts the day with the hearty but fat-controlled breakfast detailed on page 459. This meal uses 457 of the allowed calories and 13.7 grams of the permitted fat content, leaving to be eaten later in the day 1853 calories and 65.1 grams of fat.

Lunch — consisting of 1/6 the pasta with peppers recipe (page 100), 1/4 the salad in the style of the Marches recipe (page 417), a chunk of French bread, a fresh peach, and a cup of tea or coffee with 1 teaspoon sugar — totals 720 calories and 16.9 grams of fat, leaving for the rest of the day 1133 calories and 48.2 grams of fat.

If the evening meal begins with a prima piatto of 2 ounces pasta (209 calories, 0.7 grams of fat) and 2 tablespoons pesto (page 426) (133 calories, 13.5 grams of fat), there are still 791 calories and 34.0 grams of fat in the day's ration. How will these be distributed? Should he save something for a bedtime snack? Does he want a salad? Should there be a rich dessert and a less rich main course, or should he have fruit for dessert and use more of the calories and fat in the main course? For that matter, should lunch be reconsidered? Or perhaps the subject might have had a smaller breakfast, for example the Indian dosa with a cup of tea; the "saving" would have amounted to 286 calories and 10.4 grams of fat. Obviously, these questions will be answered differently by different persons and by the same person on different days.

Let us continue with our example. A main course consisting of ¼ of the fillet of sole primavera recipe (page 212), ⅙ of the recipe for potato balls (page 367), and ½ of the recipe for steamed asparagus (page 341) accounts for 659 calories and 31.5 grams of fat, leaving 132 calories and 2.5 grams of fat. Four ounces of dry white wine (100 calories, 0 fat) bring the subject to the end of the allowable calories for the day. We have actually limited the calories from fat to 29 percent, an improvement over the 30 percent for which we were aiming. Note, however, that we ran out of calories without providing a dessert. Many people would be perfectly happy to go without; those who would not, have various options available. They could eat smaller portions, they could substitute less caloric recipes for one or more of those in the example, or they could be physically more active than the sedentary example we have chosen.

We would not like to leave the impression with you that the numbers given are anything more than rough approximations, even though we have "measured" down to a tenth of gram. The data upon which the numbers are based are from limited tests on foodstuffs that vary according to freshness, source, season, and a great variety of other factors. Despite these imperfections, the data do offer the best guide we have to diet design.

You will note from the table below, which summarizes the nutritional data of the day's food, that each recipe satisfies the requirement that saturated fat be no more than ⅓ the total fat and that there be at least as much polyunsaturated fat. Some of the recipes in this book do not live up to this requirement. They may be used despite this, provided there is an excess of polyunsaturated fat in other recipes or foods to offset the excess of saturated fat in a particular item.

Viewing the whole day's food in tabular form makes it easy to see how foods that must be limited in amount can be integrated into the day's menu without violating the overall requirements. This applies even to red meat and cheese. It is also clear that the 150 milligrams of cholesterol in 100 grams of shrimp, the 220 milligrams in 100 grams of squid, and the 145 milligrams of cholesterol in 100 grams of chicken gizzard are well within the 300 milligrams limitation for cholesterol and can readily be tolerated, provided there is not much other cholesterol in the day's food. The unique feature of shrimp, squid and gizzards is that the addition to total fat is very small at the same time the addition to total cholesterol is large.

	Calories	Cholest	Protein	Carbo	Fat	Sat	Mono	Poly
Breakfast summarized (see pages 458–60)	457	2	26.3	57.2	13.7	2.7	1.7	5.1
⅙ recipe pasta with peppers	456	0	13.7	78.9	10.7	0.9	5.5	2.1
¼ recipe salad Marches style	89	0	2.3	9.4	4.9	0.6	2.6	1.1
1 slice French bread	102	0	3.2	19.4	1.1			
1 peach	58	0	0.9	13.9	0.2			
1 tsp. sugar	15	0		4.0				
2 oz. pasta	209	0	7.1	42.6	0.7			
2 Tb. pesto	133	0	1.8	2.3	13.5	1.1	4.8	6.1
½ recipe sole primavera	319	86	33.9	18.1	12.3	1.1	3.3	5.3
½ recipe steamed asparagus	154	16	3.6	8.2	12.8	3.8	2.7	5.2
¼ recipe potato balls	186	0	5.2	27.5	6.4	0.5	3.2	1.6
4 oz. dry white wine	100	0		4.8				
TOTALS	2278	104	98.0	286.3	76.3	10.7	23.8	26.5

Nutritional Data for 100 Gram Amounts of Commonly Used Foods

ITEMS & USEFUL MEASURES		CALORIES	CHOLEST.	PROTEIN	CARBO.	FAT	SAT.	MONO.	POLY.	NOTES
allspice, ground 1 tsp = 1.9 g.		263	0	0.1	50.5	8.7	2.6	0.7	2.4	
almonds 1 c., whole = 142 g. 1 c., chopped = 130 g. 1 c., sliced = 95 g.		598	0	18.6	16.9	54.2	4.3	36.3	10.8	
amaranth leaves		36	0	3.5	5.2	0.5	—	—	—	
anchovies 1 canned fillet = 4 g. Substitute 2 fillets for 1 salted anchovy		176	55	19.2	0.3	10.3	4.0	3.0	3.0	
anise seeds 1 tsp. = 2.1 g.		337	0	17.6	35.4	15.9	—	9.8	3.2	
apple, peeled 1 c., sliced = 110 g. 1 c., chopped = 125 g.		54	0	0.2	13.5	0.3	—	—	—	
arrowroot 1 Tb. = 8 g.		363	0	—	87.5	—	—	—	—	
artichoke, globe	max. min.	47 9	0	2.9	note 1	0.1	—	—	—	1

artichoke, Jerusalem
 	
 1 lb. = 13 oz.
  peeled = 3 c., sliced
  or chopped (raw)
	max.
	min.
		75
		7
			0	2.3	note 1	0.1	—	—	—	1

artichoke hearts		35	0	2.4	8.2	—	—	—	—	

asparagus
 14 spears 9–10″
  × ½–¾″ = 1 lb.
 1 c. trimmed pieces =
  150 g.
		26	0	2.5	4.3	0.2	—	—	—	

avocado 3 c. pieces = 1 lb.		167	0	2.1	4.7	16.4	3.3	7.4	2.1	

Cholest. = cholesterol in milligrams; carbo. = carbohydrate in grams; sat. = saturated fatty acids in grams; mono. = monounsaturated fatty acids in grams; poly. = polyunsaturated fatty acids in grams; protein and fat are in grams.
0 = none at all; a dash indicates that there is too little to record, none, or that data is not available. Many of the breakdowns are incomplete. Most of the time the total fat is more than the sum of the sat., mono., and poly. components because there are other classes of fats and because the breakdowns are incomplete. Many of the plant products have no separation into component fats; there is probably more polyunsaturated than saturated fat in the great majority of these.
1 lb. = 454 g. or 4.54 × 100 g.; ¾ lb. = 3.4 × 100 g.; ½ lb. = 2.3 × 100 g.; ¼ lb. = 1.1 × 100 g.
Abbreviations used: c. = cup; Tb. = tablespoon; tsp. = teaspoon; lb. = pound; g. = gram; med. = medium

[1]The major carbohydrate in fresh artichoke is nondigestible inulin, which is progressively converted to assimilable sugars in storage.

Nutritional Data for 100 Gram Amounts of Commonly Used Foods

ITEMS & USEFUL MEASURES	CALORIES	CHOLEST.	PROTEIN	CARBO.	FAT	SAT.	MONO.	POLY.	NOTES
baking powder 1 tsp. = 3 g.	78	0	0.1	18.9	—	—	—	—	
banana 1 med. (8¾" × 1¹³/₃₂") = 175 g., of which 119 g. are edible	85	0	1.1	21.7	0.2	—	—	—	
barley, pearl, light 1 c. = 200 g.	349	0	8.2	78.3	1.0	—	—	—	
basil, dried 1 tsp. = 1.4 g.	251	0	14.4	43.2	4.0	—	—	—	
basil, fresh 1 c. = 35 g.	40	0	2.3	9.7	0.6	—	—	—	
bass, freshwater approx. 31% edible	104	55	18.9	—	2.6	1.0	1.0	—	
bass, striped	105	55	18.9	—	2.7	1.0	1.0	—	
bay leaf	—	—	—	—	—	—	—	—	2
beans, broad, dried (fava beans) 1 c. = 130 g.	338	0	25.1	51.5	1.7	—	—	—	3
beans, broad, fresh (fava beans) 1 c. = 45 g.	105	0	8.4	15.6	0.4	—	—	—	
beans, common white 1 c. Great Northern = 180 g. 1 c. pea (navy) = 205 g. 1 c. raw beans = 3 c. cooked	340	0	22.3	57.0	1.6	—	—	—	3
beans, lima, dried 1 c. Fordhooks = 180 g. 1 c. baby limas = 190 g.	345	0	20.4	59.7	1.6	—	—	—	3
beans, lima, fresh 1 c. = 155 g.	123	0	8.4	20.3	0.5	—	—	—	
beans, pinto (calico) 1 c. = 190 g.	349	0	22.9	59.4	1.2	—	—	—	3

[2] Bay leaf should always be removed after cooking lest it be inadvertently swallowed and perforate the intestine; no food value need be calculated.

[3] 1 c. of dried beans expands to about 3 c. when cooked.

Nutritional Data for 100 Gram Amounts of Commonly Used Foods

ITEMS & USEFUL MEASURES	CALORIES	CHOLEST.	PROTEIN	CARBO.	FAT	SAT.	MONO.	POLY.	NOTES
beans, red 1 c. = 185 g.	343	0	22.5	57.7	1.5	—	—	—	3
beans, snap or green 4 c. = 1 lb. (4 servings)	32	0	1.9	6.1	0.2	—	—	—	
beef, chuck	158	68	21.3	—	7.4	3.6	3.3	0.1	4
beef, flank steak	144	68	21.6	—	5.7	2.7	2.5	0.1	4
beef, foreshank	141	68	21.6	—	5.4	2.6	2.4	0.1	4
beef, hind shank	134	68	21.7	—	4.6	2.2	2.0	0.1	4
beef, round	135	68	21.6	—	4.7	2.3	2.1	0.1	4
beer	48	0	0.6	4.4	—	—	—	—	5

beet greens
1 pound yields 11 oz.
  trimmed greens = 8 c.
  loosely packed =
  1½ c. cooked
	24	0	2.2	3.3	0.3	—	—	—	

beet root
5 med. beets (2–2½″
  size), trimmed = 1 lb.
1 lb. = 2½ c. cooked
  (refuse is 30%)
	43	0	1.6	9.1	0.1	—	—	—	

blueberries	62	0	0.7	13.8	0.5	—	—	—	
bluefish 51% edible	117	55	20.5	—	3.3	1.0	—	1.0	
bread, Italian 1 slice = 30 g.	276	0	9.1	56.2	0.8	—	—	—	
breadcrumbs, dried 1 c. = 100 g.	392	0	12.6	73.1	4.6	1.1	2.1	1.2	
breadcrumbs, fresh 1 c. = 45 g.	271	0	8.7	50.4	3.1	—	—	—	
broccoli 1 bunch = ½–1½ lbs. 1 lb. = 4 c. flowerettes weighing 220 g.	32	0	3.6	4.4	0.3	—	—	—	

[4] All beef cuts are choice grade, separable fat removed.

[5] Each gram of alcohol represents 6.9 calories. If, however, the alcoholic beverage is added to a recipe before cooking, the alcohol is assumed to boil off and contribute nothing to the nutritional total.

Nutritional Data for 100 Gram Amounts of Commonly Used Foods

ITEMS & USEFUL MEASURES	CALORIES	CHOLEST.	PROTEIN	CARBO.	FAT	SAT.	MONO.	POLY.	NOTES
Brussels sprouts 1 lb. = 1¼"–1½" diameter sprouts	45	0	4.9	6.7	0.4	—	—	—	
butter 1 stick = ½ c. = 113.4 g. 1 Tb. = 14.2 g.	717	219	0.9	0.1	81.1	50.5	23.4	3.0	
butterfish 51% edible	169	55	18.1	—	10.2	2.0	—	2.0	
buttermilk 1 c. = 245 g.	36	2	3.6	5.1	0.1	—	—	—	6
cabbage 1 lb. = 5 c. sliced or shredded	24	0	1.3	4.6	0.2	—	—	—	
cantaloupe	30	0	0.7	7.2	0.1	—	—	—	
capers	No figures available.								
capon	See figures for chicken.								
caraway seeds 1 tsp. = 2.0 g.	333	0	19.8	37.3	14.6	0.6	7.1	3.3	
cardamon, ground 1 tsp. = 2.1 g.	311	0	10.8	57.2	6.7	0.7	0.9	0.4	
carp 30% edible	115	55	18.0	—	4.2	1.0	—	1.0	
carrots 1 lb. = 3¼ c. sliced, chopped, or grated 1 med. carrot = 50 g.	42	0	1.1	8.7	0.2	—	—	—	
cashews 1 c. = 140 g.	561	0	17.2	27.9	45.7	7.8	32.0	3.2	
catfish approx. 44% edible	103	55	17.6	—	3.1	1.0	—	1.0	
cauliflower 1 med. = 1½ lbs. 100 g. trimmed = 1 c. pieces	27	0	2.7	4.2	0.2	—	—	—	

[6]Cultured from skim milk.

Nutritional Data for 100 Gram Amounts of Commonly Used Foods

ITEMS & USEFUL MEASURES	CALORIES	CHOLEST.	PROTEIN	CARBO.	FAT	SAT.	MONO.	POLY.	NOTES
caviar, sturgeon 1 Tb. = 16 g.	262	300	26.9	3.3	15.0	—	—	—	

celeriac
1 lb. whole =
  ½ lb. trimmed =
  2 c. chopped
	40	0	1.8	7.2	0.3	—	—	—	

celery 1 stalk 8 × 1½″ = 40 g. 1 c. raw = 100 g.	17	0	0.9	3.3	0.1	—	—	—	
celery seeds 1 tsp. = 2.0 g.	392	0	18.1	29.5	25.3	2.2	15.9	3.7	

chard, Swiss
1 lb. = ½ lb. ribs and
  ½ lb. leaves,
  i.e., 1–1½ servings of each
	25	0	2.4	3.8	0.3	—	—	—	

cheeses									
cottage, 1% fat 1 c., unpacked = 226 g.	72	9	12.4	2.7	1.0	0.6	0.3	—	

cottage, creamed,
  4½% fat
  1 c., unpacked = 210 g.
  4½% fat
	103	15	12.5	2.7	4.5	2.9	1.3	0.1	

Gorgonzola	No figures available; see Roquefort.								
Mozzarella	281	78	19.4	2.2	21.6	13.2	6.6	0.8	
Parmesan 1 Tb. = 5g.	456	113	41.6	3.7	30.0	19.1	8.7	0.7	
Ricotta	174	51	11.3	3.0	13.0	8.3	3.6	0.4	
Romano	387	104	31.8	3.6	26.9	17.1	7.8	0.6	
Roquefort	369	90	21.5	2.0	30.6	19.3	8.5	1.3	
chervil, dried 1 tsp. = 0.6 g.	237	0	23.2	37.8	3.9	—	—	—	

chestnuts, dried
1 c. = ⅜ lb.;
  when soaked overnight
  use volume called for
  in recipe
	377	0	6.7	76.1	4.1	—	2.0	1.0	

chestnuts, fresh 1 lb. in shell = 13 oz. shelled = 2⅓ c.	194	0	2.9	41.0	1.5	—	0.7	0.4	
chicken, dark meat 1 c. chopped = 140 g.	130	91	20.6	—	4.7	1.5	1.8	0.9	7

Nutritional Data for 100 Gram Amounts of Commonly Used Foods

ITEMS & USEFUL MEASURES	CALORIES	CHOLEST.	PROTEIN	CARBO.	FAT	SAT.	MONO.	POLY.	NOTES
chicken, white meat 1 c. chopped = 140 g.	117	67	23.4	—	1.9	—	—	—	7
chicken gizzard 1 c. pieces cooked = 145 g.	113	145	20.1	0.7	2.7	1.0	1.0	—	
chick peas, dried (Ceci beans, garbanzos) 100 g. = 1/2 c. 1 c. raw = 3 c. cooked 1 20-oz. can = 2 1/4 c., drained	360	0	20.5	56.0	4.8	0.4	2.4	1.7	3
chicory 1 lb. = 4 c. cut up = 1 c. cooked	15	0	1.0	2.7	0.1	—	—	—	
chili pepper, green excluding seeds	37	0	1.3	7.3	0.2	—	—	—	
chili pepper, red excluding seeds	65	0	2.3	13.5	0.4	—	—	—	
chili powder 1 tsp. = 2.6 g.	314	0	12.3	32.4	16.8	—	—	—	
chives 1 Tb. chopped = 3 g.	28	0	1.8	4.7	0.3	—	—	—	
cinnamon, ground 1 tsp. = 2.3 g.	261	0	3.9	55.5	3.2	0.7	0.5	0.5	
clam meat 4 cherrystones or 5 littlenecks = 70 g.	80	90	11.1	5.9	0.9	—	—	—	
cloves 1 tsp. = 2.1 g.	323	0	6.0	51.6	20.1	4.4	—	—	
cod, fresh 31% edible	78	50	17.6	—	0.3	—	—	—	
cod, dried	130	82	29.0	—	0.7	—	—	—	
collard greens leaves only 1 lb. with stems = 1/2 lb. stemmed = 7-8 cups packed leaves = 1 1/2 c. cooked	45	0	4.8	6.3	0.8	—	—	—	

[7]Of a whole chicken, approximately 20% is light meat and 20% dark meat.

Nutritional Data for 100 Gram Amounts of Commonly Used Foods

ITEMS & USEFUL MEASURES	CALORIES	CHOLEST.	PROTEIN	CARBO.	FAT	SAT.	MONO.	POLY.	NOTES
coriander, dried leaf 1 tsp. = 0.6 g.	279	0	21.8	41.7	4.8	—	—	—	
coriander seeds 1 tsp. = 1.8 g.	298	0	12.4	25.9	17.8	1.0	13.6	1.8	
corn 1 c. kernels = 165 g.; 　45% of corn on cob 　is cob.	96	0	3.5	21.4	1.0	—	—	—	
Cornish hens	No figures available; similar to chicken.								
cornmeal 1 c. = 122 g.	355	0	9.2	72.1	3.9	0.4	1.3	1.7	
cornstarch 1 Tb. = 8 g.	362	0	0.3	87.6	—	—	—	—	
crab, steamed 1 c. pieces = 155 g.	93	100	17.3	0.5	1.9	—	—	—	
cream, ½ & ½ 1 c. = 242 g.	130	37	3.0	4.3	11.5	7.2	3.3	0.4	
cream, heavy whipping 1 c. = 238 g.	345	137	2.1	2.8	37.0	23.0	10.7	1.4	
cream, light coffee 1 c. = 240 g.	211	66	3.0	4.3	20.6	11.3	6.8	0.6	
cream, light whipping 1 c. = 239 g.	292	111	2.2	3.0	30.9	19.3	9.1	0.9	
cream substitute	See Polyperx.								
cranberry beans	See beans, pinto.								
cucumber 1 8 × 2″ = ½ lb. = 　2 c. slices	14	0	0.6	2.9	—	—	—	—	
cumin seed 1 tsp. = 2.1 g.	375	0	17.8	33.7	22.3	—	—	—	
dandelion greens 1 c. loose greens = 105 g.	45	0	2.7	7.6	0.7	—	—	—	
dates 1 c. chopped = 178 g.	274	0	2.2	70.6	0.5	—	—	—	

Nutritional Data for 100 Gram Amounts of Commonly Used Foods

ITEMS & USEFUL MEASURES	CALORIES	CHOLEST.	PROTEIN	CARBO.	FAT	SAT.	MONO.	POLY.	NOTES
duck meat, domestic approx. ⅓ of the duck is meat	165	81	21.4	—	8.2	2.0	2.0	2.0	
duck meat, wild approx. ⅓ of the duck is meat	123	80	20.0	—	4.3	1.3	1.2	0.6	
eel	233	55	15.9	—	18.3	4.0	7.0	—	
Egg Beaters ¼ c. = 60 g. = equivalent of 1 large egg	50	0	10.0	1.6	—	—	—	—	
Egg Replacer 1 tsp. = 2.8 g.	357	0	—	71.4	—	—	—	—	8
egg whites white of 1 large egg = 33 g.	49	0	10.1	1.2	—	—	—	—	
eggplant 1 lb. diced = 4 c. raw = 2 c. cooked	25	0	1.2	4.7	0.2	—	—	—	
endive 1 lb. = 4 c. cut up = 1 c. cooked	15	0	1.0	2.7	0.1	—	—	—	
escarole 1 lb. = 4 c.	20	0	1.7	3.2	0.1	—	—	—	

fennel leaves
1 lb. = 12 oz. trimmed =
    2½ to 3 c. chopped
    or sliced, 2¼ c. cooked
	28	0	2.8	4.6	0.4	—	—	—	

fennel seeds 1 tsp. = 2.0 g.	345	0	15.8	36.6	14.9	0.5	9.9	1.7	
filberts 1 c. whole, shelled filberts = 135 g.	634	0	12.6	13.7	62.4	3.1	33.7	10.0	
flounder/sole approx. ⅓ of the fish is edible	79	50	16.7	—	0.8	—	—	—	
flour, all-purpose wheat 1 c. = 137 g.	364	0	10.5	75.8	1.0	—	—	—	
flour, whole wheat 1 c. = 120 g.	333	0	13.3	68.7	2.0	—	—	—	

[8]Jolly Joan Egg Replacer contains arrowroot, potato starch, tapioca flour, modified vegetable gums, and cereal-free leavening.

Nutritional Data for 100 Gram Amounts of Commonly Used Foods

ITEMS & USEFUL MEASURES	CALORIES	CHOLEST.	PROTEIN	CARBO.	FAT	SAT.	MONO.	POLY.	NOTES

frogs' legs
a pair of frozen legs
  averages 80 g. of which
  65% is edible
	73	50	16.4	—	0.3	—	—	—	

garlic 1 clove = 3 g. = 1 tsp. chopped	137	0	6.2	29.3	0.2	—	—	—	
gelatin, dry	335	0	85.6	—	0.1	—	—	—	
ginger, dried ground 1 tsp. = 1.8 g.	347	0	9.1	64.9	6.0	—	—	—	
ginger, fresh 1 Tb. chopped = 5 g.	49	0	1.4	8.4	1.0	—	—	—	
grapefruit	41	0	0.5	10.4	0.1	—	—	—	
grapes ·	69	0	1.3	15.1	1.0	—	—	—	
guinea hen approx. 64% edible	110	63	20.6	—	2.5	—	—	—	
haddock 48% edible	79	60	18.3	—	0.1	—	—	—	
halibut 59% edible	100	50	20.9	—	1.2	—	—	—	
honey 1 c. = 339 g.	304	0	0.3	82.3	—	—	—	—	
horse meat	121	—	20.5	—	3.7	—	—	—	
horseradish ½ lb. raw = 1½ c., grated	87	0	3.2	17.3	0.3	—	—	—	

lamb, leg, choice,
  trimmed of
  separable fat
	130	71	19.9	—	5.0	2.8	1.8	0.2	

leeks 1 large = 75 g. 1 med. = 50 g. 1 c., chopped = ¼ pound	52	0	2.2	9.9	0.3	—	—	—	

lemon juice
4 average lemons weigh
  1 pound and yield
  ¾ c. juice
	25	0	1.2	10.7	0.3	—	—	—	

lemon peel	No figures available.								

Nutritional Data for 100 Gram Amounts of Commonly Used Foods

ITEMS & USEFUL MEASURES	CALORIES	CHOLEST.	PROTEIN	CARBO.	FAT	SAT.	MONO.	POLY.	NOTES
lentils 1 c. = 190 g.	340	0	24.7	56.2	1.1	—	—	—	
lettuce 1 large, 2 medium, or 3 small leaves = 15 g.	14	0	1.2	2.0	0.2	—	—	—	
lime juice 1 Tb. = 15.4 g.	26	0	0.3	9.0	0.1	—	—	—	
liqueurs, fruit-flavored	320	0	—	30.0	—	—	—	—	5
lobster approx. ¼ the weight of a raw lobster is edible meat	91	77	16.9	0.5	1.9	—	—	—	
mackerel 54% edible	191	95	19.0	—	12.2	4.0	4.0	4.0	
mako shark	No figures available; see swordfish.								
mango	66	0	0.7	15.9	0.4	—	—	—	
margarine 1 Tb. = 14 g.	714	0	—	—	78.6	14.3	—	28.6	9
marjoram, dried 1 tsp. = 0.6 g.	271	0	12.7	42.5	7.0	—	—	—	
milk, evap. skim 1 c. = 256 g.	80	4	7.2	11.2	0.3	—	—	—	
milk, non-fat dry	363	8	35.9	52.3	0.8	0.4	0.2	—	
milk, skim 5 level Tbs. = 22.7 g. and reconstitutes to 1 c. fluid skim milk.	35	2	3.4	4.9	0.2	0.1	—	—	
milk, whole 1 c. = 244 g.	64	14	3.3	4.7	3.7	2.3	1.1	0.1	
mint, dried 1 Tb. = 1.3 g.	276	0	22.4	41.3	4.4	—	—	—	
monkfish 45% edible	81	35	15.5	1.4	1.5	—	—	—	
mullet 53% edible	146	55	19.6	—	6.9	2.0	2.0	—	

[9]Data are for Fleischmann's corn oil stick margarine.

Nutritional Data for 100 Gram Amounts of Commonly Used Foods

ITEMS & USEFUL MEASURES	CALORIES	CHOLEST.	PROTEIN	CARBO.	FAT	SAT.	MONO.	POLY.	NOTES
mushrooms, dried	275	0	12.5	59.5	1.6	—	—	—	
mushrooms, fresh 1 c. = 70 g.	28	0	2.7	3.6	0.3	—	—	—	
mussels 12 mussels in shell = 1 lb., yielding 131 g. of meat	95	50	14.4	3.2	2.2	—	—	—	
mustard greens 1 lb. of leaves = 14-16 c.	31	0	3.0	4.5	0.5	—	—	—	
mustard, prepared 1 tsp. = 5 g.	75	0	4.7	5.4	4.4	—	—	—	
nutmeg 1 tsp = 2.2 g.	525	0	5.8	45.3	36.3	25.9	3.2	0.4	
oats, rolled 1 serving = 28 g. = 1/3 c.	390	0	14.2	67.0	7.4	1.6	2.4	3.0	
ocean perch 31% edible	95	55	19.0	—	1.5	—	—	—	
octopus	73	124	15.3	—	0.8	—	—	—	
oil, corn 1 Tb. = 13.6 g.	884	0	—	—	100.0	12.7	24.2	58.7	10
oil, olive 1 Tb. = 13.5 g.	884	0	—	—	100.0	13.5	73.7	8.4	10
oil, peanut 1 Tb. = 13.5 g.	884	0	—	—	100.0	18.0	47.0	29.0	10
oil, safflower 1 Tb. = 13.6 g.	884	0	—	—	100.0	9.1	12.1	74.5	10

[10]As far as we know, the nutritional content of all olive oils is very similar, but flavor and use vary considerably. For cooking it is best to use an oil that is light in both flavor and color, such as Sasso, Calistro Francesconi, or Filippo Berio, all of which are packed in Italy. They can be mixed with an oil such as safflower both to affect the balance of saturated and polyunsaturated fats in the diet and to offset the tendency for olive oil to become heavier and heavier the longer the cooking time.

A second category of oils includes three Italian oils—Colavita, Siala, and Madre Sicilia—and Goya, a Spanish oil. These deep yellow oils should be used raw, for example in salads, or to add flavor at the very end of the cooking.

A third category of olive oils is now becoming available in the United States—the bright green extra virgin oils. Stronger in flavor than the lighter oils but not as strong as the heavy oils, they should be used only raw for their divine flavor. They are quite expensive. We can recommend Amastra, Antinori, Raineri, and Badia a Coltibuono.

We suggest that olive oil not be used for frying; corn, peanut, and safflower oils are superior for that.

Nutritional Data for 100 Gram Amounts of Commonly Used Foods

ITEMS & USEFUL MEASURES	CALORIES	CHOLEST.	PROTEIN	CARBO.	FAT	SAT.	MONO.	POLY.	NOTES
oil, soy 1 Tb. = 13.6 g.	884	0	—	—	100.0	14.4	23.3	57.9	
oil, sunflower 1 Tb. = 13.6 g.	884	0	—	—	100.0	10.3	19.5	65.7	
oil, walnut 1 Tb. = 13.6 g.	884	0	—	—	100.0	9.1	22.8	63.3	
okra 1 lb. yields 10-12 oz. trimmed okra = 3-4 c., sliced	36	0	2.4	6.6	0.3	—	—	—	
olives, dried 10 med. = 24 g.	338	0	2.2	4.9	35.8	3.9	27.2	2.5	
olives, green 10 large olives = 46 g.	116	0	1.4	—	12.7	1.4	9.7	0.9	
olives, ripe 10 med. mission olives = 40 g.	184	0	1.2	1.7	20.1	2.2	15.3	1.4	
onion blossoms	No figures available; see squash flowers.								
onions 1 large = 340 g. 1 med. = 180 g. 1 small = 50 g. 4 c., sliced = 454 g.	38	0	1.5	8.1	0.1	—	—	—	
oranges 1 c. peeled and trimmed = 86 g.	49	0	1.0	11.7	0.2	—	—	—	
orange juice 1 c. = 248 g.	45	0	0.7	10.3	0.2	—	—	—	
oregano, dried 1 tsp. = 1.5 g.	306	0	11.0	49.5	10.3	2.7	0.7	5.2	
oyster meat meat is 10% of total weight	66	50	8.4	3.3	1.8	—	—	—	
parsley, dried 1 Tb. = 1.3 g.	276	0	22.4	41.3	4.4	—	—	—	
parsley, fresh 1 Tb., chopped = 3.5 g.	44	0	3.6	7.0	0.6	—	—	—	

Nutritional Data for 100 Gram Amounts of Commonly Used Foods

ITEMS & USEFUL MEASURES	CALORIES	CHOLEST.	PROTEIN	CARBO.	FAT	SAT.	MONO.	POLY.	NOTES
parsnips	76	0	1.7	15.5	0.5	—	—	—	
pasta Depending on shape and size, 1 c. small pasta = 100 to 160 g.	369	0	12.5	74.9	1.2	—	—	—	
peaches 1 peeled, 2¾ inch diameter = 175 g.	38	0	0.6	9.1	0.1	—	—	—	
peanuts 1 c. chopped = 144 g.	568	0	26.3	15.7	48.4	10.0	20.0	14.0	
pears 1 average = 180 g.	61	0	0.7	13.9	0.4	—	—	—	
peas, blackeyed 1 c. = 145 g.	127	0	9.0	20.0	0.5	—	—	—	
peas, dried 1 c. = 200 g.	340	0	24.1	55.4	1.3	—	—	—	
peas, fresh 1 c. = 145 g. 1 lb. peas in pods yields 1 c. peas	84	0	6.3	12.4	0.4	—	—	—	
peas in pods 1 c. = 170 g.	54	0	3.4	12.0	0.2	—	—	—	
pecans 1 c. chopped = 118 g.	687	0	9.2	12.3	71.2	5.0	44.9	14.2	
pepper, black 1 tsp. = 2.1 g.	255	0	11.0	51.7	3.3	1.3	1.4	1.5	11
pepper, white 1 tsp. = 2.4 g.	296	0	10.4	64.3	2.1	—	—	—	
peppers, chili (green)	37	0	1.3	7.3	0.2	—	—	—	
peppers, chili (red)	65	0	2.3	14.5	0.4	—	—	—	
peppers, green 3 peppers 4 × 3″ = 454 g. = 1½ c. trimmed and seeded	22	0	1.2	3.4	0.2	—	—	—	
peppers, red (flakes)	318	0	12.0	31.8	17.3	3.3	2.8	8.4	

[11]Sat., mono., and poly. components exceed total fat because of exclusion of piperine from total fat.

Nutritional Data for 100 Gram Amounts of Commonly Used Foods

ITEMS & USEFUL MEASURES	CALORIES	CHOLEST.	PROTEIN	CARBO.	FAT	SAT.	MONO.	POLY.	NOTES
peppers, red 3 peppers 4 × 3″ = 454 g. = 1½ c. trimmed and seeded	65	0	2.3	13.5	0.4	—	—	—	
pheasant 61% edible	151	98	24.3	—	5.1	2.0	2.0	1.0	
pine nuts (pignolias) 1 Tb. = 5 g.	552	0	31.1	10.7	47.4	2.0	26.0	8.0	
pike 26% edible	88	89	18.3	—	1.1	—	—	—	
pimiento	27	0	0.9	5.2	0.5	—	—	—	
pistachio nuts 1 c. in shells = 110 g., yields ½ c. nuts = 55 g.	594	0	19.3	17.1	53.7	5.4	34.9	10.2	
pollack 45% edible	95	55	20.4	—	0.9	—	—	—	
Polyperx ½ c. = 120 g.	192	0	1.2	16.8	14.4	2.4	—	4.8	
pompano approx. 44% of the fish is edible	166	55	18.8	—	9.5	2.0	—	2.0	
porgy/scup 41% edible	112	55	19.0	—	3.4	1.0	1.0	—	
pork	189	62	20.1	—	11.4	4.1	4.8	1.0	
potato 1 lb. = 2 med. baking, or 3 med. boiling, or 10–12 small new	76	0	2.1	16.6	0.1	—	—	—	
preserves, fruit 1 c. sliced = 165 peeling loss = 8% 1 Tb. = 20 g.	272	0	0.6	69.0	0.1	—	—	—	
purslane	21	0	1.7	2.9	0.4	—	—	—	
rabbit meat Rabbit is about 43% edible	162	65	21.0	—	8.0	3.0	3.0	1.0	
radicchio	No figures available.								

Nutritional Data for 100 Gram Amounts of Commonly Used Foods

ITEMS & USEFUL MEASURES	CALORIES	CHOLEST.	PROTEIN	CARBO.	FAT	SAT.	MONO.	POLY.	NOTES
radish ½ lb. = 2 c. sliced	17	0	1.0	2.9	0.1	—	—	—	
raisins 1 c. = 145 g.	289	0	2.5	76.5	0.2	—	—	—	
rape 1 lb. = 14–16 c. packed loosely = 4 c. cooked	No figures available; use mustard greens.								
red/gray snapper 52% edible	93	55	19.8	—	0.9	—	—	—	
rice, raw white 1 c. = 185 g.	363	0	6.7	80.1	0.4	—	—	—	
rosemary, dried 1 tsp. = 1.2 g. 1 tsp. dried = 1 Tb. fresh	331	0	4.9	46.4	15.2	—	—	—	
rucola	No figures available; use watercress.								
saffron 1 tsp. = 0.7 g.	310	0	11.4	61.5	5.9	—	—	—	
sage 1 tsp. = 0.7 g.	315	0	10.6	42.7	12.7	7.0	1.9	1.8	
salmon, fresh	217	39	22.5	—	13.4	4.0	4.0	—	
salmon, smoked	176	38	21.6	—	9.3	3.0	3.0	—	
sardines, fresh	160	112	19.2	—	8.6	2.0	—	2.0	
savory, ground 1 tsp. = 1.4 g.	272	0	6.7	53.5	5.9	—	—	—	
scallions 1 med., trimmed = 15 g. 1 small, trimmed = 5 g. 100 g. = 1 c., chopped	45	0	1.1	9.5	0.2	—	—	—	
scallops	81	35	15.3	3.3	0.2	—	—	—	
scrod	78	50	17.6	—	0.3	—	—	—	12
shallots 1 Tb., chopped = 10 g.	72	0	2.5	16.1	0.1	—	—	—	

[12] Figures given are for cod. Scrod may also be young haddock.

Nutritional Data for 100 Gram Amounts of Commonly Used Foods

ITEMS & USEFUL MEASURES	CALORIES	CHOLEST.	PROTEIN	CARBO.	FAT	SAT.	MONO.	POLY.	NOTES
shell beans 1 c. = 155 g.	123	0	8.4	20.3	0.5	—	—	—	
shrimp 69% edible	91	150	18.1	1.5	0.8	—	—	—	
skate	98	55	21.5	—	0.7	—	—	—	
smelts 55% edible	98	55	18.6	—	2.1	—	—	—	
snow peas 1 c. = 170 g.	53	0	3.4	12.0	0.2	—	—	—	
soy sauce 1 Tb. = 18 g.	68	0	5.6	9.5	1.3	—	—	—	
spinach 568 g. (1 1/4 lbs.) cooked = 1 c. 1 c. fresh, chopped = 55 g.	26	0	3.2	4.3	0.3	—	—	—	
squab An average squab weighs 258 g. and is 65% edible flesh	142	98	17.5	—	7.5	2.0	2.7	1.6	
squash, summer 1 lb. = 3 1/2 c., sliced or 1 1/4–1 1/2 c., mashed	19	0	1.1	3.6	0.1	—	—	—	
squash, winter 1 lb. = 2 c. cooked	50	0	1.4	11.0	0.3	—	—	—	
squash flowers	27	0	1.9	5.2	0.5	—	—	—	
squid approx. 50% of a squid is edible 1 small = 115 g. 1 med. = 227 g. 1 large = 345 g.	84	220	16.4	1.5	0.9	—	—	—	
stock of fish, veal, beef, turkey, or chicken	—	—	—	—	—	—	—	—	13
strawberries 1 c. whole berries = 149 g.	37	0	0.7	7.1	0.5	—	—	—	

[13]All stocks are assumed to have no caloric value when refrigerated and skimmed of fat.

Nutritional Data for 100 Gram Amounts of Commonly Used Foods

ITEMS & USEFUL MEASURES	CALORIES	CHOLEST.	PROTEIN	CARBO.	FAT	SAT.	MONO.	POLY.	NOTES
sturgeon, fresh Raw sturgeon sections with bones and skin are 85% edible	94	55	18.1	—	1.9	—	—	—	
sturgeon, smoked	149	95	31.2	—	1.8	—	—	—	
sugar, brown 1 c., packed = 220 g.	373	0	—	96.4	—	—	—	—	
sugar, white 1 c., packed = 200 g.	385	0	—	99.5	—	—	—	—	
sweet potato Raw sweet potatoes have about 19% refuse	114	0	1.7	25.6	0.4	—	—	—	
swordfish	118	55	19.2	—	4.0	1.0	1.0	—	
teal approx. 60% edible	123	80	20.0	—	4.3	1.3	1.2	0.6	
teriyaki sauce	—	—	—	—	—	—	—	—	
thyme, ground 1 tsp. = 1.4 g.	276	0	9.1	45.3	7.4	2.7	0.5	1.2	
tomato, fresh ripe 2 large or 3 med. or 8-9 plum or 24 cherry = 1 lb. = 2 c. chopped.	22	0	1.1	4.2	0.2	—	—	—	
tomato, green	24	0	1.2	4.6	0.2	—	—	—	
tomato paste 1 c. = 262 g.	82	0	3.4	17.7	0.4	—	—	—	
tripe, beef	100	68	19.1	—	2.0	1.0	0.9	—	
trout, rainbow 49% edible	195	55	21.5	—	11.4	3.0	2.0	—	
tuna, bluefin	145	57	25.2	—	4.1	1.0	1.0	—	
tuna, canned in oil	197	65	28.8	—	8.2	2.2	1.7	1.7	14
tuna, canned in water	127	63	28.0	—	0.8	—	—	—	15
tuna, yellowfin	133	56	24.7	—	3.0	1.0	1.0	—	

[14]Drained solids.

Nutritional Data for 100 Gram Amounts of Commonly Used Foods

ITEMS & USEFUL MEASURES	CALORIES	CHOLEST.	PROTEIN	CARBO.	FAT	SAT.	MONO.	POLY.	NOTES
turkey, dark meat 1 c. cooked pieces = 140 g.	128	75	20.9	—	4.3	1.0	2.0	1.0	16
turkey, white meat 1 c. cooked pieces = 140 g.	116	60	24.6	—	1.2	—	—	—	16
turnip greens 1 lb. = 9 oz. leaves = 9–10 c. packed = 1½ to 2 c. cooked.	28	0	3.0	4.2	0.3	—	—	—	
turnips 1 lb. = 4 c. chopped or grated or 2 c. mashed	30	0	1.0	5.7	0.2	—	—	—	
vanilla extract	—	—	—	—	—	—	—	—	17
veal chops 1 chop = ¼ lb. meat	156	71	19.7	—	8.0	3.8	3.6	0.2	
veal, chuck	173	71	19.1	—	10.0	4.8	4.4	0.2	
veal, foreshank	131	71	20.1	—	5.0	2.4	2.2	0.1	
veal, round	139	71	19.9	—	6.0	2.9	2.6	0.1	
venison, lean	126	65	21.0	—	4.0	2.5	1.0	0.1	
vinegar, cider 1 Tb. = 15 g.	14	0	—	5.9	—	—	—	—	
vinegar, distilled 1 Tb. = 15 g.	12	0	—	5.0	—	—	—	—	
walnuts each walnut half = 2 g. 1 Tb. chopped = 8 g. 1 c. chopped = 125 g.	651	0	14.8	13.7	64.0	4.5	9.6	39.7	
watercress 1 c. loose = 35 g. 1 c. chopped = 125 g.	19	0	2.2	2.3	0.3	—	—	—	
watermelon 1 c. pieces = 160 g.	26	0	0.5	6.1	0.2	—	—	—	

[15]Solids and liquid.

[16]Each pound of turkey yields about 150 g. of white meat and 132 g. of dark meat.

[17]Assumed to have no calories except for the alcohol (35%); see note 5.

Nutritional Data for 100 Gram Amounts of Commonly Used Foods

ITEMS & USEFUL MEASURES	CALORIES	CHOLEST.	PROTEIN	CARBO.	FAT	SAT.	MONO.	POLY.	NOTES
wheat bran 1 Tb. = 2.5 g.	213	0	16.0	52.8	4.6	1.0	1.0	3.0	
wheat germ 1 Tb. = 6 g.	363	0	26.6	44.2	10.9	1.6	3.1	4.7	
whitebait 75% edible	105	55	18.3	—	3.0	1.0	1.0	—	
whitefish 47% edible	155	55	18.9	—	8.2	3.0	3.0	—	

whiting
1 med. whiting =
  ½ pound
  approx. 44% is edible
	105	55	18.3	—	3.0	1.0	1.0	—	

wine, dry 1 fluid oz. = 29 g.	85	0	0.1	4.2	—	—	—	—	5
wine, sweet 1 fluid oz. = 30 g.	137	0	0.1	7.7	—	—	—	—	5
yam	101	0	2.1	22.3	0.2	—	—	—	
yeast, dry active 1 envelope = 1 Tb. = 7 g.	282	0	36.9	38.9	1.6	—	—	—	
yogurt, low-fat	62	8	5.7	7.5	1.3	—	—	—	

zucchini
3 small or 1½–2 med. =
  1 lb. = 4 c. grated or
  3½ c. chunks or slices
	17	0	1.2	3.0	0.1	—	—	—	

zucchini blossoms	No figures available; see squash flowers.								

Advice from E.G. about
Some Essential Italian Ingredients

Anchovies: If possible, get anchovies in an Italian neighborhood market, where they come packed in salt in a large tin; buy as much as needed. Simply use your fingers wash the salt off and pull the fillets off the bone. If you have a few left over, fillet them and cover them with olive oil; they will be good for a few days. The anchovies that you find in the supermarkets packed in oil in small cans are alright if used immediately, although they are not as sweet and delicate tasting as the Italian salted kind. But if you try to store them, the flesh gets dark and dry and the flavor becomes much too strong. So use them up immediately or you'll have to throw out what's left in the can.

Olive Oil: A light oil, such as Sasso, Berio, Old Monk, or James Plagniol, should be used for cooking, but sparingly. The heavier, richer oils, such as Madre Sicilia, Amastra, Il Torro, and Goya, are best used raw as a flavoring agent and binder at the last minute—after a dish has been cooked—or in salads. The very best oils for this purpose would be the extra virgin olive oil. My favorites are Badia a Coltibuono, Amastra, Castello di Volpaia, and Colavita.

Olives: Dried black olives, known as Greek olives, are not really Greek—they come from Sicily. When any of these recipes calls for olives, unless a green olive is specified, you should use the dried black olives readily available in supermarkets in jars.

Tomatoes, canned: Always use whole canned tomatoes, canned in their own juices—not in a puree or sauce. The purees vary greatly in quality and invariably made from inferior tomatoes. My recipes provide the right balance of body and flavor, and adding a puree would destroy that. For information about canning your own tomatoes, see page 378.

Tomato Paste: As you can see, I rarely call for tomato paste in this book. It is much too acidic and tinny tasting, particularly the kind sold in small cans all over this country. In rural Italy when tomato paste is used, it is usually homemade—sun-dried tomatoes covered in oil—or purchased in small quantities from a large container. It is therefore much sweeter; nevertheless, it is still used sparingly. You should learn to cook Italian food without being dependent on tomato paste, which overwhelms any sauce.

INDEX

acorn squash, baked, 376
agnello brodettato, 329
albacore, fresh, on a skewer, 174
almond sauce, 427–8
American Cancer Society, 7
American Heart Association, 7, 10
amino acids, *see* proteins
anchovy/ies
  about, 504
  with Brussels sprouts, 351
  and clams with spaghettini, 115
  in peppers stuffed my way, 398–9
  in spaghetti Norcia style, 95
  in vermicelli harlot style, 107
  on vermicelli with oil and garlic, 81
anitra
  brodo di, 43
  petti di, alla griglia, 284
  querque dula a modo mio, 283–4
antipasto
  about, 15–16
  caponata Sicilian style, 33–4
  clams, stuffed, I & II, 20, 21
    Genoa style, III, 21
  eggplant, 34–5
  fava bean, 37–8
  fish salad I & II, 22–3
  mushroom(s)
    stuffed with raisins and sherry,
      32–3
    stuffed with veal and walnuts,
      32
  mussel and scallop salad, 24
  omelet, open faced, with asparagus
    and spinach, 36–7

antipasto (*continued*)
  oysters: in green sauce, 19–20; with
    pesto, 19
  rice balls ("little oranges"), 35
  scallop salad, 25
  shellfish on toast, 16–17
  shrimp and pepper salad, 25–6
  smoked fish salad, 26–7
  squid
    and scallops on a skewer, 18
    and shrimp on a skewer, 17–18
  string bean and squid salad, 27–8
  stuffed olives Ascoli style, 30–2
  tripe salad, 30
  walnut spread on grilled bread, 38
antipasto
  di fave, 37–8
  di melanzane, 34–5
appetizers, about, 15; *see* antipasto
aragosta
  all'Americana, 188
  brodo di, 52
  al forno, 187
  con patate, 189
arancini, 35, 166–7
Arborio rice, 151
artichoke(s)
  baked, 338–9
  hearts
    fried, 340–41
    and lamb with turnips, 329
    with shrimp, 206
    with veal, 311–12
    with veal and rigatoni, 136–7
  Jewish style, 339

artichoke(s) (*continued*)
    with tomato and basil, 340
Artusi, Pellegrino
    *La Scienza in Cucina e L'arte de Mangiar
        Bene,* 348
arugola, *see* rucola
asparagi
    al forno, 343
    frittata di, 36-7
    in padella, 342
    in pastella, 342
    al vapore, 341
asparagus
    baked, 343
    with chicken breasts and shrimp, 265
    fish, mushrooms, and shrimp with
        pasta, 130-31
    fried in batter, 342
    with meatballs, 321-2
    mushrooms and clams with pasta,
        116-17
    and mushrooms with penne, 82
    in open-faced omelet with spinach,
        36-7
    salad, 409
    sautéed, 342
    and spinach with ground beef in pizza
        (*var.*), 465
    steamed, 341
    with veal and potatoes, 317-18
    and whiting, baked, 230
avocado and tunafish salad, 420

baccalà
    con broccoletti di rape, 182-3
    alla Fiorentina, 183
basil
    in light pesto, 426
    in pesto (farfalle with pesto), 71-2
    in pesto sauce, 426
    and tomato with artichokes, 340
bass
    freshwater, baked, 174-5
    striped, in a paper bag, I & II,
        175-7
bean(s)
    dried (white)
        with broccoletti di rape, 349-50
        with eggplant, 359
        with flank steak, 292-3
        with pasta, 82-3

bean(s) (*continued*)
    soup: and corn, 63-4; Frankowitch,
        60-61; and lentil, 62; with rice,
        56-7; Tuscan, 61-2
    with veal, 317
    green
        and broccoli salad, 410
        broccoli and potato salad, 410-11
        with chicken breasts and
            mushrooms, 264

        ratatouille, 345
        string bean and squid salad, 27-8
        Venetian style, 343
        with zucchini and potatoes, 344
    lima, *see* lima bean(s)
    pole, with potatoes and tomatoes,
        344-5
    shell, boiled, 346
beef
    boeuf saignant à la ficelle, 289-90
    boiled, 289-90
        with beef soup, 290-91
    braised, 294
    chili con carne, 296
    cutlets, stuffed, 295-6
    escalopes of ground beef, 298
    flank steak grilled with white beans,
        292-3
    ground, with asparagus and spinach in
        pizza (*var.*), 465
    meatballs, 297
    meatloaf, 299-300
    pepper steak, grilled, 291-2
    on a skewer, 291
    with snow peas, 293
    stew, 298-9
    in wine, 295
beer sauce on broiled chicken, 243
beet
    and carrot salad, 413-14
    and potato salad, 413
bieta con patate, 355
blackeyed peas with rape, 365
blood pressure and heart attack, 13-14
blood pudding, an adventure with, 443-4
blowfish, baked, 177-8
boeuf saignant à la ficelle, 289-90
Boghosian, Marilyn, 5
Boghosian, Varujan, 5
    pasta with hot pepper sauce, 97

Boghosian, Varujan (*continued*)
    pasta primavera, 79
Boghosian's pasta al l'Arrabbiata, 97
Boni, Ada, 45, 348
    Il Talismano della Felicita, 45
borlotti lessi, 346
braciolette ripiene, 295, 303
brandy
    and marsala with pheasant and
        mushrooms, 284–5
    and shellfish on rigatoni, 117–18
branzino al cartoccio, 176–7
bread
    chicken baked in, Tuscany style,
        261–3
    cooked with rucola and potatoes,
        374
    grilled with walnut spread, 38
    Roman garlic, I & II, 39
    squab baked in, 281–2
bread (homemade)
    Ellie Giobbi's Italian-style, 462–3
    Judith Jones's basic loaf, 463–4
breadcrumbs with vermicelli, 111
breakfast
    about, 457
    continental, 459
    high calorie, 458
    low calorie, 459
    substitutions in, 458–9
broccoletti di rape
    about, 347–8
    with beans, 349–50
    with salt cod, 182–3
    with spaghettini, 85–6
    for other recipes see also under rape
broccoletti di rape, 347–8
    con fagioli, 349–50
    con orecchiette, 87
broccoli
    with chicken and pasta, 261
    with chicken wings and potatoes,
        269–70
    with linguine, 84
    with monkfish, 193–4
    and mussels baked with fish, 197–8
    with pasta, 83–4
    with potatoes, 368
    with rape and potatoes, 349
    rice, and lima beans, 164–5
    with rigatoni for fifty people, 149–50

broccoli (*continued*)
    salad, 409–10
        and green bean, 410
        green bean and potato, 410–11
    with shrimp and chicken breasts,
        207–8
    with stuffed squid, 217
    and tomatoes, fresh, with pasta, 85
    with tuna, 346–7
    and tuna with pasta, 132
    and tuna in pizza with black olives
        (*var.*), 465
    and veal with pizza, 464–5
    with yams, 347
broccoli
    insalata di, 409–10
    con patate dolci Americane, 347
    con tonno, 346–7
brodetto of fish mariner style, 232–3
brodetto
    di frutta di mare, 206–7
    di pesce alla marinara, 232–3
bruschetta, 39
Brussels sprouts
    with anchovies, 351
    with potatoes, 350
busecca (*trippa alla Milanese*), 324–5
butterfly pasta with smoked salmon,
    123–4

cabbage
    with potatoes, 351–2
    savoy, with tripe, 327
    steamed, 352
    stuffed
        with tomatoes, 390–91
        whole with veal, 391
    and veal soup, 67–8
cake
    calorie table for, 467
    spicy carrot (R.W.), 456
calamari
    fritti, 215–16
    ripieni, 217, 218
    ripieni alla Fiorentina, 216
    in umido, 219
calcionetti, 452–3
caloric equivalents of activities,
    474–5
    table for, 477

calories
in individual foods (tables for),
484–503
in snacks (tables for), 467–9
candy, calorie table for, 467
cannelloni, 145
cantaloupe and mango sherbet, 449
capelli d'angelo alla Tomasso, 118
capers
in caponata Sicilian style, 33–4
in stuffed peppers my way, 398–9
in vermicelli harlot style, 107
caponata Sicilian style, 33–4
caponata alla Siciliana, 33–4
capons
about, 274–5
stuffed, 275–6
cappe sante, 202
alla griglia, 199–200
con piselli, 201
cappone ripieno, 275–6
carbohydrates
definition of, 9
fibers, 9
in individual foods, 484–502
starches, 9
see also sugars
carbonated beverages, calorie table for,
467
carciofi
cuori di, fritto, 340–41
alla giudia, 339
con pomodore e basilico, 340
stufati, 338–9
Carnacini, Luigi, 348
Carolina long-grain rice, 151
carrot(s)
and beet salad, 413–14
cake, spicy (R.W.), 456
with veal and peas, 319–20
casserole, squab in a, 279–80
catfish in carpione, 178–9
in Etruscan Fish Stew, 233
cauliflower
fried, 353–4
Marches style, 353
with penne, 88–9
salad, 414
with spaghetti, 88
cavoletti di bruxelles
con acciughe, 351

cavoletti di bruxelles (continued)
con patate, 350
cavolfiore
fritto, 353–4
insalata di, 414
alla Marchigiana, 353
cavolo
imbottito al pomodori, 390–91
imbottito al vitello, 391
con patate, 351–2
a vapore, 352
celery with potatoes, tomatoes, and
onions, 370
celery root, purée of, 354
cervo
bistecche di, 330
alla griglia, 330–31
cetrioli al forno, 355–6
champagne peach sherbet, 450
cheese
about, 469–70
Gorgonzola with rigatoni, 110–11
Pecorino Romano, 470
ricotta with spaghetti, 109–10
St. Otho, 470
substitute for, *see* Countdown
cheesecakes, individual (R.W.), 453
chestnuts
with chicken, 250
and mushrooms with pasta, 93–4
chicken
about, 239
soaking in salt, 239
baked, 246
in bread Tuscany style, 261–3
in clay, 241–2
balls, 269
breast(s)
broiled, 258
with eggplant, 266–7
grilled, 258–9
with mushrooms and green beans,
264
with peppers, onions, mushrooms,
and tomatoes, 259
with shrimp and asparagus, 265
with shrimp and broccoli,
207–8
stuffed, Florentine, 266
broiled, 241
with beer sauce, 243

chicken (*continued*)
  broth, 41
  with chestnuts, 250
  country style, 247
  and crabmeat tempura, 267–8
  croquettes, 263–4
  cutlets, 268
  deviled, 255–6
  feet with mushroom sauce, 273
  with 41 cloves of garlic, 249
  gizzards with eggplant, 274
  grilled with mustard, 243–4
  with honey, 251–2
  lean, Canzanese style, 245–6
  legs, stuffed, 271–2
  Lombardy style, 244
  with mushrooms, onions, and fresh
       fennel, 248
  with mussels, 254
  with pasta, 138–9
  with pasta and broccoli, 261
  and pasta dinner, 256–7
  Piedmontese style, 245
  with risotto, 259–60
  roast, stuffed, 240
  with saffron, 250–51
  salad, I & II, 418–19
  with shellfish, 252–3
  soup
      corn with, 58–9
      dumpling, 42
  wings
      with mussels, 270–71
      with potatoes and broccoli, 269–70
chick pea soup, I & II, 64–5
  and lentil, 66
chili con carne, 296
cholesterol
  and blood levels, 8
  in breakfast, 458–9
  and caffeine, 458
  and carbohydrates, 9
  definition of, 9–10
  and fats, 10
  and fatty acids, 10
  and heart attacks, 7
  in individual foods, 484–503
  limitation of dietary, 11
  lipoprotein, 10
  and strokes, 7
  and weight, 10–11

Christmas turnovers, 452–3
Chrysler, Walter, Jr., 252
ciciones, 170–71
cicoria
  in padella, 356–7
  con patate, 357
cipolle imbottite, 396–7
Cirque, Le (New York), 76, 241
Claiborne, Craig, 79, 149
clams
  and anchovies with spaghettini, 115
  asparagus, and mushrooms with pasta,
       116–17
  in pasta sea and mountains, 112–13
  stuffed, I & II, 20–21
      Genoa style, III, 21
  and zucchini with pasta, 115–16
codregone in umido, 228
conchigliette con patate, 102–3
coniglio
  arrosto, 331
  alla cacciatora, 333
  alla Marchigiana, 331–2
  e polenta alla Genovese, 334–5
  alla San Remese, 334
cookies
  calorie table for, 468
  dough for (R.W.), 454
  icebox (R.W.), 455
  rolled (R.W.), 455
Cornish hens with peas, 286–7
corn soup
  and bean, 63–4
  with chicken, 58–9
  and pasta, 56
coronary heart disease, definition of, 6
  see also heart attacks
Countdown, 459, 470
cozze
  alla Genovese, 21
  alla Marchigiana, 20, 21
  al vino, 196–7
crabmeat and chicken tempura, 267–8
crabs
  softshell, 179
      fried with vegetables, 180
      in a white sauce, 180–81
crackers, calorie table for, 468
cream substitute, *see* Polyperx
crocchette
  di pesce, 234

crocchette (*continued*)
  di pollo, 263–4
  di zucchini, 381
croquettes, chicken, 263–4
crostini
  con l'aglio, 38
  di mare alla Genovese, 16–17
cucumbers, baked, 355–6

dairy dressing, sour, low fat (R.W.), 461
dandelion(s)
  about, 356
  greens with potatoes, 357
  greens in a skillet, 356–7
De Cecco pasta, 70–71
desserts, about, 443–4
diabetes, 14
dieting, 474–5
dosa (R.W.), 460–61
dough for piecrusts, cookies, and
    strudel (R.W.), 454
dressing
  dairy, sour, low fat (R.W.), 461
  see also sauce(s)
duck
  breasts, broiled, 284
  soup, 43
dumplings
  chicken soup with, 42
  potato, 171–2
  see also gnocchi

eel with rice, 158
eggplant
  antipasto, 34–5
  baked, 358
  with beans, 359
  with chicken breasts, 266–7
  with chicken gizzards, 274
  and onions with ground veal in pizza
      (*var.*), 465
  pan-fried, 357–8
  with pasta, 73–4
  with sauce, 359–60
  stuffed
    Neapolitan style, 392
    with tomatoes, 393
    with veal with tomato sauce, 394–5
  with veal and peas, 312–13

eggplant (*continued*)
  and walnuts with pasta, 89–90
egg substitutes
  Egg Beaters, 36, 458
  Jolly Joan Egg Replacer, 459
egg white omelet (R.W.), 461–2
escalopes of ground beef, 298
escarole pizza, 465–6
Etruscan fish stew, 233
exercise
  calories burned in, 475, 477
  regular, 14

fagiano al marsala, 284–5
fagioli con l'occhio e rape, 365
fagiolini
  con patate e pomodoro, 344–5
  alla Veneto, 343
  con zucchini e patate, 344
farfalle
  (bows) mariner style, 128–9
  (butterflies) with pesto, 71–2
  with white truffles, 96
farfalle
  con calamari, 126–7
  alla marinara, 128–9
  al pesto, 71–2
fennel
  baked, 360
  fresh, with chicken, mushrooms, and
      onions, 248
  and tomato salad, 415
fettuccine with smoked salmon, 122–3
fettuccine al salmone affumicato, 122–3
fibers, 10
finocchio al forno, 360
fish
  about, 173
  albacore, fresh, on a skewer, 174
  assorted, fried, 238
  baked with mussels and broccoli,
      197–8
  balls
    fried, 235
    "*al pesto*," 235–6
    steamed, 236–7
  bass
    freshwater, baked, 174–5
    striped, in a paper bag, I & II,
      175–7

fish (*continued*)
blowfish, baked, 177–8
brodetto of, mariner style, 232–3
broiled and split with pesto, 177
cakes, 234
eel with rice, 158
Etruscan stew, 233
fillets
Genoa style, 184
in pasta, fisherman style, 120
flounder baked with scallions and
ginger, 186–7
fluke, baked, 184–5
fritto misto di pesce, 237
head sauce with pasta, 119–20
lemon sole poached in lettuce leaves,
214
mackerel
broiled, 189–90
marinated, 190
and scallop seviche, 191
mako shark, 205
Messina style, 231–2
monkfish
with broccoli, 193–4
broiled, 194–5
San Benedetto style, 192
in sauce, 192–3
on a skewer, 194
stew with pasta, 195–6
pompano
broiled, 198
steamed with tomato sauce, 198
red snapper
broiled, 209
steamed, 210
salad, I & II, 22–3
salt cod
with broccoli rape, 182–3
Florentine style, 183
with linguine, 104–5
sardines
fresh, broiled, 199
with perciatelli, 124–5
in a vinegar sauce, 28–9
sauce, 428
scrod
about, 202
baked with tomatoes and peppers,
203–4
fillet with potatoes, 202–3

fish (*continued*)
sea squab, baked, 177–8
shad
about, 204
broiled, 204–5
shrimp, asparagus, and mushrooms
with pasta, 130–31
skate wing
sauce on spaghettini, 125–6
soup, 53
smelts, butterflied and fried, 208–9
smoked fish, *see* smoked fish
sole, fillet of
my way, 213–14
with oregano, 211–12
poached in wine, 212
primavera, 212–13
with snow peas, 210–11
soup, 54–5
squid
about, 214–15
fried, 215–16
with pasta, 126–7
with peas, 219
scallops, and mussels with pasta,
114
and scallops on a skewer, 18
and shrimp on a skewer, 17–18
with shrimp and scallops, 206–7
and string bean salad, 27–8
stuffed: with broccoli, 217;
Florentine, 216; with polenta,
218
tempura, 219–20
stockfish
about, 220
Abruzzi style, 220–21
swordfish
Messina style, 222
on a skewer, 223–4
steak: mariner style, 223; Sicilian
style, 221–2
trout
poached, 224–5
wrapped in lettuce leaves, 225
tuna, *see* tuna/fish
whitefish, freshwater, steamed, 228
whiting
baked with asparagus, 230
baked in white wine, 230–31
fillets of, fried, 229

fish (*continued*)
    salad, 421
flank steak grilled with white beans,
    292–3
flounder baked with scallions and ginger,
    186–7
fluke, baked, 184–5
fragole al vino, 446
Framingham Study, 473
Franey, Pierre, 79, 282
    sauce moutarde aux gherkins, 434
fritto misto di pesce, about, 237
frogs' legs
    with mushrooms, 185
    in sauce, 186
fructose, 9
fruit
    desserts, 444–51
    fried, 444–5
    salad, 445–6
frutta
    fritto di, 444–5
    macedonia di, 445–6
funghi
    ripieni, 32–3
    trifolati, 363

gamberi, pollo, e broccoli neri,
    207–8
garlic
    41 cloves of, with chicken, 249
    and oil on spaghetti, 79–80
    sauce on spaghetti with mushrooms,
        80
    on vermicelli with anchovy, 80
"Gelataio, Il," 448
Gerrardo di Nola pasta, 70
ginger and scallions baked with flounder,
    186–7
Giobbi, Ellie
    Italian style bread, 462–3
glucose, 9
glycerol, 10
gnocchi
    Sardegna style, 172
    semolina from Sardinia, 170–71
gnocchi
    di patate, 171–2
    di patate alla Sarda, 172
gobione in carpone, 178–9

Gorgonzola
    and diet, 470
    with rigatoni, 110–11
green sauce, 428–9
    Genoa style, 429
    on pasta, 75
greens, salad, 408
guinea hen cooked in red wine, 285–6

heart attacks
    risk factors for, 13–14
        table for, 473
Hirshhorn, Joe and Olga, 272
honey
    with chicken, 251–2
    sauce, I & II, 429–30
horsemeat stew, 327–8
horseradish and tomato sauce,
    432
hubbard squash, baked, 376
Hunt's canned tomatoes, 97
hydrogenation, 479
hypertension, 13–14

icebox cookies (R.W.), 455
insalata
    di aragosta, 420–21
    di arancie e d'olive, 424
    di asparagi, 409
    di avogado e tonno, 420
    di barbabietole
        e carote, 413–14
        e patate, 413
    di broccoli, 409–10
    di canestrelli, 25
    di cavolfiore, 414
    di fagiolini
        e broccoli, 410
        broccoli, e patate, 410–11
        e calamari, 27–8
    di finocchi e pomodori, 415
    di frutti di mare, 24
    di funghi e pomodori, 416
    di gamberi e peperoni, 25–6
    Marchigiana, 417
    di merluzzo, 421
    mista d'estate, I & II, 387–8
    di pasta, 148–9
    di patate, 411

insalata (continued)
  con tonno, 419
  di pesce, I & II, 22–3
    affumicato, 26–7
  di piccioncini, 282–3
  di pollo, I & II, 418–19
  di pomodori e tonno, 416–17
  di riso, I & II, 422–3
    primavera, 423
  di trippa, 30
Italian Family Cooking (Edward Giobbi),
  405
Italian Home Cooking (Edward Giobbi),
  254

Jones, Judith, 6
  basic loaf bread, 463–4

Kellogg family, 458

lady peas, 364
lamb with artichoke hearts and turnips,
  329
lasagna
  green, my way, 141–3
  vegetable, 143–5
lasagne verdi a modo mio, 141–3
lattughe ripiene, 396
  in brodo, 395
leeks and potatoes, braised, 360–61
lemon sole poached in lettuce leaves,
  214
lentil(s)
  soup
    Abruzzi style, 57–8
    and bean, 62
    and chick pea, 66
    stew, 361
  with veal and pasta, 316
lettuce
  leaves
    lemon sole poached in, 214
    trout wrapped in, 225
  stuffed, in broth, 395
lima bean(s)
  baby (butter beans), 361
  broccoli, and rice, 164–5
  soup, 63

linguine
  with baccalà (salt cod), 104–5
  with broccoli, 84
  with lobsters, 122
  with scallops and pesto, 125
  Tomasso's, with lobster sauce, 121
linguine
  all'aragosta, 122
  con broccoli, 84
  alla Capestranese, 104–5
  con cappe sante, 125
  con salsa d'aragosta Tomasso, 121
lobster
  Américaine, 188
  baked, 187
  with linguine, 122
  with potatoes, 189
  salad, warm, 420–21
  sauce with Tomasso's linguine, 121
  soup, 52

macaroni
  with meat sauce, 147
  timbale of, 146–7
maccheroni al ragu, 147
Maccioni, Sirio, 76
mackerel
  broiled, 189–90
  marinated, 190
  and scallop seviche, 191
mako shark, 205
mango and cantaloupe sherbet, 449
manzo
  bistecca di
    al ferri, 291–2
    con fagioli, 290
  bollito di, 290–91
  braciolette ripiene, 295, 303
  polpette di, 297
  polpettone, 299–300
  scaloppini di, battuto, 298
  spezzato di, 298–9
  allo spiedo, 291
  al vino, 295
margarine with breakfast, 459
marinara sauce, 430–31
marò sauce, 432
marsala
  and brandy with pheasant and
    mushrooms, 284–5

marsala (continued)
    with veal, 318–19
    wine with turkey breast, 278
meat
    about, 288
    -balls, 297
        with asparagus, 321–2
        steamed veal, 320
        veal in tomato sauce, 321
    -loaf, 299–300
    sauce on macaroni, 147
    see also beef, horse . . . , lamb . . . ,
        rabbit, tripe, veal, venison
Meissel and Schadn (Vienna), 289
melanzane
    e fagioli, 359
    al forno, 358
    imbottite
        alla Napoletano, 392
        alla Siciliana, 394–5
        in padella, 357–8
        in salsa, 359–60
Mennucci pasta, 70
menu
    Italian Christmas Eve, 173
    selection, 482–3
merluzzo
    filetti di, con patate, 202–3
    al forno con asparagi, 230
    fritte, 228–9
Metropolitan Height and Weight Tables,
    476
milk and onions with spaghetti, 98–9
minestra
    di ceci, 64–5
    di fagioli e granturco, 63–4
    di lenticchie, 361
        e fagioli, 62
    di piselli, 55
    con piselli freschi, 44–5
    di riso, 164–5
    di rughetta, 50
    di zucchini, 46–7
minestrone
    about, 45
        Genoa style, I & II, 48–9
    spring, 46
minestrone
    di cavolo e vitello, 67–8
    alla Genovese, 48–9
    di primavera, 46

minestrone (continued)
    verde, 47–8
mint sauce, I & II, 433
moleche in salsa bianca, 180–81
Molisana, La pasta
monkfish
    with broccoli, 193–4
    broiled, 194–5
    San Benedetto style, 192
    in sauce, 192–3
    on a skewer, 194
    stew with pasta, 195–6
mushrooms
    about, 362
    asparagus, and clams with pasta,
        116–17
    and asparagus with penne, 82
    boletus, 362
    and chestnuts with pasta, 93–4
    with chicken breast and green beans,
        264
    with chicken breasts, peppers, onions,
        and tomatoes, 259
    and chicken with onions and fresh
        fennel, 248
    fish, shrimp, and asparagus with pasta,
        130–31
    fried, 363
    with frogs' legs, 185
    and nuts with pasta, 92–3
    in pasta sea and mountains, 112–13
    with pheasant, marsala, and brandy,
        284–5
    sauce with chicken feet, 273
    on spaghetti with garlic and oil, 80
    in spaghetti Norcia style, 95
    in spaghetti woodsman style, 98
    stuffed
        with raisins and sherry, 32–3
        with veal and walnuts, 32
    and tomato salad, 416
    with vermicelli and wine, 94
    wild, with tripe and pasta, 137–8
mussels
    and broccoli baked with fish, 197–8
    with chicken, 254
    with chicken wings, 270–71
    and scallop salad, 24
    squid, and scallops with pasta, 114
    in wine, 196–7
mustard with grilled chicken, 243–4

nasello
  filetti di, fritti, 229
  al forno, 230–31
National Diet and Heart Study, 458–9
National Heart, Lung, and Blood
      Institute, 7
noci, intingolo di, 435
Nola pasta, 70
nondairy creamers, 458
nut(s)
  and mushrooms with pasta, 92–3
  sauce, I, II, & III, 435–6
nutrients
  calculating of, 480–81
  tables for, 481–503

oat bran
  in bread, 463
  cholesterol-lowering effect of, 9
obesity and heart attacks, 13, 14
oil(s)
  and garlic on spaghetti, 79–80
  polyunsaturated, 10, 12
  vegetable, saturated
    cocoa butter, 10
    coconut, 10
    palm, 10
    palm kernel, 10
  on vermicelli with anchovy, 81
olive(s)
  about, 504
  black, broccoli and tuna in pizza (*var.*),
      465
  and orange salad, 424
  stuffed, Ascoli style, 30–2
olive oil
  about, 504
  types, 504
olive ripiene all'Ascolana, 30–2
omelets
  egg white (R.W.), 461–2
  open-faced with asparagus and spinach,
      36–7
onion(s)
  blossoms, fried, 363–4
  with chicken breasts, peppers,
      mushrooms, and tomatoes, 259
  with eggplant and ground veal in pizza
      (*var.*), 465
  and fresh fennel with chicken and

onion(s) (*continued*)
      mushrooms, 248
  and milk with spaghetti, 98–9
  and potatoes with celery and
      tomatoes, 370
  with spaghetti, 99–100
  stuffed, 396–7
  and tomato salad, 414–15
  tomato, and purslane salad, 417–18
orange and olive salad, 424
orecchiette with rape, 87
orecchiette con piselli, 100
oregano on fillet of sole, 211
Orsini, Armando, 212
osso buco, 310
  in bianco, 309
  alla Marchigiana, 310–11
osso buco Marches style, 310–11
ostriche
  al pesto, 19
  con salsa verde, 19–20
oysters
  in green sauce, 19–20
  with pesto, 19

pancotto con rughetta e patate, 374
parsley pesto, 427
pasta
  about, 69–71
    types, domestic and imported,
        70–71
  baked in parchment, 135–6
  with beans, 82–3
  Boghosian's
    with hot pepper sauce, 97
    primavera, 79
  with broccoli, 83–4
  with broccoli and tuna, 132
  butterfly, with smoked salmon, 123–4
  cannelloni, 145
  with chestnuts and mushrooms, 93–4
  with chicken, 138–9
  with chicken and broccoli, 261
  and chicken dinner, 256–7
  with clams and zucchini, 115–16
  and corn soup, 56
  with eggplant, 73–4
  with eggplant and walnuts, 89–90
  farfalle
    (bows) mariner style, 128–9

pasta (*continued*)
- (butterflies) with pesto, 71-2
- with white truffles, 96
- fettuccine with smoked salmon, 122-3
- fisherman style, 120
- with fish head sauce, 119-20
- in a green sauce, 75
- with green tomatoes, 90-91
- homemade
  - green lasagna my way, 141-3
  - tortelloni, 139-41
- linguine
  - with baccalà (salt cod), 104-5
  - with broccoli, 84
  - with lobsters, 122
  - with scallops and pesto, 125
  - Tomasso's, with lobster sauce, 121
- macaroni
  - with meat sauce, 147
  - timbale of, 146-7
- mariner style, 106-7
- with monkfish stew, 195-6
- with mushrooms, asparagus, and clams, 116-17
- with mushrooms, fish, shrimp, and asparagus, 130-31
- with mushrooms and nuts, 92-3
- with mussels, squid, and scallops, 114
- penne
  - with asparagus and mushrooms, 82
  - with cauliflower, 88-9
  - with green tomatoes, 91-2
  - in the manner of Porto d'Ascoli, 133-4
  - with rucola pesto, 103-4
  - with spinach, 74-5
  - with tuna, 132-3
- with peppers, 100-101
- perciatelli with sardines, 124-5
- primavera, I, II, & III, 77-8
  - origins of, 76
- with rape, 86-7
- rape with orecchiette, 87
- rigatoni
  - with broccoli for fifty people, 149-50
  - with Gorgonzola, 110-11
  - with shellfish and brandy, 117-18
  - with veal and artichoke hearts, 136-7
- salad, 148-9

pasta (*continued*)
- rucola, with spaghetti, 148
- sea and mountains, 112-13
- shells
  - with peas, 100
  - with potatoes, 102-3
  - with shrimp, 131-2
  - with shrimp and pesto, 129-30
  - with smoked trout, 134-5
- spaghetti
  - with cauliflower, 88
  - with garlic and oil sauce and mushrooms, 80
  - Norcia style, 95
  - with oil and garlic, 79-80
  - with onions, 99-100
  - with onions and milk, 98-9
  - with pepper sauce, 102
  - with ricotta, 109-10
  - with rucola, 104
  - woodsman style, 98
- spaghettini
  - with broccoletti di rape, 85-6
  - with clams and anchovies, 115
  - primavera, 77-8
    - Genoa style, 78-9
  - with skate wing sauce, 125-6
  - with tomato sauce, 106
  - with zucchini blossom sauce, 108
- with squid, 126-7
- stuffed peppers, 400
- with tomatoes, fresh, and broccoli, 85
- trenette with pesto sauce, 72-3
- with tripe and wild mushrooms, 137-8
- with veal and lentils, 316
- vegetable lasagna, 143-5
- vermicelli
  - with breadcrumbs, 111
  - harlot style, 107
  - with mushrooms and wine, 94
  - with oil, garlic, and anchovy, 81
  - piquant, Calabria style, 112
- with walnut sauce, 108-9

pasta
- *e broccoli*, 83-4
- *con broccoli e tonno*, 132
- *al cartoccio*, 135-6
- *con castagne e funghi*, 93-4
- *e fagioli*, 82-3
- *con funghi, asparagi, e vongole*, 116-17

pasta (continued)
  con funghi e noci, 92–3
  funghi, pesce, gamberi, e asparagi,
      130–31
  con gamberi, 131–2
  con gamberi al pesto, 129–30
  alla macchiata, 70
  mare e monti, 112–13
  alla Marinara, 106–7
  con le melanzane, 73–4
  con melanzane e noci, 89–90
  al peperoni, 100–101
  alla pescarese, 120
  con petti di pollo, 138–9
  e pollo, 256–7
  con i pomodori verdi, 90–91
  con le rape, 86–7
  con salsa di noci, 108–9
  con salsa di pomodoro fresco e broccoli, 85
  in salsa verde, 75
  con sugo di testa di pesce, 119–20
  trippa e porcini, 137–8
  alla trota affumicata, 134–5
  con vongole e zucchini, 115–16
patate
  con broccoli, 368
  coccoli di, 367
  al forno con pomodori, 367
  fritte, 370
  ripiene, 400
    al' forno, 401–2
  al rosmarino, 368
  con sedano, pomodori, e cipolle, 370
Pastificio del Verde, Fara San Martino
    pasta, 70
pea(s)
  with Cornish hens, 286–7
  with pasta shells, 100
  and scallop soup, 51–2
  with scallops, 201
  soup, dried, 55
  soup, fresh, 44–5
  with squid, 219
  in stuffed squab, 280–81
  with veal and carrots, 319–20
  with veal and eggplant, 312–13
  with veal and rice balls, 166–7
  see also blackeyed peas. . . , lady peas,
    and snow peas
peach(es)
  champagne sherbet, 450

peach(es) (*continued*)
  in fruit salad, 445–6
  poached with raspberry sauce, 445
  tart, 450–51
  in wine, 446–7
pears
  in caponata Sicilian style, 33–4
  in port, 447
  stuffed, 448
penne
  with asparagus and mushrooms, 82
  with cauliflower, 88–9
  with green tomatoes, 91–2
  in the manner of Porto d'Ascoli,
    133–4
  with rucola pesto, 103–4
  with spinach, 74–5
  with tuna, 132–3
penne
  con asparagi, 82
  e cavolfiore, 88–9
  con frutti di mare, 114
  con pesto rucola, 103–4
  con i pomodori verdi, 91–2
  alla Porto d'Ascoli, 133–4
  con salsa di spinaci, 74–5
  al tonno, 132–3
peperoni
  arrostiti, 365–6
  fritti alla San Benedetto, 366–7
  imbotiti alla Fiorentina, 399–400
  ripieni
    a modo mio, 398–9
    di pasta, 400
    di tonno, 398
    di vitello, 397–8
pepper(s)
  with chicken breasts, onions,
    mushrooms, and tomatoes, 259
  fried San Benedetto style, 366–7
  hot
    sauce, I & II, 437–8
    sauce with Boghosian's pasta, 97
  with pasta 100–101
  roasted, 365–6
  sauce with spaghetti, 102
  and shrimp salad, 25–6
  stuffed
    Florentine style, 399–400
    my way, 398–9
    with pasta, 400

pepper(s) (*continued*)
with tuna, 398
with veal, 397–8
and tomatoes with baked scrod, 203–4
pepper steak, grilled, 291–2
perch, freshwater, in Etruscan fish stew,
233
perciatelli con le sarde, 124–5
perciatelli with sardines, 124–5
pere ripiene, 448
pesce
alla brace con pesto, 177
brodetto di, alla marinara, 232–3
crocchette di, 234
filetti di, alla Genovese, 184
al forno con cozze e broccoli, 197–8
al forno con pomodori e peperoni,
203–4
fritto misto di, 237
frutta di mare, 206–7
insalata di, 22, 23
affumicato, 26–7
alla Messinese, 231–2
polpette fritte di, 235
rospo
con i broccoli, 193–4
alla griglia, 194–5
con pasta, 195–6
alla San Benedettese, 192
alla spiedo, 194
al sugo, 192–3
spada
alla Marinara, 223
Messinese, 222
alla spiedo, 223–4
trance di, alla Siciliana, 221–2
zuppa di, 54–5
pesche
con lamponi, 445
al vino, 446–7
pesto, 426
about, 425–6
preserving of, 425–6
with farfalle (butterflies), 71–2
on fish broiled and split, 177
light, 426
with oysters, 19
parsley, 427
rucola, with penne, 103–4
sauce with trenette, 72–3
and scallops with linguine, 125

pesto (*continued*)
and shrimp with pasta, 129–30
pesto di magro, 426
pheasant with marsala, brandy, and
mushrooms, 284–5
piccione
in pane, 281–2
ripieno, 280–81
pie(s)
calorie table for, 469
crusts, dough for (R.W.), 454
pineapple in fruit salad, 445–6
pine nuts
in nut sauce I, 435
in stuffed peppers my way, 398–9
pinzimonio, 36
pistachio sauce, 437
pizza
of escarole, 465–6
with ground lean beef with asparagus
and spinach (*var.*), 465
with ground veal, eggplant, and onions
(*var.*), 465
with tuna, broccoli, and black olives
(*var.*), 465
with veal and broccoli, 464–5
pizza
rustica, 464–5
di scarola, 465–6
polenta
about, 167–8
country style, 168–9
grilled, 170
with rabbit Genoa style, 334–5
stuffed squid, 218
polenta
alla campagnola, 168–9
pollo
ali di
con muscoli, 270–71
con patate e broccoli neri,
269–70
in bianco con risotto, 259–60
brodo di, 41
gnocchetti, 42
alla campagnola, 247
Canzanese magro, 245–6
con castagnie, 250
cotolette di, 268
crocchette di, 263–4
alla diavola, 255–6

pollo (*continued*)
   al forno, 246
   con frutta di mare, 252–3
   con funghi e finocchio, 248
   grigliato con senape, 243–4
   alla Lombardia, 244
   al miele, 251–2
   con muscoli, 254
   nel pane alla Toscana, 261–3
   petto di
      con gli asparagi, 265
      alla Fiorentina, 266
      con funghi e fagiolini verdi, 264
      alla griglia, 258
      con melanzane, 266–7
      in umido, 259
   alla Piemontese, 245
   polpette di, 269
   regaglie di, con melanzane, 274
   allo spiedo, 241
      con birra, 243
   al vapore, 255
   con zafferano, 250–51
   alla zingara, 242
polpette di
   manzo, 297
      con gli asparagi, 321–2
   pesce in umido, 236–7
   pollo, 267
   vitello
      in brodo, 66–7
      buttute, 323
      in sugo di pomodori, 321
      al vapore, 320
polpettone, 299–300
   di patate, 371
Polyperx, 458–9
pommes boulangère, 369
pomodori
   fritto di, verdi, 380
   alla griglia, 378–9
   imbottiti, 402–3
   con pane tostato, 379–80
   ripieni alla Trasteverina, 402
pompano
   broiled, 198
   steamed with tomato sauce, 198
porri brasati e patate, 360–61
port with pears, 447
Post, C. W., 458
potassium and blood pressure, 6

potato(es)
   baked with tomatoes, 367
   baker style, 369
   balls, 367
   and beet salad, 413
   with bread and rucola, 374
   with broccoli, 368
   with Brussels sprouts, 350
   with cabbage, 351–2
   with celery, tomatoes, and onions,
      370
   with chicken wings and broccoli,
      269–70
   with dandelion greens, 357
   dumplings, 171–2
   fried, 370
   with green beans and zucchini, 344
   and leeks, braised, 360–61
   loaf, 371
   with lobster, 189
   with pole beans and tomatoes, 344–5
   with rape and broccoli, 349
   with rice, 161
   with rosemary, 368
   salad
      and beet, 413
      green bean and broccoli, 410–11
      and tuna, 419
      warm, 411
   and scrod fillet, 202–3
   with shells, 102–3
   and spinach, 375
   stew, with lentils, 361
   stuffed, I & II, 400–402
   with Swiss chard, 355
   and turnips, baked, 380–81
   with veal and asparagus, 317–18
   with veal stew, 314–15
   with zucchini, 382–3
poulet avec quarante-et-un gousses d'ail, 249
poultry, *see under* capons, chicken,
      Cornish hens . . . , duck, guinea
      hen . . . , pheasant . . . , squab(s),
      teal . . . , *and* turkey
Prince pasta, 70
proteins (amino acids)
   definitions of, 9
   in individual foods (tables for),
      484–503
   lipoprotein cholesterol, 10
      high density (HDL), 10

proteins (amino acids) (*continued*)
    low density (LDL), 10
purée of celery root, 354
purslane, tomato, and onion salad,
    417–18

rabbit
    fried, 335–6
    hunter style, 333
    Marches style, I & II, 331–2
    with polenta, Genoa style, 334–5
    roast, 331
    San Remo style, 334
radicchio
    about, 371–2
    braised, 372
radicchio brasato, 372
raisins
    in peppers stuffed my way, 398–9
    in stuffed mushrooms with sherry,
        32–3
rane
    con i funghi, 185
    in salsa, 186
rapa al forno con patate, 380–81
rape (broccoletti di)
    with blackeyed peas, 365
    with broccoli and potatoes, 349
    with orecchiette, 87
    with pasta, 86–7
    see also broccoletti di rape
raspberry
    sauce with poached peaches, 445
    sherbet, 448–9
ratatouille of green beans, 345
ratatouille di fagiolini, 345
redroot
    about, 373
    in padella, 373–4
red snapper
    broiled, 209
    steamed, 210
ribollita, 61–2
rice
    balls
        "little oranges," 35
        with veal and peas, 166–7
    basic, steamed, 160
    with bean soup, 56–7
    with broccoli and lima beans, 164–5

rice (*continued*)
    with eel, 158
    with potatoes, 161
    for risotto, 151
    salad, I & II, 422–3
        spring, 423
    with tomatoes, 161–2
    with tuna, 165–6
    Valtellina style, 163–4
    see also risotto
ricotta with spaghetti, 109–10
rigatoni
    with broccoli for fifty people, 149–50
    with Gorgonzola, 110–11
    with shellfish and brandy, 117–18
    with veal and artichoke hearts, 136–7
rigatoni
    con broccoli per cinquanta persone, 149–50
    con frutti di mare al brandy, 117–18
    al gorgonzola, 110–11
    con sugo di vitello, 136–7
riso
    e bisati, 158
    e patate, 161
    e pomodori, 161–2
    al tonno, 165–6
risotto
    about, 151
    baked, 160
    Certosa style, 162–3
    with chicken, 259–60
    country style, 152–3
    with fava beans (broad beans), 159
    with lemon, 155
    mariner style, 155–6
    Milanese style, 152
    Padua style, 154
    Piedmontese style, 153–4
    with shellfish Genoa style, 157
risotto
    alla Certosina, 162–3
    con le fave, 159
    al forno, 160
    con frutti di mare alla Genovese, 157
    al limone, 155
    alla Marinara, 155–6
    alla Milanese, 152
    alla Padovana, 154
    alla Piemontese, 153–4
    alla rustica, 152–3
    alla Valtellinese, 163–4

Roman
  egg drop soup, 42–3
  garlic bread, I & II, 39
Ronzoni pasta, 70
rosemary with potatoes, 368
rucola
  cooked with bread and potatoes, 374
  pesto with penne, 103–4
  salad with spaghetti, 148
  soup, 50
  with spaghetti, 104

St. Otho cheese, 470
saffron with chicken, 250–51
Sailhac, Alain, 241
salad
  about, 408
    greens for, 408
  asparagus, 409
  avocado and tunafish, 420
  beet and carrot, 413–14
  beet and potato, 413
  broccoli, 409–10
  cauliflower, 414
  chicken, I & II, 418–19
  fennel and tomato, 415
  fish, I & II, 22–3
  fish, smoked, 26–7
  fruit, 445–6
  green bean and broccoli, 410
  green bean, broccoli, and potato,
    410–11
  lobster, warm, 420–21
  mushroom and tomato, 416
  mussel and scallop, 24
  Niçoise, 411–12
  orange and olive, 424
  pasta, 148–9
  potato, warm, 411
  potato and tuna, 419
  purslane, tomato, and onion, 417–18
  rice, I & II, 422–3
    spring, 423
  rucola with spaghetti, 148
  scallop, 25
  shrimp and pepper, 25–6
  squab, 282–3
  string bean and squid, 27–8
  in the style of the Marches, 417
  tomato and onion, 414–15

salad (*continued*)
  tripe, 30
  tuna and tomato, 416–17
  whiting, 421
salmon, smoked
  with butterfly pasta, 123–4
  with fettuccine, 122–3
salsa
  alla campagnola, 440–41
  cruda, 439
  alle mandorle, 427–8
  alla marinara, 430–31
  alla menta, 433
  di miele, 430
    (*Pimice*), 429–30
  alla noci, 436
  di peperoni piccanti, 437–8
  per il pesce, 428
  alla pistacchio, 437
  di pomodoro, 440
  di prezzemolo, 427
  di rafano e pomodoro, 432
  alla senape, 434–5
  di spinaci, 438–9
  tartufata, 441
  tonnato, 442
  verde, 428–9
    alla Genovese, 429
salt (sodium)
  intake, 6
  restricting of, 14
salt cod
  with broccoli rape, 182–3
  Florentine style, 183
  with linguine, 104–5
sarde alla graticola, 199
sardelle in carpione, 28–9
sardines
  fresh, broiled, 199
  with perciatelli, 124–5
  in a vinegar sauce, 28–9
sauce(s)
  about, 425
  almond, 427–8
  ancient Sicilian recipe for boiled fish,
    442
  for fish, 428
  green, 428–9
    Genoa style, 429
  honey, I & II, 429–30
  horseradish and tomato, 432

sauce(s) (continued)
  marinara, 430–31
  marò, 432
  mint, I & II, 433
  moutarde aux gherkins, Pierre Franey's, 434
  mustard, 434–5
  nut, I, II, & III, 435–6
  pepper, hot, 437–8
  pesto, 426
    light, 426
    parsley, 427
  pistachio, 437
  raw, 439
  spinach, 438–9
  tomato, 440
    country style, 440–41
  truffled, 441
  tuna, 442
sauerkraut, 352–3
scallions and ginger baked with flounder, 186–7
scallop(s)
  bay, 202
  and mackerel seviche, 191
  and mussel salad, 24
  with peas, 201
  and pesto with linguine, 125
  salad, 25
  sea
    grilled, 199–200
    teriyaki, 200–201
  soup, 50–51
  squid, and mussels with pasta, 114
  and squid with shrimp, 206–7
  and squid on a skewer, 18
scallopini
  escalope of ground beef, 298
  of venison, grilled, 330–31
scampi alla San Benedettese, 206
scomberi
  di ferri, 189–90
  in saor, 190
scrod
  about, 202
  baked with tomatoes and peppers, 203–4
  fillet with potatoes, 202–3
sea squab (blowfish), baked, 177–8
semolina
  about, 69

semolina (continued)
  gnocchi from Sardinia, 170–71
Senate Select Committee on Nutrition and Human Needs, 10
sepe alla Veneziana, 181–2
seviche of mackerel and scallops, 191
shad
  about, 204
  broiled, 204–5
shell beans, boiled, 346
shellfish
  clams
    and anchovies with spaghettini, 115
    asparagus, and mushrooms with pasta, 116–17
    stuffed, I & II, 20–21; Genoa style, III, 21
    and zucchini with pasta, 115–16
  cuttlefish Venetian style, 181–2
  lobster
    Américaine, 188
    baked, 187
    with linguine, 122
    with potatoes, 189
    salad, warm, 420–21
    sauce with Tomasso's linguine, 121
    soup, 52
  mixed
    and brandy on rigatoni, 117–18
    with chicken, 252–3
    with risotto Genoa style, 157
    on toast, 16–17
  mussels
    and broccoli baked with fish, 197–8
    with chicken, 254
    with chicken wings, 270–71
    and scallop salad, 24
    squid, and scallops with pasta, 114
    in wine, 196–7
  oysters
    in green sauce, 19–20
    with pesto, 19
  scallop(s)
    bay, 202
    and mackerel seviche, 191
    and mussel salad, 24
    with peas, 201
    and pesto with linguine, 125
    salad, 25
    sea: grilled, 199–200; teriyaki, 200–201

scallop(s) (*continued*)
    soup, 50–51
    squid and mussels with pasta, 114
    and squid on a skewer, 18
shrimp
    with artichoke hearts, 206
    with chicken breasts and asparagus, 265
    with chicken breasts and broccoli, 207–8
    fish, asparagus, and mushrooms with pasta, 130–31
    with pasta, 131–2
    and pepper salad, 25–6
    and pesto with pasta, 129–30
    with squid and scallops, 206–7
    and squid on a skewer, 17–18
shells with potatoes, 102–3
sherbet
    champagne peach, 450
    mango and cantaloupe, 449
    raspberry, 448–9
    watermelon with sliced strawberries, 449–50
sherry and raisins in stuffed mushrooms, 32–3
shrimp
    with artichoke hearts, 206
    with chicken breasts and asparagus, 265
    with chicken breasts and broccoli, 207–8
    fish, asparagus, and mushrooms with pasta, 130–31
    with pasta, 131–2
    and pepper salad, 25–6
    and pesto with pasta, 129–30
    with squid and scallops, 206–7
    and squid on a skewer, 17–18
skate wing
    sauce on spaghettini, 125–6
    soup, 53
skewer, on a
    albacore or tuna, 174
    beef, 291
    monkfish, 194
    squid and scallops, 18
    squid and shrimp, 17–18
    swordfish, 223–4
smelts, butterflied and fried, 208–9

smoked fish
    salad, 26–7
    salmon
        with butterfly pasta, 123–4
        with fettuccine, 122–3
    sturgeon in salad, 26–7
smoking and heart attack, 13
snacks, calorie tables for, 467–8
snow peas
    with fillet of sole, 210–11
    sautéed, 364–5
sogliola, filetti di
    affogato, 212
    a modo mio, 213–14
    oreganato, 211–12
    primavera, 212–13
sole, fillet of
    my way, 213–14
    oregano, 211
    poached in wine, 212
    primavera, 212–13
    with snow peas, 210–11
sopa de mazorca con pollo, 58–9
sorbetto
    di lamponi, 448–9
    di melone e fragole, 449–50
    di melone e mango, 449
soup
    about, 40
    bean
        and corn, 63–4
        Frankowitch, 60–61
        with rice, 56–7
        Tuscan, 61–2
    chicken
        broth, 41
        with corn, 58–9
        dumpling, 42
    chick pea, I & II, 64–5
    duck, 43
    fava bean and zucchini, 49–50
    fish, 54–5
    Florentine style, 59
    lentil
        and bean, 62
        and chick pea, 66
    lobster, 52
    minestrone, 45–6
        Genovese style, I & II, 48–9
    pasta and corn, 56
    pea, 55

soup (*continued*)
  fresh, 44–5
  Roman egg drop, 42–3
  rucola, 50
  scallop, 50–51
  and pea, 51–2
  skate wing, 53
  spring style, 44
  veal balls in, 66–7
  veal and cabbage, 67–8
  vegetable, green, 47–8
  zucchini, 46–7
spaghetti
  with cauliflower, 88
  with garlic and oil sauce garnished
      with mushrooms, 80
  Norcia style, 95
  with oil and garlic, 79–80
  with onions, 99–100
  with onions and milk, 98–9
  with pepper sauce, 102
  with ricotta, 109–10
  with rucola, 104
  with rucola salad, 148
  woodsman style, 98
spaghetti
  aglio e olio, 79–80
  alla boscaiola, 98
  con cipolle, 99–100
  con cipolle e latte, 98–9
  con insalata di rucola, 148
  alla Nursina, 95
  con ricotta, 109–10
  alla rughetta, 104
  con salsa di peperoni, 102
  chi vruoccoli arriminata, 88
spaghettini
  with broccoletti di rape, 85–6
  with clams and anchovies, 115
  primavera, Genoa style, 78–9
  primavera II, 77–8
  with skate wing sauce, 125–6
  with tomato sauce, 106
  with zucchini blossom sauce, 108
spaghettini
  con broccoletti di rape, 85–6
  primavera alla Genovese, 78–9
  di salsa di fiori di zucchini, 108
  al sugo, 106
  al sugo di razza, 125–6
  con vongole e acciughe, 115

spaghetti squash, 376–7
spezzatino
  con melanzane e piselli, 312–13
  di vitello e carciofi, 311–12
  di vitello con piselli e carote, 319–20
spezzato
  di vitello
  con fagioli, 317
  al marsala, 318–19
  con patate, 314–15
spiedini
  di frutti di mare, 17–18
  di tonno, 174
Spiga Doro pasta, 70
Spiga pasta, 70
spigola al cartoccio, 175–6
spinach
  asparagus, and ground beef with pizza
      (*var.*), 465
  Genoa style, 375–6
  in open-faced omelet with asparagus,
      36–7
  with penne, 74–5
  and potatoes, 375
  sauce, 438–9
spinaci
  alla Genovese, 375–6
  con patate, 375
  salsa di, 438–9
squab(s)
  baked in bread, 281–2
  in a casserole, 279–80
  in polenta country style, 168
  salad, 282–3
  stuffed with peas, 280–81
squash
  acorn, baked, 376
  hubbard, baked, 376
  spaghetti, 376–7
  see also zucchini
squid
  about, 214–15
  fried, 215–16
  with pasta, 126–7
  with peas, 219
  scallops, and mussels with pasta,
      114
  and scallops with shrimp, 206–7
  and scallops on a skewer, 18
  and shrimp on a skewer, 17–18
  and string bean salad, 27–8

squid (*continued*)
  stuffed
    with broccoli, 217
    Florentine, 216
    with polenta, 218
  tempura, 219–20
starches (polysaccharides), 9
stew
  beef, 298–9
    in wine, 295
  Etruscan fish, 233
  horsemeat, 327–8
  monkfish with pasta, 195–6
  turkey wing, 278–9
  veal
    with mushrooms, 313
    with potatoes, 314–15
    Riato, 314
stoccafisso all' Abruzzese, 220–21
stockfish
  about, 220
  Abruzzi style, 220–21
straciatella alla Romana, 42–3
stracotto, 294
strawberry(ies)
  in fried fruit, 444–5
  sliced, with watermelon sherbet, 449–50
  in wine, 446
stress, 13, 14
string bean and squid salad, 27–8
strokes, 7
strudel (R.W.), 454–5
  dough for, 454
sturgeon in smoked fish salad, 26–7
sucrose (cane sugar), 9
sugars
  carbohydrates, 9
  disaccharides, 9
  glucose, 9
  monosaccharides, 9
  polysaccharides, 9
  sucrose, 9
Swiss chard
  about, 354–5
  with potatoes, 355
swordfish
  Messina style, 222
  on a skewer, 223–4
  steak
    mariner style, 223

swordfish (*continued*)
  Sicilian style, 221–2

tacchino
  ali di, in umido, 278–9
  arrosto ripiene, 276–7
  filetti di,
    al marsala, 278
    alla Nerone, 277–8
tart, peach, 450–51
teal my way, 283–4
tegamaccio Etrusco, 233
timbale of macaroni, 146–7
timballo di maccheroni, 146–7
toast, tomatoes on, 379–80
tomato(es)
  about
    canned, 504
    canning of, 378
    fresh, 377–8
    kinds for planting, 377
    skinning and seeding, 378
    sulphur dust on, 378
  baked with potatoes, 367
  and basil with artichokes, 340
  broiled, I & II, 378–9
    zucchini stuffed, 402–3
  with chicken breasts, peppers,
      mushrooms, and onions, 259
  fresh, with broccoli in pasta, 85
  green
    fried, 380
    with pasta, 90–91
    with penne, 91–2
  and peppers with baked scrod, 203–4
  with pole beans and potatoes, 344–5
  with potatoes, celery, and onions, 370
  with rice, 161–2
  salad
    with fennel, 415
    with mushroom, 416
    with onion, 414–15
    with onion and purslane, 417–18
    with tuna, 416–17
  sauce, 440
    country style, 440–41
    with horseradish, 432
    marinara, 430–31
    with spaghettini, 106
    on steamed pompano, 198

tomato(es) (*continued*)
    with veal balls, 321
    on veal-stuffed eggplant, 394–5
    stuffed Trastevere style, 402
    stuffing for
        cabbage, 390–91
        eggplant, 393
    on toast, 379–80
tonno
    alla Genovese, 226
    polpettone di, 227
    spiedini di, 174
torresani in tecia, 279–80
torta di pesche, 450–1
tortelloni, 139–41
trenette with pesto sauce, 72–3
trennette al pesto, 72–3
triglycerides, 9, 10
    see also oil(s)
tripe
    Milan style, 324–5
    Roman style, 325–6
    salad, 30
    with savoy cabbage, 327
    and wild mushrooms with pasta,
        137–8
trippa
    con cavolo, 327
    alla Milanese (busecca), 324–5
    alla Romana, 325–6
trota
    u foglie di lattuga, 225
    in umido, 224–5
trout
    poached, 224–5
    smoked
        in fish salad, 26–7
        with pasta, 134–5
    wrapped in lettuce leaves, 225
truffled sauce, 441
truffles (white) with farfalle, 96
tuna/fish
    and avocado salad, 420
    with broccoli, 346–7
    with broccoli and black olives in pizza
        (*var.*), 465
    and broccoli with pasta, 132
    fresh
        Genoa style, 226
        on a skewer, 174
    loaf, 227

tuna/fish (*continued*)
    in pasta with beans, 82
    with penne, 132–3
    with rice, 165–6
    salad
        with potato, 419
        with tomato, 416–17
    sauce, 442
    stuffing for
        peppers, 398
        zucchini, 405
tunnied veal (*vitello tonnato*), 323–4
turkey
    breast with marsala wine, 278
    breasts, Nero style, 277–8
    roast, 276–7
    wing stew, 278–9
turnips
    and artichoke hearts with lamb, 329
    and potatoes, baked, 380–81
turnovers, Christmas, 452–3
Tuscan bean soup, 61–2
type A behavior, 14

U.S. Bureau of Fisheries, 11

veal
    about, 288
    with artichoke hearts, 311–12
    and artichoke hearts with rigatoni,
        136–7
    balls in soup, 66–7
    birds, Genoa style, 302–3
    and broccoli with pizza, 464–5
    and cabbage soup, 67–8
    chops
        with broccoli, 306–7
        broiled, I & II, 304
        Ciociara style, 305–6
        grilled, 305
        in a paper bag, 308–9
        with peppers, 307–8
        sautéed, 306
    cutlets
        broiled, 301
        Milan style, 302
        stuffed, 303
    with eggplant and onions in pizza
        (*var.*), 465

veal (*continued*)
  with eggplant and peas, 312–13
  with lentils and pasta, 316
  with marsala, 318–19
  meatballs
    about, 320
    with asparagus, 321–2
    steamed, 320
    in tomato sauce, 321
  osso buco Marches style, 310–11
  patties, 323
  with peas and carrots, 319–20
  and peas with rice balls, 166–7
  piccata, 300
  with potatoes and asparagus, 317–18
  shanks, 310
    in a wine sauce, 309
    in a skillet, 301
  stew
    with mushrooms, 313
    with potatoes, 314–15
    Riato, 314
  stuffing for
    cabbage, 391
    eggplant with tomato, 394–5
    mushrooms with walnuts, 32
    onions, 396–7
    peppers, 397–8
    zucchini, 404, 405
  tunnied (*vitello tonnato*), 323–4
  with white beans, 317
vegetable(s)
  about, 337
  found, 389
  lasagna, 143–5
  mixed, I & II, 385–6
  soup, green, 47–8
  summer, mixed, 387–8
  tempura, 388–9
  winter, mixed, 388
vegetarian/ism, 337–8, 341–2
venison
  scallopini, grilled, 330–31
  steaks, broiled or grilled, 330
verdura
  mista, 385–6
  misto di invernale, 388
  trovata, 389
vermicelli
  with breadcrumbs, 111
  harlot style, 107

vermicelli (*continued*)
  with mushrooms and wine, 94
  with oil, garlic, and anchovy, 81
  piquant, Calabria style, 112
vermicelli
  aglio e olio, 81
  alla carrettiera, 94
  con la mollica, 111
  piccanti alla Calabrese, 112
  alla puttanesca, 107
Vernges, John, 76
vitello
  braciolette ripiene, 303–4
  costolette di,
    con broccoli, 306–7
    al cartoccio, 308–9
    al ferri, 304
    alla griglia, 305
    alla Milanese, 302
    in padella, 306
    e peperoni, 307–8
  con lenticchie e pasta, 316
  in padella, 301
  con patate e asparagi, 317–18
  piccata, di, 300
  spezzatino di,
    e carciofi, 311–12
    con piselli e carote, 319–20
  spezzato di,
    con fagioli, 317
    al marsala, 318–19
    con patate, 314–15
  all uccelletto alla Genovese, 302–3

walnut(s)
  and eggplant with pasta, 89–90
  in nut sauce, I, II, & III, 435–6
  with pasta, 108–9
  spread on grilled bread, 38
  in stuffed mushrooms with veal, 32
watermelon sherbet with sliced
    strawberries, 449–50
Wechsberg, Joseph, *Blue Trout and Black*
    Truffles, 289
weight
  and height tables, 476
  ideal, 11, 474
whitefish, freshwater, steamed, 228
whiting
  baked with asparagus, 230

whiting (*continued*)
  baked in white wine, 230-31
  fillets of, fried, 229
  fried, 228-9
  salad, 421
wine
  with beef, 295
  fillet of sole, poached in, 212
  mussels cooked in, 196-7
  with peaches, 446-7
  red, with guinea hen, 285-6
  sauce with veal shanks, 309
  with strawberries, 446
  with vermicelli and mushrooms, 94
  white, whiting, baked in, 230-31

yams with broccoli, 347

zogghiu, 442
zucca, fiori di, ripiene, 405-6
zucchini
  baked, I & II, 384-5
  baked, stuffed, 403-4
  blossoms
    fried, 383
    sauce with spaghettini, 108
    stuffed, 405-7
    stuffed and fried, 383
      Roman style, 406-7
  and clams with pasta, 115-16
  and fava bean soup, 49-50

zucchini (*continued*)
  grated with onion, 382
  with green beans and potatoes, 344
  patties, fried, 381
  with potatoes, 382-3
  soup, 46-7
  stuffed
    with tuna, 405
    with veal, 404
  stuffing for broiled tomatoes, 402-3
zucchini
  crochette di, 381
  fiori di
    fritto, 383
    impottiti, 383, 407; *alla Romana*,
      406-7
  al forno, 384-5
  grattati alla cipolla, 382
  imbottiti al forno, 403-4
  e patate, 382-3
  ripiene, 404-5
zuppa
  di ceci, 65
  di fagioli alla Frankowitch, 60-1
  di fagioli alla Romana, 56-7
  di fave e zucchini, 49-50
  Fiorentina, 59
  di lenticche Abruzzese, 57-8
  di pasta e granturco alla Marchigiana,
    56
  di pesce, 54-5
  primavera, 44
  di razza, 53

A NOTE ABOUT THE AUTHORS

Edward Giobbi was born in Waterbury, Connecticut, of Italian immigrant parents. A well-known artist, he has always been interested in good food and has come to be recognized by Craig Claiborne and others in the food community as one of the most talented cooks around today. His first cookbook, *Italian Family Cooking*, was published in 1971. He and his family live in Katonah, New York.

Richard Wolff was born in Boston, Massachusetts, and graduated from the Harvard University Medical School in 1950. A cardiologist at Beth Israel Hospital, Dr. Wolff has also served on the faculty of the Harvard University Medical School for many years. In addition, he has a private practice in Brookline, where he and his family live.

A NOTE ON THE TYPE

The text of this book was set in a film version of Perpetua, designed by the British artist Eric Gill (1882–1940) and cut by The Monotype Corporation, London, in 1928–1930. Perpetua is a contemporary letter of original design, without any direct historical antecedents. The shapes of the roman letters basically derive from stonecutting, a form of lettering in which Gill was eminent. The italic is essentially an inclined roman. The general effect of the type face in reading sizes is one of lightness and grace. The larger display sizes of the type are extremely elegant and form what is probably the most distinguished series of inscriptional letters cut in the present century.

Composed by Superior Type, Champaign, Illinois. Printed and bound by Murray Printing Company, Westford, Massachusetts.

Designed by Roberta Savage.